BASIC Problem Solving

Structured Programming Using Microsoft BASIC

PENNY FANZONE

Essex Community College
Baltimore, Maryland

THOMAS D. HANKINS

West Virginia College of Graduate Studies
Institute, West Virginia

CARL DIEKHANS

Northern Nevada Community College
Elko, Nevada

Mitchell Publishing, Inc.
Watsonville, California

Desktop Publishing Service: C. Morales, Arizona Publication Service
Printed by: R. R. Donnelley & Sons
Product Development: Raleigh S. Wilson
Production Management: Greg Hubit
Sponsoring Editor: Raleigh S. Wilson
Text and Cover Design: Detta Penna

Printed in the United States of America
10 9 8 7 6 5 4 3 2

Library of Congress Card Catalog No.: 88-61877
ISBN: 0-394-39323-6

To our parents

Dorothy and Leon Smith

Floyd Hankins
Ruth and Calvin Hankins

Helen and Aloys Diekhans

Brief Contents

Detailed Contents

Chapter Four

Variables, Data Types, and Arithmetic   55

Chapter Five

Programming Structures and Boolean Expressions   84

Chapter Six

Introduction to Files and Sequential File Processing   108

Chapter Seven

Report Design   125

Chapter Eight

Screen Design   152

Chapter Nine

Control Break Processing   192

Chapter Ten

Table Processing   229

Chapter Fourteen

Random Files   368

Chapter Fifteen

Random Files—Indexing, Inquiry, and Update   391

Chapter Sixteen

Calling Program Modules from Disk   421

Preface

BASIC Problem Solving: Structured Programming Using Microsoft BASIC is a revision of *Business BASIC*. This new edition is due primarily to two factors: first, the many instructors who have told us how much they have appreciated using *Business BASIC*, and second, the popularity of BASIC as a language for teaching programming and as a major language for developing commercial applications.

In preparing the revision, we surveyed both instructors who had adopted *Business BASIC* and many who were using other texts. Adopters were asked what they liked about our text and what they would change. We asked those using other texts what they liked about their texts and what they would suggest we do to make this revision more suitable to their needs.

The survey confirmed that there is never likely to be a single best textbook for all instructors, because reactions to features are seldom, if ever, unanimous. In fact, features that some instructors strongly supported were suggested for deletion by others. Nevertheless, the survey responses did help us decide on several of the enhancements for this revision.

FEATURES

Microsoft BASIC. This remains the *de facto* standard for the BASIC language.

Introduction to computers. A new chapter (Chapter One) introduces the computer hardware and software functions and terminology. This chapter can serve either as an introduction to computer concepts and terms or as a review of them.

BASIC from the beginning. To assist beginning BASIC programmers, a new chapter (Chapter Two) introduces the BASIC editor and beginning BASIC statements and commands. Many examples to help students learn how to use the editor to develop their BASIC programs are also included in the chapter.

Structured program design and development concepts emphasized. A new chapter (Chapter Three), with *no program code*, teaches students how to design algorithms using pseudocode and structure charts. Examples to illustrate a recommended six-step development process range from a script for operating a vending machine to simple business problems. In subsequent chapters, realistic examples illustrate the application of this six-step process, continually reminding readers of its importance.

Modular techniques introduced early. Modular design concepts and implementation with GOSUB are introduced as soon as readers have enough background to consider nontrivial programs (Chapter Four).

Structured program code. All programs in the text are easy to read and easy to modify. In addition to their modular design, the programs include the following characteristics:

- Appropriate documentation at the beginning of the program

- Descriptive labels on program modules

- Use of only the standard programming structures to control program execution

- Program statements indented or aligned wherever appropriate

- Each program statement on a separate line

Data files introduced early. Because files are the primary method of accessing data in real applications, students learn to get data from sequential files (Chapter Six) as soon as they have mastered the concept of variables, the various data types, and the standard programming structures.

Example programs are realistic. From the very beginning, example programs provide solutions to problems typical in commercial programming environments, including control breaks, data validation, and file updating.

Chapters devoted to both report design and screen design. The chapters on report design (Chapter Seven) and screen design (Chapter Eight) explain the attributes of good design. Both also include new material to make them even more helpful. For example, Chapter Seven now presents guidelines for determining the space requirements for numeric fields.

Direct access (random) files. This rapidly expanding method of file processing now is the subject of two chapters. Chapter Fourteen introduces direct access files, and Chapter Fifteen explains inquiry and updating applications using indexing.

Chaining. Chapter Sixteen explains how to manage large, complex systems by chaining modules and programs.

Graphics. Complete instructions for producing graphic screens are provided in Chapter Seventeen.

Testing and Debugging. An appendix (E) offers helpful advice on these often neglected topics.

Style tips. Throughout the text, students are offered suggestions to improve their programming style.

Data disk exercises. The data disk packaged with each copy of this text contains all example programs from the text and the programs and data files needed for the end-of-chapter exercises. Following most chapters is a section called "Using the Data Disk" that provides students an opportunity to apply concepts and techniques presented in the chapter. Many of the exercises require the student to change an example program to meet new requirements and so provide realistic file maintenance experiences. These exercises are appropriate for lab session assignments.

Extensive student exercises. Questions, problems, and program assignments follow each chapter. These provide a thorough review of the chapter contents. The questions and problems are appropriate for tests and for class discussions. Some of the problems can serve as short program assignments.

Program assignments. The program assignments vary in difficulty to allow instructors flexibility in the effort they will require from students. The assignments include a narrative describing the requirements and file layouts. For some assignments that require printed output, there is a report design, and for others the student may design the report. The complete data file listed in the text for each program assignment is also on the student data disk.

Appendix topics. In addition to testing and debugging, other appendix sections provide a list of BASIC reserved words (A), an introduction to PC/MS-DOS and EDLIN (B), an ASCII code chart (C), a discussion of file transfers between BASIC programs and Lotus and dBASE (D), suggestions for debugging and testing programs (E), and examples of program documentation for two example programs (F).

Glossary. This provides a complete list of definitions for terms and concepts introduced in the text.

TEXT AND CHAPTER DESIGN

Most of the chapters use the following plan to introduce and explain their topics:

1. A general discussion of an application

2. A scenario that poses a problem for the student to solve

3. Development of a plan to solve the problem by following the steps in the program development cycle

4. Design of a program to solve the problem with emphasis on the need for interaction with the user of the program

5. Coding of the program with an explanation of the BASIC tools that apply to the problem

6. Hints for testing the program

SUPPLEMENTS

The following supplementary materials are available to adopters of this text:

Instructor's guide. This comprehensive guide contains outlines of each chapter, complete solutions to all questions, problems, and program assignments, and multiple-choice test questions.

Instructor's disk. This diskette contains solutions to all program assignments.

Penny Fanzone
Thomas D. Hankins
Carl Diekhans

Chapter One

Introduction to Computers

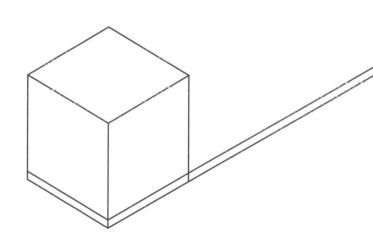

Topics

- Hardware
- Software
  Systems Software
  Applications Software
  Programming Languages

INTRODUCTION

A *computer* is an electronic device that reads data (input), transforms it (process), and reports results (output). (See Figure 1.1.) Computers are used for a wide variety of tasks. Businesses use them for applications such as word processing, accounting, inventory control, payroll, and sales forecasting. Scientists and engineers use computers for problem solving and simulations of experiments. Educators use computers as tutorial devices.

The physical parts of a computer system are the *hardware*. In general, hardware is any computer part you can see or touch. Instructions given to a computer are called *software*. An ordered set of instructions is called a *program*. The purpose of a program is to get and process data and produce specified results. *Data* are the facts used by programs.

FIGURE 1.1
The functions of a computer

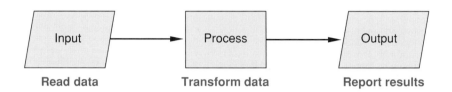

HARDWARE

A computing system normally has the following hardware components: input devices, a central processing unit, auxiliary storage devices, and output devices. Some devices can be classified as both input and output devices. Figure 1.2 shows a diagram of a typical *computer system*.

Input

An *input device* is used to enter commands, program instructions, and data into the computer. The keyboard, mouse, digitizer, optical scanner, light pen, joystick, and magnetic disk and tape unit are commonly used input devices. Sensor devices like those used in security systems and computer-controlled heating systems are also input devices.

Central Processing Unit

The *central processing unit* (CPU) can be likened to the "brain" of the computer. All instructions are processed there. The CPU is made up of a control unit, an arithmetic/logic unit, and memory.

The *control unit* routes data and instructions to and from main memory and to and from auxiliary storage. The control unit also accepts instructions, commands, and data from the input device and sends results to the output device.

The *arithmetic/logic unit* (ALU) does arithmetic calculations and compares values. Values are compared using the mathematical relationships of less than, greater than, and equal to.

One component of the memory of a computer is called the main memory, primary storage, or random-access memory (RAM). Instructions and data must be stored in RAM before they can be processed. *RAM* is measured by the number of characters that can be stored in the memory of the computer.

FIGURE 1.2
A typical computer system

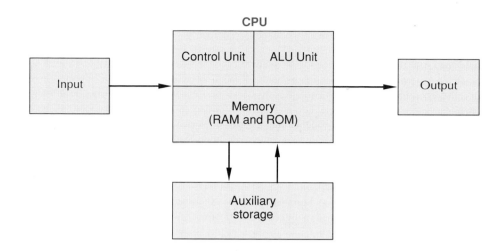

Each letter, digit, or symbol on the keyboard takes up one byte in memory. A *byte* is a set of 8 bits that represent a decimal number in binary code.

Binary code is the scheme for encoding keyboard characters using binary digits. For example, the letter *A* is assigned the decimal value 65, which corresponds to the binary value 1000001. Each binary digit in a byte is called a bit. A *bit* (*bi*nary dig*it*) is a binary 0 or 1. When you press a key on the keyboard, an 8-bit code or byte representing the key pressed is sent from the keyboard to the memory. The code used on microcomputers is the American Standard Code for Information Interchange, ASCII for short. Appendix C contains a table listing all of the decimal ASCII values and their associated characters. Figure 1.3 shows the relationship between characters, bytes, bits, and decimal (ASCII) values.

A *kilobyte* is 1024 bytes and is abbreviated 1K. To simplify calculations, 1K is usually approximated as 1000 bytes. The memory in microcomputers commonly ranges from 512K bytes to 4 megabytes (4M, or approximately 4,000,000 bytes) or more. *RAM chips* is the term given to the memory chips that make up main memory. Each chip normally holds either 64K or 256K bytes, but chips with much larger capacities are becoming common. You should know the size of RAM in your computer because computer programs have specific memory requirements.

If the power to a computer is cut off, all the instructions and data residing in main memory are lost. Memory that is erased by interrupting the power is called *volatile* memory. You can also erase programs and data from memory by issuing certain program commands.

The other component of memory is *read-only memory (ROM)*. The information in ROM is permanently stored on chips. The computer manufacturer supplies ROM, and the user cannot change the information it contains. The size of ROM varies from computer to computer, and, since it cannot be changed, its size is not an important user consideration. This type of memory is *nonvolatile*, that is, ROM retains its information when the power is cut off. RAM and ROM are considered hardware, but the instructions stored in RAM and ROM are considered software. Another name for the software stored in ROM is *firmware* (software that is built into the hardware). IBM ROM BASIC is an example of firmware.

FIGURE 1.3
Relationship between characters, bytes, bits, and ASCII values (ASCII stands for American Standard Code for Information Interchange.)

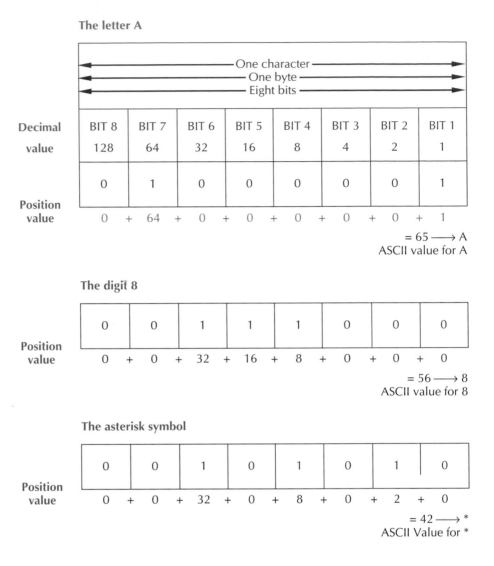

The letter A

	One character						
	One byte						
	Eight bits						

	BIT 8	BIT 7	BIT 6	BIT 5	BIT 4	BIT 3	BIT 2	BIT 1
Decimal value	128	64	32	16	8	4	2	1
	0	1	0	0	0	0	0	1
Position value	0 +	64 +	0 +	0 +	0 +	0 +	0 +	1

= 65 ⟶ A
ASCII value for A

The digit 8

	0	0	1	1	1	0	0	0
Position value	0 +	0 +	32 +	16 +	8 +	0 +	0 +	0

= 56 ⟶ 8
ASCII value for 8

The asterisk symbol

	0	0	1	0	1	0	1	0
Position value	0 +	0 +	32 +	0 +	8 +	0 +	2 +	0

= 42 ⟶ *
ASCII Value for *

Auxiliary Storage

Due to both the limited size and volatility of RAM, it is not possible or desirable to store in RAM all the software and data that you might use. More permanent storage is necessary. *Secondary storage* or *auxiliary storage* is nonvolatile. Without it, you would have to reenter the instructions and data each time you restarted your computer. Computers would not be very useful if you always had to repeat this tedious, time-consuming task. Because you can encounter problems as you work with a computer, wise users copy their work frequently to secondary storage. This precaution prevents them from having to reenter their work again if the contents of main memory are lost.

Removable magnetic disks, known best as *floppy disks* or *diskettes*, are a popular form of auxiliary storage. The two most common sizes are 5 1/4" and 3 1/2". The storage capacity of these disks ranges from 360K bytes to 1.2M bytes for the 5 1/4" size and from 720K bytes to 1.44m for the 3 1/2" disks. Before using a disk, you must format it for the computer system on which you will use it. This process is analogous to putting a reference grid on a blank sheet of paper. During formatting, the disk is divided into tracks and sectors. Each side of a 360K 5 1/4" floppy has 16 sectors with 40 tracks. A disk *directory* is set up on one of the tracks. This directory contains the names of and pertinent information about each collection of program instructions or data stored on the disk. Figure 1.4 shows the designs of 5 1/4" and 3 1/2" disks.

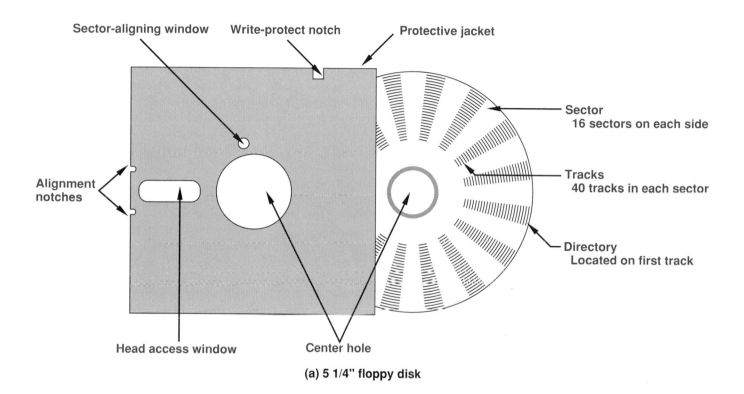

(a) 5 1/4" floppy disk

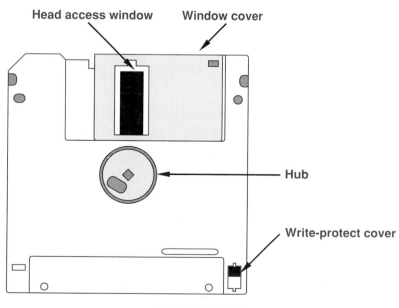

(b) 3 1/2" diskette

FIGURE 1.4   Two types of disks

The disk is in a protective jacket that should never be opened. The information is written on and read from the disk through an opening on the jacket called the head access window. The small notch on the side of the disk is the write-protect notch. If you cover the notch, the computer can read the data on the disk but cannot write data on it. This feature is useful if you do not want the data on the disk changed. If you intend to save data on the disk, however, do not cover the notch.

Another popular form of auxiliary storage is the *hard disk* or *fixed disk*. The storage capacity of these disks varies from 10M to 80M or more. Some systems can recognize only up to 40M on a hard disk. The user can subdivide the hard disk into areas called subdirectories and place each different application in its own subdirectory. Subdirectories can be erased and new ones created at the user's request. Hard disks have more storage space and allow faster operation than removable disks do.

Magnetic tape units can also be used for auxiliary storage. They are popular as a backup device for hard disk systems. *Backups* are copies of the programs and data stored on the disk. If anything should happen to the disk, you can use the tape to restore the lost programs and data to the disk. A disk may also be used to back-up other disks.

Because floppy disks are easily damaged, you should handle them with care. Keep them away from magnetic fields, heat, cold, dust, static electricity, and moisture. Store them in a vertical position so that no pressure is exerted on them. Also take care not to touch the exposed magnetic surface. Hard disks and tapes can also be damaged, but not as easily as the floppy disks. Make copies (backups) of important disks so that a copy of the information is available if you lose the information on the original disk.

Output

The main reason for using a computer is to produce output. The CPU must send the information in the computer to some type of output device. The most common output devices are the display screen or monitor and the printer. Output sent to the printer is referred to as *hard copy*, whereas output sent to the screen is called *soft copy*. Some other output devices are magnetic disk or tape units, plotters, and speakers.

Figure 1.5 shows an example of a computer system.

SOFTWARE

Software is the set of instructions that cause the hardware components to work together to produce some result. Two categories of software are systems software and applications software. *Systems software* includes the *Disk Operating System (DOS)*, compilers, interpreters, and utility programs.

DOS is a collection of programs to manage the operation of the computer. Both the DOS and the hardware are necessary for the operation of the computer system. You cannot use one without the other. Different computers may use different operating systems.

When you turn on the computer, some instructions from the DOS program named COMMAND.COM are loaded into RAM. These instructions allow the computer to function. They include directions for keeping track of all the programs and data that are available in auxiliary storage. The operating system also controls the printing operations so that information is sent to

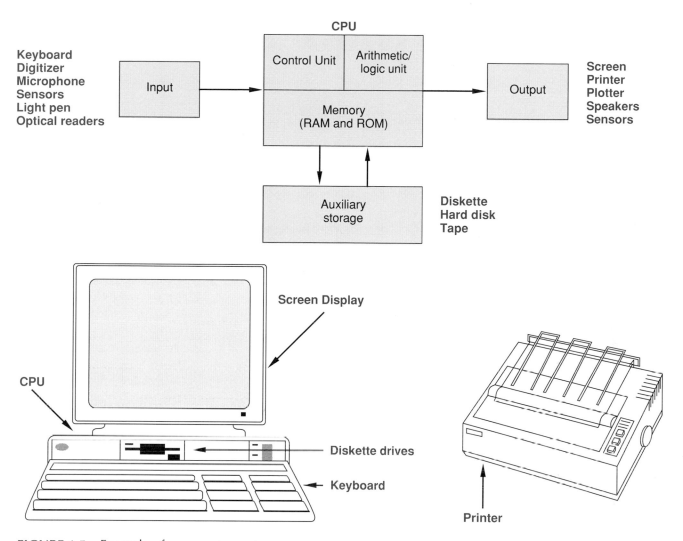

FIGURE 1.5   Example of a computer system

the printer in the proper format. The DOS makes sure that all the hardware parts work in unison and supervises the execution of applications software. The operating system also includes many utility programs, such as disk-formatting and disk-checking programs.

Applications software includes (1) prewritten packages for data base, spreadsheet, word processing, and accounting applications and (2) programs developed by the programming staff of a business or by programming consultants. Examples of the latter are in-house payroll or accounts receivable systems. Using prewritten packages, you can create and process data according to the specifications of the package. In most cases, it is less expensive to purchase prewritten packages than to maintain a programming staff or hire programming consultants. If a prewritten package does not satisfy your needs, however, you may need a program or set of programs written by programmers. This book shows you how to write your own applications software to create, process, and maintain data files. Figure 1.6 illustrates some types and uses of software.

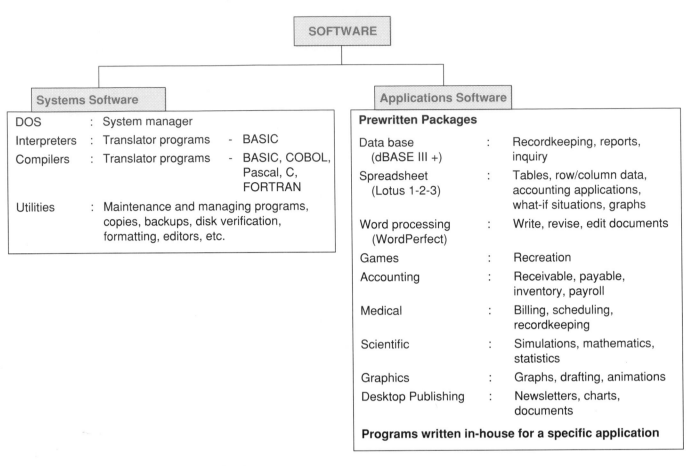

FIGURE 1.6   Some types and uses of software

Illustration

To get a better idea of how hardware and software interact, look at the following example. Suppose you are operating the computer in a business and your supervisor asks you to find the current status of an order. Figure 1.7 shows the steps you take and the actions the computer performs in response.

1. Using the keyboard (input), give the command to load the ORDER program into memory.

    Instructions from DOS direct the computer to locate the program in auxiliary storage and move it into memory. See Figure 1.7a.

2. Give the command from the keyboard to execute the ORDER program. See Figure 1.7b.

    The CPU executes the program instructions (processing) with help from DOS, then sends a message, ENTER ORDER NUMBER to the screen (output) asking for the order number. See Figure 1.7b.

3. You enter the order number 999 (input). See Figure 1.7c.

    The CPU, again with help from DOS, locates the order information from auxiliary storage and transfers it to memory (processing). See Figure 1.7c.

    Once the information is found, the CPU and DOS transfer the order information to the screen (output). See Figure 1.7c.

FIGURE 1.7
Example of steps the
computer follows

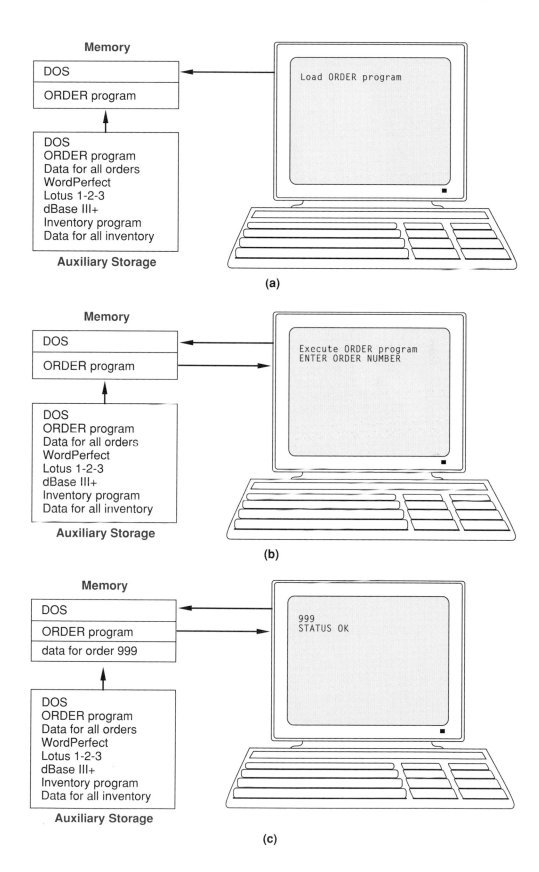

(a)

(b)

(c)

PROGRAMMING LANGUAGES

Just as people communicate with a variety of languages, programmers use different programming languages to "talk" to computers. Many different languages have been designed for different programming applications.

Programming languages can be classified as either low-level (machine-oriented) or high-level languages. The first languages used were *machine oriented*. These programs were long and tedious to write and could be used only on a specific computer. These low-level languages can be categorized as either machine language or assembly language. Machine-language programs consist of nothing but binary 0's and 1's, whereas assembly language programs use mnemonics (special codes) to represent machine-level instructions.

High-level languages were developed to make programming easier. Also, programs written in high-level languages can be transported from one type of computer to another with little or no modification. Their vocabulary resembles English. Here are some high-level programming languages and their typical applications:

Language	*Application*
COBOL, RPG	Business
FORTRAN, Pascal	Science, mathematics, engineering
LISP, Prolog	Artificial intelligence
BASIC, C, PL/1, Ada	General-purpose languages

The set of instructions that make up a program is called *code*. Instructions written in a high-level language are called *source code*. Because the CPU understands only machine language or *object code*, a *translator* program must be run to translate source code into object code. In terms of input, processing, and output, the source code is the *input* to the translator program, which *processes* (translates) the code. The *output* is the object code. See Figure 1.8.

Two types of translator programs, *compilers* and *interpreters*, are used to convert the program statements to a machine-readable format. A compiler first translates the entire program to machine language. If any syntax or translation errors are encountered, a complete listing of each error and the incorrect statement is given to the programmer. After the programmer corrects the errors, the program is compiled again. When no errors are detected, the compiled code (object code) can be executed. The machine-language version can then be saved separately so that the compiling step need not be repeated each time the program is excuted unless the original program is changed. Compiled programs run much faster than interpreted ones.

FIGURE 1.8
Translation of source code
to object code

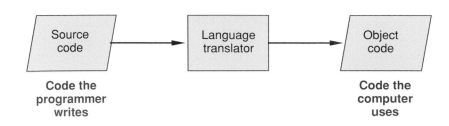

An interpreter translates and executes one source code instruction of a program at a time. Each time an instruction is executed, the interpreter uses the keywords in the source code to call prewritten machine-language routines that perform the functions specified in the source code. Whenever an error is encountered in a statement being translated, the interpreter stops running. The programmer must then fix the statement and invoke the interpreter again. After a program is free of errors, it still must be translated each time it is executed.

BASIC

BASIC is an acronym for *Beginner's All-purpose Symbolic Instruction Code*. Professors John G. Kemeny and Thomas E. Kurtz at Dartmouth College developed *BASIC* in the 1960s to give Dartmouth students a simple language for learning programming. Another advantage of most versions of BASIC for students is that it is interactive. In other words, a student sees an error or output as soon as it occurs.

Many versions of BASIC have been written since the 1960s, especially since the introduction of the microcomputer provided renewed interest in the language. BASIC is easy to learn and use, and it works well in educational settings. It can be used effectively for a variety of business and scientific applications.

Until recently, all versions of BASIC were interpreted. Microsoft BASIC and most other versions of BASIC used on microcomputers are interpreted languages. Versions of compiled BASIC on the market at this time include QuickBASIC, True BASIC, and Turbo BASIC.

Summary

- The computer is an electronic device that reads and processes data and then reports results.

- A computer system is composed of both hardware and software.

- Hardware includes input devices, the CPU, auxiliary storage, and output devices.

  □ Input devices include the keyboard, mouse, digitizer, optical scanners, joystick, light pens, sensor devices, and magnetic tape and disk units.

  □ The CPU is composed of the control unit, the ALU, and memory. Memory is made up of RAM and ROM. RAM is volatile; ROM is nonvolatile.

  □ Magnetic disks and tape units are forms of auxiliary storage. Auxiliary storage is nonvolatile.

  □ Output devices include the screen, printer, plotter, magnetic disk and tape units, and speakers. Hard copy is output sent to the printer; soft copy is output sent to the screen.

- Software includes systems software and applications software.

  □ Systems software includes DOS, compilers and interpreters, and utilities.

  □ Applications software includes prewritten packages and individualized programs written for businesses.

- Programming Languages

  □ A program is an ordered set of instructions that gets and processes data and produces specified results. Programs can be written in high-level or low-level languages.

  □ Machine language and assembly language are low-level, machine-dependent languages.

  □ High-level languages are not machine dependent. These languages are usually easier for programmers to understand and use.

  □ Interpreters and compilers are two types of translator programs that convert source code (program statements) into object code (machine-readable format). Compilers translate the entire source code into object code and then execute the machine-language instructions. Interpreters translate one source statement into machine language and then execute that instruction before going on to the next statement.

□ BASIC was developed by professors John G. Kemeny and Thomas E. Kurtz at Dartmouth College to give students an easy-to-learn, interactive programming language.

Review Questions

1. What is a computer?
2. What is hardware? What is software?
3. What is a computer program?
4. What are data?
5. Name four hardware components of a computer system.
6. Name three input devices.
7. What is the CPU? What parts make up the CPU?
8. What is RAM? ROM?
9. What is volatile memory?
10. What is nonvolatile memory?
11. What is auxiliary storage? Name three common forms of auxiliary storage.
12. What is backup? Why is it important?
13. Approximately how many bytes or characters does a formatted 40m hard disk hold?
14. What does the directory on a magnetic disk contain?
15. Define *hard copy* and *soft copy*.

16. Name three output devices.
17. Define *DOS*.
18. What are the two categories of software?
19. What software manages the operation of the computer?
20. Explain the difference between high-level languages and low-level languages.
21. Name five high-level languages and give an application for which each could be used.
22. What is the difference between source code and object code?
23. What is a translator program?
24. Explain the difference between an interpreter and a compiler.
25. Classify each of the following as hardware, systems software or applications software.
    a. Inventory program
    b. BASIC
    c. CPU
    d. ALU
    e. FORTRAN
    f. Disk-checking program
    g. Word processing programs
    h. DOS
    i. Floppy disk
    j. Hard disk
    k. Compilers
26. What does BASIC stand for?
27. List some advantages of using BASIC.
28. Take a shopping trip. Investigate the purchase of a microcomputer. Write a summary justifying what hardware and software you would purchase.

Introduction to BASIC

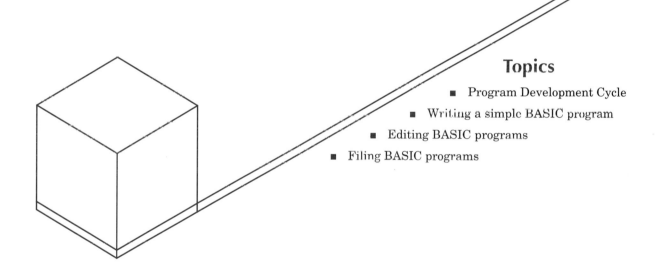

Topics

- Program Development Cycle
- Writing a simple BASIC program
- Editing BASIC programs
- Filing BASIC programs

BASIC Commands

```
AUTO
DELETE
EDIT
FILES
KILL
LIST
LLIST
LOAD/SAVE
MERGE
NAME
NEW
RENUM
RUN
SHELL
SYSTEM
TRON/TROFF
```

Program Statements

```
CLS
REM
PRINT
    SPC(n)
    TAB(n)
END
```

INTRODUCTION

In this chapter, you will plan, code, and test a simple program. The crucial word is *plan*. If you hired a construction company to build a house, you would be unhappy if the carpenters arrived without blueprints and began to erect the structure without giving thought to the result. Similarly, if you baked a cake without following a recipe and instead just guessed the ingredients, you probably would not be satisfied with the outcome.

In both cases, devoting some time to planning would produce more successful results. It is also likely that planning would reduce the time necessary to complete the tasks. The same is true of computer programs. When you write a computer program, you need to complete a series of *program planning* tasks. *Never* jump right into the coding of the instructions. Think about what you want to do first.

We will guide you through the development of a simple BASIC program following the series of steps called the *program development cycle*. This first program is very short to help you quickly become comfortable with BASIC and the microcomputer.

To write this BASIC program, you need to learn the REM, CLS, PRINT, and END statements. You will also learn how to format the output by using the comma and the TAB and SPC functions. In addition, you will learn how to correct mistakes in your programs and how to file your programs on disk for later use.

PROGRAM DEVELOPMENT CYCLE

Program development cycle is a term often used for the steps involved in planning and writing a program. The following steps are used to plan and write the sample programs in this book:

1. Define the problem.

2. Determine the output and input.

3. Design the program logic.

4. Code the program instructions.

5. Test the program.

6. Assemble the program documentation.

Define the Problem

First, review the problem description before trying to solve it. The problem definition is usually supplied by the systems designer or the user. As a student, you will probably be assigned a problem definition by your instructor. The definition helps you understand what the program is supposed to do. Usually, you, as the programmer, are not the person who will eventually use the program. Consequently, you should talk with the people who will work with the screens and use the reports that the program will generate. These people are often called the *users*. Make sure you understand exactly what they want the program to do. If you make assumptions about what the user (or your instructor) wants, you will probably not write an acceptable program the first time and will have to revise it. The time and effort needed to make such changes are very expensive for a business.

Determine the Output and Input

The programmer needs to know what the program should produce. Does the user want the output displayed on the screen or printed on paper? In what format should the messages on the screen or the report be? The programmer also needs to know what data are to be entered into the program. Will the user enter data from the keyboard, or will the program access a data file? These decisions need to be made before the programmer begins writing the program.

Notice that the output is normally specified before the input. The output is the key element in the design process. To determine exactly what data and results are required, the programmer usually reviews the output specifications first.

Design the Program Logic

The computer follows the instructions in the program *exactly*. For this reason, you need to develop an algorithm or logic plan for the solution of the problem before coding the program instructions. An *algorithm* is an ordered list of steps for solving the problem. The list of steps shows what processing must be done to get from the input to the output. This list must be in the correct sequence. Humans can interpret vague or incomplete directions. The computer, however, cannot. For example, you could follow the instruction "get a pencil from the desk." Also, if the pencil were not on the desk, you would know to look elsewhere. Computers, however, are not able to evaluate a situation and make an adjustment. They can do only what they are told.

There are several ways to represent program logic. Three are flowcharts, structure charts, and pseudocode. Flowcharts are introduced in this chapter, and structure charts and pseudocode are explained in Chapter 3. After you complete the logic design, you should review it carefully. Sometimes a procedure called "desk-checking" is helpful in finding mistakes in the logic. Desk-checking means reviewing the logic sequentially, looking for steps that are not well defined and steps that are not in correct sequence. Remember, the computer will follow the program instructions in sequence, exactly as you write them.

Code the Program Instructions

Writing the program instructions is called coding. The *code* is simply the lines of the program. The program instructions must follow the rules of the language used. BASIC programs are sometimes written on specially designed forms called *coding forms*, although most people use ordinary paper.

Test the Program

After keying the program into the computer, you *run* or *execute* it to see whether it works. At first, you may encounter a series of *syntax errors*. These are mistakes you made in implementing the rules of the language. These mistakes are often just typographical errors. Another type of error that might occur during program execution is a *run-time error*. An example of a run-time error is trying to divide a number by zero. If a program instruction requests division by zero, the computer displays an error message on the screen.

After you have corrected the syntax and run-time errors, you may generate one or more *logic errors*. Possibly nothing is printed, or only part of the result is printed, or the totals at the end of the report are incorrect. At this point you must go back and study your program. Using a technique called "playing computer" (simulating the steps the computer takes) can help you trace a logic error. To use this technique, pretend you are the computer and follow or trace the instructions in your program until you identify the mistake in the logic.

Assemble the Documentation	Program documentation is very important to a business. You may write a program, not look at it for a long time, and then be asked to revise it. *Program maintenance* is the process of revising a program. As a programmer, you will often need to update programs, sometimes programs you didn't write. If you have a definition of the problem, a description of the input and output, a sample listing, and other documentation, you can make the changes efficiently. Later chapters give more information on program documentation.

FIRST BASIC PROGRAM

Begin planning a simple program. The problem is to display the name of a store and its location (city and state) on the computer screen. The program output is:

```
Ann's Antiques
Boston, Mass
```

The program has no input.

To design the logic of the program, you will use a flowchart. A *flowchart* is a diagram or a picture of the logic of a program. Programmers use a set of standard flowcharting symbols. See Figure 2.1. When constructing a flowchart, start at the top of a page and draw the symbols from top to bottom. Plastic templates for drawing flowchart symbols are available in many bookstores and office supply shops.

Figure 2.2 shows the flowchart for this program. Note that the first step is to clear the screen because there may be output left over from a previous program. The second step is to print

```
Ann's Antiques
```

The third step is to print

```
Boston, Mass
```

To ensure that the design is correct, desk-check it. Is each step well-defined? Are any of the steps vague or confusing? Are any steps missing? Are the steps in the correct sequence? With this simple algorithm, it is easy to see that everything is OK.

Now you are ready to code the program. BASIC provides for two types of instructions: (1) commands and (2) statements. BASIC *commands* normally operate on programs and are used to control the interaction between the programmer and BASIC. There are commands for editing and executing BASIC programs as well as for creating a filing system of programs. BASIC *statements*, by contrast, operate on data and control the interaction between the user and the computer.

Any statement that is to be part of a program must begin with a line number. If you enter a statement without a line number, the computer executes the statement immediately and does not retain the statement in memory. No BASIC instruction, including the line number, may be longer than

FIGURE 2.1
Flowchart symbols and
their meanings

Symbol	Name	Meaning	Sample BASIC Statements
	Terminal	Indicates the beginning and end of the program.	END
	Input/output	Represents any input or output function. Any statement that inputs data to be processed or displays results.	INPUT PRINT LPRINT
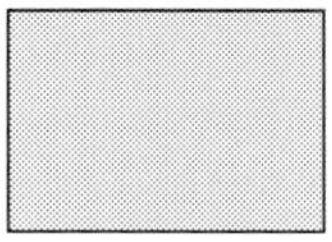	Process	Represents a defined operation, usually resulting in a change of value or location of data.	LET
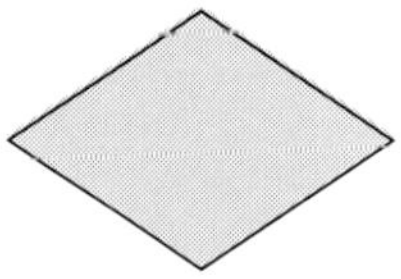	Decision	Represents a program decision allowing alternate paths based on a condition. These conditions can be evaluated as true or false.	IF/THEN/ELSE WHILE/WEND
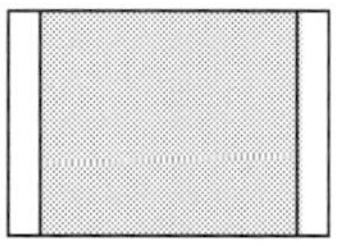	Predefined process	Represents a group of statements that together accomplish one task. Used when programs are broken into modules.	GOSUB/RETURN
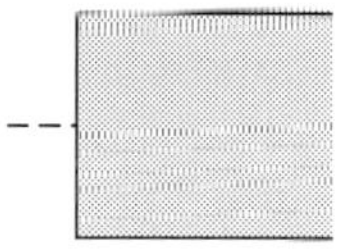	Annotation	Represents the addition of descriptive information explaining the program.	REM
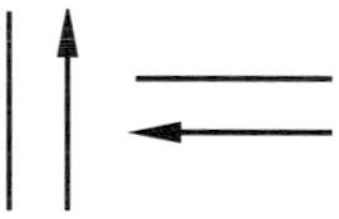	Flowlines	Used to connect symbols and represent the sequence of execution. Arrowheads are mandatory only for right-to-left and bottom-to-top flow.	
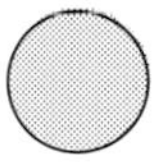	Connector	Any entry from, or exit to, another part of the flowchart, usually to eliminate lengthy flowlines and to indicate where flowlines come together.	

255 characters. A line number may be any integer in the range 0 to 65529. In BASIC, these line numbers indicate the sequence of program execution. During execution, the computer starts at the line with the lowest number line and progresses sequentially one line at a time until it is directed to stop or it encounters the last statement in the program. The programmer may enter program statements in any order. The computer arranges the statements in line number order.

Commands may also be given line numbers. If so, they are carried out during program execution. In most applications, however, commands are used to operate on a program and are entered without line numbers for immediate execution.

Figure 2.3 shows the program coded on a coding form.

Figure 2.2
Program flowchart

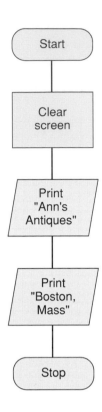

Testing the Program

Before entering the program, type the command NEW. This command erases any statements already in the computer's memory. *Caution!* If there is a program in memory, make sure you save it on disk first. Otherwise NEW will erase your work. (See the instructions for saving programs later in this chapter if you need to save an old program first.) Now enter the program as coded on the coding form. Remember to press the Enter key after each statement.

After you enter the program, or anytime you want to see results, type the command RUN. This command executes the program in the computer's memory in line number order.

Suppose that you entered the program as follows:

```
NEW
100 REM Antique Program
200 CLS
300 PRIT "Ann's Antiques"
400 PRINT "Boston, MAsss"
500 END
```

Now you type RUN to execute the program. The computer will first execute line 100, and then line 200. After it tries to execute line 300, you see the following message on the screen:

```
Syntax error in line 300
Ok
300 PRIT "Ann's Antiques"
```

The error message indicates that you have keyed in a BASIC statement incorrectly. The computer also displays the program statement that caused the error. In this case, PRINT is misspelled in line 300. To correct the mistake, move the cursor to the T in PRIT using the cursor-movement (arrow) keys. Press the Ins key and then the N. Press the Enter key. It is very important to press the Enter key after you have corrected a line because, unless you press the Enter key while the cursor is on the line being changed, the change only appears on the screen and is not registered in memory. After

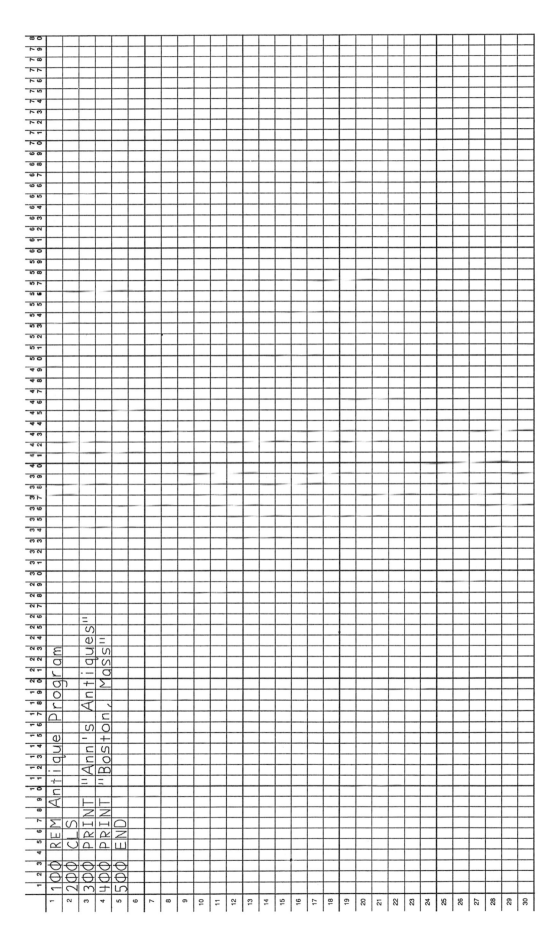

The coding form contains the following BASIC program:

```
100 REM Antique Program
200 CLS
300 PRINT "Ann's Antiques"
400 PRINT "Boston, Mass"
500 END
```

FIGURE 2.3 Coding form

moving the cursor to an open line, type RUN to test the program after the change. You will see the following:

```
Ann's Antiques
Boston, MAsss
```

The program runs without error messages, but the output is incorrect. Now you have encountered a logic error (although not a very complicated one).

When you try to find out what is wrong, you need to see the program statements. The BASIC command LIST causes the computer to display on the screen, in numeric order, the lines of the program currently in the computer's memory. After entering LIST, move the cursor to the *A* in *MAsss* (line 400) and press the lowercase a. Now move the cursor to one of the *s*'s. Press the Del key and then the Enter key. The corrected program should look as follows:

```
LIST                              ←——— Typed by the programmer
100 REM Antique Program
200 CLS
300 PRINT "Ann's Antiques"
400 PRINT "Boston, Mass"
500 END
```

When you enter the command RUN, the computer executes the program statements in this order: line 100, line 200, line 300, line 400, and, last, line 500.

You may add new lines to the program at any point. If you want to add a line between lines 300 and 400, type any line number between 300 and 400 and then the BASIC statement on any free line on the screen. For example,

```
350 PRINT "250 Harvard Ct"
```

This statement will be inserted in memory between lines 300 and 400. To see the effect of this change on the program listing, enter the BASIC command LIST.

To delete a line in a program, key in the line number and press the Enter key. For example

```
400 <Enter>
```

At this point, after adding line 350 and deleting line 400, you see the following statements after you enter the command LIST:

```
LIST                              ←——— Typed by the programmer
100 REM Antique Program
200 CLS
300 PRINT "Ann's Antiques"
350 PRINT "250 Harvard Ct"
500 END
```

To renumber the lines in the program, use the RENUM command. The command RENUM 1000,,100 renumbers the program in increments of 100 beginning with line number 1000. Note the result of using this command:

```
RENUM 1000,,100                   ←———
LIST                              ←——— Typed by the programmer
1000 REM Antique Program
1100 CLS
1200 PRINT "Ann's Antiques"
1300 PRINT "250 Harvard Ct"
1400 END
```

The command RENUM 5000,1100,50 renumbers the program starting with line number 1100 in the old program in increments of 50 beginning with line number 5000. The results of entering this command follow:

```
RENUM 5000,1100,50          ←——————
LIST                        ←—————— Typed by the programmer
1000 REM Antique Program
5000 CLS
5050 PRINT "Ann's Antiques"
5100 PRINT "250 Harvard Ct"
5150 END
```

See Table 2.1 for a summary of editing procedures.

BASIC Commands to Save and Load Programs

Now that the program is written, you may want to save it for future use. Use the SAVE command followed by a program name to store the program currently in the computer's memory on disk. The program is now in two places; it is still in memory but is now on the disk as well.

The program name may contain 1 to 8 characters and may be followed by a period and an extension of 1 to 3 characters. If you do not enter an extension, the extension .BAS is added to your program name. Be sure to make up a meaningful name so that the program will be easy to identify on the disk directory at a later time. Sample SAVE commands are:

SAVE"FIRST	Saves FIRST.BAS on the default drive
SAVE"B:PROG.ONE	Saves PROG.ONE on drive B
SAVE"A:PAYROLL	Saves PAYROLL.BAS on drive A

Some systems also require an ending quote, for example, SAVE"FIRST".

Table 2.1   Editing Procedures

Add character(s) to a line.	Move the cursor one character to the right of where you want to insert the character(s). Press the Ins key. Type the character(s) to be inserted. Press the Enter key.
Delete character(s) in a line.	Move the cursor to the character to be deleted. Press the Del key for each character to be deleted. Press the Enter key.
Change character(s) in a line.	Move the cursor to the character(s) to be changed. Key the new character(s). Press the Enter key.
Add a program line.	Key in a line number that correctly sequences the statement. Key in the program statement. Press the Enter key.
Delete a program line.	Key in the line number of the line to be deleted and press the Enter key.
Delete a sequence of program lines.	Enter the command DELETE followed by a starting line number and an ending line number separated by a hyphen (for example, DELETE 300-390). Press the Enter key.
Replace a program line.	Key in the new statement using the line number of the statement to be replaced. Press the Enter key.
Copy a program line.	Move the cursor to the line number of the statement to be copied. Change the line number and press the Enter key. This statement will be in the program twice; at the original location and the new location.
Move a program line.	Move the cursor to the line number of the statement to be moved. Change the line number and press the Enter key. Now delete the original line number. The statement will be in the program once, at the new location.

Note: The default drive is the drive (it is usually A, B, or C, depending on your computer) to which all disk commands apply unless the command designates a drive explicitly.

It is good practice to save your program regularly while you are working on it in case of a power failure or some other interruption. If you lose power, the program in memory is lost. If you have saved your program, however, you can load it back into memory from the disk. The command to retrieve a program from disk and place it in memory is LOAD followed by the program name. After you enter the LOAD command, the program is in memory as well as on the disk. Sample LOAD commands are:

LOAD"FIRST   Loads FIRST.BAS from the default drive

LOAD"B:PROG.ONE   Loads PROG.ONE from drive B

LOAD"A:PAYROLL   Loads PAYROLL.BAS from drive A

See Figure 2.4 for a schematic of the effects of SAVE and LOAD.

Remember that you change a program on disk by giving a SAVE command. If you load a program from disk and then change the program in memory, you will have two different versions of the program: the original on disk and the changed one in memory. The program on disk is *not* automatically updated. The *changed* version in memory must be saved again. When you save the new version of a program, you may give it the same name (the new version then replaces the old version) or a new name. If you use a new name, both versions will be on disk.

Sometimes you may want to save only a portion of your program, possibly so that you can insert it into other programs or use it as the shell of future programs. To save a set of lines from a program, use the LIST command with a file name. Suppose the following program is in memory:

```
100 REM Sporting Goods Program
200 CLS
300 PRINT "YORKTOWNE SPORTING GOODS"
400 PRINT "(301) 252-7800"
500 END
```

Now suppose you enter this command:

```
LIST 200-400,"A:TEL
```

Program lines 200, 300, and 400 are stored on the disk in drive A under the name TEL.BAS.

Displaying the Directory

Use the FILES command to display a directory of the programs and files stored on the disk. For example, after giving the FILES command, you may see the following on the screen:

```
FILES                              ←——— Typed by the programmer
A:\
FIRST   .BAS             PROG    .ONE
```

This screen indicates that there are two files on the disk in drive A; these files are FIRST.BAS and PROG.ONE.

See Table 2.2 for a summary of BASIC commands and Table 2.3 for examples of these commands. For a set of exercises reviewing those commands, see "Using the Data Disk" at the end of this chapter.

SAVE example

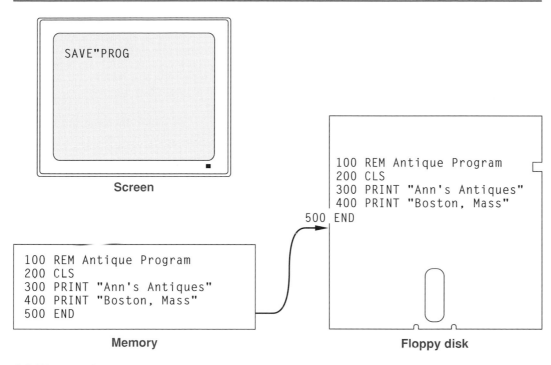

LOAD example

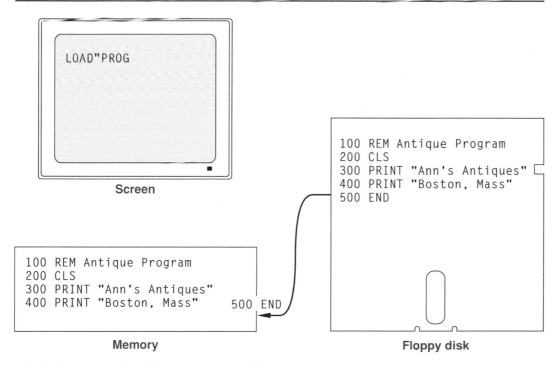

FIGURE 2.4 SAVE and LOAD commands

Table 2.2 BASIC Commands

BASIC Command	Function Key	Description
AUTO [*line#*],[*increment*]		Automatically generates and displays program line numbers; *line#* is the starting line number; *increment* is the value added to get successive line numbers; default values are 10 and 10. After giving this command, the programmer does not have to key the line numbers; just the program statements.
DELETE [*line1*] [*-line2*]		Deletes line numbers *line1* to *line2* in the program in memory.
EDIT <*line#*>		Displays the line indicated.
FILES ["*filespec*"]		Without a file specification, lists all files on default drive; otherwise, all files matching the file specification are displayed.
KILL <"*filespec*">		Erases the file from disk.
LIST [*line1*] [*-line2*] [,"*filespec*"]	F1	Displays the specified range of program lines currently in memory on the screen. If no lines are specified, the entire program is displayed. If a file is specified, the computer copies those program lines indicated to a disk file.
LLIST [*line1*] [*-line2*]	L and F1	Prints the specified range of program lines currently in memory on the printer. If no lines are specified, the entire program is printed.
LOAD <"*filespec*"> [,R]	F3	Loads the specified program into memory from disk. The R option runs the program after it is loaded.
MERGE <"*filespec*">		Merges the lines from the file specified (it must be in ASCII format) into the program currently in memory.
NAME <"*old-filespec*"> AS <"*new-filespec*">		Changes the name of file specified.
NEW		Erases the program in memory.
RENUM [*new#*] [[,*old#*] [,*increment*]]		Renumbers program lines. *New#* is the first line number in the new sequence (the default is 10); *old#* is the program line at which renumbering should begin (the default is the first line); and *increment* is the difference between successive line numbers in the new sequence (the default is 10).
RUN [*line#*]	F2	Begins execution of a program at the specified line; the default is the first line.
SAVE <"*filespec*"> [,A]	F4	Copies the program in memory to disk. The A option saves the file in ASCII format so that it can be used as a text file.
SHELL		Returns control to DOS while saving the BASIC program and variables; enter EXIT to return to BASIC from DOS.
SYSTEM		Permanently exits BASIC and returns control to DOS.
TRON	F7	Activates the program trace feature. Lists the line numbers executed during a program run (used as a debugging aid.)
TROFF	F8	Turns off the program trace feature.

Parameters inside angle brackets <> are required; those in square brackets [] are optional.

A *filespec* is used to identify program and data files on disk. A *filespec* is made up of a drive designation, a file name, and an extension (*filespec* = *drive:filename.extension*), where *drive* specifies disk drive A, B, or C (if omitted, default drive is used), *filename* may be from 1 to 8 characters, and *extension* may be from 1 to 3 characters.

The function keys may be used in place of the complete command.

Table 2.3   Examples of BASIC Commands

Example	Description
AUTO	Generates line numbers 10,20,30, . . .
AUTO 1000,100	Generates line numbers 1000,1100,1200, . . .
DELETE 200	Deletes line number 200 from the program in memory.
DELETE 200-500	Deletes all lines between 200 and 500, inclusive.
FILES	Lists all the files on the default drive.
FILES"A:	Lists all the files on drive A.
FILES"B:*.BAS	Lists all the files with the extension BAS on drive B. The asterisk (*) is called a wildcard character.
FILES"A:CHAP*.*	Lists all the files on drive A whose names begin with CHAP. Any other characters and any extension can follow CHAP.
KILL"INV.BAS	Erases the file named INV.BAS from the default drive.
LIST	Displays all the program lines in memory.
LIST 100-500	Displays all the program lines in memory between 100 and 500, inclusive.
LIST 100	Displays line 100.
LIST 100-	Displays line 100 and all the lines following 100.
LIST -100	Displays all the lines from 0 to 100, inclusive.
LIST 1000-2000,"EX1	Copies lines 1000 to 2000, inclusive, to disk and stores them under the name EX1.BAS. This can be useful if you want to store a block of code in a program under a different name.
LOAD"PAYROLL	Retrieves PAYROLL.BAS from the default drive and stores it in memory.
LOAD"PAYROLL",R	Loads PAYROLL.BAS into memory from the default drive and executes the program.
NAME"A:ACCT.BAS" AS "A:ACCOUNT.BAS"	Changes the name of ACCT.BAS on drive A to ACCOUNT.BAS.
RUN	Executes the program in memory starting with the first line.
RUN 4000	Executes the program in memory starting at line 4000.
RUN"INV	Loads INV.BAS into memory from the default drive and executes it.
SAVE"B:PROJ1	Stores the program in memory on drive B under the name PROJ1.BAS.
SAVE"B:PROJ1",A	Stores the program in memory on drive B under the name PROJ1.BAS in ASCII format.

Hard Copy Commands

Here are the commands for obtaining a paper copy of the program listing or the program output:

1. LLIST

   If you need a printed copy of the program in memory, use LLIST. LLIST causes the program in memory to be printed on hard copy.

2. Ctrl/PrtSc keys

   If you want a hard copy of the program output or the program listing, start by pressing the Ctrl and PrtSc keys. (When you use a keypress sequence—such as Ctrl/PrtSc—to give a command, press the first key and hold it down while you press the second key, and then release both keys. This procedure is identical to pressing the Shift key and a letter to type a capital letter.) After pressing the Ctrl/PrtSc keys, enter RUN to see the *output* on both the screen and the printer, and enter LIST to see the program statements on both the screen and the printer. To stop printing, press Ctrl/PrtSc again.

3. Shift/PrtSc Keys
To send any image currently on the screen to the printer, press the Shift and PrtSc keys.

PROGRAM STATEMENTS USED IN FIRST BASIC PROGRAM

REM Statement

REM signifies that a line or a portion of a line contains no instruction for the computer. Instead, it contains remarks or comments to help the reader of the program understand some aspect of the program. The single quote or apostrophe (') is an abbreviation for REM. Thus, the following two statements are equivalent:

```
100 REM Ann's Antiques
100 ' Ann's Antiques
```

A comment may be used in a line with another BASIC statement:

```
400 PRINT "Boston, Mass"  'City/State
```

You cannot, however, reverse the sequence, placing a comment before a statement on the same line. The location of the apostrophe in the following example, for instance, would cause the computer to consider the entire line a remark:

```
400' City/State    PRINT "Boston, Mass"
```

CLS Statement

Screen output is usually easier to read if the screen has nothing else on it. The CLS statement clears the screen and places the cursor in the upper left corner. The format is:

```
[line #] CLS
```

The *brackets* indicate an optional element of the statement. Remember, however, if the line # is omitted, the statement executes immediately and is not retained in memory.

PRINT Statement

The PRINT statement displays characters on the screen. A similar statement, LPRINT, sends output to the printer instead of the screen. All the rules that apply to the PRINT statement apply to the LPRINT statement as well. The general form of the PRINT statement is:

```
[line#] PRINT [list of expressions] [;] [,]
```

The value to be displayed is listed between quotes after the word PRINT, for example:

```
100 PRINT "BASIC IS EASY"
```

This statement causes this message to be displayed on the screen, starting in column 1:

```
BASIC IS EASY
```

After the message is displayed, the cursor moves to the first position of the next line on the screen. An ending semicolon, however, suppresses the carriage return. The cursor does not advance to a new line; it remains on the same line until the program encounters another PRINT command.

For example, the two-line program

```
100 PRINT "MacBeth ";
200 PRINT "BY SHAKESPEARE"
```

causes this output to be displayed on one line on the screen:

```
MacBeth BY SHAKESPEARE
```

Notice that the semicolon did not cause a space to be added between MacBeth and BY SHAKESPEARE. The necessary space was included in line 100, after MacBeth and before the ending quote.

Using the Print Zones

You can control spacing on the line by using a comma between the items to be printed. In BASIC, there are five print zones per line, each 14 columns wide. When you use commas to separate items to be printed, the computer moves to the next print zone before printing the item following the comma. Consider the following example:

```
100 PRINT "NAME", "ADDR", "AGE"
RUN
NAME          ADDR          AGE
```

The word NAME starts in column 1 of the first print zone; the word ADDR starts in column 15, the beginning of the second print zone; and the word AGE starts in column 29, the beginning of the third print zone.

Figure 2.5 contains additional examples of the PRINT statement with commas separating print items. Notice line 20 in Figure 2.5. Nothing follows the PRINT statement. *Line#* PRINT causes the cursor to move to the next

```
10 PRINT "   STUDENT LIST"
20 PRINT
30 PRINT "NAMES", "CLASS"
40 PRINT "-----", "-----"
50 PRINT "JILL", "SENIOR"
60 PRINT "LUCA", "FRESHMAN"
70 PRINT "MARK", "JUNIOR"
80 PRINT ,,"SOUTHERN HIGH SCHOOL"
90 PRINT ,"Savannah", "Georgia",, "13679"
```

```
              1             2             4             5             7
1..........5..........9..........3..........7..........0
     Zone 1        Zone 2        Zone 3        Zone 4        Zone 5

     STUDENT LIST

NAMES          CLASS
-----          -----
JILL           SENIOR
LUCA           FRESHMAN
MARK           JUNIOR
                             SOUTHERN HIGH SCHOOL
               Savannah      Georgia                     13679
```

FIGURE 2.5   PRINT statements with commas

line on the screen. If the cursor is at the beginning of a line, *line#* PRINT causes the cursor to move to the next line, creating a blank line.

TAB Function

TAB is a built-in BASIC function used to control spacing on a line. *Functions* are built-in capabilities that BASIC provides for use in program statements. The TAB function can be used only in PRINT or LPRINT statements and is written TAB(*n*). TAB is the name of the function; the expression in parentheses is called the *argument*. The argument *n* refers to a position on a line. The value *n* indicates an absolute position, not a relative one, on the screen or print line. The first position on a line is TAB(1), the thirtieth position is TAB(30), and the fiftieth position is TAB(50). Consider the following example:

```
100 PRINT TAB(10); "AMT DUE"; TAB(25); "BALANCE"
RUN
          AMT DUE        BALANCE
```

The characters AMT DUE start in column 10, and the characters BALANCE start in column 25. Note that a semicolon is placed between TAB and the value to be displayed. In this statement, the semicolon is used as a separator; typing one or more spaces would have the same result.

If the number specified in the TAB function precedes the current cursor position, the item is printed at that tab position on the next line. For example, the statement

```
100 PRINT TAB(20); "AMT DUE"; TAB(8); "BALANCE"
```

produces this output:

```
                    AMT DUE
        BALANCE
```

See Figure 2.6 for examples of PRINT statements with TAB.

```
10 PRINT TAB(23); "LOCATION REPORT"
20 PRINT
30 PRINT "NAME"; TAB(25); "TELEPHONE EXT"; TAB(45); "DEPARTMENT"
40 PRINT
50 PRINT "ADAMS"; TAB(29); "1225"; TAB(45); "CREDIT"
60 PRINT "TURNER"; TAB(29); "1446"; TAB(45); "AUDITING"
70 PRINT
80 PRINT TAB(10); "END OF REPORT"
```

```
            1         2         3         4         5         6
   1........0.........0.........0.........0.........0.........0...
                   LOCATION REPORT

   NAME                   TELEPHONE EXT     DEPARTMENT

   ADAMS                      1225          CREDIT
   TURNER                     1446          AUDITING

           END OF REPORT
```

FIGURE 2.6   PRINT statements with TAB

SPC Function

Another function that controls horizontal spacing on the line is SPC(*n*). Like the TAB function, SPC can be used only with PRINT and LPRINT statements. SPC, however, differs from TAB in that TAB moves the cursor or print pointer to an absolute position on the line, whereas SPC moves the cursor or print pointer *n* spaces to the right of the last item printed. See Figure 2.7 for examples of PRINT statements with SPC.

END Statement

The END statement should be used to signify the *logical* end of a program. When the computer executes the END statement, BASIC stops program execution. If the END statement is omitted, program execution stops when the last program statement is executed. It is not necessary, however, to make END the last statement in the program listing (that is, the statement with the highest line number). You will see examples of this in later chapters.

```
10 PRINT SPC(10); "COMPUTER BOOK INVENTORY"; SPC(4); "3/20/89"
20 PRINT
30 PRINT "BASIC"; SPC(5); "1985"
40 PRINT "C"; SPC(5); "1988"
50 PRINT "PASCAL"; SPC(5); "1987"
```

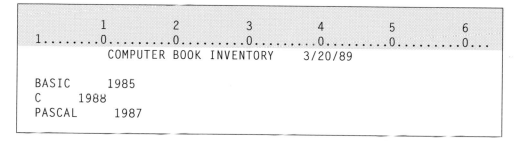

FIGURE 2.7 PRINT statements with SPC

Summary

- There are six steps to take in developing a program. Remember it is important to *think* first and code later.

  1. Define the problem the program is to solve.
     It is critical to understand the needs of the user.
  2. Determine the program's output and input.
     Again check with the user to determine that the planned output is appropriate.
  3. Design the program's logic.
     Three logic design tools are flowcharts, structure charts, and pseudocode.
  4. Code the program.
     Statements are the instructions in a BASIC program.

  Functions are built-in capabilities that BASIC provides for use with BASIC statements.

  5. Test the program.
     Correct syntax and logic errors.
     BASIC commands are useful for editing and executing programs and for program storage and maintenance.
  6. Assemble the program documentation.
     This is an important step for later program maintenance.

- The BASIC statement PRINT is used to display information on the screen. Horizontal spacing can be achieved by

  - Spaces between the quotes
  - Commas
  - SPC function
  - TAB function

■ Chapter 2 describes the following BASIC commands:

FILES A command that displays a directory of the programs and files stored on the disk.

LIST A command that displays on the screen the program lines currently in the computer's memory.

LLIST A command that prints the program lines in memory on the printer.

LOAD A command that transfers a program from secondary storage into the computer's memory.

NEW A command that erases the current program from the computer's memory, readying the system for the entry of a new program.

RENUM A command that renumbers the lines of the program currently in the computer's memory.

RUN A command that executes the program in the computer's memory.

SAVE A command that copies the program currently in the computer's memory to secondary storage.

■ Chapter 2 also describes the following BASIC statements and functions:

CLS A statement that clears the screen and places the cursor in the upper left corner of the screen.

END A statement that stops execution of the program.

LPRINT A statement that prints characters on the printer.

PRINT A statement that displays characters on the screen.

REM A statement signifying that a program line or portion of a line is a comment.

SPC(n) A function that controls horizontal spacing by moving a pointer n number of columns.

TAB(n) A function that controls horizontal spacing by moving a pointer to column n.

Review Questions

1. Why is program planning important?

2. What is the program development cycle? What are the six steps in the cycle?

3. What is meant by the term *user*?

4. What is an algorithm?

5. What is a coding form?

6. What is a syntax error?

7. What is a logic error?

8. What is meant by "playing computer"?

9. What is program maintenance?

10. Why is program documentation important?

11. What is a flowchart?

12. What are the two categories of instructions provided by BASIC? Describe when each type would be required.

13. What happens when you give an instruction without a line number?

14. What is the purpose of the line number in an instruction?

15. Describe the purpose of the following BASIC commands:

NEW RUN LOAD
LIST   SAVE FILES

16. What is the difference between LIST and LLIST?

17. How many characters may a program name have?

18. What extension is attached to a program name if the programmer does not supply one?

19. Why is it a good practice to save your program regularly while you are working on it?

20. What is the purpose of the PRINT statement?

21. What is the difference between PRINT and LPRINT?

22. What is the purpose of ending a PRINT statement with a semicolon?

23. What is the purpose of the comma in a PRINT statement?

24. Consider the statement

```
100 PRINT TAB(5); "EXCELLENT"
```

Does the TAB function cause the output EXCELLENT to be displayed five spaces to the right of the current cursor position or in column 5 of the line?

25. True or false: The two statements below are identical in effect:

```
100 PRINT "GOOD GRIEF"
100 PRINT "GOOD"; TAB(6); "GRIEF"
```

26. True or false: The two statements below are identical in effect:

```
100 PRINT "JOHNNY"; TAB(20); "APPLESEED"
100 PRINT "JOHNNY"; SPC(20); "APPLESEED"
```

27. What is the difference between the TAB and the SPC functions?

28. Why is it a good idea to use the CLS statement before displaying information on the screen?

29. Does the REM statement affect the output of the program? Why not?

30. What is the purpose of the END statement? Is this statement always mandatory in a BASIC program? What happens if the END statement is omitted?

Problems

1. Describe the tasks in each of the following flowcharts:

a.   **b.**

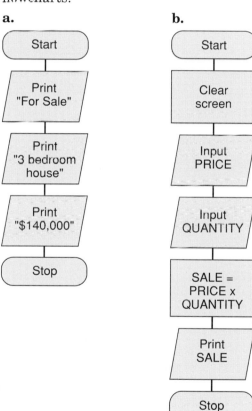

c.

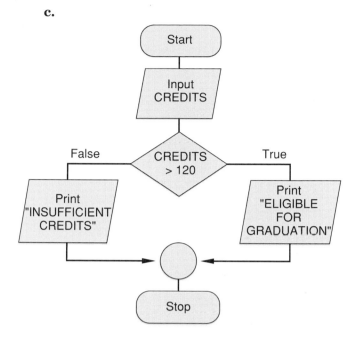

2. Draw a flowchart depicting your morning activities as you prepare for work or school.

3. Draw a flowchart illustrating the steps in making a peanut-butter- and-jelly sandwich.

4. Find the syntax errors, if any, in the following PRINT statements:

a. `10 PRINT "HOW ARE YOU? ": "COURTNEY"`

b. `10 "HAPPY NEW YEAR"`

c. `10 PRINT "WHERE ARE YOU?`

d. `10 PRINT TAB (25); "MONTHLY REPORT"`

e. `10 PRIN SPC(44); "SECTION 1"`

f. `10 PRINT ,,,,, "LAKE TAHOE"`

5. Find the logic errors, if any, in the following PRINT statements:

a. A statement to print three names on the same line, each name separated by one space from the name(s) next to it:

```
10 PRINT "JOHN"; "MARY"; "JANE"
```

b. A statement to print six words on the same line:

```
10 PRINT "one", "two", "three",
         "four","five", "six"
```

c. Two statements that print a school name and mascot on the same line:

```
10 PRINT "Hereford High School ";
20 PRINT "Bull"
```

d. A statement to print a title starting in column 20:

```
10 PRINT SPC(20); "MOVIE RATINGS"
```

e. A statement to separate a city and state by three spaces:

```
10 PRINT "Houston"; TAB(3); "Texas"
```

6. Describe the result of the following PRINT statements. Indicate in which column each item starts.

a. `10 PRINT "ESSEX"`

b. `10 PRINT TAB(5); "SPARKS";`
`      TAB(20); "MD"`

c. `10 PRINT "I LIKE ";`
`20 PRINT "BASIC"`

d. `10 PRINT`

e. `10 PRINT "NAME", "ADDR", "PHONE"`

f. `10 TAB(30)`
`20 PRINT "ALEXANDRIA"`

g. `10 PRINT TAB(15); "McArthur";`
`      TAB(6); "Park"`

h. `10 PRINT TAB(14); "Cannery Row";`
`      SPC(5); "by Steinbeck"`

7. By using different characters on the keyboard you can create "computer art." Write programs to display the following examples. Note the print columns where the output is to be displayed.

a.

	1–10	11–20	21–30
	1 2 3 4 5 6 7 8 9 0	1 2 3 4 5 6 7 8 9 0	1 2 3 4 5 6 7 8 9
01	*		
02	***		
03	*****		
04	*******		
05	*********		
06			
07	HAPPY HOLIDAYS		
08			

b.

	31–40	41–50	51–60
	1 2 3 4 5 6 7 8 9 0	1 2 3 4 5 6 7 8 9 0	1 2 3 4 5 6 7 8 9
01	XXXXX		
02	X	VX	
03	X	VV X	
04	(X O O X)		
05	X) X		
06	XXXXX		
07	XXX		
08	XX⁻⁻XX		
09	X⁻⁻⁻XX		
10	XXXXX⁻⁻)		
11	XXXXX⁻⁻)		
12	XXX⁻⁻)		
13			
14	HELLO CHARLIE BROWN		
15			

8. Write a program to print your name in block letters, as in the example shown.

```
PPPPPP            A              TTTTTTTTTTTT
P     P          A A                 T
P     P          A  A                T
PPPPPP          AAAAAAA              T
P              A      A              T
P             A        A             T
P            A          A            T
```

9. Describe what happens as each command is executed in the following sequence of commands:

```
LOAD"ACCTS
LIST 100-200
100
RUN
DELETE 300-350
LLIST 100-
SAVE"A:ACCTS
SAVE"ACCTS.REV
```

10. Write the BASIC commands to perform the following operations:

a. Erase the program currently in memory.
b. Retrieve a program named PROJ1 from the disk in drive B.
c. Display the program lines on the screen.
d. Display the lines 220 to 400, inclusive, on the screen.
e. Print hard copy of all the lines from 300 to the end of the program.

f. Display the directory for the disk in drive A.

g. Erase the program named INVENT.BAS from the disk.

h. Store the program in memory on the disk in drive A, naming it PROJ1.REV.

11.a. Write a program to print your name, street address, and city/state/zipcode on 3 consecutive lines of the screen.

b. Now change the program so that it inserts a blank line after your name and after the street address.

12. a. Write a program to print OLIVER TWIST on one line and CHARLES DICKENS on the next line.

b. Place a semicolon at the end of the first PRINT statement. What is the result of executing this program?

c. Change the semicolon to a comma. What is the result of executing this program?

13. Write a program to produce the following report. Use commas to format thc output.

```
          JOGGING RECORD

DATE            MILES        TIME

6/16/89          3           31.2
6/18/89          5           52.6
6/21/89          3           32.8
```

14. Write a program to produce the following report. Use the TAB function to center the report horizontally on the screen.

```
          GRADE REPORT

Course                    Grade

Sociology                 B
BASIC                     A
Calculus                  C
English                   B


          END OF REPORT
```

15. Write a program to produce the following report. Use the SPC function to format the output.

```
       MOVIE RATINGS

FATAL ATTRACTION          R
CINDERELLA                G
TOP GUN                   PG-13
```

Using the Data Disk

You will find a section called "Using the Data Disk" at the end of most chapters in this book. This section of each chapter gives you hands-on practice with the concepts you learned in the chapter. This first section tells you how to load BASIC; how to enter, edit, and run a BASIC program; and how to print and save a program for later use. Your instructor may have you use other commands because of differences in system requirements.

Start-up Procedure

1. Dual floppy users

   a. Insert the DOS disk in drive A.
   b. Turn on the computer if it is not already on.
   c. Enter the date and time, if necessary.
   d. Insert the data disk in drive B.
   e. After the A prompt, type

   ```
   B: <Enter>
   ```

   This command changes the default drive from A to B so that you do not have to keep typing B in all the commands that reference your data disk in drive B.

   f. When the B prompt appears, type

   ```
   A:BASICA <Enter>
   ```

   g. Now you are ready to work with BASIC.

2. Hard disk users

   a. Turn on the computer if it is not already on.
   b. Enter the date and time if necessary.
   c. Insert the data disk in drive A.
   d. After the C prompt, type

   ```
   A: <Enter>
   ```

   This command changes the default drive from C to A so that you do not have to keep typing A in all the commands that reference your data disk in drive A.

   e. When the A prompt appears, type

   ```
   C:\DOS\BASICA <Enter>
   ```

   f. Now you are ready to work with BASIC.

Entering a BASIC Program

Before entering the following program, press the Caps Lock key so that all text is in uppercase letters. BASIC does not require uppercase, but most people find uppercase easier to read. Also remember to press the Enter key when you are ready to send a statement or command to the computer.

```
NEW
10 'Sample Program
20 PRINT "RYAN MICHAEL"
30 PRINT "ESSEX COMMUNITY COLLEGE"
40 END
```

- Press the F4 function key.

- Type SAMPLE and press the Enter key.

- Enter the following:

  ```
  FILES
  ```

  Note the program SAMPLE.BAS on the directory. The extension .BAS indicates a BASIC program.

- Enter the following:

  ```
  CLS
  ```

  Note that the screen has been cleared and that the Ok prompt is in the upper left corner.

- Press the F1 function key and the Enter key to list the program.

- Press the F2 function key to execute the program.

Editing a BASIC Program

You can edit any line on the screen by (1) using the cursor-movement keys (arrow keys on the right side of the keyboard) to move the cursor to the line you want to change, (2) making the change, and (3) pressing the Enter key.

- Using the cursor-movement keys, position the cursor on line 20 under the M in MICHAEL.

- Press the Ins key.

- Type the following:

  ```
  PATRICK (space bar) <Enter>
  ```

  Line 20 now looks as follows:

  ```
  20 PRINT "RYAN PATRICK MICHAEL"
  ```

- Move the cursor to a blank screen line.

- Press F2 to test the change.

- Position the cursor on line 30 under the C in COMMUNITY.

- Press the Del key 10 times. Press Enter. Line 30 now looks as follows:

  ```
  30 PRINT "ESSEX COLLEGE"
  ```

- Move the cursor to a blank screen line. Type the following line, duplicating the misspelling:.

  ```
  25 PINT "BALTIMORE"
  ```

- Type RUN to execute the program.

- Use the Ins key to correct the syntax error in line 25.

■ Add the following lines to your program:

```
35 PRINT "MARYLAND ";
           "21237"
```

In this example, you need to place part of a program statement on a second line. You can send the cursor directly to the next line by pressing the Ctrl and J keys or the Ctrl and Enter keys.

■ Type RUN to test the changes.

■ Type the following:

```
RENUM
```

■ Type LIST (or press F1) to check the renumbering of your program.

■ Move the cursor to line 30. Change the number 30 to 40 and press the Enter key. Now move the cursor to the original line 40 (it should already be in the correct position). Change the number to 30 and press the Enter key. Type LIST to see the changes. Notice that the two program statements are now reversed.

Note: You can stop the execution of your program by pressing the Ctrl and Break keys. These keys are handy if you are ever stuck in an endless loop. This same keypress sequence interrupts the scrolling of a program listing. Pressing the Ctrl and Num Lock keys also interrupts the scrolling of a program listing. To resume the listing of the program, press any key.

Additional Practice

■ Type the following:

```
NAME"SAMPLE.BAS" AS "TEST.BAS"
```

■ Type the following to test the change:

```
FILES
```

Notice that SAMPLE.BAS no longer exists on the directory; TEST.BAS has replaced it.

■ Type the commands:

```
CLS
LIST
DELETE 20-30
LIST -40
LIST 45-
```

■ Type the following command:

```
SYSTEM
```

■ Now reload BASIC.

■ Type the command:

```
LIST
```

Notice that the BASIC program you were working on is no longer in the computer's memory.

■ Type the following commands:

```
RUN"TEST
LIST
```

Note that this program is one you saved earlier. The changes you made since then are not in the program.

■ Type the following command:

```
SHELL
```

■ Type DIR and press the Enter key.

■ Type EXIT to return to BASIC.

■ Enter the following command:

```
LIST
```

Notice that the BASIC program you were working on is still in the computer's memory. Use the SYSTEM command when you have completed your session at the computer; use SHELL if you want to return to the operating system temporarily.

■ Enter the following commands:

```
KILL"TEST.BAS
FILES
```

Notice that TEST.BAS no longer exists on the directory.

Printing

■ Enter the following commands:

```
LOAD"CH2-1.DD
LIST
```

The program is listed on the screen.

■ To display the program on the printer, type LLIST.

■ To display the program and its output on the screen and on the printer at the same time:

- Press Ctrl/PrtSc.
- Press F1 <Enter>.
  The program is listed on the screen and on the printer. Press F2. The program output is displayed on the screen and the printer.
- Press Ctrl/PrtSc to stop printing on the printer.

■ To display the image currently on the screen, press Shift/PrtSc.

- Press F2.
- Press Shift/PrtSc.

The image currently on the screen is sent to the printer.

Program Tracing

The TRON and TRACE commands are useful debugging tools. Sometimes the logic flow of a program is difficult to follow. Use the TRON command to trace the logic of a program.

- Type TRON or press the F7 function key.

- Type RUN. Notice that the line numbers of the instructions executed are listed.

- Type TROFF or press the F8 function key to turn off the trace.

END OF SESSION

Chapter Three

Program Design and Development

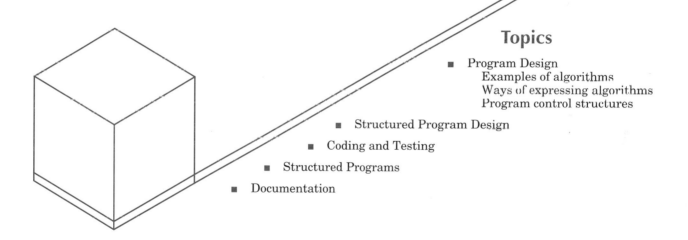

Topics

- Program Design
  Examples of algorithms
  Ways of expressing algorithms
  Program control structures
- Structured Program Design
- Coding and Testing
- Structured Programs
- Documentation

INTRODUCTION

Now that you have had a chance to work with BASIC and are comfortable with a microcomputer, you are ready to begin solving more challenging programming problems. This chapter introduces techniques that help you solve problems and design programs that are relatively easy to test and maintain. As your programs become more complex, these techniques become ever more useful.

Chapter 2 described six steps in the development of a computer program:

1. Define the problem

2. Determine the output and input

3. Design the program logic

4. Code the program

5. Test the program

6. Assemble the program documentation

If you were to interpret the term *computer programming* very narrowly, you could say that it is done only in step 4 because only at that point do you write instructions for the computer in a language it can understand.

Most programmers and most texts, including this one, use a more general definition of programming: *Computer programming* is the process of developing a reliable, revisable program that accomplishes specific objectives. Steps 3–6 are all a part of that process.

Step 3, *program design*, requires the preparation of a solution to a programming problem as defined in steps 1 and 2. This is the most difficult aspect of programming because it is the least mechanical. A major objective of this text is to help readers learn a technique, often called *structured program design*, that simplifies the job of determining solutions to programming problems. Much of this chapter is devoted to describing this technique, and subsequent chapters illustrate its use with a variety of applications.

Although our discussions of programming problems begin with program design, this is a simplification of the real world. Remember, for all nontrivial problems, the problem definition step requires considerable effort. In fact, people with different professional assignments may participate in the completion of steps 1 and 2. One or more *systems analysts* determine what the complete system (in which the program is to operate) is supposed to do. Then *system designers* specify what each individual program in the system is supposed to do. In particular, they determine what results the program is to produce and what data and information are required so that the program can produce those results.

Even though we usually provide a reasonably clear statement of each programming problem and of the specifications for the program's output and input, we emphasize that this is not where the process begins in reality. At this point (step 3) in the process, the users of the program should have already approved the specifications on which you, the programmer, are beginning to work.

PROGRAM DESIGN

Program design, step 3 in the program development cycle, is the process of specifying program logic. The objective is to develop an ordered list of actions to accomplish whatever it is that the program is supposed to do. As you learned in Chapter 2, this list is often called an *algorithm*. *Algorithm development* is another term for this process.

Examples of Algorithms

As an example of an ordered list of actions, consider what you do when you buy a canned soft drink from a vending machine:

- Get money that the machine will accept.
- Go to the machine.
- Insert the coins in the slot.
- Decide what drink to buy.
- Press the button for that variety.
- Wait for the can to appear.
- Remove the can from the dispenser.
- Retrieve and put away any change you may receive.
- Open the can.
- Enjoy the drink.
- Dispose of the can.

The position of some of the actions in this list could be interchanged; for example, you put coins in the slot after you decide what drink to buy. The order of other actions, however, is very important; you won't get a drink if you press the select button before you deposit sufficient money; you can't retrieve the drink before the can appears, and you can't drink before opening the can. When you are developing an algorithm for a computer program, you must take care to put the actions in the proper order.

Not all actions that may be required are listed in the previous paragraph; for example, the machine may not accept all of your coins, and you may have to retrieve those it won't accept and insert others. Computer programs will not be useful if you develop them from algorithms that do not incorporate all of the situations likely to occur.

Consider now the problem of calculating the sales tax and total cost of an item purchased in a retail store. Many computer programs incorporate a solution to this problem. Solving the problem requires:

1. Finding out the price of the item
2. Calculating the amount of the sales tax by multiplying the item price by the sales tax rate
3. Calculating the total cost by adding the sales tax amount to the item price

Order is also important in this example. Suppose you list the actions in this way:

1. The total cost is the sales tax plus the item price.

2. The sales tax is the item price times the sales tax rate.

3. Find out the item price.

These three steps list everything necessary to solve the problem, but you can't get a solution when you follow them in this order. In fact, you can do nothing at all because you know neither the item cost nor the amount of sales tax when you try to calculate the total cost in step 1.

Ways of Expressing Algorithms

These ordered lists of actions known as algorithms may be written in various forms. Chapter 2 introduced flowcharts as a way of expressing algorithms. The two algorithms in the preceding section are written as *informal notes*. This method is a good way to write initial versions of algorithms because you can express your thoughts in words easily in informal notes.

Another way of writing algorithms is with pseudocode, also known as *pcode*. *Pseudocode* is a list of statements written in a form very similar to computer code, but with a more relaxed syntax. The exact form of the pseudocode may vary according to the personal preference of the writer or the employer; it should, however, always be precise enough to describe what is to be done and clear enough to be understood by a person who is not a programmer. Pseudocode for the tax example might look like this:

```
ALGORITHM TO COMPUTE SALES TAX AND TOTAL ITEM COST
    sales tax rate = .05
    get item price
    sales tax = item price x sales tax rate
    total item cost = item price + sales tax
```

Program Control Structures

So far, the sample algorithms have been simple; there has been no need to repeat steps or to select among alternatives. Real-life situations frequently involve both repetition and selection. For example, consider the actions of a barber on a busy day:

```
dowhile there are customers waiting for a haircut
    say: "Who's next?"
    seat the customer who gets to the chair first
    start chatting with the customer
    fasten a bib under the customer's chin
    trim the customer's hair
    remove the bib
    allow the customer to get out of the chair
    obtain payment from the customer
    say goodbye to the customer
    stop chatting with the customer
end dowhile
```

An example of selection is this set of directions for choosing a fast-food lunch:

```
if today is a pizza day
        then choose Pizza Hut
if a taco sounds good
        then choose Taco Bell
if fish is a good idea
        then choose Long John Silver's
if a hamburger sounds good
        then if a sundae for dessert is important
                then choose McDonald's
                else if a salad bar is important
                        then choose Wendy's
```

In these two examples, the pseudocode contains *program control structures* to repeat a set of actions and to choose between alternative actions. The first example contains the structure that controls repetition; it is indicated by the words *dowhile. . .end dowhile*. The pseudocode means that the actions between "dowhile" and "end dowhile" are to be repeated as long as the conditions that follow the dowhile are true. This repetition is often called a *loop*. Because of the use of the word *dowhile*, the repetition structure is also referred to as a *dowhile* loop.

The second example illustrates the selection structure. *If, then*, and *else* are the words that implement it. The pseudocode means this: *if* some condition is true, *then* perform some action. Sometimes the pseudocode includes an alternative action that is to be performed when the condition is not true; this alternative is written in a statement beginning with *else*. Programmers frequently call this structure *IF/THEN* or *IF/THEN/ELSE*.

A more realistic problem that you solve with the selection and repetition structures is the sales tax problem modified so that the program (1) continues as long as there are items to process and (2) adds no sales tax to food items. The modified algorithm can be written in pseudocode in this way:

```
sales tax rate = .05
dowhile there are more items
        get the item price
        get the item type
        if the item type = grocery
                then total cost = item price
                else sales tax = item price x sales tax rate
                        total cost = item price + sales tax
end dowhile
```

Although there are no formal rules for writing pseudocode, we suggest the following guidelines:

1. Begin each statement on a new line

2. Use simple and short phrases, such as:

```
read quantity
write record
add 1 to total sales
```

3. Express computations in English-like statements such as:

```
net pay = gross pay - deductions
test avg = (test1 + test2 + test3) / 3
```

4. To select between alternatives, use IF/THEN/ELSE, like this:

```
if balance < 0
     then print "insufficient funds"
     else print "check approved"
```

Notice the indentation of *then* and *else*

5. To indicate the repetition of a set of actions, begin the loop with *dowhile* . . . and end it with *end dowhile*. Indent all statements within the loop. For example:

```
dowhile not end of file
     read record
     print record
end dowhile
```

STRUCTURED PROGRAM DESIGN

Solutions for complex programming problems are difficult to describe in a single pseudocode algorithm, and, once described, they are equally difficult to understand. *Structured design* is a technique that helps you to avoid both difficulties. It is an approach to problem solving in which you divide a complex problem into simpler subproblems. You apply this process to each of the subproblems until the only problems remaining cannot be subdivided again.

Figure 3.1 illustrates this "divide-and-conquer" approach to problem solving. In that example, the original programming problem has been divided into four subproblems. Of those subproblems, 1 and 4 are simple and need not be divided again. However, subproblems 2 and 3 are sufficiently complex to be decomposed; subproblem 2 is divided into three parts, and subproblem 3 is divided into two parts. These parts of a program are called *modules*. A well-designed module is a set of instructions that performs a single function in the program.

To understand this strategy of breaking down a problem into easy-to-solve parts, consider the problem of calculating an employee's pay. This problem has three major components:

1. Get the input data (hours worked and pay rate).

2. Perform the calculations.

3. Report the results.

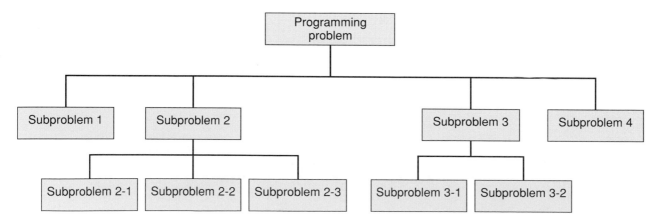

FIGURE 3.1   Problem decomposition

These three steps of obtaining data (input), processing it, and reporting the results (output) are common to the solution of many programming problems. Try this as a first-level decomposition of your programming problems, and often your problem will be defined almost completely.

Although this problem is nearly solved, step 2—perform the calculations—can be decomposed still further into two parts. (In a real situation, many calculations are required for this task, but we have simplified the requirements for this example.)

1. Calculate regular pay.

2. Calculate overtime pay.

This decomposition is illustrated in Figure 3.2. Another name for the problem-solving approach we have just described is *top-down design*. Figure 3.2 illustrates how to start at the "top" with the original problem and work "down," decomposing problems into their components on the way.

Charts like the one in Figure 3.2 are called *structure charts*, *hierarchy charts*, or *visual tables of contents* (*VTOC*s). They show the purpose of a program, identify the general steps (or functions) required to solve the programming problem, and show the relationship of those functions to one another. To understand how they do this, look at Figure 3.2 again. The top box in the chart describes the general purpose of the program. The next level (level 1) contains boxes for each of the program's primary functions. Lower-level boxes represent functions that help accomplish the tasks of higher-level modules. The structure chart for a program is analogous to an organization chart, such as the organization chart of a typical college (see Figure 3.3).

Each box in a structure chart represents a program module. Selecting the statements for a module can be difficult. All the statements in the module should contribute to accomplishing a single task. Modules that perform a single function are called functional or *cohesive*. Avoid modules of "low" cohesion that group statements only because "they had to go somewhere."

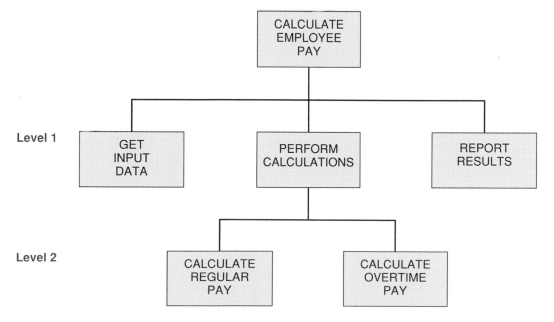

FIGURE 3.2   Structure chart for Calculate Employee Pay

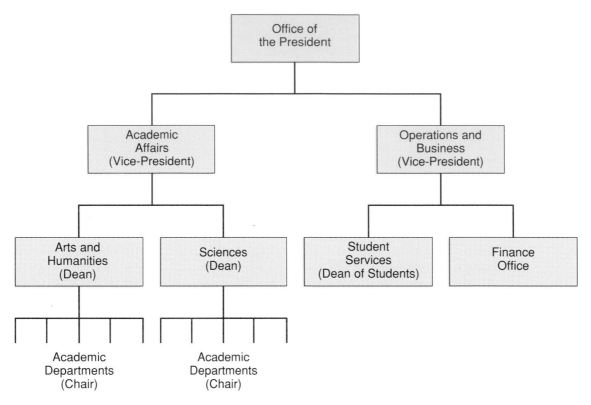

FIGURE 3.3   Organization chart for a small college

If you name the modules in your structure charts by the tasks they perform, you can recognize the ones that are cohesive. They have names like these:

```
PRINT USER INSTRUCTIONS
READ DATA
DISPLAY ERROR MESSAGES
PRINT TOTALS
CALCULATE DEDUCTIONS
```

Modules that are not cohesive have names like these:

```
READ AND WRITE   (more than one verb)
TERMINATION      (nondescriptive and time-related)
```

When writing short programs, you may not always be able to separate each function into a module without creating many one-line modules. Remember, however, that one-line modules are acceptable and are often preferable to an uncohesive, utility module.

After you identify the program modules, you can use flowcharts or pseudocode to describe the logic. Figure 3.4 shows pseudocode for the functional modules of the employee pay problem.

Programmers often use a structure chart to plan the overall organization of a program and to identify its component modules. The steps in program planning are analogous to the steps you normally follow when writing a term paper: First, outline the topics; next, write a rough draft; and worry about details like sentence structure and spelling only after these steps are completed. The list on page 47 shows the comparable steps in program development.

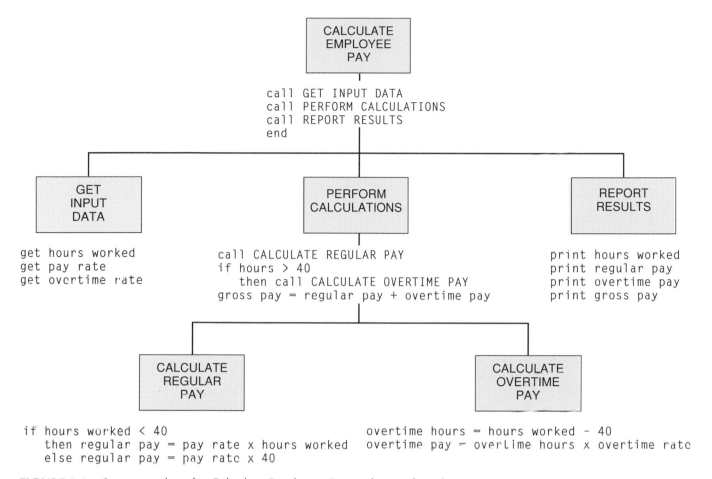

FIGURE 3.4   Structure chart for Calculate Employee Pay with pseudocode

Term Paper	Program Development
Topic outline	Structure chart
Rough draft	Pseudocode
Final draft	Coding

Validate Dates Example

Now that you know how structured design works, look at how it can help you solve the problem of validating birthdates read by the program in the form *mm-dd-yy*. The first step is to break down the problem into its input, process, and output portions. The input and output portions are both simple: The only input is the date. The only output is a message reporting the date's validity. There are, however, several components to the processing:

1. First, the appropriate portions of the input date are assigned to *Month*, *Day*, and *Year*. For example, if the input date is 05-24-70, then *Month* has the value 05, *Day* has the value 24, and *Year* has the value 70.

2. Next the values for *Month* and *Day* are tested to see if they are valid. (Assume that any combination of digits in the year position year is valid.)

This decomposition is shown at level 2 in Figure 3.5.

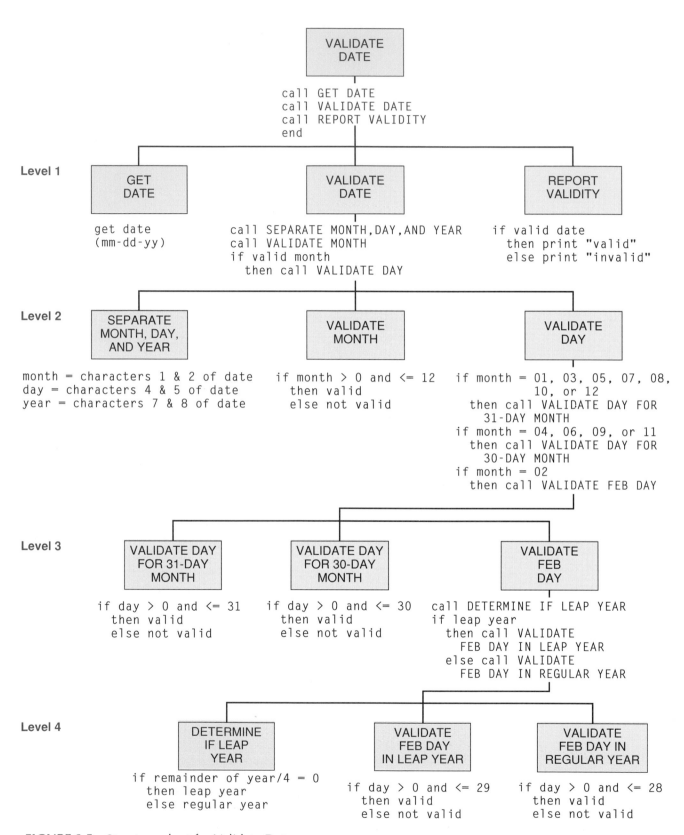

FIGURE 3.5 Structure chart for Validate Date

The validation of *Month* is simple; its value must be in the range of 01 to 12. To validate *Day*, you have to consider three different situations: months of 31 days, months of 30 days, and February. This decomposition is shown at level 3 in Figure 3.5.

A simple but effective test to see if a module should be decomposed is to identify the functions it must perform. If it must perform more than one function, it can probably be decomposed further. Three separate functions are necessary to validate *Day* if *Month* is February:

1. Determine if *Year* represents a leap year.

2. Validate *Day* for February if it is a leap year.

3. Validate *Day* for February if it is not a leap year.

Consequently, this module can be decomposed. The decomposition is shown in level 4 of Figure 3.5.

At the lowest level of decomposition, it is easy to specify the tasks the modules are to perform. It is useful to include pseudocode instructions in the structure chart, as you see in Figure 3.5. These instructions provide a complete and easy-to-grasp explanation of what a program does and how it does it. Figures like this one accompany most program illustrations in this text.

Notice that some thought is necessary to decide what processing must be done to validate dates. Also, notice that you could decompose the problem in other ways; when problems are complex, there is often no single, best solution. Finally, realize that other programmers may have attacked your problem before. As a programmer, you can adapt their algorithms to your programming situation instead of spending your time reinventing the wheel.

Structured Walk-Through

Once you have a completed program design, it is essential that you review it carefully yourself. Often, however, after you work on a program for a while, errors are no longer obvious. If you are fortunate enough to have friends or colleagues who are willing to examine what you have done, by all means take advantage of their offer. Many programming departments use a process called a *structured walk-through* to review program design. In that process, colleagues scrutinize a program design, making sure that it meets all design requirements and that the logic is correct.

CODING AND TESTING

Program *coding*, step 4 in the program development cycle, is the process of translating notes or pseudocode into BASIC or another programming language. Once you have designed the logic for your program, the coding process is usually easy.

The structure chart you created in the design process can help you organize your code. Begin your code with the highest-level module. Then you can either code the modules in each level in the order reflected on the chart (level 1, left to right, then level 2, left to right, and so on) or you can code all the modules in each top-to-bottom path, moving from left to right. Either way, the structure chart gives readers of your program a handy guide to the program's organization.

Programs written using the structured design process have proved to have fewer errors than other programs. Rarely, however, is new code ever error free. *Testing* is the process of correcting program logic and code. Errors are usually of one of two types. You saw one type illustrated in Chapter 2. Mistakes in typing the code caused the syntax errors that prevented the program from running. Because the BASIC interpreter finds syntax errors for you, they are often easy to remedy.

In Chapter 2, you also saw an example of the other type of error, an error in program logic. The incorrect output in that simple program was easy to spot and correct. Unfortunately, errors in program logic are seldom that easy to remove. One benefit of structured design is that you can integrate coding and testing by testing each module of code as you add it to a program. This process, called *top-down-testing*, is helpful because it is much easier to find logic errors in a relatively small, single-function module than it is in a complete program. (See Chapter 4 for an example of top-down testing.)

STRUCTURED PROGRAMS

If you have looked at even a few programming textbooks, you may have wondered just what a "structured" program is. Any confusion you have is certainly justified. *Structured programming* and *structured program* mean something quite different to different writers (and different instructors).

One meaning of the term *structured program* is a program with no GOTO statements. GOTO is a BASIC statement that sends program control to a line number named in the GOTO statement. The standard program control structures make GOTO statements unnecessary (see the box on the next page), and programs composed of only those structures can be thought of as "structured."

Structured programming also refers to programming using structured design techniques. The resulting programs are composed primarily of functional modules and are organized according to a structure chart.

In this text we incorporate both these meanings and considerably more when we refer to a structured program. Unless another qualifier is attached, we use both *program* and *structured program* to refer to a program with *all* of these characteristics:

1. Program logic developed with structured program design techniques

2. Appropriate documentation at the beginning of the program

3. Descriptive labels on program modules

4. Program execution controlled only with the standard programming structures

5. Program statements indented or aligned wherever appropriate

6. Each program statement on a separate line

PROGRAM CONTROL STRUCTURES AND GOTO STATEMENTS

During the first two decades of computer programming, programmers often wrote code with little thought to overall program design or to changes that might be required later. Their main goals were to have a program that worked and that used as little computer memory and computing time as possible. Altering these programs proved to be very difficult because it was so hard for the programmer making the changes to decipher the code.

An early step toward structured program design occurred at the International Colloquium on Algebraic Linguistics and Automata Theory held in Israel in 1964. There, two mathematicians named Bohm and Jacopini demonstrated that any program logic, no matter how complex, could be expressed by using a combination of just three control structures: sequence, repetition, and selection. Because of its theoretical nature, this work received very little attention at the time, but it was published in *Communication of the ACM*, journal of the Association for Computing Machinery, two years later.[1]

Two later events sparked interest in this concept of structured programming. First, in 1968, a letter by Edsger W. Dijkstra of the Netherlands to the editor of the *Communications of the ACM* attracted widespread attention.[2] Professor Dijkstra wrote that "the GOTO statement should be abolished from all higher level programming languages. . . . It is an invitation to make a mess of one's program." Dijkstra contended that the use of the GOTO statement has "disastrous effects," making a program look like a "bowl of spaghetti." At the time, few programmers would dream of writing a program without using GOTO statements, but Bohm and Jacopini had proved that it could be done.

The second event to attract interest in structured programming was the "*New York Times* Project" directed by Harlan Mills and F. Terry Baker, both IBM employees. The objective was to create an on-line information system to provide access to articles that had appeared in the newspaper. This was the first large-scale test of the use of programming structures and procedures, and it was amazingly successful. Programmer productivity was four to six times higher than was common on projects using traditional methods. The project was completed ahead of schedule and under budget estimates. The project's error rate was only 4 per 10,000 lines of code.

[1]Bohm, C. and I. Jacopini. "Flow Diagrams, Turing Machines, and Languages with Only Two Formation Rules," *Communications of the ACM*, vol. 9, no. 5 (May 1966), pp. 366–71.
[2]Dijkstra, E. W. "GOTO Statement Considered Harmful," *Communications of the ACM*, vol. 11, no. 3 (March 1968), pp. 147–48.

Programs with these characteristics have at least five very important advantages over other programs:

1. They are easier to write, and thus also quicker and cheaper to write. This is because the programming problem has been reduced to a series of easily described tasks and because just the standard programming structures are used to construct the program.

2. They are easier to read and understand. The meaningful names, formatting techniques, and the standard programming structures all contribute to this end.

3. They are easier to test. Testing is easier because they are easier to understand and because each module can be tested independently.

4. They are easier to modify. One reason for this is the programs' readability. Another is their modularity; usually only part of a program must be changed, and having each program function in a separate module simplifies making changes. Ease of modification is an especially important requirement today. Seldom does a program meet a user's needs for long. As the user's needs change, the program must change also. So much programmer time is spent in changing programs that costs for *program maintenance*, the term for changing programs to keep them current with user and system requirements, often exceed the costs of initial program development.

5. They are more reliable because they can be tested more thoroughly and can be modified more readily.

We close this section with some advice to those of you who have thoughts of becoming professional programmers. A professional programmer *must* be able to develop structured programs as we have described them. This is true because a programmer should always produce the best product possible given available time and resources, and structured programs are better than the alternatives. It is also true because a programmer is not likely to get or keep a programming job without the ability to apply a structured approach to program design and to write structured program code.

DOCUMENTATION

If you follow the guidelines for structured programs listed in the previous section, your program's documentation will be nearly complete when you finish the program. The program itself will be largely self-documenting in that someone can read and understand the program without referring to much other information.

A complete documentation package includes documentation for all steps in the program development cycle:

1. A narrative describing the purpose of the program (problem definition)

2. Input and output specifications

3. Structure chart with algorithms for program modules (program design)

4. A listing of the program and a sample run

5. A description of the testing that was done to verify that the program does what it is supposed to do

In addition, written instructions for users of the program should be a part of the documentation package. Appendix F contains sample documentation packages for Programs 4.1 and 6.1.

Summary

- *Computer programming* is the process of developing a reliable, revisable program that accomplishes specific objectives.

- *Program design* is the process of specifying program logic. The objective is to develop an ordered list of actions that will accomplish whatever it is that the program is supposed to do. This ordered list is often called an *algorithm*.

- Algorithms may be written in various forms, including informal notes, pseudocode, and flowcharts.

  - *Pseudocode* is a list of statements written in a form very similar to a computer language, but with a more relaxed syntax.

- *Programming structures* or *programming control structures* provide the means to control program execution by (1) performing one action at a time, (2) repeating a set of actions, and (3) choosing among alternative actions depending on whether specified conditions are true or false. These three programming structures can be used in combination to solve *any* programming problem.

- *Structured program design* is the technique of developing a program algorithm by repeatedly subdividing the problem until the only problems remaining cannot be subdivided. This process is also referred to as *top-down design*.

  - This decomposition can be illustrated graphically with *structure* charts, also called *hierarchy charts* and *VTOCs*.

- A *program module* is a group of related program instructions. A good module performs a single function and has a label or name reflecting its function.

- Program *coding* is the process of translating from notes or pseudocode to BASIC or another programming language.

- *Testing* is the process of correcting program logic and code.

- *Structured programs* have all of the following characteristics:

  - The program logic was developed using structured program design techniques.

  - There is appropriate documentation at the beginning of the program.

  - Each program module is identified with a descriptive label.

  - Program execution is controlled only with the standard programming structures.

  - Program statements are indented or aligned wherever appropriate.

  - Each program statement is on a separate line.

- Structured programs have at least five very important advantages over other programs:

  - They are easier, and thus quicker and cheaper, to write.

  - They are easier to test.

  - They are easier to read and understand.

  - They are easier to modify.

  - They are more reliable.

- *Program maintenance* is the process of changing programs to keep them current with user and system requirements.

- A complete documentation package for a program includes:

  - A narrative describing the purpose of the program (problem definition)

  - Input and output specifications

  - A structure chart with algorithms for program modules (program design)

  - A listing of the program and a sample run

  - A description of the testing that was done to verify that the program does what it is supposed to do

  - Written instructions for users of the program

Review Questions

1. What is computer programming? Which of the six program development steps does programming incorporate?

2. How would you define *structured program design*?

3. What is an algorithm? How does an algorithm differ from program code? Why does algorithm development precede coding?

4. Why is proper order a necessity in stating algorithms?

5. What are three ways to express algorithms?

6. How would you convince someone that careful formatting of pseudocode was important?

7. Explain why a structure chart serves as a good introduction to the reader of a program.

8. What is a program module? What makes a module cohesive? What arguments can you offer for making program modules cohesive?

9. What is a structured walk-through? What differences would you expect between programs developed using this technique and those developed without it? What would you say to colleagues who worry about having their work reviewed by others?

10. What is the objective of program testing? Why is testing normally an iterative process?

11. Using the guidelines for structured programs given in this chapter, list as many differences as you can between a structured program and an unstructured one.

12. Explain why there is much more emphasis today on developing programs that are easy to maintain than there was 20 years ago.

13. Who are the users of program documentation?

Problems

1. Write algorithms for each of the following tasks. Include instructions for selection and repetition as necessary.

   a. Ordering a pizza by phone for home delivery
   b. Making a peanut butter and jelly sandwich
   c. Brushing your teeth
   d. Getting a date with someone you've never been out with
   e. Avoiding studying for an exam
   f. Getting in a car and driving away
   g. Designing a computer program
   h. Taking a multiple-choice test
   i. Baking a cake
   j. Having lunch in a fast-food hamburger restaurant

2. Design a program to convert degrees Fahrenheit to degrees Celsius. The program should accept a Fahrenheit value, calculate the Celsius equivalent, and display the result. The formula for the conversion is:

   $$°\text{Celsius} = 5/9(°\text{Fahrenheit} - 32)$$

3. Mrs. Booth is a teacher who needs a program to calculate the average of three test scores. Design a program that lets Mrs. Booth enter these four values one at a time: student name, test score 1, test score 2, and test score 3. After accepting all the values, the program should calculate the average score and then display the student's name, the three scores, and the average score.

4. The Edsel Car Rental Company rents Edsels for $35 per day plus 10 cents per mile. Design a program that determines each customer's charge. The clerks enter the number of days a car was rented and the beginning and ending mileage. Report the number of days the car was rented, the total mileage, and the total charge.

5. At a local garage, the mechanics would like a program to calculate a customer's bill. Design a program that accepts these items: the customer's name, the cost of the parts used, the hours of labor, and the labor rate. The output is a report of the customer's name, the costs for parts and labor, the tax (6% of the cost for parts), and the total cost to the customer.

6. The mortgage department at the Putnam County Bank needs a program to calculate the monthly payment for mortgages. A formula for determining payments is:

   $$\text{Payment} = \frac{\text{Rate}(1 - \text{Rate})^N}{(1 + \text{Rate})^N - 1} \times \text{Loan amount}$$

   Design a program to:

   a. Request the mortgage officer to enter (1) the loan amount, (2) the annual interest rate, and (3) the time in years.
   b. Convert the annual interest rate to the monthly rate (by dividing the annual rate by 12 and then by 100 or by 1200).
   c. Convert the time in years to monthly payments (by multiplying by 12).
   d. Calculate the payment amount.
   e. Display the result.

7. Review program designs others have done and compare their approaches to yours.

Chapter Four

Variables, Data Types, and Arithmetic

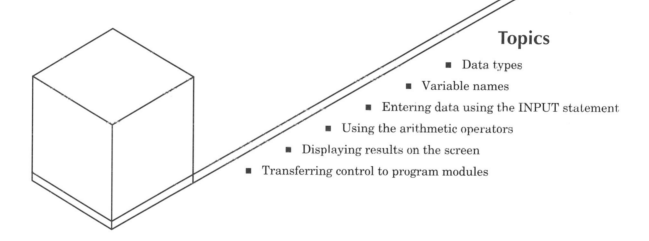

Topics

- Data types
- Variable names
- Entering data using the INPUT statement
- Using the arithmetic operators
- Displaying results on the screen
- Transferring control to program modules

Program Statements

```
GOSUB/RETURN
INPUT
LET
  CINT(n)
  INT(n)
```

INTRODUCTION

Chapter 2 described a simple program to display characters on the screen. In this chapter, we guide you through the writing of a program to accept data from the user, perform calculations, and then display the results on the screen. To write this program, you first need to learn about:

1. Two categories of data: character and numeric

2. The rules for naming variables in BASIC

3. The use of arithmetic operators

4. The following new BASIC statements: LET, INPUT, and GOSUB/ RETURN

5. The PRINT statement with numeric data

COMPONENTS OF A BASIC PROGRAM

Every language must provide a way to:

1. Specify types of data

2. Name the data elements

3. Enter, manipulate, and write data

This section describes the data types used in BASIC and the rules for naming data elements. It also gives the rules for the BASIC instructions needed to write a BASIC program that accepts data from the keyboard, performs calculations, and displays the results on the screen.

Data Types

BASIC allows for the use of two general categories of data: numeric and nonnumeric (or character) data. Nonnumeric data are the simplest to describe because they fall into a single category called a *character string*. Some examples are:

```
"9/12/84"      "S"      "Anytown, USA"
"NAMES"        "43"     "1 @ $2.20"
```

As the examples illustrate, a character string may be of varying length and may contain numbers, letters, and other characters, such as dollar signs, slashes, and spaces. The longest string that BASIC can recognize is 255 characters; the shortest is an empty string of zero characters, called a *null string* (a null string is designated by ""). These examples are enclosed in quotation marks because BASIC uses the quotes to avoid confusion between character strings and other elements of a program. The quotes are *not* part of the value of the string.

As the example "43" shows, a string may contain all digits. Sometimes this is done when a number, such as a zip code or account number, is not going to be used in a computation.

BASIC recognizes two general types of numbers: *integers*, or positive and negative whole numbers, and *real numbers*, or decimal numbers (that is, numbers that may have decimal fractions attached). Integers may be no smaller than −32768 and no larger than +32767.

There are two categories of real numbers, *single-precision* and *double-precision* numbers. The precision of a number refers to the number of digits that can be stored accurately. Single-precision numbers may be written with a decimal point and may include 7 or fewer digits. Double-precision numbers are like single-precision numbers except they may include up to 17 digits. Note the examples of each type of number.

Integers	*Real Numbers*
	Single precision
100	49.0
−340	−345.6789
2	.232323
32145	
	Double precision
	3859.1278
	9753124867554316.2
	−48.4572364

Another numeric form that the computer can display or print is *floating-point*. Floating-point numbers are expressed as multiples of some power of 10. For example, 1.7E+2 is the same as 1.7 times 10 squared, or 170. The E+2 in the number represents 10 raised to the named power (+2). Notice that in the number 1.7E+2, which has an exponent of +2, the decimal point is moved two places to the *right* to yield the number 170.

For numbers smaller than 1, a negative number follows the E and refers to 1 divided by 10 to the named power; thus 123.419E−4 is equivalent to .0123419. In this case, the exponent −4 signals that the decimal point is moved four places to the *left* to yield the number .0123419. Floating-point numbers are necessary to represent extremely large or extremely small numbers in BASIC.

In summary, there are two types of data: character and numeric. Numeric data may be expressed as integers or real numbers. A real number may be single-precision or double-precision and may be written in traditional notation or E(exponential) notation.

Variable Names

Numeric and string values can be referred to by a name. These names are called *variable names*, because the values associated with these names may be changed. BASIC associates a variable name with a storage location in the computer's memory. Whenever a variable name such as HOURLY.RATE is referenced in a program, the computer uses the value stored in the associated memory location for whatever needs to be done. For example, consider the following statement:

```
HOURLY.RATE = HOURLY.RATE + 3
```

The computer takes the value currently stored in HOURLY.RATE, adds 3 to it, and then replaces the old value with this new value in the memory location referenced by the name HOURLY.RATE. The variable name is the computer's method of referencing a value in memory. Note the association between a variable name, its value, and computer memory in Figure 4.1.

Meaningful variable names make programs easier to read and understand. BASIC makes more than adequate provision for descriptive variable names by recognizing the first 40 characters of a variable name. When writing a program, make your variable names meaningful but not so long that

FIGURE 4.1
Naming locations in
memory

HOURLY.RATE is the name of the location in memory.
The value in that location is 6.5.

HOURLY.RATE = HOURLY.RATE + 3

HOURLY.RATE is still the name of the location in memory that
you are referencing, but the value in that location is now 9.5.

keying the program is tedious. For example, if a variable name refers to an employee's net pay, use the variable name NET.PAY rather than NP. You can use widely accepted abbreviations, such as ACCT for *account*, YTD for *year-to-date*, and NUM or NO for *number*. A business may also require that specific names be used in all programs. Experience will help you develop meaningful variable names.

Variable names must begin with a letter. The other characters may be any sequence of letters, numbers, and periods. The last character of a variable name may be used to specify the type of data that the variable represents. The characters and the types they specify are shown in the next example:

Symbol	Data Type	Sample Name	Possible Value
$	Character string	CITY$	"Newport"
%	Integer	COUNTER%	32
!	Single-precision	HOURLY.PAY!	12.75
#	Double-precision	YTD.GROSS#	156320.85

You *must* attach the $ symbol to string variable names. If you do not attach any symbol to a variable name, the computer treats the value as a single-precision number.

You cannot use BASIC reserved words as variable names. This is not a serious restriction, but, if you forget about it, you may find the resulting syntax errors difficult to decipher. COLOR, DATA, ERROR, INPUT, KEY, NAME, and SPACE$ might all be descriptive of the function a variable plays in a program, but all these names generate syntax errors because they are reserved words. (Note the list of reserved words in Appendix A.)

Reserved words, however, may be used as *part* of a variable name. NEW.DATA, STUDENT.NAME$, and DATAKEY are all acceptable variable names. *Warning*: Adding a data type symbol at the end of a reserved word does *not* make it an acceptable variable name; for example, you cannot use INPUT% and COLOR$ as variable names.

One other restriction is that variable names may not begin with the letters FN because BASIC uses FN to designate a call to a function. (User-defined functions are discussed in Chapter 16.)

Here is a summary of the rules for defining variable names:

1. The name must begin with a letter, A through Z.

2. After the first letter, the other characters in the name may be any sequence of letters, numbers, and periods.

3. BASIC recognizes only the first 40 characters of a variable name.

4. The last character of a string variable name must be a $.

5. The name cannot be a reserved word, although a reserved word may be part of the name.

6. The name may not begin with FN.

It is important to note that variable names reference two categories of values. Some variable names may be assigned a constant value. A *constant* is a value that does not change during the execution of a program. The values of other variable names are assigned during program execution, and may or may not change during program execution.

LET Statement

One way to assign a value to a variable name is with the LET statement. The LET statement is BASIC's version of an *assignment* statement. Its format is:

```
[line#] [LET] <variable-name> = <expression>
```

Remember from Chapter 2 that the brackets [ ] indicate an optional element of the statement, and the angle brackets < > indicate that a valid element must be substituted for whatever is inside the angle brackets. The term *expression*, in this example, means any valid combination of constants, variables, and operators.

When BASIC encounters a LET statement, it determines the value on the right of the assignment symbol (the "equal" sign), evaluating it if necessary, and then stores that value in the memory location associated with the variable name to the left of the assignment symbol. Consider the next set of examples.

1. *Variable-name = constant*

```
100 LET FIRST.NAME$ = "RACHEL"
```

The string value "RACHEL" is placed in the memory location referenced by FIRST.NAME$, replacing any previous value in that location.

```
100 LET PAGE.LIMIT = 54
```

The numeric value 54 is placed in the memory location referenced by PAGE.LIMIT, replacing any previous value in that location.

2. *Variable-name = variable-name*

```
100 LET STATE$ = NEW.STATE$
```

The value in the memory location referenced in NEW.STATE$ is copied to the memory location referenced by STATE$. The value still remains in NEW.STATE$.

3. *Variable-name = expression*

```
100 LET PROFIT = GROSS - EXPENSES
```

The value in EXPENSES is subtracted from the value in GROSS, and the result is placed in the memory location referenced by PROFIT. The values in GROSS and EXPENSES remain unchanged. Note Figure 4.2 for a picture of what happens inside the computer when this example is executed.

Remember that the data type on the left of the LET must match the data type on the right of the statement. You cannot write a LET statement mixing string and numeric data. Type mismatch errors will occur in the following examples:

```
100 LET AVERAGE = "250"
100 LET FIRST.NAME$ = MARY
100 LET PROFIT = GROSS$ - EXPENSES
```

FIGURE 4.2
LET statement and memory locations

Possible values in memory before execution of
PROFIT = GROSS – EXPENSES

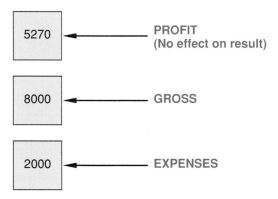

Values in memory after execution

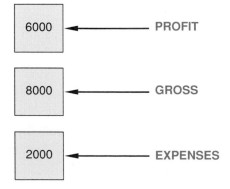

Notice that the assignment symbol, when used in a LET statement, *does not* indicate equality. The following statement illustrates this point:

```
100 LET COUNTER = COUNTER + 1
```

It is obvious that whatever COUNTER contains cannot be equal to the same value plus 1. You should read the LET statement as: COUNTER is *replaced by* the current value of COUNTER plus 1.

The word LET is optional; thus, these two BASIC statements are identical in effect:

```
100 LET PAY.RATE = 7.55
100 PAY.RATE = 7.55
```

Because the second version is simpler than the first and just as clear, we use it throughout this text.

INPUT Statement

The INPUT statement is another method of assigning a value to a variable name. It is used to halt execution of the program until the user enters a value at the keyboard. The value entered is then assigned to a variable name.

The general format of the INPUT statement is:

```
[line#] INPUT ["prompt"; or ,] <var1> [,var2] [,var-n]
```

When the computer executes the INPUT statement, it prints a question mark on a new line and waits for the user to enter a value for each variable in the list, separated by commas. The computer does not execute the next statement in the program until the user enters all the values and presses the Enter key.

Here is an example:

```
100 INPUT ANAME$
```

After the question mark appears on the screen, the user must enter a value. In this example, the user might enter:

```
? SARAH          ←——— Keyed by user
```

After the execution of this statement, the memory location referenced by ANAME$ contains the value SARAH.

The INPUT statement may be used to request more than one value. Here is another example:

```
100 INPUT EMP.NAME$, EMP.AGE
```

After the question mark appears on the screen, the user must enter two values separated by a comma. In this example, the user might enter:

```
? BAILEY,18   ←——— Keyed by user
```

Notice that the data type entered must match that of the variable name. Any string value may be entered for the variable name, EMP.NAME$, but only a numeric value may be entered for EMP.AGE. After the execution of this statement, the memory location referenced by EMP.NAME$ contains the value BAILEY, and the memory location referenced by EMP.AGE contains the value 18.

Because users of a program may not be familiar with the program's statements, a *prompt* is normally included in INPUT statements to ensure that the user knows what the program is expecting. BASIC simplifies the use of prompts by allowing them to be included in quotation marks before the variable list, as this INPUT statement shows:

```
100 INPUT "Enter account number"; ACCT.NO
RUN
Enter account number?                    ←—— Execution pauses
```

Notice the semicolon following the prompt. The effect of this semicolon is that a question mark and a space are added after the prompt.

Program execution pauses until the user enters a number and presses the Enter key. The memory location referenced by ACCT.NO contains the value that the user enters. You can suppress the question mark and the added space by using a comma instead of a semicolon after the closing quote. Thus

```
100 INPUT "Enter account number ", ACCT.NO
RUN
Enter account number 10120               ←—— Keyed by user
```

produces the prompt without the added question mark and space. Note that an ending space was added to the prompt to separate the prompt from the user's entry for readability. When designing a prompt, remember also to include sufficient information so that *the user knows how to respond*.

Another method of supplying a prompt, especially if you want the user's response to start on a new line, is to use the PRINT statement followed by an INPUT statement. Note the following example:

```
100 PRINT "Enter your name"
200 INPUT ANAME$
RUN
Enter your name
?                                        ←—— Execution pauses
```

In summary, the LET and INPUT statements are two possible methods of assigning values to variable names. The LET statement assigns a value without any interaction with the user; the INPUT statement allows the user to assign values to variable names during program execution.

Arithmetic Operators

BASIC uses a set of arithmetic operators to perform calculations. The following operators are used:

Exponentiation	^
Multiplication	*
Division	/
Integer division	\
Modulo	MOD
Addition	+
Subtraction	−

Exponentiation, or the raising of a number to a power, is indicated by the caret (^) symbol. The value on the left of the caret is raised to the power indicated by the value on the right. Note the following examples:

Operation	*Result*
4^2	16
2^8	256
2^1.2	2.297397
2^.5	1.414213
2^−2	.25
9.9^3	970.2989

As the examples illustrate, the exponent, or power to which the value on the left is raised, does not have to be a whole number, nor must it be greater than zero.

Multiplication is indicated by the asterisk (*) symbol. The following examples illustrate its use.

Operation	Result
2 * 3	6
16 * 4	64
5 * .3	1.5
33.9 * −5.2	−176.28

Division is indicated by the slash (/) symbol. The following examples illustrate its use.

Operation	Result
6 / 3	2
16 / 4	4
5 / 2	2.5
33.9 / −5.2	−6.519232
33.9 / 5.2	6.519232

There is a second type of division, called *integer division*, in BASIC. To perform this operation, the computer truncates (lops off without rounding) the dividend and the divisor to integers, and truncates any decimal portion of the quotient. The backslash (\) is the symbol for integer division. The results in the next examples allow comparison with regular division.

Operation	Result
6 \ 3	2
16 \ 4	4
5 \ 2	2
33.9 \ −5.2	−6
33.9 \ 5.2	6

In the last example, 33 (33.9 truncated) is divided by 5 (5.2 truncated) producing 6 (6.6 truncated).

BASIC also provides for an arithmetic operation known as *modulo* and indicates the operation with the symbol MOD. The modulo operation produces the integer remainder of integer division. This can be handy at times; for example, in the following list only the years with a zero value from the modulo operation are leap years:

Operation	Result
1939 MOD 4	3
1940 MOD 4	0
1954 MOD 4	2
1956 MOD 4	0

In the first example, 1939 is divided by 4, giving a result of 484 with a remainder of 3. In the second example, 1940 is divided by 4, producing a quotient of 485 with no remainder.

Addition and subtraction are indicated in BASIC by the familiar + and − symbols.

Operation	Result
4 + 2	6
5 + 7	12
7.1 + 2.3	9.4
8 + −6	2
4 − 3	1
9 − 6	3
9.3 − 5.1	4.2
8 − −6	14
5 − 7	−2

Precedence

BASIC evaluates an arithmetic expression according to a specific order of precedence of the arithmetic operators. The order is the same as you may have learned in math classes. The order is:

Precedence Level

^	Exponentiation	High
* /	Multiplication and division	
\	Integer division	↓
MOD	Modulo	
+ −	Addition and subtraction	Low

You can think of precedence evaluation as happening this way: The computer scans the expression from left to right one time for each precedence level. During the scan, the operations at that level are executed in left-to-right order. Consider the following expression:

```
1 + 3 * 5
```

It has the value of 16. First 3 is multiplied by 5. Next 1 is added to 15, giving a value of 16.

This next example has a value of 11:

```
20 - 3 * 6 / 2
```

First 3 is multiplied by 6. Next the product, 18, is divided by 2. Finally, 9 is subtracted from 20, giving 11.

This more complex example has a value of 4:

```
3 MOD 2 * 2 ^ 2 / 4 + 6 \ 2
```

First the 2 is raised to the second power, giving 4. Next the resulting 4 is multiplied by 2, giving 8. The 8 is then divided by 4, giving 2. Then the 6 is divided (integer division) by 2, producing 3. Next the value of 3 modulo 2, which is 1, is obtained. Finally, this value is added to the 3, obtained from the integer division. This expression, when evaluated step by step, looks like this:

```
3 MOD 2 * 2 ^ 2 / 4 + 6 \ 2
3 MOD 2 * 4     / 4 + 6 \ 2
3 MOD 8         / 4 + 6 \ 2
3 MOD 2             + 6 \ 2
3 MOD 2             + 3
1                   + 3
4
```

BASIC also allows the use of parentheses to change the order in which an arithmetic expression is evaluated. Operations enclosed in parentheses are performed before any other operations. When there is more than one set of parentheses, the evaluations are done from left to right, and if *nested* (one set of parentheses inside another set) from inside out. For example, we get a different result if we change

        1 + 3 * 5

to

        (1 + 3) * 5

The second expression is evaluated as 20. The 1 is added to the 3 first, and then the resulting 4 is multiplied by 5, giving 20.

Liberal use of parentheses is wise because they make complicated expressions more readable. Also, you do not have to remember which operation is performed first. You can use parentheses even when you do not want to change the order of precedence. For example, you could write the previous example as follows:

        1 + (3 * 5)

Even though in this case the parentheses have no effect on how the expression is evaluated, using them leaves no doubt about the order of operations.

The following example shows the use of nested parentheses:

        (6 + (5 * 4) - 1) + 7

First the 5 is multiplied by 4, giving 20. Next 6 is added to 20, giving 26, and 1 is subtracted from this result, producing 25. Finally, 7 is added to 25, giving 32.

Warning: Remember that you always need a matching number of open and close parentheses.

INT Function

While you are thinking about the arithmetic operators, also consider the INT (integer) function. INT is another example of one of BASIC's built-in functions. The INT function takes the form INT(*n*). It returns the largest integer that is not greater than *n*. The INT function may be used in any arithmetic expression. The examples in Table 4.1 show the INT function with the LET statement, but INT may be used in other instructions that permit arithmetic expression.

The INT function evaluates the positive values of X in the examples in Table 4.1 by truncating the decimal portion of the number and keeping the whole number portion of the number. The resulting integer, however, may never be larger than the original value of X. If X is -2.1, -3 is the result because -2 is larger than -2.1.

Table 4.1   INT function examples

Value of X	INT Function	Value of ANS
2.4	ANS = INT(X)	2
2.8	ANS = INT(X)	2
100	ANS = INT(X)	100
-2.1	ANS = INT(X)	-3
-2.7	ANS = INT(X)	-3

FIGURE 4.3
Negative and positive
values

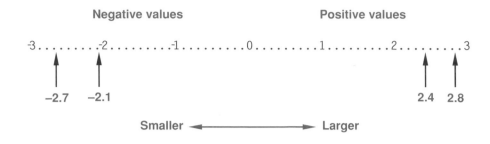

Notice that 2 is not larger than 2.4 or 2.8 on the positive side of the number line in Figure 4.3. But –2 is larger than –2.1 or –2.7 on the negative side, and so –3 is the closest integer to both –2.1 and –2.7 that is not larger than –2.1.

The INT function can be used for a variety of purposes, including rounding numbers. By *rounding*, we mean that BASIC evaluates the digit to the right of the desired place value; if that digit is 5 or greater, BASIC adds 1 to the digit immediately to the left and drops all the digits to the right of the desired place value. If the digit is less than 5, BASIC does not change the digit immediately to the left and drops all the digits to the right. The INT function can be used to round to as many decimal places as needed.

Suppose you want to round the value 38.683 to an integer. Before looking at the BASIC statements, you know the answer should be 39. In BASIC, you would write the following statements to round 38.683 to 39 and print the result:

```
100 NUM = 38.683
200 RESULT = INT(NUM + .5)
300 PRINT RESULT
RUN
 39
```

These are the steps the computer takes in line 200:

1. RESULT = INT(38.683 + .5)

2. RESULT = INT(39.183)

3. RESULT = 39

Now round this same value to one decimal position. The answer should be 38.7. In BASIC, you would write the following statements to round 38.683 to 38.7 and print the result:

```
100 NUM = 38.683
200 RESULT = INT(10 * NUM + .5) / 10
300 PRINT RESULT
RUN
 38.7
```

These are the steps the computer takes in line 200:

1. RESULT = INT(10 * 38.683 + .5) / 10

2. RESULT = INT(386.83 + .5) / 10

3. RESULT = INT(387.33) / 10

4. RESULT = 387 / 10

5. RESULT = 38.7

Remember from the discussion of parentheses that an expression within the parentheses is evaluated first. In step 1, NUM is multiplied by 10 to move the decimal point one place to the right. Then, in step 2, .5 is added to the result. In step 3 the INT function produces 387. This result is divided by 10 to move the decimal point back to the starting location.

Look at one last example of rounding. To round this same number to two decimal positions, you would write the following statements:

```
100 NUM = 38.683
200 RESULT = INT(100 * NUM + .5) / 100
300 PRINT RESULT
RUN
 38.68
```

These are the steps the computer takes in line 200:

1. RESULT = INT(100 * 38.683 + .5) / 100

2. RESULT = INT(3868.3 + .5) / 100

3. RESULT = INT(3868.8) / 100

4. RESULT = 3868 / 100

5. RESULT = 38.68

You can also use another function when you need to round a value. The CINT(n) function converts n to an integer by rounding the fractional portion. For example, the statement

```
100 PRINT CINT(2.8)
```

displays 3 when executed. Rewrite the previous examples using the CINT function.

PRINT Statement Revisited

You learned about the PRINT statement in Chapter 2, but you saw only examples of characters in quotes or character strings. You can also use the PRINT and LPRINT statements to display the values referenced by variable names and numbers.

Here is an example of the use of PRINT to display a value referenced by a variable name:

```
100 ANAME$ = "HOWARD"
200 PRINT "HELLO, "; ANAME$
RUN
HELLO, HOWARD
```

In the following example, three items are listed after PRINT: the number 7, a character string, and the number 2.

```
100 PRINT 7; "IS GREATER THAN"; 2
RUN
 7 IS GREATER THAN 2
```

Notice the space between 7 and IS in the output, even though there is no space before IS in the quoted character string of line 100. The space appears because BASIC always prints a trailing space after a number. Positive numbers are also always preceded by a space, which explains the space before the 7 and the space between THAN and 2. Negative numbers are preceded by a minus sign.

You can use the PRINT statement to evaluate numeric expressions, much as a calculator does. For instance, you can enter the following statement:

```
PRINT 3 + 4 * 6 / 2
 15
```

BASIC evaluates the expression after the statement PRINT and then displays the result on the screen. Notice that you need not give the RUN command to have the result appear on the screen. The reason is that the PRINT statement was entered without a line number. When you enter a statement without a line number, the computer executes it as soon as you press the Enter key. The PRINT statement, however, is not retained in memory after the Enter key is pressed.

See Figure 4.4 for examples of the PRINT statement using the comma and the TAB and SPC functions with numeric values and variable names.

```
10 COMPANY$ = "ACME"
20 PAYROLL = 1342.55
30 PRINT COMPANY$; " TOTAL PAYROLL IS"; PAYROLL
40 PRINT 101
50 PRINT -101
60 PRINT 8,9,,-11,12
70 COL = 12
80 PRINT TAB(COL); 78; TAB(30); -25
90 PRINT 42; SPC(COL); 36
```

```
          1    1    2         23         4  4     5      5  6              7
1........0....5....0.........90.........0..3......0......7..0.........0
 ACME TOTAL PAYROLL IS 1342.55
   101
  -101
   8            9                           -11          12
        78                -25
   42           36
```

FIGURE 4.4   PRINT statement examples.

A BASIC PROGRAM TO CONVERT DOLLARS TO LIRE

Now that you know the program design methods introduced in Chapter 3 and the rules for BASIC statements to write a program that accepts data, performs calculations, and displays the result on the screen, you can write a BASIC program following the six steps in the program development cycle.

Define the Problem

The local bank needs a program to convert U.S. dollars to Italian lire for a group traveling to Rome next month. The input to the program is the dollar amount entered by the bank clerk. No one in the group will be converting more than 999 dollars.

The program must calculate the lira equivalent, the bank charge, and the total lire given to the customer. The lira equivalent is the number of dollars entered by the bank clerk multiplied by the current exchange rate. The current exchange rate is 1280. The charge for this conversion is 5% of the lira equivalent. The total lire given to the customer is the lira equivalent minus the bank charge.

After the dollar amount is entered, the bank would like the current exchange rate, the lira equivalent, the charge for the conversion in lire, and the total lire to appear on the screen.

Determine the Output and Input

There are many preprinted forms to aid in developing the input and output specifications. For screen input and output, there is a *screen design form*. You use a screen design form to plan the placement of screen output. See Figure 4.5. The 80 positions across the top indicate the 80 columns across the screen, and the 24 rows represent the 24 available rows on the screen.

The output of this program is shown on the two screen design forms in Figure 4.5. The first screen form shows the prompt to which the user must respond. The second screen form shows the display of information that the bank clerk needs to distribute the lire to the customer. Notice that in some cases letters are placed in the blocks on the screen design form, denoting specific characters to be printed. Also notice that some blocks contain the character #. The #'s indicate numeric information, such as the dollar amount, the exchange rate, the lira equivalent, the conversion charge, and the total lire. When you are designing the screen output, you do not know what values the user will enter, and so you simply use #'s to show where the data will appear on the screen. If the program displays string information, such as the customer's name and address, you denote it by X's on the screen design form.

The input to this program is the dollar amount entered by the bank clerk.

Design the Program Logic

Note the structure chart for this program in Figure 4.6. The logic can be divided into three level-1 modules. The function of the first module is to input data. The module INPUT DOLLARS clears the screen and then asks the user to enter the dollar amount to be converted. The function of the next module is to process the data. The CALCULATE LIRE module calculates the lira equivalent, computes the conversion charge, and then calculates the total lire to be given to the customer. The function of the last module is to display the information produced. The DISPLAY RESULTS module displays the information on the screen.

We also use an additional module to call or *control* the three level-1 modules. We call this the CONTROL module. This module calls the level-1 modules.

Once the modules are identified and incorporated into a structure chart, the next step is to write the pseudocode for each module. To help you see the flow of logic, we have included the pseudocode with the structure chart in Figure 4.6.

Code the Program Instructions

Now that the input and output forms and the structure chart with the pseudocode are prepared, you are ready to write the BASIC program. Program 4.1 contains one version of the code for this program. Notice the sections before the control module: the program title, the variable name list, and the list of constants.

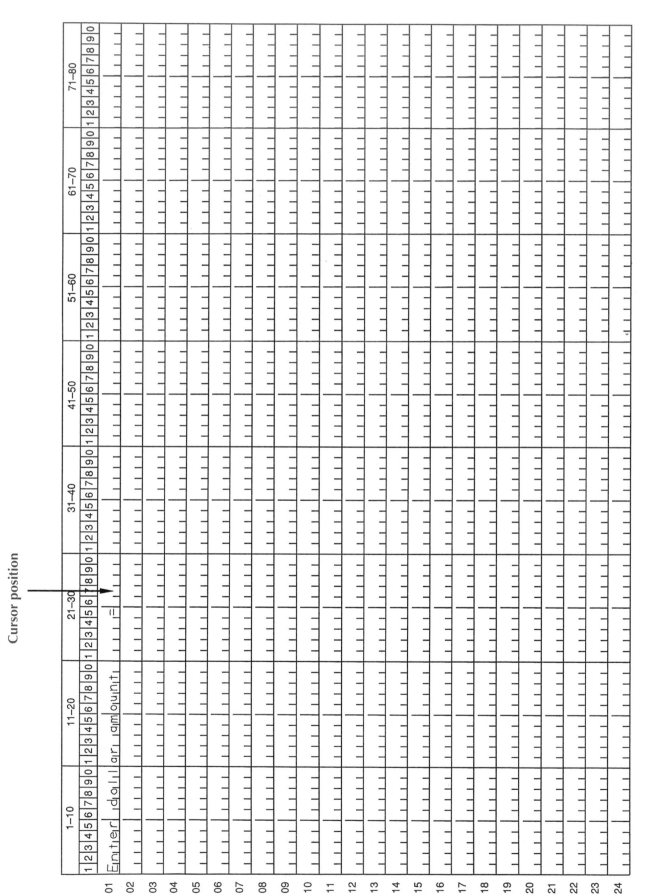

FIGURE 4.5   Screen design forms for Program 4.1

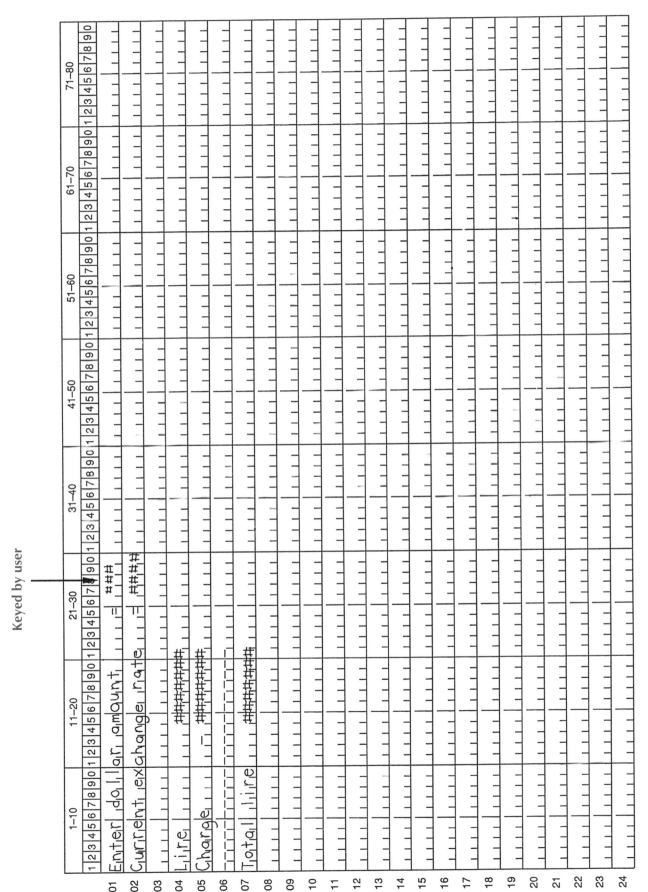

FIGURE 4.5 Screen design forms for Program 4.1 (continued)

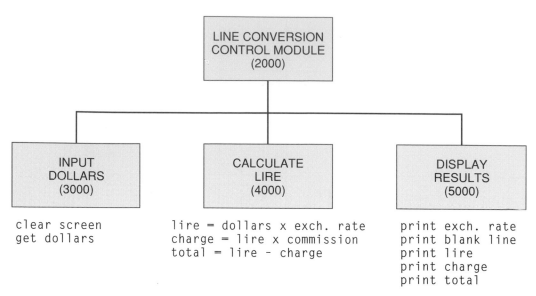

FIGURE 4.6   Structure chart and pseudocode for lire conversion program

PROGRAM 4.1

```
1000 ' PROG4-1
1010 ' ****************************
1020 ' *      LIRE CONVERSION       *
1030 ' ****************************
1040 '
1050 ' ****************************
1060 ' *         VARIABLES          *
1070 ' ****************************
1080 '
1090 ' CHARGE                  Charge for conversion
1100 ' DOLLARS                 Dollar amount entered by user
1110 ' LIRE                    Lira equivalent to dollar amount
1120 ' TOTAL                   LIRE - CHARGE
1130 '
1140 ' ****************************
1150 ' *         CONSTANTS          *
1160 ' ****************************
1170 '
1180   COMMISSION       = .05    '5% charge for conversion
1190   LIRE.PER.DOLLAR = 1280    'Exchange rate as of 5/21/88
1999 '
2000 ' ****************************
2010 ' *         CONTROL MODULE     *
2020 ' ****************************
2030 '
2040   GOSUB 3000               'Input Dollars
2050   GOSUB 4000               'Calculate Lire
2060   GOSUB 5000               'Display Results
2070   END
2999 '
3000 ' ****************************
3010 ' *         INPUT DOLLARS      *
3020 ' ****************************
3030 '
3040   CLS
3050   INPUT "Enter dollar amount    = ", DOLLARS
3060   RETURN
3999 '
```

PROGRAM 4.1
(continued)

```
4000 ' *****************************
4010 ' *        CALCULATE LIRE        *
4020 ' *****************************
4030 '
4040   LIRE   = DOLLARS * LIRE.PER.DOLLAR
4050   CHARGE = LIRE * COMMISSION
4060   TOTAL  = LIRE - CHARGE
4070   RETURN
4999 '
5000 ' *****************************
5010 ' *        DISPLAY RESULTS        *
5020 ' *****************************
5030 '
5040   PRINT "Current exchange rate   ="; LIRE.PER.DOLLAR
5050   PRINT
5060   PRINT "Lire           "; LIRE
5070   PRINT "Charge         -"; CHARGE
5080   PRINT "--------------------"
5090   PRINT "Total lire     "; TOTAL
5100   RETURN
```

The *program title* (line 1020) describes the program. This description can include any of the following documentation: a title, a brief explanation of what the program does, the name of the programmer, and the date.

The *variable name list* (lines 1050–1130) describes each variable used in the program. The values for these variables will be assigned during the execution of the program. In this section, the programmer can provide additional descriptions of or comments about the variables. Alphabetizing the variable list or placing the variables into meaningful groups makes the program easier to read.

The *list of constants* (lines 1140–1999) describes the variable names used as constants in the program and assigns them a value. Remember that these values will not change during the execution of the program. Like the variable list, the constants, if more than one, should be placed in meaningful groupings.

This list of constants has two benefits. First, it lets the reader of the program know what the values of the constants mean, instead of having to guess at the meaning of some string or number referenced in the body of the program. For example, if you changed line 4040 to

```
4040 LIRE = DOLLARS * 1280
```

the meaning of just the number 1280 may not be clear to a reader of your program. A second benefit is that changes to constant values are easier to make if the constants are grouped in one section. If a constant value must change, as LIRE.PER.DOLLAR must to keep this program current, you need to change only one easy-to-find line rather than searching for every statement in the program that uses the exchange rate.

The first module in the program is the CONTROL module, lines 2000–2999. This module acts as a traffic cop, telling the other modules when they are to execute. The control module first calls the INPUT DOLLARS module (lines 3000–3999), then the CALCULATE LIRE module (lines 4000–4999), and finally the DISPLAY RESULTS module (lines 5000–5100). The CONTROL module also serves as a table of contents for the rest of the program. Anyone reading the program can see at a glance the number of main modules in the program and the order in which they are executed.

Notice that each box in the structure chart has become a module of code in the program and that each line of pseudocode has become a program statement. You can relate the line number in the structure chart to the starting line number of the module. Notice that each module begins with a line number that is a multiple of 1000, allowing ample room to add statements without renumbering the lines. This numbering system also aids in listing the program on the screen while testing the program. You simply LIST 3000–3999, knowing you will see the entire INPUT DOLLARS module.

New BASIC Instructions

GOSUB and RETURN

To write the control module, you need to learn the GOSUB and RETURN statements. Their formats are:

```
[line#]  GOSUB <line#>
[line#]  RETURN
```

The *line#* following GOSUB refers to the first line of a module. The GOSUB statement transfers control to that module, and program execution continues from there. A RETURN statement should be the last statement in the module called by the GOSUB; when the RETURN is executed, control transfers to the statement *after* the last GOSUB executed.

Another rule of structured design is single entry/single exit. This means that the program should enter a module at only one point and exit at only one point. The GOSUB statement allows the program to transfer control to the beginning of a module. If a module contains a single RETURN as the last statement, then the module has a single exit. Although a GOSUB statement can transfer control to the middle of a module and a module can contain more than one RETURN, you should avoid this structure.

Figure 4.7 illustrates the flow of control from the control module of Program 4.1 to its subroutines and back again as each GOSUB statement is executed.

Program Readability and Ease of Use

Program 4.1 has several comments or remarks. The variables and constants used in the program, as well as the GOSUB statements, are documented. Notice the use of asterisks to highlight the major sections of the program for the reader. Comment lines will designate the general structure of later programs just as they do here. In addition, later programs will contain whatever comments are necessary to make those programs as clear as possible, yet not clutter the code.

Note the following suggestions for making a program readable and easy to use:

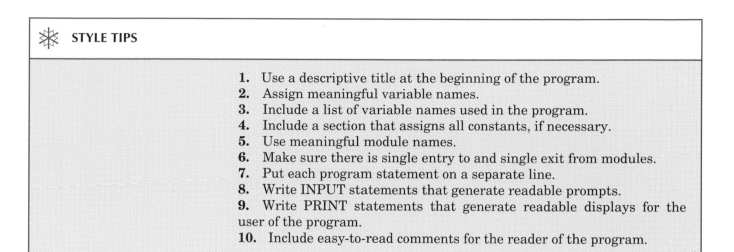

✳ **STYLE TIPS**

1. Use a descriptive title at the beginning of the program.
2. Assign meaningful variable names.
3. Include a list of variable names used in the program.
4. Include a section that assigns all constants, if necessary.
5. Use meaningful module names.
6. Make sure there is single entry to and single exit from modules.
7. Put each program statement on a separate line.
8. Write INPUT statements that generate readable prompts.
9. Write PRINT statements that generate readable displays for the user of the program.
10. Include easy-to-read comments for the reader of the program.

FIGURE 4.7
GOSUB and RETURN
statements

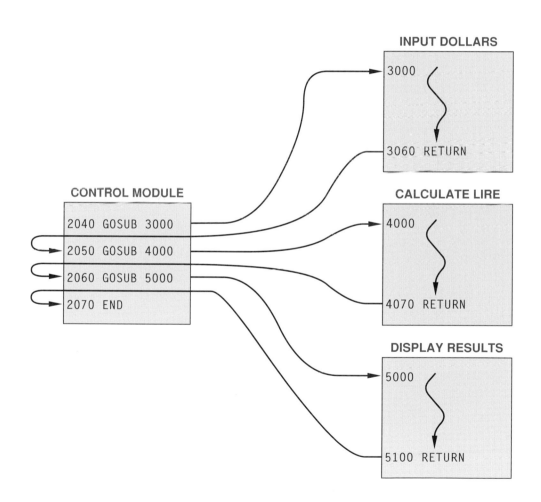

Test the Program

You can test a modular BASIC program from the top down; that is, you can code and test one module before going on to the next. If the program fails at any point, the last module tested probably caused the problem. For instance, you could code and test Program 4.1 like this:

1. Code the CONSTANTS section.

```
1140 ' ****************************
1150 ' *           CONSTANTS           *
1160 ' ****************************
1170 '
1180   COMMISSION       = .05
1190   LIRE.PER.DOLLAR = 1280
1999 '
```

2. Code the CONTROL module.

```
2000 ' ****************************
2010 ' *           CONTROL MODULE        *
2020 ' ****************************
2030 '
2040   GOSUB 3000
2050   GOSUB 4000
2060   GOSUB 5000
2070   END
2999 '
```

3. To test the CONTROL module, we will *stub in* the three level-1 modules so that we can test the overall logic before entering the code for each module. We will code an entry point, a short message to be displayed, and an exit for each of the modules.

```
3000 ' ****************************
3010 ' *           INPUT DOLLARS         *
3020 ' ****************************
3030 '
3040   PRINT "INPUT DOLLARS"
3060   RETURN
3999 '
4000 ' ****************************
4010 ' *           CALCULATE LIRE        *
4020 ' ****************************
4030 '
4040   PRINT "CALCULATE LIRE"
4070   RETURN
4999 '
5000 ' ****************************
5010 ' *           DISPLAY RESULTS       *
5020 ' ****************************
5030 '
5040   PRINT "DISPLAY RESULTS"
5100   RETURN
```

Now run the program to test the overall logic. The three messages should be displayed on the screen to indicate that the CONTROL module has called each of the three modules in the correct order and then ends.

4. Code the complete INPUT DOLLARS module, deleting the PRINT "INPUT DOLLARS" statement. Run the program to test the logic in this module.

5. Code the complete CALCULATE LIRE module, deleting the PRINT "CALCULATE LIRE" statement. Run the program to test the logic in this module.

6. Code the complete DISPLAY RESULTS module, deleting the PRINT "DISPLAY RESULTS" statement. Run the program to test the logic in this module. See Figure 4.8 for a sample output screen.

7. Add the necessary comments to the program.

At certain times you may not be sure what is happening in your program. A useful technique is to display the value of the program variables at the end of program execution. To do so, enter

```
PRINT <var1> [,var2, ...]
```

with no line number. The current values of the program variables listed in the PRINT statement will be displayed on the screen. This technique is useful to test the results of the CALCULATE LIRE module before coding the DISPLAY RESULTS module. See Appendix E for more information about program testing.

Documentation

At this point, depending on the requirements of the bank, the documentation needs to be formalized. Documentation for a program may include:

1. A narrative describing the purpose of the program (Step 1—Define the problem)

2. The input and output forms (Step 2—Determine the output and input)

3. The structure chart and possibly the pseudocode (Step 3—Design the program logic)

4. A listing of the program instructions, a sample run, and a description of the testing procedures (Step 4/Step 5—Code and test the program)

5. A user's manual with instructions for the user of the program

We have included a sample of the documentation for this program in Appendix F.

FIGURE 4.8
Sample output from
Program 4.1

```
Enter dollar amount    = 500
Current exchange rate  = 1280

Lire            640000
Charge       -  32000
---------------------
Total lire      608000
```

You will learn how to right-justify numbers in Chapter 7.

Summary

- BASIC allows for the use of two general categories of data, numeric and character. Character strings are enclosed in quotation marks and may be any combination of characters up to a length of 255. Numeric data may be expressed as integers or real numbers.

  - *Integers* may range from −32,768 to 32,767
  - *Real numbers*
    Single-precision numbers may have up to 7 digits.
    Double-precision numbers may have up to 17 digits.

- *Variables* are names of locations in the computer's memory where values may be stored. All variable names must begin with a letter that may be followed by any sequence of letters, numbers, and periods. In BASIC, variable names designate the type of data that they may reference: Variable names for

  - *string* data end with $
  - *integers* end with %
  - *single-precision* numbers end with ! or no symbol
  - *double-precision* numbers end with #

- Variable names reference two categories of values. Some variable names may be assigned a constant value, and the value of other variable names are assigned during program execution.

- In BASIC, these symbols indicate arithmetic operations:

^	Exponentiation
*	Multiplication
/	Division
\	Integer division
MOD	Modulo
+	Addition
−	Subtraction

- The INT function may be used for finding the largest integer not greater than the given number and for rounding a number to a designated number of positions. The CINT function rounds a value to an integer.

- Program 4.1 illustrates the use of BASIC statements and ways of writing a readable and easy-to-maintain program. Considerations for readability and ease of use include:

  - A descriptive title at the beginning of the program
  - Meaningful variable names
  - A list of variable names used in the program
  - A section that assigns all constants, if necessary
  - Meaningful module names
  - Single entry to and single exit from modules
  - Each program statement on a separate line
  - INPUT statements that generate readable prompts
  - PRINT statements that generate readable displays for the user of the program
  - Easy-to-read comments for the reader of the program

- Chapter 4 describes the following BASIC statements and functions:

CINT	A function that returns the rounded integer value of the argument.
GOSUB	A statement that transfers program control to a subroutine.
INPUT	A statement that assigns the value(s) entered from the keyboard to a variable name(s).
INT	A function that returns the largest integer not greater than the argument.
LET	A statement that assigns a value to a variable name.
RETURN	A statement that transfers control to the statement after the last GOSUB statement executed.

Review Questions

1. What are the two general categories of data?
2. How many characters does BASIC allow in a string?
3. What is the purpose of the quotation marks in a string?
4. Are the quotation marks considered part of the possible 255 characters in the string?
5. What are the two general types of numbers?
6. What is the difference between single-precision and double-precision numbers?
7. What is a variable name?
8. When must a variable name end with a $?
9. What is a constant?
10. In the general format of a statement, what do the brackets [ ] indicate? What do the angle brackets < > indicate?

11. Why is the LET statement called an assignment statement?

12. When do you need to use an INPUT statement?

13. What is the purpose of the prompt in the INPUT statement?

14. What is the arithmetic operator for multiplication?

15. What is the difference between regular division and integer division?

16. What does the term *precedence* mean with regard to arithmetic expressions?

17. What purpose do parentheses serve in an arithmetic expression?

18. What is the purpose of the INT function? How does it differ from the CINT function?

19. Consider the statements

```
100 NUM = 7
200 PRINT NUM; "credits"
```

In what column will the 7 be printed? The word *credits*?

20. What is the screen design form? How is it useful in program planning?

21. What is the advantage of listing the variable names at the beginning of the program?

22. What is the advantage of assigning the constants at the beginning of the program?

23. What does a GOSUB statement do?

24. Why might a subroutine that does not end with a RETURN statement produce a serious programming error? What would happen in Program 4.1 if the line 3060 did not exist? line 5100?

Problems

1. Correct, if necessary, any of the following variable names. Label variable names as string, integer, single-precision or double-precision.

   a. AREA$

   b. PAY.RATE

   c. 1NAME$

   d. PAY-HRS

   e. CTR%

   f. !CREDITS

   g. AMT#

   h. END$

   i. BILL.MONTH.AMT!

   j. DEBIT AMT

   k. T$

   l. TOTAL1

2. Correct, if necessary, the following LET statements:

   a. 100 ANS = "100"

   b. 100 ANAME$ = "Erika"

   c. 100 PAY.RATE% = 8.55

   d. 100 STATE$ = MARYLAND

   e. 100 PAY.HRS = 40

   f. 100 CR.LIMIT = 644500.58

3. Evaluate ANS in the following expressions:

   a. 100 ANS = 3 + 1

   b. 100 ANS = 1 + 4 / 2

   c. 100 ANS = (1 + 4) / 5

   d. 100 ANS = 5 * 3 - 2

   e. 100 ANS 6 - 2^2

   f. 100 ANS = 1 / 3

   g. 100 ANS = 102 MOD 4

   h. 100 ANS = 17 \ 2

4. Calculate the value of the following expressions when A = 1, B = 2, and C = 3:

   a. (A + B) / 3 + C

   b. 3 * (C^B) - 2

   c. (A + (B * C) + 10) \ 2

   d. A + B - (-B) MOD 2

   e. C * B + C * A + (A - C) + 10

5. Evaluate ANS in the following expressions:

   a. 100 ANS = INT(3.2)

   b. 100 ANS = INT(3.8)

   c. 100 ANS = INT(-3.6)

   d. 100 ANS = INT(1 / 3)

   e. 100 ANS = INT(3.8 + .5)

   f. 100 ANS = INT(100 * 5.278 + .5) / 100

   g. 100 ANS = INT(100 * 6.123 + .5) / 10

   Change the function in the previous examples to CINT. Now evaluate ANS.

6. Describe the result of the following PRINT statements. Indicate in which column each item starts.

   a. 10 PRINT 1 + 3

   b. 10 PRINT -34

   c. 10 PRINT "The answer is"; 567

   d. 10 PRINT TAB(52); 4 * 10

   e. 10 PRINT 1,2,3,4,5

7. Find the syntax errors, if any, in the following program segments:

a. 10 PRINT "Chesapeake Airlines": 103

b. 10 INPUT 10
20 PRINT 10

c. 10 INPUT NAME$
20 PRINT NAME$

d. 10 INPUT NUM1; NUM2; NUM3
20 PRINT NUM!; NUM2; NUM3

e. 10 ENTER AGE
20 PRINT AGE

f. 10 INPUT "Enter account number": ACCT

g. 10 A$ = 30
20 PRINT A$

h. 10 SALE * .5 = TAX
20 PRINT TAX

i. 10 'Convert the Fahrenheit temperature
to Celsius
20 INPUT F
30 C = 5/9(F - 32)
40 PRINT C

j. 10 INPUT ;"Enter test score #1"; TEST1
20 INPUT "Enter test score #2"; TEST2

8. Find the logic errors, if any, in the following program segments:

a. 10 'Print the number of credits
entered by the user
20 INPUT CREDITS
30 PRINT CR

b. 10 'Print the values 1 to 10 on the
same line
20 PRINT 1,2,3,4,5,6,7,8,9,10

c. 10 'Print the product of the two
numbers entered
20 PROD = NUM1 * NUM2
30 PRINT PROD
40 INPUT NUM1, NUM2

d. 10 'Print the sum of the two
numbers entered
20 INPUT NUM1
30 INPUT NUM2
40 SUM = NUM1 * NUM2
50 PRINT SUM

e. 10 'Print the sum of the two numbers
entered
20 INPUT NUM1
30 INPUT NUM2
40 SUM = NUM + NUM2
50 PRINT SUM

f. 10 'Enter name INPUT ANAME$
20 'Enter age   INPUT AGE
30 PRINT ANAME$, AGE

9. Convert the following formulas to LET statements:

a. area = length × width
b. perimeter = side1 + side2 + side3 + side4
c. volume = height × length × width
d. circle = 2pi × r^2
e. $A = \dfrac{B + C}{D}$
f. $A = \dfrac{B}{D} - \dfrac{C}{B}$
g. $X = 2Y^2 + 3Y + 8$

10. Consider the following program:

```
10 FLD1 = 10
20 FLD2 = 30
30 FLD3 = 3
99 '
100 GOSUB 1000
200 GOSUB 2000
300 GOSUB 1000
400 END
999 '
1000 FLD1 = FLD1 + 30
1010 FLD1 = FLD1 * FLD3
1020 RETURN
1999 '
2000 FLD2 = FLD1 + FLD2
2010 FLD2 = FLD2 / FLD3
2020 RETURN
```

a. How many times is module 1000 executed? How many times is module 2000 executed?
b. What is the value of FLD1 at the end of program execution? FLD2? FLD3?
c. What is the effect of deleting line 400?
d. What is the effect of deleting line 2020?

11. Refer to Figures 4.6 and 4.7. Suppose there has been a change to the program requirements. Module 4000 now calls module 6000. Change Figures 4.6 and 4.7 to reflect this change.

12. Describe what happens in the following program:

```
10 GOSUB 100
20 END
99 '
100 PRINT "HELLO"
110 GOSUB 200
120 RETURN
200 PRINT "HOW ARE YOU?"
210 GOSUB 300
220 RETURN
300 PRINT "GOODBYE"
310 RETURN
```

Program Assignments

Before writing the program code for the following program assignments, remember to first review the problem definition, determine the output and input using screen design forms, and design the program logic. You may have already designed the logic for some of the problems in Chapter 3.

1. The Footloose Shoe Company needs a program that allows the clerk to enter the price of a pair of shoes and the quantity of shoes purchased. The program then displays the total amount (price times quantity) on the screen.

   a. Write the program using semicolons in the INPUT statements and run the program. Then replace the semicolons in the INPUT statements with commas and run the program again.

   b. Modify the program so that it adds the sales tax to the total amount. (Sales tax is 5 percent of the total amount.) Display for the user:

   • PRICE times QUANTITY

   • TAX for the sale

   • TOTAL COST of the sale

2. Write a program to carry on a conversation between the user and the computer. Display a question on the screen. After the user enters an answer, display a comment using the user's response. Repeat with several questions, as in the following example. The user's responses are underlined.

   ```
   What is your name? Dan
   Hello, Dan! Where do you live? Buffalo
   I live in Buffalo, too.
   What is your favorite TV show? Cheers
   Good choice! Cheers is my favorite, too.
   ```

3. Write a program to input two numbers. Calculate the sum, the difference, the product, and the quotient. Print the answers with appropriate labels.

4. Write a program to convert the degrees in Fahrenheit to Celsius. Allow the user to input a Fahrenheit temperature, calculate the Celsius value, and display the answer.

   The formula for conversion is:

   Celsius = 5/9(Fahrenheit − 32)

5. Mrs. Booth needs a program to calculate the average of three test scores. Write a program that lets Mrs. Booth enter four values—student name, test score 1, test score 2, and test score 3—one at a time. Then display all four values plus the average on one line. Display the average as a truncated integer.

6. Some of Mrs. Booth's students are unhappy with the program calculating test scores because it truncates 89.9 to 89, preventing some students from receiving an A in the course. Change the program in assignment 5 so that it displays the average as a rounded integer.

7. The Edsel Car Rental Company rents Edsels for $35 per day plus 10 cents a mile. Write a program for the rental company so that the clerk can enter the number of days the car was rented, the mileage when the car was rented, and the mileage when the car was returned. Calculate the total charges and round the answer to two decimal positions.

8. A local shipping company needs a program to calculate the shipping charges for packages brought in by the customers. The shipping charge is 15 cents per ounce. The input to the program is how much the package weighs in pounds and ounces. The output is the weight of the package in ounces and the cost of shipping the package.

9. Write a program to calculate miles per gallon for your car. Input the miles traveled and the number of gallons of gas used and display the result rounded to one decimal position. MPG = miles driven/gallons of gas.

10. The local gas station does car repairs. The attendants at the station would like a program to calculate a customer's bill. The input to the program is the customer's name, the cost for the parts used, the hours of labor and the labor rate. The output is the customer's name; the costs for parts and labor; the tax, which is 6% of the cost for parts; and the grand total.

11. The bank is very pleased with the dollars-to-lira conversion program and now would like a program to calculate simple interest and amount due for a loan. The formulas you need are:

    ```
    Interest = principal x rate x time.yrs
    amt.due = principal + interest
    ```

    Write a program to:

    a. Request the bank clerk to enter (1) amount of the loan (principal), (2) rate, and (3) time in years. Use the PRINT statement rather than the INPUT statement to supply the prompts.

    b. Convert the rate to a decimal fraction.

    c. Calculate the interest and amt.due.

    d. Round the answers to two decimal positions.

    e. Display the results.

12. The clerks at the bank are particular about the location where the interest and amount due are displayed on the screen line. Some like to see the results at the far left of the line, some in the middle of the line, and some change their minds daily. Add an input statement to Problem 11 to allow the clerk to specify a column number. Change the PRINT statements so that the results appear in the column the clerk specifies.

13. The mortgage department at the bank needs a program to calculate the monthly payment for a mortgage. The formula you need is:

$$\text{Payment} = \frac{\text{Rate}(1 - \text{Rate})^N}{(1 + \text{Rate})^N - 1} \times \text{Loan}$$

where Payment = Monthly mortgage payment
       Rate = Monthly interest rate
       N = Number of payments in months
       Loan = Amount of loan

Write a program to:

a. Request the mortgage officer to enter (1) the loan amount, (2) the annual interest rate, and (3) the time in years.

b. Convert the annual interest rate to the monthly rate by dividing the annual rate by 12 and then by 100 (or by 1200).

c. Convert the time in years to monthly payments by multiplying by 12.

d. Calculate the payment amount.

e. Round the answer to two decimal positions.

f. Display the result.

14. The investment department of the bank has heard about your good work and would like a program to calculate how much an investor will earn if a yearly amount is put into an annuity. The formula you need is:

$$\text{Earnings} = \text{Amt} \times \frac{(1 + \text{Rate})^N - 1}{\text{Rate}}$$

where Amt = Annual amount invested
      Rate = Interest rate
      N = Number of years

Write a program to:

a. Request the investment analyst to enter (1) the annual amount invested, (2) the interest rate, and (3) the number of years.

b. Convert the rate to a decimal fraction.

c. Calculate the earnings.

d. Round the answer to two decimal positions.

e. Display the result.

Using the Data Disk

1. Insert the data disk into the disk drive.

2. Load BASIC (remember to switch the default drive first if necessary).

3. Enter the following statements without line numbers one at a time.

```
PRINT 1 + 4 - 6 / 2
PRINT 100 * 2 + 12 \ 5
PRINT 1002 MOD 4
PRINT 4^2 + (10 + 16) - (8 * 3)
```

   Note how you can use BASIC as a calculator the next time you need one.

4. Load PROG4-1.

5. Run the program, responding to the prompt with different values. Check the results with a calculator.

6. Check the newspaper for the current lira-dollar exchange rate. Change the value of LIRE.PER.DOLLAR in the program and run the program.

7. Delete line 4070. What happens when you execute the program? Replace line 4070.

8. Run the program and enter the value 99999 for the dollar amount. Change the program so that it can print larger values using standard notation.

9. Change the program so that the bank clerk also enters the customer's name and account number. Save this version of the program under the name CH4-1.DD.

10. Change the program so that it rounds the lire value to an integer.

11. Change the program so that it converts lire to dollars. Save this version of the program under the name CH4-2.DD.

12. Change the program so that it converts dollars to Japanese yen. Use 126 as the exchange rate. The commission charge is 700 yen. Save this new program under the name CH4-3.DD.

Chapter Five

Programming Structures and Boolean Expressions

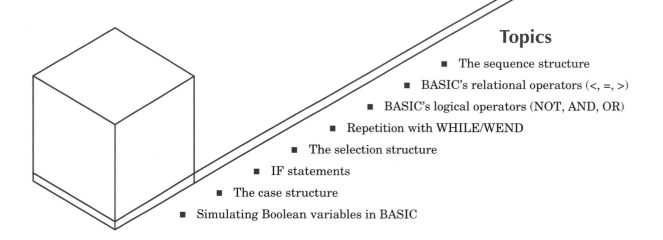

Topics

- The sequence structure
- BASIC's relational operators (<, =, >)
- BASIC's logical operators (NOT, AND, OR)
- Repetition with WHILE/WEND
- The selection structure
- IF statements
- The case structure
- Simulating Boolean variables in BASIC

Program Statements

```
WHILE/WEND
IF/THEN/ELSE
```

INTRODUCTION

You can solve any programming problem by using some combination of just three programming techniques. These techniques, or *structures*, are the building blocks of all programs. With them you can:

1. List statements in *sequence*

2. *Repeat* statements over and over

3. *Select* from among different groups of statements

By using these three structures consistently, you can write programs more quickly and with fewer errors than you might otherwise. Speed and accuracy are possible because you need to know only these three structures to write even the most complex programs. Use of the structures also helps you to separate programs into easily coded parts.

Because the structures are easily recognizable, programs you write with them will be easy for others to read and understand. This standardization is a big advantage when programs must be changed. As the programs you write get larger, you will appreciate the ease with which you can read a program after not having looked at it for a few days.

This chapter contains an explanation of the three structures and their implementation in BASIC. It also introduces Boolean expressions together with BASIC's relational and logical operators and explains how these expressions are used in the repetition and selection structures.

SEQUENCE

The sequence structure is the simplest of the three. Anyone who has written code in any programming language has used it. Sequence is nothing more than a name given to a program segment in which one or more statements are executed one after the other.

Figure 5.1 contains the pseudocode and flowchart for the sequence structure. Figure 5.2 contains an example in BASIC.

FIGURE 5.1
Sequence structure

```
statement-1
statement-2
     .
     .
     .
statement-n
```

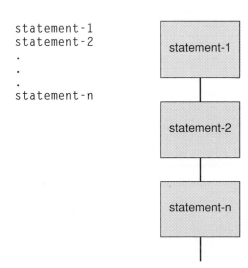

FIGURE 5.2
Sequence structure
using BASIC

```
100 CLS
110 INPUT "Enter your name ", ANAME$
120 PRINT "Your Name is ", ANAME$
130 END
```

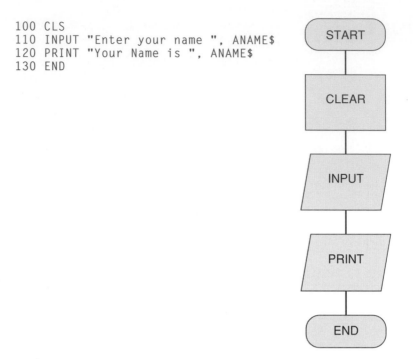

As you can see from the statements in Figure 5.2, most lines in a BASIC program are part of a sequence structure. The exceptions are comment statements and the statements (described later) that control the repetition and selection structures.

Although this structure may seem too trivial to deserve a name, sequence is essential as a building block of programs in much the same way that words are the building blocks of sentences.

BOOLEAN EXPRESSIONS

Before addressing the repetition and selection structures, you need to spend some time with the concept of Boolean expressions and the BASIC operators used to create and evaluate them. The term *Boolean* comes from the name of the nineteenth-century English mathematician, George Boole, who laid the foundation for the modern study of symbolic logic. He observed that his logic system would apply to an algebra of the numbers 1 and 0. Since all instructions to computers are expressed as combinations of 1's and 0's, Boolean algebra has received a lot of attention in recent years.

The expressions that bear Boole's name have the characteristic of being either true or false. Here are some examples in English:

- John is 12.

- John is not 12.

- John is 12 and Maria is 13.

- John is 12 or John is 13.

- John's age is less than Maria's age.

Expressions like these are important in computer programming because you can use them to signal the computer to take one action if they are true and another action if they are false. Here are some additional examples, again in English, of Boolean expressions typical of those used in computer programs:

- There are more data records to process.

- The current employee ID# is not the same as the previous employee ID#.

- The stock is a new issue, or its category is "high-tech."

- The invoice date is 3/2/89 or later, and the customer name is Silas Smith.

To write expressions like these in BASIC, you need to learn to use two additional sets of BASIC symbols, the relational operators and the logical operators.

Relational Operators

BASIC's *relational operators* are used to combine a pair of numeric or character string data values to form a Boolean expression. The six operator symbols and their meanings are listed in Table 5.1.

The values on either side of a relational operator must be either both character strings or both numeric. When the values are numeric and appear in an expression that includes arithmetic operators, the arithmetic is done before the comparison. Thus the expression

```
NUMBER * 10 > NUMBER ^ 2
```

is evaluated as true if NUMBER contains a value less than 10 and as false otherwise. (When NUMBER = 8, the expression becomes 80 > 64, which is true; when NUMBER = 9, it becomes 90 > 81, which is also true; when NUMBER = 10, the expression is 100 > 100, which is false.)

Character strings are compared in "alphabetical" order, the familiar dictionary order. A string is considered "less than" another string if it precedes the other string in alphabetical order. For example, the expressions "DATA" > "COMPUTER" and "SHOP" < "SHOPPE" are both true.

Table 5.1   The Relational Operators

Symbol	Use
=	The equal sign is used to test the equality of two items. For example, PRICE = 3.99 is true if the variable PRICE contains the numeric value 3.99 and false otherwise.
< > or > <	This is the BASIC symbol for inequality. PRICE < > 3.99 is false if the variable PRICE contains 3.99 and true otherwise.
<	This symbol means "less than." INVOICE.DATE$ < "91/03/14" is true if the invoice date precedes "91/03/14" (March 14, 1991) and false otherwise.
>	This symbol means "greater than." HOURS.WORKED > 40 is true if hours worked are greater than 40.
<= or =<	These symbols mean "less than or equal to." HOURS.WORKED <= 40 is true if the hours worked equal 40 or if the hours worked are less than 40.
>= or =>	These symbols mean "greater than or equal to." INVOICE.DATE$ >= "91/03/14" is true if the invoice date is "91/03/14" (March 14, 1991) or any date after that.

When characters are used in a string, the order of the characters is determined by the ASCII character code sequence. In that sequence, numbers come before letters, and lowercase letters follow uppercase letters. Appendix C contains a complete listing of the ASCII characters.

The following strings are arranged according to their relative positions in the ASCII code sequence:

```
&ZZ
49er
@ZZZ
A
AA
AAA
K9
Kt
```

Notice that these strings are ordered according to the first character, then the second, and so on, in the same way that lists of words are alphabetized.

Until you get used to it, ordering strings of numbers may confuse you. For instance, the expression "117232" < "71" is true because 1 precedes 7 in the ASCII code. Remember, do not consider the numeric values of the strings; instead, compare just one character at a time, from left to right, just as you would to put Jerusalem before Tokyo in an alphabetized list of cities.

Comparing strings is a useful capability. One common application is to have the computer determine if a date precedes or follows a certain date or falls within a certain range of dates, as in these examples:

```
"90/09/07" < "90/10/01"
"910101" <= "910624" <= "911231"
```

Both these expressions are true. The first says that September 9, 1990, comes before October 1, 1990. The second says that May 24, 1991, falls within the period of January 1 to December 31, 1991. Notice that a comparison of date strings works only if the dates are in the format *yymmdd*. Also, any separators must be used consistently, and there must be two digits for the year, the month, and the day.

Logical Operators

Many times decisions are based on two or more conditions. For example, suppose you want to extract from a real estate listing all colonial houses priced under $100,000. You need to examine two pieces of information, the type of house (colonial) and the price (under $100,000). BASIC provides *logical operators* to allow you to form Boolean expressions with multiple conditions such as type and price.

BASIC's AND and OR operators join pairs of expressions to form a compound expression whose value is either true or false, as in these compound expressions:

```
TYPE$ = "colonial" AND PRICE < 100000
PRICE < 100000 OR RATE < .095
```

NOT is another logical operator; it allows you to reverse the truth value of a condition, as in this expression:

```
NOT (TYPE$ = "ranch")
```

This expression is true as long as TYPE$ contains a value other than "ranch" but false when TYPE$ does contain the string "ranch".

Table 5.2 lists the values the logical operators yield for the possible true/false combinations of the expressions they join. An expression joining two conditions with AND is true *only* when both conditions are true, in the

Table 5.2   The Logical Operators

HER.AGE = 21	*NOT* (HER.AGE = 21)	
True	False	
False	True	

HER.AGE = 21	HIS.AGE = 18	(HER.AGE = 21) *AND* (HIS.AGE = 18)
True	True	True
True	False	False
False	True	False
False	False	False

HER.AGE = 21	HIS.AGE = 18	(HER.AGE = 21) *OR* (HIS.AGE = 18)
True	True	True
True	False	True
False	True	True
False	False	False

example in Table 5.2, only when HER.AGE = 21 and HIS.AGE = 18. An expression joining two conditions with OR is true *except* when both conditions are false. In Table 5.2, that exception occurs when HER.AGE = 21 is false and HIS.AGE = 18 is false.

The two expressions joined by the AND and OR operators are evaluated independently. Table 5.3 provides four examples that illustrate this process. The only compound expression that is true is the first, because it is the only one in which both conditions are true. Expressions joined with OR are evaluated in the same way, except that the compound expression is false only when both conditions are false. Substitute OR for AND in the expressions in Table 5.3 and determine the truth value of the new expressions.

Logical operators have an order of precedence: NOT, then AND, and finally OR. However, you may use parentheses to change the precedence of logical operations. We suggest you always use parentheses even when you do not wish to change the precedence, because they make complicated expressions easier to read.

Caution! Beware when using NOT in a compound expression. For instance, consider how to write a Boolean expression that is true if A has any value other than 1 or 2 and false otherwise. This expression states the condition correctly:

```
NOT (A = 1 OR A = 2)
```

By contrast, this expression does not state the condition correctly:

```
NOT (A = 1) OR NOT (A = 2)          ←——— Incorrect!
```

The second expression, instead of being true when A has a value other than 1 or 2, is always true! For example, when A = 1 the expression is evaluated as

```
NOT (true) OR NOT (false)
```

which can be reduced to

```
true OR true
```

Thus, the final value is true. If you are uncertain whether this expression is always true, try evaluating it with other numbers, including A = 2.

Table 5.3   Evaluating Compound Expressions

Situation 1			
(When TYPE$ = "colonial" and PRICE = 98000)			
	TYPE$ = "colonial"	AND	PRICE < 100000
evalutates to:	**true**	AND	**true**
which is:		**true**	
Situation 2			
(When TYPE$ = "colonial" and PRICE = 150000)			
	TYPE$ = "colonial"	AND	PRICE < 100000
evaluates to:	**true**	AND	**false**
which is:		**false**	
Situation 3			
(When TYPE$ = "contemporary" and PRICE = 89000)			
	TYPE$ = "colonial"	AND	PRICE < 100000
evaluates to:	**false**	AND	**true**
which is:		**false**	
Situation 4			
(When TYPE$ = "ranch" and PRICE = 100000)			
	TYPE$ = "colonial"	AND	PRICE < 100000
evaluates to:	**false**	AND	**false**
which is:		**false**	

To minimize error and confusion in working with compound expressions, you might want to remember these two rules, called *DeMorgan's rules* after Augustus DeMorgan, a cofounder with George Boole of symbolic logic.

- NOT (X OR Y) is equivalent to (NOT X) AND (NOT Y)
- NOT (X AND Y) is equivalent to (NOT X) OR (NOT Y)

Applying the first of these rules to the previous example produces this correct equivalent expression:

```
NOT (A = 1) AND NOT (A = 2)
```

Another technique for keeping your code readable is to use the NOT operator as little as possible. For instance, instead of writing NOT (HER.AGE = 21), use HER.AGE <> 21.

Boolean Expressions in BASIC

Using the relational and logical operators, you can write the English expressions on page 87 in BASIC; Table 5.4 lists them. BASIC expressions of this type allow programmers to tell the computer when to execute blocks of code

Table 5.4   Boolean Expressions in BASIC

English	BASIC
There are more records to process.	`MORE.RECORDS$ = "YES"`

The current employee ID# is not the same as the previous employee ID#.	`CURRENT.ID$ <> PREVIOUS.ID$`
	or
	`NOT(CURRENT.ID$ = PREVIOUS.ID$)`

The stock is a new issue or its category is "high-tech"	`(STOCK$ = "NEW") OR` `(CAT$ = "HIGH-TECH")`
The invoice date is 3/2/89 or later and the customer name is Silas Smith	`(INVOICE.DATE$ >= "89/03/02") AND` `(CUSTOMER.NAME$ = "Silas Smith")`

repeatedly and when to select blocks of code to execute. The remainder of this chapter explains how to do that using BASIC's WHILE/WEND repetition structure and IF/THEN/ELSE selection structure.

REPETITION

As a programmer, you will frequently find it necessary to direct the computer to execute sections of code over and over. This process is called *repetition* or *looping*, and the range of statements repeated is called a *loop*. Many programming problems require loops, but the most common are input/output operations and the processing of a number of records, such as records containing student grades or employee payroll information. Currency conversion (see the lire problem in Chapter 4) is another example of a frequently repeated process.

Although many people think of computers as machines that can solve complicated mathematical problems, it is their ability to perform unlimited repetitions of mundane tasks without tiring, succumbing to boredom, or complaining that has won them their place in the world of data processing.

Programmers call the standard repetition structure *dowhile*, *while-do*, or just plain *while*. Figure 5.3 contains both the flowchart and pseudocode for the *dowhile* loop. When control reaches the first statement of the loop, BASIC tests the condition to see if it is true. If it is, BASIC executes the statements in the body of the loop in sequence; if the condition is not true, control passes to the first statement after the end of the loop.

After a pass through the loop, control returns to the first statement, where the condition is tested again. As before, either the statements in the body of the loop are executed, or control passes to the first statement after the end of the loop, depending on whether or not the condition is true.

FIGURE 5.3
The dowhile loop

```
dowhile (some condition) is true
    statement-1
    statement-2
    .
    .
    .
    statement-n
end of dowhile loop
```

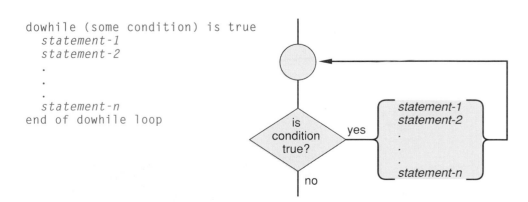

BASIC implements the while loop with two statements, WHILE and WEND (WhileEND). The code in Figure 5.4 is an excerpt from a modification of the Chapter 4 lire conversion program. Because the programmer has used WHILE/WEND, the user no longer has to run the program for every conversion. When the user finally enters −9 for the number of dollars, control passes out of the loop to statement 2070.

The value −9 was selected as a signal to exit the loop because one would not normally enter a negative value for DOLLARS in this program. Programmers often refer to values used to signal the occurrence of a condition like this as *sentinel* values, *terminating* values, or *flags*.

You should note four important points about the code in Figure 5.4:

1. The loop has only one entry point (line 2045) and one exit point (also line 2045). This is a required characteristic for the loop structure.

2. The indentation clearly indicates the boundaries of the loop. This does not matter to BASIC, but it is a great advantage for readers of the program.

3. Line 3045 has been added to the program so that the user knows how to stop the program.

4. There are two calls to the INPUT subroutine, one before the loop and one at the end of the loop. The first one is often called a *priming* or *initial* read; it obtains the value for DOLLARS used to

FIGURE 5.4
The BASIC dowhile loop

```
2000 ' ******************************
2010 ' *         CONTROL MODULE         *
2020 ' ******************************
2030 '
2035   GOSUB 3000                    'Input Dollars
2045   WHILE DOLLARS <> -9
2050       GOSUB 4000                'Calculate Lire
2060       GOSUB 5000                'Display Results
2065       GOSUB 3000                'Input Dollars
2068   WEND
2070   END
2999 '
3000 ' ******************************
3010 ' *         INPUT DOLLARS          *
3020 ' ******************************
3030 '
3040   CLS
3045   PRINT "Enter -9 to quit"
3050   INPUT "Enter dollar amount    = ", DOLLARS
3060   RETURN
3999 '
```

Line #	Action
2035	Send control to the subroutine beginning at line 3000
2045	Check to see if DOLLARS < > −9; if −9, send control to statement 2070; if not, send control to statement 2050
2050	Send control to the subroutine beginning at line 4000
2060	Send control to the subroutine beginning at line 5000
2065	Send control to the subroutine beginning at line 3000
2068	Send control to line 2045

determine whether or not to enter the loop the first time. The second INPUT, just before the end of the loop, gets the value of DOLLARS that is checked at every execution of statement 2045 after the first.

New programmers often wonder why a priming read statement is necessary. Suppose the code in Figure 5.4 were written as follows:

```
2040     ' No priming read
2045     WHILE DOLLARS <> -9
2050        GOSUB 3000              'Input Dollars
2060        GOSUB 4000              'Calculate Lire
2065        GOSUB 5000              'Display Results
2068     WEND
2070     END
```

When the user enters –9 to quit, the program prints a message reporting how many lire are equivalent to –9 dollars. To avoid such nonsense, you must call the input subroutine (to obtain the initial value of DOLLARS) *before* the WHILE statement. This way, BASIC knows whether to enter the loop. You must also call the input subroutine again at the end of the loop so that BASIC can check the next value of DOLLARS and determine whether or not to reenter the loop.

Here are some additional examples of WHILE statements and the decisions BASIC must make as it executes each one.

```
100   WHILE HOURS > 40
```

Is HOURS > 40? If so, enter the loop; if not, send control to the statement following WEND.

```
100   WHILF PRODUCT.CODE$ <> "A1"
```

Is PRODUCT.CODE$ <> "A1"? If so, enter the loop; if not, send control to the statement following WEND.

```
100   WHILE ERROR.FLAG$ = "NO"
```

Is ERROR.FLAG$ = "NO"? If so, enter the loop; if not, send control to the statement following WEND.

```
100   WHILE DAYS = 30 OR DAYS = 31
```

Is DAYS = 30 or 31? If so, enter the loop; if not, send control to the statement following WEND.

```
100   WHILE SEASON$ = "SUMMER" AND DAY$ = "FRIDAY"
```

Is SEASON$ = "SUMMER" and DAY$ = "FRIDAY"? If so, enter the loop; if not, send control to the statement following WEND.

ENDLESS LOOPS

As you construct WHILE statements, make sure that the repetitions eventually end. There are two common causes of endless loops. The first, and the easier to avoid, is omitting from the body of the loop a statement changing the value of the variable(s) tested in the WHILE statement. For example, consider this code:

```
2035    GOSUB 3000                    'Input Dollars
2045    WHILE DOLLARS <> -9
2050        GOSUB 4000                'Calculate Lire
2060        GOSUB 5000                'Display Results
2068    WEND
```

In this loop, the dollar amount always remains the same as it was on entry into the loop. Unless the initial entry is –9, the repetitions continue endlessly. (When you do create an endless loop, as you probably will at some time, you can stop the execution by pressing the Ctrl-Break or Ctrl-C key combination.)

The second common cause of endless loops is an improperly constructed Boolean expression. Suppose that you want a loop to continue as long as a variable called CHOICE$ is not equal to "N" or "n". You might try to accomplish that with a WHILE statement like this one:

```
2360   WHILE (CHOICE$ <> "n") OR (CHOICE$ <> "N")
```

Do you see the problem? This expression will *always* be true because an expression of two conditions joined with OR is false only when the conditions on *both* sides are false. In this situation, both can never be false. The correct way to write the statement is

```
2360   WHILE (CHOICE$ <> "n") AND (CHOICE$ <> "N")
```

NESTED LOOPS

Any WHILE/WEND loop may contain another loop as long as the inner loop is completely nested. *Completely nested* means that the inner loop ends before the outer loop does. BASIC places no limit on the number of loops that may be contained in an outer loop or on the level of nesting (loops within loops within loops). The following example of nested loops illustrates how indentation makes the inner loops easy to identify.

```
100  INPUT "Enter a name to display (X to quit):  ", ANAME$
110  WHILE ANAME$ <> "X"
120    CLS
130    COUNTER = 1
140    WHILE COUNTER <= 4
150      PRINT TAB(COUNTER * 3); ANAME$
160      COUNTER = COUNTER + 1
170    WEND
180    INPUT "Enter a name to display (X to quit):  ", ANAME$
190  WEND
2C0  END
```

What display will this code produce if the user enters "Erika", "Etta", "Roy", and "X"?

SELECTION

The *selection* or *choice* structure provides a way to evaluate a set of conditions and execute different sections of code depending on the value of the conditions. Because most high-level languages implement the selection structure using the key words IF, THEN, and ELSE, programmers often refer to it as the IF/THEN or IF/THEN/ELSE structure. This section explains how to use the selection structure in BASIC.

Figure 5.5 shows the pseudocode and flowchart for the selection structure. If the condition is true, the set of *statements 1–n* is executed; if the

FIGURE 5.5
The selection structure

```
if (some condition) is true
    then do
            statement-1
            statement-2
            .
            .
            .
            statement-n
    end then
    else do
            statement-a
            statement-b
            .
            .
            .
            statement-m
    end else
```

(Note that the *else* clause is optional.)

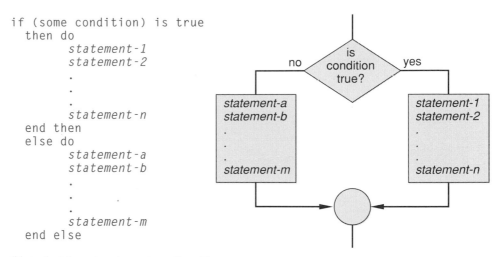

condition is false, the set of *statements a–m* is executed. Either set of statements may be a single statement. The ELSE clause is optional and may be omitted altogether. If so, an action is taken if the condition is true, but nothing is done when the condition is false.

Figure 5.6 shows code that implements the IF/THEN structure in BASIC. In this example, if the value of STUDENT.CREDITS is less than 12, then PART-TIME STUDENT is displayed on the screen. The next line, line 110, causes END OF PROGRAM to be displayed as well. If the value of STUDENT.CREDITS is 12 or greater, only the message END OF PROGRAM is displayed.

Figure 5.7 shows BASIC code that implements the IF/THEN/ELSE structure. In this example, if STUDENT.CREDITS is less than 12, then the computer displays the message PART-TIME STUDENT and, on the next line, the message END OF PROGRAM. If STUDENT.CREDITS is 12 or greater, the computer writes FULL-TIME STUDENT and END OF PROGRAM on successive screen lines.

Notice how this example illustrates the *single entry-single exit* requirement. In a structured program, whenever control enters an IF/THEN/

FIGURE 5.6
IF/THEN selection structure
using BASIC

```
100 IF STUDENT.CREDITS < 12
        THEN PRINT "PART-TIME STUDENT"
110 PRINT "END OF PROGRAM"
```

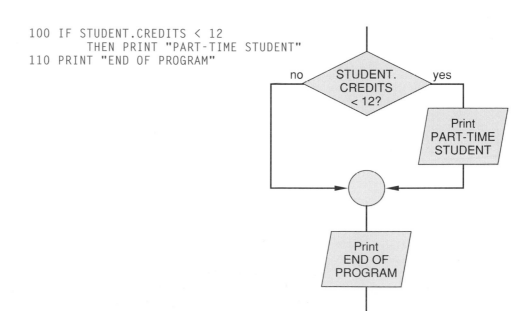

```
100 IF STUDENT.CREDITS < 12
        THEN PRINT "PART-TIME STUDENT"
        ELSE PRINT "FULL-TIME STUDENT"
110 PRINT "END OF PROGRAM"
```

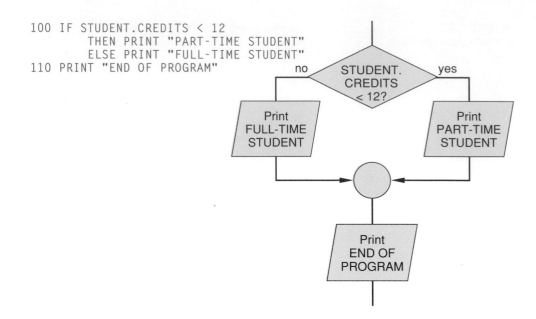

ELSE structure, the exit point for both the THEN path and the ELSE path must be the same. In this case, regardless of whether the condition in line 100 is true or false, the next line executed is line 110.

Also notice the formatting of the IF statements in Figures 5.6 and 5.7. Putting each clause of the statement on a separate line and indenting the THEN and ELSE portions allows the reader to determine quickly

1. the condition being evaluated

2. the action BASIC takes when the condition is true

3. the action it takes when the condition is false

To indent statements in this fashion, you must move the cursor to the next line *without pressing the Enter key* because pressing Enter causes BASIC to look for a new line number. The easiest way to advance the cursor to the next line without a line feed is to use the Ctrl-J (or Ctrl-Enter) key combination. You would enter statement 100 in Figure 5.7 this way:

```
100 IF STUDENT.CREDITS < 12<CTRL-J>
        THEN PRINT "PART-TIME STUDENT"<CTRL-J>
        ELSE PRINT "FULL-TIME STUDENT"<ENTER>
```

You may put multiple statements in an IF/THEN/ELSE structure after the THEN and ELSE if you separate them with a colon as in this example:

```
110 IF AGE < 18
        THEN PRINT ANAME$;" IS A MINOR."  : AGE.CODE = 1 : VOTE$ = "NO"
        ELSE PRINT ANAME$;" IS AN ADULT." : AGE.CODE = 2 : VOTE$ = "YES"
```

If AGE is less than 18, the three statements, PRINT ANAME$, AGE.CODE = 1, and VOTE$ = "NO", are executed. If AGE is greater than or equal to 18, then the statements, PRINT ANAME$, AGE.CODE = 2, and VOTE$ = "YES", are executed.

You may include as many statements after the THEN or the ELSE as space (a total of 255 characters and spaces) permits. However, combining statements in a single line makes the program more difficult to read and change.

A better way to include multiple statements in your THEN and ELSE clauses is to put the statements in subroutines and put only the GOSUB statement in the clauses. Using that approach, you can rewrite the previous example as follows:

```
.
.
.
110    IF AGE < 18
            THEN GOSUB 800
            ELSE GOSUB 900 '800=Process minor; 900=Process adult
     .
     .
     .
800 ' ****************************
810 ' *         PROCESS MINOR          *
820 ' ****************************
830 '
840    PRINT ANAME$; " IS A MINOR."
850    AGE.CODE = 1
860    VOTE$ = "NO"
870    RETURN
880 '
900 ' ****************************
910 ' *         PROCESS ADULT          *
920 ' ****************************
930 '
940    PRINT ANAME$; " IS AN ADULT."
950    AGE.CODE = 2
960    VOTE$ - "YES"
970    RETURN
```

This method is preferable for two reasons. First, it allows you to code only one statement per line, making your programs easier to read and to change. Second, it allows you to include as many statements as you wish, avoiding BASIC's 255-character statement length limit.

Table 5.5 contains some additional examples of IF statements like those you might use in your programs. Notice that in each case the statement is easy to read.

USING THE LOGICAL OPERATORS TO WRITE COMPOUND IF STATEMENTS

The logical operators allow you to write IF statements that evaluate complicated situations. Suppose you have to prepare a program for a small West Virginia college that will read a file of student records and determine the grade point average of all out-of-state (that is, not West Virginia residents) information systems majors who have completed 12 or more hours. The following statement selects the appropriate students from the file:

```
3230   IF STU.MAJOR$ = "IS" AND STU.STATE$ <> "WV" AND
           STU.CREDITS >= 12
               THEN GOSUB 4000      'Calculate GPA
```

Table 5.5   Examples of IF Statements

Statement	Result if true	Result if false
```100 IF STDNT.CAT$ = "3"``` ``` THEN PRINT "JUNIOR"```	JUNIOR is displayed.	Control passes to the next line number.

```100 IF SCORE < 60```
```   THEN PRINT "FAIL"```
```   ELSE PRINT "PASS"```
	FAIL is displayed.	PASS is displayed.

```100 IF LINE.CTR >= PAGE.LIMIT``` ``` THEN GOSUB 7000```	Control passes to line number 7000.	Control passes to the next line number.

```100 IF MATCH$ = "YES"```
```   THEN PRINT "VALID ENTRY"```
```   ELSE PRINT "ERROR": INPUT CODE$```
	VALID ENTRY is displayed.	ERROR is displayed, and the program requests a response from the user.

```100 IF HER.AGE = 20```
```   THEN```
```   ELSE PRINT "Not 21"```
	The THEN clause is empty, so control passes to the next line number.	"Not 21" is displayed.

Suppose now that the college asks you for the same information, but for information systems and computer science majors combined. This change to line 3230 provides the grade point average for the group of two majors.

```
3230   IF (STU.MAJOR$ = "IS" OR STU.MAJOR$ = "CS") AND
          STU.STATE$ <> "WV" AND STU.CREDITS >= 12
             THEN GOSUB 4000      'Calculate GPA
```

The parentheses around the two expressions joined by an OR are necessary in this example because BASIC evaluates NOTs first, then ANDs, and finally ORs. If there were no parentheses, the first expression (STU.MAJOR$ = "IS") would be joined by OR to the evaluation of the rest of the expression. To understand this evaluation sequence, assume these values for the variables: STU.MAJOR$ = "IS", STU.STATE$ = "OH", and STU.CREDITS = 6. BASIC would consider the compound expression without parentheses to have this form:

```
STU.MAJOR$ = "IS" OR STU.MAJOR$ = "CS"  AND
                     STU.STATE$ <> "WV" AND
                     STU.CREDITS >= 12
```

BASIC would evaluate the expression as true because one of the pair of expressions (STU.MAJOR$ = "IS") joined by OR is true (even though the student doesn't have 12 credits).

Table 5.6 lists more examples of IF statements that contain logical operators. Notice that parentheses can be used to enhance readability and change the precedence of operations.

CASE STRUCTURE

Programmers often encounter problems that require a choice among more than two alternatives. A selection structure for that purpose is called the *case* structure. The pseudocode and flowchart for the case structure are shown in Figure 5.8. As you can see from the figure, one of the set of possible choices is selected according to the contents of some variable or the result of evaluating some alternative. For each possible case, a set of actions is performed, although, for some cases, the action may be no action.

The simplest way to implement the case structure in BASIC is with a series of IF statements, as in the top portion of Figure 5.9. This format has

Table 5.6   Examples of IF Statements Using Logical Operators

Statement	Result if true	Result if false
100 IF NOT TEMP > 32 THEN PRINT "It's freezing"	"It's freezing" is displayed.	Control passes to the next line number.

100   IF (SELECT$ < "1") OR (SELECT$ > "4")
          THEN PRINT "ERROR"
          ELSE GOSUB 9000
	ERROR is displayed.	Control passes to line 9000.

100   IF (AGE >= 35) AND (COUNTRY$ = "USA")
          THEN PRINT "You can be president"
          ELSE PRINT "You are not eligible"
	"You can be president" is displayed.	"You are not eligible" is displayed.

100   IF (SAT > 1200 OR GPA > 3.7) AND (ACT$ = "YES")
          THEN GOSUB 4000
          ELSE PRINT "REJECT"
	Control passes to line 4000.	REJECT is displayed.

FIGURE 5.8
Case structure

```
if (some condition) =
   case-1 then do actions-1
   case-2 then do actions-2
   .
   .
   .
   case-n then do actions-n
end case
```

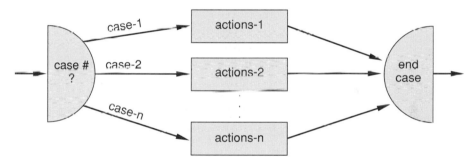

the advantage of being easy to write and understand, but it is inefficient in that every IF statement is evaluated, even after a true condition is found.

An alternative is to use nested IF statements. A *nested IF statement* contains an IF statement as part of the THEN or ELSE condition of another IF statement. Nested IFs are very efficient at selecting from among several mutually exclusive outcomes.

The bottom portion of Figure 5.9 illustrates the use of the nested IF. In that code, evaluation stops after a true condition. This code is more efficient than separate IF statements for each condition, but BASIC's statement length restriction limits its use.

When you code nested IF statements, you can maximize their efficiency by putting the most common choice first. Suppose the code in Figure 5.9 needs to check the ages of 1000 people, of whom 70% are adults, 25% are teenagers, and 5% are children. The program would run faster if you swapped the tests for adults and children; Figure 5.10 shows how many times each portion of the IF statement is executed for each of the two arrangements. Notice also that either arrangement requires fewer comparisons than separate IF statements.

FIGURE 5.9
Alternative implementations of the case structure

Using Separate IF Statements

```
100  INPUT "ENTER AGE "; AGE
110  IF  AGE <= 12                     THEN CATEGORY$ = "Child"
120  IF (AGE >  12) AND (AGE <= 17) THEN CATEGORY$ = "Teen"
130  IF  AGE >  17                     THEN CATEGORY$ = "Adult"
140  PRINT CATEGORY$
```

Using Nested IF Statements

```
100  INPUT "Enter age:  "; AGE
110  IF          AGE <= 12 THEN CATEGORY$ = "Child"
       ELSE IF AGE <= 17 THEN CATEGORY$ = "Teen"
       ELSE                    CATEGORY$ = "Adult"
120  PRINT CATEGORY$
```

Consider this example, which illustrates an important characteristic of nested IF statements.

```
930   IF condition-1
         ┌─THEN IF condition-2
         │        ┌─THEN statement-1
         │        └─ELSE statement-2
         └─ELSE statement-3
```

Each ELSE is always paired with the most recent IF/THEN that does not already have a matching ELSE, as the lines in this example illustrate.

Nested IF statements are often too long to fit in a single BASIC line, but you can implement them as a series of IF statements with compound conditions. The previous example could be written in BASIC this way:

```
930 IF condition-1 AND condition-2
       THEN statement-1
940 IF condition-1 AND NOT condition-2
       THEN statement-2
950 IF NOT condition-1
       THEN statement-3
```

FIGURE 5.10
Efficiency in nested IF statements (1000 persons; 70% adults, 25% teens, 5% children)

		Times Executed
`110  IF          AGE <= 12 THEN CATEGORY$ = "Child"`		1000
`       ELSE IF AGE <= 17 THEN CATEGORY$ = "Teen"`		950
`       ELSE                    CATEGORY$ = "Adult"`		700
	Total	2650

		Times Executed
`110  IF          AGE >  17 THEN CATEGORY$ = "Adult"`		1000
`       ELSE IF AGE >  12 THEN CATEGORY$ = "Teen"`		300
`       ELSE                    CATEGORY$ = "Child"`		50
	Total	1350

Separate IF statements

		Times Executed
`110  IF AGE <= 12          THEN CATEGORY$ = "Child"`		1000
`110  IF (AGE > 12) AND (AGE <= 17)`		
`                           THEN CATEGORY$ = "Teen"`		1000
`110  IF AGE > 17          THEN CATEGORY$ = "Adult"`		1000
	Total	3000

SIMULATING BOOLEAN VARIABLES

Some programming languages have a Boolean data type that allows only two values, true and false. As you might expect from the name, such a data type is appropriate for use in writing Boolean expressions. Although BASIC does not provide for Boolean variables, it is easy to simulate them, and doing so can improve the readability of some Boolean expressions and often reduce the amount of code. (Simulated Boolean variables are similar to Boolean variables in Pascal and level 88's in COBOL.)

In BASIC, the value 0 indicates a false expression, and the value −1 indicates a true one. (Note that although one would not normally associate −1 with a true condition, it is nevertheless the number used in BASIC.) BASIC does not allow control to enter a WHILE loop or the THEN branch of an IF statement unless it can evaluate the Boolean expression to −1.

To simulate a Boolean variable you begin by assigning −1 and 0, respectively, to the numeric variable names TRUE and FALSE (or YES and NO). Now you can assign TRUE and FALSE to other variables to indicate the status of a condition. To understand this process, consider these excerpts of code from a program that determines if a date entered by a user is valid and, if it is, prints a message:

```
1310   FALSE =  0
1320   TRUE  = -1
         .
         .
         .
3410   IF (MONTH$ >= "01") AND (MONTH <= "12")
           THEN VALID.MONTH = TRUE
           ELSE VALID.MONTH = FALSE
         .
         .
         .
4180   IF VALID.MONTH AND VALID.DAY AND VALID.YEAR
           THEN PRINT "Valid date"
```

Lines 1310 and 1320 assign BASIC's false and true values, respectively, to the variables FALSE and TRUE. Line 3410 tests the value the user enters for the variable MONTH$ and, if the value falls within the range of "01"–"12", sets the value of the VALID.MONTH to true. If the value falls outside the range of "01"–"12", the value of VALID.MONTH is set to false. (A complete program would provide validity tests for DAY and, if appropriate, for YEAR.) Finally, line 4180 tests the Boolean expression and, if all three Boolean variables are true (have the value −1), displays the message "Valid date".

By using Boolean variables in this fashion, you can make your programs much cleaner and easier to read than they are likely to be otherwise. Consider how line 4180 would look if it were written with string variables:

```
4180   IF VALID.MONTH$ = "YES" AND VALID.DAY$  = "YES"
                              AND VALID.YEAR$ = "YES"
           THEN PRINT "Valid date"
```

Boolean variables can be equally useful in dowhile loops. For example, look at the code on the next page that asks the user to enter a zip code until the zip code that is entered matches the number in line 3150.

```
1310  NO = 0
1320  YES = -1
        .
        .
        .
3140  FOUND = NO
3150  SEARCH.ZIP = 21093
3160  WHILE NOT FOUND
3170      INPUT "Enter zip code  ", ZIP
3180      IF SEARCH.ZIP = ZIP
                THEN FOUND = YES
3190  WEND
```

Summary

■ You can write any program with a combination of just three programming structures, *sequence*, *repetition*, and *selection*.

■ To write *sequence* structures, you simply write one program instruction after another in sequence.

■ *Boolean expressions* are expressions that can be only true or false. To write them, you need to use BASIC's relational and logical operators. The *relational operators* are:

=	equality	<>	inequality
<	less than	<=	less than or equal to
>	greater than	>=	greater than or equal to

■ The logical operators used in this text are NOT, AND, and OR.

■ You can implement the *repetition* structure in BASIC with the WHILE/WEND statements. This is the general form of WHILE/WEND loops:

```
line#  WHILE some condition is true
line#       statement
        .
        .
        .
line#       statement
line#  WEND
```

■ Program the *selection* structure with IF, THEN, and ELSE statements. The form for its use is:

```
line# IF some condition is true
          THEN statement(s)
          ELSE statement(s)
```

■ *Boolean variables* are variables that can store only the values true and false. By simulating this data type in BASIC, you can write statements like this one:

```
4180   IF VALID.MONTH AND VALID.DAY AND VALID YEAR
          THEN PRINT "Valid date"
```

Review Questions

1. Name the three basic programming structures.

2. What are the advantages of using just these three structures to write your programs?

3. What are Boolean expressions? Why are they an important part of computer programs?

4. What is a relational operator? Use each of BASIC's relational operators in an example.

5. What do BASIC's logical operators do? Explain the difference between the results produced by the AND and OR operators.

6. What is the order of precedence for BASIC's logical operators?

7. The meaning of compound expressions containing logical operators is seldom obvious. For instance, consider NOT(*exp1* AND *exp2*). You might expect this to be equivalent to NOT(*exp1*) AND NOT(*exp2*), but it is not. What is another way to write NOT(*exp1* AND *exp2*)?

8. What is a priming read?

9. How is a sentinel value used?

10. What is the case structure? How is it implemented in BASIC?

11. Why are nested IF/THEN/ELSE statements more efficient than multiple IF statements?

12. Why is BASIC's 255-character line length limit sometimes a problem?

13. What reasons can you give for simulating Boolean variables in BASIC? Give an example of a statement that uses such a variable.

Problems

1. Arrange these character strings in ascending order. (You will probably need to refer to the ASCII code chart in Appendix C to determine the correct order of some of the characters.)

    a. "3","18","11810","44884","33","10"

    b. "A1","1A","a1","1a"

    c. " abc","abc","!abc","#abc"

    d. "*@!x","*@!x "

2. Given these values:
    ```
    STUDENT.NUMBER$ = "A1050"
    GENDER$         = "M"
    CREDITS         = 12
    GPA             = 3.5
    SCHOLARSHIP.AMT = 1000.00
    FINES           = 50.00
    ```
    determine whether the following conditions are true or false:

    a. CREDITS < 9 OR GENDER$ = "M"

    b. CREDITS = 12 AND GPA = 3.4

    c. NOT CREDITS < 12

    d. NOT SCHOLARSHIP > 1200.00 AND
       NOT FINES > 100

    e. NOT(GENDER$ = "F" OR
       STUDENT.NUMBER = "A1050")

    f. SCHOLARSHIP - FINES = 0 OR
       FINES > 500.00

3. Write BASIC expressions to describe the following conditions. Select appropriate variable names wherever necessary.

    a. The month is February.
    b. DEPT$ contains a value different from the value in PREV.DEPT$.
    c. PERCENT is no less than 0 and no more than 100.
    d. An account is overdue.
    e. The day is not Saturday or Sunday.
    f. The culprit is either the butler or the singer.

4. Write WHILE statements to implement the following:

    a. Enter the loop when GENDER$ contains "F".
    b. Skip the loop when AGE is less than 18.
    c. Enter the loop when either SALARY or TOTAL.INCOME is greater than $60,000.
    d. Skip the loop if TEMPERATURE is in the range 98–99°F.

5. The following code is supposed to report the sales tax (given a tax rate of 5%) and the total amount due when the user enters the cost of an item. Are there any syntax errors? Logical errors? Rewrite the code to remove any errors you find, to improve the readability of the code, and to make the output easier to use.
    ```
    100 INPUT I
    110 WHILE I > 0
    120 X = I * .05
    130 Y = I + X
    140 PRINT X,Y
    150 INPUT I
    160 WEND
    ```

6. Find any syntax errors in each set of statements.

    a.
    ```
    1000   IF ANS$ = "YES"
               PRINT "OK"
    ```

    b.
    ```
    1000   IF RES$ = "NO"
    1010       THEN PRINT "STOP RUN"
    ```

    c.
    ```
    1000   IF HRS.WORKED > "40"
               THEN OT.HRS = HRS.WORKED - 40
    ```

    d.
    ```
    1000   IF PAY > 60000
               THEN PRINT "EXECUTIVE"
                   EXECS = EXECS + 1
    ```

    e.
    ```
    1000   IF A < B THEN PRINT "small"
               ELSE PRINT "BIG"
    ```

    f.
    ```
    1000   IF PAY <> OLDPAY OR > 2000
               THEN PRINT "NEW SALARY"
    ```

    g.
    ```
    1000   IF HRS.WORKED NOT > 40
               THEN PRINT "No Overtime"
    ```

7. Are the sets of code in the following groups of statements equivalent?

    Group 1

    a.
    ```
    100 IF AGE.CODE = 1
           THEN CTR = CTR + 1
           ELSE CTR = CTR - 1
    200 PRINT ANAME$
    ```

    b.
    ```
    100 IF AGE.CODE = 1
           THEN CTR = CTR + 1 : PRINT ANAME$
           ELSE CTR = CTR - 1
    ```

    Group 2

    a.
    ```
    100 IF ANAME$ = OLDNAME$
           THEN CTR = CTR + 1 : PRINT ANAME$
           ELSE PRINT ANAME$
    ```

    b.
    ```
    100 IF ANAME$ = OLDNAME$
           THEN CTR = CTR + 1
    200 PRINT ANAME$
    ```

Group 3

a. 100 IF TOTAL.AMT <= 1000
           THEN PRINT "BELOW QUOTA"

b. 100 IF NOT(TOTAL.AMT > 1000)
           THEN PRINT "BELOW QUOTA"

c. 100 IF TOTAL.AMT > 1000
           THEN
           ELSE PRINT "BELOW QUOTA"

Group 4

a. 100 IF CALC.PAY = 120 OR DEPT$ = "ENG"
           THEN PRINT "OK"
           ELSE PRINT "NOT OK"

b.

100 IF CALC.PAY <> 120 AND DEPT$ <> "ENG"
        THEN PRINT "NOT OK"
        ELSE PRINT "OK"

8. Write an IF statement to perform the following operations:

   a. Display the massage "HOORAY" if the variable GRADE$ contains the value "A".
   b. Display the message "FULL-TIME" if a student is taking more than 15 credits. Use CREDITS as the variable name.
   c. When the student is full-time (as defined in the previous exercise) and the student's major (MAJOR$) is "DP", write the student's name (STUDENT.NAME$) on the printer.
   d. Display the message "ADULT" if a person's age is 18 or greater; if the person is younger than 18, display the message "DEPENDENT". Use AGE as the variable name.

9. Rewrite the following nested IF statements as multiple IF statements using NOT's and AND's.

   a. IF *condition-1*
           THEN IF *condition-2*
                   THEN *statement-1*
                   ELSE *statement-2*
           ELSE *statement-3*

   b. IF *condition-1*
           THEN IF *condition-2*
                   THEN *statement-1*
                   ELSE IF *condition-3*
                           THEN *statement-2*
                           ELSE (nothing)
           ELSE *statement-3*

   c. IF *condition-1*
           THEN IF *condition-2*
                   THEN IF *condition-3*
                           THEN *statement-1*
                           ELSE (nothing)
                   ELSE *statement-2*

10. The variable CHECK$ should contain the value "C", "K", or "T"; any other character represents an error. Would the following IF statement correctly check for the possibility of an error? If not, change it so that it will.

    1000 IF (CHECK$ <> "C") OR
            (CHECK$ <> "K") OR (CHECK$ <> "T")
            THEN PRINT "ERROR!"

11. Write a series of IF statements to print the tax calculated according to the following table. Use the variable names EARNINGS and TAX.

Earnings	Tax
Not over $2000	Zero
Over $2000 but not over $5000	3% of the amount over $2000
Over $5000	$90 + 5% of the amount over $5000

12. Write a single nested IF statement to display the taxes as specified in the previous problem.

13. Consider this logic:

```
if boy is "Edward"
    then if girl is "Erica"
         then write "siblings"
         else if girl is "Sarah"
              then write "friends"
              else write "unknown"
```

   a. What execution will occur if the boy is "Edward" and the girl is "Erica"?
   b. What execution will occur if the boy is "Edward" and the girl is "Sarah"?
   c. What execution will occur if the boy is not "Edward"?
   d. What execution will occur if the boy is "Edward" and the girl is neither "Erica" nor "Sarah"?
   e. Change the pseudocode so that "unknown" will be written if the boy is not "Edward".

14. What reports will be printed if a user enters the temperatures and sky conditions below when running the following code?

User input

Sun:	cold	clear
Mon:	cool	ptly sunny
Tue:	warm	overcast
Wed:	hot	clear
Thu:	warm	overcast
Fri:	cold	clear
Sat:	cool	ptly sunny

Code

```
100 INPUT "Do you have weather data to enter (Y or N) "; MORE.DATA$
110 WHILE MORE.DATA$ = "Y" OR  MORE.DATA$ = "y"
120     INPUT "Enter temperature (cold/cool/warm/hot): ", TEMP$
130     INPUT "Enter sky condition (clear/ptly sunny/overcast):  ", SKY$
140     IF (TEMP$ = "cool" OR TEMP$ = "warm") AND (SKY$ <> "overcast")
            THEN LPRINT "A nice day"
            ELSE LPRINT "Perhaps tomorrow will be a nice day"
150 INPUT "Do you have more weather data to enter (Y or N): "; MORE.DATA$
160 WEND
```

Program Assignments

1. A local gift shop needs a program to calculate the pay of each employee.

   The input to the program is:

   Employee name
   Hours worked
   Pay rate

   The formulas for calculating pay are:

   $$\begin{aligned}
   \text{Gross pay} &= \text{Hours} \times \text{Rate} \\
   \text{State tax} &= 7\% \times \text{Gross pay} \\
   \text{Federal tax} &= 12\% \times \text{Gross pay} \\
   \text{FICA} &= 6.5\% \times \text{Gross pay} \\
   \text{Net pay} &= \text{Gross pay} - (\text{State tax} \\
   &\quad + \text{Federal tax} + \text{FICA})
   \end{aligned}$$

   Design a screen to display the following information for each employee:

   Employee name
   Gross pay
   State tax
   Federal tax
   FICA
   Net pay

   Write a program that allows the user to enter the data for one employee and then view the results on the screen. The program should allow the user to repeat the entry process until the user enters a signal value, and then an end-of-program message should appear on the screen.

2. Professor Zuckerman would like a program to calculate averages for his classes to shorten the time it takes him to post grades each semester. The final grade is determined by scores received on one test, a term paper, and a final. The test, for which the maximum score is 150 points, accounts for 20% of the final grade. The term paper, for which the maximum score is 100 points, accounts for 50% of the grade. The final exam, for which the maximum score is 200 points, accounts for 30% of the final grade.

   The input to the program is:

   Student name
   Score on test
   Score on the project
   Score on the final exam

   The formula for calculating a weighted average is:

   $$100 \times \left(\left(\frac{\text{test score}}{150} \times .20 \right) + \left(\frac{\text{project score}}{100} \times .50 \right) + \left(\frac{\text{final exam}}{200} \times .30 \right) \right)$$

   Design a screen to display the data entered plus the student's average. Also indicate what letter grade the student will receive.

   A = 90–100
   B = 80–89
   C = 70–79
   D = 60–69
   F = 0–59

   The program should allow Professor Zuckerman to repeat the process until he enters some predetermined value. At the end of the program, a closing message should appear on the screen.

```
                    MONKTON BANK
                    MONKTON MARYLAND

              Exchange rate =      -#
              Dollar amount = ###

      Monkton Bank

              Pounds           ###
              Commission -      ##

              Net Pounds = ###

      Bank of London

              Pounds           ###
              Commission -       #

              Net Pounds = ###


                      Best exchange rate = xxxxxxxxxxxxxxx
```

Screen design form for Program Assignment 5-3

3. A tour group is about to fly to London. Each member has the choice of exchanging his or her dollars at the local bank in Monkton or at the Bank of London. The Monkton Bank charges a 4% commission on each currency transaction. In London, the bank deducts 2 pounds per transaction.

The Monkton Bank would like a program that requests the current exchange rate once at the beginning of execution and then, for each tour member, the number of dollars to be exchanged. The program would then calculate the pounds that would be received in Monkton and the pounds that would be received in London.

The program should also print a message indicating whether the customer should exchange his or her money at the bank in Monkton or the bank in London. The bank would like the results displayed as shown on the screen design form, with the currency values rounded to a whole number. The program should allow the bank clerk to repeat this process as long as the clerk desires. At the end of the program, an end-of-program message should appear.

Use the following exchange rates when testing the program:

.5 pounds per dollar
.6 pounds per dollar

Use the screen design shown.

Using the Data Disk

1. Insert the data disk into the disk drive.

2. Load BASIC.

3. Load CH5-1.DD.

   a. Run the program. Notice that the program's output is immediately erased from the screen. Modify the program to correct this problem.
   b. Make any other modifications to the program's output that you think makes it easier to read.
   c. Save the revised program as CH5-2.DD.

4. Key in the statements in Problem 6, one at a time, and correct any syntax errors.

5. Write and test the series of IF statements you wrote to answer Problem 11. Write and test a nested IF, as specified in Problem 12, to perform the same calculations.

6. The Rough Riders Outing Club maintains an electronic bulletin board. They would like to offer a program on the bulletin board that would help prospective members determine if they would enjoy club activities. Members who stick with the club tend to have the following characteristics:

   ■ They enjoy being outdoors.

   ■ They are willing to tolerate such physical discomforts as getting wet and being bothered by insects.

   ■ They enjoy physical exercise.

   a. Write an interactive program that determines if a caller has each of these traits and then suggests whether club membership is something the caller is likely to enjoy. If the caller has all three traits, have the program report that the caller is very likely to enjoy the club; if a caller has one or two of the traits, have the program report that the caller is likely to enjoy it. If a caller has none, have the program report that the person is not likely to enjoy the club.
   b. Add a WHILE/WEND loop to the program.
   c. Save the program as CH5-3.DD.

Chapter Six

Introduction to Files and Sequential File Processing

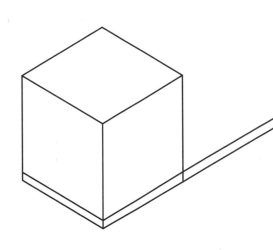

Topics

- Structure and characteristics of files
- Writing a program using a sequential input file

BASIC Statements and Functions

```
OPEN
INPUT #
EOF
CLOSE
```

INTRODUCTION

To write practical programs that require any significant amount of data input, you need to master the use of data files. So far, you have used only the INPUT statement to enter data into your programs. In actual applications, data are often entered from files stored on disks.

There are two important reasons for using files. First, many users need to process thousands or hundreds of thousands of data items, far too many to key in every time a program is run. Second, data produced by one program can become the input for another program, eliminating the need to reenter data manually.

This chapter begins with a general discussion of data file characteristics and processing. Then it introduces sequential files, the file type most often used for batch processing of data. A program example illustrates how to use sequential files for program input.

FILE CONCEPTS

A *file* is a collection of data in a defined format so that individual data items are distinguishable. A telephone book is a common example of a file in a defined format. The format is: the name to the left with the last name first, the phone number to the right, and the address between the name and number; these three items are in the same position (name, address, number) for every listing in the book. The individual names are arranged alphabetically.

File Organization

A *field* is a single data item within the file. Each field is made up of characters. A product code, a purchase price, and a transaction date are all examples of a field. Each entry or record in the telephone book has three fields: the person's name, address, and number.

A field can be either numeric or string. A numeric field can be used in computations and may contain only digits, a decimal point, or a minus sign. String fields may contain any combination of characters.

A *record* is a group of fields that contain data about a specific individual, object, or event. In the telephone book, an individual's name, address, and telephone number constitute a record. Notice that in every record in the telephone book, the fields are in the same order: name, address, number.

A *file* is a collection of related records, with each record having the same fields arranged in the same order. Common files in business computer systems are payroll, accounts payable, and inventory.

The top part of Figure 6.1 pictures an example of another familiar file, a set of checks returned with a monthly account statement. The collection of returned checks is a file. Each check is a record made up of the following fields: check number, date, payee, character amount, numeric amount, and account number.

Although each check contains different data, all the checks have the same format. Each field on the check is a set of numeric or string characters. The bottom portion of Figure 6.1 shows the check data as it might be entered in a computer file. Figure 6.2 shows how the check file's fields and records might be stored on a microcomputer diskette.

File Types

Master files contain relatively permanent data. A file of student records is an example. A student record might include fields for the student's name,

FIGURE 6.1
An example of a file of checks

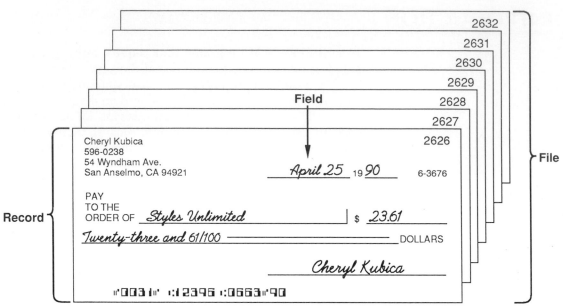

Field1	Field2	Field3	Field4
2626	23.61	04/25/90	Styles Unlimited
2627	44.44	04/25/90	Bargain Books
2628	13.76	05/01/90	Sport Mart
2629	387.67	05/01/90	People's Bank
2630	33.09	05/01/90	Gregory's Market
2631	149.75	05/01/90	Pacific Gas & Elec
2632	60.50	05/04/90	Carroll's Insurance

FIGURE 6.2
Sequential file storage on magnetic disk

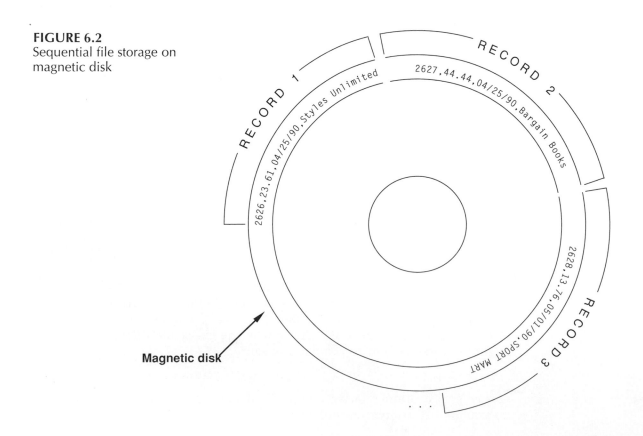

address, class, sex, credit hours completed, and grade point average (gpa). An inventory file is another example; inventory file records normally include a product number, cost, price, location, and quantity on hand.

Transaction files contain records of data activity used to update a master file. For example, at the end of each semester, many colleges create a transaction file with the data necessary to update two fields—grade point average and credit hours completed—in their student files. Similarly, files with data about sales and order transactions are necessary to update inventory files.

Record Keys

A *key* is a field in a record that either (1) identifies the record because its value is unique to that record or (2) indicates that the record belongs to a specific category of records within the file. Master file records have at least one *unique key* that distinguishes that record from all the others in the file. The check numbers in the Figure 6.1 file are a unique key. Social Security and other identification numbers are common unique keys in commercial files.

Updating a student master file provides an illustration of the use of keys that are not unique. The master file has a single record for each student, and that record is identified by a student identification number. At the end of each semester, the master file is updated with new grade reports. A transaction file contains a record for every course each student has taken. If, for example, a student took five courses, the transaction file has five transaction records with that student's ID number as a key.

File Access

Files are often referred to by the way they are organized and accessed in a computer system. In general, files are accessed sequentially, randomly (directly), or by using an index. If a majority of the records are to be processed, sequential access is usually more efficient. If a few records are to be processed or the records are processed in random order, direct access is necessary.

The records in *sequential files* are accessed sequentially, starting with the first record in the file. Each record must be stored or retrieved in consecutive order. The computer cannot access the 100th record in a sequential file without first accessing the previous 99 records. For example, reading the data for check number 2632 in Figure 6.1 requires reading through the data for checks 2626–2631 first. This is the only type of access possible for files stored on tapes.

Direct or *random-access* files allow direct access to any record. They may also be processed sequentially. Again, the telephone directory is a familiar example; you can go directly to any name in the directory without having to read through the preceding names, or you can start from the beginning of the book, examining each name in turn.

Indexed files are accessed directly using an index to reference records in a file. The index serves as a pointer to the location of the record and permits the computer to locate the record without having to read sequentially through the file. For example, to find information about file processing in this book, you may refer first to the index and then turn to the page number indicated. This method is much faster than starting on the first page and searching for information about file processing.

Some programming languages, including COBOL and RPG, support indexed organization, but BASIC does not. A combination of a sequential file, a table, and a random file can, however, be used to implement indexed files in BASIC.

File-Processing Programs

This text describes four types of file-processing programs. They are:

- Creation programs
- Update programs
- Report programs
- Inquiry programs

File-creation programs are necessary to build master files and create transaction files. Data are entered into these programs and then formatted according to the arrangement of the fields in a record. The records are then written to the file being created. These programs often contain data validation routines to verify that the data entered are correct.

File-updating programs keep the data in master files current. There are two general types of updating programs: posting and file maintenance.

Posting is the process of changing the value of one or more fields in a record. An example of posting is writing a check and adjusting the balance by subtracting the amount of the check.

File maintenance is the process of adding, deleting, and changing records in a master file. A college student file is a good example. It must be continually maintained as new students are admitted to the college, old students graduate or leave, and others change their addresses and telephone numbers.

Report programs produce reports based on the data in a file. The reports may contain a listing of all the records in the file or a summary of the data. Reports may also be classified by time. Some reports are produced at scheduled times, and others are produced only on demand.

Inquiry programs allow immediate access to a particular record in a file. For example, a bank teller may need to see a customer's current balance, or the registrar may need to see whether a student has enough credits to graduate. The need for immediate access has increased substantially in recent years.

File Compatibility

File-processing programs are seldom used in isolation. They frequently must be able to read data from a file created by another program and write data to a file for still another program to use. For this to occur, the design of the fields and records in the various files needs to be coordinated so that the programs produce compatible files.

USING SEQUENTIAL FILES

To work with the data from a sequential file, you need to do the following:

1. Let BASIC know what disk file you want to use.

2. Assign that file a reference number for use in your program.

3. Read the data, each field from each record in turn, from the beginning of the file to the end, processing the data as you read each record. Alternatively, you might read the data until you locate a particular record and then process that record.

4. Tell BASIC that you are finished using the file.

A PROGRAM EXAMPLE USING A SEQUENTIAL FILE FOR INPUT

To understand the processing of data from a sequential file, consider the following problem:

> Mr. Bauer of Lowell and Bauer, Attorneys at Law, has requested a listing of the names of the firm's clients. This client file contains client account numbers and client names. The printed report for Mr. Bauer should include a heading, a single-spaced listing of the client names, and an end-of-report message.

Determine the Output

For a printed report like this one, a print chart, like a screen design form, is a helpful design tool. The numbers across the top of the chart reference the positions on the print line. The numbers at the left of the chart refer to the lines on the page.

Printers may have anywhere from 30 to 144 or more print positions. Some printers also have variable type sizes, and the number of spaces they print on a line varies accordingly. For example, many dot-matrix printers normally print 80 characters per line, but most can also print in a condensed mode that allows 132 characters per line. The trade-off for the extra characters is decreased readability.

A report typically has three categories of lines. *Heading lines* are printed at the top to title the report and identify columns of information. *Detail lines* are those printed every time a record is processed. *Summary lines* appear at the end of a report (or of a section of a report) after the records in a file (or portion of it) have been processed. They may include numeric totals and end-of-report messages.

For the Lowell and Bauer report, you need to design a simple heading, the detail lines of the body of the report, and an end-of-report message. The print chart in Figure 6.3 shows a suitable design for this program's output.

The heading line of the print chart consists of the actual letters to be printed. A blank line separates the heading line from the detail lines. The detail lines start on line 3 of the report. Xs appear in each of the 20 blocks where data might be printed. (There are 20 Xs because a maximum of 20 characters is allowed in CLIENT.NAME$.) An X denotes that a character may be printed in a position. Which characters actually are printed depends on the contents of the file.

The three lines of Xs on this print chart indicate that more than one line will probably be printed, but the number of lines printed depends on the number of records processed. The three consecutive lines of Xs also indicate that the detail lines are single-spaced. The end-of-report message is spaced one line beyond the last detail line, and the letters to be printed are placed in the print chart blocks.

Below the print chart in Figure 6.3 is an actual report from the program so that you can see the relationship between the print chart and the program's output.

After completing the design, you ask Mr. Bauer to review your plans to ensure that this is the report he wants. In this case, he agrees that the report is, indeed, just what he needs, and he compliments you on your good work.

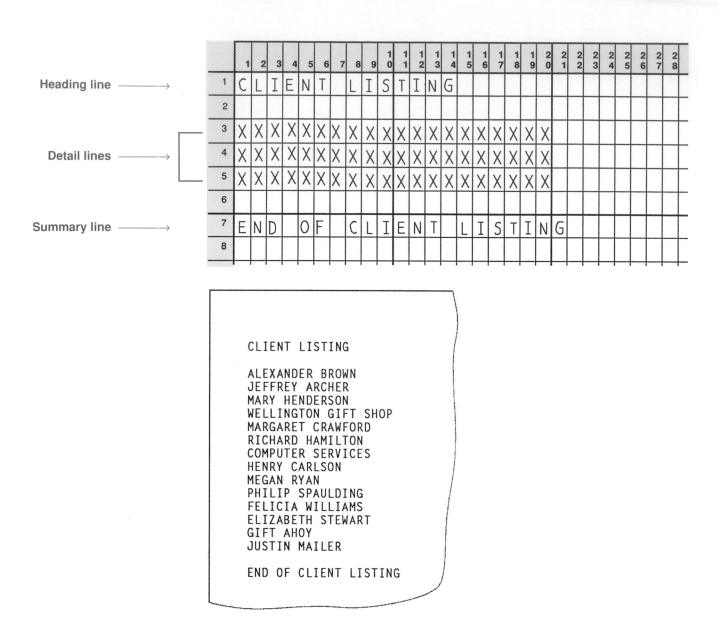

	1	2	3	4	5	6	7	8	9	10	11	12	13	14	15	16	17	18	19	20	21	22	23	24	25	26	27	28
1	C	L	I	E	N	T		L	I	S	T	I	N	G														
2																												
3	X	X	X	X	X	X	X	X	X	X	X	X	X	X	X	X	X	X										
4	X	X	X	X	X	X	X	X	X	X	X	X	X	X	X	X	X	X										
5	X	X	X	X	X	X	X	X	X	X	X	X	X	X	X	X	X	X										
6																												
7	E	N	D		O	F		C	L	I	E	N	T		L	I	S	T	I	N	G							
8																												

Heading line →

Detail lines →

Summary line →

```
CLIENT LISTING

ALEXANDER BROWN
JEFFREY ARCHER
MARY HENDERSON
WELLINGTON GIFT SHOP
MARGARET CRAWFORD
RICHARD HAMILTON
COMPUTER SERVICES
HENRY CARLSON
MEGAN RYAN
PHILIP SPAULDING
FELICIA WILLIAMS
ELIZABETH STEWART
GIFT AHOY
JUSTIN MAILER

END OF CLIENT LISTING
```

FIGURE 6.3   Report design for Lowell and Bauer

Determine the Input

The input file for the Lowell and Bauer client listing is a sequential file of records with the fields CLIENT.ACCT$ and CLIENT.NAME$, in that order. The name of the file is CLIENT.SEQ. The client name field may not exceed 20 characters, but names may be shorter than 20 characters. The client account number field, which is not used in this program, is 3 characters long.

Table 6.1 lists a set of sample records in the Lowell and Bauer file so that you can see the relationship between the record definition and the data in each record of the file. In this example, the string fields are surrounded by double quotes. The quotes are optional, and in this text, we present examples of files with and without the quotes.

Table 6.1   Description and Sample Records for CLIENT.SEQ

CLIENT.SEQ is a sequential input file

Record description:

Field name	Data length	Data type
CLIENT.ACCT$	3	String
CLIENT.NAME$	20	String

Sample records:

```
"101","ALEXANDER BROWN"
"150","JEFFREY ARCHER"
"201","MARY HENDERSON"
"301","WELLINGTON GIFT SHOP"
"360","MARGARET CRAWFORD"
"401","RICHARD HAMILTON"
"501","COMPUTER SERVICES"
"540","HENRY CARLSON"
"601","MEGAN RYAN"
"701","PHILIP SPAULDING"
"780","FELICIA WILLIAMS"
"801","ELIZABETH STEWART"
"820","GIFT AHOY"
"901","JUSTIN MAILER"
```

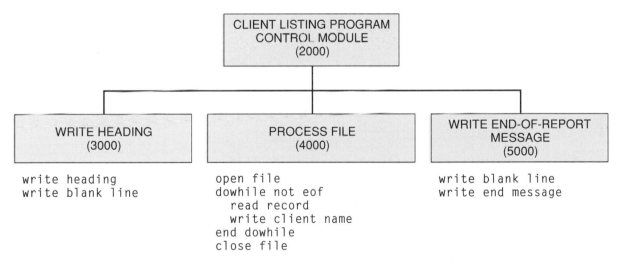

FIGURE 6.4   Logic design for Program 6.1

Design the Program Logic

The program for Mr. Bauer must:

1. Write a heading.

2. Process the file.

    a. Prepare to read the input file.
    b. Read each record.
    c. Write each name to a detail line.
    d. Close the file.

3. Write the end-of-report message.

Figure 6.4 displays a logic design for this program.

Code the Program Instructions

Now that you have completed the program design, you are ready to code the program instructions. Program 6.1 contains one possible version of the code to provide Mr. Bauer's client listing.

Line 1020 gives the program a title. Lines 1090–1120 list the variable names used in the program. The first module in the program is the CONTROL module (lines 2000–2999). This module calls the other modules in order, the WRITE HEADING module (lines 3000–3999) first, then the PROCESS FILE module (lines 4000–4999), and finally the WRITE END-OF-REPORT MESSAGE module (lines 5000–5070).

PROGRAM 6.1

```
1000 ' PROG6-1
1010 ' *****************************
1020 ' *      CLIENT LISTING        *
1030 ' *****************************
1040 '
1050 ' *****************************
1060 ' *         VARIABLES          *
1070 ' *****************************
1080 '
1090 ' CLIENT.SEQ              Client File
1100 ' Client record:
1110 '    CLIENT.ACCT$
1120 '    CLIENT.NAME$
1999 '
2000 ' *****************************
2010 ' *      CONTROL MODULE        *
2020 ' *****************************
2030 '
2040    GOSUB 3000              'Write Heading
2050    GOSUB 4000              'Process File
2060    GOSUB 5000              'Write End-of-Report Message
2070    END
2999 '
3000 ' *****************************
3010 ' *      WRITE HEADING         *
3020 ' *****************************
3030 '
3040    LPRINT "CLIENT LISTING"
3050    LPRINT
3060    RETURN
3999 '
4000 ' *****************************
4010 ' *       PROCESS FILE         *
4020 ' *****************************
4030 '
4040    OPEN "CLIENT.SEQ" FOR INPUT AS #1
4050    WHILE NOT EOF(1)
4060       INPUT #1, CLIENT.ACCT$,
                    CLIENT.NAME$
4070       LPRINT CLIENT.NAME$
4080    WEND
4090    CLOSE #1
4100    RETURN
4999 '
5000 ' *****************************
5010 ' *     WRITE END-OF-REPORT    *
5020 ' *          MESSAGE           *
5030 ' *****************************
5040 '
5050    LPRINT
5060    LPRINT "END OF CLIENT LISTING"
5070    RETURN
```

New BASIC Instructions

The OPEN statement lets BASIC know what disk file you want to read and assigns a number that refers to that file in the program. All files must be opened before they can be used for input or output.

OPEN Statement

The general form of the statement to open a sequential file is:

```
[line#] OPEN <filename> [FOR mode] AS [#] <filenumber>
```

Filename must be the name of an existing disk file or a name to be given to a new file. The name must be a valid DOS file name with from 1–8 characters; it may be followed by an extension of from 1–3 characters. The characters allowed in DOS filenames are:

```
A-Z a-z 0-9 $ & # @ ! % ` ' ( ) - { } _ ^ ~
```

Like variable names, file names should be as descriptive as possible. In this program, CLIENT describes the contents of the file, and SEQ describes the type of file.

The *mode* must be either INPUT, OUTPUT, or APPEND. APPEND is used to add to the end of an existing file. (See Chapter 8 for a discussion of APPEND.) OUTPUT is used to write to a file. (See Chapter 8.) INPUT is used to read from a file.

The number sign is optional, but *filenumber* is not; it must be an integer between 1 and the maximum number of files that can be open at one time. The default maximum is three, but you can increase that number by starting BASIC with the /F:n option. For example,

```
A>BASICA/F:6
```

allows you to have six files open at once.

Line 4040 of the program, OPEN "CLIENT.SEQ" FOR INPUT AS #1, causes the computer to search for a file on the default drive named CLIENT.SEQ and to place a pointer at the beginning of the file in preparation for a read instruction. If you want to read the file from a drive other than the current default drive, you need to put a drive designator in front of the file name, for example, "B:CLIENT.SEQ".

The AS #1 portion of line 4040 associates file number 1 with the file CLIENT.SEQ on the disk for as long as the file remains open. All other BASIC instructions that refer to the file (lines 4050, 4060, and 4090) use this number instead of the name. (This number actually references the memory buffer through which records are passed.)

The OPEN statement in line 4040 may also be written as

```
4040 OPEN "I", #1, "CLIENT.SEQ"
```

We prefer the form used in the program because it is easier to read.

INPUT # Statement

This is the statement you must use to read data from sequential files. Its general format is

```
[line#] INPUT #<filenumber>, <var1> [,var2,...,varN]
```

When the INPUT # statement in line 4060 is executed, the computer reads the two fields of the client record from the CLIENT.SEQ file and assigns their values one at a time, in order, to the listed variables, CLIENT.ACCT$ and CLIENT.NAME$.

As a programmer, you must ensure that:

1. The number of fields listed in the INPUT statement equals the number of fields in the record.

2. The type of data in the field matches the type of the variable name. For example, if the items in a field will be used later in the program with statements requiring numbers, the variable name should be numeric; if the field contains character items, the variable name must indicate a string variable.

Notice that CLIENT.ACCT$ and CLIENT.NAME$ appear on separate lines in statement 4060 to enhance readability.

EOF Function

This BASIC built-in function lets you write a WHILE/WEND loop that will exit after all of the records in the file are read. The general format of the function is

```
EOF(filenumber)
```

where filenumber refers to the number with which the file being read was opened.

EOF signals that the end of the file being read has been reached and that there are no more records to read. It must be used in line 4050 because, when a sequential file is read, an attempt to read past the last record in the file produces an INPUT PAST END error and stops program execution.

In Chapter 5, you learned that it is necessary to use a priming read (INPUT) before a WHILE/WEND loop and another read (INPUT) at the end of the loop. When the read is from a sequential file (INPUT #), the priming read is not necessary because BASIC recognizes the end-of-file *as* the last record is read rather than *after* it is read. After EOF notes the end of file, the WHILE/WEND loop is not entered again; instead, control passes to the statement following WEND. If the file is empty, the loop is not entered at all, and control passes immediately to the statement following WEND.

CLOSE Statement

When you are finished reading from the file, you should use a CLOSE statement to tell BASIC that you are finished with the file. The general format of the CLOSE statement is

```
[line #] CLOSE [[#] filenumber] [,[#]filenumber . . .]
```

This statement cancels the association between a file number and a file name. After the execution of line 4090 in Program 6.1, the number 1 is no longer associated with CLIENT.SEQ. If the program logic so required, you could open the file CLIENT.SEQ again using the same number or a different number. A CLOSE statement that specifies no numbers closes all files currently open.

It is good programming practice to close all files before executing the END statement. The NEW, RUN, and END instructions, however, automatically close any open files.

Test the Program

To test your program, run it with the file CLIENT.SEQ until you eliminate all syntax and logic errors. Check the output for accuracy. Also check the printer output for readability.

You can create your own sequential file for testing by using the DOS COPY command and sending the output to a disk file. You can do that in this way:

```
A>COPY CON CLIENT.SEQ<Enter>
101,ALEXANDER BROWN<Enter>
150,JEFFREY ARCHER<Enter>
201,MARY HENDERSON<Enter>
^Z<Enter>
```

The words on the line with the A> tell the system to copy what you enter from the console (the keyboard, in this case) to a file (on drive A) called CLIENT.SEQ. (If the file is to be placed on drive B, type B: before the file name or change to the B> prompt.) Each succeeding line you enter is then written to the file as a record. After entering the last record, end the file by pressing F6 (or Ctrl-Z) and then pressing the Enter key.

Notice that in this example the fields in the record are separated by a comma and that the strings are not enclosed in quotation marks. The commas are required to separate the fields, but the quotes are optional.

Caution! If you are exiting BASIC to create a file, be sure to save your program. If you are using a version of BASIC that supports the SHELL command, you can enter the command SHELL from BASIC. Doing so returns you to the system prompt. After you have created your file and are ready to return to BASIC, enter EXIT. SHELL is convenient because it lets you avoid having to reboot BASIC and reload your program.

OUTPUT OF PROGRAM 6.1

When CLIENT.SEQ contains the sample set of records shown in Table 6.1, Program 6.1 produces the report shown in Figure 6.3.

DOCUMENTATION

Complete documentation for this program is provided in Appendix F.

❋ **STYLE TIPS**

1. *List your file names.* At the beginning of the program, list the file and the fields in the file in the section where you list your variable names.

2. *Select meaningful file and field names.* As with variable names, select file names that describe the contents of the file. For example, label a sequential file with the extension SEQ. Begin the name of each field with the file name; this ensures that the fields are easily recognized as components of the record structure of the file.

3. *Indent for readability.* Insofar as BASIC's line length allows, placing the field names in the INPUT # statement on separate lines makes the statement easier to read.

Summary

- A *field* is a set of one or more characters. A *record* is a collection of related fields arranged in a specific order and format. A *file* is a collection of related records.

- *Master files* contain relatively permanent data.

- *Transaction files* contain records of data activity that will be used to update a master file.

- A *key* is a field in a record that either (1) identifies the record because its value is unique to that record or (2) indicates that the record belongs to a specific category of records within the file.

- Files are often referred to by the way they are organized and accessed in a computer system.

  □ The records in *sequential files* are accessed sequentially, starting with the first record in the file.

  □ *Direct* or *random-access* files allow direct access to any record. They may also be processed sequentially.

  □ *Indexed files* are accessed directly using an index to reference records in a file.

- *File-creation programs* are necessary to build master files and create transaction files.

- *File-updating programs* keep the data in master files current by posting and file maintenance. *Posting* is the process of changing the value of one or more fields in a record. *File maintenance* is the process of adding, deleting, and changing records in a master file.

- *Report programs* produce reports based on the data in a file.

- *Inquiry programs* allow immediate access to a particular record in a file.

- The chapter explains the use of these BASIC statements and functions:

CLOSE	A statement that dissociates a disk file from a BASIC program.
EOF	A function that signals when the end of a sequential file is reached.
INPUT #	A statement that reads data from sequential files.
OPEN	A statement that makes the preparations necessary for reading from or writing to a file.

Review Questions

1. What is a field? A record? A file?
2. What is a record key?.
3. List some common examples of files.
4. What are the characteristics of sequential files?
5. What are heading lines? Detail lines? Summary lines?
6. What is a print chart? How can print charts be useful in developing programs?
7. When is an OPEN statement necessary? What happens when it is executed?
8. What, if any, correspondence is there between the file number in an OPEN statement and the file number in an INPUT # statement?
9. Explain the purpose and the use of the EOF function.
10. What will happen if you do not close the files used in a program?

Problems

1. Use the following data with Program 6.1 for these problems:

   ```
   101,ALEXANDER BROWN
   150,JEFFREY ARCHER
   201,MARY HENDERSON
   301,WELLINGTON GIFT SHOP
   ```

   a. What will the computer print if line 4060 is written as

   ```
   4060  INPUT #1, CLIENT.NAME$,
                   CLIENT.ACCT$
   ```

   b. What will the computer print if line 4060 is written as

   ```
   4060 INPUT #1, CLIENT.ACCT$, CLIENT.NAME$,
                   CLIENT.ACCT$, CLIENT.NAME$
   ```

   c. What will the computer print if line 4060 is written as

   ```
   4060  INPUT #1, CLIENT.ACCT$,
                   CLIENT.NAME$,
                   CLIENT.ACCT$
   ```

2. Correct the syntax, logic, and documentation errors in this version of Program 6.1.

```
1000 ' PROG6-1
1010 ' ****************************
1020 ' *         SALES LISTING        *
1030 ' ****************************
1040 '
1050 ' ****************************
1060 ' *           VARIABLES          *
1070 ' ****************************
1080 '
1090 ' CLIENT.FILE        Client File
1100 ' Client record:
1110 '     ACCT$
1120 '     NAME$
1999 '
2000 ' ****************************
2010 ' *       CONTROL MODULE         *
2020 ' ****************************
2030 '
2040   GOSUB 4000        'Write Heading
2050   GOSUB 3000         Process File
2060   GOSUB 6000        'Write Summary Lines
2070   END
2999 '
3000 ' ****************************
3010 ' *          END OF JOB          *
3020 ' ****************************
3030 '
3040 ' LPRINT "CLIENT LISTING"
3050   LPRINT
3060   RETURN
3999 '
4000 ' ****************************
4010 ' *         PROCESS FILE         ^
4020 ' ****************************
4030 '
4040   OPEN "CLIENT.SEQ FOR OUTPUT AS #1
4050   WHILE NOT EOF(2)
4060       INPUT #1, CLIENT.NAME$,
                     CLIENT.ACCT$
4070       LPRINT CLIENT.NAME
4080   END
4090   CLOSE #1
4100   RETURN
4999 '
5000 ' ****************************
5010 ' *     WRITE END-OF-REPORT      *
5020 ' *            MESSAGE           *
5030 ' ****************************
5040 '
5050   PRINT: PRINT
5060   LPRINT "END OF CLIENT LISTING"
```

Program Assignments

1. The Baltimore division of the MAIL-USA Catalog Company needs a listing of customer name and zip codes. A sequential file contains the name and zip code of each customer. You are to design a printed report that includes a general heading, column headings, a single-spaced listing of customer names and zip codes, and an end-of-report message. The detail line should also include PARKVILLE if the zip code is 21234. Write a program to generate your report.

a. CUST.SEQ Sequential Input File
b. CUST Record:

Field Name	Data Length	Data Type
CUST.NAME$	20	String
CUST.ZIP$	5	String

c. File contents:

```
ALONZO BEAM,21234
AMANDA BLACK,21234
ALISHA CORDAY,21221
COLEMAN CORDISH,21111
BENJAMIN DAVIS,21204
CHRISTEN DERBY,21234
PHILIP DURHAM,21030
NEVIN HILLIARD,21111
CHRISTOPHER LEWIS,21111
ELLEN MCKINNEY,21234
ANDREW PARK,21221
JACK REMSON,21237
JEFFREY SNYDER,21111
SASKIA TRAILL,21234
MARK TRESS,21221
GREGORY WINTERS,21234
TIMOTHY YORK,21204
```

2. Mr. Foley needs a listing of names and grades of students in his eighth-grade social studies class. The sequential file contains the name and grade (from 0–100 percent) of each student in the class. Write a program to produce a printed report to meet the requirements on the print chart design. Notice that the letter grade is also printed on the detail line. Determine the letter grade as follows:

```
A = 90-100
B = 80-89
C = 70-79
D = 60-69
F = 0-59
```

a. STU.SEQ Sequential Input File
b. STU Record:

Field Name	Data Length	Data Type
STU.NAME$	20	String
STU.GRADE	3	Numeric

c. File contents

```
ANDREA BEDINGFIELD,95
JEREMY BROWN,89
ANNE CHAMBERS,60
KELLY DEVLIN,78
ARLO DEXTER,75
LARRY FINNEGAN,52
RENEE GUCKERT,90
JANICE KELSEY,83
JULIE LORIMAR,87
COLIN MEEKS,99
ASA NAYLOR,0
CANDICE ROLLINS,79
PETE SMITH,98
JOE-PAUL SWINSKI,70
JOSEPH WAYNE,100
```

d. The report design is shown below.

3. As a programmer for the Putnam County Bank, you are comparing the bank's mailing list for promotional materials and its master checking account file and find that many customers are not on the mailing list. On closer inspection, you find that all customers whose account numbers are greater than 2000000 and less than 4000000 have been left off the mailing list.

Write a program to print the names of all customers who are not on the mailing list. Design a report that includes a heading line, detail lines, and an end-of-report message.

a. CHECK.SEQ Sequential Input File

b. CHECK Record:

Field Name	Data Length	Data Type
CHECK.ACCT$	7	String
CHECK.NAME$	20	String
CHECK.BALANCE#	10	Numeric

c. File contents:

```
1025576,"Murry,Beverly",321.88
1030978,"Bare,F. W.",10.44
2599834,"Sturgeon,Hazel",13015.69
3728841,"Angelo,Mary",778.21
3898141,"Tierney,Jeanne",57098.02
4581787,"Reveal,John T.",3001.00
5213445,"Yao,Wei Chu",4999.11
8852601,"Eng,Joseph",929.44
```

	1	2	3	4	5	6	7	8	9	10	11	12	13	14	15	16	17	18	19	20	21	22	23	24	25	26	27	28	29	30	31	32	33	34	35	36	37	38	39
1														S	T	U	D	E	N	T		G	R	A	D	E		R	E	P	O	R	T						
2																																							
3													N	A	M	E													G	R	A	D	E						
4																																							
5			X	X	X	X	X	X	X	X	X	X	X	X	X	X	X	X	X	X	X	X	X			X		(		X	X	%	)						
6			X	X	X	X	X	X	X	X	X	X	X	X	X	X	X	X	X	X	X	X	X			X		(		X	X	X		%	)				
7			X	X	X	X	X	X	X	X	X	X	X	X	X	X	X	X	X	X	X	X	X			X		(		X	X		%	)						
8																																							
9													E	N	D		O	F		G	R	A	D	E		R	E	P	O	R	T								
10																																							

Report design for Program Assignment 6-2

Using the Data Disk

These exercises will help you learn some useful DOS commands to use when working with sequential files. Refer to Appendix B for more information.

1. Insert the data disk into the disk drive.

2. Change the default drive to the drive where the data disk is residing.

3. Using the DOS COPY command to create a file directly from the keyboard

   a. Enter the following command:

   ```
   COPY CON NAME.SEQ
   ```

   b. Enter a last name and press the Enter key. Repeat this process five times.
   c. Press the F6 function key (or the Ctrl and Z keys) and press the Enter key.
   d. You have now created a sequential data file.

4. Using the DOS TYPE command

   a. Enter the command:

   ```
   TYPE NAMF.SEQ
   ```

   b. Notice that the five last names you entered now appear on the screen. This is a useful command for viewing a data file when testing a program.

   (1)   How many records are in the NAME.SEQ file?
   (2)   How many fields are in each record?

5. Using EDLIN

   a. You can only create a file with COPY; you cannot use COPY to make any changes to a data file. However, with EDLIN you may add, delete, and change records in a data file. Refer to Appendix B for information about EDLIN.
   b. If you are using a hard disk, enter

   ```
   C:\DOS\EDLIN TEL.SEQ
   ```

   If you are using dual floppy drives, enter

   ```
   A:EDLIN TEL.SEQ
   ```

   c. The following lines will appear on the screen:

   ```
   New file
   *
   ```

   d. Press I for insert and press the Enter key. The following will appear on the screen:

   ```
   1:*
   ```

e. Type the following, pressing the Enter key at the end of each line:

```
1:*STEVENS,654-332
2:*MITCHELL,344-5654
3:*PATE,432-1009
4:*TRACEY,999-8888
```

f. Now press the Ctrl-C key combination.

g. Press E and the Enter key to end the session.

h. Now call back the file TEL.SEQ using EDLIN.

    (1)   List the file.

    (2)   Add a record to the file.

    (3)   Change a record in the file.

    (4)   Delete a record in the file.

    (5)   Save the file.

6. Using the DOS COPY command to send output to the printer

a. Enter the following command

```
COPY TEL.SEQ LPT1
```

b. Notice that you now have a hard copy of the TEL.SEQ file. This list can be handy when you are testing a program using a data file to confirm what data are in the file.

    (1)   How many records are in the data file?

    (2)   How many fields are in each record?

    (3)   How are the fields separated?

Chapter Seven

Report Design

Topics

- Components of a report
- Report design
- Preparation of summary lines

BASIC Statements and Functions

```
LPRINT USING
PRINT USING
PRINT #
STRING$(n,"x")
CHR$(n)
WIDTH
```

INTRODUCTION

Businesses utilize a variety of reports. *Detail reports* contain detailed information, usually about every record in a file. *Summary reports* contain more general information obtained by calculating totals, averages, and other summary values from the records in detail reports. *Edit reports* are used to help check the data in a file; they usually contain a listing of a file's contents and an error message for each inappropriate data item.

Reports are also often categorized by time. *Periodic reports* are generated at specified intervals, for instance, weekly, monthly, or quarterly. *Demand reports* are generated whenever they are requested. *Exception reports* are generated whenever some exceptional condition occurs.

Whatever the type, good reports must meet two requirements:

1. They must contain the information the user wants.

2. The information must be easy to read.

In this chapter, we offer suggestions for ensuring that your reports meet these requirements.

REPORT DESIGN

Every report should have a *main heading* that tells (1) the purpose of the report, (2) the date the report was run and, when relevant, (3) the time period covered in the report. Some titles can be very short, but others need to be more detailed. You must make certain that the heading contains everything the user needs to know to identify the report's purpose and the time to which it applies.

If a report is longer than one page, every page should have a title and a page number. You may abbreviate the title that appears on pages after the first, but the abbreviated title should fully identify the report. Place this heading information in a consistent location (top or bottom, in the center, flush left, or flush right) on all the organization's reports.

Each page of the report should also contain *column headings*. Avoid crowding the columns. If you need more space for a column heading, use multiple lines. If you have too many columns for the page, use a wider page or a smaller type if possible.

The body of a report is comprised of rows of *detail lines*. There is usually one detail line for each input record processed for the report. For example, a student grade report contains one detail line for each student record in the input file. For ease of reading insert a blank line after every 5 to 10 detail lines in a long report.

Reports also normally contain some *summary lines*. Counts of records and column totals are the most common. Subtotals for departments or time periods are often included. Descriptive statistics or other, more sophisticated analyses of the data may also be required.

Depending on the requirements of the user, you may be able to do several things to ensure that your reports are easy to read. The most important is to avoid crowding. Also center your report on the page. Use line and column spacing to distinguish totals and subtotals from detail lines. Finally, edit to insert commas in numeric fields where appropriate, put slashes or dashes in dates, and avoid redundant dollar signs when the column heading identifies a monetary field.

The remainder of this chapter focuses on techniques for printing detail lines and preparing summary lines. Chapters 8 and 9 continue the discussion and show examples of reports that conform to the design recommendations outlined here.

Implementing Report Design

You can use some standard techniques to simplify report generation. In this section, you learn how to format and edit print lines using BASIC's LPRINT USING statement and how to prepare standard summary lines.

Before you proceed, *design your report on a print chart*. You will save time and avoid frustration as you begin translating your design into code, especially when you are coding PRINT USING and LPRINT USING statements.

The PRINT USING and LPRINT USING Statements

BASIC's PRINT USING and LPRINT USING statements greatly simplify the formatting and editing of print lines. Like PRINT and LPRINT, PRINT US-ING directs output to the screen and LPRINT USING directs it to the printer; otherwise, the two statements function alike. The examples in this chapter use LPRINT USING. PRINT USING is discussed in connection with screen design in Chapter 8.

You can use the LPRINT USING statement to:

- Right-justify numbers (the default is left-justification)
- Align decimal points in a column of numbers
- Specify the number of decimal digits to display
- Insert the comma, *, +, −, and $ symbols in numeric fields
- Round numeric values on output
- Include string constants at any location in the print line
- Begin printing fields at a specific column number

The format for the statement is:

```
[line#] LPRINT USING <format$>; <list of expressions> [;]
```

where *format$* is a string constant or variable that normally includes special format characters. The *list of expressions* includes the string and numeric values that are to be formatted and printed. By including special formatting characters in *format$*, you can edit and format both numbers and strings.

Printing String Values

You use three characters—the backslash (\), the ampersand (&), and the exclamation point (!)—to specify the format of printed strings. Suppose you want to print the following column headings:

```
          1         2         3         4         5  ←── position
12345678901234567890123456789012345678901234567890      numbers
     Name      Rank      Serial No.
```

This code does the job:

```
1000 '12345678901234567890123456789012345678901234567890
1010 HEAD$ =
     "        \   \     \   \     \         \"
1020 LPRINT USING HEAD$; "Name","Rank","Serial No."
```

(Line 1000 is a comment line to help you see the relationship between *format$* and the print line; it is not necessary in your programs.)

The backslashes indicate the beginning and end of the string. You need to insert enough spaces between them to allow for printing as much of the string as you want. If the string is *n* characters long, then you will need to put *n*–2 blanks between the backslashes because each backslash accounts for a character in the string.

Caution! Do not confuse the backslash (\) on the left side of the keyboard with the slash (/) on the right side of the keyboard. The slash has no special meaning in a PRINT USING statement.

You could also use the & symbol to indicate the positioning of these headings:

```
1000 '           12345678901234567890123456789012345 67890
1010 HEAD$ = "          &         &         &"
1020 LPRINT USING HEAD$: "Name","Rank","Serial No."
```

The & symbol indicates that the entire string will be printed. The first string begins at the location of the first & in HEAD$. The second string begins 7 spaces after the end of the first string and *not* in position 27. The third string also begins 7 spaces after the end of the second. Six blank spaces separate the three strings because the & symbols are 7 spaces apart.

This code use the ! :

```
1000 '12345678901234567890123456789012345 67890
1010 HEAD$ =
     "         !         !        !"
1020 LPRINT USING HEAD$; "Name","Rank","Serial No."
```

and this time the output is:

```
        1         2         3         4  ←— position
12345678901234567890123456789012345 67890     numbers
        N         R         S
```

As you can see, the ! causes only the first character of the string to be printed. Use this symbol when you want to print an initial instead of an entire name.

If there are more items in the list of expressions than you have provided for in *format$*, BASIC begins again at the beginning of *format$* without skipping to a new line. The following example shows a line of code and its output directly below.

```
1000 LPRINT USING "This is & "; "IT.", "REALLY IT."
This is IT. This is REALLY IT.
```

This is also true for the numeric field designations we will discuss.

Printing Numeric Values

The symbols for editing and formatting numeric fields are #, +, –, $, $$, *, the comma, and ^^^^. The # sign is used with every numeric field representation; each # represents a single digit. To see how the # works, look at these examples of statements and their output:

Example 1

```
1000 LPRINT USING "##.##"; 23.45
```

```
23.45
```

The first example shows that BASIC inserts the digits of the number to be printed in the appropriate positions on each side of the decimal point and then prints them.

The next two examples show what happens when there are more digits to the right of the decimal point than are specified in the print field. In these cases, the decimal portion of the number is *rounded* to fit the field specification. *Caution*! Although BASIC rounds the number as it is printed, the number stored in memory is not rounded.

Example 2

```
1000 LPRINT USING "##.##"; 23.451

23.45


1000 LPRINT USING "##.##"; 2.345

 2.35
```

Notice the space before the result in the previous example. BASIC right-justifies numbers as they are printed in fields specified with the #. This allows the programmer to align decimal points in a column of numbers even if the integer portions occupy different numbers of decimal places.

Example 3

```
1000 LPRINT USING "##.##"; .234

 0.23
```

In example 3, the integer portion of the number is equal to zero, and BASIC prints the 0, even though there is no zero in line 1000.

Example 4

```
1000 LPRINT USING "##.##"; 2345.89

%2345.89
```

When the integer portion of the number is larger than the field specification, as in example 4, BASIC prints the entire number but signals an error by printing the % symbol immediately before the number.

Example 5

```
1000 LPRINT USING "##.##"; -2

-2.00
```

Example 5 shows how a negative number is handled. The printed minus sign counts as a space in the field. For that reason, if the number to be printed were –22 instead of –2, the result would be %–22.00. The % indicates the overflow in the integer portion. Also notice that, even though no zeros appear after the –2, BASIC inserts zeros when it prints the number.

Now look at example 6. As with strings, you can use a single field specification to print multiple numbers on a line:

Example 6

```
1000 LPRINT USING "###.# "; 22, 33.19, 8, 144, 86.33

 22.0  33.2   8.0 144.0  86.3
```

> Here is a summary of points to remember about using the # symbol:
>
> 1. Use enough #'s to accommodate the integer portion of the number. BASIC adds blanks to the left if the integer portion has fewer digits than you specify.
>
> 2. If the field may contain a negative number, add an extra # to accommodate the sign.
>
> 3. The # symbols to the right of the decimal signify the decimal portion of the number to be printed. Use only as many #'s to the right of the decimal point as you want decimal places printed, and BASIC will print the number rounded to those specifications.

Controlling the Sign in a Number

You can use + and − to control the signs printed with numbers. If you add the − at the end of the field, any negative numbers will be printed with a trailing rather than leading negative sign, as in example 1:

Example 1

```
1000 LPRINT USING "###-"; -242

242-
```

In this case, the − in the format line provides a space for the trailing sign in the field so that there is no overflow error. Many business reports require that negative numbers be indicated in this fashion.

A + format symbol added at the beginning or end of a field causes the sign of the number to be printed at the beginning or end, respectively, as these examples illustrate:

Example 2

```
1000 LPRINT USING "+### +##"; -237, 32
1010 LPRINT USING "###+ ##+"; -237, 32

-237 +32
237- 32+
```

Adding a Fixed Dollar Sign

You can use the $ format symbol to include dollar signs in numeric output. A single $ causes a dollar sign to be printed to the left of all characters in the field, including any blank spaces.

```
1000 LPRINT USING "$###.##  "; 22.5, 1.98, 2, 714, .49

$ 22.50 $  1.98 $  2.00 $714.00 $  0.49
```

Adding a Floating Dollar Sign

To put the dollar sign to the immediate left of the leftmost digit in the field, use $$ in *format$*. The first $ is an extra character to be printed, and the second $ replaces the leftmost #.

```
1000 LPRINT USING "$$##.##  "; 22.5, 1.98, 2, 714, .49

$22.50    $1.98    $2.00 $714.00    $0.49
```

Printing Leading Asterisks

Sometimes you may want to fill unused portions of a numeric field with something other than blanks. PRINT USING allows you to use the * to insert leading asterisks in a field. A single * acts much as a single $ does, causing one asterisk to be printed at the beginning of a field. Two asterisks replace all leading blanks with asterisks, as in example 1.

Example 1

```
1000 LPRINT USING "**#.##  "; 22.5, 1.98, 2, 714, .49

*22.50  **1.98  **2.00  714.00  **0.49
```

Notice that both asterisks, like the # symbols, provide a position for a number, and there is no overflow.

You can combine the * and $ to fill leading blanks with asterisks and print a dollar sign to the immediate left of the number, as example 2 shows.

Example 2

```
1000 LPRINT USING "**$.##  "; 22.5, 1.98, 2, 714, .49

$22.50  *$1.98  *$2.00  %$714.00  *$0.49
```

The floating dollar sign and leading asterisk combination is often used for check writing to make it difficult to alter the printed value. For that purpose, make the field large enough to accommodate several leading asterisks, as in example 3.

Example 3

```
1000 LPRINT USING "**$###########.##"; 2192

********$2192.00
```

You can rewrite example 3 to put the dollar sign before the asterisks, as in example 4.

Example 4

```
1000 LPRINT USING "$**###########.##"; 2192

$********2192.00
```

Adding a Comma

Large numbers like 2378512 are much more readable if the digits are separated into groups of three with commas. To do that simply insert a comma in the field descriptor immediately to the right of the integer portion of the field. This example illustrates the use of the comma in both integer and decimal number fields:

```
1000 LPRINT USING "########, ####,.##"; 1234567, 1234.56

1,234,567 1,234.56
```

You can also place the field descriptor comma in the exact positions that you wish commas to be printed, and you can use the comma in combination with the other numeric editing symbols. For example, incorporating the comma in the code to print a check amount makes large figures easier to read:

```
1000 LPRINT USING "**$#,###,###,###.##"; 6289309.48

******$6,289,309.48
```

Using the Exponential Format

You can print a number in exponential format by using the ^^^^ format symbol, as in this example:

```
1000 LPRINT USING "##.########^^^^"; 1234.791

 1.23479100E+03
```

Printing Format Characters

Finally, what should you do when you need to include one of the formatting or editing characters in a print line? Yet another format symbol permits that. An underscore (_) tells BASIC that the next character is to be printed and not interpreted. For example, this code causes the # character to be printed:

```
1000 LPRINT USING "Item_# = ##"; 49

Item# = 49
```

Caution! If you want to print more than one format character on a print line, you must repeat the underscore:

```
1000 LPRINT USING "Item_# = ##_*_*_*"; 49

Item# = 49***
```

Summary of Format Characters

Tables 7.1 and 7.2 provide examples of format symbols and summarize their effects.

Table 7.1   Formatting and Editing Examples

Descriptor	Entry Value	Printed Result
&	"09-07-1997"	09-07-1997
\ßßßßßßß\	"09-07-1997"	09-07-199
\ßßßßßßß\	"09-07-97"	09-07-97ß
!	"09-07-1997"	0
_\		\
##.#	22.9	22.9
##.#	2.9	ß2.9
##.#	22.98	23.0
##.#	722.98	%723.0
##.#	.9	ß0.9
##.#	−12.0	%−12.0
##.#+	18.7	18.7+
##.#−	18.7	18.7
##.#−	−18.7	18.7−
+##.#	18.7	+18.7
####,	2042	2,042
#,###	2042	2,042
#,###.####	2042.9	2,042.9000
$###.##	32.81	$ß32.81
$$##.##	32.81	ß$32.81
**$###.##	32.81	***$32.81
$**###.##	32.81	$***32.81
##.##^^^^	1099.85	1.10E+03

ß = blank in descriptor or printed result

7.2 Formatting and Editing Symbols

Symbol	Description
&	Field descriptor for a left-justified character string of variable length, starting at the location of the first &.
\ \	Field descriptor for a fixed-length character string, beginning at the left \ and ending at the right \.
!	Describes a one-character field at the location of the !. If the string to be printed has more than one character, only the first character is printed.
#	Represents a single digit position in a numeric field. Use as many as necessary to accommodate the number to be printed.
+	Added to the left or right of a numeric field descriptor, causes the sign of the number to be printed to the immediate left or right, respectively, of the number.
–	Added to the right of a numeric field descriptor, causes the negative sign to appear to the immediate right, rather than left, of a negative number.
.	Used in a numeric field descriptor to position the decimal point in the output.
,	If used to the immediate right of the integer portion of a field descriptor, causes commas to be inserted between every third digit of the printed integer portion. You can also place the field descriptor commas exactly in the position where commas are desired in the output.
$	If used as the first symbol in a numeric field descriptor, causes a left-justified dollar sign to be inserted in the printed number.
$ $	If used as the first two symbols of a numeric field descriptor, causes a dollar sign to be printed to the immediate left of the leftmost digit. One of the $ format symbols reserves a place for a digit.
*	If used as the first symbol in a numeric field descriptor, causes a left-justified asterisk to be inserted in the printed number.
* *	If used as the first two symbols in a numeric field descriptor, causes asterisks to be substituted for leading blanks. Both * format symbols reserve places for digits.
* * $	If used as the first three symbols in a numeric field descriptor, causes a dollar sign to be inserted to the immediate left of the leftmost digit and asterisks to be substituted for leading blanks.
$ * *	If used as the first three symbols in a numeric field descriptor, causes a left-justified dollar sign to appear and asterisks to be substituted for leading blanks.
^ ^ ^ ^	If used as the final four symbols in a numeric field descriptor, causes the number to be printed in exponential notation.
_	The underscore before any of the above symbols causes the symbol to be printed as a character instead of interpreted as a format symbol.

GENERATING SUMMARY INFORMATION

The three most common items in report summary lines are *counts*, *totals*, and *averages*. The processing of sequential file SALARY.SEQ illustrates the design and coding of these summary lines. The records in SALARY.SEQ contain only two fields, SALARY.ID$, an employee identification number, and SALARY.AMT, an employee's weekly salary.

Assume that the assignment is to read each record from the file, print it, and, at the end of the listing, print the total number of records read, the total of all the monthly salaries, and the average employee salary. To emphasize techniques for counting and totaling, we will limit this discussion to the portions of the program related to those activities.

Reading and printing the records of the file require a processing loop that reads a record and then prints it, continuing as long as there are records in the file. This is pseudocode for such a loop:

```
dowhile not eof (SALARY.SEQ)
      read  SALARY.ID$, SALARY.AMT
      write SALARY.ID$, SALARY.AMT
end dowhile
```

Counting

It is easy to *count* the records read from a file. Insert into this procedure a variable that is incremented by 1 during each pass through the loop. Make sure the variable contains the value of zero before the first pass. After the first pass, the variable contains 1, 2 after the second, and so on. If you call the variable RECORD.COUNT, the pseudocode now looks like this:

```
RECORD.COUNT = 0
dowhile not eof (SALARY.SEQ)
      read  SALARY.ID$, SALARY.AMT
      write SALARY.ID$, SALARY.AMT
      add 1 to RECORD.COUNT
end dowhile
```

Accumulating

Accumulating or *totaling* the salaries of the employees is no more complicated than counting because it requires almost the same procedure. This time, insert a variable that is incremented by the current value of the employee salary during each pass through the loop. Again, be sure the variable contains the value of zero when the loop is entered for the first time. If this variable is TOTAL.SALARY, the pseudocode is:

```
RECORD.COUNT = 0
TOTAL.SALARY = 0
dowhile not eof (SALARY.SEQ)
      read  SALARY.ID$, SALARY.AMT
      write SALARY.ID$, SALARY.AMT
      add 1 to RECORD.COUNT
      add SALARY.AMT to TOTAL.SALARY
end dowhile
```

Variables that perform a totaling function are often referred to as *accumulators*.

Averaging

All that remains to be done now is to calculate the average and print the three summary values. The pseudocode for these steps is simple:

```
AVERAGE.SALARY = TOTAL.SALARY / RECORD.COUNT
write RECORD.COUNT
write TOTAL.SALARY
write AVERAGE.SALARY
```

Program 7.1

Program 7.1 contains the BASIC code that implements the pseudocode for the salary report. Notice that the variables that must be set to zero at the beginning of the program are initialized in a program section called INITIALIZED VARIABLES. Having a separate section for this purpose makes it easy for readers of the program to see which variables are being initialized, to determine what initial values are assigned to those variables, and to change those values as necessary.

The variables listed in INITIALIZED VARIABLES are ones that require initial values even though those values may change as the program executes. In contrast, the values in a CONSTANTS section (there is none in Program 7.1) do *not* change during execution.

PROGRAM 7.1

```
1000 ' PROG7-1
1010 ' ****************************
1020 ' *        SALARY REPORT        *
1030 ' ****************************
1040 '
```

PROGRAM 7.1
(continued)

```
1050 ' ****************************
1060 ' *         VARIABLES           *
1070 ' ****************************
1080 '
1090 ' SALARY.SEQ               Salary File
1100 ' Salary record:
1110 '     SALARY.ID$
1120 '     SALARY.AMT
1130 '
1140 ' AVERAGE.SALARY           TOTAL.SALARY/TOTAL.RECORDS
1150 '
1160 ' ****************************
1170 ' *   INITIALIZED VARIABLES    *
1180 ' ****************************
1190 '
1200   TOTAL.RECORDS  = 0        'Total number of employees in file
1210   TOTAL.SALARY   = 0        'Total salary
1999 '
2000 ' ****************************
2010 ' *        CONTROL MODULE       *
2020 ' ****************************
2030 '
2040   GOSUB 3000                'Write Heading
2050   GOSUB 4000                'Process File
2060   GOSUB 5000                'Write Summary Lines
2070   END
2999 '
3000 ' ****************************
3010 ' *         WRITE HEADING       *
3020 ' ****************************
3030 '
3040   LPRINT " SALARY REPORT"
3050   LPRINT
3060   LPRINT "ID        AMOUNT"
3070   LPRINT
3080   RETURN
3999 '
4000 ' ****************************
4010 ' *          PROCESS FILE       *
4020 ' ****************************
4030 '
4040   OPEN "SALARY.SEQ" FOR INPUT AS #1
4050   WHILE NOT EOF(1)
4060       INPUT #1, SALARY.ID$,
                     SALARY.AMT
4070       LPRINT USING "\\           ###.##"; SALARY.ID$,
                                                SALARY.AMT
4080       TOTAL.RECORDS = TOTAL.RECORDS + 1
4090       TOTAL.SALARY  = TOTAL.SALARY + SALARY.AMT
4100   WEND
4110   CLOSE #1
4120   RETURN
4999 '
5000 ' ****************************
5010 ' *     WRITE SUMMARY LINES     *
5020 ' ****************************
5030 '
5040   AVERAGE.SALARY = TOTAL.SALARY / TOTAL.RECORDS
5050   LPRINT
5060   LPRINT USING "TOTAL EMPLOYEES =     ##";     TOTAL.RECORDS
5070   LPRINT USING "TOTAL SALARY    = ##,###.##"; TOTAL.SALARY
5080   LPRINT USING "AVERAGE SALARY  =    ###.##"; AVERAGE.SALARY
5090   LPRINT
5100   LPRINT " END OF REPORT"
5110   RETURN
```

Determining the Field Width of Summary Values

An important aspect of report design is making sure that the space allocated for summary values accommodates the numbers being printed. Following these rules generally provides you with enough, but not too much space.

Addition

When you are adding two numbers, add 1 to the length of the longest field. Ignore the decimal points and the commas, and add room for them after applying the rule. For example, for a problem like this one

$$\begin{array}{ll} \#\#,\#\#\#.\#\# & \text{width} = 7 \\ \underline{+\ \ \#,\#\#\#.\#\#} & \text{width} = 6 \end{array}$$

you should allow a field width 8 plus 2 (for a decimal point and one comma), or a total of 10 for the output.

If you require additional commas in a larger field, increase the field size to include them also. For example, in this problem

$$\begin{array}{ll} \#\#\#,\#\#\#.\#\# & \text{width} = 8 \\ \underline{+\ \ \#\#,\#\#\#.\#\#} & \text{width} = 7 \end{array}$$

you add 1 to the longest field, yielding 9. Nine digits require another comma, and so you should make the field width 12.

When you need to allocate space for the sum of a list of numbers, add the field width of the largest number in the list to the width of the number of items in the list, as this example illustrates:

$$\begin{array}{r} \#\#\# \\ \#\#,\#\#\# \\ \#,\#\#\# \\ \underline{\#\#} \\ \#\#\#,\#\#\# \end{array}$$

The second number is the largest one in the list, and its width is 5. There are 4 numbers in the list, and the width of 4 is 1. The allocation for the total is 5 + 1 (width of number of items) + 1 (comma) = 7.

Subtraction

When subtracting, you do not need to provide spaces for additional commas. In subtraction problems, however, the result may be negative, and a space may be required for a minus sign. To be safe, follow the rule for addition and provide a field one space wider than the larger of the two fields.

Multiplication

To allocate space for a product, make the field width equal to the sum of the field widths of the numbers being multiplied, as in this example:

$$\begin{array}{ll} \#\#.\#\# & \text{width} = 4 \\ \underline{x\ \ \#\#\#.\#\#} & \text{width} = 5 \\ \#,\#\#\#,\#\#\#.\#\# \end{array}$$

The allocation is 4 + 5 = 9 plus an additional 3 spaces for the decimal point and two commas.

Division

You may need to display either the quotient or the remainder. For the quotient, use the field width of the dividend.

	Dividend	**Divisor**		**Quotient**
Division:	###.##	/ ##.#	$\longrightarrow$	###.##
Field widths:	5	3		5 + 1 (decimal point)

To display the remainder, use the field width of the divisor, in this example, 3.

GENERATING A REPORT

This section illustrates the use of the report formatting techniques you learned in earlier sections of this chapter. The example shows how to incorporate report design techniques into the steps of the program development process.

Define the Problem

The Putnam County Bank needs a listing of the records in a sequential file containing the checks and deposits for the week. The report should include headings, formatted detail lines for each record, and summary lines showing the total number and amount of checks and deposits.

Describe the Output

The output is a report listing each check and deposit record and including summary totals at the end. The print chart in Figure 7.1 shows the report format for Program 7.2.

The print chart conforms to earlier suggestions: The title identifies the contents of the report and the time to which it applies. The columns are evenly spaced and centered on the page. A blank line separates the summary lines from the body of the report.

Determine the Input

The input to the program is a sequential file of account transactions called TRANS.SEQ. Table 7.3 shows the format of the records in the file.

Design the Program Logic

Among the variables necessary for Program 7.2 are counters for the number of checks and deposits and accumulators for the total amount of checks and deposits. The program's INITIALIZED VARIABLES section sets the counters and accumulators to zero.

The WRITE HEADING module prints the main and column headings and defines the format strings for the check and deposit detail lines.

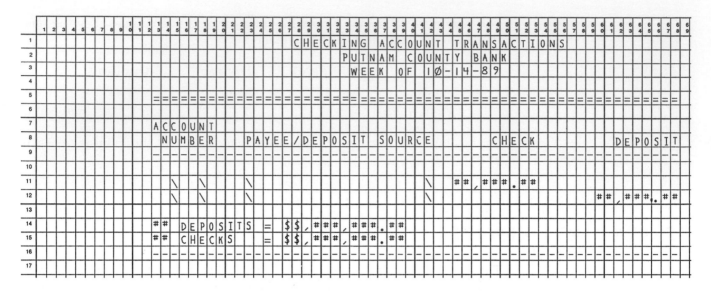

FIGURE 7.1 Report design for Program 7.2

Table 7.3 **Description and Sample Records for TRANS.SEQ**

TRANS.SEQ is a sequential input file

Record description:

Field Name	Data Length	Data Type
TRANS.CODE$	1	String
TRANS.ACCT$	4	String
TRANS.COMMENT$	20	String
TRANS.AMT	8	Numeric (#####.##)

Sample records:

```
"D","3203","DFH Resource Inc",768.51
"C","1900","WVFLBA",436.20
"C","3203","Jones Appliance",106.95
"C","1450","Gulf Oil",48.84
"C","1906","Buffalo Shopping Ctr",45.27
"C","1705","United Fund",40.00
"C","1906","A A Vaughn",7.00
"C","1003","Riverside VW",578.42
"D","1705","Westinghouse",998.75
"C","3217","Town & Country Vet",118.00
"C","1450","Cash",40.00
"C","1023","Eleanor IGA",29.84
"C","1003","Shirt Shack",8.14
"C","1506","Appalachian Power",37.80
"C","1108","Denise Burke",230.84
```

The following pseudocode describes the processing module:

```
open file
dowhile not eof
     read record
     if code = "C"
           then
                add 1 to check counter
                add check amount to check total
                write check detail line
```

```
            else
                add 1 to deposit counter
                add deposit amount to deposit total
                write deposit detail line
        end dowhile
        close file
```

Because the THEN and ELSE clauses have several statements each, you cannot enter them all in a single, easy-to-read IF/THEN/ELSE statement. Instead, add two new modules to the program, a subroutine to process checks and another to process deposits.

The PROCESS FILE module reads and processes records until it reaches the end of the file. Once it reads a record, it decides if the record is a deposit or a check record and then calls either PROCESS CHECKS or PROCESS DEPOSITS. (TRANS.CODE$ for checks is the character "C"; for deposits, the character "D".)

The WRITE SUMMARY LINES module prints the summary values.

Figure 7.2 contains the program structure chart and pseudocode for each program module.

Code the Program Instructions

The STRING$ Function

There is one new function used in Program 7.2.

The lines of code that print the report heading use a built-in function, STRING$, for printing a string of characters. (See lines 3080, 3140, and

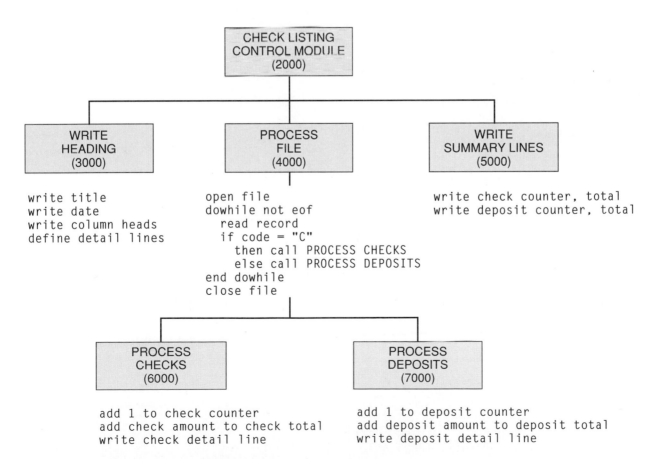

FIGURE 7.2 Structure chart with pseudocode for Program 7.2

PROGRAM 7.2

```
1000 ' PROG7-2
1010 ' *******************************
1020 ' *         CHECK LISTING        *
1030 ' *******************************
1040 '
1050 ' *******************************
1060 ' *          VARIABLES           *
1070 ' *******************************
1080 '
1090 ' TRANS.SEQ                  Transaction File
1100 ' Transaction record:
1110 '     TRANS.CODE$
1120 '     TRANS.ACCT$
1130 '     TRANS.COMMENT$
1140 '     TRANS.AMT
1150 '
1160 ' CHECK.DETAIL$              Format for check detail line
1170 ' DEPOSIT.DETAIL$            Format for deposit detail line
1180 '
1190 ' *******************************
1200 ' *    INITIALIZED VARIABLES     *
1210 ' *******************************
1220 '
1230   CHECK.CTR       = 0      'Total number of checks
1240   DEPOSIT.CTR     = 0      'Total number of deposits
1250   TOTAL.CHECKS#   = 0      'Total amount of checks
1260   TOTAL.DEPOSITS# = 0      'Total amount of deposits
1999 '
2000 ' *******************************
2010 ' *         CONTROL MODULE        *
2020 ' *******************************
2030 '
2040   GOSUB 3000                'Write Heading
2050   GOSUB 4000                'Process File
2060   GOSUB 5000                'Write Summary Lines
2070   END
2999 '
3000 ' *******************************
3010 ' *          WRITE HEADING        *
3020 ' *******************************
3030 '
3040   LPRINT TAB(28); "CHECKING ACCOUNT TRANSACTIONS"
3050   LPRINT TAB(33); "PUTNAM COUNTY BANK"
3060   LPRINT TAB(34); "WEEK OF 10-14-89"
3070   LPRINT
3080   LPRINT TAB(13); STRING$(56,"=")
3090   LPRINT
3100   LPRINT
       "                ACCOUNT"
3110   LPRINT
       "                NUMBER   PAYEE/DEPOSIT SOURCE       CHECK        DEPOSIT"
3120   CHECK.DETAIL$ =
       "                \ \      \                     \   ##,###.##"
3130   DEPOSIT.DETAIL$ =
       "                \ \      \                     \               ##,###.##"
3140   LPRINT TAB(13); STRING$(56,"-")
3150   LPRINT
3160   RETURN
3999 '
4000 ' *******************************
4010 ' *          PROCESS FILE         *
4020 ' *******************************
4030 '
4040   OPEN "TRANS.SEQ" FOR INPUT AS #1
4050   WHILE NOT EOF(1)
4060      INPUT #1, TRANS.CODE$,    TRANS.ACCT$,
                    TRANS.COMMENT$, TRANS.AMT
```

PROGRAM 7.2   (continued)

```
4070         IF TRANS.CODE$ = "C"
                 THEN GOSUB 6000
                 ELSE GOSUB 7000  '(6000 = Process Checks  7000 = Process Deposits)
4080      WEND
4090      CLOSE #1
4100      RETURN
4999 '
5000 ' *****************************
5010 ' *      WRITE SUMMARY LINES       *
5020 ' *****************************
5030 '
5040      LPRINT
5050      LPRINT TAB(13); USING "## DEPOSITS = $$,###,###.##"; DEPOSIT.CTR,
                                               TOTAL.DEPOSITS#
5060      LPRINT TAB(13); USING "## CHECKS   = $$,###,###.##"; CHECK.CTR,
                                               TOTAL.CHECKS#
5070      LPRINT TAB(13); STRING$(56,"-")
5080      RETURN
5999 '
6000 ' *****************************
6010 ' *          PROCESS CHECKS        *
6020 ' *****************************
6030 '
6040      CHECK.CTR     = CHECK.CTR + 1
6050      TOTAL.CHECKS# = TOTAL.CHECKS# + TRANS.AMT
6060      LPRINT USING CHECK.DETAIL$; TRANS.ACCT$,
                                   TRANS.COMMENT$,
                                   TRANS.AMT
6070      RETURN
6999 '
7000 ' *****************************
7010 ' *          PROCESS DEPOSITS      *
7020 ' *****************************
7030 '
7040      DEPOSIT.CTR     = DEPOSIT.CTR + 1
7050      TOTAL.DEPOSITS# = TOTAL.DEPOSITS# + TRANS.AMT
7060      LPRINT USING DEPOSIT.DETAIL$; TRANS.ACCT$,
                                     TRANS.COMMENT$,
                                     TRANS.AMT
7070      RETURN
```

5070.) The first argument to STRING$ tells how many times to print the character; the second argument tells what character to print. Thus, STRING$(56,"=") prints 56 equal symbols. Notice that the character used as the second argument must be enclosed in quotes. This function is useful if you are not using preprinted forms and want to dress up your report.

✳ **STYLE TIPS**

Notice the INITIALIZED VARIABLES section in this program. It is helpful to the reader of the program to see what variables are being used as counters and accumulators.

The format strings for the check and deposit detail lines are defined in lines 3120 and 3130. They appear immediately after line 3110 so that the reader of the program listing can see their relationship to the column headings defined in line 3110.

Notice that the dollar signs are printed only before the total checks and deposits and not with every TRANS.AMT in the detail line.

Test the Program

When Program 7.2 is run with the TRANS.SEQ file containing the sample records in Table 7.3, the program prints the report shown in Figure 7.3.

FIGURE 7.3
Report generated by
Program 7.2

```
                     CHECKING ACCOUNT TRANSACTIONS
                          PUTNAM COUNTY BANK
                          WEEK OF 10-14-89


     =========================================================

     ACCOUNT
     NUMBER   PAYEE/DEPOSIT SOURCE      CHECK        DEPOSIT
     ---------------------------------------------------------

       3203   DFH Resource Inc                        768.51
       1900   WVFLBA                    436.20
       3203   Jones Appliance           106.95
       1450   Gulf Oil                   48.84
       1906   Buffalo Shopping Ctr       45.27
       1705   United Fund                40.00
       1906   A A Vaughn                  7.00
       1003   Riverside VW              578.42
       1705   Westinghouse                            998.75
       3217   Town & Country Vet        118.00
       1450   Cash                       40.00
       1023   Eleanor IGA                29.84
       1003   Shirt Shack                 8.14
       1506   Appalachian Power          37.80
       1108   Denise Burke              230.84

      2 DEPOSITS =     $1,767.26
     13 CHECKS   =     $1,727.30
     ---------------------------------------------------------
```

Alternate Report Design

Like all programs, this one could have been written in a variety of ways. Figure 7.4 illustrates an alternate design for the report produced by a modified version of Program 7.2. The totals for checks and deposits are printed under the appropriate column of numbers with the decimal points aligned. Only a few changes needed to be made to the WRITE SUMMARY LINES module to create a different format for the summary lines.

ALTERNATIVES FOR PROGRAM OUTPUT

The discussion thus far has assumed that report output will always be sent to a standard 80-column printer. There are other alternatives that you may find useful; this section introduces some of them.

Writing the Report to Disk

Program 7.2 sends its report to a printer. An alternative is to write the report to a disk file. This allows you to print the report as often as necessary without rerunning the program. You can also use a text editor to make changes in the report or insert it into another document.

FIGURE 7.4
Alternate design for the
report produced by
Program 7.2

```
                         CHECKING ACCOUNT TRANSACTIONS
                               PUTNAM COUNTY BANK
                               WEEK OF 10-14-89


        ========================================================

        ACCOUNT
        NUMBER   PAYEE/DEPOSIT SOURCE       CHECK        DEPOSIT
        --------------------------------------------------------

          3203   DFH Resource Inc                        768.51
          1900   WVFLBA                    436.20
          3203   Jones Appliance           106.95
          1450   Gulf Oil                   48.84
          1906   Buffalo Shopping Ctr       45.27
          1705   United Fund                40.00
          1906   Λ A Vaughn                  7.00
          1003   Riverside VW              578.42
          1705   Westinghouse                            998.75
          3217   Town & Country Vet        118.00
          1450   Cash                       40.00
          1023   Eleanor IGA                29.84
          1003   Shirt Shack                 8.14
          1506   Appalachian Power          37.80
          1108   Denise Burke              230.84

         2 DEPOSITS =                                  $1,767.26
        13 CHECKS    =                    $1,727.30
        --------------------------------------------------------
```

Few modifications are necessary to write the report from Program 7.2 to a disk file. To send it to a file called TRANS.REP, do the following:

- Add this line: 3035 OPEN "TRANS.REP" FOR OUTPUT AS #2

- Change every instance of LPRINT to PRINT #2,

- Add this line: 5075 CLOSE #2

PRINT

The DOS commands TYPE and PRINT are useful tools for displaying a report stored on disk. PRINT sends its output to the printer. To use it, enter the following lines:

```
A>PRINT TRANS.REP    (if TRANS.SEQ is on drive A)
A>PRINT B:TRANS.SEQ (if TRANS.SEQ is on drive B)
```

This message appears:

```
A>Name of list device [PRN]:
```

You can either press the Enter key or enter LPT1 if your printer is on port 1. The report (or records) in TRANS.REP will then be printed on the printer.

Another way to print a sequential file is with the DOS COPY command. Either of these examples will work:

```
A>COPY filename PRN
```

```
A>COPY filename LPT1
```

Remember that COPY is an internal command and PRINT is an external command.

TYPE

The TYPE command sends its output to the screen. To use it, enter the following lines:

```
A>TYPE TRANS.REP      (if TRANS.SEQ is on Drive A)
A>TYPE B:TRANS.REP   (if TRANS.SEQ is on Drive B)
```

The report in TRANS.REP will be displayed on the screen.

Condensing the Report

In the beginning of this chapter we mentioned that if you did not have enough room for your report, you could either redesign the report or condense the print. If your machine prints 80 columns per page of normal print and more columns when the print is smaller, you may sometimes want to condense the print size to lengthen the print line. Use the following BASIC code to do that:

```
100 LPRINT CHR$(15)
200 WIDTH "LPT1:",132
300 TEST$ = STRING$(100,"T")
400 LPRINT TEST$
```

LPRINT CHR$(15) condenses the print size on most dot-matrix printers, and the WIDTH statement increases the LPT1 (line printer—port 1) print line to 132 characters. Any value up to 255 is acceptable as the second parameter of the WIDTH statement. Line 400 will cause 100 T's to be printed on a line that normally accommodates a maximum of 80 characters.

If this code does not work for your printer, try modifying line 100. CHR$($n$) is a BASIC built-in function that returns a single-string character equivalent in ASCII code to the numeric argument n, and 15 is the numeric argument for condensing the print on some printers. Other printers use other codes. Check your user's manual for the code required for your printer, and substitute it for the 15.

To return to normal print mode, execute the following statements:

```
700 LPRINT CHR$(18)
710 WIDTH "LPT1:", 80
```

Summary

- A good business report (1) must contain the information the user wants and (2) must be easy to read.

- A report consists of heading lines, detail lines, and summary lines.

- The *main heading* should identify the report's purpose and the time to which it applies. That information, or an abbreviated form of it, should be on every page of the report.

- *Column headings* should identify different sets of information in the body of the report.

- These headings should be included on each page as well. The body of the report is comprised of rows of *detail lines* that correspond to records in the files being processed.

- *Summary lines* at the end of the report should provide the user with useful totals and an end-of-report message.

- To make reports attractive and readable:

   1. Do not crowd the report. If you need more room, redesign the report or use a smaller print or wider paper.

   2. Center the report on the page.

3. When necessary, format the data in the detail lines to make the information attractive and readable.

4. Use line and column spacing to distinguish summary information from the body of the report.

5. Save time and avoid frustration by designing the form of your report on a print chart.

■ PRINT USING and LPRINT USING are BASIC statements that simplify the formatting and editing of print lines. Edit character strings and numbers to produce more readable reports.

■ *Counting* and *accumulating* are common operations for preparing summary information for reports. Programs 7.1 and 7.2 use both these operations to generate reports.

■ The PRINT # statement allows you to send a formatted report to a disk file. By saving the report on disk, you can reprint the report as often as necessary without having to rerun the program.

■ This chapter describes the following BASIC statements and functions:

CHR$(*n*) — A function that returns a single-string character equivalent in ASCII code to the numeric argument *n*. For example, 100 LPRINT CHR$ (65) causes the letter A to be printed. Check Appendix C for other ASCII codes.

LPRINT USING — A statement to format and edit character and numeric data sent to the printer.

PRINT USING — A statement to format and edit character and numeric data to be displayed on the screen.

PRINT # — A statement to write data sequentially to disk.

STRING$(*n*,"*x*") — A function for printing a string of characters. The first argument, *n*, determines how many times the character is printed. The second argument, "*x*", determines what character is printed. For example, 100 LPRINT STRING$(25,"+") causes 25 plus signs to be printed.

WIDTH — A statement to set the output line width.

Review Questions

1. What different types of reports do businesses use?

2. What are the two major requirements for a business report?

3. What are the characteristics of a good report heading?

4. What is a detail line?

5. What information can summary lines include?

6. Why should you use a print chart to design your report?

7. What is the purpose of the LPRINT USING statement?

8. What is the difference between LPRINT US-ING and PRINT USING?

9. What are the three format characters used for printing string values?

10. Will the statement

```
100 LPRINT USING "##.##"; PAY.AMT
```

round PAY.AMT if PAY.AMT contains more than 2 decimals?

11. Suppose an LPRINT USING statement produces the output %7964.30. What is the significance of the % in the output?

12. What is the difference between a fixed dollar sign and a floating dollar sign?

13. Why would a business want to fill unused portions of a numeric field with something other than blanks?

14. What is the difference between counting and accumulating?

15. Why should counters and accumulators be initialized to zero?

16. Give rules of thumb for allocating space for the results of addition, multiplication, subtraction, and division.

17. Could you reverse lines 4080 and 4090 of Program 7.1 without changing the output of the program? What would happen if you placed 4080 before 4060? 4090 before 4060?

18. Why is it sometimes necessary to use the GOSUB statement in an IF statement?

19. What output will the following statement generate?

```
100 LPRINT TAB(10); STRING$(5,"?")
```

20. What output will the following statement generate?

```
100 LPRINT CHR$(70)
```

21. What is an advantage of sending a report to a disk file?

22. Explain a way to print (on the printer) a report stored in a disk file.

Problems

1. Write the results of the following LPRINT USING statements. If necessary, use ƀ to indicate a blank. (Some of the examples contain syntax errors.)

a. `100 LPRINT USING "###.#"; 289.9`

b. `100 LPRINT USING "\   \"; "PARIS"`

c. `100 LPRINT USING "\   \"; "ROME"`

d. `100 LPRINT USING "\   \"; "MUNICH"`

e. `100 LPRINT USING "$##.##"; 5.623`

f. `100 LPRINT USING "$##.##"; .838`

g. `100 LPRINT`
`   USING "!"; "APRIL", "MAY", "JUNE"`

h. `100 LPRINT USING "&"; 12`

i. `100 LPRINT`
`   USING "TOTAL = $$#,###.##"; 100.92`

j. `100 LPRINT USING "/   /"; "LONDON"`

k. `100 LPRINT`
`   USING "VALUE = +##.###_!"; 40.9287`

l. `100 LPRINT USING "####,.##"; 1323.9`

m. `100 LPRINT USING`
`   "AMOUNT OF SALE = ###.##_***"; 399.98`

n. `100 LPRINT USING "#,###.##"; 145.82`

o. `100 LPRINT USING "**$#,###.##"; 1.22`

p. `100 LPRINT USING "##.##", 4426.32`

q. `100 LPRINT`
`   USING "$**#,###.###-"; 4426.32`

r. `100 LPRINT`
`   USING "$**#,###.###-"; -4426.32`

s. `100 LPRINT USING "$$#,###.###"; 26.32`

t. `100 LPRINT USING "$#,###.###"; 26.32`

2. Write LPRINT USING statements to display the value of ANAME$ in position 10 of the print line as follows:

a. All of ANAME$ is displayed.

b. Only the first character of ANAME$ is displayed.

c. The first five characters of ANAME$ are displayed.

3. Write one field descriptor that can be used for each set of the following values:

a. $4,293.25
$62,342.00   Field descriptor: _____
$1.50

b.   293.462–
25.603   Field descriptor: _____
42.892–

c. $***5,602.29 *
$*425,809.60 *   Field descriptor: _____
$*****402.80 *

4. Display your name on the screen using the CHR$ function. Check the ASCII chart in Appendix C for the values. Use both uppercase and lowercase letters.

5. If you use the following values for SALARY.ID$ and SALARY.AMT in Program 7.1, what will the computer print?

SALARY.ID$	SALARY.AMT
10	50.60
15	100.20
42	230.40

6. You can use the TYPE command to display the contents of a sequential file. This is a convenient way to review the input of a program you are testing. Use the TYPE command to display a sequential file stored on your disk.

7. Change Program 7.2 to produce the report in Figure 7.4.

8. What will be printed if you assign TRANS.COMMENT$ in Program 7.2 the value "State Board of Higher Education"?

9. Write a program to list the cost of 1–50 copies of a software program. The first copy costs $19.99. Copies 2–9 cost $18.99 each. Copies 10–29 cost $17.99 each. Copies 30–50 cost $15.99 each. The list should look like this:

Number of Copies	Cost
1	$ 19.99
2	38.98
·	·
·	·
·	·
50	849.51

Program Assignments

1. The national sales manager of the MAIL-USA Catalog Company needs a sales commission report. A sequential file contains department number, salesperson name, and sales amount for each salesperson. Design a report that includes heading lines, detail lines, and summary lines. In addition, dress up the report by adding lines using the STRING$ function to separate the parts of the report. The heading lines should include a general heading and column headings. The detail line should include department number, salesperson name, sales amount (may be a negative value), and commission. The commission is 10% of the sales amount. However, if the SALE.AMT is less than zero, the commission is zero. The summary lines should include total salespersons, total sales amount, average sales amount, total commission, and average commission.

   a. SALE.SEQ   Sequential Input File

   b. SALE record:

Field Name	Data Length	Data Type
SALE.DEPT$	3	String
SALE.NAME$	20	String
SALE.AMT	7	Numeric (####.##)

   c. File contents:

   ```
   101,JOSEPH BISHOP,100.55
   101,PAUL BURKE,800.34
   101,MARGE HACKETT,4000.32
   101,BETH FOSTER,8000.88
   101,JULIA JEFFERSON,-800.87
   101,DANIEL MUNN,200.76
   101,BARBARA TIPTON,1203.76
   223,PATRICK COLLINS,199.67
   223,KYLE DURKEE,1500.75
   223,SCOTT HURLOCK,234.50
   223,BRIAN LUIRE,50.89
   223,MIGUEL PEREZ,344.57
   223,NANCY SYMANS,2003.89
   455,GEORGE FASSIO,-900.76
   455,CHARLES HOWARD,0
   455,KEVIN MCBAIN,100.98
   455,VIRGINIA MURRAY,6500.50
   455,CAROL PALM,1300.45
   455,KRISTEN SCHUETZ,1600.78
   455,LEON SMITH,675.80
   455,DANIEL THOMAS,0
   455,CARL TROSS,-450.98
   455,LINDSEY WEST,2400.68
   455,STEPHANIE WYATT,2500.75
   455,ROBERT XANDER,500.98
   ```

2. The stock brokers at Futures, Inc., need a stock report. A sequential file contains the stock number and name, number of shares purchased, per-share purchase price and the per-share price, at which the stock was sold. If the selling price (STK.SELL) is zero, the stock has not been sold. Write a program to produce the printed report designed on the print chart.

   The heading lines include the general heading plus the column headings. The date in the heading should be entered by the user.

   The detail lines include the fields on the record plus the total cost, the total sale, and the gain or loss. The total cost of the stock is calculated by multiplying the purchase price by the number of shares (STK.BUY * STK.SHARES). The total sale of the stock is calculated by multiplying the selling price of the stock by the number of shares (STK.SELL * STK.SHARES). The gain or loss is calculated by subtracting the total cost from the total sale of the stock. The total sale and the loss or gain are calculated only for those stocks that do not have a zero value in the selling price (STK.SELL).

   The summary totals include the total stocks, the total shares, the total cost of the stocks, the total sale of the stocks, the total loss, and the total gain plus an end message.

   a. STK.SEQ   Sequential Input File

   STK record:

Field Name	Data Length	Data Type
STK.NO	3	Numeric (###)
STK.NAME$	15	String
STK.SHARES	3	Numeric (###)
STK.BUY	3	Numeric (###)
STK.SELL	3	Numeric (###)

   b. File contents:

   ```
   102,Allegis,100,84,0
   108,Ashton Tate,100,16,14
   115,Chase,230,26,32
   123,Coca Cola,230,40,52
   276,Compaq,560,25,0
   345,Disney,100,62,60
   432,Ford,150,43,82
   498,Genrad,100,7,10
   541,IBM,800,113,0
   687,Kellogg,200,52,64
   701,Lotus,140,24,20
   786,Marriot,100,32,20
   799,McCormick,100,46,0
   801,Sony,180,41,33
   ```

```
849,TWA,150,27,35
852,Westinghouse,110,43,62
902,Xerox,400,56,0
```

c. The report design is shown below.

3. The Hereford lacrosse team needs a report of team statistics. A sequential file contains the name, position, and uniform number of each player plus the total goals and assists for the season. Write a program to produce a report for the team. You design the report.

The heading lines include the general heading plus the column headings.

The detail lines include the fields on the record plus the percentage of goals and assists for each player. The percentage of goals is the player's goals divided by the total goals for the team. The percentage of assists is the player's assists divided by the total assists for the team. Round the percentages to an integer.

The summary totals include the total players, the total goals, and the total assists plus an end message.

a. LAX.SEQ   Sequential file

LAX record:

Field Name	Data Length	Data Type
LAX.NUM	2	Numeric (##)
LAX.NAME$	20	String
LAX.POS$	2	String
LAX.GOALS	3	Numeric (###)
LAX.ASSTS	3	Numeric (###)

b. File contents:

```
2,HOWARD CAUGHTY,A,10,2
3,DOUG PORTA,A,12,13
4,GEOFF MOORE,G,0,0
5,TOM SOLTER,A,8,2
7,TODD SCHOLTZ,M,0,0
10,ROBERT HOUGH,G,0,0
13,SHANE CURREY,M,0,4
14,JOHN CARROLL,M,2,1
15,TODD PATTERSON,M,3,1
16,CHRIS LEWIS,M,9,12
19,RUSTY ROBERTS,D,0,0
20,CHRIS COOPER,M,6,3
21,MATT BECK,D,0,2
22,JUSTIN SCHUETZ,A,9,2
23,CHIP MARSHALL,D,0,0
26,CARTER RUSSELL,D,0,0
29,COURTNEY CARR,D,0,1
32,WALTER BECKER,D,0,0
33,RYAN FANZONE,M,14,10
35,ANDY WARNER,M,0,2
36,ROGER MUNN,M,1,1
38,CHRIS WESS,A,0,2
40,COLIN MEEKS,D,0,1
42,KEN WAGONER,D,1,0
```

4. The credit department at Berrenger's Department Store needs a report of overdue accounts. The sequential file contains the account number, name, last payment date, and current balance for each customer with an account at the store. The first three fields of the file contain date information. Field 1 contains the over-90-days date, field 2 contains the over-60-days

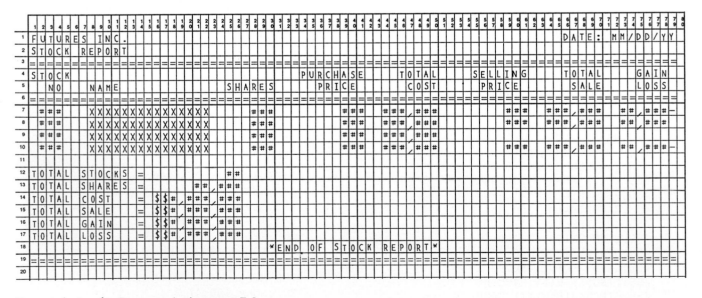

Report design for Program Assignment 7.2

date, and field 3 contains the over-30-days date. The dates are in the *yymmdd* format. For each record in the file, compare the last payment date to see whether the account is over 30 days due, over 60 days due, or over 90 days due. For example, if the last payment date is equal or prior to the over-90-days due date, the account is 90 days overdue. Of course, some accounts are current (all dates after the over-30-days due date). Write a program to produce the printed report designed on the print chart.

a. CR.SEQ Sequential Input File

CR record:

Field Name	Data Length	Data Type
DAY.90	6	Numeric (yymmdd)
DAY.60	6	Numeric (yymmdd)
DAY.30	6	Numeric (yymmdd)
CR.ACCT$	4	String
CR.NAME$	20	String
CR.DATE	6	Numeric (yymmdd)
CR.BAL	7	Numeric

b. File contents:

```
900401
900501
900601
1122,CAROLINE ANDERS,900615,110.85
1234,JERRY AYERS,900615,100.25
1345,ERICH BLACK,900609,500.85
2347,WALKER BURL,900401,1009.90
2365,PATRICK CALLAHAN,900601,200.39
2389,JENNA COLEMAN,900617,400.55
2430,VINCENT CONWAY,900512,400.76
2435,DIANE DIBERNARDO,900415,300.45
2440,THOMAS FOUNDS,900510,1500.54
2445,STEPHEN FULLER,900507,430.80
2890,SHARON HARDESTY,900610,900.78
3889,GUY HARLEE,900115,90.85
3992,JOYCE HARNER,900612,499.78
3998,CASSANDRA HARRIS,900301,700.40
4556,REBECCA JAMES,900530,45.75
4680,TONI KASKO,900510,800.32
4778,ALICE KNESS,900425,200.98
5667,CLINTON KNIGHT,900620,200.98
6111,MARTIN MALPAS,900618,300.50
6233,DAVID NOVOTNY,900605,600.43
6332,DONALD PERSY,900419,2.30
6448,RICHARD PITT,900620,400.78
6556,WAVERLY QUINCY,900214,1200.98
6788,ADA ROBINSON,900512,765.90
6878,JEFFREY SAVOYE,900420,500.67
7112,JACQUE SHELDON,900215,900.45
7148,PHYLIS SMITH,900405,100.12
7150,KATHLEEN SULLIVAN,900523,1200.45
7223,THERESA TRUSCOTT,900605,50.46
8760,MICHAEL WINTERS,900328,199.60
8899,ELAINE YOUNG,900520,344.67
```

c. The report design is shown below.

Report design for Program Assignment 7.4

Using the Data Disk

1. Insert the data disk into the disk drive.

2. Load BASIC.

3. In the textbook, turn to the first problem in the "Problems" section. Enter each statement listed with a different line number. Also change all LPRINT statements to PRINT statements. Now run this program. Correct any of the statements that produce error messages. Note the results to confirm your understanding of PRINT USING.

4. Load CH7-1.DD.

   a. Run the program. The output is the client listing report produced in Chapter 6 (Program 6.1). The only changes are (1) all the LPRINT statements have been changed to PRINT statements so that program testing is easier and (2) a CLS command was added to make the report more readable on the screen.
   b. Change CH7-1.DD so that it prints a blank line after every four detail lines. Test your changes.
   c. Switch to DOS using the SHELL command after the changes have been tested.
   d. Using EDLIN, delete any two records from the CLIENT.SEQ file so that the file has a total of 12 records.
   e. Switch back to BASIC using the EXIT command.
   f. Test the revised CH7-1.DD again. If the report has more than one blank line between the last detail line and the end message, revise your code.
   g. Save the revised program under the name CH7-2.DD.

5. Load PROG7-1.

   a. Change PROG7-1 so that the report is printed in condensed print size and the print size is changed back to normal after the report is printed. Also add TAB(80) to all the LPRINT statements to test the WIDTH statement.
   b. Now change PROG7-1 so that the report is saved on disk. Use SALARY.REP as the name of the report on disk.
   c. Switch to DOS using the SHELL command.
   d. Use the command COPY SALARY.REP LPT1 to check the results.
   e. After switching back to BASIC, save the revised program using the name CH7-3.DD.

6. The Rough Riders Outing Club likes the program you prepared for them to use on their bulletin board (CH5-3.DD), but would like it enhanced. Load CH5-3.DD.

   a. Members who stick with the club tend to have the following characteristics:

□ They enjoy being outdoors.

□ They are willing to tolerate such physical discomforts as getting wet, and being bothered by insects.

□ They enjoy physical exercise.

□ They are able to change plans at last minute.

□ They don't mind being away from phones and televisions for several days at a time.

□ They like to try new activities, such as horseback riding, sailing, and caving.

Modify your program so that it determines if a caller has each of these traits and then suggests whether club membership is something the caller is likely to enjoy. Base the suggestion on the number of positive answers:

$$6 \text{ positives } = \text{ very likely}$$
$$4\text{–}5 \text{ positives } = \text{ probably}$$
$$\text{fewer than } 4 \text{ positives } = \text{ not likely}$$

b. Save your new program as CH7-4.DD

7. The disk jockeys on a local radio station need a program to help them program their shows. Write a program that accepts the title of each program segment and the time (in minutes and seconds) that each segment runs and then reports the time remaining to be filled. The program should begin with a request for the total time to be allocated. Then it should continue asking for the program segment information until the time is filled or the user decides to quit. At the end of the program, display the number of titles entered and the total time allocated. Save this program as CH7-5.DD.

Screen Design

Topics

- Programs to create sequential files
- Screen use during data entry
- Screen display of reports
- Design and use of menus

Program Statements and Functions

```
INKEY$
INPUT$(n)
KEY OFF/KEY ON
LINE INPUT
LOCATE
ON n GOSUB
WRITE #
```

INTRODUCTION

Many of the programs you will write will be *interactive*—programs that require the user to enter from the keyboard some or all of the input to the program. Some of these programs will be *data entry* programs for which the user will enter data to create or update a file.

Other interactive programs require the user to select from a list of potential functions that the program can perform. This list of choices has the same format as a restaurant menu; for this reason, this list of options presented on the screen is called a *menu*. Some programs are controlled by the menu; these programs are sometimes called *menu-driven* programs. For example, the menu for a vocabulary drill program might look like this:

```
VOCABULARY QUIZ

    1  Synonyms
    2  Antonyms
    3  Homonyms
    4  Exit

SELECT A NUMBER (1, 2, 3, OR 4)
```

All interactive programs present the user with prompts and await the user's response. Good programs allow the user to recognize input requirements easily and to enter the requested input with a minimum of effort. The design of screen displays to help the user is the theme of this chapter.

The chapter begins with an example of a data entry program to create or append to a sequential file. The second program displays a report on the screen. The third program displays a copy of an order form on the screen to facilitate data entry from a business form. Finally, the fourth is a menu-driven program that displays either of two reports on the screen, depending on the user's selection.

People make mistakes, so whenever the user is to enter data from the keyboard, you as the programmer should do whatever is necessary to minimize user errors. All of Chapter 11 is devoted to this important topic of *data validation*. The programs in this chapter, however, are based on the unrealistic assumption that users always respond correctly to program prompts.

DATA ENTRY

An easy-to-write data entry program prompts the user to enter the data field by field. The sample program presented here uses this approach to create a sequential file of billing records for a law firm.

Define the Problem

The firm of Lowell and Bauer needs a billing file to use with a program that prepares a billing report. This file should be a sequential file with the following fields:

- Account number of the client to be billed
- Name of the client to be billed
- Number of hours to be charged to the client
- Billing rate

Mrs. Murphy, the office secretary, will be entering the data. She has no previous data entry experience. Consequently, the program should be as easy to use as possible.

Describe the Output

The program must write the billing record of each client to a disk file. Since the file will contain billing records, its name is BILL.SEQ; BILL describes its contents, and the extension .SEQ describes the file type. The records in the file BILL.SEQ are in this format:

```
BILL.SEQ  Sequential Output File
BILL  record description:
```

Field Name	Data Length	Data Type
BILL.ACCT$	3	String
BILL.NAME$	20	String
BILL.HRS	3	Numeric (###)
BILL.RATE	5	Numeric (##.##)

Another output item, an end-of-program message, will be helpful to Mrs. Murphy. When she enters a Q to indicate that she is finished entering billing records, a screen message will report the end of data entry and the number of records written to the disk file, as follows:

```
Creation of BILL.SEQ complete
Total records = ##
```

Determine the Input

Input to the program will be through the keyboard. Mrs. Murphy must type the data for each field in every client's billing record. The prompts in Figure 8.1 let her know when to enter each data item. Remember that the user of the program must have some way to signal the end of the process: Mrs. Murphy will enter a Q for "Client account number" when she has finished entering the billing records.

At this point, Mrs. Murphy should review the plans to see if this approach seems reasonable to her and discuss any possible changes she may want.

Design the Program Logic

This program consists of two level-1 modules. The first level-1 module, CREATE FILE, controls the task of creating the billing file. The other level-1 module, WRITE SUMMARY LINES, displays on the screen the end-of-program message and total number of records in the file.

The module CREATE FILE calls in three additional modules. INPUT ACCT NUMBER displays a prompt on the screen requesting the client's account number. This module is used as the "priming read" for the loop and is called again each time a new account number is required. After the user

FIGURE 8.1
Screen design form for
Program 8.1

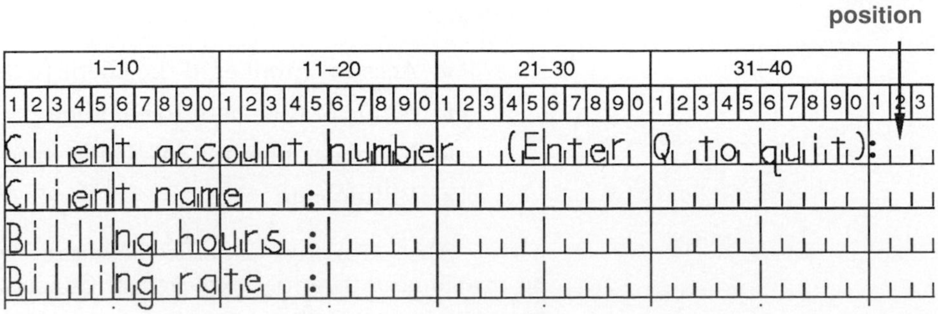

enters the client's account number, the module INPUT DATA requests the remaining data needed to create the client's record. After the user enters the client name, hours billed, and billing rate, the WRITE RECORD module writes the record to the file and increments the record counter. This process is repeated until the user enters Q as the account number. Before exiting the CREATE FILE module, BASIC closes the client file.

Figure 8.2 shows the structure chart and pseudocode for Program 8.1.

Code the Program Instructions

Program 8.1 is a listing of the program code to create BILL.SEQ. It contains some new statements and some familiar statements used in a new way.

OPEN Statement

The rules for opening a file for output are almost the same as the rules for opening a file for input. The difference is that the FOR option is written FOR OUTPUT. FOR OUTPUT in line 3040 designates the file name inside quotation marks as an output file.

When you use OPEN with the FOR OUTPUT option, BASIC places a pointer at the beginning of the file in preparation for writing to the file. If the file named in the OPEN statement does not exist, BASIC creates one. *CAUTION!* If the file does exist, its contents are destroyed when you open it for output. The file number is associated with the file name for as long as the file remains open, just as with a file opened for input.

Line 3040 may also be written as

```
3040  OPEN "O",#1,"BILL.SEQ"
```

FIGURE 8.2
Logic design for
Program 8.1

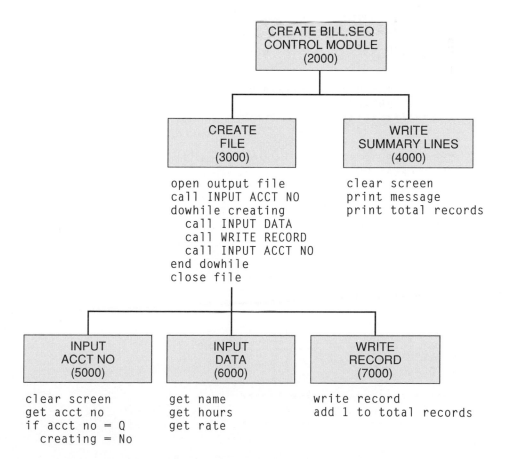

PROGRAM 8.1

```
1000 ' PROG8-1
1010 ' *****************************
1020 ' *       CREATE BILL.SEQ       *
1030 ' *****************************
1040 '
1050 ' *****************************
1060 ' *         VARIABLES          *
1070 ' *****************************
1080 '
1090 ' BILL.SEQ                Billing File
1100 ' Billing record:
1110 '     BILL.ACCT$
1120 '     BILL.NAME$
1130 '     BILL.HRS
1140 '     BILL.RATE
1150 '
1160 ' *****************************
1170 ' *         CONSTANTS          *
1180 ' *****************************
1190 '
1200   YES = -1                'Value for true
1210   NO  =  0                'Value for false
1220 '
1230 ' *****************************
1240 ' *   INITIALIZED VARIABLES    *
1250 ' *****************************
1260 '
1270   CREATING = YES          'Set CREATING flag to true
1280   TOTAL.RECORDS = 0       'Total records in the file
1999 '
2000 ' *****************************
2010 ' *       CONTROL MODULE       *
2020 ' *****************************
2030 '
2040   GOSUB 3000              'Create File
2050   GOSUB 4000              'Write Summary Lines
2060   END
2999 '
3000 ' *****************************
3010 ' *         CREATE FILE        *
3020 ' *****************************
3030 '
3040   OPEN "BILL.SEQ" FOR OUTPUT AS #1
3050   GOSUB 5000              'Input Acct No
3060   WHILE CREATING
3070     GOSUB 6000            'Input Data
3080     GOSUB 7000            'Write Record
3090     GOSUB 5000            'Input Acct No
3100   WEND
3110   CLOSE #1
3120   RETURN
3999 '
4000 ' *****************************
4010 ' *    WRITE SUMMARY LINES     *
4020 ' *****************************
4030 '
4040   CLS
4050   PRINT "Creation of BILL.SEQ complete"
4060   PRINT "Total records ="; TOTAL.RECORDS
4070   RETURN
4999 '
5000 ' *****************************
5010 ' *        INPUT ACCT NO       *
5020 ' *****************************
5030 '
```

PROGRAM 8.1 (continued)

```
5040    CLS
5050    INPUT "Client account number  (Enter Q to quit): ", BILL.ACCT$
5060    IF (BILL.ACCT$ = "Q") OR (BILL.ACCT$ = "q")
              THEN CREATING = NO
5070    RETURN
5999 '
6000 ' *****************************
6010 ' *           INPUT DATA            *
6020 ' *****************************
6030 '
6040    INPUT "Client name   : ", BILL.NAME$
6050    INPUT "Billing hours : ", BILL.HRS
6060    INPUT "Billing rate  : ", BILL.RATE
6070    RETURN
6999 '
7000 ' *****************************
7010 ' *            WRITE RECORD          *
7020 ' *****************************
7030 '
7040    WRITE #1, BILL.ACCT$, BILL.NAME$,
                   BILL.HRS,    BILL.RATE
7050    TOTAL.RECORDS = TOTAL.RECORDS + 1
7060    RETURN
```

WRITE # Statement

The general format of the WRITE # statement is:

```
[line#] WRITE #<filenumber, var1> [,var2, . . ., varN]
```

Line 7040 causes the system to write the four fields of the billing record to the BILL.SEQ file, assigning the values of BILL.ACCT$, BILL.NAME$, BILL.HRS, and BILL.RATE to the record in that order.

The WRITE # statement causes the data to be written to the file with commas between the fields and with quotation marks around the strings. All leading and trailing spaces or zeros within a field are deleted. This statement also generates a carriage return/line feed after the last field in the record is written.

Keep these facts in mind when you use the WRITE # statement:

1. The number of variables listed in the WRITE # statement must equal the number of fields in the record.

2. The type of data in the field must match the type of the variable name: If the field contains numeric values that will be used with statements requiring numbers, you must follow the rules for naming numeric variables when you assign a name to that field. Follow the rules for naming string variables if the field contains string values.

CLOSE Statement

The CLOSE statement for an output file causes the final records to be written from the buffer to the disk, adds an end-of-file marker to the end of the file just created, and ends the association between the file and the file number.

Note the use of the Boolean variable in line 3060 to control the WHILE/WEND loop. In line 1270, the flag CREATING is assigned the value −1, indicating true. CREATING remains true until the user enters Q and line 5060 assigns the value NO (0) to the flag, stopping execution of the loop.

Test the Program

Now suppose Mrs. Murphy enters the following data:

Client Acct	Client name	Hours	Rate
101	ALEXANDER BROWN	20	55.00
150	JEFFREY ARCHER	18	40.50
201	MARY HENDERSON	10	55.00
301	WELLINGTON GIFT SHOP	30	75.00
360	MARGARET CRAWFORD	0	75.00
401	RICHARD HAMILTON	5	40.50
501	COMPUTER SERVICES	40	75.00
540	HENRY CARLSON	20	55.00
601	MEGAN RYAN	8	55.75
701	PHILIP SPAULDING	25	80.00
780	FELICIA WILLIAMS	0	55.00
801	ELIZABETH STEWART	15	40.50
820	GIFT AHOY	12	75.00
901	JUSTIN MAILER	24	80.00

In response, the program creates this file:

```
"101","ALEXANDER BROWN",20,55
"150","JEFFREY ARCHER",18,40.5
"201","MARY HENDERSON",10,55
"301","WELLINGTON GIFT SHOP",30,75
"360","MARGARET CRAWFORD",0,75
"401","RICHARD HAMILTON",5,40.5
"501","COMPUTER SERVICES",40,75
"540","HENRY CARLSON",20,55
"601","MEGAN RYAN",8,55.75
"701","PHILIP SPAULDING",25,80
"780","FELICIA WILLIAMS",0,55
"801","ELIZABETH STEWART",15,40.5
"820","GIFT AHOY",12,75
"901","JUSTIN MAILER",24,80
```

Note the differences between the data as Mrs. Murphy entered them and the data in the file. Commas now separate the fields, and quotation marks enclose the string data. All leading and trailing spaces or zeros within a field have been deleted.

While testing a program that creates a file, enter just two or three records to begin with, until you determine if the program is working properly. As soon as you get the program to process your test set correctly, test the program with a full set of data.

As you are testing a program that creates a file, the system commands TYPE and PRINT are useful for displaying the records of a data file, such as BILL.SEQ. Remember to use these commands from the system prompt.

FOR APPEND

Mrs. Murphy already has a problem with Program 8.1. Sometimes she is not able to enter all the billing information in one sitting. Of course, when she enters Q for QUIT, the billing file is closed. If she runs Program 8.1 later, the previous billing file is erased, and she has to start from scratch. Here is a solution for her. Change line 3040 to

```
3040 OPEN "BILL.SEQ" FOR APPEND AS #1
```

FOR APPEND specifies sequential file output mode and positions the file pointer after the last record in the file. Any new records will be added to the file beginning at that point. The previous records in the file remain unchanged.

✳ **STYLE TIPS**

1. Make prompts easy to read and understand. The prompts Mrs. Murphy sees on the screen are concise but still indicate what action she should take. Notice the prompts request only one field at a time (for instance, Client name). Mrs. Murphy does not have to enter all four fields separated by commas in response to a single prompt. Although it simplifies her job, this method of data entry is slow. After Mrs. Murphy develops skill and confidence in using the program, she may request a faster way to create the billing file. At that time, you may decide to change the program so that she can enter all four fields with a single entry.

2. Provide a display that helps the user. With the current program, Mrs. Murphy sees only the responses for one billing record. Before she enters the next billing record, the screen is cleared. She likes the simplicity of the screen and the fact that potentially sensitive information does not remain on the screen for long after she enters it. Mrs. Murphy may find, however, that she would like the information to remain on the screen after she has entered a record. In this way, if she loses her place, the last record she entered is still on the screen. To make this adjustment, just change line 5040 to PRINT, which inserts a blank line between records as they are entered. Also add CLS before line 3050 to clear the screen before the initial prompt.

3. Minimize the keystrokes required for user responses. To exit the program, Mrs. Murphy has to enter only a Q rather than the word QUIT.

4. Be flexible in the responses you will accept from the user. When entering a Q to quit, Mrs. Murphy may enter either an uppercase or lowercase Q.

If you open a file that does not exist and specify FOR APPEND mode, the system creates a file just as if you had opened it for output. A file opened FOR APPEND mode must be closed like any other open file.

Suppose these records are in the file before Mrs. Murphy runs the revised Program 8.1:

```
"101","ALEXANDER BROWN",20,55
"150","JEFFREY ARCHER",18,40.5
"201","MARY HENDERSON",10,55
```

Now suppose that Mrs. Murphy enters the following data while running the version of Program 8.1 with the FOR APPEND mode:

401	RICHARD HAMILTON	5	40.50
501	COMPUTER SERVICES	40	75.00

BILL.SEQ now contains these records:

```
"101","ALEXANDER BROWN",20,55
"150","JEFFREY ARCHER",18,40.5
"201","MARY HENDERSON",10,55
"401","RICHARD HAMILTON",5,40.5
"501","COMPUTER SERVICES",40,75
```

Mrs. Murphy has one more request. Sometimes she would like to run Program 8.1 in output mode and sometimes in append mode. She also would like to give the file a different name each month.

To accommodate Mrs. Murphy's request, you can add the following lines to Program 8.1:

```
3032   CLS
3034   INPUT "Enter file mode: A or O ", MODE$
3036   INPUT "Enter file name:        ", FILE$
3040   OPEN MODE$,#1,FILE$
```

SCREEN REPORT

The reports that programs generate can be written on a hard copy device, such as a printer; on a secondary storage device, such as a floppy disk; or on the screen. In this section, you develop a program that writes a report on the screen.

Define the Problem

Now that Mrs. Murphy has run the program to create the billing file, Lowell and Bauer want a client billing report displayed on the screen. The report is to include headings, detail lines, and summary lines. The heading lines include the name of the law firm, the type of report, and column headings. The detail lines contain the client account number and name, hours billed, billing rate, and current amount billed. (The current amount billed is the billing rate multiplied by the billing hours.) At the end of the report, the total number of clients billed, total hours billed, and total amount billed are displayed.

Describe the Output

Figure 8.3 illustrates the format of the report. In this screen design form, the heading information is centered at the top of the form, and X's and #'s represent the detail line information. The formatted summary lines, which include totals for number of clients, number of hours, and amount billed, are at the bottom.

Determine the Input

The input for this program is the sequential file BILL.SEQ created by Program 8.1.

Design the Program Logic

The program is organized into three level-1 modules:

1. The WRITE HEADING module sets the line counter to zero, clears the screen, and displays the heading lines on the screen. The line counter is incremented every time a detail line is printed. When the line counter reaches 10, the program pauses, the screen is cleared, another heading is displayed, and the line counter is reset to zero.

2. The PROCESS FILE module contains the logic to be repeated until all the billing records have been processed.

   a. The BILL.SEQ file is opened.
   b. For each record input in the file:
      (1) The total amount of the bill is calculated.
      (2) The module WRITE DETAIL LINE is called.
      (3) The module UPDATE TOTALS is called.

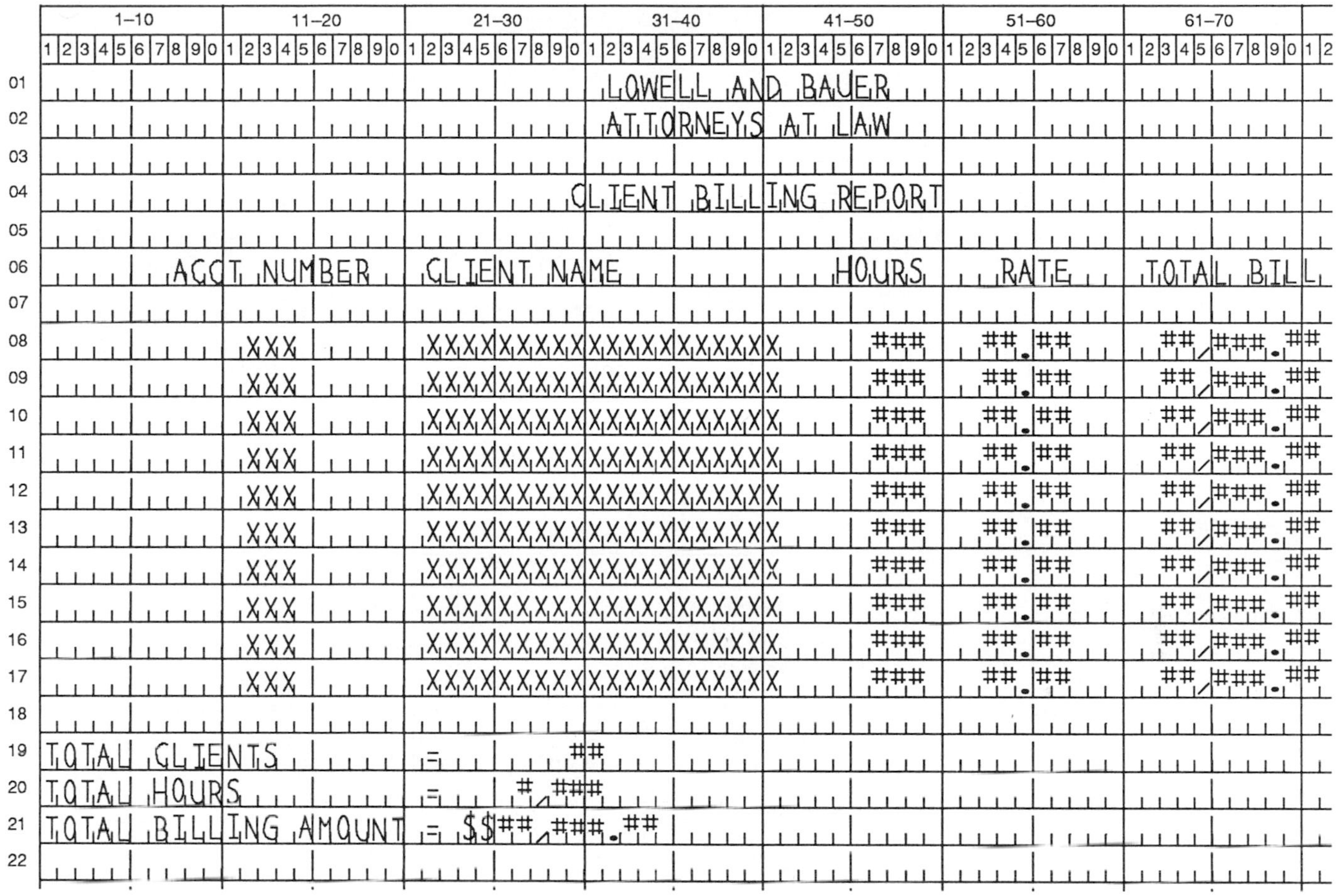

FIGURE 8.3 Screen design form for Program 8.2

c. The BILL.SEQ file is closed.

3. The WRITE SUMMARY LINES module displays the totals at the end of the report.

The WRITE DETAIL LINE module called by the PROCESS FILE module first checks to see whether it is time to print another heading. If the line counter is equal to the screen limit, the PAUSE SCREEN module is called. This module causes the program to pause until the user is ready to view a new screen. When the user presses any key on the keyboard, the WRITE HEADING module is called. Whether a new heading is displayed or not, the detail line is displayed, and the line counter is incremented by one.

The UPDATE TOTALS module called by the PROCESS FILE module increments the counters and accumulators that are displayed at the end of the report.

Figure 8.4 shows the structure chart and pseudocode for Program 8.2. The shading in the upper right corner of the WRITE HEADING module indicates that it is called from more than one place in the program.

Code the Program Instructions

Program 8.2 shows the code to implement the design for the client billing report. The program contains one new BASIC statement and one new BASIC function.

FIGURE 8.4
Logic design for
Program 8.2

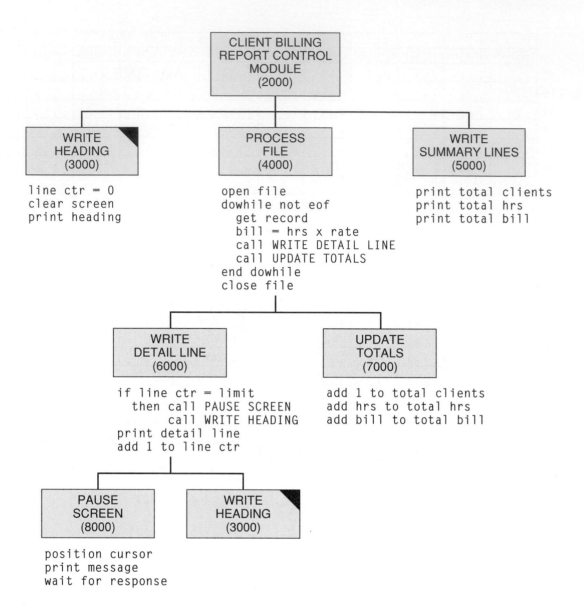

LOCATE

Notice line 8040. This statement positions the cursor on the screen.
The general format for the LOCATE statement is:

    [*line#*] LOCATE [*row*] [,*col*] [,*cursor,start,stop*]

You can use the LOCATE statement to position the cursor on the screen in preparation for a PRINT or INPUT statement. The word *row* refers to the rows on the screen (the horizontal lines on the screen form); *row* must be a number from 1 to 25. The word *col* refers to the columns on the screen (the vertical lines on the screen design form); *col* must be a number from 1 to 80.
    Look at these examples:

    100 LOCATE 12,35

This statement positions the cursor in the 35th column of the 12th row.

    100 LOCATE 20,10

This statement positions the cursor in the 10th column of the 20th row.

PROGRAM 8.2

```
1000 ' PROG8-2
1010 ' *****************************
1020 ' *    CLIENT BILLING REPORT    *
1030 ' *****************************
1040 '
1050 ' *****************************
1060 ' *           VARIABLES           *
1070 ' *****************************
1080 '
1090 ' BILL.SEQ                    Billing File
1100 ' Billing record:
1110 '     BILL.ACCT$
1120 '     BILL.NAME$
1130 '     BILL.HRS
1140 '     BILL.RATE
1150 '
1160 ' CALC.BILL.AMT               BILL.HRS * BILL.RATE
1170 ' DETAIL$                     Format for detail line
1180 ' LINE.CTR                    Line counter
1190 ' PAUSE$                      Screen pause
1200 '
1210 ' *****************************
1220 ' *           CONSTANTS           *
1230 ' *****************************
1240 '
1250   SCREEN.LIMIT = 10          'Maximum number of lines per screen
1260 '
1270 ' *****************************
1280 ' *   INITIALIZED VARIABLES    *
1290 ' *****************************
1300 '
1310   TOTAL.CLIENTS  = 0         'Total number of clients in file
1320   TOTAL.HRS      = 0         'Total hours
1330   TOTAL.BILL.AMT = 0         'Total billing amount
1999 '
2000 ' *****************************
2010 ' *         CONTROL MODULE         *
2020 ' *****************************
2030 '
2040   GOSUB 3000                 'Write Heading
2050   GOSUB 4000                 'Process File
2060   GOSUB 5000                 'Write Summary Lines
2070   END
2999 '
3000 ' *****************************
3010 ' *         WRITE HEADING          *
3020 ' *****************************
3030 '
3040   LINE.CTR = 0
3050   CLS
3060   PRINT TAB(32); "LOWELL AND BAUER"
3070   PRINT TAB(32); "ATTORNEYS AT LAW"
3080   PRINT
3090   PRINT TAB(30); "CLIENT BILLING REPORT"
3100   PRINT
3110   PRINT TAB(8);
          "ACCT NUMBER   CLIENT NAME            HOURS    RATE    TOTAL BILL"
3120   DETAIL$ =
          "    \  \        \                  \   ###    ##.##    ##,###.##"
3130   PRINT
3140   RETURN
3999 '
4000 ' *****************************
4010 ' *         PROCESS FILE          *
4020 ' *****************************
4030 '
4040   OPEN "BILL.SEQ" FOR INPUT AS #1
```

PROGRAM 8.2 (continued)

```
4050    WHILE NOT EOF(1)
4060        INPUT #1, BILL.ACCT$, BILL.NAME$,
                        BILL.HRS,  BILL.RATE
4070        CALC.BILL.AMT = BILL.HRS * BILL.RATE
4080        GOSUB 6000              'Write Detail Line
4090        GOSUB 7000              'Update Totals
4100    WEND
4110    CLOSE #1
4120    RETURN
4999 '
5000 ' ******************************
5010 ' *     WRITE SUMMARY LINES     *
5020 ' ******************************
5030 '
5040    PRINT
5050    PRINT USING "TOTAL CLIENTS          =        ##";    TOTAL.CLIENTS
5060    PRINT USING "TOTAL HOURS            =    #,###";    TOTAL.HRS
5070    PRINT USING "TOTAL BILLING AMOUNT = $$##,###.##"; TOTAL.BILL.AMT
5080    RETURN
5999 '
6000 ' ******************************
6010 ' *      WRITE DETAIL LINE      *
6020 ' ******************************
6030 '
6040    IF LINE.CTR = SCREEN.LIMIT
            THEN GOSUB 8000:
                 GOSUB 3000        'Pause Screen : Write Heading
6050    PRINT TAB(8); USING DETAIL$; BILL.ACCT$, BILL.NAME$,
                            BILL.HRS,   BILL.RATE,
                            CALC.BILL.AMT
6060    LINE.CTR = LINE.CTR + 1
6070    RETURN
6999 '
7000 ' ******************************
7010 ' *         UPDATE TOTALS        *
7020 ' ******************************
7030 '
7040    TOTAL.CLIENTS  = TOTAL.CLIENTS + 1
7050    TOTAL.HRS      = TOTAL.HRS + BILL.HRS
7060    TOTAL.BILL.AMT = TOTAL.BILL.AMT + CALC.BILL.AMT
7070    RETURN
7999 '
8000 ' ******************************
8010 ' *          PAUSE SCREEN        *
8020 ' ******************************
8030 '
8040    LOCATE 23,27
8050    PRINT "PRESS ANY KEY TO CONTINUE"
8060    PAUSE$ = INPUT$(1)
8070    RETURN
```

```
100 LOCATE 50,50
```

The last statement, however, causes an error because the value of row may not exceed 25.

The other parameters of the LOCATE statement are explained in the discussion of Program 8.3.

INPUT$ Function

The general format of the INPUT$ function is:

```
{line#] <var$> = INPUT$(<n>[#]filenumber])
```

This function returns a string of *n* characters read from the keyboard or from the file referenced by *filenumber*. You may use any string variable name for *var\$* (PAUSE\$ is used in line 8060). PAUSE\$ = INPUT\$(1) causes the program to halt until the user presses any key. It is not necessary to press the Enter key, although Enter may be the key pressed. Neither the cursor nor the user's response appears on the screen, as they do when the INPUT statement is used. The value of the key pressed is stored in *var\$*.

Since you cannot include a prompt with INPUT\$, line 8060 must be preceded by a PRINT statement with a prompt that lets the user know what the program expects. In this case, the prompt PRESS ANY KEY TO CONTINUE tells the person at the keyboard how to continue to the next screen of the report.

The number inside the parentheses in the INPUT\$ function indicates how many keys are to be pressed before program execution continues. If line 8060 were rewritten as

```
8060 PAUSE$ = INPUT$(2)
```

the user would need to enter two characters from the keyboard to have the program resume.

INKEY\$ Variable

Like INPUT\$, INKEY\$ can be used to halt the program until the user presses a key on the keyboard. The following routine could be substituted for line 8060 of Program 8.2.

```
8060 CHECK$ = ""
8062 WHILE CHECK$ = ""
8064     CHECK$ = INKEY$
8066 WEND
```

The value of INKEY\$ is the character of the last key pressed or the null string ("") before a key is pressed. In this routine, INKEY\$ equals the null string as long as no characters are entered from the keyboard. As soon as a character key is pressed, INKEY\$ contains that character, and that value is assigned to CHECK\$, ending the WHILE/WEND loop.

The general format of INKEY\$ is simply

```
[line#] <var$> = INKEY$
```

Test the Program

When the data Mrs. Murphy used to create BILL.SEQ are entered, the program directs the computer to display the two screens shown in Figure 8.5.

Remember that it is best to test a program like this one with only a few records at first. You can use COPY CON or EDLIN to create a small test file.

❄ **STYLE TIPS**

1. Make prompts readable. Visually isolate the prompt PRESS ANY KEY TO CONTINUE from the report so that the prompt attracts the user's attention. Always place prompts in the same position on the screen so that the user knows where to look for them.

2. Minimize input responses. When you use INPUT\$, the user does not have to press the Enter key. Remember, though, that the INPUT\$ function gives the user no opportunity to change an entry. If it is important for the user to be able to correct a response, use the INPUT statement instead.

```
                            LOWELL AND BAUER
                            ATTORNEYS AT LAW

                          CLIENT BILLING REPORT

      ACCT NUMBER    CLIENT NAME          HOURS    RATE     TOTAL BILL

          101        ALEXANDER BROWN        20     55.00      1,100.00
          150        JEFFREY ARCHER         18     40.50        729.00
          201        MARY HENDERSON         10     55.00        550.00
          301        WELLINGTON GIFT SHOP   30     75.00      2,250.00
          360        MARGARET CRAWFORD       0     75.00          0.00
          401        RICHARD HAMILTON        5     40.50        202.50
          501        COMPUTER SERVICES      40     75.00      3,000.00
          540        HENRY CARLSON          20     55.00      1,100.00
          601        MEGAN RYAN              8     55.75        446.00
          701        PHILIP SPAULDING       25     80.00      2,000.00



                    PRESS ANY KEY TO CONTINUE
```

```
                            LOWELL AND BAUER
                            ATTORNEYS AT LAW

                          CLIENT BILLING REPORT

      ACCT NUMBER    CLIENT NAME          HOURS    RATE     TOTAL BILL

          780        FELICIA WILLIAMS        0     55.00          0.00
          801        ELIZABETH STEWART      15     40.50        607.50
          820        GIFT AHOY              12     75.00        900.00
          901        JUSTIN MAILER          24     80.00      1,920.00


      TOTAL CLIENTS        =        14
      TOTAL HOURS          =       227
      TOTAL BILLING AMOUNT =  $14,805.00
```

FIGURE 8.5   Screen output from Program 8.2

DATA ENTRY USING A FORM SCREEN

It is not difficult to reproduce the layout of a business form on the screen. In this section, you will use the screen display of a customer order form for a data entry application.

Define the Problem

At Capshaw Enterprises, the sales staff fill out a standardized form when they take orders (see Figure 8.6). This customer order form then becomes a *source document* for the data entry department. The data entry personnel enter the data from the order form, and each order becomes an order record in the sequential order file. The staff would like a program to simplify data entry by displaying a replica of a blank order on the screen.

FIGURE 8.6
Customer order form for
Capshaw Enterprises

```
                    CAPSHAW ENTERPRISES
                        P.O. BOX 1224
                    SUNNYVALE, OHIO 45234

                                    Date: _____

    Customer's Name:  _____

    Address: _____

    City: _____  State: _____

    Zip Code: _____

    Telephone: _____

    Account Number: _____      Order Number: _____

    Amount Due: _____        Shipping Date: _____
```

Describe the Output

The program's output will be a sequential file of order records with each record corresponding to a customer order. The format of the file is as follows:

```
ORDER.SEQ  Sequential Output File
ORDER  record description:
```

Field Name	Data Length	Data Type
ORDER.NO$	4	String
ORDER.DATE$	8	String
ORDER.ACCT$	5	String
ORDER.NAME$	30	String
ORDER.ADDR$	20	String
ORDER.CITY$	10	String
ORDER.ST$	2	String
ORDER.ZIP$	5	String
ORDER.TEL$	8	String
ORDER.SHIP.DATE$	8	String
ORDER.AMT	7	Numeric (####.##)

The program also shows the user a screen replica of the customer order form shown in Figure 8.6. Figure 8.7 shows this screen design.

Determine the Input

Input to the program comes from the keyboard. The staff will enter the data from the order form onto the screen field by field. At the end of each order, the following prompt is displayed:

```
Do you want to enter another order (Y/N)?
```

By pressing Y, the clerk causes a fresh order form to be displayed on the screen. If N is pressed, the following prompt appears:

```
Do you have more orders to enter   (Y/N)?
```

This safety feature protects the clerk who incorrectly presses N in response to the previous prompt but would like to enter more orders before

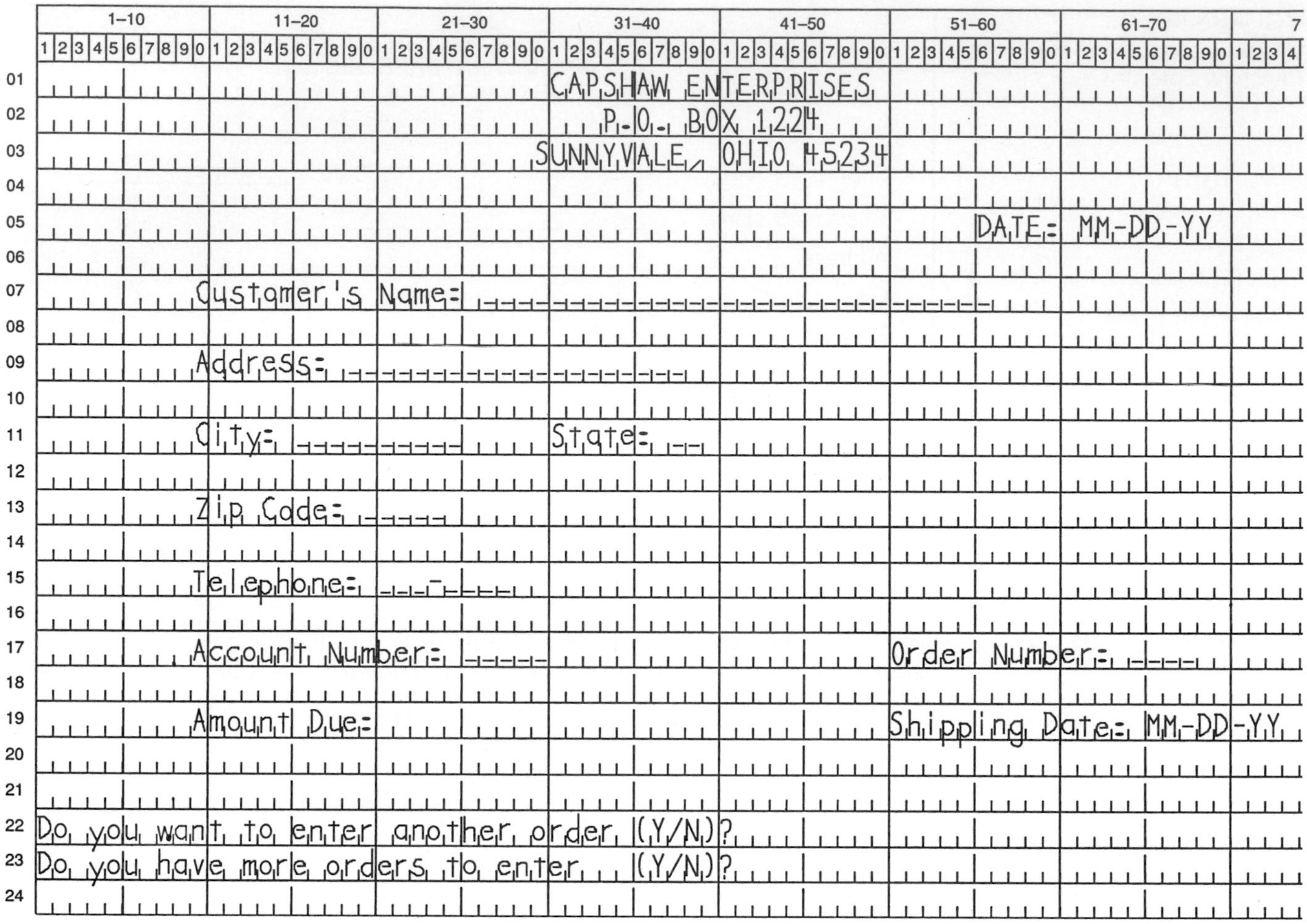

FIGURE 8.7 Screen design form for Program 8.3

closing the file. If, at this point, the clerk presses Y, a new order form appears on the screen. If the clerk presses N once more, the following message appears:

```
Creation of ORDER.SEQ complete
Total records = ##
```

Design the Program Logic

This program consists of two level-1 modules. The first level-1 module, CRE-ATE FILE, controls the task of creating the order file. First it opens the file, then it displays the order form, inputs the data, and writes the record until the user requests the stopping of the loop, and then it closes the file. The other level-1 module, WRITE SUMMARY LINES, displays on the screen the end-of-program message and number of records in the file.

The module CREATE FILE calls in three additional modules. DISPLAY SCREEN displays the order form on the screen. After the form is displayed, the ENTER DATA module prompts the user to enter the necessary data. After the data are entered, the WRITE RECORD module writes the record to the file and increments the record counter. This process is repeated until the user enters N in response to "Do you have more orders to enter (Y/N)?".

Figure 8.8 shows the structure chart and pseudocode for Program 8.3.

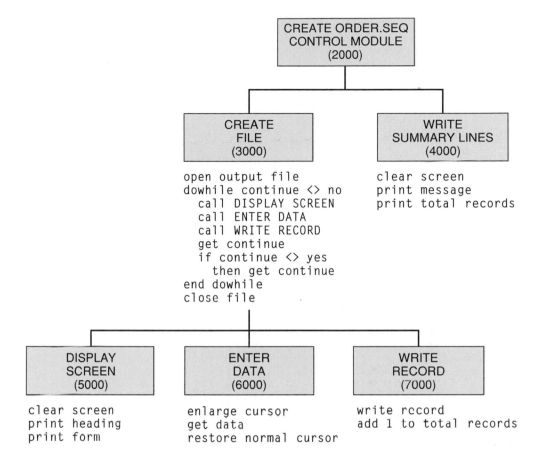

FIGURE 8.8
Logic design for
Program 8.3

Code the Program Instructions

LOCATE Statement Revisited

Program 8.3 implements the design in Figure 8.8; it contains some new BASIC statements and some familiar statements used in a new way.

Earlier in this chapter, you learned how to use the LOCATE statement to position the cursor on the screen, but you did not learn its three optional parameters. Here is the format of LOCATE again:

```
[line#] LOCATE [row] [,col] [,cursor,start,stop]
```

You can use the parameters *cursor*, *start*, and *stop* to specify the characteristics of the cursor.

The *cursor* parameter indicates whether the cursor is visible or not. While a program is running, the cursor is normally off. The underscore cursor associated with the INPUT statement, however, is still on. Using a 0 as this parameter makes the cursor invisible, and using a 1 causes the cursor to remain visible.

If you want the cursor to be larger than it normally is, you may use the *start* and *stop* parameters to design your own cursor. You create a cursor by turning on *scan lines*, which are numbered from 0 at the top to 7 (Color/Graphics Monitor Adapter) or 13 (Monochrome Display) at the bottom. The parameter *start* designates the cursor-start scan line. The parameter *stop* designates the cursor-stop line.

In line 6040, the statement LOCATE ,,1,3,5 creates a visible cursor larger than the default size. This larger cursor makes it easier for the clerks to keep track of their places on the form as they enter data. The first two commas in the statement cause the *row* and *col* parameters to be skipped.

PROGRAM 8.3

```
1000 ' PROG8-3
1010 ' *****************************
1020 ' *        CREATE ORDER.SEQ      *
1030 ' *****************************
1040 '
1050 ' *****************************
1060 ' *          VARIABLES           *
1070 ' *****************************
1080 '
1090 ' ORDER.SEQ                 Order File
1100 ' Order record:
1110 '     ORDER.NO$
1120 '     ORDER.DATE$
1130 '     ORDER.ACCT$
1140 '     ORDER.NAME$
1150 '     ORDER.ADDR$
1160 '     ORDER.CITY$
1170 '     ORDER.ST$
1180 '     ORDER.ZIP$
1190 '     ORDER.TEL$
1200 '     ORDER.SHIP.DATE$
1210 '     ORDER.AMT
1220 '
1230 ' *****************************
1240 ' *   INITIALIZED VARIABLES     *
1250 ' *****************************
1260 '
1270    CONTINUE$      = "Y"       'Enter another record flag
1280    TOTAL.RECORDS = 0          'Total records in file
1999 '
2000 ' *****************************
2010 ' *        CONTROL MODULE        *
2020 ' *****************************
2030 '
2040    GOSUB 3000                'Create File
2050    GOSUB 4000                'Write Summary Lines
2060    END
2999 '
3000 ' *****************************
3010 ' *          CREATE FILE         *
3020 ' *****************************
3030 '
3040    OPEN "ORDER.SEQ" FOR OUTPUT AS #1
3050    WHILE (CONTINUE$ <> "N") AND (CONTINUE$ <> "n")
3060        GOSUB 5000                'Display Screen
3070        GOSUB 6000                'Enter Data
3080        GOSUB 7000                'Write Record
3090        LOCATE 22,1
3100        INPUT "Do you want to enter another order (Y/N)"; CONTINUE$
3110        IF (CONTINUE$ <> "Y") AND (CONTINUE$ <> "y")
              THEN INPUT "Do you have more orders to enter   (Y/N)"; CONTINUE$
3120    WEND
3130    CLOSE #1
3140    RETURN
3999 '
4000 ' *****************************
4010 ' *    WRITE SUMMARY LINES       *
4020 ' *****************************
4030 '
4040    CLS
4050    PRINT "Creation of ORDER.SEQ complete"
4060    PRINT "Total records ="; TOTAL.RECORDS
4070    RETURN
4999 '
```

PROGRAM 8.3   (continued)

```
5000 ' *****************************
5010 ' *        DISPLAY SCREEN       *
5020 ' *****************************
5030 '
5040    CLS
5050    PRINT TAB(31); "CAPSHAW ENTERPRISES"
5060    PRINT TAB(34); "P.O. BOX 1224"
5070    PRINT TAB(30); "SUNNYVALE, OHIO 45234"
5080    PRINT
5090    PRINT TAB(56); "Date: MM-DD-YY"
5100    PRINT
5110    PRINT TAB(10); "Customer's Name: "; STRING$(30,"_")
5120    PRINT
5130    PRINT TAB(10); "Address: "; STRING$(20, "_")
5140    PRINT
5150    PRINT TAB(10); "City: "; STRING$(10, "_"); TAB(31); "State: __"
5160    PRINT
5170    PRINT TAB(10); "Zip Code: _____"
5180    PRINT
5190    PRINT TAB(10); "Telephone: ___-____"
5200    PRINT
5210    PRINT TAB(10); "Account Number: _____"; TAB(51); "Order Number: ____"
5230    PRINT
5240    PRINT TAB(10); "Amount Due:"; TAB(51); "Shipping Date: MM-DD-YY"
5250    RETURN
5999 '
6000 ' *****************************
6010 ' *          ENTER DATA        *
6020 ' *****************************
6030 '
6040    LOCATE ,,1,3,5               'Larger cursor
6050    LOCATE  5,62 : INPUT "",  ORDER.DATE$
6060    LOCATE  7,27 : LINE INPUT ORDER.NAME$
6070    LOCATE  9,19 : INPUT "",  ORDER.ADDR$
6080    LOCATE 11,16 : INPUT "",  ORDER.CITY$
6090    LOCATE 11,38 : INPUT "",  ORDER.ST$
6100    LOCATE 13,20 : INPUT "",  ORDER.ZIP$
6110    LOCATE 15,21 : INPUT "",  ORDER.TEL$
6120    LOCATE 17,26 : INPUT "",  ORDER.ACCT$
6130    LOCATE 17,65 : INPUT "",  ORDER.NO$
6140    LOCATE 19,22 : INPUT "",  ORDER.AMT
6150    LOCATE 19,66 : INPUT "",  ORDER.SHIP.DATE$
6160    LOCATE ,,,7                 'Set cursor to normal size
6170    RETURN
6999 '
7000 ' *****************************
7010 ' *          WRITE RECORD      *
7020 ' *****************************
7030 '
7040    WRITE #1, ORDER.NO$,   ORDER.DATE$,      ORDER.ACCT$, ORDER.NAME$,
                  ORDER.ADDR$, ORDER.CITY$,      ORDER.ST$,   ORDER.ZIP$,
                  ORDER.TEL$,  ORDER.SHIP.DATE$, ORDER.AMT
7050    TOTAL.RECORDS = TOTAL.RECORDS + 1
7060    RETURN
```

The cursor parameter 1 designates a visible cursor; the start parameter 3 designates the third line as the start scan line; and the stop parameter 5 designates the fifth line as the stop scan line. Figure 8.9 shows a diagram of the cursor produced by the LOCATE ,,1,3,5 statement. In line 6160, LOCATE ,,,7 resets the cursor to its normal size.

FIGURE 8.9
Cursors showing scan lines

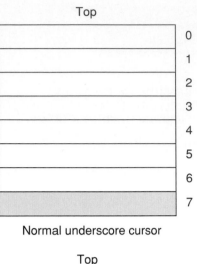

Normal underscore cursor

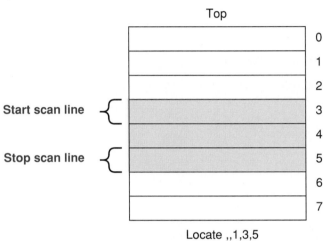

Locate ,,1,3,5

A two-part cursor can be useful in drawing attention to the current screen position. You can create a two-part cursor with the following statement:

```
100 LOCATE ,,1,6,1
```

Figure 8.10 shows a diagram of that cursor. This cursor is "on" from scan line 6 to scan line 1 and "off" from scan line 2 through scan line 5. Two-part cursors are especially easy to see.

FIGURE 8.10
Two-part cursor

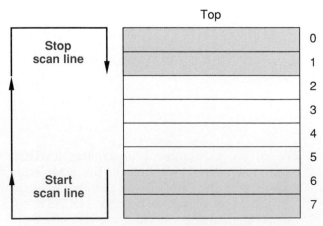

Locate ,,1,6,1

LINE INPUT Statement

The general format of the LINE INPUT statement is:

```
[line#] LINE INPUT ["prompt";] <var$>
```

LINE INPUT is used to enter a string of characters that may include commas or quotation marks. In BASIC, commas and quotation marks are used as delimiters in many situations. For that reason, they cause errors when entered in response to an INPUT statement. Any characters may be entered in response to LINE INPUT; however, only one string variable may be included in each statement. This example shows a program segment containing LINE INPUT, the output that segment produces, and the user's response, which contains quotation marks and commas as part of the input string.

```
100 LINE INPUT "Enter title: "; TITLE$
110 PRINT TITLE$
RUN
Enter title: "PROGRAMMING" by Kelly, Kelly, and Kelly
"PROGRAMMING" by Kelly, Kelly, and Kelly
```

Notice that the LINE INPUT does not prompt the user with a question mark.

In Program 8.3, line 6060 uses LINE INPUT to accept the value of ORDER.NAME$ because that value may include commas.

✳ STYLE TIPS

1. Be consistent in how the user responds. When the user responds to the two messages:

```
Do you want to enter another order (Y/N)?
Do you have more orders to enter   (Y/N)?
```

Y in both cases indicates more orders are to be entered, and N indicates the process has been completed. Both prompts use the same format (Y/N) to prompt the user for a YES or NO response.

2. Don't allow a user's response to produce drastic results. For example, in Program 8.3, the data entry clerk has a second chance to keep the file open if the clerk mistakenly enters an N in response to the message: "Do you want to enter another order (Y/N)?".

3. If the format for a response is not obvious, supply the user with the required format. In Program 8.3, the prompt specifies the format for the dates fields because dates can be entered in a variety of formats. Also, the underline characters indicate how many characters can be entered in that field. For example, the state field has two underline characters, indicating to the user that only two characters should be entered in the state field.

4. Use a cursor that is easy to see. In Program 8.3, the displayed form shows a number of fields on the screen at the same time. The larger cursor helps the data entry clerk to keep track of his or her position on the screen.

INPUT Statement Revisited

The ENTER DATA module in Program 8.3 uses a series of compound statements containing LOCATE and INPUT. These INPUT statements have a null, or empty, prompt (indicated by the pair of double quote marks with no spaces between them). The null prompt is necessary to suppress the question mark that BASIC would otherwise display in this situation.

Test the Program

Figure 8.11 shows five source documents and the ORDER.SEQ file they create.

FIGURE 8.11
Five source documents and the file they create

CAPSHAW ENTERPRISES
P.O. BOX 1224
SUNNYVALE, OHIO 45234

Date: *10-10-88*

Customer's Name: *Mike Johns, Inc*
Address: *3220 Elm St*
City: *Reno*　　　State: *N V*
Zip Code: *89814*
Telephone: *784-5647*
Account Number: *A1003*　　Order Number: *1001*
Amount Due: *300.10*　　　Shipping Date: *10-15-88*

CAPSHAW ENTERPRISES
P.O. BOX 1224
SUNNYVALE, OHIO 45234

Date: *10-10-88*

Customer's Name: *Dorothy Smith*
Address: *5 Market Pl*
City: *Pittsburgh*　　　State: *P A*
Zip Code: *31256*
Telephone: *522-1804*
Account Number: *A0999*　　Order Number: *1002*
Amount Due: *810.25*　　　Shipping Date: *10-20-88*

CAPSHAW ENTERPRISES
P.O. BOX 1224
SUNNYVALE, OHIO 45234

Date: *10-11-88*

Customer's Name: *Boston, Stover, and Sims Assoc*
Address: *10 Main St*
City: *Cape Cod*　　　State: *MA*
Zip Code: *43325*
Telephone: *687-5543*
Account Number: *BS002*　　Order Number: *1003*
Amount Due: *60.00*　　　Shipping Date: *11-29-88*

FIGURE 8.11
(continued)

```
                    CAPSHAW ENTERPRISES
                       P.O. BOX 1224
                    SUNNYVALE, OHIO 45234

                                    Date: 10-11-88

    Customer's Name: Ryan Michael
    Address: 4777 Heilo Dr
    City: Honolulu              State: HI
    Zip Code: 78923
    Telephone: 344-1998
    Account Number: A4009          Order Number: 1004
    Amount Due: 995.80             Shipping Date: 11-19-88
```

```
                    CAPSHAW ENTERPRISES
                       P.O. BOX 1224
                    SUNNYVALE, OHIO 45234

                                    Date: 10-11-88

    Customer's Name: Carter, Carter, and Katz
    Address: 455 Berry La
    City: Albany                State: NY
    Zip Code: 56489
    Telephone: 566-7676
    Account Number: B6778          Order Number: 1005
    Amount Due: 100.55             Shipping Date: 12-17-88
```

```
"1001","10-10-88","A1003","Mike Johns, Inc","3220 Elm St",
    "Reno","NV","89814","784-5647","10-15-88",300.1
"1002","10-10-88","A0999","Dorothy Smith","5 Market Pl",
    "Pittsburgh","PA","31256","522-1804","10-20-88",810.25
"1003","10-11-88","B5002","Boston, Stover, and Sims Assoc","10 Main St",
    "Cape Cod","MA","43325","687-5543","11-29-88",60
"1004","10-11-88","A4009","Ryan Michael","4777 Heilo Dr",
    "Honolulu","HI","78923","344-1998","11-19-88",995.8
"1005","10-11-88","B6778","Carter, Carter, and Katz","455 Berry La",
    "Albany","NY","56489","566-7676","12-17-88",100.55
```

MENU DESIGN

Individual programs can be written to produce the various reports a firm might use. The people needing these reports, however, may find it convenient to use a single program that provides them a menu of report options and produces the report they select. This section describes such a menu-driven program.

Define the Problem

Now that Capshaw Enterprises has an order file available, the sales staff would like a program that will generate the information they routinely need regarding orders for the month. In this case, they need two reports. One will allow the salespersons to view all the orders. The other will allow them to see all orders that exceed some dollar amount, which they enter at run time.

This program should first display a menu listing the available options, then display the report selected, and then return to the menu in case the salesperson wants to display another report. The sales staff would, in addition, like the ability to print the report.

Describe the Output

Figure 8.12 presents the screen designs for the program. These include the program menu and the format for the two reports. The report formats are identical except for the general title of the report. One report has the heading ORDER INFORMATION; the other report has the heading SELECTED ORDERS.

Determine the Input

The input for the program is the ORDER.SEQ file created in Program 8.3 and, if the "LIST SELECTED ORDERS" option is selected, an amount entered from the keyboard.

The user must respond to the following prompt if he or she selects the "LIST SELECTED ORDERS" option:

```
Enter amount due (####.##)
```

Design the Program Logic

The logic of the CONTROL MODULE is different from the logic of previous control modules. The CONTROL MODULE calls the DISPLAY MENU module and then calls the appropriate module to implement the user's choice. In this program, the user's options are:

1. Listing all orders

2. Listing selected orders based on amount due

3. Exiting the program

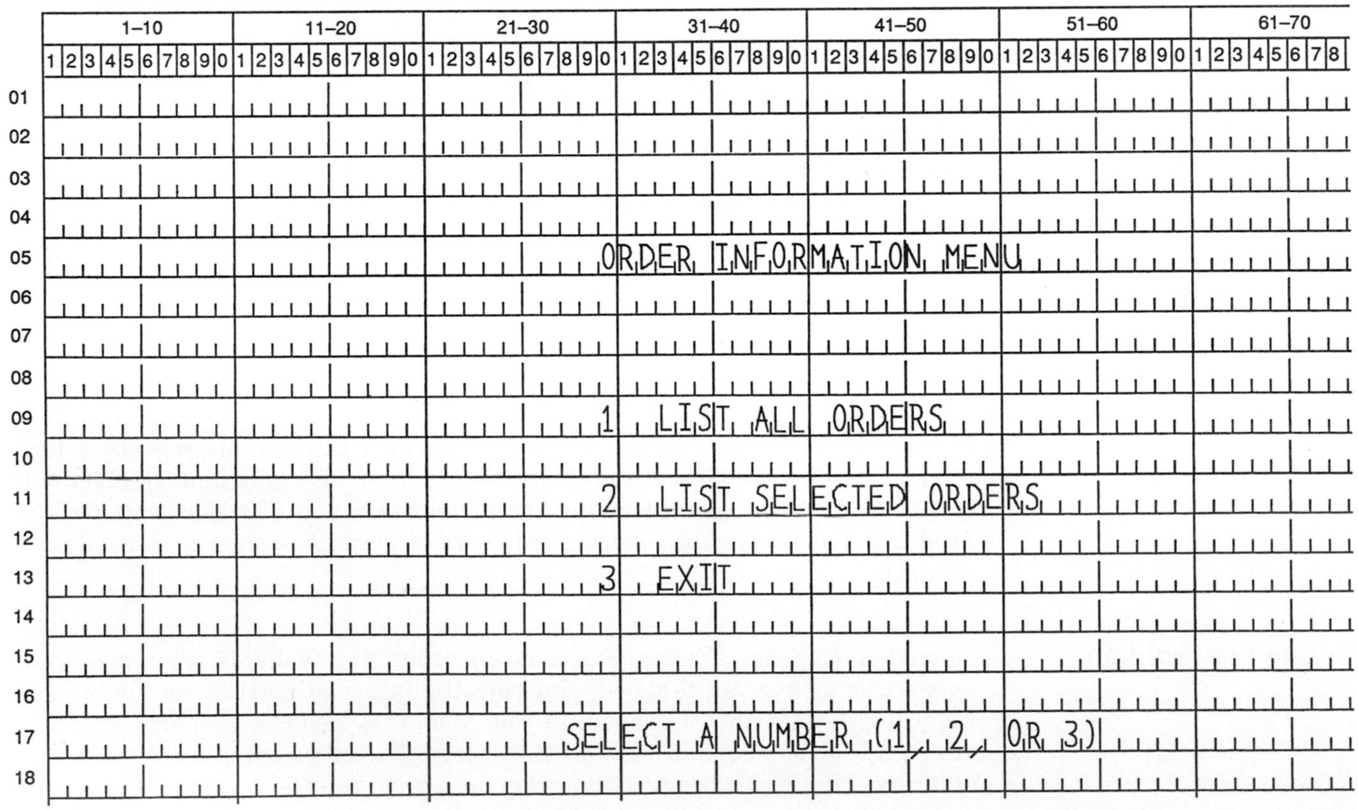

FIGURE 8.12   Screen design forms for Program 8.4

The selection logic here is an example of the case structure described in Chapter 5.

If the LIST ALL ORDERS module is called, a heading is printed, the file is opened, the order records are read and displayed until the end-of-file is reached, and then the file is closed. Control returns to the CONTROL MODULE, and the menu is presented again.

If the LIST SELECTED ORDERS module is called, a dollar amount is accepted from the user; a heading is printed; the file is opened; the order records are read and any record that contains an amount greater than the amount entered by the user is printed until the end-of-file is reached; and then the file is closed. Control returns to the CONTROL MODULE, and the menu is presented again.

If the *EXIT* module is called, an end-of-program message is displayed, and program execution stops.

The structure chart and pseudocode in Figure 8.13 show the program logic.

```
                 1-10        11-20       21-30       31-40       41-50       51-60       61-70
01                                        CAPSHAW ENTERPRISES
02                                           P. O. BOX 1224
03                                  SUNNYVALE, OHIO 45234
04                                                                        Heading
05
06                                       XXXXXXXXXXXXXXXXX
07
08     ORDER NO.    ACCT. NO.    NAME                                            AMOUNT DUE
09
10        XXXXX       XXXXXX    XXXXXXXXXXXXXXXXXXXXXXXXXXXXXXXXXXX          #,###.##
11        XXXXX       XXXXXX    XXXXXXXXXXXXXXXXXXXXXXXXXXXXXXXXXXX          #,###.##
12        XXXXX       XXXXXX    XXXXXXXXXXXXXXXXXXXXXXXXXXXXXXXXXXX          #,###.##
13
14
15
16
17
18
19
20
21
22              Press SHIFT PRTSC-KEYS for paper copy
23                  Press any key to continue
24
```

FIGURE 8.12   (continued)

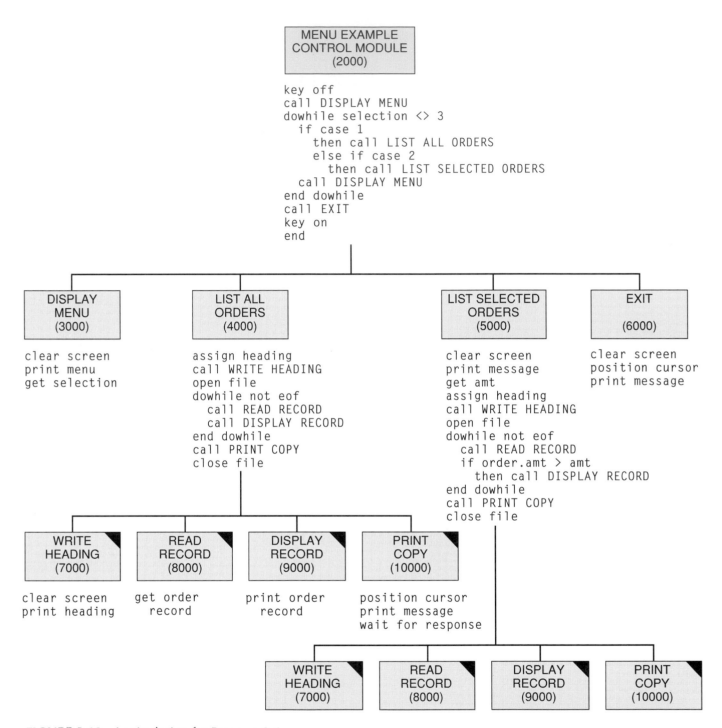

FIGURE 8.13   Logic design for Program 8.4

Code the Program Instructions

Program 8.4 implements the logic design in Figure 8.13 and demonstrates the following new BASIC statements and features.

ON GOSUB Statement

The general format for this statement is:

```
[line#] ON <n> GOSUB <line#> [,line# , . . .., line#]
```

This statement causes the program to branch to one of the specified line numbers, depending on the value of *n*. The parameter *n* may be any numeric value from 0 to 255. In the statement

100 ON CHOICE GOSUB 1000,2000,3000,4000

program control passes to line 1000 if CHOICE equals 1, to line 2000 if CHOICE equals 2, to line 3000 if CHOICE equals 3, and to line 4000 if CHOICE equals 4. If CHOICE is zero or greater than 4, then program execution continues with the line number following line 100. If a negative number is entered, execution stops and an error message is displayed. The RETURN statement in the modules called will cause control to transfer to the line number following line 100.

PROGRAM 8.4

```
1000 ' PROG8-4
1010 ' *****************************
1020 ' *          MENU EXAMPLE          *
1030 ' *****************************
1040 '
1050 ' *****************************
1060 ' *            VARIABLES           *
1070 ' *****************************
1080 '
1090 ' ORDER.SEQ                    Order File
1100 ' Order record:
1110 '     ORDER.NO$
1120 '     ORDER.DATE$
1130 '     ORDER.ACCT$
1140 '     ORDER.NAME$
1150 '     ORDER.ADDR$
1160 '     ORDER.CITY$
1170 '     ORDER.ST$
1180 '     ORDER.ZIP$
1190 '     ORDER.TEL$
1200 '     ORDER.SHIP.DATE$
1210 '     ORDER.AMT
1220 '
1230 ' HEADING$                     Report heading
1240 ' DETAIL$                      Format for detail line
1250 ' PAUSE$                       Screen pause
1260 ' SELECT.AMT                   User"s amount due selection
1999 '
2000 ' *****************************
2010 ' *          CONTROL MODULE          *
2020 ' *****************************
2030 '
2040    KEY OFF
2050    GOSUB 3000                   'Display Menu
2060    WHILE SELECTION <> 3
2070        ON SELECTION GOSUB 4000,5000        'List All Orders
                                                'List Selected Orders
2080        GOSUB 3000               'Display Menu
2090    WEND
2100    GOSUB 6000                   'Exit
2110    KEY ON
2120    END
2999 '
3000 ' *****************************
3010 ' *          DISPLAY MENU          *
3020 ' *****************************
3030 '
3040    CLS
3050    LOCATE  5,30
3060    PRINT "ORDER INFORMATION MENU"
3070    LOCATE  9,30
```

PROGRAM 8.4 (continued)

```
3080    PRINT "1  LIST ALL ORDERS"
3090    LOCATE 11,30
3100    PRINT "2  LIST SELECTED ORDERS"
3110    LOCATE 13,30
3120    PRINT "3  EXIT"
3130    LOCATE 17,28
3140    INPUT "SELECT A NUMBER (1, 2, OR 3) ", SELECTION
3150    RETURN
3999 '
4000 ' *****************************
4010 ' *        LIST ALL ORDERS        *
4020 ' *****************************
4030 '
4040    HEADING$ = "ORDER INFORMATION"
4050    GOSUB 7000                   'Write Heading
4060    OPEN "ORDER.SEQ" FOR INPUT AS #1
4070    WHILE NOT EOF(1)
4080        GOSUB 8000               'Read Record
4090        GOSUB 9000               'Display Record
4100    WEND
4110    GOSUB 10000                  'Print Copy
4120    CLOSE #1
4130    RETURN
4999 '
5000 ' *****************************
5010 ' *     LIST SELECTED ORDERS     *
5020 ' *****************************
5030 '
5040    CLS
5050    PRINT "THIS SELECTION WILL DISPLAY ALL ORDERS"
5060    PRINT "THAT EXCEED THE AMOUNT YOU ENTER"
5070    PRINT
5080    INPUT "Enter amount due (####.##) ", SELECT.AMT
5090 '
5100    HEADING$ = " SELECTED ORDERS"
5110    GOSUB 7000                   'Write Heading
5120    OPEN "ORDER.SEQ" FOR INPUT AS #1
5130    WHILE NOT EOF(1)
5140        GOSUB 8000               'Read Record
5150        IF ORDER.AMT > SELECT.AMT
                    THEN GOSUB 9000  'Display Record
5160    WEND
5170    GOSUB 10000                  'Print Copy
5180    CLOSE #1
5190    RETURN
5999 '
6000 ' *****************************
6010 ' *              EXIT              *
6020 ' *****************************
6030 '
6040    CLS
6050    LOCATE 12,20
6060    PRINT "PROGRAM COMPLETE"
6170    RETURN
6999 '
7000 ' *****************************
7010 ' *         WRITE HEADING         *
7020 ' *****************************
7030 '
7040    CLS
7050    PRINT TAB(31); "CAPSHAW ENTERPRISES"
7060    PRINT TAB(34); "P.O. BOX 1224"
7070    PRINT TAB(30); "SUNNYVALE, OHIO 45234"
7080    PRINT
7090    PRINT
```

PROGRAM 8.4 (continued)

```
7100    PRINT TAB(32); HEADING$
7110    PRINT
7120    PRINT TAB(5);
           "ORDER NO    ACCT NO    NAME                            AMOUNT DUE"
7130    DETAIL$ =
           "  \  \        \    \      \                    \    #,###.##"
7140    PRINT
7150    RETURN
7999    '
8000    ' ****************************
8010    ' *         READ RECORD         *
8020    ' ****************************
8030    '
8040    INPUT #1, ORDER.NO$,    ORDER.DATE$,      ORDER.ACCT$, ORDER.NAME$,
                  ORDER.ADDR$, ORDER.CITY$,      ORDER.ST$,   ORDER.ZIP$,
                  ORDER.TEL$,  ORDER.SHIP.DATE$, ORDER.AMT
8050    RETURN
8999    '
9000    ' ****************************
9010    ' *         DISPLAY RECORD        *
9020    ' ****************************
9030    '
9040    PRINT TAB(5); USING DETAIL$; ORDER.NO$,    ORDER.ACCT$,
                                     ORDER.NAME$, ORDER.AMT
9050    RETURN
9999    '
10000   '****************************
10010   '*          PRINT COPY         *
10020   '****************************
10030   '
10040   LOCATE 22,20
10050   PRINT "Press SHIFT-PRTSC KEYS for paper copy"
10060   PRINT TAB(25); "Press any key to continue"
10070   PAUSE$ = INPUT$(1)
10080   RETURN
```

✳ **STYLE TIPS**

1. **Give every menu a heading that clearly defines the menu's topics.** For example, ORDER INFORMATION MENU tells the user that this menu contains options pertaining to orders placed with Capshaw Enterprises.

2. **Make the menu options clear.** State the choices in the menu concisely but clearly. Use words that the user will understand; avoid computer jargon whenever possible. One of the choices should always allow the user to exit the menu or the program. EXIT, STOP, and QUIT are all appropriate names for the option to leave the menu program.

3. **Make the prompt instructions clear and readable.** The prompt should be displayed away from the body of the menu, and it should be descriptive enough so that the user knows how to respond.

4. **Use submenus when necessary.** If a menu becomes too crowded, the main menu can call another menu. The same rules for menu design apply, except that when the user exits a submenu, the program should return the user to the previous menu.

Shift-PrtSc Keys

Line 10050 displays the message

```
Press SHIFT-PRTSC KEYS for paper copy
```

When the user holds down a Shift key and presses the PrtSc (Print Screen) key, the current screen display is sent to the printer.

KEY ON/KEY OFF
Statements

If you do not want the function key menu (1LIST, 2RUN, 3LOAD, etc.) to be displayed on the 25th line of the screen, enter the KEY OFF statement. KEY OFF in line 2040 causes the 25th line on the screen to be blank so that the function key menu does not appear on the screen or hard copy report. The function keys associated with this menu are, however, still available for use. KEY ON in line 2110 causes the function key menu to reappear on the screen.

Test the Program

If you use the ORDER.SEQ file you created in Program 8.3, Program 8.4 will generate the screens shown in Figure 8.14.

```
                         ORDER INFORMATION MENU


                    1   LIST ALL ORDERS

                    2   LIST SELECTED ORDERS

                    3   EXIT



                 SELECT A NUMBER (1, 2, OR 3)
```

```
                      CAPSHAW ENTERPRISES
                        P.O. BOX 1224
                    SUNNYVALE, OHIO 45234

                       ORDER INFORMATION

    ORDER NO   ACCT NO   NAME                         AMOUNT DUE

       1001    A1003     Mike Johns, Inc                 300.10
       1002    A0999     Dorothy Smith                   810.25
       1003    B5002     Boston, Stover, and Sims Assoc   60.00
       1004    A4009     Ryan Michael                    995.80
       1005    B6778     Carter, Carter, and Katz        100.55




                 Press SHIFT-PRTSC KEYS for paper copy
                     Press any key to continue
```

FIGURE 8.14   Screens generated by Program 8.4

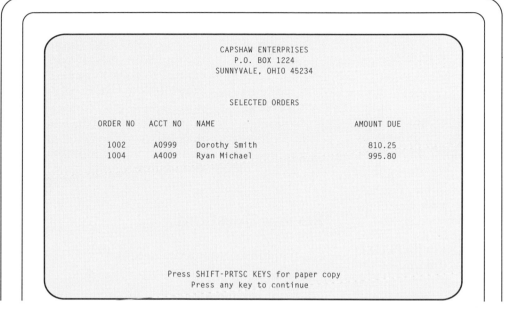

```
                        CAPSHAW ENTERPRISES
                          P.O. BOX 1224
                        SUNNYVALE, OHIO 45234

                          SELECTED ORDERS

      ORDER NO   ACCT NO   NAME                        AMOUNT DUE

        1002     A0999     Dorothy Smith                  810.25
        1004     A4009     Ryan Michael                   995.80




                Press SHIFT-PRTSC KEYS for paper copy
                    Press any key to continue
```

FIGURE 8.14   (continued)

Summary

- *Interactive programs* require some form of input from the user. One type of interactive program allows users to create or update a file; these are called *data entry* programs.

- A *menu-driven* program allows the user to choose from a list or *menu* of options. For example, the menu for an arithmetic drill program might look like this:

```
        ARITHMETIC PRACTICE

        1   ADDITION
        2   SUBTRACTION
        3   MULTIPLICATION
        4   DIVISION
        5   STOP

SELECT A NUMBER (1, 2, 3, 4, or 5)
```

- Design your prompts and the responses you expect from the user so that the user understands the prompts easily and can respond with the minimum of keystrokes.

- Make prompts easy for the user to see and understand by:

  1. Separating them from other material with blank lines.

  2. Displaying them in a consistent format and position.

  3. Clearing the screen if it has become cluttered and the old text is no longer useful to the user.

  4. Specifying a field format or maximum length.

  5. Being flexible in accepting responses.

  6. Not allowing a response to produce drastic results.

- You can use the LOCATE statement to write at any location on the screen. For example

```
LOCATE 12,40
PRINT "HI"
```

  causes H to appear in column 40 and I in column 41 of screen line 12. The LOCATE statement also allows you to modify the cursor form. For example

```
LOCATE ,,1,3,5
```

  produces a cursor that is three times taller than the normal cursor. Such modifications help the user of interactive programs find the cursor on the screen.

- When input from the user might contain commas or quotation marks, the INPUT statement will not work. The BASIC statement to use in those instances is LINE INPUT. In the following example, the LINE INPUT statement accepts the entire location description the user enters, even though a comma is included in the response.

```
100 LINE INPUT "Where do you live? "; LOCATION$
200 PRINT LOCATION$
RUN
Where do you live? 18 Mile Creek Rd., near Buffalo
18 Mile Creek Rd., near Buffalo
```

- You can send the screen display to the printer by holding down a Shift key and pressing the PrtSc (Print Screen) key once.

- Opening a file for output prepares a file to which the computer can write. If a file with the name specified in the OPEN statement already exists on the disk, opening it for output destroys its contents. Opening a file using the FOR APPEND option, however, adds records to the end of the current file.

- The WRITE # statement writes data to a sequential file, as in the example from Program 8.1:

```
WRITE #1, BILL.ACCT$, BILL.NAME$,
        BILL.HRS,   BILL.RATE
```

When you are using WRITE #, be careful to specify as many variables as there are fields in the record and to avoid data type mismatch errors (that is, specify variable names of the same data types as those in the respective fields of the record).

- Chapter 8 describes the following new BASIC instructions:

INKEY$ A variable that contains the value of the character of the last key pressed or, before a key is pressed, of the null string (" ").

INPUT$(n) A function that causes the program to halt until the user presses n keys.

KEY OFF A statement that causes the 25th screen line to be blank so that the function key menu is not displayed.

KEY ON A statement that causes the function key menu to reappear on the screen.

LINE INPUT A statement used to enter a string of characters that may include commas and quotation marks.

LOCATE A statement that positions the cursor on the screen and controls the visibility and size of the cursor.

ON n GOSUB A statement that branches to one of the specified line numbers depending on the value of n. The RETURN statement of the module called will cause control to pass to the statement following the ON n GOSUB.

WRITE # A statement that causes data to be written to the file with commas between the fields and with quotation marks at either end of the strings.

Review Questions

1. What is an interactive program?

2. What is the purpose of data entry?

3. What is a menu?

4. What is a menu-driven program?

5. What are two characteristics of good interactive programs?

6. How does a screen design form differ from a print chart?

7. When the statement

```
OPEN "AFILE.TXT" FOR OUTPUT AS #1
```

is executed, what happens to the contents of AFILE.TXT if a file by that name already exists on the current disk?

8. What are the differences among the following statements:

```
OPEN "DOC.TXT" FOR INPUT AS #1
OPEN "DOC.TXT" FOR OUTPUT AS #1
OPEN "DOC.TXT" FOR APPEND AS #1
```

9. What will the contents of a sequential file look like after this statement is executed:

```
WRITE #1, FIELD1, FIELD2$, FIELD3
```

Assume that FIELD1 = 27, FIELD2$ = RUTH, and FIELD3 = 44.80.

10. What determines the number of variable names in a WRITE # statement? Do you have to worry about matching variable names with data types?

11. How can you format a WRITE # statement to make it more readable?

12. What is the purpose of the CLOSE statement when you create or append to a sequential file?

13. Do INPUT$ and INKEY$ serve the same function?

14. When would you use INPUT instead of INPUT$?

15. What can you do to make it easy for the user to respond to prompts?

16. For what types of fields do you think the data entry person needs to see a format?

17. What is a source document?

18. Why might you want to design a cursor rather than use the default cursor? Explain how you can change the form of the cursor.

19. How does the LINE INPUT statement differ from the INPUT statement? When might you need to use LINE INPUT?

20. Why would you require the user to verify that he or she is finished before allowing the program to end?

21. Why is it good practice to allow the user to enter y or Y for YES? Why not have the user enter the entire word YES?

22. For the following statement

    `20 ON N GOSUB 100,200,300`

    what will happen if N = 4?

23. How can you send a copy of the display on the screen to the printer? What happens if the printer is not turned on?

24. Why, when you print a display from the screen, would you want to have given the KEY OFF instruction?

25. In BASIC, if the function key menu is not displayed on the screen, can you still use the function keys to enter the commands LOAD, SAVE, and RUN?

26. What are some characteristics of a good menu?

27. Why is it important to include an exit option in a menu?

Problems

1. List possible prompts to replace the prompt (Enter Q to quit) in Program 8.1.

2. Change Program 8.1 so that the prompts are centered on the screen.

3. Describe the results of executing the following OPEN statements:

   a. `OPEN "INPUT.SEQ" FOR INPUT AS #1`

   b. `OPEN "A:PAY.SEQ" FOR INPUT AS #1`

   c. `OPEN "ACCT.SEQ" FOR APPEND AS #2`
      (ACCT.SEQ does not exist on the disk.)

   d. `OPEN "ACCT.SEQ" FOR APPEND AS #2`
      (ACCT.SEQ already exists as a file on the disk.)

   e. `OPEN "C:SALARY.SEQ" FOR OUTPUT AS #3`

   f. `OPEN NEW.FILE$ FOR OUTPUT AS #1`

   g. `OPEN "I",#1,"ACCT.SEQ"`

   h. `OPEN "O",#1,"B:INV.SEQ"`

   i. `OPEN "FILE.SEQ" FOR OUTPUT AS #1`
      (FILE.SEQ already exists as a file on the disk.)

   j. `OPEN "STUDENT.SEQ" FOR INPUT AS #1`
      (STUDENT.SEQ does not exist on the disk.)

4. List possible prompts to replace the prompt (Y/N) in Program 8.3.

5. Modify Program 8.4 so that the user can view the next screen by pressing any key when a report occupies more than one screen.

Program Assignments

1. The local library in Mission Hills plans to computerize the status of overdue books. The library needs a program to create a book file and a second program to list the books and their status.

Program 1

Write a program to create a sequential file named LIB.SEQ. This program should allow the user to enter data by responding to prompts on the screen. At the end of the program, display a message and the number of records in the file.

The library file consists of the following fields:

LIB.SEQ Sequential File
LIB Record:

Field Name	Data Length	Data Type
LIB.TITLE$	30	String
LIB.AUTHOR$	20	String
LIB.DATE$	8	String (YY/MM/DD)
LIB.NO$	4	String

LIB.DATE$ is the date the book is due back to the library. If the field is blank, the book is on the library shelf. LIB.NO$ is the library card number of the borrower. If the field is blank, the book is on the library shelf.

Enter the data from the table on page 186 to create the file (Note that the author field contains commas.)

Data for Program Assignment 1

LIB.TITLE$	LIB.AUTHOR$	LIB.DATE$	LIB.NO$
East of Eden	Steinbeck, John	89/10/08	T344
Gone with the Wind	Mitchell, Margaret		
Rage of Angels	Sheldon, Sidney	89/10/16	A331
The Great Gatsby	Fitzgerald, F. Scott	89/10/15	B335
War and Peace	Tolstoy, Leo	89/10/02	T442
Rebecca	DuMaurier, Daphne	89/10/08	T344
The Iliad	Homer		
A Farewell to Arms	Hemingway, Ernest		
Kaleidoscope	Steele, Danielle	89/10/20	S446
Texas	Michener, James	89/10/16	H667
The Fountainhead	Rand, Ayn	89/10/14	J789
Love Story	Segal, Erich		
Patriot Games	Clancy, Tom		
Great Expectations	Dickens, Charles		
Catch-22	Heller, Joseph	89/10/07	K986

Program 2

Display the file in a report format. Note the screen design format given to you on page 187 indicating the placement of the heading lines, the format of the detail lines, and the necessary summary lines. This program should first request a date from the user (enter 89/10/14). This date is used to determine whether a book is overdue or not. If the date in the file for books on loan precedes the date entered by the user, the book is overdue. If the book is overdue, place asterisks to the right of the detail line. The totals should include total books, total books on loan, and total books overdue. Display 10 detail lines per screen and be sure to use page numbers.

2. Successories, Inc., is planning to expand to the United States from its home location in Paris. The company has had success selling expensive fashion accessories not only in its Paris boutique but also in such cities as London, Rome, and Vienna. The company, after surveying major cities in the United States, has decided to open its first American store in your hometown. One of the first tasks for the data processing department is to create an inventory file. Successories needs two programs.

Program 1

The first program should create a sequential inventory file. The user enters the data to create INV.SEQ by responding to prompts on the screen. At the end of the program, display a message and the number of records in the file.

Allow the user the ability to enter the name of the file at the beginning of the run as well as the mode of the file (output or append).

The INV.SEQ file consists of the following fields:

INV.SEQ Sequential File
INV Record:

Field Name	Data Length	Data Type
INV.DEPT$	4	String
INV.CODE$	3	String
INV.NUM$	3	String
INV.NAME$	16	String
INV.ON.HAND	3	Numeric (###)
INV.PRICE	8	Numeric (#####.##)
INV.ON.ORDER	3	Numeric (###)

Enter the data on page 187 to create the file.

Program 2

Display the inventory file. After creating the INV.SEQ file, write a program to display the file on the screen in a report format. The heading should include a general title, column headings, a date entered by the user, and page numbers. The detail lines should include the fields in the inventory record and the inventory cost (INV.ON.HAND * INV.PRICE). Display 12 records per screen. The summary lines should include the total cost of the inventory products and the total records in the file after all the records have been displayed.

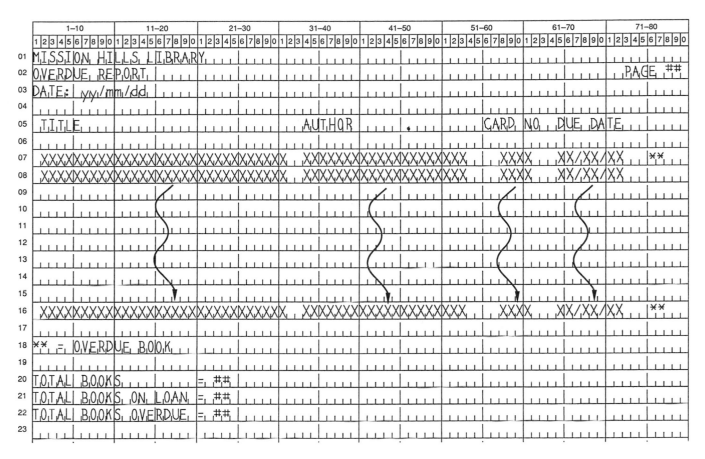

Screen design form for Program Assignment 8-1

Data for Program Assignment 2

Dept	Product Code	Product Number	Product Name	On Hand	Unit Price	On Order
1010	210	426	Silver bracelets	30	100.20	0
1010	210	329	Silver necklaces	2	1200.95	1
1010	210	746	Silver earrings	12	88.99	0
1010	210	123	Stickpins	7	500.89	2
1010	210	545	Silver rings	10	999.99	0
1010	350	828	Amalfi shoes	40	85.66	20
1010	350	260	Nickol shoes	32	98.99	10
1010	350	739	Red Cr shoes	50	54.99	0
1010	520	743	Leather bags	12	345.99	0
1010	520	843	Suede bags	0	299.89	10
1010	750	234	Straw hats	10	45.96	0
1010	750	128	Felt hats	12	134.99	0
1010	750	478	Knit hats	20	50.99	10
1010	750	489	Wool hats	12	99.99	10
2020	210	489	Gold bracelets	4	16299.99	0
2020	210	466	Gold necklaces	3	10877.95	1
2020	210	566	Gold rings	2	9112.89	0
2020	420	111	Silk scarves	20	340.55	20
2020	420	050	Tie scarves	50	78.00	30
2020	420	231	Bow scarves	10	62.88	5
2020	420	321	Wool scarves	12	98.89	15
3030	870	156	Wool capes	9	545.66	3
3030	920	862	Suede coats	3	14870.00	0

3. In addition to an inventory file, Successories also needs an employee file.

The employee file consists of the following fields:

EMP.SEQ   Sequential File
EMP Record:

Field Name	Data Length	Data Type
EMP.SSN$	9	String
EMP.DATE$	8	String (mm/dd/yy)
EMP.FIRST$	12	String
EMP.MID$	1	String
EMP.LAST$	15	String
EMP.ADDR1$	20	String (street address)
EMP.ADDR2$	20	String (city,state)
EMP.ZIP$	5	String
EMP.AREA$	3	String
EMP.TEL$	8	String
EMP.BIRTH$	8	String (mm/dd/yy)
EMP.SEX$	1	String
EMP.REF$	30	String

a. Design a screen to match the employment form used by the personnel department. Remember to supply the format for the user's response when appropriate.

b. After designing a screen, write a program to create the employee file from the data entered by the personnel department. Design a unique cursor to help the people in personnel keep track of the current position on the screen.

c. Use the LINE INPUT statement to enter data for city/state and for the employment reference.

d. After the user has completed entering the data, display an end message and the number of records written to the file.

e. Make up test data to create ten records. Use the TYPE or COPY command to check the sequential output file.

4. Mr. Dumont, the director of the new Successories store, wants one program that will allow him to see (1) the employment information for anyone in the employment file, (2) selected product codes in the inventory file, and (3) any items on order in the inventory file.

SUCCESSORIES, INC.
Leaders in Fashion Accessories

Employment Application

Date _____

Social Security Number _____

First Name _____ Middle Initial _____ Last Name _____

Street Address_____

City/State   _____

Zip Code   _____

Area Code _____ Telephone Number _____

Date of Birth _____   Sex (M or F)_____

Reference _____

Employment Application Form for Program Assignment 3

Write a menu-driven program for Mr. Dumont that:

a. Allows him to enter a Social Security number and then displays the employment information on file (use the EMP.SEQ file created in program assignment 3) for that employee. If Mr. Dumont does not know the Social Security number, give him the option of entering the employee's last name. Process the file only until a match is found. (You may want to use a submenu.)

b. Allows him to enter a product code and then displays all the inventory records for that product code (use the INV.SEQ file created in program assignment 2). Display the total number of records listed at the end of the report.

c. Display all the records with a value greater than zero in the on-order field. For each record, also display the on-order cost (INV.ON.ORDER * INV.PRICE). Display the total on-order cost at the end of the report.

5. Write a menu program to convert currency. Use the following menu choices:

```
(1)   Dollars to French francs
(2)   Dollars to Canadian dollars
(3)   Dollars to Mexican pesos
(4)   Dollars to Japanese yen
```

After the user selects an option, clear the screen and prompt for the amount to be converted. After converting the dollars, display the converted amount. Find the current conversion rates in the newspaper. For help, refer to the lire problem in Chapter 4.

6. Futures, Inc., needs to display a menu from which the stock brokers can select different reports. Design a menu that allows the broker to pick from the following options:

a. *List of stocks in the file.* If this option is selected, display the fields in each of the stocks in STK.SEQ (described in Program Assignment 7.2 on page 147.). For each stock, list all the fields in the record. At the end of the report, print the total number of stocks listed.

b. *List stocks sold for a loss.* If this option is selected, display all stocks that were sold at a loss. In addition to displaying the fields in the record, display the dollar loss for each stock. The dollar loss is the total sale of the stock minus the total cost. At the end of the report, print the total number of stocks listed and the total loss.

c. *List stocks sold for a gain.* If this option is selected, display all stocks that were sold for a gain. In addition to displaying the fields in the record, display the dollar gain for each stock. The dollar gain is the total sale of the stock minus the total cost. At the end of the report, print the total number of stocks listed and the total gain.

d. *Calculate loss or gain for a stock.* If this option is selected, request that the user enter a stock number and the current selling price of that stock. Calculate the current value of the stock by multiplying the current selling price by the number of shares. Calculate the cost of the stock by multiplying the purchase price by the number of shares (STK.BUY * STK.SHARES). Finally, calculate the loss or gain by subtracting the cost value from the current value. Display the stock number and name, the purchase price and number of shares, the selling price entered by the user, the current value and the loss or gain.

7. The credit department at Berrenger's Department store needs to display their overdue accounts on the screen. Design a menu that allows the clerk to view the accounts over 30 days due, the accounts over 60 days due, and the accounts over 90 days due. Display the total accounts overdue and the total overdue for the time period at the end of the report. After the screen is displayed, give the clerk a chance to print the information on the printer. Use the CR.SEQ file from Program Assignment 7.4 on page 148–149.

8. The Hereford Lacrosse team needs a program that allows the team manager to create a file of player statistics, append new players to the file, list the team statistics, and display the statistics about a particular player. Write a menu-driven program with the following options:

a. *Create a file.* This option allows the user to enter the data field by field to create the LAX.SEQ file described in Program Assignment 7.3 on page 148. Warn the user of this option that any current file may be destroyed, and allow the user to exit to the menu without creating a file. Also request that the user enter the name of the file. After the file is created, display the total number of records in the file.

b. *Add to a file.* This option allows the user to add records to the file. After the records are added, display the total number of records added to the file.

c. *List the team statistics.* This option allows the user to see a display of the records in the file. List every field in the record. At the end of the report, display the total number of players, total goals, and total assists. Display 10 players per screen.

d. *Display statistics of individual players.* This option allows the user to enter a player's number. In response, the computer displays the information on the file concerning this player. Also display the percentage of goals and assists this player has made. The percentage of goals is the player's goals divided by the total goals for the team. The percentage of assists is the player's assists divided by the total assists for the team.

9. Write a program that displays four multiple-choice questions a user is to answer. The program should:

a. Display general instructions for answering the questions and then allow the user to press any key to continue.

b. Display each question one at a time. If the answer is correct, a message should be displayed. If the answer is incorrect, the correct answer should be displayed. Allow the user to press any key to continue.

c. Display the number of correct answers after all four questions have been asked.

Using the Data Disk

1. Insert the data disk into the disk drive.

2. Load BASIC (change the default drive first if necessary).

3. Load PROG8-1.

   a. You can use a string variable name instead of the file name in the OPEN statement. For example:

   ```
   OPEN FILE$ FOR OUTPUT AS #1
   ```

   Mrs. Murphy would like to create a series of sequential files labeled BILL1.SEQ, BILL2.SEQ, etc., that she will merge together later (Chapter 13). Change PROG8-1 to allow Mrs. Murphy to enter the name of the file she wants to create. After running the new version of the program, be sure you check the output. To do this, switch to DOS using the SHELL command and use the type command followed by the name of the file to view the newly created file.

   b. Now that Mrs. Murphy is proficient at entering data from the keyboard, she has asked if there is any way to speed up the process. Modify PROG8-1 so that she can enter an entire record and then press the Enter key.

   c. Use the LOCATE statement to create a different cursor for this program.

   d. Save this version of the program under the name CH8-1.DD.

4. Load PROG8-4.

   a. Change PROG8-4 so that when the user selects option 2 from the menu, the amount due entered by the user is displayed in the heading of the report.

   b. Change PROG8-4 so that the user must enter a 4 character password before either report is displayed on the screen. The password entered by the user should not be displayed on the screen.

   c. Change PROG8-4 so that

   (1) An entry is added to the menu allowing the user to look at a single order.
   (2) After selecting this new option, the user may enter an order number to see the order information displayed on the screen.
   (3) An appropriate message is printed if the order is not found in the file.

   d. Save this version of the program under the name CH8-2.DD.

Chapter Nine

Control Break Processing

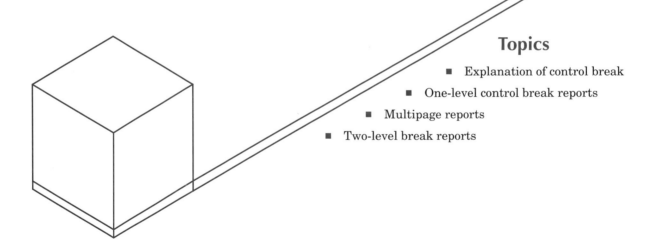

Topics

- Explanation of control break
- One-level control break reports
- Multipage reports
- Two-level break reports

BASIC Variables

```
DATE$
TIME$
```

INTRODUCTION

So far, the formats of the printed reports produced by the sample programs have been like the format of the Berrenger's Department Store report shown in Figure 9.1. That report has one set of headings, uninterrupted detail lines, and summary information at the end. The only total in this report is total sales for the quarter. Total quarterly sales figures are important information for Berrenger's, but the report would have been more useful to the store's management if it had also listed monthly sales totals.

The main purpose of this chapter is to explain how to write programs that create reports with subtotals, such as monthly sales at Berrenger's Department Store. Programs that produce subtotals are commonly called *control break programs*.

The first program in this chapter creates a single-page report for Berrenger's that includes subtotals for monthly sales as well as total sales for the quarter. The second program, a modification of the first, produces multi-page reports. The final control break program provides Berrenger's with subtotals for each department as well as for each month.

DEFINING CONTROL BREAK

A program that creates reports with monthly subtotals must check the value of the month field each time it reads a record. Whenever it reads a month different from the previous month, the program interrupts the printing of detail lines and prints the monthly total. This pause in the processing of records because of a change in a designated field is called a *control break*. Figure 9.2 illustrates the relationship between the records in a file and a report with monthly subtotals.

Any field in a record can be designated as the field that signals a break. The field so designated is called a *control field*. Notice that the records in the file must be ordered according to the values of the control field. The process of arranging the records in some order is called *sorting*, and files are described as being sorted on one or more fields. (Chapter 12 discusses sorting in detail.) To produce the report in Figure 9.2, you need to sort the input file on the month field.

The three programs in this chapter show the steps necessary to implement control break processing.

ONE-LEVEL CONTROL BREAK

Programs that generate reports with subtotals calculated from records grouped according to a single-control field implement a *one-level* control break. The program in this section is a one-level control break program.

Define the Problem

Mr. Berrenger has learned that it is possible for his reports to provide monthly totals. He has requested that you write a program to include monthly totals beginning with the next report.

Describe the Output

This program's output will be a report with the quarterly and monthly sales information Mr. Berrenger requested. The print chart in Figure 9.3 illustrates its format.

FIGURE 9.1
A report without control breaks

```
                    SALES REPORT
              BERRENGER'S DEPARTMENT STORE
                     05-12-1990

    MONTH   DEPT    SALESPERSON       SALES

      1     311    L DERBYSHIRE        500.12
      1     311    M JEFFERSON          40.56
      1     311    J SAMUELS           600.99
      1     312    H BLESSING        1,000.50
      1     312    G MALLONEE          675.50
      1     312    K MCCREADY          400.36
      1     312    M QUILL             300.99
      1     315    J ANDREWS           300.15
      1     315    D MAYER             200.75
      2     311    L DERBYSHIRE        899.50
      2     311    M JEFFERSON       1,000.65
      2     311    J SAMUELS            50.75
      2     312    H BLESSING           30.34
      2     312    G MALLONEE          900.45
      2     312    K MCCREADY          400.20
      2     312    M QUILL               0.00
      2     315    J ANDREWS            90.90
      2     315    D MAYER             700.65
      3     311    L DERBYSHIRE        700.80
      3     311    M JEFFERSON         200.80
      3     311    J SAMUELS           400.55
      3     312    H BLESSING           70.60
      3     312    G MALLONEE        2,000.85
      3     312    K MCCREADY          600.14
      3     312    M QUILL             300.15
      3     315    J ANDREWS           700.85
      3     315    D MAYER             200.99

              FINAL TOTAL    $13,269.09***


            ***END OF REPORT***
```

Determine the Input

The input will be Berrenger's sequential sales file, SALES.SEQ:

```
SALES.SEQ  Sequential Input File
SALES  record description:
```

Field Name	Data Length	Data Type
SALES.MTH	2	Numeric (##)
SALES.DEPT$	3	String
SALES.NAME$	14	String
SALES.AMT	8	Numeric (#####.##)

Remember that this file must be sorted on SALES.MTH; otherwise, the report will be a mess.

Design the Program Logic

Designing a successful control break program requires careful attention to the details of the task the program is to perform. Beginning programmers often have trouble with these programs because they try to code them before they fully understand the logic required to implement a control break.

```
                    SALES REPORT
           BERRENGER'S DEPARTMENT STORE
                     05-12-1990
```

MONTH	DEPT	SALESPERSON	SALES
1	311	L DERBYSHIRE	500.12
1	311	M JEFFERSON	40.56
1	311	J SAMUELS	600.99
1	312	H BLESSING	1,000.50
1	312	G MALLONEE	675.50
1	312	K MCCREADY	400.36
1	312	M QUILL	300.99
1	315	J ANDREWS	300.15
1	315	D MAYER	200.75
		MONTHLY.TOTAL	$4,019.92**
2	311	L DERBYSHIRE	899.50
2	311	M JEFFERSON	1,000.65
2	311	J SAMUELS	50.75
2	312	H BLESSING	30.34
2	312	G MALLONEE	900.45
2	312	K MCCREADY	400.20
2	312	M QUILL	0.00
2	315	J ANDREWS	90.90
2	315	D MAYER	700.65
		MONTHLY.TOTAL	$4,073.44**
3	311	L DERBYSHIRE	700.80
3	311	M JEFFERSON	200.80
3	311	J SAMUELS	400.55
3	312	H BLESSING	70.60
3	312	G MALLONEE	2,000.85
3	312	K MCCREADY	600.14
3	312	M QUILL	300.15
3	315	J ANDREWS	700.85
3	315	D MAYER	200.99
		MONTHLY.TOTAL	$5,175.73**
		FINAL TOTAL	$13,269.09***

*** END OF REPORT***

SALES.SEQ file

Control Field (SALES.MTH)

Record 1 →	1	311	L DERBYSHIRE	500.12
Record 2 →	1	311	M JEFFERSON	40.56
Record 3 →	1	311	J SAMUELS	600.99
	1	312	H BLESSING	1000.50
	1	312	G MALLONEE	675.50
	1	312	K MCCREADY	400.36
	1	312	M QUILL	300.99
	1	315	J ANDREWS	300.15
Record 9 →	1	315	D MAYER	200.75
Record 10 →	2	311	L DERBYSHIRE	899.50
	2	311	M JEFFERSON	1000.65
	2	311	J SAMUELS	50.75
	2	312	H BLESSING	30.34
	2	312	G MALLONEE	900.45
	2	312	K MCCREADY	40C.20
	2	312	M QUILL	0.00
	2	315	J ANDREWS	90.90
Record 18 →	2	315	D MAYER	700.65
Record 19 →	3	311	L DERBYSHIRE	700.80
	3	311	M JEFFERSON	200.80
	3	311	J SAMUELS	400.55
	3	312	H BLESSING	70.60
	3	312	G MALLONEE	2000.85
	3	312	K MCCREADY	600.14
	3	312	M QUILL	300.15
	3	315	J ANDREWS	700.85
Record 27 →	3	315	D MAYER	200.99

FIGURE 9.2   Relationship between records and subtotals

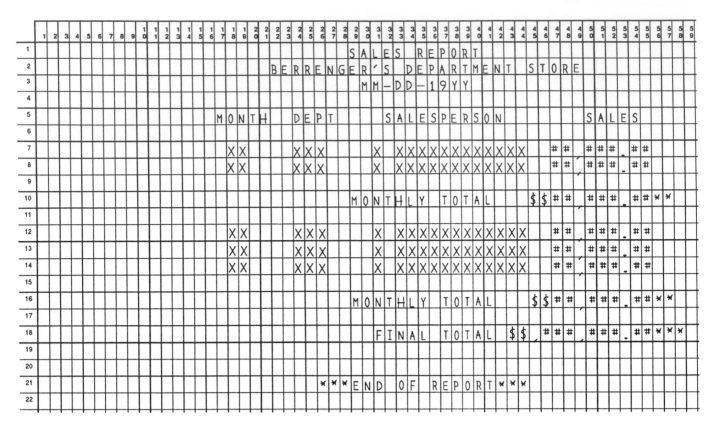

FIGURE 9.3 Print chart for Program 9.1

To avoid problems, begin by considering what the program must do. For each month it must:

- Initialize a monthly sales total to zero.
- Assign the current sales month to a variable so that the computer can compare each record read to determine whether a new month has been encountered.
- Process all the records for the current month.
- Write the monthly sales total.
- Increment the final total by the monthly sales total.

Also, for each record in the current month the program must:

- Write the detail line.
- Increment the monthly sales total by the sales amount.

See Table 9.1 for a diagram of this logic.

The structure chart and pseudocode for each module is shown in Figure 9.4. This figure represents a complete design for Program 9.1. The SET UP MONTH module is executed once for every new month in the file, the PROCESS RECORDS module is executed for every record in that month, and the WRAP UP MONTH module is executed once for every month. In addition to these sets of functions, the program requires the WRITE HEADING module to write the heading lines at the top of the report, the READ RECORD module to get a record, and the WRITE SUMMARY LINES module to print the final total and end message at the end of the report.

Take time to work through the logic illustrated in Figure 9.4 carefully. As you do that, notice the following essential points of this design:

1. The monthly sales total is set to zero for each new month in the SET UP MONTH module. The final total is set to zero only once, in the INITIALIZED VARIABLES section.

2. The save variable, SAVE.MTH, is set to the current sales month each time a new month is encountered in the file. Each time a record is read, the sales month, SALES.MTH, is compared to SAVE.MTH to determine whether all the records for the current month have been processed. A control break occurs when the value in SAVE.MTH is different from the value in SALES.MTH.

3. A call to READ RECORD from PROCESS MONTHS reads the first record. After reading this first record, the SET UP MONTH module is called, which sets SAVE.MTH equal to SALES.MTH. This ensures that SAVE.MTH will have the same value as SALES.MTH during the first pass through PROCESS RECORDS. In this way, the first record will not cause a control break, and a subtotal will not be printed before any detail lines are printed.

Table 9.1   One-Level Control Break

PROCESS MONTHS Level-1 Control Field		PROCESS RECORDS Records in the File
do for each month		
1. set month total to 0		
2. process all the records for this month	⟶	do for each record 1. write detail line
		2. add sales amt to month total
3. write month total	⟵	end
4. add month total to final total		
end		

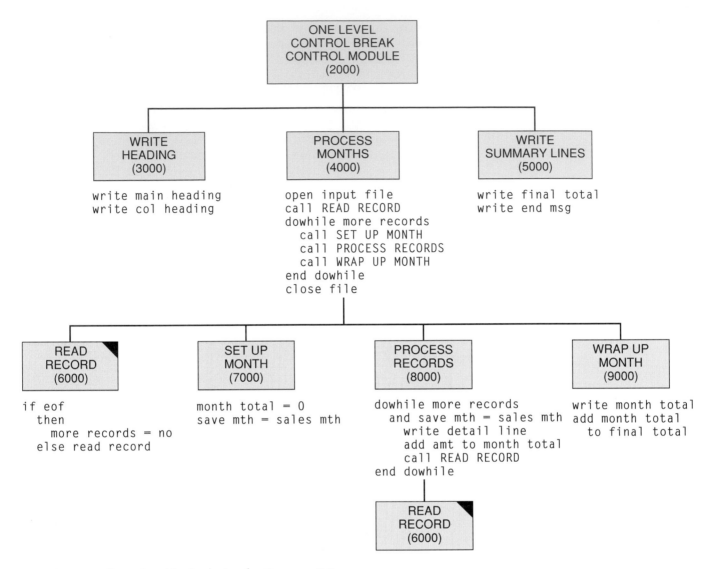

FIGURE 9.4 Completed logic design for Program 9.1

4. The PROCESS FILE module calls the READ RECORD module only once (the priming read). The PROCESS RECORDS module calls READ RECORD for the rest of the records in the file. Because this program processes the file with a priming read, you need a flag to signal the end of processing. This flag is named MORE.RECORDS.

5. In the WRAP UP MONTH module, the monthly sales total is printed and used to increment the final total *after* the transactions for that month have been processed.

Code the Program Instructions

Program 9.1 lists the code to implement the design in Figure 9.4 and introduces one new BASIC reserved word.

PROGRAM 9.1

```
1000 ' PROG9-1
1010 ' *****************************
1020 ' *    ONE LEVEL CONTROL BREAK   *
1030 ' *****************************
1040 '
1050 ' *****************************
1060 ' *          VARIABLES           *
1070 ' *****************************
1080 '
1090 ' SALES.SEQ                 Sales File
1100 ' Sales Record:
1110 '     SALES.MTH
1120 '     SALES.DEPT$
1130 '     SALES.NAME$
1140 '     SALES.AMT
1150 '
1160 ' DETAIL$                   Format for detail line
1170 ' MONTHLY.TOTAL#            Total sales for the month
1180 ' SAVE.MTH                  Value of SALES.MTH in current group
1190 '
1200 ' *****************************
1210 ' *          CONSTANTS           *
1220 ' *****************************
1230 '
1240   YES = -1                  'Value for true
1250   NO  =  0                  'Value for false
1260 '
1270 ' *****************************
1280 ' *   INITIALIZED VARIABLES      *
1290 ' *****************************
1300 '
1310   FINAL.TOTAL# = 0          'Total sales for the report
1320   MORE.RECORDS = YES        'Flag for reading records
1999 '
2000 ' *****************************
2010 ' *        CONTROL MODULE        *
2020 ' *****************************
2030 '
2040   GOSUB 3000                'Write Heading
2050   GOSUB 4000                'Process Months
2060   GOSUB 5000                'Write Summary Lines
2070   END
2999 '
3000 ' *****************************
3010 ' *         WRITE HEADING        *
3020 ' *****************************
3030 '
3040   LPRINT TAB(29); "SALES REPORT"
3050   LPRINT TAB(22); "BERRENGER'S DEPARTMENT STORE"
3060   LPRINT TAB(30); DATE$
3070   LPRINT
3080   LPRINT TAB(17); "MONTH  DEPT    SALESPERSON        SALES"
3090   LPRINT
3100   DETAIL$ =       " ##    \ \    \                \  ##,###.##"
3110   RETURN
3999 '
4000 ' *****************************
4010 ' *         PROCESS MONTHS       *
4020 ' *****************************
4030 '
4040   OPEN "SALES.SEQ" FOR INPUT AS #1
4050   GOSUB 6000                'Read Record
4060   WHILE MORE.RECORDS
4070      GOSUB 7000             'Set Up Month
4080      GOSUB 8000             'Process Records
```

PROGRAM 9.1 (continued)

```
4090       GOSUB 9000              'Wrap Up Month
4100    WEND
4110    CLOSE #1
4120    RETURN
4999 '
5000 ' ****************************
5010 ' *     WRITE SUMMARY LINES     *
5020 ' ****************************
5030 '
5040    LPRINT TAB(31);
              USING "FINAL TOTAL $$,###,###.##_*_*_*"; FINAL.TOTAL#
5050    LPRINT
5060    LPRINT
5070    LPRINT TAB(26); "***END OF REPORT***"
5080    RETURN
5999 '
6000 ' ****************************
6010 ' *          READ RECORD          *
6020 ' ****************************
6030 '
6040    IF EOF(1) THEN MORE.RECORDS = NO
                  ELSE INPUT #1, SALES.MTH,   SALES.DEPT$,
                                  SALES.NAME$, SALES.AMT
6050    RETURN
6999 '
7000 ' ****************************
7010 ' *         SET UP MONTH         *
7020 ' ****************************
7030 '
7040    MONTHLY.TOTAL# = 0
7050    SAVE.MTH = SALES.MTH
7060    RETURN
7999 '
8000 ' ****************************
8010 ' *        PROCESS RECORDS        *
8020 ' ****************************
8030 '
8040    WHILE MORE.RECORDS AND (SAVE.MTH = SALES.MTH)
8050       LPRINT TAB(17); USING DETAIL$; SALES.MTH,   SALES.DEPT$,
                                  SALES.NAME$, SALES.AMT
8060       MONTHLY.TOTAL# = MONTHLY.TOTAL# + SALES.AMT
8070       GOSUB 6000              'Read Record
8080    WEND
8090    RETURN
8999 '
9000 ' ****************************
9010 ' *         WRAP UP MONTH         *
9020 ' ****************************
9030 '
9040    LPRINT
9050    LPRINT TAB(29);
              USING "MONTHLY.TOTAL    $$##,###.##_*_*"; MONTHLY.TOTAL#
9060    LPRINT
9070    FINAL.TOTAL# = FINAL.TOTAL# + MONTHLY.TOTAL#
9080    RETURN
```

DATE$

DATE$ provides the current date in the heading of Berrenger's Sales Report. DATE$ is a variable that contains the system date; that is the date entered in the format mm-dd-yyyy when DOS was loaded. For example, if the system date is March 21, 1989,

```
10 PRINT DATE$
```

causes 03-21-1989 to be displayed on the screen. Check line 3060 in Program 9.1 for DATE$.

You may also use DATE$ to change the system date from within the program by assigning a value to it. For example,

```
10 DATE$ = "10-16-1989"
```

changes the system date to October 16, 1989. You can make this variable assignment, like any other, with input from the keyboard or from a file.

The system accepts two alternate date formats; you may replace either or both of the dashes with slashes (/). You may also enter only the last two digits of the year, and BASIC will supply the missing "19."

TIME$

TIME$ displays the system time. If the current time is 1:30 and 14 seconds P.M.,

```
10 PRINT TIME$
```

causes 13:30:14 to be displayed on the screen. Notice that TIME$ keeps 24-hour time rather than distinguishing between A.M. and P.M.

You can assign a value to TIME$ to change the system time, just as you can assign a value to DATE$. Thus

```
10 TIME$ = "10:18"
```

changes the system time to 10:18 A.M.

Note: Unless your computer has a calendar/clock or you enter values for the time and date from the keyboard when you boot the computer, the values contained in DATE$ and TIME$ are meaningless.

Test the Program

Below is a listing of Berrenger's sales file, SALES.SEQ. When run with this file, Program 9.1 generates the report shown in Figure 9.2. The program writes monthly totals at the end of each month's sales transactions and a total of all sales at the end of the report.

```
1,"311","L DERBYSHIRE",500.12      3,"311","L DERBYSHIRE",700.80
1,"311","M JEFFERSON",40.56        3,"311","M JEFFERSON",200.80
1,"311","J SAMUELS",600.99         3,"311","J SAMUELS",400.55
1,"312","H BLESSING",1000.5        3,"312","H BLESSING",70.60
1,"312","G MALLONEE",675.5         3,"312","G MALLONEE",2,000.85
1,"312","K MCCREADY",400.36        3,"312","K MCCREADY",600.14
1,"312","M QUILL",300.99           3,"312","M QUILL",300.15
1,"315","J ANDREWS",300.15         3,"315","J ANDREWS",700.85
1,"315","D MAYER",200.75           3,"315","D MAYER",200.99
2,"311","L DERBYSHIRE",899.5
2,"311","M JEFFERSON",1000.65
2,"311","J SAMUELS",50.75
2,"312","H BLESSING",30.34
2,"312","G MALLONEE",900.45
2,"312","K MCCREADY",400.2
2,"312","M QUILL",0
2,"315","J ANDREWS",90.9
2,"315","D MAYER",700.65
```

MULTIPAGE REPORT

The examples so far make no provision for reports that are longer than one page. This is shortsighted, since files like Berrenger's may have hundreds or thousands of records. In this section, you learn what to include in a program to produce attractive and easy-to-read reports of more than one page.

Define the Problem

Mr. Berrenger appreciated the information Program 9.1 provided him, but he would like the program modified so that it prints the report with about 32 lines on a page. He also wants headings and page numbers on every page.

Describe the Output

Each page of the report will contain a main heading, including a page number, and column headings. There will be a maximum of 32 lines per page. Figure 9.5 shows a partial print chart for the program. The only change is the page number in the upper right corner.

Determine the Input

The input for this program is the same sequential file used in Program 9.1.

Design the Program Logic

After 32 lines have been printed, the program must:

1. Signal the printer to go to a new page.

2. Print the page number and headings for the new page before resuming the printing of detail lines.

The counter for the lines must be incremented every time a line or lines are printed. The line counter is incremented when the heading is printed, when a detail line is printed, and when the monthly totals are printed. The PROCESS MONTH module checks the value of the line counter on each pass, and, when that value becomes equal to or greater than 32, calls the WRITE HEADING module to print the headings for a new page.

Since every call to the headings module corresponds to a new page, the page counter can be incremented there. For the same reason, it is appropriate for the headings module to signal the printer to advance to a new page.

Figure 9.6 illustrates the design modifications to Program 9.1 to produce the reports in the form Mr. Berrenger wants.

Code the Program Instructions

Program 9.2 implements the design in Figure 9.6. Notice the following about Program 9.2:

1. The number of lines per page is established in the CONSTANTS section (line 1280). The program checks the actual count (LINE.CTR) against the page limit in the PROCESS RECORDS month loop (line 8050), and, if the count equals or exceeds 32, it calls the headings module.

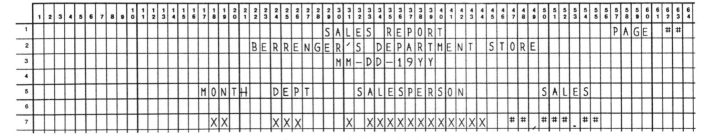

FIGURE 9.5 Print chart for Program 9.2

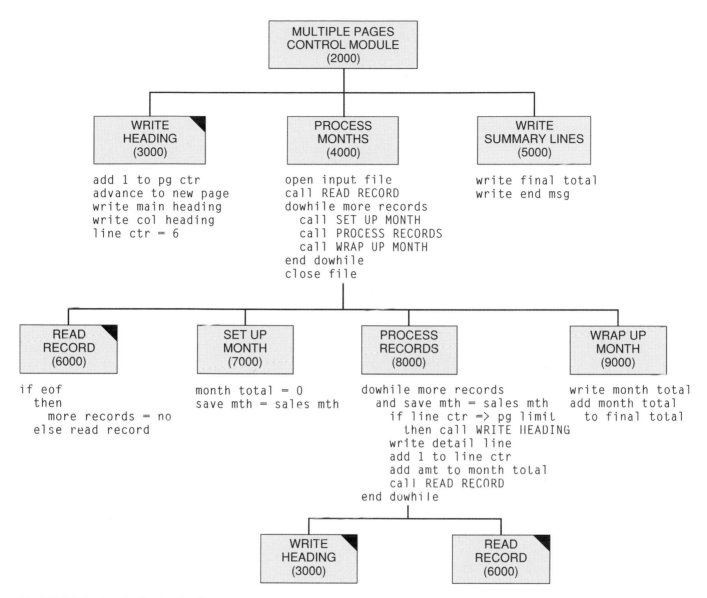

FIGURE 9.6 Logic design for Program 9.2

2. Note the order of actions in the PROCESS RECORDS module. The check for a new page precedes the writing of a detail line. Ordering the functions in this way ensures that monthly subtotals appear on the same page as at least one of the detail lines being totaled. Also, at least one detail line will be printed on the last page with the final totals. If space on the report is critical, however, then you should evaluate the line counter before every print statement in the program.

3. Notice how the program signals the printer to go to a new page. In line 1270, NEW.PAGE$ is given the value of CHR$(12), which is the ASCII symbol for a form feed. Although this may not work with all printers, it is among the most widely used printer control symbols. When first testing the program, delete the LPRINT NEW.PAGE$ instruction (line 3050) to avoid wasting paper during your initial runs.

PROGRAM 9.2

```
1000 ' PROG9-2
1010 ' ******************************
1020 ' *        MULTIPLE PAGES       *
1030 ' ******************************
1040 '
1050 ' ******************************
1060 ' *           VARIABLES         *
1070 ' ******************************
1080 '
1090 ' SALES.SEQ                Sales File
1100 ' Sales Record:
1110 '     SALES.MTH
1120 '     SALES.DEPT$
1130 '     SALES.NAME$
1140 '     SALES.AMT
1150 '
1160 ' DETAIL$                  Format for detail line
1170 ' LINE.CTR                 Line counter
1180 ' MONTHLY.TOTAL#           Total sales for the month
1190 ' SAVE.MTH                 Value of SALES.MTH in current group
1200 '
1210 ' ******************************
1220 ' *           CONSTANTS         *
1230 ' ******************************
1240 '
1250    YES = -1                'Value for true
1260    NO  =  0                'Value for false
1270    NEW.PAGE$  = CHR$(12)   'ASCII character for new page (form feed)
1280    PAGE.LIMIT = 32         'Maximum number of lines per page
1290 '
1300 ' ******************************
1310 ' *   INITIALIZED VARIABLES     *
1320 ' ******************************
1330 '
1340    FINAL.TOTAL# = 0        'Total sales for the report
1350    PAGE.CTR     = 0        'Page number counter
1360    MORE.RECORDS = YES      'Flag for reading records
1999 '
2000 ' ******************************
2010 ' *        CONTROL MODULE       *
2020 ' ******************************
2030 '
2040    GOSUB 3000              'Write Heading
2050    GOSUB 4000              'Process Months
2060    GOSUB 5000              'Write Summary Lines
2070    END
2999 '
3000 ' ******************************
3010 ' *        WRITE HEADING        *
3020 ' ******************************
3030 '
3040    PAGE.CTR = PAGE.CTR + 1
3050    LPRINT NEW.PAGE$
3060    LPRINT TAB(29); "SALES REPORT"; TAB(57); USING "PAGE ##"; PAGE.CTR
3070    LPRINT TAB(22); "BERRENGER'S DEPARTMENT STORE"
3080    LPRINT TAB(30); DATE$
3090    LPRINT
3100    LPRINT TAB(17); "MONTH  DEPT     SALESPERSON        SALES"
3110    LPRINT
3120    DETAIL$ =        " ##    \ \     \               \  ##,###.##"
3130    LINE.CTR = 6
3140    RETURN
3999 '
4000 ' ******************************
4010 ' *         PROCESS MONTHS      *
4020 ' ******************************
4030 '
```

PROGRAM 9.2   (continued)

```
4040    OPEN "SALES.SEQ" FOR INPUT AS #1
4050    GOSUB 6000                  'Read Record
4060    WHILE MORE.RECORDS
4070       GOSUB 7000               'Set Up Month
4080       GOSUB 8000               'Process Records
4090       GOSUB 9000               'Wrap Up Month
4100    WEND
4110    CLOSE #1
4120    RETURN
4999 '
5000 ' *****************************
5010 ' *      WRITE SUMMARY LINES     *
5020 ' *****************************
5030 '
5040    LPRINT TAB(31);
                USING "FINAL TOTAL $$,###,###.##_*_*_*"; FINAL.TOTAL#
5050    LPRINT
5060    LPRINT
5070    LPRINT TAB(26); "***END OF REPORT***"
5080    RETURN
5999 '
6000 ' *****************************
6010 ' *          READ RECORD         *
6020 ' *****************************
6030 '
6040    IF EOF(1) THEN MORE.RECORDS = NO
                ELSE INPUT #1, SALES.MTH,   SALES.DEPT$,
                                    SALES.NAME$, SALES.AMT
6050    RETURN
6999 '
7000 ' *****************************
7010 ' *          SET UP MONTH        *
7020 ' *****************************
7030 '
7040    MONTHLY.TOTAL# = 0
7050    SAVE.MTH = SALES.MTH
7060    RETURN
7999 '
8000 ' *****************************
8010 ' *        PROCESS RECORDS       *
8020 ' *****************************
8030 '
8040    WHILE MORE.RECORDS AND (SAVE.MTH = SALES.MTH)
8050       IF LINE.CTR => PAGE.LIMIT
                THEN GOSUB 3000          'Write Heading
8060       LPRINT TAB(17); USING DETAIL$; SALES.MTH,   SALES.DEPT$,
                                    SALES.NAME$, SALES.AMT
8070       LINE.CTR = LINE.CTR + 1
8080       MONTHLY.TOTAL# = MONTHLY.TOTAL# + SALES.AMT
8090       GOSUB 6000                  'Read Record
8100    WEND
8110    RETURN
8999 '
9000 ' *****************************
9010 ' *          WRAP UP MONTH       *
9020 ' *****************************
9030 '
9040    LPRINT
9050    LPRINT TAB(29);
                USING "MONTHLY.TOTAL    $$##,###.##_*_*"; MONTHLY.TOTAL#
9060    LPRINT
9070    LINE.CTR = LINE.CTR + 3
9080    FINAL.TOTAL# = FINAL.TOTAL# + MONTHLY.TOTAL#
9090    RETURN
```

4. Notice that the line count includes headings, detail lines, subtotal lines, and blank lines. This is typical of business reports. The program includes the headings in the line count by setting LINE.CTR equal to 6 after the headings are printed (line 3130). The summary lines are not included in the line count for this program. Enough room was available for the final totals. If space is critical, each summary line can be counted and the page limit tested before the summary lines are printed.

5. The program tests for a line count that is greater than, not just equal to, 32 (line 8050) because the line counter is not always incremented by 1. In this program, the subtotals require three lines, and the line counter is incremented by 3 (line 9070). Consequently, the statement in line 8050 would not always work if it were written as LINE.CTR = 32. For example, the line counter could jump from 30 to 33, an equal condition would not occur, and a new set of page headings would never be printed.

6. Finally, at the end of the report, the message ***END OF REPORT*** is printed. An end-of-report message appears in most of the sample programs. This message is especially helpful when you are printing long reports because it is easy to differentiate the end of one report from the beginning of the next report being printed. Also, persons reading the report know by this message that they have a complete version.

Test the Program

Figure 9.7 shows the report the program generates when it is run with the SALES.SEQ file used previously in Program 9.1.

TWO-LEVEL CONTROL BREAK

Now that you have mastered a one-level control break, you can continue to the next level. Here, you learn how to generate subtotals within subtotals.

Define the Problem

Mr. Berrenger found the monthly subtotals so useful that he now wants to know the monthly sales figures for each of his departments. Figure 9.8 illustrates the relationship between the records in a file and a report with department and monthly subtotals.

Describe the Output

The output will be similar to the report generated by Program 9.2, except that there will be subtotals for every department. Figure 9.9 shows the format of the report plotted on a print chart.

Determine the Input

The input for this program is the same sequential file used for Program 9.1.

In a two-level control break program, the two control fields always have a *major/minor relationship* to one another. The minor field is sorted inside the sort of the major field. In this program, SALES.MTH is the major control field because the entire file is arranged by month; that is, all sales occurring in one month are grouped together. SALES.DEPT$ is a minor field because the records are arranged by department within each month. Look at Figure 9.8 to confirm this relationship between the two fields for yourself.

FIGURE 9.7
Multipage report generated
by Program 9.2

```
                    SALES REPORT              PAGE 1
              BERRENGER'S DEPARTMENT STORE
                     05-12-1990

       MONTH   DEPT    SALESPERSON        SALES

         1     311    L DERBYSHIRE        500.12
         1     311    M JEFFERSON          40.56
         1     311    J SAMUELS           600.99
         1     312    H BLESSING        1,000.50
         1     312    G MALLONEE          675.50
         1     312    K MCCREADY          400.36
         1     312    M QUILL             300.99
         1     315    J ANDREWS           300.15
         1     315    D MAYER             200.75

               MONTHLY.TOTAL        $4,019.92**

         2     311    L DERBYSHIRE        899.50
         2     311    M JEFFERSON       1,000.65
         2     311    J SAMUELS            50.75
         2     312    H BLESSING           30.34
         2     312    G MALLONEE          900.75
         2     312    K MCCREADY          400.20
         2     312    M QUILL               0.00
         2     315    J ANDREWS            90.90
         2     315    D MAYER             700.65

               MONTHLY.TOTAL        $4,073.44**

         3     311    L DERBYSHIRE        700.80
         3     311    M JEFFERSON         200.80
```

```
                    SALES REPORT              PAGE 2
              BERRENGER'S DEPARTMENT STORE
                     05-12-1990

       MONTH   DEPT    SALESPERSON        SALES

         3     311    J SAMUELS           400.55
         3     312    H BLESSING           70.60
         3     312    G MALLONEE        2,000.85
         3     312    K MCCREADY          600.14
         3     312    M QUILL             300.15
         3     315    J ANDREWS           700.85
         3     315    D MAYER             200.99

               MONTHLY.TOTAL        $5,175.73**

               FINAL TOTAL        $13,269.09***


           ***END OF REPORT***
```

All records with 1 in the Month field appear first. Within that set, all records with 311 in the Department field come first, all with 312 come second, and so on.

Another way to designate control fields is by their level. In the SALES.SEQ file used with the programs in this chapter, SALES.MTH is the *first-level* control field and SALES.DEPT$ is the *second-level* control field.

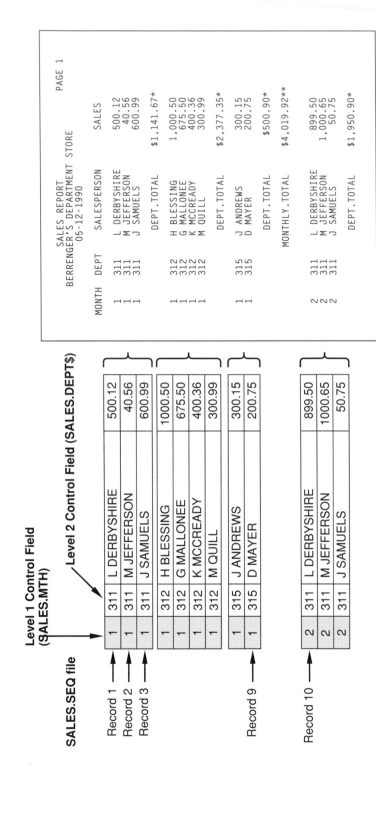

SALES REPORT
BERRENGER'S DEPARTMENT STORE
05-12-1990   PAGE 1

MONTH	DEPT	SALESPERSON	SALES
1	311	L DERBYSHIRE	500.12
1	311	M JEFFERSON	40.56
1	311	J SAMUELS	600.99
		DEPT.TOTAL	$1,141.67*
1	312	H BLESSING	1,000.50
1	312	G MALLONEE	675.50
1	312	K MCCREADY	400.36
1	312	M QUILL	300.99
		DEPT.TOTAL	$2,377.35*
1	315	J ANDREWS	300.15
1	315	D MAYER	200.75
		DEPT.TOTAL	$500.90*
		MONTHLY.TOTAL	$4,019.92**
2	311	L DERBYSHIRE	899.50
2	311	M JEFFERSON	1,000.65
2	311	J SAMUELS	50.75
		DEPT.TOTAL	$1,950.90*

SALES.SEQ file

Level 1 Control Field (SALES.MTH)

Level 2 Control Field (SALES.DEPT$)

			SALES
Record 1 →	1	311	L DERBYSHIRE	500.12
Record 2 →	1	311	M JEFFERSON	40.56
Record 3 →	1	311	J SAMUELS	600.99
	1	312	H BLESSING	1000.50
	1	312	G MALLONEE	675.50
	1	312	K MCCREADY	400.36
	1	312	M QUILL	300.99
Record 9 →	1	315	J ANDREWS	300.15
	1	315	D MAYER	200.75
Record 10 →	2	311	L DERBYSHIRE	899.50
	2	311	M JEFFERSON	1000.65
	2	311	J SAMUELS	50.75

FIGURE 9.8 Relationship between records and two levels of and subtotals

```
                    SALES REPORT
              BERRENGER'S DEPARTMENT STORE                    PAGE 2
                      05-12-1990

MONTH  DEPT  SALESPERSON            SALES

  2    312   H BLESSING              30.34
  2    312   G MALLONEE             900.45
  2    312   K MCCREADY             400.20
  2    312   M QUILL                  0.00
                    DEPT.TOTAL   $1,330.99*

  2    315   J ANDREWS              90.90
  2    315   D MAYER               700.65
                    DEPT.TOTAL     $791.55*

                 MONTHLY.TOTAL   $4,073.44**

  3    311   L DERBYSHIRE          700.80
  3    311   M JEFFERSON           200.80
  3    311   J SAMUELS             400.55
                    DEPT.TOTAL   $1,302.15*

  3    312   H BLESSING             70.60
  3    312   G MALLONEE          2,000.85
  3    312   K MCCREADY            600.14
  3    312   M QUILL               300.15
                    DEPT.TOTAL   $2,971.74*
```

```
                    SALES REPORT
              BERRENGER'S DEPARTMENT STORE                    PAGE 3
                      05-12-1990

MONTH  DEPT  SALESPERSON            SALES

  3    315   J ANDREWS             700.85
  3    315   D MAYER               200.99
                    DEPT.TOTAL     $901.84*

                 MONTHLY.TOTAL   $5,175.73**

                  FINAL TOTAL  $13,269.09***

                ***END OF REPORT***
```

2	312	H BLESSING	30.34
2	312	G MALLONEE	900.45
2	312	K MCCREADY	400.20
2	312	M QUILL	0.00
2	315	J ANDREWS	90.90
2	315	D MAYER	700.65

Record 18 →

3	311	L DERBYSHIRE	700.80
3	311	M JEFFERSON	200.80
3	311	J SAMUELS	400.55
3	312	H BLESSING	70.60
3	312	G MALLONEE	2000.85
3	312	K MCCREADY	600.14
3	312	M QUILL	300.15

Record 19 →

3	315	J ANDREWS	700.85
3	315	D MAYER	200.99

Record 27 →

FIGURE 9.8 (continued)

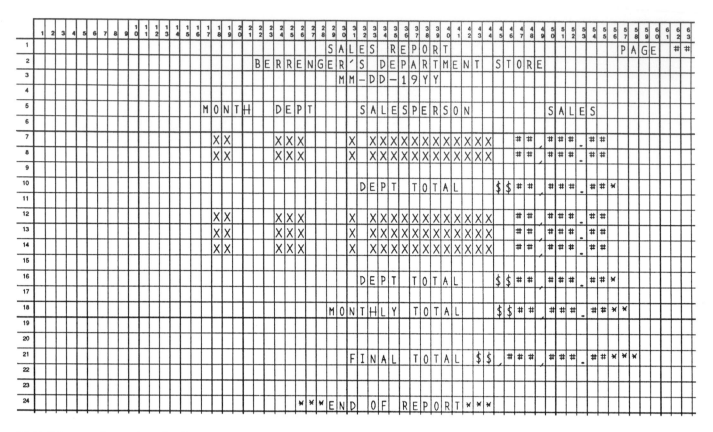

FIGURE 9.9   Print chart for Program 9.3

Design the Program Logic

This program requires only a simple extension of the logic of Programs 9.1 and 9.2. As before, for each month, the program must:

- Initialize a monthly sales total to zero.
- Assign the current sales month to a variable.
- Process all the departments for the month.
- Write the monthly sales total.
- Increment the final total by the monthly sales total.

Now, during the current month for each department, the program must do the following:

- Initialize a department total to zero.
- Assign the current department to a variable so that the computer can compare each record read to determine whether a new department has been encountered.

■ Process all the records for this department.

■ Write the department sales total for the month.

■ Increment the monthly sales total by the department total.

Also, for each record in the current department during the current month, the program must:

■ Write the detail line.

■ Increment the department sales total by the sales amount.

Just as in Program 9.1, each of the groups of processing functions can represent a module in the program. Table 9.2 illustrates the relationship between the modules that process the records in the file, including the way the called modules supply values needed by the calling module.

Figure 9.10 shows the final design for this two-level control-break program.

Code the Program Instructions

Program 9.3 contains no new instructions, just three new modules to process the departments. Note these new modules. Module PROCESS DEPTS (8000–8999) processes the departments for each month. The module SET UP DEPT (10000–10999) initializes DEPT.TOTAL# and SAVE.DEPT for each new department. Finally, the module WRAP UP DEPT (12000–12090) prints the department total and increments the line counter and monthly total.

Table 9.2   Two-Level Control Break

PROCESS MONTHS Level-1 Control Field	PROCESS DEPTS Level-2 Control Field	PROCESS RECORDS Records in the File
do for each month 1. set month total to 0		

2. process all the depts for
     this month ⟶
	do for each dept
	  1. set dept total to 0	

	2. process all the records
	     for this dept ⟶
		do for each record
		  1. write detail line

		2. add sales amt to dept total
	3. write dept total ⟵	end
	4. add dept total to month total	
3. write month total ⟵	end	
4. add month total to final total		
end		

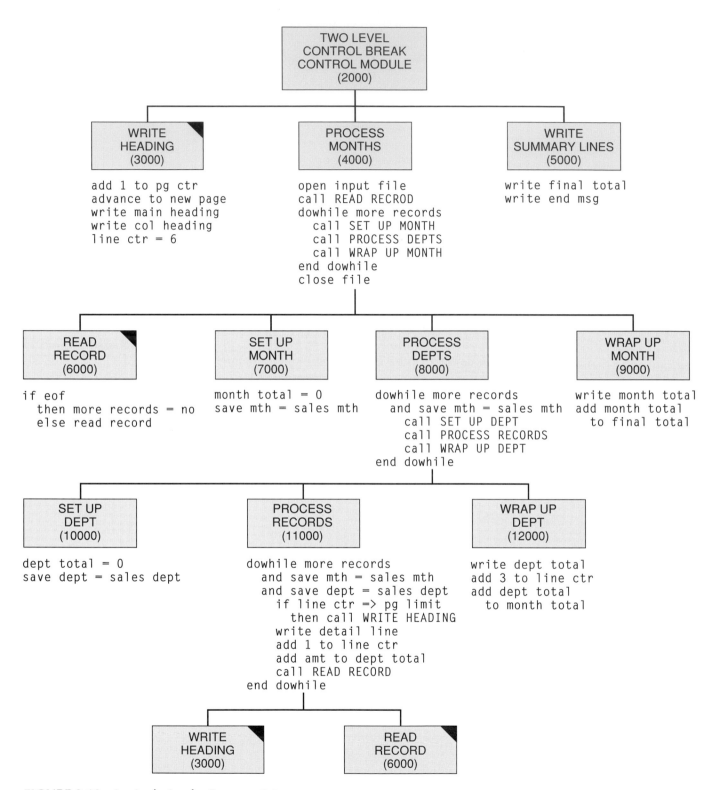

FIGURE 9.10   Logic design for Program 9.3

Test the Program   Figure 9.8 shows the report Program 9.3 will generate from the SALES.SEQ file used previously.

PROGRAM 9.3

```
1000 ' PROG9-3
1010 ' *****************************
1020 ' *   TWO LEVEL CONTROL BREAK   *
1030 ' *****************************
1040 '
1050 ' *****************************
1060 ' *          VARIABLES          *
1070 ' *****************************
1080 '
1090 ' SALES.SEQ                 Sales File
1100 ' Sales Record:
1110 '     SALES.MTH
1120 '     SALES.DEPT$
1130 '     SALES.NAME$
1140 '     SALES.AMT
1150 '
1160 ' DETAIL$                   Format for detail line
1170 ' LINE.CTR                  Line counter
1180 ' DEPT.TOTAL#               Total sales for the department
1190 ' MONTHLY.TOTAL#            Total sales for the month
1200 ' SAVE.DEPT$                Value of SALES.DEPT$ in current group
1210 ' SAVE.MTH                  Value of SALES.MTH in current group
1220 '
1230 ' *****************************
1240 ' *          CONSTANTS          *
1250 ' *****************************
1260 '
1270   YES = -1                  'Value for true
1280   NO  =  0                  'Value for false
1290   NEW.PAGE$  = CHR$(12)     'ASCII character for new page (form feed)
1300   PAGE.LIMIT = 32           'Maximum number of lines per page
1310 '
1320 ' *****************************
1330 ' *   INITIALIZED VARIABLES   *
1340 ' *****************************
1350 '
1360   FINAL.TOTAL# = 0          'Total sales for the report
1370   PAGE.CTR    = 0           'Page number counter
1380   MORE.RECORDS = YES        'Flag for reading records
1999 '
2000 ' *****************************
2010 ' *          CONTROL MODULE          *
2020 ' *****************************
2030 '
2040   GOSUB 3000                'Write Heading
2050   GOSUB 4000                'Process Months
2060   GOSUB 5000                'Write Summary Lines
2070   END
2999 '
3000 ' *****************************
3010 ' *          WRITE HEADING          *
3020 ' *****************************
3030 '
3040   PAGE.CTR = PAGE.CTR + 1
3050   LPRINT NEW.PAGE$
3060   LPRINT TAB(29); "SALES REPORT"; TAB(57); USING "PAGE ##"; PAGE.CTR
3070   LPRINT TAB(22); "BERRENGER'S DEPARTMENT STORE"
3080   LPRINT TAB(30); DATE$
3090   LPRINT
3100   LPRINT TAB(17); "MONTH   DEPT    SALESPERSON        SALES"
3110   LPRINT
3120   DETAIL$ =        " ##    \ \     \              \   ##,###.##"
3130   LINE.CTR = 6
3140   RETURN
3999 '
```

PROGRAM 9.3 (continued)

```
4000 ' ******************************
4010 ' *         PROCESS MONTHS         *
4020 ' ******************************
4030 '
4040    OPEN "SALES.SEQ" FOR INPUT AS #1
4050    GOSUB 6000                'Read Record
4060    WHILE MORE.RECORDS
4070       GOSUB 7000             'Set Up Month
4080       GOSUB 8000             'Process Depts
4090       GOSUB 9000             'Wrap Up Month
4100    WEND
4110    CLOSE #1
4120    RETURN
4999 '
5000 ' ******************************
5010 ' *      WRITE SUMMARY LINES      *
5020 ' ******************************
5030 '
5040    LPRINT TAB(31);
              USING "FINAL TOTAL $$,###,###.##_*_*_*"; FINAL.TOTAL#
5050    LPRINT
5060    LPRINT
5070    LPRINT TAB(26); "***END OF REPORT***"
5080    RETURN
5999 '
6000 ' ******************************
6010 ' *          READ RECORD          *
6020 ' ******************************
6030 '
6040    IF EOF(1) THEN MORE.RECORDS = NO
                 ELSE INPUT #1, SALES.MTH,   SALES.DEPT$,
                                 SALES.NAME$, SALES.AMT
6050    RETURN
6999 '
7000 ' ******************************
7010 ' *          SET UP MONTH         *
7020 ' ******************************
7030 '
7040    MONTHLY.TOTAL# = 0
7050    SAVE.MTH = SALES.MTH
7060    RETURN
7999 '
8000 ' ******************************
8010 ' *          PROCESS DEPTS        *
8020 ' ******************************
8030 '
8040    WHILE MORE.RECORDS AND (SAVE.MTH = SALES.MTH)
8050       GOSUB 10000            'Set Up Dept
8060       GOSUB 11000            'Process Records
8070       GOSUB 12000            'Wrap Up Dept
8080    WEND
8090    RETURN
8999 '
9000 ' ******************************
9010 ' *          WRAP UP MONTH        *
9020 ' ******************************
9030 '
9040    LPRINT TAB(29);
              USING "MONTHLY.TOTAL    $$##,###.##_*_*"; MONTHLY.TOTAL#
9050    LPRINT
9060    LPRINT
9070    LINE.CTR = LINE.CTR + 3
9080    FINAL.TOTAL# = FINAL.TOTAL# + MONTHLY.TOTAL#
9090    RETURN
9999 '
```

PROGRAM 9.3 (continued)

```
10000  '*****************************
10010  '*          SET UP DEPT          *
10020  '*****************************
10030  '
10040   DEPT.TOTAL# = 0
10050   SAVE.DEPT$ = SALES.DEPT$
10060   RETURN
10999  '
11000  '*****************************
11010  '*         PROCESS RECORDS        *
11020  '*****************************
11030  '
11040   WHILE MORE.RECORDS AND (SAVE.MTH   = SALES.MTH)
                           AND (SAVE.DEPT$ = SALES.DEPT$)
11050       IF LINE.CTR => PAGE.LIMIT
               THEN GOSUB 3000           'Write Heading
11060       LPRINT TAB(17); USING DETAIL$; SALES.MTH,   SALES.DEPT$,
                                       SALES.NAME$, SALES.AMT
11070       LINE.CTR = LINE.CTR + 1
11080       DEPT.TOTAL# = DEPT.TOTAL# + SALES.AMT
11090       GOSUB 6000                   'Read Record
11100   WEND
11110   RETURN
11999  '
12000  '*****************************
12010  '*          WRAP UP DEPT          *
12020  '*****************************
12030  '
12040   LPRINT
12050   LPRINT TAB(32);
           USING "DEPT.TOTAL    $$##,###.##_*"; DEPT.TOTAL#
12060   LPRINT
12070   LINE.CTR = LINE.CTR + 3
12080   MONTHLY.TOTAL# = MONTHLY.TOTAL# + DEPT.TOTAL#
12090   RETURN
```

Summary

- Programs that generate business reports with subtotals are often referred to as *control-break programs*. A *control break* is a pause in the processing of records because of a change in a designated field. This designated field is called a *control field*. To work properly, a control-break program must use an input file that is sorted on the control field.

- There may be any number of control fields, but each field has a unique *level*.

  1. The field on which the entire file is ordered is the *first-level* control field.

  2. The *second-level* control field is used to order the records with identical values in the first-level control field.

3. You can write a program with many levels; each level is major in relationship to the subsequent level.

For example, in the following file, Income Category is the first-level control field, and Location Code is the second.

Location Code	Income Category	Balance
A	1	420
A	1	270
B	1	468
A	2	640
B	2	335
B	2	219
A	3	198

Control-break programs are nested processing loops. The logic outline for a two-level control-break program to generate the total balance by Income Category (first-level control field) and balance totals for each Location Code (second-level control field) looks as shown at the bottom of the page.

- Multipage reports should have headings and a page number on each page. A program that generates a multipage report must count lines as it prints them so that it can determine when to start a new page.

- DATE$ and TIME$ are BASIC variables that contain the values of the system date and time, respectively. You can change the system values by assigning new values to these variables. For example

```
10 DATE$ = 09-17-89
```

sets the system date to September 17, 1989.

Review Questions

1. What is the purpose of control-break processing?

2. What is a control break?

3. What is a control field?

4. Why must an input file for a control-break program be in a particular order?

5. What does it mean to sort a file "on" a field? How can you know which field(s) a file should be sorted on?

6. Could the PROCESS RECORDS module in Program 9.1 be included in the code for the PROCESS MONTHS module? If your answer is yes, why do you think the programmer didn't put it there?

7. Why is the call to the PROCESS RECORDS module in Program 9.1 necessary before the WRAP UP MONTH module can write a monthly total?

8. In Program 9.1, FINAL.TOTAL# is initialized to zero in the INITIALIZED VARIABLES section. Why can't you initialize MONTHLY.TOTAL# to zero in that section as well?

9. How would you correct the system date before running a program?

10. How could you use TIME$ to measure how long a program takes to run?

11. What is the new page signal (form feed) for the printer you use?

12. Why should a report have a heading on every page?

13. Why does line 8050 of Program 9.2 use the greater than or equal to comparison operator instead of just the equal sign?

14. Why is an end-of-report message useful?

15. What is the difference between a one-level and a two-level control break?

16. What does it mean to say that fields are in a "major/minor" relationship? How can you determine the major field by looking at a listing of a file? The minor field?

17. Can there be more than one major control field? Can there be more than one first-level control field?

```
do for each income category
    .
    .
    .
    do for each location code (for current income category)
        .
        .
        .
        do for each record (for current location code within
                        current income category)
            .
            .
            .
        end do
    end do
end do
```

18. Are the three process modules in Program 9.3 nested? If so, diagram the nested relationship.

Problems

1. In Program 9.1, what would happen if module READ RECORD were called from the PROCESS RECORDS module at line 8045 (that is, new line 8045 would be GOSUB 6000) and the calls to the READ RECORD module in lines 4050 and 8070 were deleted? Trace the logic of the program using the data in the input file.

2. Trace the logic of Program 9.1 using a version of SALES.SEQ that contains no records. Create a file with no records using EDLIN to confirm your solution.

3. Trace the logic of Program 9.1 using a version of SALES.SEQ that is not in SALES.MTH order. Create a file using COPY CON or EDLIN to confirm your solution.

4. Modify Program 9.2 so that the line counter is checked for the page limit before any set of lines is printed.

5. Add a field, called Location, to the SALES.SEQ file. Suppose that the file is sorted by Department within Location within Month. Write the pseudocode for this three-level control-break program. You can test your logic using the instructions in "Using the Data Disk."

Debugging Clinic

1. The following report was generated by Program 9.2 before it was running correctly. Find the errors in the report and correct the errors in the program listing that follows the report.

```
SALES REPORT                          PAGE  1
         BERRENGER'S DEPARTMENT STORE

MONTH   DEPT    SALESPERSON        SALES

   1    311     L DERBYSHIRE
   1    311     M JEFFERSON
   1    311     J SAMUELS
   1    312     H BLESSING
   1    312     G MALLONEE
   1    312     K MCCREADY
   1    312     M QUILL
   1    315     J ANDREWS
   1    315     D MAYER

                MONTHLY TOTAL      $200.75**

   2    311     L DERBYSHIRE
   2    311     M JEFFERSON
   2    311     J SAMUELS
   2    312     H BLESSING
   2    312     G MALLONEE
   2    312     K MCCREADY
   2    312     M QUILL
   2    315     J ANDREWS
   2    315     D MAYER

                MONTHLY TOTAL      $700.65**

   3    311     L DERBYSHIRE
   3    311     M JEFFERSON
```

```
SALES REPORT                          PAGE  2
         BERRENGER'S DEPARTMENT STORE

MONTH   DEPT    SALESPERSON        SALES

   3    311     J SAMUELS
   3    312     H BLESSING
   3    312     G MALLONEE
   3    312     K MCCREADY
   3    312     M QUILL
   3    315     J ANDREWS
   3    315     D MAYER

                MONTHLY TOTAL      $200.99**

                FINAL TOTAL       $1,102.39***


           ***END OF REPORT***
```

Debugging Clinic #1 Report

Debugging Clinic #1 Program

```
1000 ' PROG9-2  (Test Version)
1210 ' *****************************
1220 ' *          CONSTANTS            *
1230 ' *****************************
1240 '
1250   YES = -1                'Value for true
1260   NO  =  0                'Value for false
1270   NEW.PAGE$  = CHR$(12)    'ASCII character for new page (form feed)
1280   PAGE.LIMIT = 32          'Maximum number of lines per page
1290 '
1300 ' *****************************
1310 ' *    INITIALIZED VARIABLES    *
1320 ' *****************************
1330 '
1340   FINAL.TOTAL# = 0         'Total sales for the report
1350   PAGE.CTR    = 0         'Page number counter
1360   MORE.RECORDS = YES       'Flag for reading records
1999 '
2000 ' *****************************
2010 ' *        CONTROL MODULE         *
2020 ' *****************************
2030 '
2040   GOSUB 3000               'Write Heading
2050   GOSUB 4000               'Process Months
2060   GOSUB 5000               'Write Summary Lines
2070   END
2999 '
3000 ' *****************************
3010 ' *         WRITE HEADING          *
3020 ' *****************************
3030 '
3040   PAGE.CTR = PAGE.CTR + 1
3050   LPRINT NEW.PAGE$
3060   LPRINT TAB(15); "SALES REPORT"; TAB(57); USING "PAGE ##"; PAGE.CTR
3070   LPRINT TAB(22); "BERRENGER'S DEPARTMENT STORE"
3090   LPRINT
3100   LPRINT TAB(17); "MONTH  DEPT    SALESPERSON       SALES"
3110   LPRINT
3120   DETAIL$ =         " ##    \ \     \              \  ##,###.##"
3130   LINE.CTR = 6
3140   RETURN
3999 '
4000 ' *****************************
4010 ' *          PROCESS MONTHS       *
4020 ' *****************************
4030 '
4040   OPEN "SALES.SEQ" FOR INPUT AS #1
4050   GOSUB 6000               'Read Record
4060   WHILE MORE.RECORDS
4070      GOSUB 7000            'Set Up Month
4080      GOSUB 8000            'Process Records
4090      GOSUB 9000            'Wrap Up Month
4100   WEND
4110   CLOSE #1
4120   RETURN
4999 '
5000 ' *****************************
5010 ' *      WRITE SUMMARY LINES     *
5020 ' *****************************
```

Debugging Clinic #1 Program (continued)

```
5030  '
5040     LPRINT TAB(31);
                 USING "FINAL TOTAL $$,###,###.##_*_*_*"; FINAL.TOTAL#
5050     LPRINT
5060     LPRINT
5070     LPRINT TAB(26); "***END OF REPORT***"
5080     RETURN
5999  '
6000  ' ****************************
6010  ' *         READ RECORD            *
6020  ' ****************************
6030  '
6040     IF EOF(1) THEN MORE.RECORDS = NO
                     ELSE INPUT #1, SALES.MTH,    SALES.DEPT$,
                                   SALES.NAME$, SALES.AMT
6050     RETURN
6999  '
7000  ' ****************************
7010  ' *         SET UP MONTH          *
7020  ' ****************************
7030  '
7040     MONTHLY.TOTAL# = 0
7050     SAVE.MTH = SALES.MTH
7060     RETURN
7999  '
8000  ' ****************************
8010  ' *       PROCESS RECORDS         *
8020  ' ****************************
8030  '
8040     WIITLE MORE.RECORDS AND (SAVE.MTH = SALES.MTH)
8050         IF LINE.CTR => PAGE.LIMTT
                     IHEN GOSUB 3000         'Write Heading
8060         LPRINT TAB(17); USING DETAIL$; SALES.MTH,    SALES.DEPT$,
                                            SALES.NAME$
8070         LINE.CTR = LINE.CTR + 1
8080         MONTHLY.TOTAL# = MONTHLY.TOTAL + SALES.AMT
8090         GOSUB 6000                      'Read Record
8100     WEND
8110     RETURN
8999  '
9000  ' ****************************
9010  ' *        WRAP UP MONTH          *
9020  ' ****************************
9030  '
9040     LPRINT
9050     LPRINT TAB(29);
                 USING "MONTHLY.TOTAL    $$##,###.##_*_*"; MONTHLY.TOTAL#
9060     LPRINT
9070     LINE.CTR = LINE.CTR + 3
9080     FINAL.TOTAL# = FINAL.TOTAL# + MONTHLY.TOTAL#
9090     RETURN
```

2. The following report was generated by Program 9.3 before it was running correctly. Find the errors in the report and correct the errors in the program listing that follows the report.

```
                SALES REPORT              PAGE   0
           BERRENGER'S DEPARTMENT STORE
                  05-12-1990

    MONTH   DEPT    SALESPERSON         SALES

      1     311    L DERBYSHIRE          500
      1     311    M JEFFERSON            41
      1     311    J SAMUELS             601

                   DEPT TOTAL       $1,141.67*

      1     312    H BLESSING          1,001
      1     312    G MALLONEE            676
      1     312    K MCCREADY            400
      1     312    M QUILL               301

                   DEPT TOTAL       $2,377.35*

      1     315    J ANDREWS             300
      1     315    D MAYER               201

                   DEPT TOTAL         $500.90*

                 MONTHLY TOTAL       $2,200.15

      2     311    L DERBYSHIRE          900
      2     311    M JEFFERSON         1,001
      2     311    J SAMUELS              51

                   DEPT TOTAL       $1,950.90*
```

```
                SALES REPORT              PAGE   1
           BERRENGER'S DEPARTMENT STORE
                  05-12-1990

    MONTH   DEPT    SALESPERSON         SALES

      2     312    H BLESSING             30
      2     312    G MALLONEE            900
      2     312    K MCCREADY            400
      2     312    M QUILL                 0

                   DEPT TOTAL       $1,330.99*

      2     315    J ANDREWS              91
      2     315    D MAYER               701

                   DEPT TOTAL         $791.55*

                 MONTHLY TOTAL         $822.04

      3     311    L DERBYSHIRE          701
      3     311    M JEFFERSON           201
      3     311    J SAMUELS             401

                   DEPT TOTAL       $1,302.15*

      3     312    H BLESSING             71
      3     312    G MALLONEE          2,001
      3     312    K MCCREADY            600
      3     312    M QUILL               300

                   DEPT TOTAL       $2,971.74*
```

Note: The operator had to stop the printing because the program was in an endless loop.

```
                SALES REPORT              PAGE   2
           BERRENGER'S DEPARTMENT STORE
                  05-12-1990

    MONTH   DEPT    SALESPERSON         SALES

      3     315    J ANDREWS             701

                   DEPT TOTAL         $700.85*

                   DEPT TOTAL           $0.00*

                   DEPT TOTAL           $0.00*

                   DEPT TOTAL           $0.00*
```

Debugging Clinic #2 Report

Debugging Clinic #2 Program

```
1000 ' PROG9-3 (Test Version)
1230 ' *****************************
1240 ' *         CONSTANTS           *
1250 ' *****************************
1260 '
1270   YES = -1                  'Value for true
1280   NO  =  0                  'Value for false
1290   NEW.PAGE$  = CHR$(12)     'ASCII character for new page (form feed)
1300   PAGE.LIMIT = 32           'Maximum number of lines per page
1310 '
1320 ' *****************************
1330 ' *   INITIALIZED VARIABLES    *
1340 ' *****************************
1350 '
1360   FINAL.TOTAL# = 0          'Total sales for the report
1370   PAGE.CTR     = 0          'Page number counter
1380   MORE.RECORDS = YES        'Flag for reading records
1999 '
2000 ' *****************************
2010 ' *         CONTROL MODULE     *
2020 ' *****************************
2030 '
2040   GOSUB 3000                'Write Heading
2050   GOSUB 4000                'Process Months
2060   GOSUB 5000                'Write Summary Lines
2070   END
2999 '
3000 ' *****************************
3010 ' *         WRITE HEADING       *
3020 ' *****************************
3030 '
3040   LPRINT NEW.PAGE$
3050   LPRINT TAB(29); "SALES REPORT"; TAB(57); USING "PAGE ##"; PAGE.CTR
3060   LPRINT TAB(22); "BERRENGER'S DEPARTMENT STORE"
3070   LPRINT TAB(30); DATE$
3080   LPRINT
3090   LPRINT TAB(17); "MONTH  DEPT    SALESPERSON       SALES"
3100   LPRINT
3110   DETAIL$ =        " ##    \ \    \              \  ##,###"
3120   LINE.CTR = 6
3130   PAGE.CTR = PAGE.CTR + 1
3140   RETURN
3999 '
4000 ' *****************************
4010 ' *         PROCESS MONTHS      *
4020 ' *****************************
4030 '
4040   OPEN "SALES.SEQ" FOR INPUT AS #1
4050   GOSUB 6000                'Read Record
4060   WHILE MORE.RECORDS
4070      GOSUB 7000             'Set Up Month
4080      GOSUB 8000             'Process Depts
4090      GOSUB 9000             'Wrap Up Month
4100   WEND
4110   CLOSE #1
4120   RETURN
4999 '
```

Debugging Clinic #2 Program (continued)

```
5000 ' *****************************
5010 ' *     WRITE SUMMARY LINES     *
5020 ' *****************************
5030 '
5040    LPRINT TAB(31);
              USING "FINAL TOTAL $$,###,###.##_*_*_*"; FINAL.TOTAL#
5050    LPRINT
5060    LPRINT
5070    LPRINT TAB(26); "***END OF REPORT***"
5080    RETURN
5999 '
6000 ' *****************************
6010 ' *           READ RECORD           *
6020 ' *****************************
6030 '
6040    IF EOF(1) THEN MORE.RECORDS = NO
                   ELSE INPUT #1, SALES.MTH,    SALES.DEPT$,
                                  SALES.NAME$, SALES.AMT
6050    RETURN
6999 '
7000 ' *****************************
7010 ' *           SET UP MONTH           *
7020 ' *****************************
7030 '
7040    MONTHLY.TOTAL# = 0
7050    SAVE.MTH = SALES.MTH
7060    RETURN
7999 '
8000 ' *****************************
8010 ' *           PROCESS DEPTS           *
8020 ' *****************************
8030 '
8040    WHILE MORE.RECORDS AND (SAVE.MTH = SALES.MTH)
8050       GOSUB 10000          'Set Up Dept
8060       GOSUB 11000          'Process Records
8070       GOSUB 12000          'Wrap Up Dept
8080    WEND
8090    RETURN
8999 '
9000 ' *****************************
9010 ' *           WRAP UP MONTH           *
9020 ' *****************************
9030 '
9040    LPRINT TAB(29);
              USING "MONTHLY.TOTAL    $$##,###.##**"; MONTHLY.TOTAL#
9050    LPRINT
9060    LPRINT
9070    LINE.CTR = LINE.CTR + 3
9080    FINAL.TOTAL# = FINAL.TOTAL# + MONTHLY.TOTAL#
9090    RETURN
9999 '
10000 '*****************************
10010 '*           SET UP DEPT           *
10020 '*****************************
10030 '
10040  DEPT.TOTAL# = 0
10050  SAVE.DEPT$ = SALES.DEPT$
10060  RETURN
10999 '
```

Debugging Clinic #2 Program (continued)

```
11000 '*****************************
11010 '*          PROCESS RECORDS          *
11020 '*****************************
11030 '
11040   WHILE NOT EOF(1) AND (SAVE.MTH  = SALES.MTH)
                         AND (SAVE.DEPT$ = SALES.DEPT$)
11050       IF LINE.CTR => PAGE.LIMIT
               THEN GOSUB 3000          'Write Heading
11060       LPRINT TAB(17); USING DETAIL$; SALES.MTH,   SALES.DEPT$,
                                     SALES.NAME$, SALES.AMT
11070       LINE.CTR = LINE.CTR + 1
11080       DEPT.TOTAL# = DEPT.TOTAL# + SALES.AMT
11090       GOSUB 6000                  'Read Record
11100   WEND
11110   RETURN
11999 '
12000 '*****************************
12010 '*          WRAP UP DEPT          *
12020 '*****************************
12030 '
12040   LPRINT
12050   LPRINT TAB(32);
               USING "DEPT.TOTAL    $$##,###.##_*"; DEPT.TOTAL#
12060   LPRINT
12070   LINE.CTR = LINE.CTR + 3
12080   MONTHLY.TOTAL# = MONTHLY.TOTAL# + SALES.AMT
12090   RETURN
```

Program Assignments

1. Carroll County needs a bidding report listing the bids on parcels of land the county wishes to sell. Write a program using the sequential file BID.SEQ, which is sorted by parcel number. This report is to be displayed on the screen and should not exceed 24 lines. Write a program to:

    a. Display a heading, including the current date and time (use DATE$ and TIME$).
    b. Display column headings for parcel number, bid number, name, and amount.
    c. Display each field in every record.
    d. Print the total number of bids at the end of each parcel number group.
    e. After the report is displayed on the screen, allow the user to print a hard copy.

    The sequential file BID.SEQ contains four fields in the following order: parcel number, bid number, name, and amount. The file contents are:

    ```
    1087,455,Mary Miller,167500
    1087,221,Kim English,171300
    1087,764,Willie White,72999.99
    1497,231,George Adams,65678.95
    1497,165,Fred Paris,65345
    ```

    ```
    1497,455,Mary Miller,72000
    5131,165,Fred Paris,23590.95
    5131,343,Susie Wong,19775
    ```

2. The national sales manager of the MAIL-USA Catalog Company (you wrote a program for him in Chapter 7) needs a sales report by department. Write a program using the sequential file SALE.SEQ described in Program Assignment 7.1. The file is sorted by department number. Use it to produce the following report.

    a. The heading includes a general title, the current date (use DATE$), page number, and column headings. Print 20 lines per page.
    b. The detail lines include the department number, the salesperson, and the sales amount. "Group-indicate" the department number. (Group-indicate means that an item is printed only on the *first* occurrence after a control break or at the top of a new page.)
    c. At the end of the department group, print the total sales and the average sales for the department.
    d. At the end of the report, print the total sales and average sales for all the departments.
    e. The report design is shown on the next page.

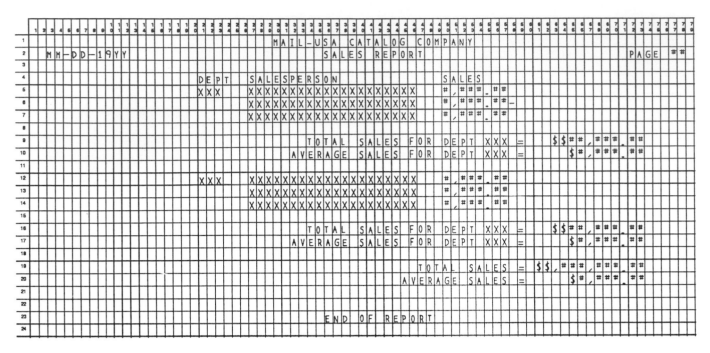

Screen design form for Program Assignment 9.2

3. Successories, Inc., needs a program that prints inventory costs by product code within department number. Write a program using INV.SEQ sequential file from Program Assignment 8.2. The file is sorted by product code within department number. Use it to produce the following report.

  a. The heading includes a general title, the current date (use DATE$), page numbers, and column headings.

  b. Print each new department group on a new page. The maximum lines per page is 25.

  c. The detail lines include the department number, product code, product number, number on hand, price, and inventory cost (INV.ON.HAND * INV.PRICE).

  d. Note that the department number and product code are group-indicated (printed only at the beginning of each new group or new page).

  e. Print the total inventory cost at the end of each product code and department number group. At the end of the report, print the total inventory cost for the report.

  f. The report design is shown on the next page.

4. Spring Nursery needs a monthly sales report. Write a program using the sequential file PL.SEQ, which is sorted by plant type (PL.TYPE) within store number (PL.STORE) within territory (PL.TER). The program should produce the following report.

  a. The heading includes a general title, the current date (use DATE$), the current time (use TIME$), page number, and column headings. Print 50 lines per page.

  b. The detail lines include the plant name, quantity, price, and total sales. The total sales is the result of multiplying PL.QTY by PL.PRICE.

  c. Print the name of the territory in the title for each new territory. The field PL.TER contains a code which is described in the record description. Print the store number once at the beginning of each new store, and print the plant type once at the beginning of each new group. The field PL.TYPE contains a code. The code is described in the record description.

  d. At the end of each plant type print the total sales for the group. At the end of each store number group, print the total sales. And at the end of each territory, print the total sales for the group. Print a grand total at the end of the report.

  e. PL.SEQ Sequential File

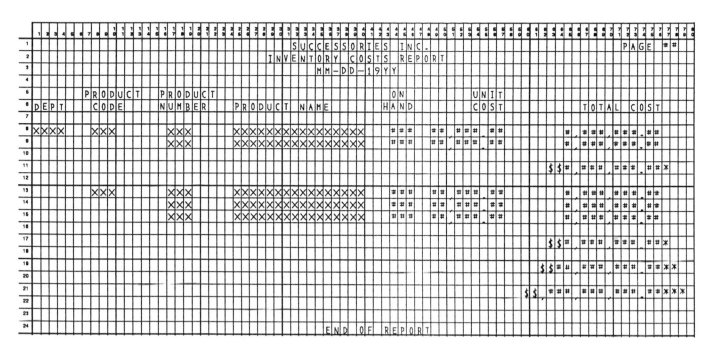

Screen design form for Program Assignment 9.3

PL record:

Field Name	Data Length	Data Type
PL.TER	1	Numeric
1 = NORTHERN		
2 = SOUTHERN		
PL.STORE	2	Numeric (##)
PL.TYPE	1	Numeric
1 = FLOWERS		
2 = PERENNIALS		
3 = VEGETABLES		
4 = HERBS		
PL.NAME$	12	String
PL.QTY	3	Numeric (###)
PL.PRICE	4	Numeric (#.##)

f. File contents:

```
1,1,1,Ageratum,100,1.75
1,1,1,Aster,150,1.5
1,1,1,Dahlia,90,1.65
1,1,1,Impatiens,200,1.75
1,1,1,Marigold,500,1.5
1,1,1,Petunia,224,1.75
1,1,1,Snapdragon,78,1.85
1,1,2,Baby's breath,93,1.25
1,1,2,Shasta daisy,104,1.25
1,1,2,Sweet william,321,1.25
1,1,3,Broccoli,789,1.65
1,1,3,Eggplant,345,1.75
1,1,3,Green pepper,654,1.45
1,1,3,Lettuce,678,1.65
1,1,3,Tomato,985,1.5
```

```
1,1,4,Basil,43,.75
1,1,4,Oregano,56,.75
1,1,4,Parsley,76,.75
1,1,4,Sage,9,.65
1,1,4,Thyme,15,.65
1,2,1,Ageratum,312,1.75
1,2,1,Aster,99,1.5
1,2,1,Dahlia,65,1.65
1,2,1,Impatiens,399,1.75
1,2,1,Marigold,987,1.5
1,2,1,Petunia,103,1.75
1,2,1,Snapdragon,112,1.85
1,2,2,Baby's breath,53,1.25
1,2,2,Shasta daisy,0,1.25
1,2,2,Sweet william,134,1.25
1,2,3,Broccoli,842,1.65
1,2,3,Eggplant,114,1.75
1,2,3,Green pepper,543,1.45
1,2,3,Lettuce,876,1.65
1,2,3,Tomato,890,1.5
1,2,4,Basil,56,.75
1,2,4,Oregano,12,.75
1,2,4,Parsley,1,.75
1,2,4,Sage,86,.65
1,2,4,Thyme,10,.65
1,3,1,Ageratum,0,1.75
1,3,1,Aster,203,1.5
1,3,1,Dahlia,99,1.65
1,3,1,Impatiens,703,1.75
1,3,1,Marigold,989,1.5
1,3,1,Petunia,506,1.75
1,3,1,Snapdragon,435,1.85
1,3,2,Baby's breath,102,1.25
1,3,2,Shasta daisy,25,1.25
```

```
1,3,2,Sweet william,331,1.25          2,1,4,Basil,0,.75
1,3,3,Broccoli,678,1.65               2,1,4,Oregano,43,.75
1,3,3,Eggplant,50,1.75                2,1,4,Parsley,54,.75
1,3,3,Green pepper,748,1.45           2,1,4,Sage,89,.65
1,3,3,Lettuce,983,1.65                2,1,4,Thyme,24,.65
1,3,3,Tomato,904,1.5                  2,2,1,Ageratum,243,1.75
1,3,4,Basil,32,.75                    2,2,1,Aster,764,1.5
1,3,4,Oregano,56,.75                  2,2,1,Dahlia,819,1.65
1,3,4,Parsley,82,.75                  2,2,1,Impatiens,432,1.75
1,3,4,Sage,63,.65                     2,2,1,Marigold,534,1.5
1,3,4,Thyme,3,.65                     2,2,1,Petunia,421,1.75
2,1,1,Ageratum,78,1.75                2,2,1,Snapdragon,312,1.85
2,1,1,Aster,345,1.5                   2,2,1,Baby's breath,29,1.25
2,1,1,Dahlia,398,1.65                 2,2,2,Shasta daisy,200,1.25
2,1,1,Impatiens,653,1.75              2,2,2,Sweet william,89,1.25
2,1,1,Marigold,903,1.5                2,2,3,Broccoli,817,1.65
2,1,1,Petunia,902,1.75                2,2,3,Eggplant,543,1.75
2,1,1,Snapdragon,756,1.85             2,2,3,Green pepper,302,1.45
2,1,1,Baby's breath,0,1.25            2,2,3,Lettuce,987,1.65
2,1,2,Shasta daisy,44,1.25            2,2,3,Tomato,876,1.5
2,1,2,Sweet william,32,1.25           2,2,4,Basil,0,.75
2,1,3,Broccoli,706,1.65               2,2,4,Oregano,15,.75
2,1,3,Eggplant,287,1.75               2,2,4,Parsley,45,.75
2,1,3,Green pepper,716,1.45           2,2,4,Sage,43,.65
2,1,3,Lettuce,804,1.65                2,2,4,Thyme,49,.65
2,1,3,Tomato,706,1.5
```

g. The report design is shown on the next page.

```
                                        SPRING NURSERY
                                        MM-DD-19YY                          PAGE  ##
                                        HH:MM:SS

XXXXXXXX TERRITORY

      STORE  ##

                              NAME          QUANTITY    PRICE         TOTAL
            FLOWERS
                              XXXXXXXXXXXX    ###       #.##        #,###.##
                              XXXXXXXXXXXX    ###       #.##        #,###.##

                                                               $$#,###.##

            PERENNIALS
                              XXXXXXXXXXXX    ###       #.##        #,###.##
                              XXXXXXXXXXXX    ###       #.##        #,###.##

                                                               $$#,###.##

            VEGETABLES
                              XXXXXXXXXXXX    ###       #.##        #,###.##
                              XXXXXXXXXXXX    ###       #.##        #,###.##

                                                               $$#,###.##

            HERBS
                              XXXXXXXXXXXX    ###       #.##        #,###.##
                              XXXXXXXXXXXX    ###       #.##        #,###.##

                                                               $$#,###.##

                              STORE  ##  TOTAL  =       $$#,###.##
                      XXXXXXXX TERRITORY  TOTAL  =   $$,###,###.##
                                    GRAND  TOTAL  =  $$#,###,###.##
                              END OF REPORT
```

Screen design form for Program Assignment 9.4

Using the Data Disk

1. Insert the data disk into the disk drive.

2. Load BASIC.

3. Load PROG9-1

   a. Modify Program 9.1 so that it prints a summary report including only the monthly totals and final total, not the detail lines.
   b. Add the necessary code to print the total salespersons and the average sales for each month. Also print the average sales for the quarter.
   c. Save this version of the program under the name CH9-1.DD.

4. Load PROG9-3.

   a. Line 3050 of Program 9.3, LPRINT NEW.PAGE$, causes printing to begin on a new page. You may want the user to adjust the paper before the first page of the report is printed so that a blank sheet of paper is not wasted. After that, the program controls the advancing to a new page. Modify Program 9.3 to tell the user to adjust the paper for the first page of the report.
   b. Add a field, called Location, to the SALES.SEQ file. Location is a field containing four characters. The file should be sorted by department within location within month. Modify Program 9.3 to print totals by department, by location, and by month. Create a test file named SALES.REV for this program.
   c. Add the code to group-indicate the control fields.
   d. Save this version of the program under the name CH9-2.DD.

Chapter Ten

Table Processing

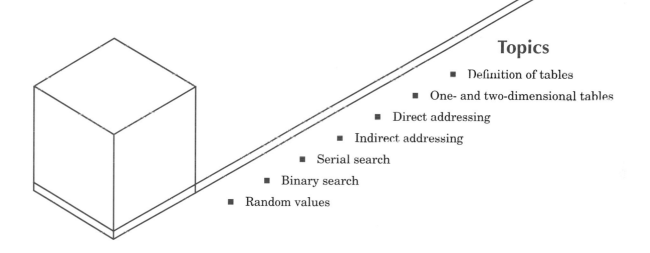

Topics

- Definition of tables
- One- and two-dimensional tables
- Direct addressing
- Indirect addressing
- Serial search
- Binary search
- Random values

BASIC Statements

```
DIM
FOR/NEXT
OPTION BASE
RND function (RANDOMIZE TIMER)
READ/DATA
RESTORE
```

INTRODUCTION

People frequently find it convenient to refer to persons or things that are related in some way as a group instead of naming each item in the group individually. When people speak of "my bridge club," "the Cincinnati Bengals," or the "streets of Atlanta," listeners understand, even though the members of the group go unnamed. This ability certainly makes communication easier.

Because such generalization is convenient, a similar ability has been built into most programming languages. In BASIC, a special kind of variable, called an *array* or *subscripted* variable, allows you to reference collections of similar items. In business programming applications, these collections of related items are called *tables*. This chapter describes two new sets of BASIC statements needed for table processing and then defines tables and explores some applications using tables. Also included in this chapter is a discussion of the random number function.

BASIC STATEMENTS USED FOR TABLE PROCESSING

Before you tackle programs that require table processing, you need to learn some new BASIC statements. First you will learn the general rules for using these new statements, and then, in the following section, you'll see them used in table processing programs.

READ and DATA Statements

Like INPUT and LET, READ and DATA statements provide a method of assigning values to variables. The general format of these statements is:

```
[line#] READ <var1> [,var2, . . . var-n]
[line#] DATA <value1> [,value2, . . . value-n]
```

READ and DATA statements are always used together, as in the following example:

```
10 READ ANAME$,PAY
20 PRINT ANAME$,PAY
30 DATA CARSON,340
RUN
CARSON          340
```

Line 10 causes the system to search for the program's first DATA statement (line 30), then read the first value (CARSON) into ANAME$ and the second value (340) into PAY. If you changed line 10 to

```
10 READ ANAME$,PAY,TAX
```

you would get an OUT OF DATA error because the DATA statement contains no value for the variable TAX.

If you want to print a list of names and wages, you can create a loop:

```
10 READ ANAME$,PAY
20 WHILE ANAME$ <> "ENDOFDATA"
30     PRINT ANAME$,PAY
40     READ ANAME$,PAY
50 WEND
60 END
```

```
100 DATA CARSON,340
110 DATA STEVENS,600
120 DATA LORIN,260
130 DATA ENDOFDATA,0
RUN
CARSON          340
STEVENS         600
LORIN           260
```

Line 10 is a priming read that gets the first two values in the first DATA statement. The WHILE statement checks whether ANAME$ has the value "ENDOFDATA". If it does, the program ends. If ANAME$ does not have the value "ENDOFDATA", then two values are printed and line 40 reads the next two values in the DATA statement.

Note the steps BASIC takes when you run this program.

Line#	Action
10	ANAME$ = "CARSON", PAY = 340
20	Check to see if ANAME$ <> "ENDOFDATA" It is not, so the body of the loop is executed.
30	CARSON and 340 are displayed.
40	ANAME$ = "STEVENS", PAY = 600
50	Control is transferred to line 20.
20	Check to see if ANAME$ <> "ENDOFDATA" It is not, so the body of the loop is executed.
30	STEVENS and 600 are displayed.
40	ANAME$ = "LORIN", PAY = 260
50	Control is transferred to line 20.
20	Check to see if ANAME$ <> "ENDOFDATA" It is not, so the body of the loop is executed.
30	LORIN and 260 are displayed.
40	ANAME$ = "ENDOFDATA", PAY = 0
50	Control is transferred to line 20.
20	Check to see if ANAME$ <> "ENDOFDATA" It is equal to "ENDOFDATA", so control is transferred to line 60.
60	Stop the program.

The last data items (line 130) are used to stop the loop. "ENDOFDATA" and 0 are not a name and a pay to be printed; this set of values signals the end of the data and ends the loop. Any data values may be used to terminate the loop as long as they are not values that might occur in the list to be printed.

Even though the value 0 in line 130 was not checked, it is necessary to include some numeric value in that position because each time the READ statement in the program is executed, it causes two values to be read. Without the 0 in line 130, the system would have produced an OUT OF DATA message.

DATA statements may have up to 255 characters, but the data may be distributed over several DATA statements as well. These are two alternative ways to write the data for the sample program.

```
100 DATA CARSON,340,STEVENS,600,LORIN,260,ENDOFDATA,0

100 DATA CARSON
110 DATA 340
120 DATA STEVENS
130 DATA 600
140 DATA LORIN
150 DATA 260
160 DATA ENDOFDATA
170 DATA 0
```

Here is a review of how READ and DATA statements work:

1. The READ statement takes values, in order, from the DATA statement and assigns them to the corresponding variables in its variable list.

2. The DATA statement may be, but need not be, located next to the READ statement. A READ statement triggers a search of the program statements, starting with the first line of the program, until a DATA statement is found.

3. If the number of variables in the READ statement exceeds the number of values in the DATA statements, the computer will report an OUT OF DATA error message. Extra data values, however, are ignored.

4. It is important to note that the READ statement is executed, but the DATA statement is not.

READ statement variables can be numeric or string, but the values in the DATA statements must be of the same types specified in their accompanying READ statements. Thus, if you use a numeric variable name in the READ statement, you must have numeric values in the DATA statement. String values in a DATA statement may be enclosed in quotation marks, but the quotes are not required. Quotation marks are necessary only when the value in the DATA statement contains an embedded comma.

RESTORE Statement

The RESTORE statement is used in conjunction with the READ and DATA statements. The general format of this statement is:

```
[line#] RESTORE [line#]
```

The execution of this statement

```
1070 RESTORE
```

causes BASIC to go to the first item of the first DATA statement when the next READ statement is executed. This allows you to access the contents of DATA statements more than once.

You are not likely to use the RESTORE statement often, but the following program shows an example of its usefulness.

```
100 TOTAL = 0
110 '
120 READ ANAME$,PAY
130 WHILE ANAME$ <> "ENDOFDATA"
140     TOTAL = TOTAL + PAY
```

```
150       READ ANAME$,PAY
160 WEND
170 '
180 RESTORE
190 READ ANAME$,PAY
200 WHILE ANAME$ <> "ENDOFDATA"
210      PERCT = INT(PAY / TOTAL * 100 + .5)
220      PRINT NAME$, PAY, PERCT; "%"
230      READ ANAME$,PAY
240 WEND
250 END
260 '
270 DATA CARSON,340
280 DATA STEVENS,600
290 DATA LORIN,260
300 DATA ENDOFDATA,0
RUN
CARSON          340              28 %
STEVENS         600              50 %
LORIN           260              22 %
```

In this program, the set of data in lines 270–300 is read twice. The first loop (lines 120–160, including the priming read) reads the data to total the pay for all the names in the data list. After the total has been accumulated, the percent of the total paid to each person can be calculated. Before the second loop (lines 190–240, including the priming read) can access the data again from the beginning, the RESTORE in line 180 must be executed. Without that RESTORE statement, the program generates an OUT OF DATA message when line 190 is executed.

Take a few minutes and "play computer" with this program to verify the results.

When a line number is included in the RESTORE statement, the next READ statement accesses the first item in the specified DATA statement. For example, if line 180 were written as RESTORE 290, only the output for LORIN would be printed.

In summary, READ/DATA statements provide another method for assigning values to variables in a BASIC program. With this method the data values are part of the program; the user does not enter them, and they are not part of a shared data file.

FOR/NEXT Statements

Until now, WHILE/WEND statements have been used for all loops. FOR/NEXT statements, however, provide another way to write a dowhile loop. They use a built-in counting procedure to repeat a series of instructions a specified number of times. The general format is:

```
[line#] FOR <loop.ctr = initial.value TO stop.value> [STEP increment]
    .
    .   (Body of loop)
    .
[line#] NEXT [loop.ctr]
```

where

loop.ctr   is a numeric variable that functions as a counter;

initial.value   is a numeric expression used as the initial value of *loop.ctr*;

stop.value   is a numeric expression that BASIC compares with the value of *loop.ctr* to determine whether to execute the statements in the loop; and *increment*   is a numeric expression added to *loop.ctr* each time the NEXT statement is executed. If *increment* is omitted, 1 is automatically added to *loop.ctr*.

This four-line program, displayed with its output, shows how a FOR/NEXT loop works.

```
10 FOR CTR = 1 TO 3
20    PRINT "HAPPY BIRTHDAY!"
30 NEXT CTR
40 END
RUN
HAPPY BIRTHDAY!
HAPPY BIRTHDAY!
HAPPY BIRTHDAY!
```

The loop extends from line 10 to line 30. The number of times BASIC executes these three lines depends on the numbers in line 10. CTR is the variable name for *loop.ctr*. The first number, 1, is the value BASIC assigns to CTR the first time the loop is executed (*initial.value*). The second number, 3, is the stopping value (*stop.value*) or test value; BASIC executes the code in the loop when CTR has this or any smaller value, but not when the value of CTR exceeds 3. Because STEP is omitted in line 10, the value 1 is added to CTR at the end of each cycle in the loop. The steps BASIC takes when you run this program are shown in the box below.

Line#	Action
10	Set CTR to 1 and check to see if the new value is greater than 3. It is not, so the body of the loop is executed.
20	Print HAPPY BIRTHDAY!
30	Add 1 to the value of CTR (now = 2) and send control to line 10.
10	Check to see if CTR is greater than 3. It is not, so the body of the loop is executed.
20	Print HAPPY BIRTHDAY!
30	Add 1 to the value of CTR (now = 3) and send control to line 10.
10	Check to see if CTR is greater than 3. It is not, so the body of the loop is executed.
20	Print HAPPY BIRTHDAY!
30	Add 1 to the value of CTR (now = 4), and send control to line 10.
10	Check to see if CTR is greater than 3. It is, so send control to the statement following the NEXT statement.
40	Stop the program.

Loop control with FOR/NEXT is similar to loop control with WHILE/WEND. The major difference is that a FOR/NEXT loop automatically initializes and increments the counter. Compare the previous FOR/NEXT code with this WHILE/WEND loop.

```
10 CTR = 1
20 WHILE CTR <= 3
30     PRINT "HAPPY BIRTHDAY!"
40     CTR = CTR + 1
50 WEND
60 END
RUN
HAPPY BIRTHDAY!
HAPPY BIRTHDAY!
HAPPY BIRTHDAY!
```

Notice that in the WHILE/WEND loop two additional statements are needed to do the same job: Line 10 is needed to initialize the counter, and line 40 is needed to increment the counter. Thus, FOR/NEXT is easier to use when you are coding a loop controlled by a counter.

The following two examples illustrate the use of the STEP option in FOR/NEXT statements:

```
10 FOR CTR = 4 TO 10 STEP 2
20     PRINT CTR
30 NEXT CTR
RUN
 4
 6
 8
 10
```

In this program, CTR starts with a value of 4. Line 20 is executed, and line 30 adds a value of 2 to CTR. This process is repeated until CTR is greater than 10 (the stop value). What additional value would be printed if you added the following statement to this program?

```
40 PRINT CTR
```

The STEP value can be negative as well as positive. When it is negative, the loop continues until the loop counter is less than the stopping value. Note the output of this program:

```
10 FOR CTR = 10 TO 4 STEP -3
20     PRINT CTR
30 NEXT CTR
RUN
 10
 7
 4
```

In this case, CTR starts with a value of 10. Line 20 is executed, and line 30 subtracts 3 from CTR. This process is repeated until CTR is less than 4.

In the next program, line 20 will never be executed because the initial value of CTR is 2, a value *already* greater than the stopping value of 1.

```
10 FOR CTR = 2 TO 1
20     PRINT CTR
30 NEXT CTR
40 PRINT "STOP"
RUN
STOP
```

You may use numeric variable names instead of constant values in a FOR/NEXT loop. Note in the next example how the values of *initial.value*, *stop.value*, and *increment* can be changed with each execution of the program.

```
10 INPUT "Enter initial value"; INIT.VAL
20 INPUT "Enter stopping value"; STOP.VAL
30 INPUT "Enter increment"; INCR
40 FOR LOOP.CTR = INIT.VAL TO STOP.VAL STEP INCR
50     PRINT "HELLO"
60 NEXT LOOP.CTR
```

In summary, WHILE/WEND statements may be used for all loop processing, but FOR/NEXT statements provide an easier way to write a counter-controlled loop.

TABLES

Now back to table processing. A *table* is a collection of related items of the same data type referenced by the same variable name. BRIDGE.CLUB$, BENGAL$, and ATLANTA.STREET$ are appropriate BASIC names to refer to the groups "my bridge club," "the Cincinnati Bengals," and "streets of Atlanta." To reference a collection of numbers, such as exams scores, you might use EXAM.SCORES; to reference state population figures, you might use POPULATION#.

Although BASIC stores the values of individual variables at various locations in the computer's memory, the values for all the items in a table are kept in consecutive storage locations. This storage method makes it efficient for the computer to access first one part of a table and then the next. As you will see later, these storage areas exist even for "empty" parts of the table.

You might be wondering how a programmer can refer to individual items in the table by using only one variable name. The answer is that table names have an additional part that single value variables don't. This additional part is a set of parentheses enclosing one or more numbers, called *subscripts*. (For this reason, elements in a table are sometimes referred to as *subscripted variables*.) Subscripts identify the location of a particular data item within the group. For example, if table MONTH$ contains the months of the year, MONTH$(2) contains "February"; MONTH$(5), "May"; and so on.

Consider another example: an alphabetical list of the 50 states, as shown on the left of Figure 10.1. Suppose these data are stored in order in a table appropriately named STATE.TBL$; STATE indicating state, and TBL indicating table. You reference the third state in the table as STATE.TBL$(3). Because the state names are arranged alphabetically, the value of STATE.TBL$(3) is "ARIZONA". Figure 10.1 illustrates how subscripts are used to store and reference the list of states.

FIGURE 10.1
Table of states

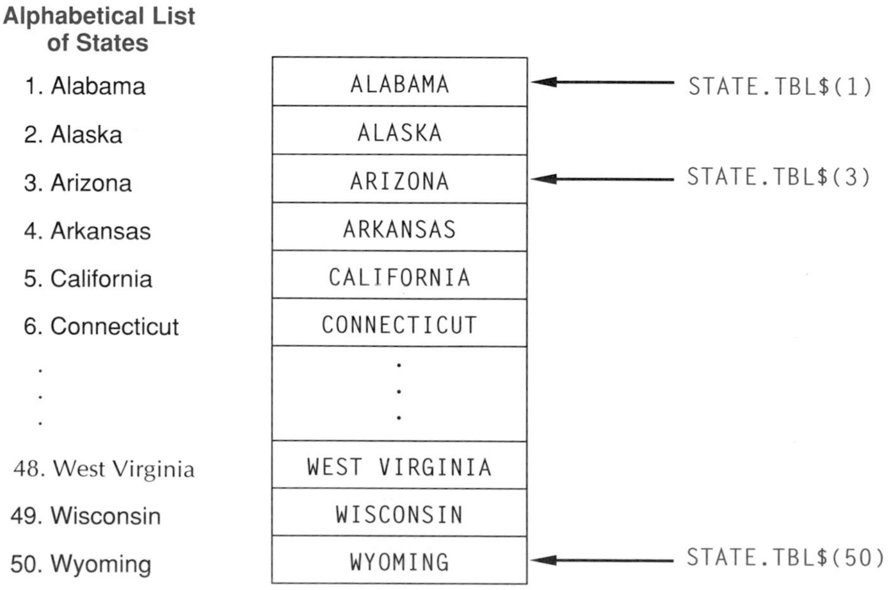

Alphabetical List of States		
1. Alabama	ALABAMA	← STATE.TBL$(1)
2. Alaska	ALASKA	
3. Arizona	ARIZONA	← STATE.TBL$(3)
4. Arkansas	ARKANSAS	
5. California	CALIFORNIA	
6. Connecticut	CONNECTICUT	
.	.	
.	.	
.	.	
48. West Virginia	WEST VIRGINIA	
49. Wisconsin	WISCONSIN	
50. Wyoming	WYOMING	← STATE.TBL$(50)

Storing related data items in tables has two important advantages over referencing each item individually. The first you already know: You need use only one variable name, even to reference hundreds or thousands of values. The second advantage is that tables cut down enormously on the amount of code you must write to refer to a set of values. You must reference individual variables separately, but you can reference the items in a table using one variable name whose subscript changes inside a loop.

For example, suppose you want to print the names of the 50 states. If you use unique variable names, you need to write 50 statements of the form PRINT ALABAMA\$, PRINT ALASKA\$, and so on. You can, however, print the contents of STATE.TBL\$ with just these three lines of code:

```
10 FOR CTR = 1 TO 50
20    PRINT STATE.TBL$(CTR)
30 NEXT CTR
```

TABLE PROCESSING FUNCTIONS

Three general types of functions are required in table processing—those that (1) define the table, (2) load values into the table, and (3) use or manipulate the values in the table.

Defining the Table

Defining a table simply means (1) selecting a name for the table, (2) specifying its data type, and (3) specifying the maximum number of data items it may contain. In BASIC, you do this with the DIM statement.

The general format for the DIM (dimension) statement is:

```
[line#] DIM <var1(subscripts)> [, . . . var-n(subscripts)]
```

This statement lets you list all of the table names you want to use. The variable name designates the data type. The integer value you put in parentheses after each name as a subscript tells BASIC how big the table is to be, and the system reserves consecutive storage space for that number of items. You may use a numeric variable name instead of an integer value for the subscript.

If a table name is used without a DIM statement, the maximum value of the subscript is assumed to be 10. In that case, if a subscript greater than 10 is used, a SUBSCRIPT OUT OF RANGE error occurs. That same error message appears whenever a program executes a statement containing a variable with a subscript larger than the value specified in the DIM statement.

A table may be defined only once in a program. If you attempt to define it again, a DUPLICATE DEFINITION error appears. BASIC allows the user to select the value of the first subscript in a table. For now, assume that the first subscript in all tables is 1.

Here are some examples of DIM statements:

```
10 DIM STATE.TBL$(50)
```
STATE.TBL\$ is the name of a table with space for 50 string items.

```
10 DIM NAME.TBL$(N)
```
NAME.TBL\$ is the name of a table with space for N string items.

```
10 DIM TAX.TBL(100)
```
TAX.TBL is the name of a table with space for 100 numeric items.

```
10 DIM PRICE.TBL(60), PROD.TBL$(60)
```
PRICE.TBL is the name of a table with space for 60 numeric items, and PROD.TBL$ is the name of a table with space for 60 string items.

Loading Values into the Table

The DIM statement just allocates space for the table. You may load values into a table by using any of the methods for assigning values to variables, including INPUT, INPUT #, LINE INPUT, and READ/DATA.

READ/DATA statements are frequently used to supply the values for program tables. The INPUT statement, however, is used if the values in the table will be changed frequently. For example, if the prices of a set of items change daily, each morning a clerk may enter the prices interactively. In this instance, the INPUT statement is used to load the values into the table.

Files are often loaded into tables to decrease processing time because the computer can reference data in memory faster than it can access data on disk. When you write a program that must frequently read data from a disk file, you should consider whether the program would run faster if the data were read from the file into a table and then processed from the table.

Using the Table

After the program assigns data values to the table, you need to consider three questions when using the table in a program:

1. What data value is the program looking for in the table?

2. If the value is found in the table, what processing steps should be taken?

3. If the value is not found in the table, what processing steps should be taken?

ONE-DIMENSIONAL TABLE USING DIRECT ADDRESSING

Start with an easy problem: Write a program that asks the user to enter a number from 1 to 12. In response, the program displays on the screen the name of the month corresponding to that number. For example, if the user presses 5, the program displays MAY.

This program will contain a table with the names of the months in calendar order. The table will have 12 *rows* of information with one data item, the name of the month, in each row. This kind of table, with one data item per row, is called a *one-dimensional* table or list.

This type of table can also be described as a *positionally-organized* table that can be *addressed directly*. This means that the row numbers in the table have a direct relationship to the contents of the rows. For example, MAY is the fifth month of the year and the fifth item in the table.

Figure 10.2 illustrates how the table is used in the program. The code to implement the simple specifications is listed in Program 10.1.

FIGURE 10.2
Direct addressing

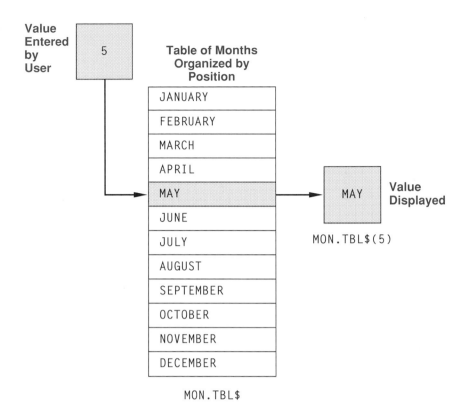

The DEFINE TABLE section defines the table. The DIM statement (line 1160) allocates space for 12 entries or 12 rows of data because 12 is the value of ROWMAX.

The LOAD TABLE module assigns values to the rows in the table. The FOR/NEXT loop (lines 3040–3060) reads data into each row. Notice the advantage of tables in this situation. Instead of using 12 variable names and 12 READ statements to store the names of the months, you need only 1 variable name, MON.TBL$, and 1 READ statement.

The months are stored in consecutive rows because the subscript (ROW) changes by one each time through the FOR/NEXT loop. JANUARY is stored in MON.TBL$(1); FEBRUARY, in MON.TBL$(2); and so on until DECEMBER is stored in MON.TBL$(12).

In the PROCESS TABLE module, the user is asked to enter a number from 1 to 12 (line 4050). This number is placed in the subscript variable ROW. If the user enters 9, the ROW is 9. Since SEPTEMBER is the ninth month in the table, SEPTEMBER appears on the screen.

Because this table is organized positionally, you do not have to search the table for the month. Instead, you can directly address the month in the table by using the number the user supplies as the table subscript.

 Style and Efficiency Tips

1. Use descriptive variable names. When assigning variable names to tables, you may want to use the word TABLE or the abbreviation TBL in the variable name. For example, the table of months is called MON.TBL$. Because tables are made up of rows, use the word ROW as the subscript name when referencing the table.

(continued on page 241)

Program 10.1

```
1000 ' PROG10-1
1010 ' *****************************
1020 ' *       MONTH CONVERSION       *
1030 ' *****************************
1040 '
1050 ' *****************************
1060 ' *           VARIABLES          *
1070 ' *****************************
1080 '
1090 ' ROW                            Table subscript
1100 '
1110 ' *****************************
1120 ' *          DEFINE TABLE        *
1130 ' *****************************
1140 '
1150   ROWMAX = 12                 'Number of rows in table
1160   DIM MON.TBL$(ROWMAX)        'Table of months
1170 '
1180 ' *****************************
1190 ' *          DATA FOR TABLE      *
1200 ' *****************************
1210 '
1220 '          MONTH.TBL$(ROW)
1230 '
1240   DATA     JANUARY
1250   DATA     FEBRUARY
1260   DATA     MARCH
1270   DATA     APRIL
1280   DATA     MAY
1290   DATA     JUNE
1300   DATA     JULY
1310   DATA     AUGUST
1320   DATA     SEPTEMBER
1330   DATA     OCTOBER
1340   DATA     NOVEMBER
1350   DATA     DECEMBER
1999 '
2000 ' *****************************
2010 ' *          CONTROL MODULE      *
2020 ' *****************************
2030 '
2040   GOSUB 3000                  'Load Table
2050   GOSUB 4000                  'Process Table
2060   END
2999 '
3000 ' *****************************
3010 ' *           LOAD TABLE         *
3020 ' *****************************
3030 '
3040   FOR ROW = 1 TO ROWMAX
3050       READ MON.TBL$(ROW)
3060   NEXT ROW
3070   RETURN
3999 '
4000 ' *****************************
4010 ' *          PROCESS TABLE       *
4020 ' *****************************
4030 '
4040   CLS
4050   INPUT "Enter month 1-12 ", ROW
4060   PRINT "The month is "; MON.TBL$(ROW)
4070   RETURN
```

STYLE AND EFFICIENCY TIPS (*continued from page 239*)

2. When you define a table, use a numeric variable to indicate the number of entries in the table. Use the variable ROWMAX to reference the maximum number of entries or rows in a table. In this example, ROWMAX is always 12, but in other table problems the number of rows in a table may change. Set ROWMAX equal to the number of entries in the table. Then, when the number of entries in the table changes, you need to change only the value of ROWMAX. For instance, suppose you write a program that loads and processes a table of product codes. It would be inefficient to search the program for all the statements that specify the number of entries in the table each time the number of product codes changes.

3. Put DATA statements in a separate section. Place the DATA statements in a separate section near the beginning of your program. You may need to change the data in the list, and the DATA statements are easy to find here. Also, because the READ statement searches for DATA statements beginning with the first line of the program, the closer you put the DATA statements to the beginning of the program, the more efficiently your program will run.

4. Consider using a single DATA statement for each data set. Placing one DATA set per line makes your program easy to read and change.

5. Consider using integer variables. Although the counter used with FOR/NEXT statements may be any real number, you usually use an integer value for table applications. Your program will be more efficient if you attach the % suffix to variable names that will always have integer values. For example, you could rewrite the FOR/NEXT loop in the module LOAD TABLE as follows:

```
3040 FOR ROW% = 1 TO ROWMAX%
3050     READ MON.TBL$(ROW%)
3060 NEXT ROW%
```

6. Your programs will execute faster if you do not list the name of the counter variable in the NEXT statement. BASIC always pairs a NEXT with the nearest preceding FOR that is not already paired. For example, you could replace 3060 NEXT ROW% with 3060 NEXT.

ONE-DIMENSIONAL TABLES USING INDIRECT ADDRESSING

Now, try a program that uses two tables: a table of last names and a table with corresponding zip codes. When a user enters a name, the zip code corresponding to that name appears on the screen. If the name entered is not in the table, an appropriate message appears.

In this problem, the user supplies a *search argument* (a name). The program looks through the table to match the search argument with one of the values in the table, called a *table argument*. Each table argument has a corresponding zip code; the zip codes are the *table functions* corresponding to each table argument. Review Figure 10.3 to understand these new terms more fully.

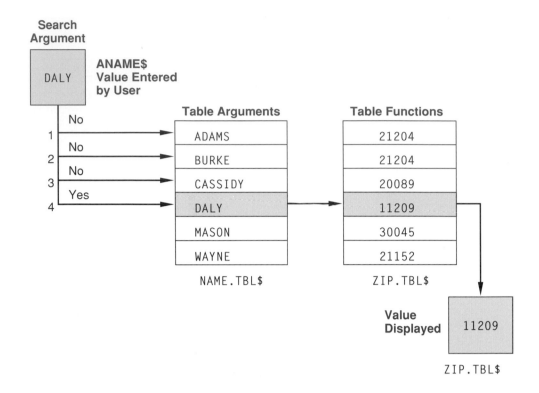

Unlike the table of months in Program 10.1, these two tables are not positionally organized and so cannot be addressed directly. Rather, they are *argument organized* and must be *addressed indirectly*.

The logic for one approach to searching a table organized by argument is:

```
set flag = false
set subscript to 1
dowhile (flag = false) and (subscript <= max subscript)
     if search argument = table(subscript)
          then set flag to true
          else add 1 to subscript
end dowhile
if flag = true
     then process match
     else process error
```

This is called a *serial* or *sequential* search because it begins at the start of the table and examines each row in turn.

Program 10.2 contains the code for this program. Notice that the module DEFINE TABLES again defines the tables with DIM statements, and a FOR/NEXT loop loads the table in the LOAD TABLES module.

Program 10.2

```
1000 ' PROG10-2
1010 ' *****************************
1020 ' *     NAMES AND ZIP CODES     *
1030 ' *****************************
1040 '
1050 ' *****************************
1060 ' *          VARIABLES          *
1070 ' *****************************
1080 '
```

Program 10.2 (continued)

```
1090 '  ANAME$                     Name entered by user
1100 '  MATCH$                     Flag for finding match in table
1110 '  ROW                        Table subscript
1120 '
1130 '  *****************************
1140 '  *         DEFINE TABLES          *
1150 '  *****************************
1160 '
1170    ROWMAX = 6                 'Number of rows in tables
1180    DIM NAME.TBL$(ROWMAX)      'Table of names
1190    DIM ZIP.TBL$(ROWMAX)       'Table of zip codes
1200 '
1210 '  *****************************
1220 '  *         DATA FOR TABLES        *
1230 '  *****************************
1240 '
1250 '            NAME.TBL$(ROW)       ZIP.TBL$(ROW)
1260 '
1270    DATA    ADAMS,             21204
1280    DATA    BURKE,             21204
1290    DATA    CASSIDY,           20089
1300    DATA    DALY,              11209
1310    DATA    MASON,             30045
1320    DATA    WAYNE,             21152
1999 '
2000 '  *****************************
2010 '  *        CONTROL MODULE          *
2020 '  *****************************
2030 '
2040    GOSUB 3000                 'Load lables
2050    GOSUB 4000                 'Search Table
2060    END
2999 '
3000 '  *****************************
3010 '  *         LOAD TABLES            *
3020 '  *****************************
3030 '
3040    FOR ROW = 1 TO ROWMAX
3050        READ NAME.TBL$(ROW),
                ZIP.TBL$(ROW)
3060    NEXT ROW
3070    RETURN
3999 '
4000 '  *****************************
4010 '  *         SEARCH TABLE           *
4020 '  *****************************
4030 '
4040    CLS
4050    INPUT "Enter name ", ANAME$
4060 '
4070    MATCH$ = "NO"
4080    ROW = 1
4090    WHILE (MATCH$ = "NO") AND (ROW <= ROWMAX)
4100        IF ANAME$ = NAME.TBL$(ROW)
                THEN MATCH$ = "YES"
                ELSE ROW = ROW + 1
4110    WEND
4120 '
4130    IF MATCH$ = "YES"
            THEN PRINT "The zip code for "; ANAME$; " is "; ZIP.TBL$(ROW)
            ELSE PRINT "The zip code is unavailable"
4140    RETURN
```

In SEARCH TABLE, ANAME$ is the search argument and NAME.TBL$(ROW) is the table argument. ZIP.TBL$(ROW) is the table function. MATCH$ is the flag that signals a match between the search argument and the table argument.

Before the loop is entered, MATCH$ has the value "NO". The WHILE/WEND loop checks the table arguments one row at a time, starting at the beginning of the table and ending when a match occurs or the end of the table is reached. The IF statement in 4130 checks for a match, and, if a match is found, prints the zip code for the matching name.

If the program executes the WHILE/WEND loop six times (the value of ROWMAX), control transfers to line 4130. In this case, MATCH$ still equals "NO", and the message "The zip code is unavailable" appears.

❋ Efficiency Tips

1. Consider ordering tables by usage frequency. Sometimes, some table entries are referenced more frequently than others. For faster processing, place the most frequently referenced entries at the beginning of the table.

2. Use the OPTION BASE statement. In a table dimensioned as T$(14), 15 rows are available. Even though it is not used in the examples, row 0 is the first row in the table. The OPTION BASE statement lets you set the lower boundary value of the table to 1 instead of the default 0, thereby avoiding unused table space. For example, in Program 10.2, you could add the statement

```
1175 OPTION BASE 1
```

and neither NAME.TBL$ or ZIP.TBL$ will have a row 0. The OPTION BASE statement must precede any definition or use of tables in the program. Note, however, that it is sometimes useful to have row 0 in a table. For example, suppose your table contained numbers of laboratory mice found to have 0 tumors, 1 tumor, 2 tumors, and so on. In this case, it's advantageous to have the number of tumors correspond to the row in the table.

ONE-DIMENSIONAL TABLES USING A SEQUENTIAL FILE FOR DATA

In the first two examples, READ and DATA statements were used to load the values into the tables. Sometimes, however, you will want to put a sequential file into a table for faster processing, as in the following example.

A local toy store needs a program to use each day that will perform the following processing:

1. Allow the clerks to enter a product code when a customer calls to place an order.

2. After finding the matching product code in the product file, print the name of the product and allow the clerk to enter the quantity the customer wants to order.

3. Keep a running total of the quantity ordered for each product code.

4. If a match is not found in the product file, print a message to the clerk.

5. At the end of the day, generate a printed report listing the product codes, product names, the total quantity for each product code, and the total quantity for all product codes.

The sequential file contains two string fields: product code and product name. Because the product file will be accessed continually throughout the day, the product codes will be put into a code table and the product names into a name table. Also needed is a third table to hold the quantities ordered for each product code. See Figure 10.4 for a diagram of these three tables.

The general logic for loading a table from a sequential file is as follows:

```
open file
set subscript to 0
dowhile not eof
     add 1 to subscript
     read record into table(s)
end dowhile
close file
```

The logic for finding a match in the table is the same as in Program 10.2.

The code for the program is listed in Program 10.3. In the DEFINE TABLES module, the subscript variable ROWMAX is an estimate of the number of rows in the table. When you assign a value to that variable, remember to select a number large enough to hold all the records in the file.

In the LOAD TABLES module, the tables are loaded in a WHILE/WEND loop because the number of records in the file is not known. Because a WHILE/WEND loop does not count the number of times through the loop, as the FOR/NEXT loop does, a counter is necessary to keep track of the actual number of rows in the table. The INPUT # statement reads the two fields in each record and places the first field in CODE.TBL\$(ROW) and the second field in NAME.TBL\$(ROW).

The third table, which keeps track of the quantity ordered for each product code, is used as an accumulator. For this reason, each of its rows must be initialized to zero.

After the file has been read and loaded into the tables, ROWMAX, the maximum number of rows in the table, is set equal to ROW. At this time (line 3120), ROW contains the actual number of rows used in the table.

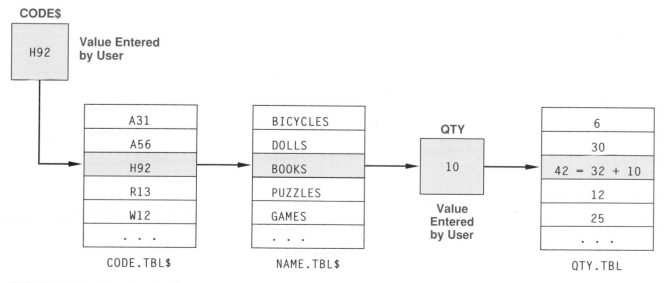

FIGURE 10.4   Toy store tables

Program 10.3

```
1000 ' PROG10-3
1010 ' ****************************
1020 ' *       TOY STORE REPORT        *
1030 ' ****************************
1040 '
1050 ' ****************************
1060 ' *           VARIABLES           *
1070 ' ****************************
1080 '
1090 ' PROD.SEQ                   Product File
1100 ' Prod Record:
1110 '      CODE.TBL$             Code field becomes table of product codes
1120 '      NAME.TBL$             Name field becomes table of product names
1130 '
1140 ' CODE$                      Code entered by user
1150 ' DETAIL$                    Format for detail line
1160 ' MATCH$                     Flag for finding match in table
1170 ' QTY                        Quantity entered by user
1180 ' ROW                        Table subscript
1190 '
1200 ' ****************************
1210 ' *    INITIALIZED VARIABLES    *
1220 ' ****************************
1230 '
1240   QTY.TOTAL = 0              'Total quantity for report
1250 '
1260 ' ****************************
1270 ' *         DEFINE TABLES         *
1280 ' ****************************
1290 '
1300   ROWMAX = 100              'Estimated number of rows in tables
1310   DIM CODE.TBL$(ROWMAX)     'Table of product codes from file
1320   DIM NAME.TBL$(ROWMAX)     'Table of product names from file
1330   DIM QTY.TBL(ROWMAX)       'Table of product quantities
1999 '
2000 ' ****************************
2010 ' *         CONTROL MODULE         *
2020 ' ****************************
2030 '
2040   GOSUB 3000                'Load Tables
2050   GOSUB 4000                'Process Inquiries
2060   GOSUB 5000                'Print Report
2070   END
2080 '
3000 ' ****************************
3010 ' *           LOAD TABLES           *
3020 ' ****************************
3030 '
3040   OPEN "PROD.SEQ" FOR INPUT AS #1
3050   ROW = 0
3060   WHILE NOT EOF(1)
3070       ROW = ROW + 1
3080       INPUT #1, CODE.TBL$(ROW),
                     NAME.TBL$(ROW)
3090       QTY.TBL(ROW) = 0
3100   WEND
3110   CLOSE #1
3120   ROWMAX = ROW
3130   RETURN
3999 '
4000 ' ****************************
4010 ' *       PROCESS INQUIRIES        *
4020 ' ****************************
4030 '
```

Program 10.3 (continued)

```
4040    CLS
4050    INPUT "Enter Product Code or S to stop ", CODE$
4060    WHILE (CODE$ <> "S") AND (CODE$ <> "s")
4070        MATCH$ = "NO"
4080        ROW = 1
4090        WHILE (MATCH$ = "NO") AND (ROW <= ROWMAX)
4100            IF CODE$ = CODE.TBL$(ROW)
                    THEN MATCH$ = "YES"
                    ELSE ROW = ROW + 1
4110        WEND
4120        IF MATCH$ = "YES"
                THEN GOSUB 6000
                ELSE PRINT "Invalid Product Code - Please enter again"
4130        PRINT
4140        INPUT "Enter Product Code or S to stop ", CODE$
4150    WEND
4160    RETURN
4999    '
5000    ' *****************************
5010    ' *          PRINT REPORT         *
5020    ' *****************************
5030    '
5040    LPRINT TAB(14); "TOY REPORT"
5050    LPRINT TAB(12); "FOR "; DATE$
5060    LPRINT
5070    LPRINT    "PRODUCT CODE    PRODUCT NAME    QUANTITY"
5080    LPRINT
5090    DETAIL$ = "   \ \           \             \        ###"
5100    '
5110    FOR ROW = 1 TO ROWMAX
5120        LPRINT USING DETAIL$; CODE.TBL$(ROW),
                                  NAME.TBL$(ROW),
                                  QTY.TBL(ROW)
5130        QTY.TOTAL = QTY.TOTAL + QTY.TBL(ROW)
5140    NEXT ROW
5150    '
5160    LPRINT
5170    LPRINT TAB(23); USING "TOTAL = ##,###"; QTY.TOTAL
5180    RETURN
5999    '
6000    ' *****************************
6010    ' *         UPDATE QUANTITY       *
6020    ' *****************************
6030    '
6040    PRINT "How many "; NAME.TBL$(ROW); " do you want to order?"
6050    INPUT QTY
6060    QTY.TBL(ROW) = QTY.TBL(ROW) + QTY
6070    RETURN
```

The module PROCESS INQUIRIES searches the CODE.TBL$ serially each time a product code is entered. Whenever the user enters a product code in response to the prompt "Enter Product Code or S to stop", CODE.TBL$ is searched for a match. If a match is found, the search is terminated, and QTY.TBL is updated in the module UPDATE QUANTITY. If BASIC finds no match after examining every entry in CODE.TBL$, the message "Invalid Product Code - Please enter again" appears on the screen.

When the orders for the day have been completed, the clerk enters S or s in response to the prompt "Enter Product Code or S to stop". Then the last module, PRINT REPORT, is executed. This module generates a report including a heading, detail lines, and a total. The detail lines are the entries in each of the three parallel tables, listed one row at a time.

Program 10.3 produced the following report:

```
                        TOY  REPORT
                    FOR 08-27-1989

     PRODUCT CODE     PRODUCT NAME    QUANTITY

         A31            BICYCLES          6
         A56            DOLLS            30
         H92            BOOKS            42
         R13            PUZZLES          12
         W12            GAMES            25

                             TOTAL  =    115
```

TWO-DIMENSIONAL TABLE

Until now, you have been using one-dimensional tables, tables in which each row has only one data item. Another way to describe those tables is to say that they have only one *column* of data. Single-column tables have one *dimension*.

You can load and use tables with multiple dimensions. In a *two-dimensional* table, each row has more than one data item, or, equivalently, more than one column of data. You reference the data items in a two-dimensional table in the same way as those in a one-dimensional table, except that you must specify two subscripts, one for each dimension.

Consider these examples:

TEST.SCORES(13,4)   This might refer to the score of the 13th student on the fourth exam.

STATE.FLOWER$(48,2)   This could contain the name of the state flower of the 48th state. Column one could be the name of the state.

The first subscript in the table name always refers to the *row* of the table; the second, to the *column*. Remember (ROW,COL).

BASIC allows tables with up to 255 dimensions, but only one- and two-dimensional tables are ordinarily used in business data processing.

To appreciate the use of a two-dimensional table, you can rewrite Program 10.2 with one two-dimensional table instead of two one-dimensional tables. See Figure 10.5 for an illustration of the two-dimensional table, NAME.TBL$, which has two columns of information. The first column contains names, and the second contains zip codes.

Program 10.4 is a version of Program 10.2 modified to contain one two-dimensional table. The DIM statement in the module DEFINE TABLE now has two variables. The first variable, ROWMAX, defines how many rows are in the table, and the second variable, COLMAX, defines how many columns are in each row. In this program, NAME.TBL$ has six rows, with each row having two columns of data, for a total of 12 data items.

FIGURE 10.5
A two-dimensional table

	Column 1	Column 2
Row 1	ADAMS	21204
Row 2	BURKE	21204
Row 3	CASSIDY	20089
Row 4	DALY	11209
Row 5	MASON	30045
Row 6	WAYNE	21152

NAME.TBL$

```
NAME.TBL$(6,1) = "WAYNE"
NAME.TBL$(3,2) = "20089"
```

To load the table using READ/DATA statements, the program uses *nested* FOR/NEXT loops, one FOR/NEXT loop inside another. When loops are nested, each loop must use a different variable name as a counter, and the NEXT statement for the inside loop must appear before the NEXT statement for the outside loop.

Notice the nested loops in this code:

```
10 PRINT "COL 1", "COL 2"
20 FOR A = 1 TO 2
30     FOR B = 1 TO 4
40         PRINT A,B
50     NEXT B
60 NEXT A
70 END
RUN
COL 1          COL 2
 1              1
 1              2
 1              3
 1              4
 2              1
 2              2
 2              3
 2              4
```

Line 10 prints the column headings. Line 20 sets A equal to 1. Line 30 sets B equal to 1. The inside loop is executed four times before line 60 is executed. After line 60, A equals 2. Line 30 is executed again, and B is set to its starting value, 1. The inside loop is executed another four times before line 60 is executed again. Because A now equals 3, line 20 sends control to line 70, and the program stops.

Notice that, in nested FOR/NEXT loops, every time the outside loop is executed once, the inside loop is executed as many times as necessary to exceed the stopping value.

In the LOAD TABLE module of Program 10.4, the nested FOR/NEXT loop loads the table a row at a time. Row 1, Col 1 first, then Row 1, Col 2, then Row 2, Col 1, then Row 2, Col 2, then Row 3, Col 1, and so on until the table is loaded.

Notice that, in the module SEARCH TABLE, NAME.TBL$(ROW,1) refers to all of the names in the table, and NAME.TBL$(ROW,2) refers to all of the zip codes.

Program 10.4

```
1000 ' PROG10-4
1010 ' ******************************
1020 ' *      NAMES AND ZIP CODES      *
1030 ' ******************************
1040 '
1050 ' ******************************
1060 ' *           VARIABLES           *
1070 ' ******************************
1080 '
1090 ' ANAME$                    Name entered by user
1100 ' COL                       Column subscript
1110 ' MATCH$                    Flag for finding match in table
1120 ' ROW                       Row subscript
1130 '
1140 ' ******************************
1150 ' *          DEFINE TABLE          *
1160 ' ******************************
1170 '
1180   ROWMAX = 6                      'Number of rows in table
1190   COLMAX = 2                      'Number of columns in table
1200   DIM NAME.TBL$(ROWMAX,COLMAX)    'Table of names and zip codes
1210 '
1220 ' ******************************
1230 ' *          DATA FOR TABLE          *
1240 ' ******************************
1250 '
1260 '           NAME.TBL$(ROW,1)     NAME.TBL$(ROW,2)
1270 '
1280   DATA    ADAMS,                21204
1290   DATA    BURKE,                21204
1300   DATA    CASSIDY,              20089
1310   DATA    DALY,                 11209
1320   DATA    MASON,                30045
1330   DATA    WAYNE,                21152
1999 '
2000 ' ******************************
2010 ' *          CONTROL MODULE          *
2020 ' ******************************
2030 '
2040   GOSUB 3000                'Load Table
2050   GOSUB 4000                'Search Table
2060   END
2070 '
3000 ' ******************************
3010 ' *           LOAD TABLE           *
3020 ' ******************************
3030 '
3040   FOR ROW = 1 TO ROWMAX
3050       FOR COL = 1 TO COLMAX
3060           READ NAME.TBL$(ROW,COL)
3070       NEXT COL
3080   NEXT ROW
3090   RETURN
3999 '
4000 ' ******************************
4010 ' *           SEARCH TABLE           *
4020 ' ******************************
4030 '
4040   CLS
4050   INPUT "Enter name ", ANAME$
4060 '
```

Program 10.4 (continued)

```
4070    MATCH$ = "NO"
4080    ROW = 1
4090    WHILE (MATCH$ = "NO") AND (ROW <= ROWMAX)
4100       IF ANAME$ = NAME.TBL$(ROW,1)
              THEN MATCH$ = "YES"
              ELSE ROW = ROW + 1
4110    WEND
4120    '
4130    IF MATCH$ = "YES"
           THEN PRINT "The zip code for "; ANAME$ ;" is "; NAME.TBL$(ROW,2)
           ELSE PRINT "The zip code is unavailable"
4140    RETURN
```

ANOTHER TWO-DIMENSIONAL EXAMPLE

In the previous sample program, there was really no advantage to using one two-dimensional table instead of two one-dimensional tables. Two-dimensional tables, however, are useful when you want to analyze numeric data either by row or by column.

In Chapter 9, by using control-break logic, you created a sales report for Berrenger's Department Store with totals by department within month (Program 9.3). You can place these totals in a two-dimensional table named SALES.TBL#. Figure 10.6 shows these totals in the two-dimensional table.

Now suppose Berrenger's sales director wants a report that shows the data as they are contained in SALES.TBL# and that also shows the department totals for each quarter (column totals) and sales totals for each month (row totals).

Program 10.5 produces the report shown in Figure 10.7. Notice that, in the module TOTALS BY MONTH, all the columns in a row are processed before the next row is started. In the TOTALS BY DEPT module, all the rows in a column are processed before the next column is started.

FIGURE 10.6
Berrenger's sales report totals loaded into a table

	Dept 311	Dept 312	Dept 315
Month 1	1141.67	2377.35	500.90
Month 2	1950.90	1330.99	791.55
Month 3	1302.15	2971.74	901.84

SALES.TBL#

FIGURE 10.7
Report produced by Program 10.5

```
                  BERRENGER'S DEPARTMENT STORE
                         SALES REPORT

MONTH        DEPT 311       DEPT 312       DEPT 315        TOTALS

  1          1,141.67       2,377.35         500.90      4,019.92
  2          1,950.90       1,330.99         791.55      4,073.44
  3          1,302.15       2,971.74         901.84      5,175.73

TOTALS       4,394.72       6,680.08       2,194.29
```

Program 10.5

```
1000 ' PROG10-5
1010 ' ******************************
1020 ' *          SALES REPORT          *
1030 ' ******************************
1040 '
1050 ' ******************************
1060 ' *            VARIABLES            *
1070 ' ******************************
1080 '
1090 ' ROW                     Row subscript
1100 ' COL                     Column subscript
1110 ' SALES.TOTAL#            Total sales
1120 '
1130 ' ******************************
1140 ' *          DEFINE TABLE          *
1150 ' ******************************
1160 '
1170     ROWMAX = 3                     'Number of rows in table
1180     COLMAX = 3                     'Number of columns in table
1190     DIM SALES.TBL#(ROWMAX,COLMAX)  'Table of sales numbers
1200 '
1210 ' ******************************
1220 ' *         DATA FOR TABLE         *
1230 ' ******************************
1240 '
1250 '            SALES.TBL#(ROW,1)    SALES.TBL#(ROW,2)    SALES.TBL#(ROW,3)
1260 '
1270     DATA    1141.67,             2377.35,             500.90
1280     DATA    1950.90,             1330.99,             791.55
1290     DATA    1302.15,             2971.74,             901.84
1999 '
2000 ' ******************************
2010 ' *         CONTROL MODULE         *
2020 ' ******************************
2030 '
2040     GOSUB 3000                 'Load Table
2050     GOSUB 4000                 'Write heading
2060     GOSUB 5000                 'Totals by Month
2070     GOSUB 6000                 'Totals by Dept
2080     END
2999 '
3000 ' ******************************
3010 ' *           LOAD TABLE           *
3020 ' ******************************
3030 '
3040     FOR ROW = 1 TO ROWMAX
3050         FOR COL = 1 TO COLMAX
3060             READ SALES.TBL#(ROW,COL)
3070         NEXT COL
3080     NEXT ROW
3090     RETURN
3999 '
4000 ' ******************************
4010 ' *          WRITE HEADING          *
4020 ' ******************************
4030 '
4040     CLS
4050     PRINT
4060     PRINT
4070     PRINT TAB(26); "BERRENGER'S DEPARTMENT STORE"
4080     PRINT TAB(34); "SALES REPORT"
4090     PRINT
4100     PRINT
```

Program 10.5 (continued)

```
4110    PRINT TAB(8);
            "MONTH        DEPT 311        DEPT 312        DEPT 315        TOTALS"
4120    PRINT
4130    RETURN
4999 '
5000 ' *****************************
5010 ' *       TOTALS BY MONTH       *
5020 ' *****************************
5030 '
5040    FOR ROW = 1 TO ROWMAX
5050        SALES.TOTAL# = 0
5060        PRINT TAB(10); ROW;
5070 '
5080        FOR COL = 1 TO COLMAX
5090            PRINT USING "        ###,###.##"; SALES.TBL#(ROW,COL);
5100            SALES.TOTAL# = SALES.TOTAL# + SALES.TBL#(ROW,COL)
5110        NEXT COL
5120 '
5130        PRINT TAB(62); USING "#,###,###.##"; SALES.TOTAL#
5140    NEXT ROW
5150    RETURN
5999 '
6000 ' *****************************
6010 ' *       TOTALS BY DEPT       *
6020 ' *****************************
6030 '
6040    PRINT
6050    PRINT TAB(7); "TOTALS";
6060    FOR COL = 1 TO COLMAX
6070        SALES.TOTAL# = 0
6080 '
6090        FOR ROW = 1 TO ROWMAX
6100            SALES.TOTAL# = SALES.TOTAL# + SALES.TBL#(ROW,COL)
6110        NEXT ROW
6120 '
6130        PRINT USING "     #,###,###.##"; SALES.TOTAL#;
6140    NEXT COL
6160    RETURN
```

BINARY SEARCH

In the previous examples, the tables were searched serially, starting at the beginning of the table and continuing until either a match was found or the end of the table was reached. A serial search is more efficient for short tables, but not for ones with ten rows or more.

For longer tables arranged in alphabetical or numeric order, a *binary search* is very efficient. In a binary search, the row at the middle of the table is checked first. If a match is found, the search ends. Otherwise, the program determines whether the table argument needed is in the upper half of the table or the lower half. The half of the table containing the table argument is again halved and the search continues as before. The name *binary* refers to this process of dividing by two.

This problem illustrates a binary search: A local credit company needs a program to display the current credit limit of any customer. Even though the company does not have many customers, a binary search method will be used to find a match in the table of customer account numbers. When the program finds a match, the credit limit for that customer account is displayed. Figure 10.8 diagrams the binary search process in this context.

FIGURE 10.8
Diagram of a binary search

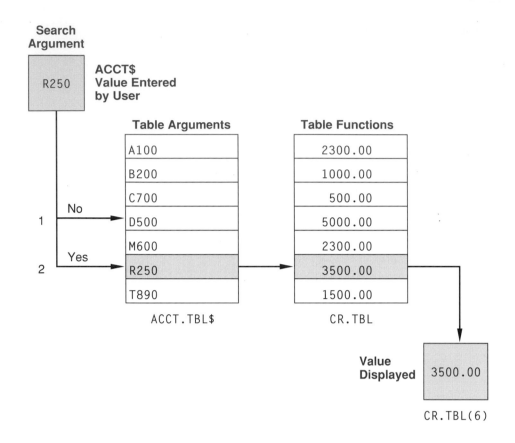

The general logic for a binary search is as follows:

```
flag = false
set min subscript
set max subscript
dowhile (flag = false) and (min subscript <= max subscript)
     subscript = integer((min subscript + max subscript)/2)
     if search argument < table(subscript)
          then max subscript = subscript - 1
          else if search argument > table(subscript)
                  then min subscript = subscript + 1
                  else flag = true
end dowhile
if flag = true
     then process data
     else process error
```

Program 10.6 displays the credit limit for customers.

Program 10.6
```
1000 ' PROG10-6
1010 ' ***************************
1020 ' *  ACCTS AND CREDIT LIMITS  *
1030 ' ***************************
1040 '
1050 ' ***************************
1060 ' *          VARIABLES          *
1070 ' ***************************
1080 '
```

Program 10.6   (continued)

```
1090 ' ACCT$                     Acct number entered by user
1100 ' MATCH$                    Flag for finding match in table
1110 ' ROW                       Table subscript
1120 ' ROWMIN                    First row of table
1130 '
1140 ' ****************************
1150 ' *        DEFINE TABLES        *
1160 ' ****************************
1170 '
1180   ROWMAX = 7                'Number of rows in tables
1190   DIM ACCT.TBL$(ROWMAX)     'Table of acct numbers
1200   DIM CR.TBL(ROWMAX)        'Table of credit limits
1210 '
1220 ' ****************************
1230 ' *       DATA FOR TABLES       *
1240 ' ****************************
1250 '
1260 '           ACCT.TBL$(ROW)       CR.TBL(ROW)
1270 '
1280   DATA     A100,              2300.00
1290   DATA     B200,              1000.00
1300   DATA     C700,               500.00
1310   DATA     D500,              5000.00
1320   DATA     M600,              2300.00
1330   DATA     R250,              3500.00
1340   DATA     T890,              1500.00
1999 '
2000 ' ****************************
2010 ' *        CONTROL MODULE        *
2020 ' ****************************
2030 '
2040   GOSUB 3000                'Load Tables
2050   GOSUB 4000                'Process Inquiry
2060   END
2999 '
3000 ' ****************************
3010 ' *         LOAD TABLES         *
3020 ' ****************************
3030 '
3040   FOR ROW = 1 TO ROWMAX
3050       READ ACCT.TBL$(ROW),
               CR.TBL(ROW)
3060   NEXT ROW
3070   RETURN
3999 '
4000 ' ****************************
4010 ' *        PROCESS INQUIRY        *
4020 ' ****************************
4030 '
4040   CLS
4050   INPUT "Enter acct number ", ACCT$
4060 '
4070   MATCH$ = "NO"
4080   ROWMIN = 1
4090   WHILE (MATCH$ = "NO") AND (ROWMIN <= ROWMAX)
4100       ROW = INT((ROWMIN + ROWMAX)/2)
4110       IF            ACCT$ < ACCT.TBL$(ROW) THEN ROWMAX = ROW - 1
               ELSE IF ACCT$ > ACCT.TBL$(ROW) THEN ROWMIN = ROW + 1
               ELSE                              MATCH$ = "YES"
4120   WEND
4130 '
4140   IF MATCH$ = "YES"
           THEN PRINT USING "The credit limit is #,###.##"; CR.TBL(ROW)
           ELSE PRINT "The credit limit is unavailable"
4150   RETURN
```

If the user enters account number R250, the variables in Program 10.6 have the following values at the start of the search in module PROCESS IN-QUIRY.

```
ROWMIN = 1
ROWMAX = 7
ACCT$ = "R250"
MATCH$ = "NO"
```

After pass 1 (statements 4090–4120), this is the situation:

```
4100 ROW = INT((1 + 7)/2)                       ———→ 4
4110 IF "R250" <  ACCT.TBL$(4)                   ———→ false
        ELSE IF "R250" > ACCT.TBL$(4)            ———→ true
        THEN ROWMIN = 4 + 1                      ———→ 5
```

This is the situation after pass 2 (statements 4090–4120):

```
4100 ROW = INT((5 + 7)/2)                        ———→ 6
4110 IF "R250" < ACCT.TBL$(6)                    ———→ false
        ELSE IF "R250" > ACCT.TBL$(6) ———→ false
        ELSE MATCH$ = "YES"                      ———→ match$ = "yes"
```

Locating the table argument, R250, took two passes. Had a serial search been used, the program would have made six passes before finding a match. Of course, the serial search will find a match for A100 in one pass. The relative efficiency of a binary search, however, increases rapidly as the size of the table increases. For example, in a table of 20 items requested with equal frequency, a serial search *averages* ten comparisons, while a binary search makes a *maximum* of five comparisons. For a similar table of 200 items, the number of comparisons is 100 and 8, respectively.

RND FUNCTION

The function RND returns a number between 0 and 1. This means that any number from 0 to 1, but not 0 or 1, is as likely to come up as any other. Of course, values between 0 and 1 are decimal fractions. The general expression for finding a random number that is an integer rather than a decimal value is:

```
R = INT(N * RND + L)
```

where R = random number

N = number of values in the range
    N = (high.value.in.range – low.value.in.range + 1)

L = lowest number in the range (low.value.in.range)

For example, you could use the following expression to print a random number between 1 and 6, including 1 and 6:

```
R = INT(6 * RND + 1)
```

N is 6 because there are six digits between 1 and 6, inclusive $(6 - 1 + 1 = 6)$, and L is 1 because 1 is the lowest digit in the range.

If you want to display five random numbers within the range 1 through 6, the following code would do the job:

```
10 FOR CTR = 1 TO 5
20     R = INT(6 * RND + 1)
30     PRINT R
40 NEXT CTR
RUN
```

```
1
4
6
5
5
```

Note that duplicate random numbers are possible.

The random number generator is started by a *seed number*, which controls the sequence of numbers generated. If the random number generator is not "reseeded," the RND function returns the same sequence of random numbers each time the program is run. To change the sequence of random numbers every time the program is run, place the statement RANDOMIZE TIMER before the segment of code using the RND function. RANDOMIZE reseeds the random number generator. The TIMER function returns a single-precision number representing the number of seconds elapsed since system reset. Since this value is always changing, it is used to reseed the random number generator every time the program is run.

For example, the following code selects 3 random numbers from 4 to 10. The RANDOMIZE TIMER statement is included to ensure that the sequence of numbers changes with each run.

```
10 RANDOMIZE TIMER
20 FOR CTR = 1 TO 3
30     R = INT(7 * RND + 4)
40     PRINT R
50 NEXT CTR
```

Read the following problem and see if you can find a solution: The auditor has arrived at your company. She wants you to write a program to select 15 accounts at random for her to review. The accounts are numbered sequentially from 100 to 900. Be sure the program does not duplicate any account numbers (a table is required).

Summary

- A table is a group of related string or numeric data items referenced by a single variable name. The separate data items are distinguished by *subscripts*, as in TABLE(4) where the 4 refers to the fourth item in the table.

- A table with one data item (or column) in each row is *one dimensional*. A table with more than one data item (or column) in each row is *two dimensional*. The advantages of table processing are:

  1. The programmer can use one subscripted variable name to refer to many data items.
  2. The amount of code needed to process related data items is greatly reduced.
  3. Placing the data in a file into a table greatly increases processing speed.

- The functions involved in using a table are:

  1. Defining the data type and size of the table
  2. Loading the table with values
  3. Using or manipulating values in the table

- Tables may be organized by *position* or by *argument*. Tables organized by position are processed by *direct addressing*. Tables organized by argument are processed by *indirect addressing* with either a serial search or a binary search.

- During a *serial* or *sequential search*, the computer starts at the beginning of the table and examines the items one at a time until the value sought is found or the end of the table is reached.

- A *binary search* starts at the middle of the table. If the value sought is in the middle row, the search ends; otherwise, the program determines whether the value sought is in the upper or lower half of the table. The half of the table that should contain the value is halved, and the search continues as before until a match is found or the entire table has been searched. Before a binary search can be applied, the table must be arranged in numeric or alphabetic order.

- Chapter 10 describes the following BASIC statements and functions:

  DIM A statement that allocates space in memory for a table.

FOR/NEXT   An alternative way to implement the repetition structure. The statements between the FOR statement and the NEXT statement are repeated the number of times specified by the variables in the FOR statement.

OPTION BASE   A statement that lets the programmer change the lower boundary of a table to something other than the default value of zero.

READ/DATA   Statements that are always used together to assign values to variables. The READ statement takes values in order from the DATA statement and assigns them to the corresponding variables in its variable list.

RESTORE   A statement that resets the DATA pointer to the beginning of the DATA list. After a RESTORE statement is executed, the next READ statement reads the first item in the program's first DATA statement.

RANDOMIZE TIMER   RANDOMIZE reseeds the random number generator with the TIMER value, a number representing the number of seconds that have elapsed since system reset.

RND   This function returns a number between 0 and 1, not including the digits 0 and 1. Any number is as likely to come up as any other.

Review Questions

1. Are the READ and DATA statements always used together? Why?

2. Compare the advantages of storing data in a DATA statement and storing data in a file.

3. When do READ/DATA statements generate an OUT OF DATA error message?

4. What might be the purpose of the last value(s) in a set of DATA statements?

5. What is the purpose of the RESTORE statement?

6. Can you use the RESTORE statement more than once in a program?

7. What is the general purpose of FOR/NEXT statements?

8. When is it advantageous to use FOR/NEXT rather than WHILE/WEND statements to control a loop?

9. Explain the following code:

```
100 FOR DELAY = 1 to 1000
200 NEXT DELAY
```

When would you use these statements?

10. What is a table?

11. What is a subscript?

12. What are the advantages of storing data in a table?

13. What are the major concerns in defining a table?

14. What is the purpose of the DIM statement?

15. What will happen if a table is not dimensioned?

16. Can you allocate more space in a table than is used by the program?

17. Can you dimension more than one table in a DIM statement?

18. How can you load values into a table?

19. What is a one-dimensional table?

20. How can you tell from the variable name that a table is one dimensional?

21. What does the term *row* mean in reference to a table?

22. What is a positionally organized table? Give an example.

23. What is an argument organized table? Give an example.

24. What is the relationship among a search argument, table argument, and table function?

25. What is a serial search?

26. How can you organize a table so that the serial search is as efficient as possible?

27. Why would you use the OPTION BASE statement?

28. Why would you read a data file into a table?

29. What is a two-dimensional table?

30. What does the term *column* mean in reference to a table?

31. What is a nested FOR/NEXT loop?

32. What is a binary search?

33. Can you use a binary search on any table? Why not?

34. When would you use the RND function?

35. Why is it necessary to reseed the random number generator?

Problems

1. What will the following programs print?

   a.
   ```
   10 READ STUDENT$,CREDITS
   20 PRINT STUDENT$,CREDITS
   30 DATA SULLIVAN,82
   ```

   b.
   ```
   10 READ STUDENT$,CREDITS
   20 WHILE STUDENT$ <> "EXIT"
   30     PRINT STUDENT$,CREDITS
   40     READ STUDENT$,CREDITS
   50 WEND
   60 DATA SULLIVAN,82
   70 DATA MARSHALL,43
   80 DATA O'BRIEN,12
   90 DATA EXIT,-9
   ```

   c.
   ```
   10 WHILE STUDENT$ <> "EXIT"
   20     READ STUDENT$,CREDITS
   30     PRINT STUDENT$,CREDITS
   40 WEND
   50 DATA SULLIVAN,82,MARSHALL,43,
          O'BRIEN,12,EXIT,-9
   ```

   d.
   ```
   10 READ STUDENT$,CREDITS
   20 WHILE STUDENT$ = "SULLIVAN"
   30     PRINT STUDENT$
   40     READ STUDENT$,CREDITS
   50 WEND
   60 DATA SULLIVAN,82,MARSHALL,43
   70 DATA O'BRIEN,12,EXIT,-9
   ```

   e.
   ```
   10 READ CREDITS
   20 WHILE CREDITS <> -9
   30     PRINT CREDITS
   40     READ CREDITS
   50 WEND
   60 DATA SULLIVAN,82
   70 DATA MARSHALL,43
   80 DATA O'BRIEN,12
   90 DATA EXIT,-9
   ```

   f.
   ```
   10 TOT.SALARY = 0
   20 DATA.COUNT = 0
   30 RESTORE
   40 READ EMP$,SALARY,RATE
   50 WHILE RATE <> -9
   60     TOT.SALARY =
              TOT.SALARY + SALARY
   70     DATA.COUNT = DATA.COUNT + 1
   80     READ EMP$,SALARY,RATE
   90 WEND
   100 RESTORE
   110 READ EMP$,SALARY,RATE
   120 WHILE SALARY <> -9
   130     PCT = (SALARY / TOT.SALARY) * 100
   140     PRINT
              USING "\     \     ###%"; EMP$,PCT
   150     READ EMP$,SALARY,RATE
   160 WEND
   170 AVG = TOT.SALARY / DATA.COUNT
   180 PRINT USING "###"; AVG
   190 END
   200 DATA JONES,100,6.50
   210 DATA SMITH,400,7.20
   220 DATA -9,-9,-9
   ```

2. What will the following programs print?

   a.
   ```
   10 FOR CTR = 1 TO 4
   20     PRINT CTR
   30 NEXT CTR
   40 PRINT CTR
   ```

   b.
   ```
   10 FOR CTR = 1 TO 20 STEP 4
   20     PRINT CTR
   30 NEXT CTR
   40 PRINT CTR
   ```

   c.
   ```
   10 FOR CTR = 5 TO 1 STEP -1
   20     PRINT CTR
   30 NEXT CTR
   40 PRINT CTR
   ```

   d.
   ```
   10 TOT = 0
   20 FOR CTR = 1 TO 3
   30     TOT = TOT + 1
   40     PRINT TOT
   50 NEXT CTR
   60 PRINT TOT
   ```

   e.
   ```
   10 TOT = 0
   20 FOR CTR = 1 TO 3
   30     PRINT TOT
   40     TOT = TOT + 1
   50 NEXT CTR
   60 PRINT TOT
   ```

3. What will the following programs print?

   a.
   ```
   10 FOR CTR = 1 TO 3
   20     READ ACCT$
   30     PRINT ACCT$
   40 NEXT CTR
   50 DATA A105,B402,C302
   ```

   b.
   ```
   10 FOR CTR = 1 TO 3
   20     READ TITLE$,QTY,PRICE
   30     PRINT TITLE$,QTY,PRICE
   40 NEXT CTR
   50 DATA COBOL,34
   60 DATA PASCAL,67
   70 DATA BASIC,400
   80 DATA RPG,20
   ```

   c.
   ```
   10 FOR CTR = 1 TO 3
   20     READ ACCT$
   30     PRINT ACCT$
   40 NEXT CTR
   50 DATA A105,B402
   ```

d.
```
10 FOR CTR = 1 TO 4
20    READ TAX.TABLE(CTR)
30 NEXT CTR
40 PRINT TAX.TABLE(3)
50 DATA 30.33,46.78,20.89,42.31
```

4. What will the following programs print?

a.
```
10 FOR OUTLOOP = 1 TO 4
20    FOR INLOOP = 1 TO 3
30       PRINT OUTLOOP,INLOOP
40    NEXT INLOOP
50 NEXT OUTLOOP
```

b.
```
10 FOR OUTLOOP = 2 TO 6
20    FOR INLOOP = 1 TO 2
30       PRINT INLOOP,OUTLOOP
40    NEXT INLOOP
50 NEXT OUTLOOP
```

5. A WHILE/WEND loop could be used in all of the following situations. When would a FOR/NEXT loop also be appropriate?

a. Find the total annual contributions to a church, given the contributions for each month of the year.

b. Get data from a user at the keyboard until there are no more to enter.

c. Calculate the average score on the arithmetic test for the students in Mrs. Bias's fifth-grade class. The information is on a data file.

d. Calculate the average temperature for the day, given a temperature for each hour in the day.

e. Print the employee number, name, and salary for each of the 32 salaried employees of Genstar, Inc.

6. Write a program to display the following graph for the local elementary school to help monitor the sale of candy bars.

```
            Candy Bar Sales

Monday      $20  *******************
Tuesday     $10  **********
Wednesday   $5   *****
Thursday    $25  ************************
Friday      $9   *********
```

Store the names of the days of the week and the sales for each day in DATA statements. Each * on the graph indicates one dollar in sales; thus, if the sales on Tuesday are seven dollars, display seven *'s. (Hint: Use FOR/NEXT loops.)

7. Suppose table T has the following values:

```
T(1) = 2        T(5) = 5
T(2) = 4        T(6) = 3
T(3) = 1        T(7) = 7
T(4) = 0        T(8) = 2
```

What values will be in table T after the following routine:

```
10 FOR SUB = 2 TO 8
20    T(SUB) = T(SUB-1) + T(10-SUB)
30 NEXT SUB
```

Add the code to print the values in table T. Print four values on one line.

8. a. Using the following program code, diagram the table PROFIT.TBL showing the location of the values.

```
100 ROWMAX = 4
110 DIM PROFIT.TBL(ROWMAX)
120 FOR ROW = 1 TO ROWMAX
130    READ PROFIT.TBL(ROW)
200 NEXT ROW
210 DATA 10000
220 DATA 10987
230 DATA 86500
240 DATA 4300
```

b. Using the values in PROFIT.TBL, what will the following additional program code print?

```
300 FOR ROW = 2 TO ROWMAX
310    PRINT PROFIT.TBL(ROW)
320 NEXT ROW
```

c. Using the values in PROFIT.TBL, what will the following additional program code print? How many values in the table were checked before a match was found?

```
400 ROW = 3
410 PRINT PROFIT.TBL(ROW)
```

9. a. Using the following program code, diagram the tables CITY.TBL$ and AIR.FARE.TBL, showing the location of the values.

```
100 ROWMAX = 7
110 DIM CITY.TBL$(ROWMAX)
120 DIM AIR.FARE.TBL(ROWMAX)
130 FOR ROW = 1 TO ROWMAX
140    READ CITY.TBL$(ROW),
              AIR.FARE.TBL(ROW)
150 NEXT ROW
200 DATA CHICAGO,140
210 DATA OKLAHOMA CITY,218
220 DATA DENVER,240
230 DATA CHEYENNE,420
240 DATA SAN FRANCISCO,298
250 DATA DALLAS,248
260 DATA BOSTON,89
```

b. Using the values in CITY.TBL$ and AIR.FARE.TBL, what will the following additional program code print?

```
300 CITY$ = "SAN FRANCISCO"
310 MATCH$ = "NO"
320 ROW = 1
330 WHILE (MATCH$ = "NO") AND
          (ROW <= ROWMAX)
340    IF CITY$ = CITY.TBL$(ROW)
           THEN MATCH$ = "YES"
           ELSE ROW = ROW + 1
350 WEND
360 PRINT AIR.FARE.TBL(ROW)
```

c. How many values in the table were checked before a match was found?

d. What would be printed if CITY$ = "MILWAUKEE"?

e. Modify the program code in 9b to print a message if no match is found.

f. Suppose that inquiries about air fares are received in this order of frequency:

```
BOSTON
OKLAHOMA CITY
CHICAGO
CHEYENNE
DENVER
SAN FRANCISCO
DALLAS
```

How would you change the DATA statements to improve efficiency of the table search?

g. How could the program place the most frequently checked items at the beginning of the table?

h. Change the code so that Boolean variables are used for the MATCH$ variable.

10. a. Using the following program code, diagram the table, showing the location of the values.

```
100 ROWMAX = 6
110 COLMAX = 4
120 EXP.TABLE(ROWMAX,COLMAX)
130 FOR ROW = 1 TO ROWMAX
140    FOR COL = 1 TO COLMAX
150        READ EXP.TABLE(ROW,COL)
160    NEXT COL
170 NEXT ROW
200 DATA 100.25,500.60,35.50,46.50
210 DATA 125.60,842.78,46.70,0
220 DATA 118.40,678.23,35.50,0
230 DATA 98.55,1000.20,38.90,25.00
240 DATA 102.45,980.76,42.75,0
250 DATA 105.60,1200.98,35.50,0
```

b. This table represents a six-month budget. The rows of the table represent the first six months of the year. The columns represent monthly bills in the following order: utilities (gas and electricity), VISA, telephone, and medical. Write a routine that requests the user to enter a month from 1 to 6 and then prints the bills for the month and their total.

c. Modify the code in problem 10b so that the name of the month is printed. For example, if the user enters 1, the program should print JANUARY. Use a table for the names of the months.

d. Write a routine that requests the user to enter a number from 1 to 4 and then prints the bills in that category for the six months as well as the total. Be sure to let the user know that the categories are as follows:

```
1 = Utilities
2 = VISA
3 = Telephone
4 = Medical
```

11. The following values are in STUDENT.TBL$ and GPA.TBL:

```
ARMACOST        3.63
BELSINGER       2.40
CONNORS         3.21
FARLEY          4.00
HAINES          2.30
JENNINGS        1.20
KANE            0.24
KERRY           2.96
MOORE           3.40
NORRIS          2.98
PARSONS         2.87
RAINES          3.12
SCANNELL        3.99
STARLING        2.53
TANYARD         3.00
VANSANT         2.50
WILSON          2.34
```

a. Write a program that requests a name and then does a binary search to find a match. When a match is found, the program should display the GPA of that student.

b. Using the tables at the beginning of this problem, diagram the path of the search to find RAINES.

c. How many names in STUDENT.TBL$ are checked before a match for RAINES is found? How many names would be checked in a serial search?

12. Write the pseudocode for a program to determine a customer's discount based on his or her credit rating. Here is the discount schedule:

Credit Rating	Discount
1	2%
2	5%
3	7%
4	10%

The program should request the user to enter a credit rating from 1 to 4 and a sales amount. Then the program should determine the new amount of sale by multiplying the amount of sale by the discount and then subtracting the discount amount from the amount of sale. Last, the program should display the discount amount and the new amount of sale.

Program Assignments

1. The records office at Sussex County College needs a program that displays a student's Social Security number if the name is entered, or the student's name if the Social Security number is entered. Write a program that:

   a. Displays a menu on the screen with two options plus the exit option. The two options are:

   ```
   1.   Find Social Security number
   2.   Find name
   ```

   b. If option 1 is selected, the user must enter a name. In response, the program searches a table to find the Social Security number. If option 2 is selected, the user must enter a Social Security number. In response, the program searches a table to find the name. In either case, if no match is found, the program should display a message to the user.

   c. After completing either option, the program returns to the menu and allows the user to select another option.

   d. Use READ/DATA statements to load the program tables with the following names and Social Security numbers:

Solter, Thomas	222-34-1200
Talbot, Gregory	231-32-5612
Heymann, Celeste	212-83-2314
Anderson, Avis	211-43-1233
Gerth, Janet	211-23-2113
Radabaugh, Jeanne	321-22-5467
Lambros, Gail	211-56-7788
Lehnert, Alice	211-34-6789

2. The local astrologist needs a program that displays the zodiac sign when the month and day of birth are entered. The birth month and day must be entered in the format *mmdd*. The program should run until the astrologist stops it. Here is the chart for birth dates and zodiac signs:

March 21 – April 19	Aries
April 20 – May 20	Taurus
May 21 – June 20	Gemini
June 21 – July 22	Cancer
July 23 – August 22	Leo
August 23 – September 22	Virgo
September 23 – October 22	Libra
October 23 – November 21	Scorpio
November 22 – December 21	Sagittarius
December 22 – January 19	Capricorn
January 20 – February 18	Aquarius
February 19 – March 20	Pisces

3. The local fast-food restaurant—O'Fast's—needs a program to calculate the total amount due from each customer. Here is a list of keys to press for each item sold:

Key	Item	Price
1	Hamburger	1.79
2	Cheeseburger	1.89
3	Fr Fries	.69
4	Milkshake	.98
5	Coke	.59
6	Sprite	.59
7	Sundae	.79

   Write a program to:

   a. Display a message requesting the item ordered and then the quantity of that item. The user must press a number from 1 to 7, depending on the item ordered, and then enter a quantity for that item. For example,

   ```
   Press number for item  7
   Enter quantity         2
   ```

   (This entry means that a customer is ordering two sundaes.) This process should continue until the user presses –1 to quit, indicating that the order is complete. Remember to display a screen chart of the numbers associated with the items and their prices for the user.

   b. The name of each item ordered, the quantity, and the total should be printed on the printer after the user enters –1 for quit. Also print the tax, which is 6%, and the final total.

   c. Next, the user must enter the amount of money received from the customer. In response, the program should display on the screen the change the customer is to receive.

   d. This process is repeated until the manager of the store enters –9 for program exit.

   e. Use a table to determine the name of the item and the price. Also use a table to keep track of a customer's order.

4. In Chapter 8, (page 186), you wrote a program to display the inventory file for Successories, Inc. The user could press any key to look at the next page of the report. The user, however, could not "page backward" to view previous screens. Modify this program assignment to:

a. Load the inventory file into a table.

b. Allow the user to press a key to page forward to view the next 12 records.

c. Allow the user to press another key to page backward to view the previous 12 records.

d. Allow the user to press a key to terminate the program.

5. Successories, Inc., needs a program to print a payroll register. Using the payroll file PAY.SEQ, write a program to:

a. Print a general heading that includes the current date and page number and column headings.

b. Print a detail line for each payroll record that includes the fields on the record (employee number, tax class, hours worked, and pay rate) plus gross pay, state tax, federal tax, FICA, and net pay. Assume that the data in the file are correct. The formulas are:

gross pay = PAY.HRS × PAY.RATE
state tax = state rate (from table) × gross pay
federal tax = federal rate (from table) × gross pay
FICA = .065 × gross pay
net pay = gross pay − (state tax + federal tax + FICA)

c. Use the following tables:

TAX CLASS	STATE TAX	FEDERAL TAX
T3	.03	.13
T5	.05	.15
T7	.07	.17
T9	.09	.19

d. Print 20 lines per page.

e. Store the following summary line messages and totals in tables and print them at the end of the report:

```
Total employees
Total gross pay
Total net pay
Total state tax
Total federal tax
Total FICA
```

f. Use the following file format and file contents (assume the data are valid):

PAY.SEQ Sequential File
PAY Record:

Field Name	Data Length	Data Type
PAY.NO$	4	String
PAY.CLASS$	2	String
PAY.HRS	3	Numeric (###)
PAY.RATE	4	Numeric (##.##)

File contents:

```
1223,T3,40,5.45
1233,T3,35,5.45
2344,T9,60,9.50
3444,T3,32,6.80
3889,T5,39,7.80
4009,T9,55,10.80
4667,T5,42,7.80
4998,T3,40,8.80
5001,T7,62,6.50
5225,T9,54,8.95
5667,T7,40,7.40
5772,T9,35,12.65
6007,T3,32,5.45
6556,T3,20,6.00
6778,T3,20,5.00
6999,T5,32,8.80
7005,T7,38,8.99
7332,T9,40,12.34
7665,T5,35,7.90
7889,T3,20,5.50
8009,T5,40,9.90
8443,T7,40,7.40
8776,T3,20,5.45
8993,T3,20,5.45
9001,T9,42,10.95
9556,T7,50,9.99
9889,T5,32,7.40
```

6. Professor Holden would like to check her students' grades and current test averages. In addition, if a name or grade is incorrect, she would like to be able to change it. Write a program to:

a. Read a sequential file named GRADE.SEQ into tables.

b. Allow Professor Holden to enter a name. If a match is found, display the student's name, three test scores, and the average test score. If a match is not found, display a message.

c. Allow Professor Holden to change the student's name or any of the test scores. Save these changes in the tables.

d. Write the data in the tables to the disk as an updated GRADE.SEQ when Professor Holden is finished. Note that the original contents will be destroyed. Use the TYPE command to check GRADE.SEQ before the update and then after the update.

e. Use this file format:

GRADE.SEQ Sequential File
GRADE Record:

Field Name	Data Length	Data Type
GRADE.NAME$	15	String
GRADE.TEST1	3	Numeric (###)
GRADE.TEST2	3	Numeric (###)
GRADE.TEST3	3	Numeric (###)

Use the system commands COPY CON or EDLIN to create a file for testing.

f. Extra credit: Add a routine to the program that creates a backup file for GRADE.SEQ before GRADE.SEQ is changed.

7. Berg's Metal Company uses the following table to determine shipping charges:

Pounds	Area 1	2	3	4
0–50	10.00	25.00	45.00	70.00
51–100	20.00	38.00	60.00	85.00
101–200	35.00	55.00	80.00	105.00
201–300	65.00	88.00	115.00	140.00
301–400	100.00	120.00	145.00	170.00
401–500	125.00	150.00	175.00	210.00

Write a program that:

a. Allows the user to enter the shipping weight and the area number (1,2,3, or 4).

b. Displays the shipping charges for that order.

c. Allows the user to enter a value to terminate the program.

d. Displays a message to the user at the end of the program.

Make up test data for each combination of area number and shipping weight.

8. Sussex County College needs a program to collect data and report the results of the teacher evaluations. Write a program to:

a. First enter an instructor's code number and then display prompts on a screen requesting one of five possible responses to a statement. There are six statements. After each

statement the user enters 1, 2, 3, 4, or 5. The statements are:

(1) Did the instructor know the material?
(2) Did the instructor test fairly?
(3) Did the instructor provide a variety of assignments?
(4) Did the instructor encourage classroom discussion?
(5) Did the course meet your expectations?
(6) Would you take another class from this instructor?

The possible responses are:

1 = Agree strongly
2 = Agree somewhat
3 = Disagree somewhat
4 = Disagree strongly
5 = Undecided

b. Keep track of the responses to each of the statements in a table.

c. The program should run until the user stops recording responses for an instructor.

d. After the user stops entering data for an instructor, print a summary report of the results. Use the format shown below.

MEAN is the average response given. For example, a mean of 1.5 indicates that the average response fell between 1 and 2. After you have completed Chapter 12, add the mode to the report. MODE is the value which occurs most often. There can be more than one mode for a set of numbers.

9. Chesapeake Airlines is a small commuter airline. Each plane seats 20 passengers in five rows of four seats each. Passengers may reserve a seat when purchasing their tickets. The airplane layout is as follows:

```
                    RESULTS OF TEACHER EVALUATIONS
                          (instructor's code)

                               RESPONSES
        STATEMENT
        NUMBER          1    2    3    4    5           MEAN

            1          ####  ####  ####  ####  ####      #.#
            2          ####  ####  ####  ####  ####      #.#
            3          ####  ####  ####  ####  ####      #.#
            4          ####  ####  ####  ####  ####      #.#
            5          ####  ####  ####  ####  ####      #.#
            6          ####  ####  ####  ####  ####      #.#
```

Report format for Assignment 8-d

Front

Row 1	A B	C D
	A B	C D
	A B	C D
	A B	C D
Row 5	A B	C D

Rear

Write a program that presents the airline clerk with a menu that offers these choices:

SEAT REQUEST
SEAT ASSIGNMENTS
STANDBY LIST

a. If the selection is SEAT REQUEST, the program should:

(1) Let the passenger request a seat by indicating a row and a letter.
(2) Place the passenger's last name in that seat position (table) if the seat is available. Names are limited to 10 characters.
(3) Ask the passenger for another selection if the seat is occupied.
(4) Assign the next empty seat starting with Row 1 Seat A, then Row 2 Seat A, etc., if the passenger does not have a choice.
(5) Print a message and place the passenger on a standby list (another table) if the plane is full.

b. If the selection is SEAT ASSIGNMENTS, the program should:

(1) Display the plane layout with the passenger names inserted, as follows:

Seat Assignments

Row	Seat A	Seat B	Seat C	Seat D
1	JEFFERS	**********	CONNORS	DAVIS
2	**********	VICKERS	**********	JOHNSON
3	BOGDAN	CARROLL	**********	HALL
4	KIMMEL	**********	DARNELL	O'SHEA
5	**********	SHINSKY	**********	**********

(2) Display the number of empty seats available. Note the empty seats are designated by 10 "*".

c. If the selection is STANDBY LIST, the program should:

(1) Display the list of names on standby as follows:

STANDBY LIST

1. GENTRY
2. AVERY
3. THOMPSON
4. HAZARD

(2) Display an appropriate message if no one is on the standby list.

d. Test the program with

(1) Fewer than 20 passengers.
(2) Exactly 20 passengers.
(3) More than 20 passengers.

Using the Data Disk

1. Insert the data disk into the disk drive.

2. Load BASIC.

3. FOR/NEXT loops

   a. Write a program using a FOR/NEXT loop to print your name 12 times on the screen.
   b. Press F7 to turn on the program trace feature and run the program again.
   c. Press F8 to turn off the trace.
   d. Write a program to print your name 12 times on the screen, indenting your name by two spaces each time so that your name appears on a diagonal down the screen.
   e. Write a program to print all the integers from 13 to 93 ending with a three.
   f. Enter the following program, described earlier in the chapter:

   ```
   NEW
   10 INPUT "Enter initial value"; INIT.VAL
   20 INPUT "Enter stopping value"; STOP.VAL
   30 INPUT "Enter increment"; INCR
   40 FOR LOOP.CTR = INIT.VAL TO STOP.VAL STEP INCR
   50     PRINT "HELLO"
   60 NEXT LOOP.CTR
   ```

   Test the program using different values.

4. Nested FOR/NEXT loops

   a. Write a FOR/NEXT loop to display an asterisk six times on one line. You must use the string "*" (not the string "******"). Your output should look as follows:

   ```
   ******
   ```

   b. Now add the code to display three lines of six asterisks. Your output should look as follows:

   ```
   ******
   ******
   ******
   ```

   c. Write a program using a nested FOR/NEXT loop to display the multiplication tables. Your output should look like this:

```
      0    1    2    3    4    5    6    7    8    9   10
-----------------------------------------------------------
 0 |  0    0    0    0    0    0    0    0    0    0    0
 1 |  0    1    2    3    4    5    6    7    8    9   10
 2 |  0    2    4    6    8   10   12   14   16   18   20
 3 |  0    3    6    9   12   15   18   21   24   27   30
 4 |  0    4    8   12   16   20   24   28   32   36   40
 5 |  0    5   10   15   20   25   30   35   40   45   50
 6 |  0    6   12   18   24   30   36   42   48   54   60
 7 |  0    7   14   21   28   35   42   49   56   63   70
 8 |  0    8   16   24   32   40   48   56   64   72   80
 9 |  0    9   18   27   36   45   54   63   72   81   90
10 |  0   10   20   30   40   50   60   70   80   90  100
```

Save this program under the name CH10-1.DD.

5. Load PROG10-1.

Change this program so that the user is presented with a menu with these two options plus an exit:

```
Enter month number
Enter month name
```

If the user selects the first option, the program should request the month number and print the corresponding month name. If the user selects the second option, the program should request the month name and print the corresponding month number. Save this program under the name CH10-2.DD.

6. Write a program to help customers find the aisle and shelf number for different products in Peter's Grocery Store. The food is organized as follows:

		Shelf				
		1	**2**	**3**	**4**	**5**
Aisle	1	Butter	Cheese	Eggs	Yogurt	Milk
	2	Lettuce	Peppers	Apples	Bananas	Oranges
	3	Rolls	Bread	Donuts	Cake	Cookies
	4	Coke	Pepsi	7-Up	Sprite	Lemonade

If a customer enters the item Milk, the computer should display:

```
Aisle 1
Shelf 5
```

If the item is not available in the store, the computer should print a message. The program should run until Peter enters a value to stop execution. Save the program under the name CH10-3.DD.

7. Test the frequency of the values that come up when you roll a pair of dice. In a table, keep track of the number of times the combinations of 2 through 12 occur. Use the RND function to select numbers 2 to 12. After "rolling the dice" 100 times, display the total number of times each number 2 through 12 was rolled.

Chapter Eleven

Data
Validation

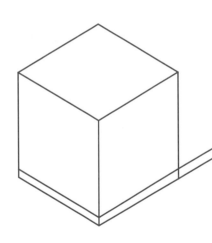

Topics

- The need for checking input data
- Control totals
- Validating data in a sequential file and creating an edit (error) report
- Validating data as they are entered from the keyboard and creating a sequential file of valid data
- Validating data in a sequential file and creating both an edit (error) report and a sequential file containing valid data

BASIC Functions

```
ASC(a$)
INSTR(n,a$,b$)
LEFT$(a$,n)
LEN(a$)
MID$(a$,m,n)
RIGHT$(a$,n)
SPACE$(n)
STR$(n)
VAL(a$)
```

BASIC Statements

```
BEEP
MID$
```

INTRODUCTION

Implicit in the programs you have seen so far is the assumption that all data files contain only valid data. This assumption is not realistic. People, even professionals trained in data entry, make mistakes. Data should always be checked for errors before they are used to generate reports, create files, or update existing files. The process of checking or editing data is called *data validation*.

This chapter begins with a discussion of various techniques used to discover errors. These techniques are illustrated in three different applications using sequential files. The first program checks the data in a sequential file and produces an edit report listing the data as well as error messages for the invalid data. The second program checks the data as they are entered from the keyboard to create a file of valid data. The third program checks the data in a sequential file, produces an edit report different in design from the report in the first sample program, and creates a sequential file of valid data.

TYPES OF DATA CHECKS

You can test data with two types of checks. One is to compare a data item against a list of acceptable entries. A second is to determine if the data item is at least a reasonable one. In both cases, a data item that passes all the checks can still be incorrect. For example, a clerk entering data in a personnel file may mistakenly press F rather than M to denote the gender of an employee. F is an allowable response, but incorrect in this instance. No program can prevent this type of error.

Whenever practical, determine if the entry is among a set of allowable responses; for example 1990 might be the only acceptable entry in a year field. If you cannot test against a list of acceptable entries, then test the field to see if the entry is reasonable. The following are among the most useful such tests:

1. *Presence.* Is there anything at all in the field? If the person entering the data presses the Enter key without first typing the appropriate information, such as name or address, the field will be empty. For some string fields, this may be the only relevant test.

2. *Class.* Are the characters in the field all numeric or all alphabetic? Very often a field should contain characters of one of these types or the other, but not both. Tax rate fields, for example, should contain only digits, and only letters are appropriate in a field containing two-character state abbreviations.

3. *Range.* Is the number in a field within a specified range? Dates are commonly tested this way. For example, is the entry in the month field in the range 1 to 12?

4. *Limit.* Does the number in a field exceed some maximum acceptable value? For example, the payroll checks of some companies may not exceed a certain value. (This is a special case of a range check in which only one end of the range is checked.)

5. *Length.* Were the expected number of characters entered into the field? For example, a five-digit zip code should contain exactly five characters.

6. *Self-checking digit.* Some or all of the digits in numeric fields can be manipulated to produce an additional digit appended to the end of the entry. The calculation is repeated during the validation; if the same extra digit is not produced, an error must have occurred during data entry.

The modulus-11 method makes effective use of a self-checking digit to discover errors. To apply it, follow these steps:

1. Begin at the right and assign a weight or checking factor in the range of 2 to 7 to each digit in the field. Assign the rightmost digit a weight of 2, the next a weight of 3, and so on, until you have assigned a weight to all of the digits in the field. If you assign the weight of 7 before reaching the leftmost digit, then begin again with 2 and continue as before.

    For example, the employee number 345-67-8910 should receive these weights:

Employee Number	3	4	5	6	7	8	9	1	0
Weights		4	3	2	7	6	5	4	3	2

2. Multiply each digit in the field by its weight factor.

3. Add the products obtained in step 2.

4. Find the modulo value (the remainder after division by 11) of the sum obtained in step 3.

5. Subtract the value obtained in step 4 from 11. If that value has one digit, use it as the self-checking digit. If the value has two digits, use the rightmost digit as the self-checking digit.

Here these steps are applied to the employee number 345-67-8910:

Employee Number	3	4	5	6	7	8	9	1	0
1. Weights		4	3	2	7	6	5	4	3	2
2. Products		12	12	10	42	42	40	36	3	0
3. Sum of products	197									
4. Modulo 11 of sum	10									
5. 11 − modulo value	1									
6. Resulting self-checking number	345-67-8910<u>1</u>									

CONTROL TOTALS

The control totals at the end of an edit report are used to verify the contents of a file. *Control totaling* or *batch balancing* helps the user to determine whether the data in the file are correct. If the data are not correct, control totaling helps the user to determine where the error may be. Some examples of helpful totals are record counts, field totals, and batch totals.

Record Counts

At the end of an edit report, the total records in the file, the total records in error, and the total valid records should be printed. The user can then check the totals. If the total number of records is less than expected, the user must check for the missing records. If the total number of records is larger than expected, possibly a record was entered more than once.

Field Totals

Control totals can be produced for all numeric fields in a record. These totals represent accumulations of entries in numeric fields containing dollar amounts or quantities. These totals are checked at the end of a validation run for accuracy.

Another type of control total is a hash total. A *hash total* is the sum of entries in numeric fields containing numbers that are not usually totaled, such as account numbers or part numbers. Although this value is meaningless, it can help verify the correctness of the numbers in a field.

Batch Totals

If large groups of records are processed, a single count of all records or a field total for the entire group may be insufficient to trace an error. Batch totals help the user find a missing record or an extra record in a very large file. For example, the records in the sales file for Berrenger's (Chapter 9) are grouped by department number. You might want to print the total number of records for each department as well as total records for the file. These totals help you locate which department group has the incorrect number of records if a discrepancy occurs. For control purposes, you can assign a batch number to groups of records in a file. Then you can verify counts of the records and field totals in each batch or control group after the data are validated.

Control totaling or batch balancing is a two-part process. Record counts, field totals, and batch totals must be calculated before the data validation program is run. After the data validation program is run, the user or the control clerk determines whether the report control totals agree with the previous totals. The user may also enter the control totals at the beginning of the program run. The program then compares the totals entered with the calculated totals and prints appropriate messages.

VALIDATING A SEQUENTIAL FILE AND WRITING AN EDIT REPORT

When data in a file is checked, each field entry in each record is checked against a set of allowable and reasonable responses. If a field in the file contains incorrect data, a message is reported to help the user, possibly a clerk in the data entry department, correct the entry. A report listing the fields in each record with an error message next to each incorrect entry helps the user correct the entries. Control totals at the end of the report also help the user verify the contents of the file. The example to illustrate these techniques is a program for a college professor.

Define the Problem

Professor Chamberlain has created a sequential file of student names and grades. Before he posts the grades, he wants to ensure that the file contains the correct information.

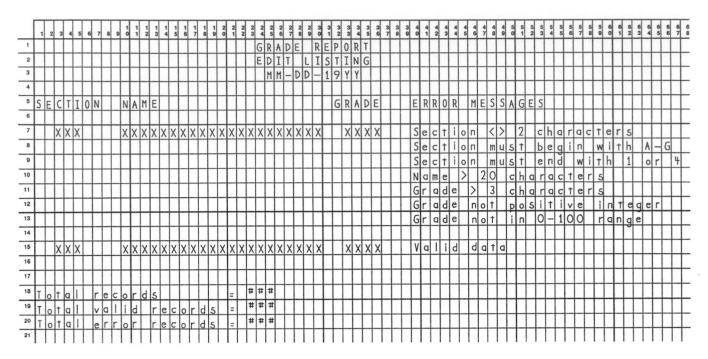

The chart shows columns numbered 1 through 68 across the top, with rows numbered 1 through 21 down the left side.

Row 1: GRADE REPORT
Row 2: EDIT LISTING
Row 3: MM-DD-19YY
Row 5: SECTION NAME GRADE ERROR MESSAGES
Row 7: XXX XXXXXXXXXXXXXXXXXXXX XXXX Section <> 2 characters
Row 8: Section must begin with A-G
Row 9: Section must end with 1 or 4
Row 10: Name > 20 characters
Row 11: Grade > 3 characters
Row 12: Grade not positive integer
Row 13: Grade not in 0-100 range
Row 15: XXX XXXXXXXXXXXXXXXXXXXX XXXX Valid data
Row 18: Total records = ###
Row 19: Total valid records = ###
Row 20: Total error records = ###

FIGURE 11.1 Report design for Program 11.1

Describe the Output

The output is the edit report shown on the print chart in Figure 11.1. The report includes headings; a listing of the data currently in the file; appropriate error messages identifying incorrect data; and totals for all records, valid records, and erroneous records. Notice that the string lengths for each of the fields on the detail line are one space longer than the maximum length of the fields. Thus, when a field exceeds its limit, the first of the extra characters is printed.

Determine the Input

The input is the sequential file of grades that Professor Chamberlain created, STUDENT.SEQ, which has this format:

STUDENT.SEQ   Sequential Input File

STUDENT record description:

Field Name	Data Length	Data Type
STUDENT.SECTION$	2	String
STUDENT.NAME$	20	String
STUDENT.GRADE$	3	String of digits

Design the Program Logic

In this program, the processing consists of checking each field in each record and totaling the record counts. For the sake of simplicity, the sample program does not include the logic for generating multiple pages, although an error report could have more than one page. These are the checks the program is to make for each field:

Check of STUDENT.SECTION$ Field

1. The entry must be exactly 2 characters long.

2. The first character of the entry must be an uppercase letter between A and G, inclusive.

3. The second character must be the digit 1 or the digit 4.

*Check of
STUDENT.NAME$
Field*

1. The entry must be no longer than 20 characters.

*Check of
STUDENT.GRADE$
Field*

1. The entry must be no longer than three digits.

2. The entry must contain only digits (0–9).

3. The numeric value of the string entry must be in the range of 0 to 100.

The structure chart and pseudocode for Program 11.1 are shown in Figure 11.2.

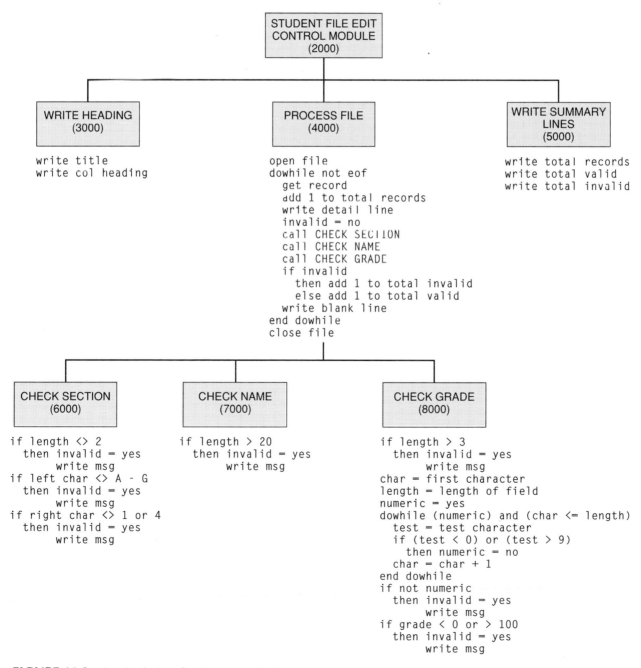

FIGURE 11.2   Logic design for Program 11.1

Program 11.1

```
1000 ' PROG11-1
1010 ' *****************************
1020 ' *       STUDENT FILE EDIT        *
1030 ' *****************************
1040 '
1050 ' *****************************
1060 ' *           VARIABLES            *
1070 ' *****************************
1080 '
1090 ' STUDENT.SEQ                 File of student records
1100 ' Student record:
1110 '     STUDENT.SECTION$
1120 '     STUDENT.NAME$
1130 '     STUDENT.GRADE$
1140 '
1150 ' CHAR                    Counter in numeric check
1160 ' DETAIL$                 Format for detail line
1170 ' INVALID                 Flag to indicate error
1180 ' LENGTH                  Temporary area used for length in numeric check
1190 ' NUMERIC                 Flag to indicate numeric error
1200 ' TEST$                   Temporary variable used in numeric check
1210 '
1220 ' *****************************
1230 ' *           CONSTANTS            *
1240 ' *****************************
1250 '
1260   YES = -1                  'Value for true
1270   NO  =  0                  'Value for false
1280   COL = 40                  'TAB position for messages
1290 '
1300 '          MESSAGES
1310 '
1320   MSG1$ = "Valid data"
1330   MSG2$ = "Section <> 2 characters"
1340   MSG3$ = "Section must begin with A-G"
1350   MSG4$ = "Section must end with 1 or 4"
1360   MSG5$ = "Name > 20 characters"
1370   MSG6$ = "Grade > 3 characters"
1380   MSG7$ = "Grade not positive integer"
1390   MSG8$ = "Grade not in 0-100 range"
1400 '
1410 ' *****************************
1420 ' *     INITIALIZED VARIABLES     *
1430 ' *****************************
1440 '
1450   TOTAL.INVALID = 0         'Total error records in file
1460   TOTAL.RECORDS = 0         'Total number of records in file
1470   TOTAL.VALID   = 0         'Total valid records in file
1999 '
2000 ' *****************************
2010 ' *          CONTROL MODULE        *
2020 ' *****************************
2030 '
2040   GOSUB 3000                'Write Heading
2050   GOSUB 4000                'Process File
2060   GOSUB 5000                'Write Summary Lines
2070   END
2999 '
3000 ' *****************************
3010 ' *           WRITE HEADING        *
3020 ' *****************************
3030 '
3040   LPRINT TAB(24); "GRADE REPORT"
3050   LPRINT TAB(24); "EDIT LISTING"
3060   LPRINT TAB(25); DATE$
```

Program 11.1   (continued)

```
3070    LPRINT
3080    LPRINT    "SECTION    NAME                            GRADE    ERROR MESSAGES"
3090    DETAIL$ = "  \ \     \                    \  \  \"
3100    LPRINT
3110    RETURN
3999 '
4000 ' *****************************
4010 ' *         PROCESS FILE         *
4020 ' *****************************
4030 '
4040    OPEN "STUDENT.SEQ" FOR INPUT AS #1
4050    WHILE NOT EOF(1)
4060        INPUT #1, STUDENT.SECTION$,
                      STUDENT.NAME$,
                      STUDENT.GRADE$
4070        TOTAL.RECORDS = TOTAL.RECORDS + 1
4080        LPRINT USING DETAIL$; STUDENT.SECTION$,
                                  STUDENT.NAME$,
                                  STUDENT.GRADE$;
4090        INVALID = NO
4100        GOSUB 6000              'Check Section
4110        GOSUB 7000              'Check Name
4120        GOSUB 8000              'Check Grade
4130        IF INVALID THEN  TOTAL.INVALID = TOTAL.INVALID + 1
                      ELSE   LPRINT TAB(COL); MSG1$:
                             TOTAL.VALID = TOTAL.VALID + 1
4140        LPRINT
4150    WEND
4160    CLOSE #1
4170    RETURN
4999 '
5000 ' *****************************
5010 ' *      WRITE SUMMARY LINES      *
5020 ' *****************************
5030 '
5040    LPRINT
5050    LPRINT USING "Total records       = ###"; TOTAL.RECORDS
5060    LPRINT USING "Total valid records = ###"; TOTAL.VALID
5070    LPRINT USING "Total error records = ###"; TOTAL.INVALID
5080    RETURN
5999 '
6000 ' *****************************
6010 ' *        CHECK SECTION         *
6020 ' *****************************
6030 '
6040    IF LEN(STUDENT.SECTION$) <> 2
            THEN INVALID = YES:
                 LPRINT TAB(COL); MSG2$
6050 '
6060    IF   (LEFT$(STUDENT.SECTION$,1) < "A")
          OR (LEFT$(STUDENT.SECTION$,1) > "G")
               THEN INVALID = YES: LPRINT TAB(COL); MSG3$
6070 '
6080    IF     (RIGHT$(STUDENT.SECTION$,1) <> "1")
           AND (RIGHT$(STUDENT.SECTION$,1) <> "4")
               THEN INVALID = YES: LPRINT TAB(COL); MSG4$
6090    RETURN
6999 '
7000 ' *****************************
7010 ' *          CHECK NAME          *
7020 ' *****************************
7030 '
7040    IF LEN(STUDENT.NAME$) > 20
            THEN INVALID = YES:
                 LPRINT TAB(COL); MSG5$
```

Program 11.1 (continued)

```
7050    RETURN
7999    '
8000    ' ****************************
8010    ' *         CHECK GRADE          *
8020    ' ****************************
8030    '
8040    IF LEN(STUDENT.GRADE$) > 3
              THEN INVALID = YES:
                    LPRINT TAB(COL); MSG6$
8050    '
8060    CHAR    = 1
8070    LENGTH  = LEN(STUDENT.GRADE$)
8080    NUMERIC = YES
8090    WHILE (NUMERIC) AND (CHAR <= LENGTH)
8100        TEST$ = MID$(STUDENT.GRADE$,CHAR,1)
8110        IF (TEST$ < "0") OR (TEST$ > "9")
                  THEN NUMERIC = NO
8120        CHAR = CHAR + 1
8130    WEND
8140    IF NOT NUMERIC
              THEN INVALID = YES:
                    LPRINT TAB(COL); MSG7$
8150    '
8160    IF   (VAL(STUDENT.GRADE$) < 0)
          OR (VAL(STUDENT.GRADE$) > 100)
                THEN INVALID = YES: LPRINT TAB(COL); MSG8$
8170    RETURN
```

Code the Program Instructions

Program 11.1 is the code based on the structure chart in Figure 11.2. The following BASIC built-in functions allow you to code the string evaluations required for this program.

LEN The LEN function returns the number of characters in a string, including any blanks and unprintable characters.

```
10 A$ = "11 Hunt Farms Ct."
20 PRINT LEN(A$)
RUN
 17
```

**LEFT$** LEFT$(A$,N) returns a string of the leftmost N characters of A$. N may not be larger than 255.

```
10 A$ = "Data Processing"
20 PRINT LEFT$(A$,4)
RUN
Data
```

**RIGHT$** RIGHT$(A$,N) returns a string of the rightmost N characters of A$. Again, N may not be larger than 255.

```
10 A$ = "Data Processing"
20 PRINT RIGHT$(A$,4)
RUN
sing
```

**MID$**   MID$(A$,M[,N]) returns part of the string A$. The string returned is N characters long, beginning with the Mth character in A$. N may range from 0 to 255 and M from 1 to 255. If N is omitted or if fewer than N characters are to the right of the Mth character, all rightmost characters are returned.

```
10 A$ = "Data Processing"
20 PRINT MID$(A$,6,7)
RUN
Process
```

LEFT$, RIGHT$, and MID$ are useful functions when you need to evaluate a character or characters within a variable. See Table 11.1 for more examples of these functions.

VAL   VAL(A$) returns the numeric value of A$. If the first character of A$ is not numeric, VAL(A$) returns 0.

```
10 A$ = "56.8"
20 PRINT VAL(A$)
RUN
 56.8
```

VAL("56.8") is treated as a numeric value. Notice the leading space inserted before the printed value. Here is an example of the use of this function in a mathematical expression:

```
10 A$ = "25.67"
20 T = VAL(A$) + 3
30 PRINT T
RUN
 28.67
```

In the next example, only the number 12 is printed because once BASIC encounters a nonnumeric character, BASIC ignores the rest of the string.

```
10 A$ = "12 Chester Ct"
20 PRINT VAL(A$)
RUN
 12
```

Several aspects of Program 11.1 warrant comment. Notice that the messages are assigned in the CONSTANTS section of the program. If you need to change the program messages, you can find them easily in one section of the program.

The INPUT # statement in line 4060 specifies only string variable names. Because the data in the file may be invalid, string variable names must be used. If a numeric variable name is used and if that field contains nonnumeric data, the system gives the field a value of zero. In that case, the value printed on the edit report would not reflect the actual contents of the field, and, if zero were an acceptable value, the program would not signal an error.

Table 11.1   Examples of LEFT\$, RIGHT\$, and MID\$

Statement	Result
Assume A\$ = GARBAGE IN GARBAGE OUT (GIGO)	
100 T\$ = LEFT\$(A\$,10)	T\$ = GARBAGE IN
110 T\$ = LEFT\$(A\$,1)	T\$ = G
120 T\$ = LEFT\$(A\$,280)	Illegal function call
130 T\$ = LEFT\$(A\$,0)	T\$ = null character
200 T\$ = RIGHT\$(A\$,6)	T\$ = (GIGO)
210 T\$ = RIGHT\$(A\$,1.8)	T\$ = O) (A decimal value is rounded.)
220 T\$ = RIGHT\$(A\$,–2)	Illegal function call
300 T\$ = MID\$(A\$,12,11)	T\$ = GARBAGE OUT
310 T\$ = MID\$(A\$,24)	T\$ = (GIGO)
320 T\$ = MID\$(A\$,100,4)	T\$ = null character

Note the LPRINT statement in line 4080. This statement ends with a semicolon so that the first error message or the valid data message will be printed on the same line as the data. The constant COL (line 1280) is used as the TAB argument in the statements to print the error messages. That way, if you decide to change the starting position of the error messages on the report, you have to change only one value in the program. Also note that the program does not perform any format editing of the data such as right-justifying the grade field; that should be done only *after* the data are validated and any needed data corrections are made.

Notice the use of a flag to decide what action the program takes. The error flag INVALID is set to NO (line 4090) before the modules to check the fields are called. Whenever an error is detected in the processing of a record, INVALID is set to YES. After all fields are checked, INVALID is checked (line 4130) to determine which counter, TOTAL.INVALID or TOTAL.VALID, should be incremented.

Look at the three modules that perform the validation checks.

1. In the CHECK SECTION module, LEN is used to check the length of the field. If the section is not equal to two characters (line 6040), the program sets the invalid flag to YES and prints a message. LEFT\$ is used to check that the leftmost character of the section field is an uppercase letter from A to G (line 6060). RIGHT\$ is used to check that the rightmost character is a 1 or a 4 (line 6080).

2. The only check in the CHECK NAME module is for length. Although STUDENT.NAME\$ could have been checked for uppercase and lowercase letters, note that one of the names in the data is JOHN DALY 3RD (see Figure 11.3). Sometimes a name may contain a number.

3. In the CHECK GRADE module, LEN is used just as in the other two modules. In addition, MID\$ is used within a dowhile loop (lines 8090–8130) to determine whether all of the characters are digits; that is, whether each character has an ASCII value within

the range of "0" to "9". If the character being checked is not in the range of 0 to 9, then the flag NUMERIC is set to NO, indicating a nonnumeric character. The variables LENGTH and TEST\$ are used to make the purpose of the WHILE and IF statements easy to read. The WHILE/WEND loop processes the field one character at a time until a nonnumeric character is found or all the characters have been checked.

Finally, VAL is used to determine whether the numeric value of the string is in the range 0 to 100. The VAL function evaluates the numeric value of a string variable. Remember, however, that the VAL function evaluates the characters in a string variable only until a nonnumeric value is encountered. If an entry contains nonnumeric characters, no error message is printed. For instance, the lines with *8, ZZ, and XXXX in the grade field do not cause the message "Grade not in 0–100 range" to be printed (see Figure 11.3). The reason no error message was printed is that VAL evaluated each of the entries beginning with a nonnumeric character as 0. (Can you think of a way to modify Program 11.1 so that the message "Grade not in 0–100 range" is printed when the field contains nonnumeric characters?)

Notice that more than one error message appears when a grade is not in the range 0–100. Likewise, an error in a section entry may generate more than one error message. In each case, one message would have been sufficient to signal an error in the field. Sometimes, however, messages that describe the error further—such as "Grade > 3 characters" or "Grade not positive integer"—are helpful to the user. Be sure to check with the user of the error report to see whether the error messages are sufficiently specific. Also, some users may want only the invalid records printed on the report and not the valid records.

Test the Program

Assume that Professor Chamberlain's student grade file, STUDENT.SEQ, contains the following data:

```
A1,PHILIP SMITH,99
I1,JANINE POWELL,*8
F3,ANN JACKSON,196
B4,JOHN DALY 3RD,-3
1A,MICHAEL BLAIR,ZZ
C1,,.92
XXX,XXXXXXXXXXXXXXXXXXXXX,XXXX
B1,LAURA SMITH,95
```

(Professor Chamberlain is remarkably unskilled in data entry!) When the program is run with these data, the report shown in Figure 11.3 is printed.

At the end of the report for Professor Chamberlain, the total records in the file, total valid records, and total invalid records are shown. These totals tell Professor Chamberlain whether he has included all his students. If the total number of records is less than the number of students, he needs to check which students he omitted. If the total is larger than the number of students, he should check whether he entered a name more than once.

```
                          GRADE REPORT
                          EDIT LISTING
                          07-07-1989
   SECTION   NAME              GRADE   ERROR MESSAGES
    A1       PHILIP SMITH       99     Valid data
    I1       JANINE POWELL      *8     Section must begin with A-G
                                       Grade not positive integer

    F3       ANN JACKSON       196     Section must end with 1 or 4
                                       Grade not in 0-100 range

    B4       JOHN DALY 3RD      -3     Grade not positive integer
                                       Grade not in 0-100 range

    1A       MICHAEL BLAIR      ZZ     Section must begin with A-G
                                       Section must end with 1 or 4
                                       Grade not positive integer

    C1                         .92     Grade not positive integer

    XXX      XXXXXXXXXXXXXXXXXX XXXX    Section <> 2 characters
                                       Section must begin with A-G
                                       Section must end with 1 or 4
                                       Grade > 3 characters
                                       Grade not positive integer

    B1       LAURA SMITH        95     Valid data

   Total records       =   8
   Total valid records =   2
   Total error records =   6
```

FIGURE 11.3 Output of Program 11.1

VALIDATING DURING DATA ENTRY

Data can be validated as they are entered from the keyboard. They need not be stored in a file and checked later. Again, a program for Professor Chamberlain illustrates the techniques.

Define the Problem

Professor Chamberlain wants to create the file STUDENT.SEQ, but this time he would like each field checked as he enters the data from the keyboard. In addition, he noticed that the previous grade report (Figure 11.3) showed no error message when he forgot to enter a name. This time, he wants the program to check for the presence of data. To verify the data, he plans to use his calculator to sum the grade field. The program should print a hash total of the grades.

Describe the Output

The final output of this program is the disk file STUDENT.SEQ and a message displayed on the screen at the end of processing. The message should report the creation of the file, the number of records written to the file, and the total value of the grade field.

Determine the Input

The input will be Professor Chamberlain's responses to screen prompts. After entering all the necessary information, the professor must enter the letter N in response to the prompt "Enter record (Y/N)?" to end the input portion of the program.

The following example shows the program's prompts and some error messages generated by Professor Chamberlain's responses to those prompts.

```
Student Section? A2
Section must end with 1 or 4

Student Section? A1
Student Name   ? Elaine Bright
Student Grade  ? 1111
Grade > 3 characters
Grade not in range 0-100

Student Grade  ? 83
```

Design the Program Logic

The processing will include all the checks for errors included in Program 11.1 plus a check for the presence of data in each of the three fields. The program will also need to count the number of records written to the file and to accumulate the values in the grade field in order to report these totals in a screen message at the end of the program. Review the structure chart and pseudocode for Program 11.2 in Figure 11.4.

Code the Program Instructions

Program 11.2 is one solution to Professor Chamberlain's request for a data entry program. This program includes one new statement, BEEP. BEEP causes the computer's speaker to sound for one quarter of a second.

```
100 IF CHK.BAL < 0
        THEN BEEP
```

The ASCII code for the beep is 7 (see the ASCII code chart in Appendix C), so this code also produces a beep:

```
100 IF CHK.BAL < 0
        THEN PRINT CHR$(7)
```

We recommend the first version because the purpose of the statement is obvious to the reader.

Look at the CREATE FILE module. The outer WHILE/WEND loop continues as long as the user presses Y to indicate that there are more records to enter. Once in the loop, there is a FOR/NEXT loop to check the fields in a record. The variable NO.OF.ITEMS contains 3 in this program because there are three fields to check (see line 1490). The first time through the loop, the variable ITEM contains the value 1, and so statement 3110 sends control to the CHECK SECTION module. On return from that module the computer checks the error flag INVALID to see whether the field was entered correctly. If INVALID = YES the computer executes the inner WHILE/WEND loop again, returning to the CHECK SECTION module. If the section field is valid, ITEM is incremented by 1 to become 2. After line 3110 is executed, control passes to the CHECK NAME module. On return from that module, the error flag INVALID is checked. After the name is entered correctly, the process is repeated a third time for the grade field.

This WHILE/WEND, FOR/NEXT, WHILE/WEND loop structure may appear confusing at first. But note how easy it would be to add the code necessary to check another field if a fourth field were added to the record. Just change NO.OF.ITEMS to 4, add a module number to line 3110, and add the module to check the new field.

Also, notice that the computer sounds a beep whenever the program detects an error (line 3120). The beep alerts the person at the keyboard that a field has been entered incorrectly. The beep is especially helpful if the user

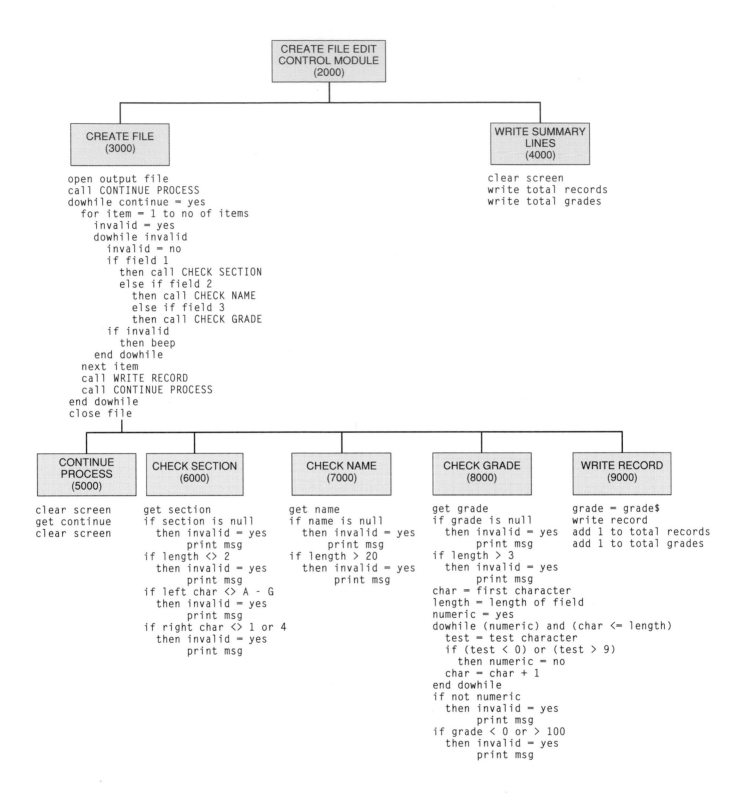

FIGURE 11.4   Logic design for Program 11.2

Program 11.2

```
1000 ' PROG11-2
1010 ' *****************************
1020 ' *       CREATE FILE EDIT        *
1030 ' *****************************
1040 '
1050 ' *****************************
1060 ' *           VARIABLES           *
1070 ' *****************************
1080 '
1090 ' STUDENT.SEQ               File of student records
1100 ' Student record:
1110 '     STUDENT.SECTION$
1120 '     STUDENT.NAME$
1130 '     STUDENT.GRADE
1140 '
1150 ' CHAR                     Counter in numeric check
1160 ' CONTINUE$                Process record flag
1170 ' INVALID                  Flag to indicate error
1180 ' ITEM                     Counter in FOR/NEXT loop
1190 ' LENGTH                   Temporary area used for length in numeric check
1200 ' NUMERIC                  Flag to indicate numeric error
1210 ' STUDENT.GRADE$           Storage for STUDENT.GRADE before edit
1220 ' TEST$                    Temporary variable used in numeric check
1230 '
1240 ' *****************************
1250 ' *           CONSTANTS           *
1260 ' *****************************
1270 '
1280   NULL$ = ""               'Empty string
1290   YES  = -1                'Value for true
1300   NO  =  0                 'Value for false
1310 '
1320 '          ERROR MESSAGES
1330 '
1340   MSG1$  = "Missing section"
1350   MSG2$  = "Section <> 2 characters"
1360   MSG3$  = "Section must begin with A-G"
1370   MSG4$  = "Section must end with 1 or 4"
1380   MSG5$  = "Missing name"
1390   MSG6$  = "Name > 20 characters"
1400   MSG7$  = "Missing grade"
1410   MSG8$  = "Grade > 3 characters"
1420   MSG9$  = "Grade not positive integer"
1430   MSG10$ = "Grade not in 0-100 range"
1440 '
1450 ' *****************************
1460 ' *     INITIALIZED VARIABLES     *
1470 ' *****************************
1480 '
1490   NO.OF.ITEMS   = 3        'Number of fields to check in record
1500   TOTAL.GRADES  = 0        'Total of grade field
1510   TOTAL.RECORDS = 0        'Total records in file
1999 '
2000 ' *****************************
2010 ' *        CONTROL MODULE         *
2020 ' *****************************
2030 '
2040   KEY OFF
2050   GOSUB 3000               'Create File
2060   GOSUB 4000               'Write Summary Lines
2070   KEY ON
2080   END
2999 '
```

PROGRAM 11.2 (continued)

```
3000 ' ******************************
3010 ' *           CREATE FILE          *
3020 ' ******************************
3030 '
3040   OPEN "STUDENT.SEQ" FOR OUTPUT AS #1
3050   GOSUB 5000                'Continue Process
3060   WHILE (CONTINUE$ = "Y") OR (CONTINUE$ = "y")
3070      FOR ITEM = 1 TO NO.OF.ITEMS
3080           INVALID = YES
3090           WHILE INVALID
3100              INVALID = NO
3110              ON ITEM GOSUB 6000, 7000, 8000  'Check Section
                                                  'Check Name
                                                  'Check Grade
3120              IF INVALID
                     THEN BEEP: PRINT
3130           WEND
3140      NEXT ITEM
3150      GOSUB 9000               'Write Record
3160      GOSUB 5000               'Continue Process
3170   WEND
3180   CLOSE #1
3190   RETURN
3999 '
4000 ' ******************************
4010 ' *      WRITE SUMMARY LINES     *
4020 ' ******************************
4030 '
4040   CLS
4050   PRINT "Creation of STUDENT.SEQ complete"
4060   PRINT "Total records ="; TOTAL.RECORDS
4070   PRINT
4080   PRINT
4090   PRINT "Total value of grade field ="; TOTAL.GRADES
4100   RETURN
4999 '
5000 ' ******************************
5010 ' *      CONTINUE PROCESS       *
5020 ' ******************************
5030 '
5040   CLS
5050   INPUT "Enter record (Y/N)"; CONTINUE$
5060   CLS
5070   RETURN
5999 '
6000 ' ******************************
6010 ' *           CHECK SECTION         *
6020 ' ******************************
6030 '
6040   INPUT "Student Section"; STUDENT.SECTION$
6050   IF STUDENT.SECTION$ = NULL$
          THEN INVALID = YES:
                PRINT MSG1$
6060 '
6070   IF LEN(STUDENT.SECTION$) <> 2
          THEN INVALID = YES:
                PRINT MSG2$
6080 '
6090   IF   (LEFT$(STUDENT.SECTION$,1) < "A")
         OR (LEFT$(STUDENT.SECTION$,1) > "G")
                THEN INVALID = YES: PRINT MSG3$
6100 '
```

PROGRAM 11.2 (continued)

```
6110 · IF      (RIGHT$(STUDENT.SECTION$,1) <> "1")
          AND (RIGHT$(STUDENT.SECTION$,1) <> "4")
              THEN INVALID = YES: PRINT MSG4$
6120   RETURN
6999 '
7000 ' ****************************
7010 ' *         CHECK NAME         *
7020 ' ****************************
7030 '
7040   INPUT "Student Name   "; STUDENT.NAME$
7050   IF STUDENT.NAME$ = NULL$
          THEN INVALID = YES:
              PRINT MSG5$
7060 '
7070   IF LEN(STUDENT.NAME$) > 20
          THEN INVALID = YES:
              PRINT MSG6$
7080   RETURN
7999 '
8000 ' ****************************
8010 ' *         CHECK GRADE        *
8020 ' ****************************
8030 '
8040   INPUT "Student Grade  "; STUDENT.GRADE$
8050   IF STUDENT.GRADE$ = NULL$
          THEN INVALID = YES:
              PRINT MSG7$
8060 '
8070   IF LEN(STUDENT.GRADE$) > 3
          THEN INVALID = YES:
              PRINT MSG8$
8080 '
8090   CHAR    = 1
8100   LENGTH  = LEN(STUDENT.GRADE$)
8110   NUMERIC = YES
8120   WHILE (NUMERIC) AND (CHAR <= LENGTH)
8130      TEST$ = MID$(STUDENT.GRADE$,CHAR,1)
8140      IF (TEST$ < "0") OR (TEST$ > "9")
              THEN NUMERIC = NO
8150      CHAR = CHAR + 1
8160   WEND
8170   IF NOT NUMERIC
          THEN INVALID = YES:
              PRINT MSG9$
8180 '
8190   IF   (VAL(STUDENT.GRADE$) < 0)
        OR (VAL(STUDENT.GRADE$) > 100)
              THEN INVALID = YES: PRINT MSG10$
8200   RETURN
8999 '
9000 ' ****************************
9010 ' *         WRITE RECORD       *
9020 ' ****************************
9030 '
9040   STUDENT.GRADE = VAL(STUDENT.GRADE$)
9050   WRITE #1, STUDENT.SECTION$,
              STUDENT.NAME$,
              STUDENT.GRADE
9060   TOTAL.RECORDS = TOTAL.RECORDS + 1
9070   TOTAL.GRADES  = TOTAL.GRADES + STUDENT.GRADE
9080   RETURN
```

does not look at the screen while entering data. *Caution!* Remember to check with the user about including the beep in a program. Some users find this noise irritating rather than helpful.

Notice that the variable list contains two similar variables, STUDENT.GRADE and STUDENT.GRADE$. STUDENT.GRADE$ functions as storage for characters entered as a grade until they are validated. A string variable must be used for this purpose because an attempt to enter non-numeric characters into a numeric variable will generate the screen message ?REDO FROM START, at which point the user must enter a new value.

The writer of Program 11.2 could have used the numeric variable STUDENT.GRADE in the INPUT statement in line 8040 and deleted the grade checking statements. The system message ?REDO FROM START, however, is not descriptive, and the user may have trouble correcting the error. Also, the CHECK GRADE module does not allow grades that contain decimal positions or grades outside the range 0–100. Without the CHECK GRADE module, these errors would go undetected.

Once the program determines that the grade is valid, it uses the VAL function to assign the numeric equivalent of STUDENT.GRADE$ to STUDENT.GRADE (line 9040) and writes STUDENT.GRADE to the file along with the other two fields (line 9050).

A new feature of Program 11.2 is the use of NULL$ to test for the presence of characters in each field. NULL$ is set equal to the null string in line 1280 and then used to check that the user has entered a value in each field (lines 6050, 7050, and 8050).

Test the Program

The output of this program is the disk file STUDENT.SEQ and an end-of-job message written on the screen. Although STUDENT.SEQ contains valid data, remember that the contents of each field are not necessarily accurate. The program accepts B1 as the section even when A1 is the correct section. It accepts meaningless names like "XXXXXXXXX". If the grade is mistakenly entered as 89 rather than 98, however, the hash total produced by the program should be different than the total calculated by Professor Chamberlain. This difference in control totals should alert Professor Chamberlain to the fact that a grade was entered incorrectly. Thus, even though the program cannot detect all possible errors, it allows Professor Chamberlain to avoid many of his usual data entry errors.

WRITING VALID DATA TO AN OUTPUT FILE

When a file is edited, the valid data are sometimes placed in a file during the edit run. The incorrect records are corrected and later added to the valid sequential file. Also, when editing a file, you may have limited space on the report for error messages. Instead of printing the error messages next to each incorrect record, you may have to print a code for each incorrect field. If you use this method, you must print a key to the error codes at the end of the report. Also, your report is more readable if you highlight the fields in error. Putting asterisks next to the entry or underlining it with asterisks are common ways to highlight errors. The program to illustrate these techniques is to be developed for Lowell and Bauer, Attorneys at Law.

Define the Problem

Lowell and Bauer need a program to validate the data in their billing file and produce an edit report and a new sequential billing file containing only valid data.

Describe the Output

The output will be a sequential file with valid data and an edit report listing. The sequential output file has this format:

BILL-OUT.SEQ   Sequential Output file
BILL record description:

Field Name	Data Length	Data Type
BILL.ACCT$	3	String
BILL.NAME$	20	String
BILL.HRS	3	Numeric (###)
BILL.RATE	5	Numeric (##.##)

Figure 11.5 shows a print chart for the edit report. The string lengths to be printed are defined as they are in Program 11.1; they contain one space

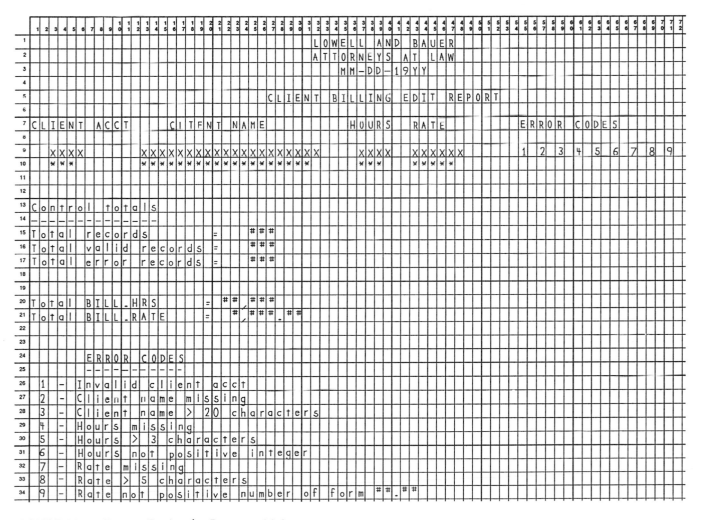

FIGURE 11.5   Report Design for Program 11.3

more than the maximum allowable field length so that the first of any extra characters can be printed. Again, the numeric fields in the detail lines are not edited (justified, dollar signs added, and so on) in the edit report because they may be invalid.

The report differs from the edit report generated by Program 11.1 in that it highlights the fields in error with asterisks and lists only error codes on the detail lines with an explanation of the error codes at the end of the report.

Determine the Input

The input is the billing file. Its format is:

BILL-IN.SEQ   Sequential Input File
BILL record description:

Field Name	Data Length	Data Type
BILL.ACCT$	3	String
BILL.NAME$	20	String
BILL.HRS$	3	String
BILL.RATE$	5	String

Design the Program Logic

This program must check each field in each record to validate the data. These are the checks to be performed for each field:

Check of BILL.ACCT$ Field

The sequence of characters in the field must match a character set in a table of valid client account numbers. Because a set of allowable responses exists, it is not necessary to perform any other checks unless the user requests them.

Check of BILL.NAME$ Field

1. There must be an entry in the field (presence).

2. The entry can have a maximum of 20 characters.

Check of BILL.HRS$ Field

1. There must be an entry in the field (presence).

2. The maximum length is three characters.

3. The entry must be a positive integer.

Check of BILL.RATE$ Field

1. There must be an entry in the field (presence).

2. The maximum length is five characters, including the decimal point.

3. The entry must be a positive numeric value, with a maximum integer value of 99 and a maximum decimal value of .99.

The structure chart and pseudocode for Program 11.3 are shown in Figure 11.6.

Code the Program Instructions

Program 11.3 represents one way to validate the BILL-IN.SEQ file.

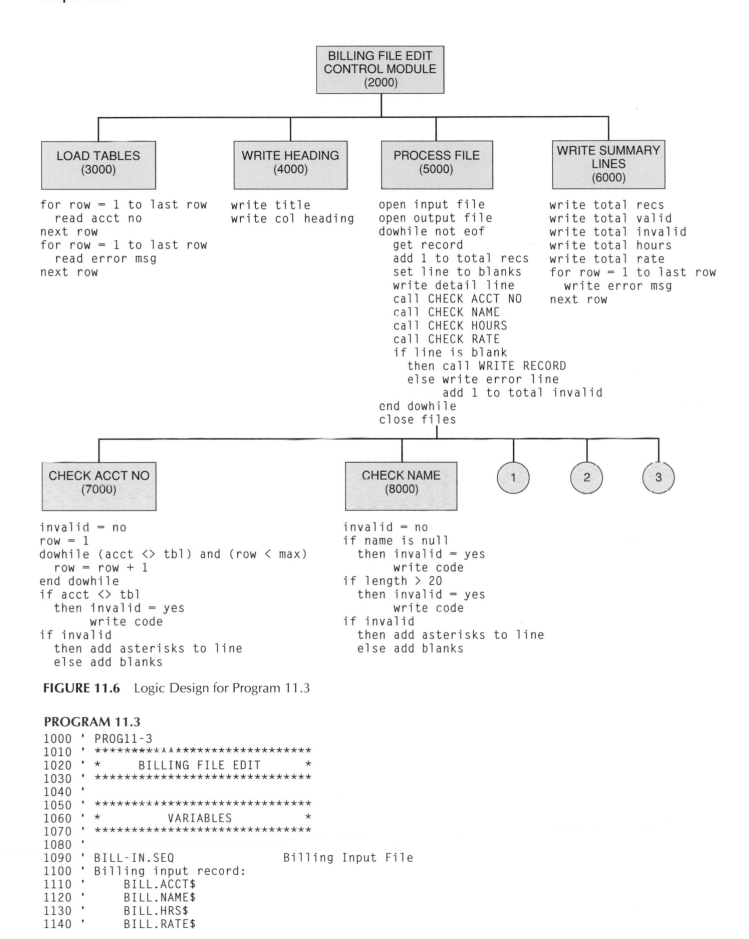

FIGURE 11.6   Logic Design for Program 11.3

PROGRAM 11.3
```
1000 ' PROG11-3
1010 ' ****************************
1020 ' *      BILLING FILE EDIT      *
1030 ' ****************************
1040 '
1050 ' ****************************
1060 ' *          VARIABLES          *
1070 ' ****************************
1080 '
1090 ' BILL-IN.SEQ              Billing Input File
1100 ' Billing input record:
1110 '      BILL.ACCT$
1120 '      BILL.NAME$
1130 '      BILL.HRS$
1140 '      BILL.RATE$
```

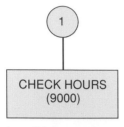

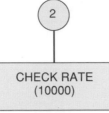

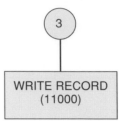

```
invalid = no                    INVALID = NO                    hours = hours$
if hours is null                if rate is null                 rate = rate$
  then invalid = yes              then invalid = yes            write record
      write code                      write code                add 1 to total valid
if length > 3                   if length > 5                   add hours to total hours
  then invalid = yes              then invalid = yes            add rate to total rate
      write code                      write code
test = hours                    find decimal position
length = length of field        integer = integer values
call NUMERIC CHECK              decimal = decimal values
if not numeric                  if (integers > 2) or (decimals > 2)
  then invalid = yes              then numeric = no
      write code                  else test = rate
if invalid                            length = length of field
  then add asterisks to line          call NUMERIC CHECK
  else add blanks               if not numeric
                                  then invalid = yes
                                      write code
                                if invalid
                                  then add asterisks to line
                                  else add blanks
```

```
NUMERIC
CHECK
(12000)
```

```
char = first character
numeric = yes
dowhile (numeric) and
        (char <= length)
  if (test char < 0) or
     (test char > 9)
    then numeric = no
  char = char + 1
end dowhile
```

```
NUMERIC
CHECK
(12000)
```

FIGURE 11.6   Logic Design for Program 11.3 (continued)

PROGRAM 11.3   (continued)

```
1150 '
1160 ' BILL-OUT.SEQ                Billing output file
1170 ' Billing output record:
1180 '     BILL.ACCT$
1190 '     BILL.NAME$
1200 '     BILL.HRS
1210 '     BILL.RATE
1220 '
1230 ' CHAR                        Counter in numeric check
1240 ' DECIMAL$                    Decimal portion in BILL.RATE$
1250 ' DEC.POS                     Position of decimal point
1260 ' DETAIL$                     Format for detail line
1270 ' INTEGER$                    Integer portion of BILL.RATE$
1280 ' INVALID                     Flag to indicate error
1290 ' LENGTH                      Temporary area used for length in numeric check
1300 ' NUMERIC                     Flag to indicate numeric error
1310 ' ROW                         Table subscript
1320 '
```

PROGRAM 11.3 (continued)

```
1330 ' ******************************
1340 ' *          CONSTANTS            *
1350 ' ******************************
1360 '
1370   COL = 55                    'TAB position for error codes
1380   NULL$ = ""                  'Empty string
1390   YES = -1                    'Value for true
1400   NO  =  0                    'Value for false
1410 '
1420 '        "*" FOR ERROR LINE
1430 '
1440   BLANK$  = SPACE$(47)
1450   BLANK1$ = SPACE$(5)
1460   AST1$   = SPACE$(2) + STRING$(3,"*")
1470   BLANK2$ = SPACE$(27)
1480   AST2$   = SPACE$(7) + STRING$(20,"*")
1490   BLANK3$ = SPACE$(7)
1500   AST3$   = SPACE$(4) + STRING$(3,"*")
1510   BLANK4$ = SPACE$(8)
1520   AST4$   = SPACE$(3) + STRING$(5,"*")
1530 '
1540 ' ******************************
1550 ' *    INITIALIZED VARIABLES   *
1560 ' ******************************
1570 '
1580   TOTAL.INVALID = 0      'Total error records in file
1590   TOTAL.RECORDS = 0      'Total number of records in file
1600   TOTAL.INVALID = 0      'Total valid records in file
1610   TOTAL.HRS    = 0       'Total of valid BILL.HRS
1620   TOTAL.RATE   = 0       'Total of valid BILL.RATE
1630 '
1640 ' ******************************
1650 ' *        DEFINE TABLES       *
1660 ' ******************************
1670 '
1680   CLIENTMAX = 15              'Number of clients in table
1690   DIM CLIENT.TBL$(CLIENTMAX)  'Table of client acct numbers
1700   MSGMAX    = 9               'Number of error messages
1710   DIM MSG.TBL$(MSGMAX)        'Table of error messages
1720 '
1730 ' ******************************
1740 ' *        DATA FOR TABLES     *
1750 ' ******************************
1760 '
1770 '          CLIENT.TBL$(ROW)
1780 '
1790   DATA     101, 150, 201, 301, 360
1800   DATA     401, 501, 540, 601, 701
1810   DATA     780, 801, 820, 901, 955
1820 '
1830 '          MSG.TBL$(ROW)
1840 '
1850   DATA     Invalid client acct
1860   DATA     Client name missing
1870   DATA     Client name > 20 characters
1880   DATA     Hours missing
1890   DATA     Hours > 3 characters
1900   DATA     Hours not positive integer
1910   DATA     Rate missing
1920   DATA     Rate > 5 characters
1930   DATA     Rate not positive number of form ##.##
1999 '
```

PROGRAM 11.3 (continued)

```
2000 ' *****************************
2010 ' *       CONTROL MODULE       *
2020 ' *****************************
2030 '
2040    GOSUB 3000                'Load Tables
2050    GOSUB 4000                'Write Heading
2060    GOSUB 5000                'Process File
2070    GOSUB 6000                'Write Summary Lines
2080    END
2999 '
3000 ' *****************************
3010 ' *          LOAD TABLES        *
3020 ' *****************************
3030 '
3040    FOR ROW = 1 TO CLIENTMAX
3050        READ CLIENT.TBL$(ROW)
3060    NEXT ROW
3070 '
3080    FOR ROW = 1 TO MSGMAX
3090        READ MSG.TBL$(ROW)
3100    NEXT ROW
3110    RETURN
3999 '
4000 ' *****************************
4010 ' *          WRITE HEADING       *
4020 ' *****************************
4030 '
4040    LPRINT TAB(32); "LOWELL AND BAUER"
4050    LPRINT TAB(32); "ATTORNEYS AT LAW"
4060    LPRINT TAB(35); DATE$
4070    LPRINT
4080    LPRINT TAB(27); "CLIENT BILLING EDIT REPORT"
4090    LPRINT
4100    LPRINT
           "CLIENT ACCT    CLIENT NAME         HOURS   RATE        ERROR CODES"
4110    LPRINT
4120    DETAIL$ =
           "  \  \         \                  \    \   \ \     \"
4130    RETURN
4999 '
5000 ' *****************************
5010 ' *          PROCESS FILE        *
5020 ' *****************************
5030 '
5040    OPEN "BILL-IN.SEQ"  FOR INPUT  AS #1
5050    OPEN "BILL-OUT.SEQ" FOR OUTPUT AS #2
5060    WHILE NOT EOF(1)
5070        INPUT #1, BILL.ACCT$, BILL.NAME$,
                    BILL.HRS$,  BILL.RATE$
5080        TOTAL.RECORDS = TOTAL.RECORDS + 1
5090        ASTLINE$ = NULL$
5100        LPRINT USING DETAIL$; BILL.ACCT$, BILL.NAME$,
                               BILL.HRS$,  BILL.RATE$;
5110        GOSUB  7000            'Check Acct No
5120        GOSUB  8000            'Check Name
5130        GOSUB  9000            'Check Hours
5140        GOSUB 10000            'Check Rate
5150        LPRINT
5160        IF ASTLINE$ = BLANK$
               THEN GOSUB 11000
               ELSE LPRINT ASTLINE$: TOTAL.INVALID = TOTAL.INVALID + 1
5170        LPRINT
5180    WEND
5190    CLOSE #1, #2
```

PROGRAM 11.3   (continued)

```
5200    RETURN
5999  '
6000  ' *****************************
6010  ' *      WRITE SUMMARY LINES      *
6020  ' *****************************
6030  '
6040    LPRINT
6050    LPRINT "Control totals"
6060    LPRINT "--------------"
6070    LPRINT USING "Total records        =    ###"; TOTAL.RECORDS
6080    LPRINT USING "Total valid records  =    ###"; TOTAL.VALID
6090    LPRINT USING "Total error records  =    ###"; TOTAL.INVALID
6100    LPRINT
6110    LPRINT
6120    LPRINT USING "Total BILL.HRS      = ##,###";    TOTAL.HRS
6130    LPRINT USING "Total BILL.RATE     =  #,###.##"; TOTAL.RATE
6140    LPRINT
6150    LPRINT
6160    LPRINT TAB(7); "ERROR CODES"
6170    LPRINT TAB(7); "-----------"
6180    LPRINT
6190    FOR ROW = 1 TO MSGMAX
6200        LPRINT USING "##"; ROW;
6210        LPRINT " - "; MSG.TBL$(ROW)
6220    NEXT ROW
6230    RETURN
6999  '
7000  ' *****************************
7010  ' *          CHECK ACCT NO          *
7020  ' *****************************
7030  '
7040    INVALID = NO
7050    ROW = 1
7060    WHILE (BILL.ACCT$ <> CLIENT.TBL$(ROW)) AND (ROW < CLIENTMAX)
7070        ROW = ROW + 1
7080    WEND
7090    IF BILL.ACCT$ <> CLIENT.TBL$(ROW)
            THEN INVALID = YES:
                LPRINT TAB(COL); "1";
7100  '
7110    IF INVALID
            THEN ASTLINE$ = ASTLINE$ + AST1$
            ELSE ASTLINE$ = ASTLINE$ + BLANK1$
7120    RETURN
7999  '
8000  ' *****************************
8010  ' *          CHECK NAME          *
8020  ' *****************************
8030  '
8040    INVALID = NO
8050    IF BILL.NAME$ = NULL$
            THEN INVALID = YES:
                LPRINT TAB(COL+2); "2";
8060  '
8070    IF LEN(BILL.NAME$) > 20
            THEN INVALID = YES:
                LPRINT TAB(COL+4); "3";
8080  '
8090    IF INVALID
            THEN ASTLINE$ = ASTLINE$ + AST2$
            ELSE ASTLINE$ = ASTLINE$ + BLANK2$
8100    RETURN
8999  '
```

PROGRAM 11.3   (continued)

```
9000 ' *****************************
9010 ' *           CHECK HOURS          *
9020 ' *****************************
9030 '
9040    INVALID = NO
9050    IF BILL.HRS$ = NULL$
            THEN INVALID = YES:
                LPRINT TAB(COL+6); "4";
9060 '
9070    IF LEN(BILL.HRS$) > 3
            THEN INVALID = YES:
                LPRINT TAB(COL+8); "5";
9080 '
9090    TEST$  = BILL.HRS$
9100    LENGTH = LEN(BILL.HRS$)
9110    GOSUB 12000                  'Numeric Check
9120    IF NOT NUMERIC
            THEN INVALID = YES:
                LPRINT TAB(COL+10); "6";
9130 '
9140    IF INVALID
            THEN ASTLINE$ = ASTLINE$ + AST3$
            ELSE ASTLINE$ = ASTLINE$ + BLANK3$
9150    RETURN
9999 '
10000 '*****************************
10010 '*           CHECK RATE           *
10020 '*****************************
10030 '
10040    INVALID = NO
10050    IF BILL.RATE$ = NULL$
            THEN INVALID = YES:
                LPRINT TAB(COL+12); "7";
10060 '
10070    IF LEN(BILL.RATE$) > 5
            THEN INVALID = YES:
                LPRINT TAB(COL+14); "8";
10080 '
10090    DEC.POS = INSTR(BILL.RATE$,".")
10100    IF DEC.POS <> 0 THEN INTEGER$ = LEFT$(BILL.RATE$,DEC.POS - 1):
                              DECIMAL$ = MID$(BILL.RATE$,DEC.POS + 1)
                          ELSE INTEGER$ = BILL.RATE$: DECIMAL$ = NULL$
10110    IF (LEN(INTEGER$) > 2) OR (LEN(DECIMAL$) > 2)
            THEN NUMERIC = NO
            ELSE TEST$ = INTEGER$ + DECIMAL$: LENGTH = LEN(TEST$): GOSUB 12000
10120    IF NOT NUMERIC
            THEN INVALID = YES:
                LPRINT TAB(COL+16); "9";
10130 '
10140    IF INVALID
            THEN ASTLINE$ = ASTLINE$ + AST4$
            ELSE ASTLINE$ = ASTLINE$ + BLANK4$
10150    RETURN
10999 '
11000 '*****************************
11010 '*          WRITE RECORD          *
11020 '*****************************
11030 '
11040    BILL.HRS  = VAL(BILL.HRS$)
11050    BILL.RATE = VAL(BILL.RATE$)
11060    WRITE #2, BILL.ACCT$, BILL.NAME$,
                   BILL.HRS,   BILL.RATE
11070    TOTAL.VALID = TOTAL.VALID + 1
11080    TOTAL.HRS   = TOTAL.HRS + BILL.HRS
11090    TOTAL.RATE  = TOTAL.RATE + BILL.RATE
```

PROGRAM 11.3   (continued)
```
11100  RETURN
11999  '
12000  '*****************************
12010  '*        NUMERIC CHECK        *
12020  '*****************************
12030  '
12040  CHAR = 1
12050  NUMERIC = YES
12060  WHILE (NUMERIC) AND (CHAR <= LENGTH)
12070     IF (MID$(TEST$,CHAR,1) < "0") OR (MID$(TEST$,CHAR,1) > "9")
              THEN NUMERIC = NO
12080        CHAR = CHAR + 1
12090  WEND
12100  RETURN
```

This program uses the function STRING$ introduced in Chapter 7, introduces the functions SPACE$ and INSTR, and uses string concatenation.

**SPACE$**   SPACE$(N) returns N number of spaces. The following code and output illustrate the effect of the SPACE$ function.

```
10 PRINT "SHOGUN"; SPACE$(5); "CLAVELL"
RUN
SHOGUN     CLAVELL
```

Notice that five spaces are placed between SHOGUN and CLAVELL. SPACE$ is used in Program 11.3 to enter spaces in the print line that causes errors to be underlined. For example, after

```
1440   BLANK$ = SPACE$(47)
```

is executed, BLANK$ contains 47 spaces.

SPC, a function introduced in Chapter 2, is similar to SPACE$. SPC, like TAB, however, can be used only in PRINT and LPRINT statements. SPACE$ can be used with any string expression.

**STRING$**   For review, STRING$(N,X) returns a string of length N whose characters have the ASCII code of X.

```
10 A$ = STRING$(5,70)  '70 = ASCII code for "E"
20 PRINT A$
RUN
EEEEE
```

Line 10 could also be written as A$ = STRING$(5,"E").

STRING$ is used in Program 11.3 to enter asterisks in a print line. For example, after

```
1460   AST1$ = SPACE$(2) + STRING$(3,"*")
```

is executed, AST1$ contains two blanks plus three asterisks.

Concatenation

Notice the plus (+) sign in line 1460. Two or more strings may be joined using BASIC's concatenation operator, the plus sign. *Concatenation*, from the Latin word for chain, means a linking or joining together. The following code illustrates its use:

```
10 ANAME$ = "BILL"
20 SYMBOL$ = " & "
30 BNAME$ = "COO"
40 PHRASE$ = ANAME$ + SYMBOL$ + BNAME$
50 PRINT PHRASE$
RUN
BILL & COO
```

INSTR

INSTR([N,]A$,B$) searches for the first occurrence of string B$ in A$ and returns the position at which the match is found. The optional numeric variable N denotes the position at which the search of A$ starts. If N is omitted, the search starts with the first position of the string. If there are no occurrences of B$ in A$, INSTR returns a value of zero.

```
10 T$ = "T"
20 X$ = "IT'S TIME"
30 PRINT INSTR(X$,T$)
RUN
 2
10 N = 3
20 T$ = "T"
30 X$ = "IT'S TIME"
40 PRINT INSTR(N,X$,T$)
RUN
 6
```

See Table 11.2 for more examples of the INSTR function.

Program 11.3 builds two report lines for each record. The first line echoes the data and prints appropriate error codes. If there are errors, the second line underlines with asterisks any fields containing an error. The program uses the STRING$ and SPACE$ functions and the concatenation operator to construct the second line, ASTLINE$, from a set of constant strings defined in the CONSTANTS section. ASTLINE$ must be reset to the null string before each new record is validated (line 5090). If ASTLINE$ contains a blank line, indicating no asterisks for highlighting errors, then the fields are valid and the program writes the record to the output file BILL-OUT.SEQ (module 11000).

The program stores the valid client account numbers and error messages in tables. The tables are constructed in the LOAD TABLES module

Table 11.2   Examples of the INSTR function

Statement	Result
Assume A$ = "HOME ON THE RANGE"	
100 N = INSTR(1,A$,"M")	N = 3
200 N = INSTR(A$,"M")	N = 3
300 N = INSTR(5,A$,"O")	N = 6
400 N = INSTR(A$,"J")	N = 0
500 N = INSTR(A$,"THE")	N = 9

```
10090  DEC.POS = INSTR(BILL.RATE$,".")
10100  IF DEC.POS <> 0 THEN INTEGER$ = LEFT$(BILL.RATE$,DEC.POS - 1):
                            DECIMAL$ = MID$(BILL.RATE$,DEC.POS + 1)
                       ELSE INTEGER$ = BILL.RATE$: DECIMAL$ = NULL$
10110  IF (LEN(INTEGER$) > 2) OR (LEN(DECIMAL$) > 2)
          THEN NUMERIC = NO
          ELSE TEST$ = INTEGER$ + DECIMAL$: LENGTH = LEN(TEST$): GOSUB 12000
```

What are the values of DEC.POS, INTEGER$, and DECIMAL$ for the following values of BILL.RATE$:

```
                        12.47
                        56.999
                        897.32
                        A5.67
                        75
                          .43
```

In line 10100, can DECIMAL$ = RIGHT$(BILL.RATE$,LEN(BILL.RATE$) - DEC.POS) replace
DECIMAL$ = MID$(BILL.RATE$,DEC.POS + 1)?

FIGURE 11.7   Checking Numeric Values with Decimal Positions

using READ and DATA statements in a FOR/NEXT loop. Notice the shortened method of searching the client table in lines 7050–7090. This method eliminates the need for a flag like MATCH$, used in Chapter 10. Some people, however, do not find this shortcut quite as readable. The message table is used in lines 6190–6220. This FOR/NEXT loop prints the error messages at the end of the report.

Most of the validation checks are similar to those in the first two programs except for the code to check BILL.RATE$. Notice the BASIC code in Figure 11.7. The INSTR function is used to find the decimal point in the string BILL.RATE$. That location is stored in DEC.POS (line 10090). For the case of DEC.POS <> 0, the program assigns the portion of the string to the left of the decimal to INTEGER$ and the portion to the right of the decimal to DECIMAL$ (line 10100). If DEC.POS = 0 (that is, if there are no decimals), the program assigns all of the string to DECIMAL$ and assigns the empty NULL$ to DECIMAL$. The program then checks INTEGER$ and DECIMAL$ to see if they have more than two characters; if so, the numeric flag is set to NO. Finally, INTEGER$ and DECIMAL$ are concatenated (line 10110) and checked in the NUMERIC CHECK module to verify that they contain only digits.

Test the Program

Assume BILL-IN.SEQ contains these records:

```
101,ALEXANDER BROWN,20,55
999,MARY HENDERSON,,55
301,WELLINGTON GIFT SHOP,3009,
XXXX,XXXXXXXXXXXXXXXXXXXX,XXXX,XXXXXX
,RICHARD HAMILTON,.555,40.5
501,,40,755.5
601,MEGAN RYAN,-8,55.756
701,PHILIP SPAULDING,25,80
888,ELIZABETH STEWART,15,40.5
```

If so, the output of Program 11.3 will be the edit report shown in Figure 11.8. The contents of output file BILL-OUT.SEQ will be

```
"101","ALEXANDER BROWN",20,55
"701","PHILIP SPAULDING",25,80
```

```
                        LOWELL AND BAUER
                        ATTORNEYS AT LAW
                          07-27-1989

                   CLIENT BILLING EDIT REPORT

  CLIENT ACCT      CLIENT NAME        HOURS   RATE      ERROR CODES

     101         ALEXANDER BROWN        20    55

     999         MARY HENDERSON               55        1     4
     ***                                ***

     301         WELLINGTON GIFT SHOP  3009                       5   7
                                       ***   *****

     XXXX        XXXXXXXXXXXXXXXXXXXXX  XXXX  XXXXXX    1   3   5 6   8 9
     ***         ********************   ***   *****

                 RICHARD HAMILTON       .555  40.5      1       5 6
     ***                                ***

     501                                 40   755.5      2                9
                 ********************          *****

     601         MEGAN RYAN             -8    55.756             6     8 9
                                        ***   *****

     701         PHILIP SPAULDING        25   80

     888         ELIZABETH STEWART       15   40.5      1
     ***


  Control totals
  --------------
  Total records       =      9
  Total valid records =      2
  Total error records =      7


  Total BILL.HRS    =      45
  Total BILL.RATE   =     135.00


        ERROR CODES
        -----------

   1 - Invalid client acct
   2 - Client name missing
   3 - Client name > 20 characters
   4 - Hours missing
   5 - Hours > 3 characters
   6 - Hours not positive integer
   7 - Rate missing
```

FIGURE 11.8   Output of Program 11.3

Table 11.3 summarizes some of the string functions available in BASIC.

Table 11.3   String Functions

Function	Description
ASC(A$)	Returns the ASCII code, a numeric value, for the first character in A$. ASC is the inverse of CHR$. Example: `PRINT ASC("B")` `66`
CHR$(N)	Returns a single string character equivalent in ASCII code to N. CHR$ is the inverse of ASC. Example: `PRINT CHR$(66)` `B`
INPUT$(N)	Returns a string of N characters from the keyboard. Example: `TEST$ - INPUT$(2)` `XY` (if XY were the 2 characters entered)
INSTR(N,A$,B$)	Returns the beginning position of B$ in A$. The optional numeric variable N sets the position for starting the search of A$. If there are no occurrences of B$ in A$, INSTR returns a value of zero. Example: `PRINT INSTR(3,"DATA","A")` `4`
LEFT$(A$,N)	Returns a string of the leftmost N characters of A$. Example: `PRINT LEFT$("ACCOUNTING",3)` `ACC`
LEN(A$)	Returns the number of characters in A$, including any blanks and unprintable characters. Example: `PRINT LEN("TEACHER")` `7`
MID$(A$,M,N)	Returns a string of length N characters from A$ beginning with the Mth character. If N is omitted or if fewer than N characters are to the right of the Mth character, all rightmost characters are returned. Example: `PRINT MID$("FINANCIAL",4,3)` `ANC`
RIGHT$(A$,N)	Returns a string of the rightmost N characters of A$. Example: `PRINT RIGHT$("REPORT",4)` `PORT`
SPACE$(N)	Returns N number of spaces. Example: `PRINT SPACE$(3); "MERRY"` `MERRY`
STR$(N)	Returns the string equivalent of N. Example: `PRINT STR$(123.44)` `123.44`
STRING$(N,A$)	Returns a string of N length whose characters have the ASCII code of the first character of A$. Example: `PRINT STRING$(5,"Z")` `ZZZZZ`
VAL(A$)	Returns the numeric equivalent of A$. Example: `PRINT VAL("123.44")` `123.44`

Note that when the function does not end with a $, a number is returned rather than a string.

Summary

- The first step in many data processing applications is the creation of a file that will be used later to generate reports or update existing files. If the data in this file are incorrect, the reports produced later or the files updated with these data will be erroneous and of little value to the user. Consequently, all data should be checked for errors when first entered. The process of checking or editing data is called *data validation*.

- There are two ways to check data:

  1. Compare an entry against a list of acceptable responses.

  2. Determine if the entry is a reasonable one. Tests for reasonableness include:
     - **a.** Presence
     - **b.** Class
     - **c.** Range
     - **d.** Limit
     - **e.** Length
     - **f.** Shelf-checking digit

- *Control totals* are also used to verify the contents of a file. These types of control totals can be used:

  1. Record counts

  2. Field totals

  3. Batch totals

- When editing a sequential file for valid data, you can design a report that lists the fields in error and gives error messages for each type of error. The error messages can be listed next to each record, or a set of codes can be printed adjacent to erroneous records. If error codes are used, a key explaining these codes should be printed at the end of the report. Check with the users of the edit report to ensure that the messages you are providing are useful and sufficiently specific.

- Data can also be verified as they are entered from the keyboard. After the data have passed all the checks in the program, the record can be written to a file.

- You have used many BASIC built-in string functions in this chapter as well as previous chapters. Table 11.3 summarizes some of the string functions available in BASIC.

Review Questions

1. What is data validation?

2. Why is data validation important?

3. What are the two general ways to validate data?

4. Define and give an example of each of the following data checks:
   - **a.** Presence
   - **b.** Class
   - **c.** Range
   - **d.** Limit
   - **e.** Length
   - **f.** Self-checking digit

5. What are control totals?

6. How are control totals used? Why is batch balancing a two-part process?

7. Define and give an example of each of the following types of control totals:
   - **a.** Record counts
   - **b.** Field totals
   - **c.** Batch totals

8. What is an edit report?

9. Compare the two different edit report designs presented in this chapter. What are the advantages and disadvantages of each report design?

10. What is the purpose of the LEN function?

11. Compare the LEFT$, RIGHT$, and MID$ functions.

12. Should you always use the BEEP statement to signal a user's error? In what other applications would the BEEP statement be useful?

13. What is the purpose of the INSTR function?

14. What is meant by concatenation?

15. Compare the VAL and STR$ functions.

16. Why should you validate any entry keyed by the user?

Problems

1. What is the output of the following programs?

   a.
   ```
   10 A$ = "COMPUTER"
   20 PRINT MID$(A$,3,2)
   ```

   b.
   ```
   10 A$ = "FALLSWAY"
   20 PRINT LEFT$(A$,5)
   30 PRINT LEN(A$)
   ```

c.
```
10 A$ = "GEORGE "
20 B$ = "WASHINGTON"
30 PRINT RIGHT$(B$,3)
40 PRINT A$ + B$
50 PRINT LEN(A$ + B$)
```

d.
```
10 A$ = SAMANTHA SIMMONS"
20 B$ = "S"
30 PRINT INSTR(A$,B$)
40 PRINT INSTR(5,A$,"A")
```

e.
```
10 A$ = "84 ELM DRIVE"
20 PRINT VAL(A$)
30 B = 156.78
40 PRINT LEN(STR$(B))
```

f.
```
10 A$ = SPACE$(10) + STRING$(5," ")
                   + STRING$(2,"%")
20 PRINT A$
```

2. Write two routines:

   a. Allow the user to enter a number. Then calculate the check digit using modulus-11 and display it.

   b. Allow the user to enter a number with the check digit. Calculate what the check digit should be and compare it to the check digit entered. If the check digits are different, display a message.

3. Berg's Metal Company assigns its customers a five-digit account number. The first four digits are assigned from a list of available numbers. The fifth digit is assigned so that the sum of the five digits is divisible by nine.

   For example, if the first four digits of the assigned number are 4173, then the fifth digit must be 3, since:

   $$4 + 1 + 7 + 3 = 15$$
   $$15 + 3 = 18$$

   The addition of 3 makes the sum 18, which is divisible by 9. Write a program that will supply the fifth digit of an account number when it is selected from the available list. Use the following list of available numbers:

3174	4892	8147	9171	8318
4276	1135	8917	5562	3236

4. Write a routine to print any given string in reverse order.

5. Write the following routines:

   a. For any given string, convert all the lowercase letters to uppercase letters.

   b. For any given string, convert all the uppercase letters to lowercase letters.

   c. For a name field, make sure the first letter of each part of the name is capitalized and the rest of the name is lowercase. For example, if the name is kATHLEEN ANN urbanski, change to Kathleen Ann Urbanski. Some of the fields contain first, middle, and last names, and others contain only first and last names. In each case, there is only one space between each part of the name.

   d. Modify part c so that if there is more than one space between two parts of the name, the extra spaces are deleted.

6. Check the following code:

   ```
   100 PRINT "Do you want to continue?  Enter Y or N"
   110 INPUT CONTINUE$
   120 IF CONTINUE$ = "Y" OR CONTINUE$ = "y"
            THEN GOSUB 1000
   ```

   Change the code so that if the user enters YE or YES or any word starting with a "Y" or "y," the program will execute the module starting with line number 1000.

7. Using READ and DATA statements, write a routine that will convert names from the first-last form to the last-first form. Use the following data:

   ```
   DOLLY MADISON
   THOMAS JEFFERSON
   PAUL REVERE
   ```

   After converting the names, they should should be printed as follows:

   ```
   MADISON, DOLLY
   JEFFERSON, THOMAS
   REVERE, PAUL
   ```

8. A simple method for encoding a message is to substitute another character for each letter.

   a. Write a routine to encode a statement by exchanging every letter in the statement for its code. Use this code:

Character	Code	Character	Code
A	<	O	/
B	)	P	\
C	7	Q	_
D	$	R	%
E	&	S	(
F	3	T	=
G	^	U	;
H	*	V	'
I	!	W	2
J	@	X	+
K	9	Y	:
L	+	Z	5
M	>	-	.
N	?	blank	#

   b. Using the previous code, decode the following statement:

   !(#%<7&#=/#+&<%?#<$#)&^;?

9. Using READ and DATA statements, display only the city names that begin with the letter H. The names in the DATA statements are:

```
BARSTOW
CUMBERLAND
HAGERSTOWN
EDMOND
FORT WORTH
HELENA
HURRICANE
```

Now write a routine to display all the names in a right-justified column.

10. Write a routine to count the S's in any string variable. Test your routine with the following data:

```
MANASSAS
MARYLAND
SEBRING
```

11. Write a program to convert the system date provided by the computer into the following forms:

- Month Day, Year   example July 7, 1990
- Day Month Year   example 7 July 1990

12. Write a routine to center the title of a report. Test your routine with the following titles:

```
EDIT REPORT
ACCOUNTS RECEIVABLE REPORT
PAYROLL REGISTER
```

13. The charge for a telegram is based on the number of words used in the message plus a base cost. Write a program to compute the cost of a message if the first 10 words cost 25 cents each, and the remaining words cost 15 cents each. The base charge is $3.85. Test your program with this message:

Hello! Having a great time. The weather is wonderful. Wish you were here. Love, Tim

14. Write a program to count the occurrences of a substring in a string. Request that the user enter a phrase and a set of characters. The program will count the number of times the set of characters occurs in the phrase and display the result. A sample run might look like this:

```
Enter phrase        row row row your boat
Enter character set row
row occurs 3 times
```

15. The INSTR function can be used to search a string for one character or a set of characters. The MID$ *statement* is used for substring replacement. The MID$ function returns a substring, but the MID$ statement replaces a series of characters within a string with a designated substring. The general format is:

```
MID$(A$,M [,N]) = S$
```

where A$ is the string that will have its characters replaced, M is the position at which the replacement begins, N is the number of characters to replace, and S$ is the replacement substring. For example,

```
100 S$ = "EI"
200 A$ = "RECIEVE"
300 MID$(A$,4,2) = S$
400 PRINT A$
RUN
RECEIVE
```

Using the INSTR function and the MID$ statement, write a program to search and replace characters in a line of text. Request the user to enter the following data:

a. The line of text.
b. The characters to search for.
c. The characters to use for replacement.

After the program searches for the designated characters and replaces them, the program should print the new line of text. A sample run might look like this:

```
Enter text               two little two late
Enter search characters        two
Enter replacement characters   too
Old text = two little two late
New text = too little too late
```

Program Assignments

1. The Spencer Insurance Company needs a program to determine whether a customer's payment is late or not. The input to the program is the following file, which contains valid data:

INS-IN.SEQ (sequential input file)
INS record:

Field Name	Data Length	Data Type
INS.CUST.NO	6	Numeric ######
INS.PAY	7	Numeric ####.##
INS.DATE	6	Numeric ddmmyy

The output is a screen report listing the information in the records of all customers who are late plus the late charge. The late charge is 3% of INS.PAY. Note the screen design as shown below.

Also, an output file is created with the following data:

INS-OUT.SEQ   (sequential output file)
INS Record

Field Name	Data Length	Data Type
INS.CUST.NO	6	Numeric ######
INS.CHG	6	Numeric ###.##

The INS.CHG is 3% of INS.PAY.

The program should read each record and compare the payment date (INS.DATE) to the current date. Assume the current date is October 12, 1990. Set DATE$ to this value before testing the program. Any payment date greater than the current date indicates a late payment. If the payment is late, print the information on the screen and write a record to the INS-OUT.SEQ file. If the payment is not late, read the next record.

To compare the dates, remember that both dates must be in the *yymmdd* format.

The file contents are as follows:

```
INS-IN.SEQ
    112683,100.41,091090
    132221,250.63,300990
    233367,400.03,121090
    454432,99.73,241090
    477899,43.21,051090
    489933,345.67,301090
    654431,300.23,011190
    765489,500.54,100890
```

2. In Chapter 8, the second program assignment was to create an inventory file for Successories, Inc. The user entered data by responding to a set of prompts on the screen. Modify this program to validate each field before the program writes the inventory record.

The fields in the INV.SEQ sequential output file are shown in the table on the next page.

	1–10	11–20	21–30	31–40	41–50	51–60	61–70
01				SPENCER INSURANCE COMPANY			
03		Customer				Late	
04		Number	Payment	Date	Charge		
06		######	# ###.##	dd-mm-yy	###.##		
19		Total late payments = ##					
20		Total late charges = $$,###.##					

Screen design for Program Assignment #1

INV.SEQ sequential ouput file fields

Field Name	Data Length	Data Type	Constraints
INV.DEPT$	4	String	Must be one of these values: 1010, 2020, 3030
INV.CODE$	3	String	Must be one of these values: 210, 350, 420, 520, 750, 870, 920
INV.NUM$	3	String	Must be one of these values: If INV.CODE$ = 210 123, 329, 382, 426, 466, 489, 566, 545, 746 If INV.CODE$ = 350 260, 739, 828 If INV.CODE$ = 420 050, 111, 231, 321 If INV.CODE$ = 520 743, 843 If INV.CODE$ = 750 128, 149, 234, 327, 329, 455 478, 489, 899 If INV.CODE$ = 870 156 If INV.CODE$ = 920 367, 466, 862

To validate INV.NUM$, you must check INV.CODE$. For example, if INV.CODE$ is 520, then INV.PROD$ must be 743 or 843. Hint: Use a two-dimensional table to store the values of INV.CODE$ and INV.NUM$.

Field Name	Data Length	Data Type	Constraints
INV.NAME$	16	String	Cannot be greater than 16 characters
INV.ON.HAND	3	Numeric	Must be in ### format Must be positive value
INV.PRICE	7	Numeric	Must be in #####.## format Must be positive value

INV.ON.ORDER	3	Numeric	Must be in ### format
			Must be positive value
			If INV.NUM$ = 466
			    then INV.ON.ORDER
			    cannot be greater than 4

First determine the necessary checks and appropriate error messages and then modify the program in Chapter 8 to:

a. Validate the user's response.
b. Display error messages.
c. Allow the user to enter the data again if the entry is incorrect.
d. Write the record to the INV.SEQ when the data are correct.

Prepare test data to check all possible errors.

3. Harley Clocks, Ltd., needs a program to validate accounts receivable payments before applying the payments to the master accounts receivable file. A file called HCL-AR.SEQ has been created. The data, however, need to be edited, a file of valid payments must be created, and an error report must be generated.

The fields in the HCL-AR.SEQ sequential input file are shown in the following table.

HCL-AR.SEQ sequential input file fields

Field Name	Data Length	Data Type	Constraints
HCL.AR.ACCT	4	String	Must be in the master file.
HCL.AR.AMT	8	Numeric	Must be in the format of ####.##. Should not be less than the minimum payment, which is 20% of the account balance on the master file.
HCL.AR.DATE	8	String	Month must be 1–12
			Day must be 1–28, 1–30, or 1–31, depending on the month.
			Year must be same as year in DATE\$ (1989 for the data file supplied)

The HCL-AR.SEQ payments file also includes batch records. In front of each batch of payments in the file is a record with the following data:

Field 1 = B (code for batch record)
Field 2 = Batch number assigned by control clerk
Field 3 = Record count in batch

Assume the batch records are valid.

The output of this program is a sequential output file called HCL-ARV.SEQ and an error report. The HCL-ARV.SEQ sequential output file has the following format:

Field Name	Data Length	Data Type
HCL.ARV.ACCT	4	String
HCL.ARV.AMT	8	Numeric #####.##
HCL.ARV.DATE	6	Numeric *yymmdd*

The error report should include headings with each batch on a new page, detail lines with error messages or error codes, subtotals at the end of each batch, and summary lines at the end of the report. At the end of each batch of records, the following totals are to be printed. The last total should appear only when necessary.

```
Total error records
Total valid records
Batch record count
Total records processed
Difference between batch record count
    and total records processed
```

The summary totals at the end of the report should include:

```
Total error records
Total valid records
Total record count
```

First determine the necessary checks and design the error report. Then write a program to:

a. Read the necessary accounts receivable master file fields into tables. The format of the master file is:

HCL-MAST.SEQ (sequential input file)
HCL-MAST record:

Field Name	Data Length	Data Type
HCL.MAST.ACCT\$	4	String
HCL.MAST.NAME\$	20	String
HCL.MAST.BAL	8	Numeric #####.##
HCL.MAST.DATE	6	Numeric *yymmdd*
HCL.MAST.CR	5	Numeric #####

b. Print each batch on a new page.
c. Read each record in the HCL-AR.SEQ file.

(1) Check the account number against the master account numbers in the table.
(2) Check that HCL.AR.AMT contains numeric data in ####.## format and make sure that the amount is not less than 20% of the balance in the master file. (Use the master records in the table again.)
(3) Check that the month is a string between 01–12.
Check that the day is not larger than the number of days in the specified month. For example, the maximum days in June is 30.
(4) Check that the year is 1989.

d. If the record is invalid, print the data in the record with appropriate error messages or codes.

e. If the record is valid, print the data in the record on the error report and write the data to HCL-ARV.SEQ. Note that the format of the date changes.

f. At the end of each batch, print the necessary totals.

g. At the end of the report, print the necessary totals.

File contents:

HCL-MAST.SEQ

```
A100,PATRICIA WINN,100.55,890830,2500
A199,GINGER NORRIS,362.96,890818,2500
A205,MARTIN WEBSTER,640.74,890801,2300
A250,LUIS HERNANDEZ,200.62,890815,2500
B788,PATRICK SWAYZEE,980.70,890801,3000
C260,JENNIFER NOLAN,6000.90,890702,10000
D650,BRANDON SCHISLER,500.99,890615,2300
J500,DENNIS AMELL,870.54,890812,2300
K428,GLENN REYNOLDS,600.38,890814,2500
K657,GARY UMSTEAD,879.56,890813,3000
M828,BERNARD GAVIN,1000.76,890715,10000
M999,PAMELA MCDONOUGH,422.99,890612,2300
N402,BARBARA JONES,2000.80,890815,2500
P492,DAVID RANSONE,487.62,890512,3000
P566,JEFFREY VITTER,788.89,890815,2300
```

```
Q492,JOAN HAMILTON,0,890805,1200
S378,PAUL STITZ,650.99,890830,2500
S460,DONNA DAUBERT,500.30,890830,2300
S899,JOSEPH SEFA,100.20,890704,3000
T100,BRIANA MARIS,0,890123,1200
T600,MICHAEL GECKLE,1000.65,890817,3000
```

HCL-AR.SEQ

```
B,1,5
A100,100.55,9-20-89
A250,200.62,9-9-89
T600,1000.65,10-1-89
M828,840.82,9-30-89
S460,500.30,10-2-89
B,2,4
J460,323.82,9-31-89
C260,6000.90,14-30-89
T6,360.X2,9-18-89
B,3,6
,400.20,10-32-78
N402,100,
J500,,#-14-89
K428,420.567,10-P3-89
S378,320.62,9-18-89
P492,487.62,922-89
T600,980.00,10-1-89
B788,A80.70,10-2-7
k657,888879.56,10-14-89
```

Using the Data Disk

1. Insert the data disk into the disk drive.

2. Load BASIC (change the default drive first if necessary).

3. After loading CH11-1.DD:

   a. List the program. It should look as follows:

   ```
   1000 'CH11-1.DD
   1010 FIRST$ = "The Adventure of the Devil's Foot"
   1020 SEC$ = "by Arthur Conan Doyle"
   1030 NUM = 2
   1040 PRINT LEN(FIRST$)
   1050 PRINT LEN(SEC$)
   1060 PRINT LEN(NUM)
   1070 PRINT LEN(STR$(NUM))
   1080 PRINT VAL(FIRST$)
   1090 PRINT LEFT$(FIRST$,5)
   1100 PRINT RIGHT$(FIRST$,NUM)
   1110 PRINT RIGHT$(SEC$,256)
   1120 PRINT LEFT$(SEC$,1.2)
   1130 PRINT LEFT$(SEC$,1.7)
   1140 PRINT MID$(FIRST$,5,9)
   1150 PRINT ASC(LEFT$(FIRST$,1))
   1160 PRINT ASC("A")
   1170 PRINT INSTR(SEC$,"C")
   1180 PRINT INSTR(FIRST$,"D")
   1190 PRINT INSTR(10,FIRST$,"e")
   1200 PRINT INSTR(SEC$,"X")
   1210 PRINT INSTR(SEC$,"Arthur")
   1220 PRINT MID$(FIRST$,NUM * 3,NUM * 20)
   1230 PRINT MID$(SEC$,4)
   1240 PRINT LEFT$(FIRST$,13) + " " + LEFT$(SEC$,3) +
             RIGHT$(SEC$,5)
   ```

   b. First predict what will be displayed and then run the program to test your prediction. Some of the statements are not valid and need to be corrected.

4. Using READ and DATA statements, display only the words that begin with the prefix PRE or end with the suffix ION. Place an asterisk (*) next to any words that begin with PRE *and* end with ION. Test your routine with the following data:

   ```
   PRECAUTION
   ELECTION
   PRECISE
   CARELESS
   PREDICTION
   PREPARATION
   ```

   Save the program under the name CH11-2.DD.

5. Write a program to check that any string the user enters contains only letters, either uppercase or lowercase. If the string contains a character other than a letter, display the message ENTRY CONTAINS NON-ALPHABETIC CHARACTERS; otherwise, display the message ALPHABETIC ENTRY. Save the program under the name CH11-3.DD.

6. Write a routine to input a string of words and count the number of words in the string. After counting the words, display the total number of words and the average number of letters per word. Save the program under the name CH11-4.DD.

7. A palindrome is a word or phrase that is spelled the same from right to left as from left to right. The word is derived from a Greek word meaning "running back again." For example, *noon* is a palindrome but *soon* is not. Write a program that requests the user to enter a string of characters and determines whether the string is a palindrome. Use the following data to test the routine:

```
NOON
SOON
12344321
COBOL
HANNAH
RADAR
BASIC IS SPOKEN HERE
MADAM IM ADAM
12345678
ABLE WAS I ERE I SAW ELBA
```

Save the program under the name CH11-5.DD.

8. After loading PROG11-1, modify it as follows:

   a. Dress up the report using the STRING$ function.
   b. Add the code necessary to print multiple pages. Print 40 lines per page.
   c. Using EDLIN, add more records to the data file STUDENT.SEQ.
   d. Within each check module, stop printing error messages after an error is found.
   e. Save the revised program under the name CH11-6.DD

9. After loading PROG11-2, modify it as follows:

   a. List module 3000–3999. Notice line 3035. This line was added so that the file could be named by you and the current STUDENT.SEQ is not destroyed.
   b. Add another field to the STUDENT.SEQ file. Determine what checks need to be made to validate the field. Add the necessary code to the program.
   c. Allow the user to enter the total for TOTAL.GRADES calculated manually and then compare that total to the total calculated by the computer. Display a message to the user indicating whether the totals agree.
   d. Save the revised program under the name CH11-7.DD.

10. Chapter 8 introduced the subject of menu design. The CONTROL module in Program 8.4 calls different modules depending on the selection the user makes. That program, however, does not print an error message when the user selects a number not available on

the menu. Instead, if the user selects an incorrect numeric option in Program 8.4, the menu is redisplayed on the screen and the user makes another selection. A better programming practice is to display an error message to let the user know that a requested option is not available. Also, when a user selects an incorrect option, the system should not waste time displaying a fresh copy of the menu. Instead, the menu should remain on the screen, and the program should display an error message and allow the user to press another key. Review Program 8.4 and add the code to validate the user's selection from a set of options in a menu.

a. Load PROG 8-4.
b. List lines 3000–3999 (the DISPLAY MENU module).
c. Be sure to change SELECTION to SELECTION$ so that the message ?REDO FROM START does not appear when a nonnumeric value is entered.
d. Add the code to validate the user's selection.
e. Make sure that the menu does not scroll off the screen if the user enters multiple invalid responses.
f. Save the program under the name CH11-8.DD.

Chapter Twelve

Sorting

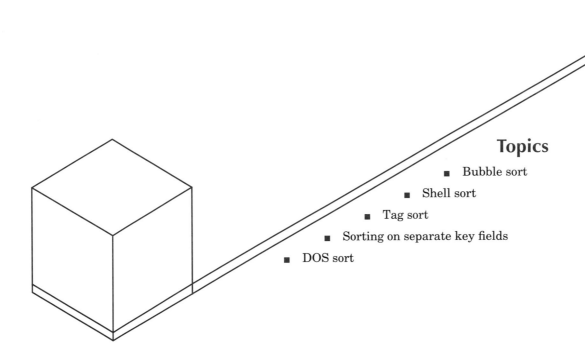

Topics

- Bubble sort
- Shell sort
- Tag sort
- Sorting on separate key fields
- DOS sort

BASIC Statements

```
LINE INPUT #
SWAP
```

INTRODUCTION

Whenever the input to a program is from sequential files, the records in those files usually are arranged in some specific order. You saw examples of this requirement in the control-break programs of Chapter 9. The process of arranging records in a specific order is called *sorting*.

The Sorted File column in Table 12.1 is an example of a file whose records are arranged in a specific order. In this case, all the records with the same first field (month) are grouped together. Within each of those groups, the files are ordered by the second field (department).

As this example shows, the records in a file may be arranged according to one or more fields, called key fields. One or more fields may be used as key fields to arrange the records in a file. Any field in a record may be a key field; it does not necessarily have to be the first field in a record.

For any key, records may be arranged in either ascending or descending order. *Ascending* and *descending* have their usual meanings when applied to numeric fields. When applied to string fields, *ascending* refers to increasing values in the ASCII code sequence and *descending* to decreasing ASCII code values. The typical dictionary (alphabetic) order is an ascending sort.

The quickest way to sort a file is to read it into the computer's memory and sort it there. This type of sort is often referred to as a *memory* sort because the sorting is done in the computer's random-access memory. This approach works well for files that hold 60K bytes or less, but larger files cannot fit into memory areas recognizable by BASIC.

This chapter presents some memory-sorting algorithms and explains how you can use them to order sequential files. A short discussion of the use of the DOS SORT command concludes the chapter.

All memory-sort programs follow these three steps:

1. Read the records from the unsorted file into a table.

2. Rearrange the records in the table so that they are in the desired order.

3. Write the sorted table to a file.

Each sort program in this chapter has modules to implement these steps. The read and write modules are the same in all of the programs; only the sort module, which rearranges the records, is different.

BUBBLE SORT

Although the bubble sort is not very efficient, it is a good introduction to sorting because it is easy to understand. The more efficient Shell sort that follows is based on a modification of the bubble-sort algorithm.

In a bubble sort, adjacent items in a list are examined. The positions of any pair that is out of order are exchanged or swapped. For example, if you perform a series of such swaps on the list of numbers on the left of Figure 12.1, you produce the sorted list on the right.

Perform the exchanges by working from the top of the list to the bottom. The first two elements are 5 and 10; they are in order, and so you don't need to swap them. The next pair, 10 and 18, is also in order and need not be swapped. The next pair, 18 and 7, is out of order, so swap the items, as

Table 12.1 Unsorted and sorted sales records

Unsorted File	Sorted File
1,"315","J ANDREWS",300.15	1,"311","J SAMUELS",600.99
2,"315","J ANDREWS",90.9	1,"311","L DERBYSHIRE",500.12
3,"315","J ANDREWS",700.85	1,"311","M JEFFERSON",40.56
1,"312","H BLESSING",1000.5	1,"312","G MALLONEE",675.5
2,"312","H BLESSING",30.34	1,"312","H BLESSING",1000.5
3,"312","H BLESSING",70.6	1,"312","K MCCREADY",400.36
1,"311","L DERBYSHIRE",500.12	1,"312","M QUILL",300.99
2,"311","L DERBYSHIRE",899.5	1,"315","D MAYER",200.75
3,"311","L DERBYSHIRE",700.8	1,"315","J ANDREWS",300.15
1,"311","M JEFFERSON",40.56	2,"311","J SAMUELS",50.75
2,"311","M JEFFERSON",1000.65	2,"311","L DERBYSHIRE",899.5
3,"311","M JEFFERSON",200.8	2,"311","M JEFFERSON",1000.65
1,"312","G MALLONEE",675.5	2,"312","G MALLONEE",900.45
2,"312","G MALLONEE",900.45	2,"312","H BLESSING",30.34
3,"312","G MALLONEE",2000.85	2,"312","K MCCREADY",400.2
1,"315","D MAYER",200.75	2,"312","M QUILL",0
2,"315","D MAYER",700.65	2,"315","D MAYER",700.65
3,"315","D MAYER",200.99	2,"315","J ANDREWS",90.9
1,"312","K MCCREADY",400.36	3,"311","J SAMUELS",400.55
2,"312","K MCCREADY",400.2	3,"311","L DERBYSHIRE",700.8
3,"312","K MCCREADY",600.14	3,"311","M JEFFERSON",200.8
1,"312","M QUILL",300.99	3,"312","G MALLONEE",2000.85
2,"312","M QUILL",0	3,"312","H BLESSING",70.6
3,"312","M QUILL",300.15	3,"312","K MCCREADY",600.14
1,"311","J SAMUELS",600.99	3,"312","M QUILL",300.15
2,"311","J SAMUELS",50.75	3,"315","D MAYER",200.99
3,"311","J SAMUELS",400.55	3,"315","J ANDREWS",700.85

FIGURE 12.1
Sorting by exchanging adjacent items

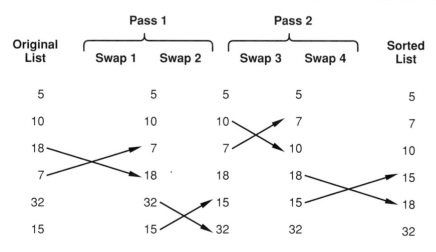

the arrows in Figure 12.1 indicate (Swap 1). The pair 18 and 32 is in order, but you need to swap the last pair of items, 32 and 15 (Swap 2). This completes one pass down the list.

Because some items in the list are still out of order, begin the comparison process again at the top of the list. The first pair to swap is 7 and 10 (Swap 3). The next pair out of order is 18 and 15. After you swap them (Swap 4), the list is sorted in ascending order.

To develop a computer algorithm for the bubble sort, you need to examine this process in detail and decide exactly what is happening. First, consider the swaps. You can describe them in terms of the order of the items in the list:

```
if item(row) > item(row+1)
  then swap item(row) with item(row+1)
```

This means that if an item in a row is greater than the item in the next row, the two items are to be exchanged, but if the first item is equal to or less than the item in the next row, nothing need be done.

How many times must the system do this? If there are n items in the list, there must be a comparison for item(1) with item(2) through item(n-1) with item(n). This requires n-1 comparisons of adjacent items. You can specify this number of comparisons in the algorithm by writing:

```
for row = 1 to n-1
  if item(row) > item(row+1)
    then swap item(row) with item(row+1)
next row
```

After n-1 comparisons, one pass through the list is completed, and the list is arranged as shown after Swap 2 in Figure 12.1. Notice that the list is nearer to being sorted, but the job is not yet finished. A complete sort requires continued application of the algorithm. In this example, one more pass produces the two additional exchanges (Swap 3 and Swap 4) necessary to sort the list fully.

The number of passes necessary to sort a list depends on the list's contents. Any list can be sorted in n-1 passes. (Try it with a list of numbers arranged in descending order.) Thus, this algorithm will sort a list completely:

```
for pass = 1 to n-1
  for row = 1 to n-1
    if item(row) > item(row+1)
      then exchange item(row) with item(row+1)
  next row
next pass
```

Although this algorithm works, it may perform many more comparisons than are necessary. The sort continues for (n-1) times (n-1) comparisons, even if the list is sorted to begin with. By using a flag and a dowhile loop, you can create a more efficient bubble-sort algorithm.

A list is sorted if no exchanges of adjacent pairs are necessary. Use the Boolean variable *swapping* as a flag to report any swaps during a pass. Set *swapping* to no before the loop is entered; set it to yes when an exchange occurs. The inner portion of the algorithm thus becomes

```
swapping = no
for row = 1 to n-1
  if item(row) > item(row+1)
    then exchange item(row) with item(row+1)
        swapping = yes
next row
```

Now, when the inner loop ends, you can check the value of *swapping*; if the value of *swapping* is yes, another cycle through the inner loop is required, and *swapping* must be reset to no. If the value of *swapping* is no, there were no swaps during the last pass: The items are in order, and the sort is finished.

Use a dowhile loop based on the value of *swapping* to control the number of cycles through the inner loop. Be sure to set *swapping* equal to yes before entering this loop.

Here is the complete algorithm:

```
swapping = yes
dowhile swapping
    swapping = no
    for row = 1 to n-1
        if item(row) > item(row+1)
            then exchange item(row) with item(row+1)
                    swapping = yes
    next row
end dowhile
```

Figure 12.2 contains a flowchart of this algorithm.

The sales records for Berrenger's Department Store illustrate the application of this and other sorting algorithms in this chapter. Here is a typical record:

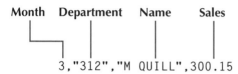

Month   Department   Name   Sales

```
3,"312","M QUILL",300.15
```

You will sort an unsorted file of sales records into the order required for the control-break processing of Chapter 9; that is, you will sort records by month and by department within month.

This sort will be simple because the major and minor sort fields are the first and second fields, respectively, in the record. A statement of the form

```
if record1 > record2
    then . . .
```

performs the needed comparison because it ensures that the months and the departments are both in the proper order.

Figure 12.3 shows the structure chart and pseudocode for a bubble-sort program. Program 12.1 is based on that design. The program's implementation of the design is straightforward, but the program does contain two new BASIC statements.

SWAP

The SWAP statement exchanges the contents of two variables of the same data type. Its form is

```
[line#] SWAP <variable1, variable2>
```

This statement allows you to write line 4080 as follows:

```
IF SALE.TBL$(ROW) > SALE.TBL$(ROW + 1)
    THEN SWAP SALE.TBL$(ROW), SALE.TBL$(ROW + 1)
```

You might be interested in knowing how the SWAP function works, since not all languages and not all versions of BASIC have a SWAP statement. To perform the exchange without SWAP, you must put one of the values to be exchanged into a temporary storage area, set the variable whose value was stored equal to the other, and then set the latter one equal to the value in temporary storage. Using this technique, you would write line 4080 like this:

```
IF SALE.TBL$(ROW) > SALE.TBL$(ROW+1)
    THEN TEMP$ = SALE.TBL$(ROW):
        SALE.TBL$(ROW) = SALE.TBL$(ROW+1):
        SALE.TBL$(ROW+1) = TEMP$
```

The temporary storage area must be of the same data type as that of the variables you will be swapping.

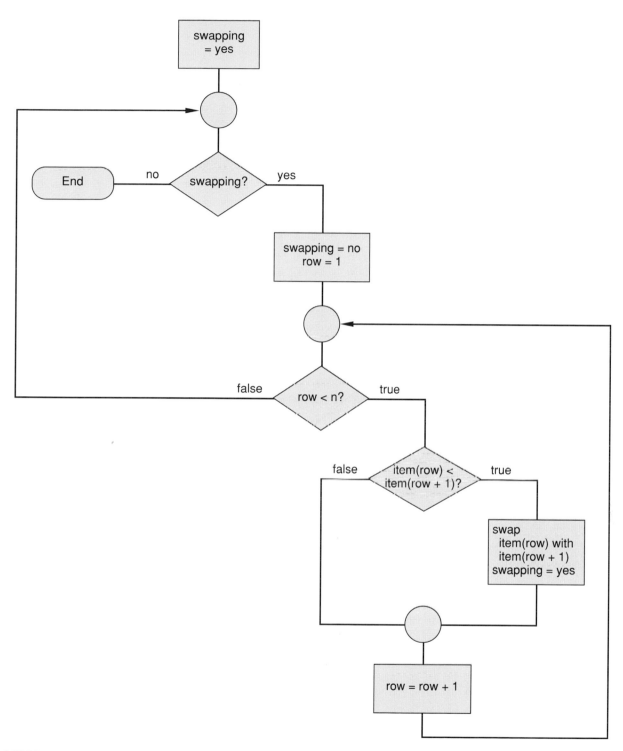

FIGURE 12.2 Flowchart for the bubble-sort algorithm

LINE INPUT #

The LINE INPUT # statement works just like the LINE INPUT statement introduced in Chapter 8 except that it is designed to read from a sequential file. Its general form is:

```
[line#] LINE INPUT <#filenumber, variable$>
```

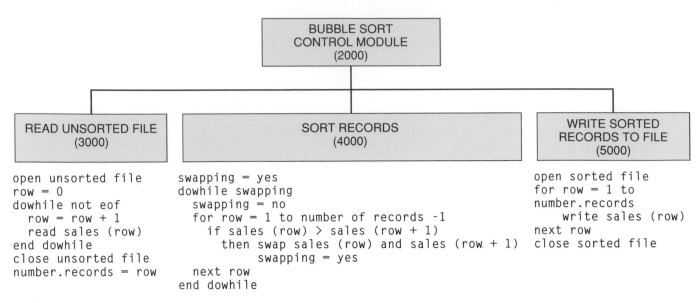

FIGURE 12.3   Structure chart and pseudocode for Program 12.1

Program 12-1

```
1000 ' PROG12-1
1010 ' *****************************
1020 ' *          BUBBLE SORT           *
1030 ' *****************************
1040 '
1050 ' *****************************
1060 ' *            VARIABLES            *
1070 ' *****************************
1080 '
1090 ' SALES-IN.SEQ               File of unsorted sales records
1100 ' SALES.SEQ                  File of sorted sales records
1110 ' SALES-IN and SALES record:
1120 '      SALES.MTH
1130 '      SALES.DEPT$
1140 '      SALES.NAME$
1150 '      SALES.AMT
1160 '
1170 ' NUMBER.OF.RECORDS          Number of records to sort
1180 ' ROW                        Table subscript
1190 ' SWAPPING                   Flag to indicate a swap of records
1200 '
1210 ' *****************************
1220 ' *            CONSTANTS            *
1230 ' *****************************
1240 '
1250    YES = -1                 'Value for true
1260    NO  =  0                 'Value for false
1270 '
1280 ' *****************************
1290 ' *           DEFINE TABLE          *
1300 ' *****************************
1310 '
1320    DIM SALE.TBL$(100)       'Table of sales records
1999 '
2000 ' *****************************
2010 ' *          CONTROL MODULE         *
2020 ' *****************************
2030 '
2040    GOSUB 3000               'Read Unsorted File
2050    GOSUB 4000               'Sort Records
```

Program 12-1   (continued)

```
2060    GOSUB 5000                    'Write Sorted Records to File
2070    END
2999 '
3000 ' ****************************
3010 ' *    READ UNSORTED FILE    *
3020 ' ****************************
3030 '
3040    OPEN "SALES-IN.SEQ" FOR INPUT AS #1
3050    ROW = 0
3060    WHILE NOT EOF(1)
3070        ROW = ROW + 1
3080        LINE INPUT #1, SALE.TBL$(ROW)
3090    WEND
3100    CLOSE #1
3110    NUMBER.OF.RECORDS = ROW
3120    RETURN
3999 '
4000 ' ****************************
4010 ' *       SORT RECORDS       *
4020 ' ****************************
4030 '
4040    SWAPPING = YES
4050    WHILE SWAPPING
4060        SWAPPING = NO
4070        FOR ROW = 1 TO NUMBER.OF.RECORDS - 1
4080            IF SALE.TBL$(ROW) > SALE.TBL$(ROW + 1)
                    THEN SWAP SALE.TBL$(ROW), SALE.TBL$(ROW + 1):
                        SWAPPING = YES
4090        NEXT ROW
4100    WEND
4110    RETURN
4999 '
5000 ' ****************************
5010 ' *    WRITE SORTED RECORDS  *
5020 ' *           TO FILE        *
5030 ' ****************************
5040 '
5050    OPEN "SALES.SEQ" FOR OUTPUT AS #2
5060    FOR ROW = 1 TO NUMBER.OF.RECORDS
5070        PRINT #2, SALE.TBL$(ROW)
5080    NEXT ROW
5090    CLOSE #2
5100    RETURN
```

Program 12.1 contains a LINE INPUT # statement in line 3080. Its purpose is to read a record from a file called SALES-IN.SEQ into SALE.TBL$(ROW). (SALES-IN.SEQ contains the same records as SALES.SEQ, but they are not arranged in the order needed for Berrenger's control-break programs.) Notice that LINE INPUT # reads an entire line including quotes and commas. For example, after line 3080 is executed, SALE.TBL$(1) will contain:

```
1,"315","J ANDREWS",300.15
```

Table 12.1 contains an unsorted set of Berrenger's records and the sorted set produced by Program 12.1.

SHELL SORT

Because the bubble sort is quite slow, it is not suitable for large files. A more efficient alternative is the Shell sort, named after its designer, Donald Shell.

A. Gap = 4

item		swap	swap	no swap	swap
1	P	D	D	D	D
2	T	T	H	H	H
3	C	C	C	C	C
4	F	F	F	F	B
5	D	P	P	P	P
6	H	H	T	T	T
7	S	S	S	S	S
8	B	B	B	B	F

B. Gap = 2

item	Pass 1						Pass 2					
	swap	swap	no swap	no swap	no swap	swap	no swap	no swap	no swap	swap	no swap	no swap
1	D	C	C	C	C	C	C	C	C	C	C	C
2	H	H	B	B	B	B	B	B	B	B	B	B
3	C	D	D	D	D	D	D	D	D	D	D	D
4	B	B	H	H	H	H	H	H	H	H	F	F
5	P	P	P	P	P	P	P	P	P	P	P	P
6	T	T	T	T	T	T	F	F	F	F	H	H
7	S	S	S	S	S	S	S	S	S	S	S	S
8	F	F	F	F	F	F	T	T	T	T	T	T

C. Gap = 1

item	swap	no swap	no swap	no swap	swap	no swap	no swap
1	C	B	B	B	B	B	B
2	B	C	C	C	C	C	C
3	D	D	D	D	D	D	D
4	F	F	F	F	F	F	F
5	P	P	P	P	P	H	H
6	H	H	H	H	H	P	P
7	S	S	S	S	S	S	S
8	T	T	T	T	T	T	T

FIGURE 12.4 Shell sort (underlined items are being compared)

The Shell sort is similar to the bubble sort in that it compares pairs of items in the list and exchanges their values if they are out of order. It differs from the bubble sort in that it compares pairs of items that are varying distances apart instead of comparing only adjacent ones. During the first pass through the list, this distance or *gap* is half the number of items in the list; next, it is a quarter of the number of items; and so on until adjacent items are compared, just as in the bubble sort.

To understand the varying gap between the items compared, consider this eight-item list:

```
Item#:  1  2  3  4  5  6  7  8
Item:   P  T  C  F  D  H  S  B
```

In the first pass, items 1 and 5 (four places apart, or half of all the items in the list) are compared, as are items 2 and 6, 3 and 7, and 4 and 8. Pairs that are out of order are swapped as shown in Figure 12.4A.

In the next pass, items two places apart (1 and 3, 2 and 4, and so on) are compared. Pairs that are out of order are swapped as shown in Figure 12.4B. Finally, the sort ends with a comparison of adjacent items. The exchanges are shown in Figure 12.4C.

Because the size of the gap between the items compared is variable, a nested loop must be added to the bubble-sort algorithm. Here is the Shell-sort algorithm:

```
gap = number.of.items \ 2
dowhile gap > 0
    last = number.of.items - gap
    swapping = yes
    dowhile swapping
        swapping = no
        for row = 1 to last
            if item(row) > item(row + gap)
                then swap item(row) with item(row + gap)
                    swapping = yes
        next row
    end dowhile
    gap = gap \ 2
end dowhile
```

In the algorithm, *gap* is always defined by integer division by 2, a process that eventually produces a gap equal to 1. The variable *last* contains the item number at which the comparisons stop. For example, in the list of 8 items, *last* initially contains 8 minus *gap*, which is 4; that means the last comparison in a pass with a *gap* of 4 is of items 4 and 8. Similarly, in a pass with a *gap* of 2, items 6 and 8 are the last pair compared.

The *swapping* flag serves the same function as it does in the bubble sort; it allows passes to continue for each gap until there are no more swaps.

Programs 12.1 and 12.2 sort Berrenger's SALES-IN.SEQ file identically. The difference between the two programs is speed.

PROGRAM 12.2

```
1000 ' PROG12-2
1010 ' ****************************
1020 ' *           SHELL SORT          *
1030 ' ****************************
1040 '
1050 ' ****************************
1060 ' *           VARIABLES           *
1070 ' ****************************
1080 '
1090 ' SALES-IN.SEQ                File of unsorted sales records
1100 ' SALES.SEQ                   File of sorted sales records
1110 ' Sales-in and Sales record:
1120 '       SALES.MTH
1130 '       SALES.DEPT$
1140 '       SALES.NAME$
1150 '       SALES.AMT
1160 '
1170 ' GAP                         Variable value for sort comparisons
1180 ' LAST                        Last row to use in comparison loop
1190 ' NUMBER.OF.RECORDS           Number of records to sort
1200 ' ROW                         Table subscript
1210 ' SWAPPING                    Flag to indicate a swap of records
```

PROGRAM 12.2 (continued)

```
1220 '
1230 ' ******************************
1240 ' *          CONSTANTS           *
1250 ' ******************************
1260 '
1270   YES = -1                    'Value for true
1280   NO  =  0                    'Value for false
1290 '
1300 ' ******************************
1310 ' *          DEFINE TABLE        *
1320 ' ******************************
1330 '
1340   DIM SALE.TBL$(100)          'Table of sales records
1999 '
2000 ' ******************************
2010 ' *          CONTROL MODULE      *
2020 ' ******************************
2030 '
2040   GOSUB 3000                  'Read Unsorted File
2050   GOSUB 4000                  'Sort Records
2060   GOSUB 5000                  'Write Sorted Records to File
2070   END
2999 '
3000 ' ******************************
3010 ' *      READ UNSORTED FILE      *
3020 ' ******************************
3030 '
3040   OPEN "SALES-IN.SEQ" FOR INPUT AS #1
3050   ROW = 0
3060   WHILE NOT EOF(1)
3070       ROW = ROW + 1
3080       LINE INPUT #1, SALE.TBL$(ROW)
3090   WEND
3100   CLOSE #1
3110   NUMBER.OF.RECORDS = ROW
3120   RETURN
3999 '
4000 ' ******************************
4010 ' *          SORT RECORDS        *
4020 ' ******************************
4030 '
4040   GAP = NUMBER.OF.RECORDS \ 2
4050   WHILE GAP > 0
4060       LAST = NUMBER.OF.RECORDS - GAP
4070       SWAPPING = YES
4080       WHILE SWAPPING
4090           SWAPPING = NO
4100           FOR ROW = 1 TO LAST
4110               IF SALE.TBL$(ROW) > SALE.TBL$(ROW + GAP)
                        THEN SWAP SALE.TBL$(ROW), SALE.TBL$(ROW + GAP):
                             SWAPPING = YES
4120           NEXT ROW
4130       WEND
4140       GAP = GAP \ 2
4150   WEND
4160   RETURN
4999 '
5000 ' ******************************
5010 ' *    WRITE SORTED RECORDS      *
5020 ' *            TO FILE           *
5030 ' ******************************
5040 '
5050   OPEN "SALES.SEQ" FOR OUTPUT AS #2
5060   FOR ROW = 1 TO NUMBER.OF.RECORDS
5070       PRINT #2, SALE.TBL$(ROW)
5080   NEXT ROW
5090   CLOSE #2
5100   RETURN
```

TAG OR INDEX SORT

The process of swapping records consumes much of the time required for a sort; the larger the record, the longer the exchanges take. One way to make the Shell sort even more efficient is not to swap the records. Instead, simply swap the order in which you want the records written to the sorted file.

To understand this process, consider the unsorted list of letters J, C, M, R, T, S, shown in Figure 12.5, a representation of a sort table in the computer's memory (Table). Next to it is another table containing the order in which the records are to be written to the sorted file. Because the table on the right stores subscripts of the one on the left (Table), this table is called *Sub*.

Only two exchanges are necessary to sort the table: The letter in Table(1) should be swapped with the letter in Table(2), and the letter in Table(5) should be swapped with the one in Table(6). However, in place of those swaps, corresponding swaps are made in Sub(row). The items in Table can now be written to the sorted file in this order:

Order to Write	Item to Write	Item
1	Table(2)	C
2	Table(1)	J
3	Table(3)	M
4	Table(4)	R
5	Table(6)	S
6	Table(5)	T

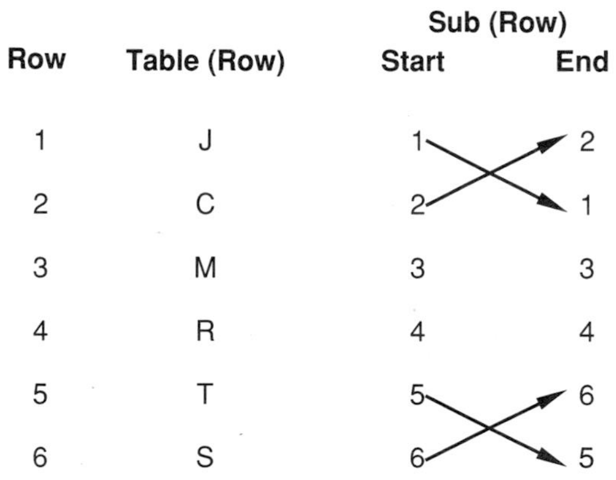

FIGURE 12.5
Tag sort

Row	Table (Row)	Sub (Row) Start	End
1	J	1	2
2	C	2	1
3	M	3	3
4	R	4	4
5	T	5	6
6	S	6	5

Notice that the subscript in each Table(row) is just the contents of Sub(row). You can specify the sorted order by writing nested subscripts in this way:

Order to Write	Item to Write
1	Table(Sub(1)) [= Table(2) = C]
2	Table(Sub(2)) [= Table(1) = J]
3	Table(Sub(3)) [= Table(3) = M]
4	Table(Sub(4)) [= Table(4) = R]
5	Table(Sub(5)) [= Table(6) = S]
6	Table(Sub(6)) [= Table(5) = T]

When you use the nested subscripts, the algorithm to write the items to the sorted file is:

```
for row = 1 to number.of.items
       write Table(Sub(row)) to sorted file
next row
```

You still need an algorithm to exchange the contents of the subscript table. Because the sort is a Shell sort, you can modify that algorithm's *if* statement to incorporate the nested subscripts, Sub(row), and to swap the contents of Sub rather than those of Table.

```
if Table(Sub(row)) > Table(Sub(row + gap))
    then swap Sub(row) and Sub(row + gap)
```

Figure 12.6 contains the pseudocode for the new module to initialize the subscript table and the two tag-sort modules that differ from those of the Shell sort. Program 12.3 is the listing for the tag sort. Like the two previous programs, it generates the sorted file, SALES.SEQ, listed in Table 12.1.

FIGURE 12.6
A Tag Sort Algorithm

```
FILL SUB TABLE    for row = 1 to number.of.records
   (4000)             sub(row) = row
                  next row


SORT RECORDS    gap = number.of.records \ 2
   (5000)       dowhile gap > 0
                    last = number.of.records - gap
                    swapping = yes
                    dowhile swapping
                        swapping = no
                        for row = 1 to last
                          if table(sub(row)) > table(sub(row + gap))
                              then swap sub(row) with sub(row + gap)
                                     swapping = yes
                        next row
                    end dowhile
                    gap = gap \ 2
                end dowhile


WRITE SORTED    open sales.seq for output
RECORDS TO      for row = 1 to number.of.records
    FILE            write sales(sub(row))
   (6000)       next row
                close sales.seq
```

Program 12-3

```
1000 ' PROG12-3
1010 ' *****************************
1020 ' *          TAG SORT         *
1030 ' *****************************
1040 '
1050 ' *****************************
1060 ' *          VARIABLES        *
1070 ' *****************************
1080 '
1090 ' SALES-IN.SEQ             File of unsorted sales records
1100 ' SALES.SEQ               File of sorted sales records
1110 ' Sales-in and Sales record:
1120 '     SALES.MTH
1130 '     SALES.DEPT$
1140 '     SALES.NAME$
1150 '     SALES.AMT
1160 '
1170 ' GAP                     Variable interval for sort comparisons
1180 ' LAST                    Last row to use in comparison loop
1190 ' NUMBER.OF.RECORDS       Number of records to sort
1200 ' ROW                     Table subscript
1210 ' SWAPPING                Flag to indicate a swap of subscripts
1220 '
1230 ' *****************************
1240 ' *          CONSTANTS        *
1250 ' *****************************
1260 '
1270   YES = -1                'Value for true
1280   NO  =  0                'Value for false
1290 '
1300 ' *****************************
1310 ' *        DEFINE TABLES      *
1320 ' *****************************
1330 '
1340   DIM SALE.TBL$(100)      'Table of sales records
1350   DIM SUB(100)            'Table containing order to write records
1999 '
2000 ' *****************************
2010 ' *        CONTROL MODULE     *
2020 ' *****************************
2030 '
2040   GOSUB 3000              'Read Unsorted File
2050   GOSUB 4000              'Fill SUB Table
2060   GOSUB 5000              'Sort Records
2070   GOSUB 6000              'Write Sorted Records to File
2080   END
2999 '
3000 ' *****************************
3010 ' *      READ UNSORTED FILE   *
3020 ' *****************************
3030 '
3040   OPEN "SALES-IN.SEQ" FOR INPUT AS #1
3050   ROW = 0
3060   WHILE NOT EOF(1)
3070       ROW = ROW + 1
3080       LINE INPUT #1, SALE.TBL$(ROW)
3090   WEND
3100   CLOSE #1
3110   NUMBER.OF.RECORDS = ROW
3120   RETURN
3999 '
```

Program 12-3 (continued)

```
4000 ' ****************************
4010 ' *        FILL SUB TABLE        *
4020 ' ****************************
4030 '
4040   FOR ROW = 1 TO NUMBER.OF.RECORDS
4050       SUB(ROW) = ROW
4060   NEXT ROW
4070   RETURN
4999 '
5000 ' ****************************
5010 ' *        SORT RECORDS        *
5020 ' ****************************
5030 '
5040   GAP = NUMBER.OF.RECORDS \ 2
5050   WHILE GAP > 0
5060       LAST = NUMBER.OF.RECORDS - GAP
5070       SWAPPING = YES
5080       WHILE SWAPPING
5090           SWAPPING = NO
5100           FOR ROW = 1 TO LAST
5110               IF SALE.TBL$(SUB(ROW)) > SALE.TBL$(SUB(ROW + GAP))
                        THEN SWAP SALE.TBL$(SUB(ROW)), SALE.TBL$(SUB(ROW + GAP)):
                             SWAPPING = YES
5120           NEXT ROW
5130       WEND
5140       GAP = GAP \ 2
5150   WEND
5160   RETURN
5999 '
6000 ' ****************************
6010 ' *     WRITE SORTED RECORDS     *
6020 ' *            TO FILE            *
6030 ' ****************************
6040 '
6050   OPEN "SALES.SEQ" FOR OUTPUT AS #2
6060   FOR ROW = 1 TO NUMBER.OF.RECORDS
6070       PRINT #2, SALE.TBL$(SUB(ROW))
6080   NEXT ROW
6090   CLOSE #2
6100   RETURN
```

SHELL SORT ON SEPARATE KEY FIELDS

The sorts you have seen so far have all compared entire records just as they were written in the file. More often you will need to sort files using only some of the fields as keys. Also, the order in which these keys are applied may be different from the order in which the fields appear in the file.

For example, suppose Miss Lo, Berrenger's sales manager, would like a report that shows how her staff performed each month. The report must list the salespersons by amount of monthly sales. To simplify the program design, you will list the employee with the lowest sales for the month first.

The two fields that contain the information needed for this sort are SALES.MTH and SALES.AMT. SALES.MTH must be the first key so that January sales are listed first, then February sales, and so on. One way to sort on these two fields is to convert them both to strings and then concatenate them with the month string first. This would produce a key for row 1 of the SALES-IN.SEQ file with the value "1300.15", and your code for the comparisons would look like this:

```
IF key(ROW) > key(ROW + GAP)
   THEN SWAP record(row), record(row + gap)
```

The program must read the four fields of each record separately and then create the key string by combining the first and fourth fields. You can use a two-dimensional sort table and store each field in a separate column in the table.

Some complications arise when you use this composite string value for the sort. The length of SALES.AMT varies considerably, and SALES.MTH may be either one or two digits. Before combining the two field values for the record comparisons, you need to standardize the field values by adding leading blanks and trailing zeros as necessary.

Now that you know the general program requirements, look at the more detailed aspects of the program's design. First, to differentiate this program's output from the output of earlier ones (SALES.SEQ), call the output file SALESOUT.SEQ. The table storing the records will have two dimensions, ROW and COL.

Because you need to read each field of the input records separately, you must use INPUT # instead of LINE INPUT #. Also, because the items in a table must all be of the same data type, read the first and fourth fields, SALES.MTH and SALES.AMT, into temporary variables, called TEMP.MTH and TEMP.AMT, respectively. Then convert the temporary values to strings and standardize their lengths before assigning them to their appropriate positions in the table.

To standardize the length of the month string, first determine its length. If the length is 1, add a leading blank (or zero); otherwise, do nothing.

To standardize the length of the amount string, you must check both ends of the string. For even-dollar amounts (no cents), TEMP.AMT will have no decimal point or trailing zeros. Likewise, it will have no trailing zero for cents that are even multiples of ten. Find out what trailing zeros, if any, are missing, and add them, like this:

```
SALE.TBL$(ROW, 4) = STR$(TEMP.AMT)
IF TEMP.AMT = INT(TEMP.AMT)
   THEN SALE.TBL$(ROW,4) = SALE.TBL$(ROW,4) + ".00"
   ELSE IF INT(TEMP.AMT * 10) = TEMP.AMT * 10
      THEN SALE.TBL$(ROW,4) = SALE.TBL$(ROW,4) + "0"
```

The first THEN clause adds the decimal point and two trailing zeros if the input number is an integer. The ELSE clause checks whether there is only one decimal digit; if so, the final THEN clause adds the single trailing zero. (Depending on your system, you may have to reformat this statement so that it occupies no more than three lines.)

The smaller sales will be shorter than the larger sales because there will be fewer digits to the left of the decimal. After adding any necessary zeros to the right of the decimal point, pad the string on the left with leading blanks (or zeros) until the string is nine characters long. Do that by using the LEN function as follows:

```
WHILE LEN(SALE.TBL$(ROW, 4)) < 9
   SALE.TBL$(ROW, 4) = " " + SALES.TBL$(ROW, 4)
WEND
```

Nine is the standardized length because nine digits accommodate a leading blank for the sign, 5 integer digits, the decimal point, and the two decimal digits of TEMP.AMT (that is, the format #####.## specification plus the leading sign).

With these changes made, the modifications of the Shell sort module are nearly done. The only remaining changes are in the inner dowhile loop. It must begin by initializing the two keys. Then, if there is to be a swap, all four of the corresponding fields in the records must be swapped. Here is the code for that inner loop:

```
FOR ROW = 1 TO LAST
    KEY1$ = SALE.TBL$(ROW,1) + SALE.TBL$(ROW,4)
    KEY2$ = SALE.TBL$(ROW+GAP,1) + SALE.TBL$(ROW+GAP,4)
    IF KEY1$ > KEY2$
        THEN FOR COL = 1 TO 4:
            SWAP SALE.TBL$(ROW,COL), SALE.TBL$(ROW+GAP,COL):
            NEXT COL: SWAPPING = YES
NEXT ROW
```

Some minor changes in the output are also necessary. Convert SALE.TBL$(ROW, 1) and SALE.TBL$(ROW, 4) back to numbers. (You can use the variable names TEMP.MTH and TEMP.AMT again.) Then write to the output file with PRINT # USING so that the file will be ready for inclusion in a report for the sales manager.

The structure chart and pseudocode for the program are in Figure 12.7; some variable names have been abbreviated there to save space. Subroutine 6000 is the module to convert the month value to a two-character string. Subroutine 7000 is the module to convert SALES.AMT to a nine-character string.

Program 12.4 shows the code to implement the pseudocode. The file (SALESOUT.SEQ) that results when the program is run with SALES-IN.SEQ as input is listed in Table 12.2.

Table 12.2   Output of Program 12.4

1	311	M	JEFFERSON	40.56
1	315	D	MAYER	200.75
1	315	J	ANDREWS	300.15
1	312	M	QUILL	300.99
1	312	K	MCCREADY	400.36
1	311	L	DERBYSHIRE	500.12
1	311	J	SAMUELS	600.99
1	312	G	MALLONEE	675.50
1	312	H	BLESSING	1000.50
2	312	M	QUILL	0.00
2	312	H	BLESSING	30.34
2	311	J	SAMUELS	50.75
2	315	J	ANDREWS	90.90
2	312	K	MCCREADY	400.20
2	315	D	MAYER	700.65
2	311	L	DERBYSHIRE	899.50
2	312	G	MALLONEE	900.45
2	311	M	JEFFERSON	1000.65
3	312	H	BLESSING	70.60
3	311	M	JEFFERSON	200.80
3	315	D	MAYER	200.99
3	312	M	QUILL	300.15
3	311	J	SAMUELS	400.55
3	312	K	MCCREADY	600.14
3	311	L	DERBYSHIRE	700.80
3	315	J	ANDREWS	700.85
3	312	G	MALLONEE	2000.85

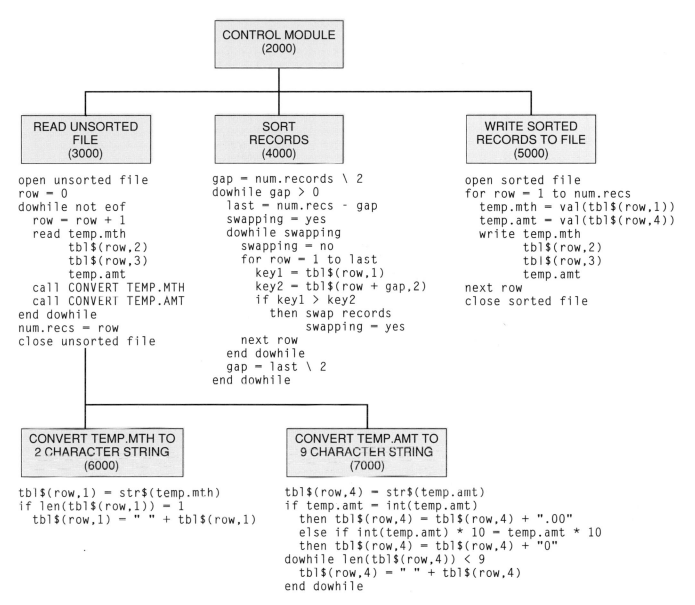

FIGURE 12.7 Structure chart and pseudocode for Program 12.4

PROGRAM 12.4

```
1000 ' PROG12-4
1010 ' *****************************
1020 ' *   SHELL SORT WITH SEPARATE   *
1030 ' *          KEY FIELDS          *
1040 ' *****************************
1050 '
1060 ' *****************************
1070 ' *           VARIABLES          *
1080 ' *****************************
1090 '
1100 ' SALES-IN.SEQ            File of unsorted sales records
1110 ' SALESOUT.SEQ            File of sorted sales records
1120 ' Sales-in and Salesout record:
1130 '     SALES.MTH
1140 '     SALES.DEPT$
1150 '     SALES.NAME$
1160 '     SALES.AMT
```

PROGRAM 12.4 (continued)

```
1170 '
1180 ' GAP                     Variable value for sort comparisons
1190 ' KEY$1, KEY2$            Key field = SALES.MTH + SALES.AMT
1200 ' LAST                    Last subscript to use in comparison loop
1210 ' NUMBER.OF.RECORDS       Number of records to sort
1220 ' ROW, COL                Subscripts for SALE.TBL$
1230 ' SWAPPING                Flag to indicate a swap of records
1240 ' TEMP.AMT                Temporary variable for SALES.AMT
1250 ' TEMP.MTH                Temporary variable for SALES.MTH
1260 '
1270 ' *****************************
1280 ' *        CONSTANTS          *
1290 ' *****************************
1300 '
1310   YES = -1                 'Value for true
1320   NO  =  0                 'Value for false
1330 '
1340 ' *****************************
1350 ' *        DEFINE TABLES      *
1360 ' *****************************
1370 '
1380   DIM SALE.TBL$(100,4)      'Table of sales records
1999 '
2000 ' *****************************
2010 ' *        CONTROL MODULE     *
2020 ' *****************************
2030 '
2040   GOSUB 3000                'Read Unsorted File
2050   GOSUB 4000                'Sort Records
2060   GOSUB 5000                'Write Sorted Records to File
2070   END
2999 '
3000 ' *****************************
3010 ' *      READ UNSORTED FILE   *
3020 ' *****************************
3030 '
3040   OPEN "SALES-IN.SEQ" FOR INPUT AS #1
3050   ROW = 0
3060   WHILE NOT EOF(1)
3070       ROW = ROW + 1
3080       INPUT #1, TEMP.MTH, SALE.TBL$(ROW,2), SALE.TBL$(ROW,3), TEMP.AMT
3090       GOSUB 6000             'Convert TEMP.MTH to 2 Character String
3100       GOSUB 7000             'Convert TEMP.AMT to 9 Character String
3110   WEND
3120   CLOSE #1
3130   NUMBER.OF.RECORDS = ROW
3140   RETURN
3990 '
4000 ' *****************************
4010 ' *        SORT RECORDS       *
4020 ' *****************************
4030 '
4040   GAP = NUMBER.OF.RECORDS \ 2
4050   WHILE GAP > 0
4060       LAST = NUMBER.OF.RECORDS - GAP
4070       SWAPPING = YES
4080       WHILE SWAPPING
4090           SWAPPING = NO
4100           FOR ROW = 1 TO LAST
4110               KEY1$ = SALE.TBL$(ROW,1) + SALE.TBL$(ROW,4)
4120               KEY2$ = SALE.TBL$(ROW+GAP,1) + SALE.TBL$(ROW+GAP,4)
4130               IF KEY1$ > KEY2$ THEN
                       FOR COL = 1 TO 4: SWAP SALE.TBL$(ROW,COL),
                           SALE.TBL$(ROW+GAP,COL) : NEXT COL : SWAPPING = YES
4140           NEXT ROW
```

PROGRAM 12.4   (continued)

```
4150          WEND
4160          GAP = GAP \ 2
4170       WEND
4180       RETURN
4999    '
5000    ' *****************************
5010    ' *      WRITE SORTED RECORDS      *
5020    ' *            TO FILE             *
5030    ' *****************************
5040    '
5050       OPEN "SALESOUT.SEQ" FOR OUTPUT AS #2
5060       FOR ROW = 1 TO NUMBER.OF.RECORDS
5070          TEMP.MTH = VAL(SALE.TBL$(ROW,1))
5080          TEMP.AMT = VAL(SALE.TBL$(ROW,4))
5090          PRINT #2, USING
                "## \ \    \            \ #####.##";
                TEMP.MTH; SALE.TBL$(ROW,2); SALE.TBL$(ROW,3); TEMP.AMT
5100       NEXT ROW
5110       CLOSE #2
5120       RETURN
5999    '
6000    ' *****************************
6010    ' *         CONVERT TEMP.MTH        *
6020    ' *     TO 2 CHARACTER STRING       *
6030    ' *****************************
6040    '
6050       SALE.TBL$(ROW,1) = STR$(TEMP.MTH)
6080    ' Pad with a leading blank, if necessary:
6090       IF LEN(SALE.TBL$(ROW, 1)) = 1
              THEN SALE.TBL$(ROW, 1) = " " + SALE.TBL$(ROW,1)
6100       RETURN
6999    '
7000    ' *****************************
7010    ' *         CONVERT TEMP.AMT        *
7020    ' *     TO 9 CHARACTER STRING       *
7030    ' *****************************
7040    '
7050       SALE.TBL$(ROW,4) = STR$(TEMP.AMT)
7060    ' Add trailing zeros, if necessary:
7070       IF TEMP.AMT = INT(TEMP.AMT) THEN SALE.TBL$(ROW,4)=SALE.TBL$(ROW,4)+".00"
              ELSE IF INT(TEMP.AMT * 10) = TEMP.AMT * 10
                   THEN SALE.TBL$(ROW,4) = SALE.TBL$(ROW,4) + "0"
7080    ' Pad with leading blanks, if necessary:
7090       WHILE LEN(SALE.TBL$(ROW,4)) < 9
7100          SALE.TBL$(ROW,4) = " " + SALE.TBL$(ROW,4)
7110       WEND
7120       RETURN
```

THE DOS SORT COMMAND

A built-in DOS command gives you another alternative when you need to perform a memory sort. It is easy to use and fast, but it is not very flexible. However, the DOS sort works well with files whose key fields are adjacent, as they are in the file SALES-IN.SEQ used in Programs 12.1, 12.2, and 12.3. In cases like these, one line of instructions entered from the DOS prompt can tell the operating system all it needs to know to do the job! The equivalent to any of the first three programs of this chapter is:

```
A>SORT < SALES-IN.SEQ > SALES.SEQ
```

The less-than symbol tells the operating system where to get the records to sort, and the greater-than symbol tells it what to do with them after they are sorted. The above statement translates to "read the records in SALES-IN.SEQ, sort them, and then write them to SALES.SEQ."

You can use two options with the SORT command. If you insert /R immediately after the word SORT, DOS sorts in reverse (descending) order. For example,

```
A>SORT /R < SALES-IN.SEQ > SALES.SEQ
```

will sort the records from SALES-IN.SEQ in order from March (3) to January (1), then write the sorted records into SALES.SEQ.

The other option is to add /+*n* at the end of the command, where *n* is the number of the character in the record at which the sort is to begin. The command

```
A>SORT < SALES-IN.SEQ > SALES.SEQ /+12
```

will create a SALES.SEQ file arranged in order of the salespersons' last names. See Table 12.1 to confirm that the last names do begin at the 12th character of the records in SALES-IN.SEQ. Quotes and commas count. *Caution*: You *must* insert the plus sign before the position number; otherwise the file will be sorted by the first character in the record.

The DOS sort is very fast. It sorts the SALES.SEQ file in about half the time the tag sort, the fastest of this chapter's BASIC programs, requires. However, it has limitations. Like the BASIC sorts, the DOS sort works with limited memory; it will not process files occupying more than 63K. It is also not very flexible; if you wish to sort on key fields that are not adjacent (as Program 12.4 does) you would probably be better off writing your own program.

In addition to the DOS SORT command, other prewritten sort programs may suit your needs. Look first for such ready-to-run programs because they will save you programming time and because they are fast. Nevertheless, when your sort is a complex one, with some keys in ascending order and others in descending order, you are likely to have to write a new program.

Summary

- Sequential files often must be arranged or *sorted* in a particular order before they are processed; that was the case with the files used in Chapter 9 for control-break processing.

- *Memory sorts* are those done in the computer's memory. The basic steps in this process are:

  1. Read the records from an unsorted file into a table.

  2. Rearrange the records in the table so that they are in the desired order.

  3. Write the sorted table to a file.

- The three sorting algorithms described in this chapter are:

  1. Bubble-sort (easy to understand and code, but slow)

  2. Shell sort (more complex than the bubble sort, but faster)

  3. Shell sort of tags (still more complex, but much faster for large records)

- The sort available with PC/MS-DOS is very fast, but it is limited to files of 63K or smaller and is not very flexible.

- New BASIC instructions introduced in this chapter are:

LINE INPUT #   A statement that reads an entire line from a sequential file to a string variable.

SWAP   A statement that exchanges the values of two variables of the same type.

Review Questions

1. When is it necessary to sort sequential files?

2. What is a memory sort?

3. What three steps are involved in every memory sort?

4. What is the purpose of the SWAP statement?

5. When would you use LINE INPUT # instead of INPUT #?

6. What does the variable GAP refer to in the Shell sort? How does it vary during the sorting process?

7. The tag-sort algorithm is very similar to the Shell-sort algorithm. What makes the tag sort faster? When would it be especially advantageous to use the tag sort instead of the Shell sort?

8. What are the advantages and disadvantages of the DOS sort?

9. Explain why each of the operations performed by the subroutine beginning on line 7000 of Program 12.4 are necessary.

Problems

1. Write code to sort the following table according to its row values. Be sure that you do not mix up the numbers in the rows. Whenever two rows have the same value in a corresponding column, you will need to sort on the next element of the row.

		Original Table col				Sorted Table col		
		(1)	**(2)**	**(3)**	**(4)**	**(1)**	**(2)**	**(3)**	**(4)**
	(1)	9	4	7	6	2	5	1	3
	(2)	2	5	4	9	2	5	4	3
	(3)	8	7	7	1	2	5	4	9
	(4)	2	5	1	3	7	2	2	1
row	**(5)**	9	4	7	2	8	6	1	0
	(6)	8	6	1	0	8	6	2	1
	(7)	2	5	4	3	8	7	7	1
	(8)	7	2	2	1	9	4	7	2
	(9)	8	6	2	1	9	4	7	6

2. Using the techniques described in Chapter 10, write a program to generate 500 three-digit numbers at random. Store the numbers in a sequential file. Sort this file using the bubble sort, the Shell sort, and the DOS sort to determine how long each sort takes.

3. Assign the letters A through Z the integer values 1 through 26, respectively. Using the techniques described in Chapter 10, generate 100 five-character strings at random. Sort the strings and print both the sorted and unsorted lists of strings.

4. Create two lists containing 100 six-digit integers, one list in random order and the other with only 10% of the items out of order. (Use a text editor to move 10% of the items in the sorted list.) Order the lists with the bubble sort, the Shell sort, the tag sort, and the DOS sort. Record how long each sort took.

5. Repeat the comparisons in problem 4 with lists of 200 and 500 integers.

6. Run Program 12.4 with the SALES-IN.SEQ file as input. Use a word processor or text editor to prepare a memo to Berrenger's sales manager, Miss Natasha Lo, and load the SALES-IN.SEQ file in the appropriate place in the memo.

Program Assignments

1. Almost Heaven Products, Inc., maintains a master inventory file that lists items available at each of its plants. Management would like a report that provides inventory information for each unit in each plant and for each plant in each of the corporate divisions.

   a. Write a program that arranges the data in the file in the proper order for the report. Use *division* as the first key field, *plant* as the second key field, and *unit* as the third key field.

   b. The file is AHP-INV.SEQ; each record has the following structure:

Field Name	**Length**	**Data Type**
AHP.INV.DIV	1	String
AHP.INV.PLANT	1	String
AHP.INV.UNIT	2	String
AHP.INV.STOCK.NO	3	String
AHP.INV.PART.NO	4	String
AHP.INV.QTY	4	Numeric (####)
AHP.INV.PRICE	6	Numeric (###.##)

   c. Run your program with the following data:

Division	Plant	Unit	Stock	Part	Quantity	Price
A	3	34	451	1234	550	2.25
C	7	25	571	7321	225	3.50
C	9	34	132	4589	85	7.90
B	6	17	657	1123	120	3.85
A	3	9	876	9812	90	16.75
A	2	12	554	5436	356	.95
B	6	3	665	2131	125	3.15
C	9	25	756	3334	75	9.50
A	1	2	812	4112	230	1.50
A	1	4	333	1988	145	3.30
C	7	4	411	2367	110	5.65
B	6	7	350	3456	50	8.75

d. List your file to test your program's output.

2. Commercial Innovations of the Kanawha Valley, Inc., keeps data about its employees on a sequential file. Mr. Howard, the personnel manager, would like a report that lists job titles in alphabetical order and, for each job title, the employees holding the title arranged from highest to lowest salary. Write a program to:

a. Arrange the records in the employee file in the order necessary for Mr. Howard's report.

b. Prepare the report with appropriate headings and page numbers.

c. Print no more than 20 lines of the report body on a single page.

d. The employee file is CI-EMP.SEQ. The file format is as follows:

Field Name	Length	Data Type
CI.EMP.ID$	4	String
CI.EMP.NAME$	20	String
CI.EMP.TITLE$	20	String
CI.EMP.HIRE.DATE$	6	String (*mmddyy*)
CI.EMP.SALARY	7	Numeric (####.##)

e. Run your program with the following CI-EMP.SEQ records:

```
1001,"SULLIVAN, RHONDA",PROGRAMMER/
    ANALYST,102276,2371.80
1020,"HESCHT, JEFF",PROGRAMMER,120383,
    1431.00
1033,"BLANKENSHIP, MARY",SYSTEMS
    ANALYST,030181,3011.42
1045,"SULLIVAN, JENNIFER",PROGRAMMER,
    091085,1300.00
1058,"NEASE, ALAN",PROG. SUPERVISOR,
    062381,1985.66
1061,"TUCKER, THOMAS",SYSTEMS
    ENGINEER,081878,3712.49
1068,"PARSONS, TERRI ANN",PROGRAMMER,
```

```
    043080,1888.91
1071,"PARSONS, CANDY",PROGRAMMER,
    040381,1721.80
1075,"TUCKER, K. L.",PROGRAMMER/
    ANALYST,110188,2019.20
1077,"FELLEURE, JENNIFER",PROGRAMMER,
    010585,1250.00
1084,"WOODS, WENDY",SYSTEMS ANALYST,
    040179,3191.47
1088,"FELLEURE, STEPHANIE",PROGRAMMER,
    070783,1458.00
1093,"MASER, GRETCHEN",PROGRAMMER,
    081285,1250.00
1095,"BADGELY, TAMMY",PROGRAMMER,
    081585,1250.00
1099,"LEGG, CHARLES",SYSTEMS ENGINEER,
    020176,3905.00
2003,"TUCKER, TIMOTHY",PROGRAMMER,
    061283,1738.48
2006,"TOLLEY, LISA",PROGRAMMER/
    ANALYST,091777,2191.00
2010,"HESCHT, JENNIFER",PROGRAMMER,
    030884,1313.89
2013,"HUDSON, KIM",PROGRAMMER,051284,
    1300.32
2017,"BLANKENSHIP, LAURA",PROGRAMMER,
    120183,1359.44
2019,"NELSON, SUSAN",PROGRAMMER,
    111286,1200.00
2029,"HARRIS, MARK",PROGRAMMER/
    ANALYST,090785,1987.25
2036,"HALLBACK, MARIA",PROGRAMMER,
    020181,1730.17
2040,"YOUNG, TAMRA",PROGRAMMER,030780,
    1850.12
2044,"LEONG, JOE",PROGRAMMER,070778,
    2015.88
```

3. Make these modifications to the program you wrote for programming assignment 9 in Chapter 10:

a. Add another table to your program to store the passenger name and seat assignment.

b. Add a Passenger List option to the menu.

c. When the user selects the Passenger List option, have the program sort the table entries by name and display the alphabetical passenger list in this format:

Passenger List

Name	Row	Seat
Bogdan	3	A
Carroll	3	B

. . . .

d. Run your program with the following records:

Name	Row	Seat
Jeffers, B	1	A
Conners, A	1	C
Davis, P	1	D
Vickers, M	2	B
Johnson, D	2	D
Criner, G	3	A
Hall, H	3	D
Kimmell, C	C	A
Scholl, L	4	B
Darnell, B	4	C
Darnell, S	4	D
Shinsky, A	5	B
Yao, W	5	D

Using the Data Disk

1. Put the data disk in the disk drive.

   a. Enter the DOS command:

   `COPY SALES-IN.SEQ SALES-IN.CPY`

   b. Enter the DOS command:

   `TYPE SALES-IN.CPY`

   c. Enter the DOS command:

   `[SORT < SALES-IN.CPY > SALESORD.CPY]`

   d. Enter the DOS command:

   `TYPE SALESORD.CPY`

2. Load PROG12-2.

   a. Change line 5050 so that the output file is SALES2.SEQ.
   b. Run the program with the SALES-I2.SEQ file and examine the output file. Why doesn't the sort work correctly with this file?
   c. Modify the program so that it will work correctly when the input file has both one- and two-digit months.
   d. Save the program as CH12-1.DD.

3. Load PROG12-2.

   a. Modify the program so that it will sort the file SALES-IN.SEQ in order of sales from lowest to highest.
   b. Continue to change the program so that it writes the name, sales amount, and department of each record on the screen. The result will be a list of salespersons in increasing order of sales.
   c. Now make the list appear on the screen in decreasing order.
   d. Save the program as CH12-2.DD.

4. Load PROG12-4. Modify the program so that it lists the sales for each month in decreasing order (from highest to lowest). Save the program as CH12-3.DD.

Chapter Thirteen

Sequential File Updating

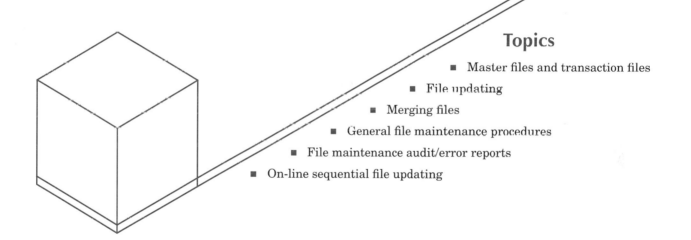

Topics

- Master files and transaction files
- File updating
- Merging files
- General file maintenance procedures
- File maintenance audit/error reports
- On-line sequential file updating

INTRODUCTION

A *master file* is a file of records that contains relatively permanent data. Lowell and Bauer's client file (CLIENT.SEQ), described in Chapter 6, is an abbreviated example of a master file. That firm's actual master file of client records would include additional items, such as address, telephone number, and place of employment. The file might also include some items that change often, such as a client's current balance.

Regardless of whether the data are relatively permanent (name and address, for example) or changed periodically (current balance, for example), you will sometimes need to change items to bring the master file up to date. The process of changing a master file to reflect the current status of a business is called *file updating*.

A *transaction file* contains data about individual events or transactions. You can use the data in transaction files to calculate summary information that may be kept in master files. For example, Lowell and Bauer's billing file (BILL.SEQ) is a transaction file; using the data in BILL.SEQ, you can calculate clients' current balances for inclusion in the client master file. *Posting* is the process of accumulating totals, such as current balance, and using them to update the master file.

Another type of transaction file contains records for file maintenance. *File maintenance* is the process of making any of the three following changes to the relatively permanent data in the master file:

1. Adding a new record to the file

2. Removing a record from the file

3. Changing the contents of one or more fields in an existing record

File maintenance differs from posting in two ways: First, it may change the number of records in the file. Second, file maintenance does not involve accumulating current balances. Both types of file updating—file maintenance and file posting—may be done in the same program, however.

The important characteristics of sequential file updating are:

1. A sequential file is updated with two input files, a master file and a transaction file. The master file contains the records before any changes are made. The transaction file contains the information needed for making the changes.

2. Both the master file and transaction file must be sorted on the same control field or key field. For example, Lowell and Bauer's master client file and the transaction file of changes could both be sorted on the field CLIENT.ACCT$.

3. File maintenance requires that the transaction file include a code indicating what action the program should take: add a record to the master file, delete a record from the master file, or change a master file record. For example, here are some codes that you might use:

```
A = Add
C = Change
D = Delete
```

These codes become a minor control field on which the transaction file is sorted. To understand why, suppose that Lowell and Bauer acquire a new client; thus, an Add transaction is required. As the law clerk reviews the client information, she notices that the name of the new client is misspelled. At this point, a Change transaction is required. During file updating, the Change transaction must be processed after the Add transaction; otherwise, the file will not contain the record to be changed.

4. The output from a sequential file update consists of a new master file and an *audit report*, which lists the update actions, record counts, and any applicable error messages. Audit reports provide an audit trail if discrepancies arise. Any incorrect transactions must be corrected and resubmitted later.

5. Each record in the old (input) master file must be rewritten to the new (output) master file, even if no changes have been made. Consequently, sequential file processing is inefficient if there are few changes to the master file. It is a good technique, however, when there is substantial activity on the master file. *Activity* refers to the percentage of master records that are updated during a processing run.

In this chapter, Program 13.1 illustrates a way to merge two files. *Merging* files means combining two or more files (sorted in the same order) into a single file. You will need to apply the logic used to merge files when you write a program to update a sequential file. Both Programs 13.2 and 13.3 perform file maintenance. Program 13.2 updates a file but makes no provision for incorrect transaction codes in the transaction file; the programmer assumes all the information has been validated beforehand. Program 13.3 provides an error report if the user attempts to (1) add a record that is already in the master file or (2) delete or change a record that is not already in the master file. The chapter concludes with a discussion of on-line updating of a sequential master file.

MERGING TWO FILES

In sequential file updating, an old master file is merged with the transaction file to create the new master file. Before creating a program to update a sequential file, consider the process of merging two files.

Define the Problem

Mrs. Murphy from Lowell and Bauer has created two separate billing files and now wants a single billing file. She has asked you to write a program that will merge the two files.

Describe the Output and Determine the Input

Figure 13.1 shows the format of the three files and a systems chart illustrating the relationship among them. BILL1.SEQ and BILL2.SEQ are the input files; they both must be sorted on the billing account number field (BILL.ACCT$). BILL3.SEQ is the output file; it contains the records from both input files arranged in order by billing account numbers.

BILL1.SEQ (sequential input file)
BILLING Record:

Field Name	Data Length	Data Type
BILL1.ACCT$	3	String
BILL1.NAME$	20	String
BILL1.HRS	3	Numeric (###)
BILL1.RATE	5	Numeric (##.##)

BILL2.SEQ (sequential input file)
BILLING Record:

Field Name	Data Length	Data Type
BILL2.ACCT$	3	String
BILL2.NAME$	20	String
BILL2.HRS	3	Numeric (###)
BILL2.RATE	5	Numeric (##.##)

BILL3.SEQ (sequential output file)
BILLING Record:

Field Name	Data Length	Data Type
BILL3.ACCT$	3	String
BILL3.NAME$	20	String
BILL3.HRS	3	Numeric (###)
BILL3.RATE	5	Numeric (##.##)

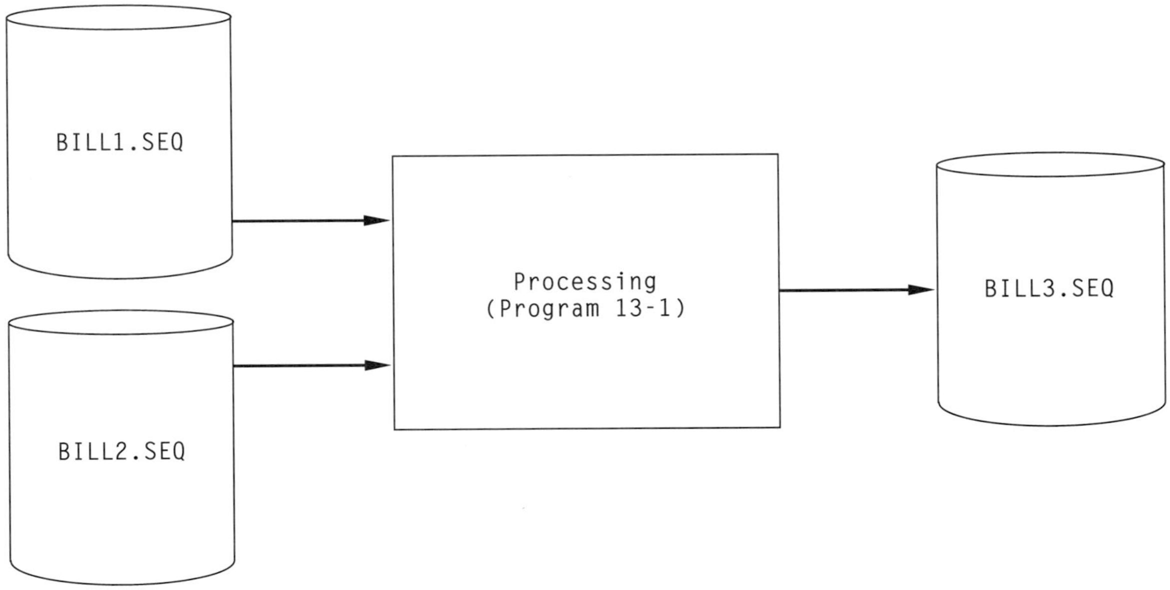

FIGURE 13.1   Format of billing files for Program 13.1

The program also displays a message when the merge is complete and, for control purposes, gives the following record counts:

```
Records in BILL1.SEQ
Records in BILL2.SEQ
Records in BILL3.SEQ
```

Design the Program Logic

The program is divided into two level-1 modules, MERGE FILES and WRITE SUMMARY LINES. The MERGE FILES module first opens the three files and then reads the first record from each input file. A record must be read from each file before the dowhile loop that compares the billing account numbers.

In the dowhile loop, the billing account number from BILL1.SEQ is compared with the billing account number from BILL2.SEQ. If the billing account number from BILL1.SEQ is less than the billing account number from BILL2.SEQ, the module calls WRITE BILL3.SEQ FROM BILL1.SEQ and READ BILL1.SEQ. The first module writes a record to the output file using the record from BILL1.SEQ, and the second module reads another record from the BILL1.SEQ file to replace the record just written. If the billing account number from BILL1.SEQ is not less than the billing account number from BILL2.SEQ, the MERGE FILES module calls WRITE BILL3.SEQ FROM BILL2.SEQ and READ BILL2.SEQ. The first module writes a record to the output file using the record from BILL2.SEQ, and the second module reads another record from the BILL2.SEQ file to replace the record just written. If the billing account numbers are equal, it does not matter which input file is used for writing the output record.

This process of comparing billing account numbers and writing to the output file continues until the program comes to the end of both files. Because one file will end before the other, you need to continue the loop until the second file ends so that BILL3.SEQ contains all the records from both files. You can use a variable with the value CHR$(255) to accomplish this. CHR$(255) is the highest ASCII value possible (see Appendix C).

The control field, billing account number, is three characters long so put CHR$(255) in each of the three billing account number positions of the last record of each input file. Note that both the READ modules place the value CHR$(255) in the billing account field when the end of file is reached. When the end of one file is reached, the remaining billing account numbers in the other file will always be less than the billing account number of the completed file because no billing account number can be greater than CHR$(255). The dowhile loop stops when the billing account number in both files contains CHR$(255).

The WRITE SUMMARY LINES module displays the end-of-program message and the record counts.

Figure 13.2 shows the structure chart and pseudocode for this program. Also review Table 13.1, which summarizes what happens in these three situations:

1. BILL1.ACCT$ < BILL2.ACCT$

2. BILL1.ACCT$ = BILL2.ACCT$

3. BILL1.ACCT$ > BILL2.ACCT$

Code the Program Instructions

Program 13.1 provides a way to merge two files. There are no new BASIC statements in this program. Note, however, the use of CHR$(255). In the CONSTANTS section, HIGH.VALUES$ is the variable used to hold the *highest value* in the ASCII collating sequence. It is set to STRING$(3,CHR$(255)) in line 1340. HIGH.VALUES$ is used to control the WHILE/WEND loop in lines 3110–3130. As long as both billing account numbers are not equal to HIGH.VALUES$, the merge process continues. Lines 5040 and 6040 place HIGH.VALUES$ in the billing account number if the end of the file has been reached.

Notice that the CLOSE statement in line 3150 is not followed by any file numbers. Remember that in this case all currently opened files are closed. This statement could have also been written as follows:

```
3150 CLOSE #1,#2,#3
```

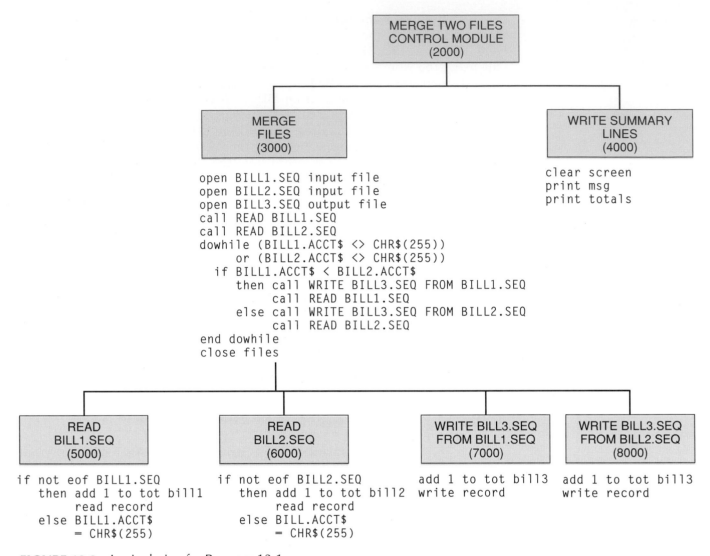

FIGURE 13.2 Logic design for Program 13.1

Table 13.1 **Merge processing**

	BILL1.ACCT$ < BILL2.ACCT$	BILL1.ACCT$ = BILL2.ACCT$	BILL1.ACCT$ > BILL2.ACCT$
Write Billing 3 Record from Billing 1 Record	Yes	No	No
Write Billing 3 Record from Billing 2 Record	No	Yes	Yes
Read BILL1.SEQ.	Yes	No	No
Read BILL2.SEQ	No	Yes	Yes

PROGRAM 13.1

```
1000 ' PROG13-1
1010 ' *****************************
1020 ' *        MERGE TWO FILES        *
1030 ' *****************************
1040 '
1050 ' *****************************
1060 ' *          VARIABLES          *
1070 ' *****************************
1080 '
1090 ' BILL1.SEQ                    Billing Input File
1100 ' Billing Record:
1110 '      BILL1.ACCT$
1120 '      BILL1.NAME$
1130 '      BILL1.HRS
1140 '      BILL1.RATE
1150 '
1160 ' BILL2.SEQ                    Billing Input File
1170 ' Billing Record:
1180 '      BILL2.ACCT$
1190 '      BILL2.NAME$
1200 '      BILL2.HRS
1210 '      BILL2.RATE
1220 '
1230 ' BILL3.SEQ                    Billing Output File
1240 ' Billing Record:
1250 '      BILL3.ACCT$
1260 '      BILL3.NAME$
1270 '      BILL3.HRS
1280 '      BILL3.RATE
1290 '
1300 ' *****************************
1310 ' *          CONSTANTS          *
1320 ' *****************************
1330 '
1340   HIGH.VALUES$ = STRING$(3,CHR$(255))    'Highest possible value in
                                               collating sequence
1350 '
1360 ' *****************************
1370 ' *   INITIALIZED VARIABLES   *
1380 ' *****************************
1390 '
1400   TOTAL.BILL1 = 0          'Total input records  in BILL1.SEQ
1410   TOTAL.BILL2 = 0          'Total input records  in BILL2.SEQ
1420   TOTAL.BILL3 = 0          'Total output records in BILL3.SEQ
1999 '
2000 ' *****************************
2010 ' *        CONTROL MODULE        *
2020 ' *****************************
2030 '
2040   GOSUB 3000              'Merge Files
2050   GOSUB 4000              'Write Summary Lines
2060   END
2999 '
3000 ' *****************************
3010 ' *          MERGE FILES          *
3020 ' *****************************
3030 '
3040   OPEN "BILL1.SEQ" FOR INPUT  AS #1
3050   OPEN "BILL2.SEQ" FOR INPUT  AS #2
3060   OPEN "BILL3.SEQ" FOR OUTPUT AS #3
3070 '
3080   GOSUB 5000              'Read BILL1.SEQ
3090   GOSUB 6000              'Read BILL2.SEQ
```

PROGRAM 13.1 (continued)

```
3100  '
3110     WHILE (BILL1.ACCT$ <> HIGH.VALUES$) OR (BILL2.ACCT$ <> HIGH.VALUES$)
3120        IF BILL1.ACCT$ < BILL2.ACCT$
                  THEN GOSUB 7000: GOSUB 5000
                  ELSE GOSUB 8000: GOSUB 6000
3130     WEND
3140  '
3150     CLOSE
3160     RETURN
3999  '
4000  ' *****************************
4010  ' *      WRITE SUMMARY LINES      *
4020  ' *****************************
4030  '
4040     CLS
4050     PRINT TAB(26); "File merge complete."
4060     PRINT TAB(26); USING "Records in BILL1.SEQ =  ##"; TOTAL.BILL1
4070     PRINT TAB(26); USING "Records in BILL2.SEQ =  ##"; TOTAL.BILL2
4080     PRINT TAB(26); USING "Records in BILL3.SEQ = ###"; TOTAL.BILL3
4090     RETURN
4999  '
5000  ' *****************************
5010  ' *         READ BILL1.SEQ         *
5020  ' *****************************
5030  '
5040     IF NOT EOF(1) THEN TOTAL.BILL1 = TOTAL.BILL1 + 1:
                        INPUT #1, BILL1.ACCT$,BILL1.NAME$,BILL1.HRS,BILL1.RATE
                  ELSE BILL1.ACCT$ = HIGH.VALUES$
5050     RETURN
5999  '
6000  ' *****************************
6010  ' *         READ BILL2.SEQ         *
6020  ' *****************************
6030  '
6040     IF NOT EOF(2) THEN TOTAL.BILL2 = TOTAL.BILL2 + 1:
                        INPUT #2, BILL2.ACCT$,BILL2.NAME$,BILL2.HRS,BILL2.RATE
                  ELSE BILL2.ACCT$ = HIGH.VALUES$
6050     RETURN
6999  '
7000  ' *****************************
7010  ' *        WRITE BILL3.SEQ        *
7020  ' *        FROM BILL1.SEQ         *
7030  ' *****************************
7040  '
7050     TOTAL.BILL3 = TOTAL.BILL3 + 1
7060     WRITE #3, BILL1.ACCT$, BILL1.NAME$,
                  BILL1.HRS,   BILL1.RATE
7070     RETURN
7999  '
8000  ' *****************************
8010  ' *        WRITE BILL3.SEQ        *
8020  ' *        FROM BILL2.SEQ         *
8030  ' *****************************
8040  '
8050     TOTAL.BILL3 = TOTAL.BILL3 + 1
8060     WRITE #3, BILL2.ACCT$, BILL2.NAME$,
                  BILL2.HRS,   BILL2.RATE
8070     RETURN
```

To understand the logic of this program, take some time to "play computer." Suppose that BILL1.SEQ contains the records

```
"206","CHRISTY ANDERSON",12,80
"503","KIRA PETERSON",14,40
```

and BILL2.SEQ contains the records

```
"105","MICHELLE GECZY",10,75
"602","RONALD JONES",20,80
"660","RIDGELY BRYANT",15,80
```

What does BILL3.SEQ contain at the end of the program run? What are the record counts?

Test the Program

Figure 13.3 shows the contents of BILL3.SEQ after the merge using the input shown in BILL1.SEQ and BILL2.SEQ. Notice the record counts displayed after the merge is completed. Record counts from file merges and updates are very useful control data.

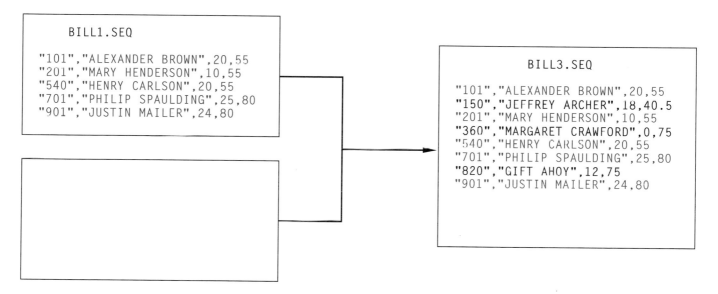

```
        BILL1.SEQ

"101","ALEXANDER BROWN",20,55
"201","MARY HENDERSON",10,55
"540","HENRY CARLSON",20,55
"701","PHILIP SPAULDING",25,80
"901","JUSTIN MAILER",24,80
```

```
        BILL3.SEQ

"101","ALEXANDER BROWN",20,55
"150","JEFFREY ARCHER",18,40.5
"201","MARY HENDERSON",10,55
"360","MARGARET CRAWFORD",0,75
"540","HENRY CARLSON",20,55
"701","PHILIP SPAULDING",25,80
"820","GIFT AHOY",12,75
"901","JUSTIN MAILER",24,80
```

The following totals are displayed on the screen at the end of Program 13.1:

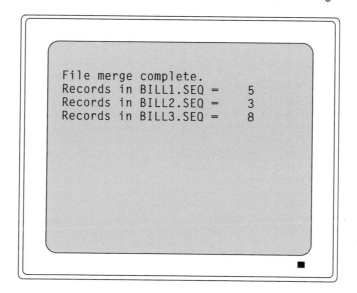

```
File merge complete.
Records in BILL1.SEQ =    5
Records in BILL2.SEQ =    3
Records in BILL3.SEQ =    8
```

FIGURE 13.3 Output from Program 13.1

UPDATING A MASTER FILE

Now that you are familiar with the process of merging two sequential files, consider a program to update the file during the merge process.

Define the Problem

A local jewelry store, Briana's, has a master file of customer account information. This file needs updating; new accounts must be added, certain names and discounts must be changed, and dormant accounts must be deleted. A transaction file with the maintenance data already exists.

Describe the Output and Determine the Input

Figure 13.4 shows the formats of the master file, the transaction file, and the new master file. (The records contain few fields so that the example will not be too complex; also, the data in both files have been previously validated.) The old master file is sorted by account number (OLDMAST.ACCT$). The transaction file is sorted by TRAN.CODE$ (transaction code) within TRAN.ACCT$ (account number). The account number is the unique field or key on which the update is based. The output of this program is the updated master file plus a set of control totals displayed on the screen.

FIGURE 13.4
Formats of files for
Program 13.2

TRAN.SEQ   (sequential input file)
TRAN record:

Field Name	Data Length	Data Type
TRAN.CODE$	1	String
TRAN.ACCT$	4	String
TRAN.NAME$	20	String
TRAN.DISC	2	Numeric (##)
TRAN.CODE$	= A for add record	
TRAN.CODE$	= C for change name or discount	
TRAN.CODE$	= D for delete record	

OLDMAST.SEQ   (sequential input file)
OLDMAST record:

Field Name	Data Length	Data Type
OLDMAST.ACCT$	4	String
OLDMAST.NAME$	20	String
OLDMAST.DISC	2	Numeric (##)

NEWMAST.SEQ   (sequential output file)
NEWMAST record:

Field Name	Data Length	Data Type
NEWMAST.ACCT$	4	String
NEWMAST.NAME$	20	String
NEWMAST.DISC	2	Numeric (##)

Design the Program Logic

To update a master file with new records, changes, and deletions, you need to:

1. Read a record from the transaction file and the master file.
2. Set the current key equal to the smaller key.
3. If the current key is equal to the old master key:
   a. Move the old master data to the new master record.
   b. Read another old master record.
   c. Note that a record is in progress.
4. If the current key is equal to the transaction key, check for an addition, change, or deletion.
   a. If there is an addition, move the transaction data to the new master record and note that a record is in progress.
   b. If there is a change, check which fields to change and move the changes to the new master record.
   c. If there is a deletion, note that a record is not in progress.
   d. Read another transaction.
   e. Repeat until the transaction key does not equal the current key.
5. Write a new master record if a record is in progress.
6. Repeat steps 2–5 until all the records from both files are read.

The pseudocode in Figure 13.5 describes the general logic of file maintenance. This method has two important advantages: First, the program can process multiple transactions affecting the same account. For example, suppose a customer opens an account one day and closes it the next. The first transaction, Add, sets up a new master record, but the subsequent Delete changes the record in progress flag to no so that the record is never written to the new master file. The second advantage is that multiple transaction files

FIGURE 13.5
General pseudocode for file updating

```
open files
read transaction record
read old master record
select current key

dowhile current key not = high-values

    if old master key = current key
      then record in progress = yes
            set up new master record
            read old master record
      else record in progress = no

      dowhile transaction key = current key

        if tran code = add
          then set up new master record
                record in progress = yes
          else if tran code = change
                then change new master record
                else if tran code = delete
                        then record in progress = no
        read transaction record

      end dowhile

      if record in progress = yes
        then write new master record

      select next current key

end dowhile

close files
```

can be processed with this method because current key is always defined as the smallest value of all keys currently being processed.

Now, look at the structure chart and pseudocode in Figure 13.6. After the files are opened and the first record from each file is read, the UPDATE FILE module calls the SELECT CURRENT KEY module to select the first value for the variable CURRENT.KEY$. The key field or control field in this application is the account number. CURRENT.KEY$ is the smaller of the old master and transaction account numbers currently being processed. If the transaction key is less than the old master key, then CURRENT.KEY$ is set equal to the transaction key. If the transaction key is equal to the old master key, either key could be the CURRENT.KEY$, but in this example it is set to the old master key. Finally, if the transaction key is greater than the old master key, CURRENT.KEY$ is set equal to the old master key.

The dowhile loop in the module UPDATE FILE is executed until the last record in both files is read because CURRENT.KEY$ will not equal

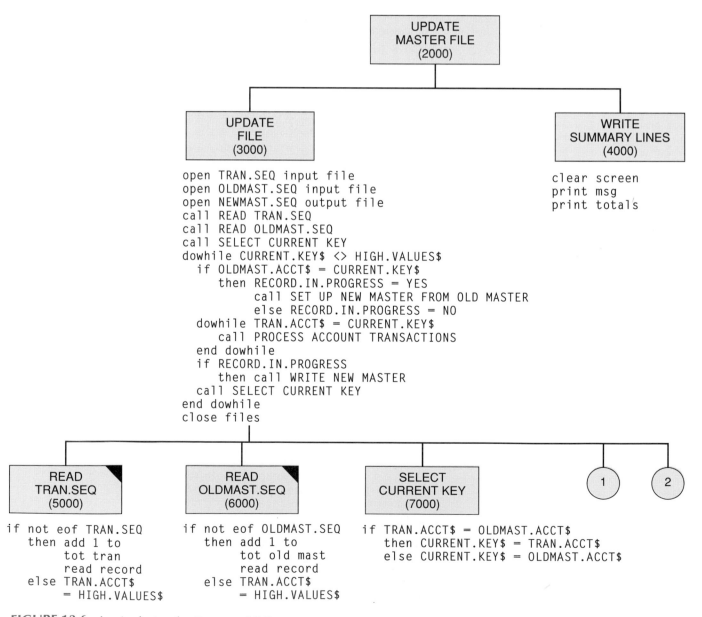

```
                              UPDATE
                           MASTER FILE
                             (2000)


          UPDATE                                    WRITE
          FILE                                   SUMMARY LINES
          (3000)                                    (4000)

open TRAN.SEQ input file                      clear screen
open OLDMAST.SEQ input file                   print msg
open NEWMAST.SEQ output file                  print totals
call READ TRAN.SEQ
call READ OLDMAST.SEQ
call SELECT CURRENT KEY
dowhile CURRENT.KEY$ <> HIGH.VALUES$
  if OLDMAST.ACCT$ = CURRENT.KEY$
    then RECORD.IN.PROGRESS = YES
         call SET UP NEW MASTER FROM OLD MASTER
         else RECORD.IN.PROGRESS = NO
  dowhile TRAN.ACCT$ = CURRENT.KEY$
    call PROCESS ACCOUNT TRANSACTIONS
  end dowhile
  if RECORD.IN.PROGRESS
    then call WRITE NEW MASTER
  call SELECT CURRENT KEY
end dowhile
close files


    READ                  READ                 SELECT              1        2
  TRAN.SEQ             OLDMAST.SEQ           CURRENT KEY
   (5000)                (6000)               (7000)

if not eof TRAN.SEQ    if not eof OLDMAST.SEQ   if TRAN.ACCT$ = OLDMAST.ACCT$
  then add 1 to          then add 1 to            then CURRENT.KEY$ = TRAN.ACCT$
       tot tran               tot old mast         else CURRENT.KEY$ = OLDMAST.ACCT$
       read record           read record
  else TRAN.ACCT$       else TRAN.ACCT$
     = HIGH.VALUES$        = HIGH.VALUES$
```

FIGURE 13.6 Logic design for Program 13.2

HIGH.VALUES$ until after the last record in the second file is read. The first statement in the dowhile loop checks whether the old master key is equal to CURRENT.KEY$. If it is, a new master record is set up, the RECORD. IN.PROGRESS flag is set to YES, and another old master record is read. The RECORD.IN.PROGRESS flag is used to determine whether a master record is in the process of being prepared for the new master file. If the old master key is not equal to CURRENT.KEY$, the RECORD.IN.PROGRESS flag is set to NO.

A nested dowhile loop processes all the transactions with the same account number or key in case a master record is being updated by more than one transaction. Within this loop, the PROCESS ACCT TRANSACTIONS module is called. This module checks the transaction code. If the code is A, a record is added to the file. If the code is C, the record is changed. Several fields in a record may need to be changed. To determine which fields to change, the program checks the fields in the transaction record for a null character. If the field is empty, the corresponding master record is not changed. If the field contains data, the master record field is changed. If the code is D, the RECORD.IN.PROGRESS flag is set to NO so that the record will not be written to the new master file.

Table 13.2 shows what happens in these three possible situations:

1. TRAN.ACCT$ < OLDMAST.ACCT$

2. TRAN.ACCT$ = OLDMAST.ACCT$

3. TRAN.ACCT$ > OLDMAST.ACCT$

Program 13.2 reflects these assumptions: First, if an Add transaction is processed, the account does not already exist. Second, if a Change or Delete

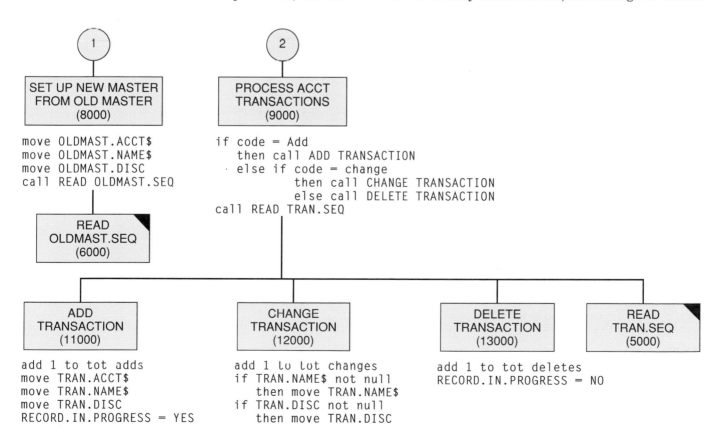

FIGURE 13.6   Logic design for Program 13.2 (continued)

Table 13.2   File maintenance processing

	TRAN.ACCT$ < OLDMAST.ACCT$	TRAN.ACCT$ = OLDMAST.ACCT$	TRAN.ACCT$ > OLDMAST.ACCT$
CURRENT.KEY$	TRAN.ACCT$	OLDMAST.ACCT$	OLDMAST.ACCT$
RECORD.IN.PROGRESS	No	Yes	Yes
Add Transaction	Yes (now RECORD.IN.PROGRESS = YES)	No	No
Change Transaction	No	Yes	No
Delete Transaction	No	Yes (now RECORD.IN.PROGRESS = NO)	No
Read TRAN.SEQ	Yes	Yes	No
Read OLDMAST.SEQ	No	Yes	Yes

transaction is processed, the account exists on the file. These assumptions are not realistic unless the transaction file is validated before Program 13.2 is run. (Program 13.3 contains the additional code to respond appropriately when these assumptions are not true.)

After the update is complete, the program displays the following control totals:

```
Total records in TRANS.SEQ
Total records in OLDMAST.SEQ
Total additions
Total changes
Total deletions
Total records in NEWMAST.SEQ
```

Code the Program Instructions

Program 13.2 is one solution to the problem of updating Briana's master file.

PROGRAM 13.2

```
1000 ' PROG13-2
1010 ' *****************************
1020 ' *     UPDATE MASTER FILE      *
1030 ' *****************************
1040 '
1050 ' *****************************
1060 ' *          VARIABLES           *
1070 ' *****************************
1080 '
1090 ' TRAN.SEQ                    Transaction Input File
1100 ' Transaction Record:
1110 '     TRAN.CODE$
1120 '     TRAN.ACCT$
```

PROGRAM 13.2   (continued)

```
1130 '     TRAN.NAME$
1140 '     TRAN.DISC
1150 '
1160 ' OLDMAST.SEQ               Old Master Input File
1170 ' Old Master Record:
1180 '     OLDMAST.ACCT$
1190 '     OLDMAST.NAME$
1200 '     OLDMAST.DISC
1210 '
1220 ' NEWMAST.SEQ               New Master Output File
1230 ' New Master Record:
1240 '     NEWMAST.ACCT$
1250 '     NEWMAST.NAME$
1260 '     NEWMAST.DISC
1270 '
1280 ' CURRENT.KEY$              Current account being processed
1290 ' RECORD.IN.PROGRESS        New master record being created
1300 '
1310 ' *****************************
1320 ' *          CONSTANTS         *
1330 ' *****************************
1340 '
1350   HIGH.VALUES$ = STRING$(4,CHR$(255))     'Highest possible value in
                                                collating sequence
1360   NULL$ = ""                             'Empty string
1370   YES = -1                               'Value for true
1380   NO  =  0                               'Value for false
1390 '
1400 ' *****************************
1410 ' *    INITIALIZED VARIABLES    *
1420 ' *****************************
1430 '
1440   TOTAL.TRAN    = 0        'Total input records in TRAN.SEQ
1450   TOTAL.OLDMAST = 0        'Total input records in OLDMAST.SEQ
1460   TOTAL.ADDS    = 0        'Total new records added to Master File
1470   TOTAL.CHGS    = 0        'Total changes to Master File
1480   TOTAL.DELS    = 0        'Total deletions to Master File
1490   TOTAL.NEWMAST = 0        'Total output records in NEWMAST.SEQ
1999 '
2000 ' *****************************
2010 ' *        CONTROL MODULE       *
2020 ' *****************************
2030 '
2040   GOSUB 3000               'Update File
2050   GOSUB 4000               'Write Summary Lines
2060   END
2999 '
3000 ' *****************************
3010 ' *           UPDATE FILE       *
3020 ' *****************************
3030 '
3040   OPEN "TRAN.SEQ"    FOR INPUT  AS #1
3050   OPEN "OLDMAST.SEQ" FOR INPUT  AS #2
3060   OPEN "NEWMAST.SEQ" FOR OUTPUT AS #3
3070 '
3080   GOSUB 5000                          'Read TRAN.SEQ
3090   GOSUB 6000                          'Read OLDMAST.SEQ
3100   GOSUB 7000                          'Select Current Key
3110 '
3120   WHILF CURRENT.KEY$ <> HIGH.VALUES$
3130       IF OLDMAST.ACCT$ = CURRENT.KEY$
              THEN RECORD.IN.PROGRESS = YES: GOSUB 8000
              ELSE RECORD.IN.PROGRESS = NO
```

PROGRAM 13.2 (continued)

```
3140        WHILE TRAN.ACCT$ = CURRENT.KEY$
3150             GOSUB 9000                      'Process Acct Transactions
3160        WEND
3170        IF RECORD.IN.PROGRESS
                 THEN GOSUB 10000                'Write New Master
3180        GOSUB 7000                           'Select Current Key
3190   WEND
3200 '
3210   CLOSE
3220   RETURN
3999 '
4000 ' *****************************
4010 ' *     WRITE SUMMARY LINES       *
4020 ' *****************************
4030 '
4040   CLS
4050   PRINT TAB(27); "File update complete."
4060   PRINT TAB(27); USING "Records in TRAN.SEQ    = ##"; TOTAL.TRAN
4070   PRINT TAB(27); USING "Records in OLDMAST.SEQ = ##"; TOTAL.OLDMAST
4080   PRINT TAB(27); USING "Additions              = ##"; TOTAL.ADDS
4090   PRINT TAB(27); USING "Changes                = ##"; TOTAL.CHGS
4100   PRINT TAB(27); USING "Deletions              = ##"; TOTAL.DELS
4110   PRINT TAB(27); USING "Records in NEWMAST.SEQ = ##"; TOTAL.NEWMAST
4120   RETURN
4999 '
5000 ' *****************************
5010 ' *          READ TRAN.SEQ          *
5020 ' *****************************
5030 '
5040   IF NOT EOF(1) THEN TOTAL.TRAN = TOTAL.TRAN + 1:
                        INPUT #1, TRAN.CODE$,TRAN.ACCT$,TRAN.NAME$,TRAN.DISC
                   ELSE TRAN.ACCT$ = HIGH.VALUES$
5050   RETURN
5999 '
6000 ' *****************************
6010 ' *          READ OLDMAST.SEQ       *
6020 ' *****************************
6030 '
6040   IF NOT EOF(2) THEN TOTAL.OLDMAST = TOTAL.OLDMAST + 1:
                        INPUT #2, OLDMAST.ACCT$, OLDMAST.NAME$, OLDMAST.DISC
                   ELSE OLDMAST.ACCT$ = HIGH.VALUES$
6050   RETURN
6999 '
7000 ' *****************************
7010 ' *       SELECT CURRENT KEY        *
7020 ' *****************************
7030 '
7040   IF TRAN.ACCT$ < OLDMAST.ACCT$
           THEN CURRENT.KEY$ = TRAN.ACCT$
           ELSE CURRENT.KEY$ = OLDMAST.ACCT$
7050   RETURN
7999 '
8000 ' *****************************
8010 ' *       SET UP NEW MASTER         *
8020 ' *          FROM OLD MASTER        *
8030 ' *****************************
8040 '
8050   NEWMAST.ACCT$ = OLDMAST.ACCT$
8060   NEWMAST.NAME$ = OLDMAST.NAME$
8070   NEWMAST.DISC  = OLDMAST.DISC
8080   GOSUB 6000              'Read OLDMAST.SEQ
8090   RETURN
8999 '
```

PROGRAM 13.2 (continued)

```
9000  ' *****************************
9010  ' *  PROCESS ACCT TRANSACTIONS *
9020  ' *****************************
9030  '
9040    IF TRAN.CODE$ = "A"               THEN GOSUB 11000
              ELSE IF TRAN.CODE$ = "C" THEN GOSUB 12000
              ELSE                             GOSUB 13000
9050    GOSUB 5000                  'Read TRAN.SEQ
9060    RETURN
9999  '
10000 '*****************************
10010 '*       WRITE NEW MASTER       *
10020 '*****************************
10030 '
10040   TOTAL.NEWMAST = TOTAL.NEWMAST + 1
10050   WRITE #3, NEWMAST.ACCT$,
                  NEWMAST.NAME$,
                  NEWMAST.DISC
10060   RETURN
10999 '
11000 '*****************************
11010 '*         ADD TRANSACTION        *
11020 '*****************************
11030 '
11040   TOTAL.ADDS = TOTAL.ADDS + 1
11050   NEWMAST.ACCT$ = TRAN.ACCT$
11060   NEWMAST.NAME$ = TRAN.NAME$
11070   NEWMAST.DISC  = TRAN.DISC
11080   RECORD.IN.PROGRESS = YES
11090   RETURN
11999 '
12000 '*****************************
12010 '*       CHANGE TRANSACTION      *
12020 '*****************************
12030 '
12040   TOTAL.CHGS = TOTAL.CHGS + 1
12050   IF TRAN.NAME$ <> NULL$
            THEN NEWMAST.NAME$ = TRAN.NAME$
12060   IF TRAN.DISC <> VAL(NULL$)
            THEN NEWMAST.DISC = TRAN.DISC
12070   RETURN
12999 '
13000 '*****************************
13010 '*       DELETE TRANSACTION      *
13020 '*****************************
13030 '
13040   TOTAL.DELS = TOTAL.DELS + 1
13050   RECORD.IN.PROGRESS = NO
13060   RETURN
```

To understand the logic of file updating, again take time to "play computer." Assume that TRAN.SEQ contains the following transactions:

```
"A","1001","ELISE BURKE",3
"D","4422",,
"C","7788","KATHLEEN JACOBS",
"C","7788","CATHERINE JACOBS",
```

Assume that OLDMAST.SEQ contains these records:

```
"2200","SCOTT FALIN",10
"4422","JACK SMOTHERS",7
"6666","ANDY McDONALD",15
"7788","KATHY JACOBS",4
"8000","MARK GIFFORD",10
```

At the end of the program run, what records does the NEWMAST.SEQ file contain? What are the record counts? What are the final values of CURRENT.KEY$ and RECORD.IN.PROGRESS?

Test the Program

Figure 13.7 shows the files after the file update is complete using the data shown in TRAN.SEQ and OLDMAST.SEQ. The new master file includes the change to account 2222; the addition of account 4444; the deletion of account 7777; and the addition of, followed by the change to, account 9999. Account numbers 1111, 3333, 6666, and 8888 were unchanged.

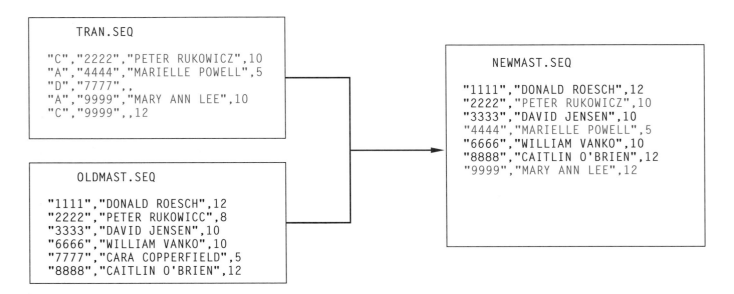

The following totals are displayed on the screen at the end of Program 13.2:

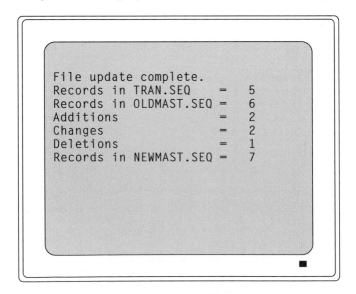

FIGURE 13.7   Sequential file output from Program 13.2

UPDATING A MASTER FILE AND GENERATING AN ERROR REPORT

Program 13.2 reflects these three assumptions:

1. If the user adds a record, that record does not already exist.

2. If the user changes a record, that record is on the master file.

3. If the user deletes a record, that record is on the master file.

Now you will learn how to revise Program 13.2 so that it responds appropriately if any of these assumptions proves false.

Define the Problem

Because the transaction code in the record may not always be correct, you need to write a program to update the master file for Briana's jewelry store and generate an error report listing the error records.

Describe the Output and Determine the Input

The file formats are the same as in Program 13.2 (see Figure 13.4). The error report contains a heading, a listing of each transaction record that cannot be processed together with a message describing the error, and summary totals at the end of the report. The print chart in Figure 13.8 specifies the error report format. To simplify the program, assume that no more than one page will be printed, but remember that error reports may be any number of pages.

Design the Program Logic

The major changes from Program 13.2 are the tests in the ADD TRANSACTION, CHANGE TRANSACTION, and DELETE TRANSACTION modules. If, in the ADD TRANSACTION module, RECORD.IN.PROGRESS is

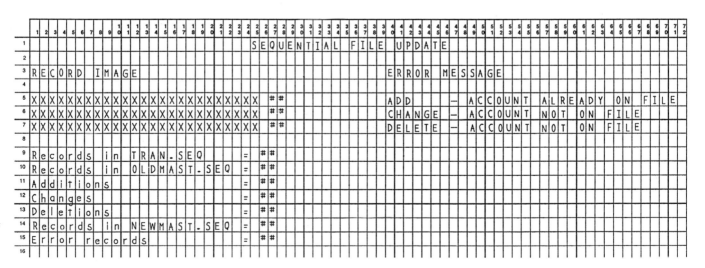

FIGURE 13.8   Report design for Program 13.3

YES, the account already exists and the program should print an error message; otherwise, the program sets up a new master record. If, in either the CHANGE TRANSACTION or DELETE TRANSACTION modules, REC-ORD.IN.PROGRESS is NO, then the account does not exist and can therefore be neither changed nor deleted. Figure 13.9 shows the general logic of this update; Figure 13.10 presents the pseudocode and structure chart for the program starting with the PROCESS ACCOUNT TRANSACTIONS module. The logic before that module is the same as in Program 13.2.

Code the Program

Program 13.3 is one solution to the problem of updating a file while taking into account possible errors in the transaction records.

FIGURE 13.9
General pseudocode for file updating with invalid Add, Change, and Delete transactions

```
open files
read transaction record
read old master record
select current key

dowhile current key not = high-values

    if old master key = current key
       then record in progress = yes
            set up new master record
            read old master record
       else record in progress = no

      dowhile transaction key = current key

        if tran code = add
           then if record in progress = yes
                   then error
                   else set up new master record
                        record in progress = yes

        else if tran code = change
           then if record in progress = no
                   then error
                   else change new master record

        else if tran code = delete
           then if record in progress = no
                   then error
                   else record in progress = no


        read transaction record

      end dowhile

      if record in progress = yes
         then write new master record

      select next current key

end dowhile

close files
```

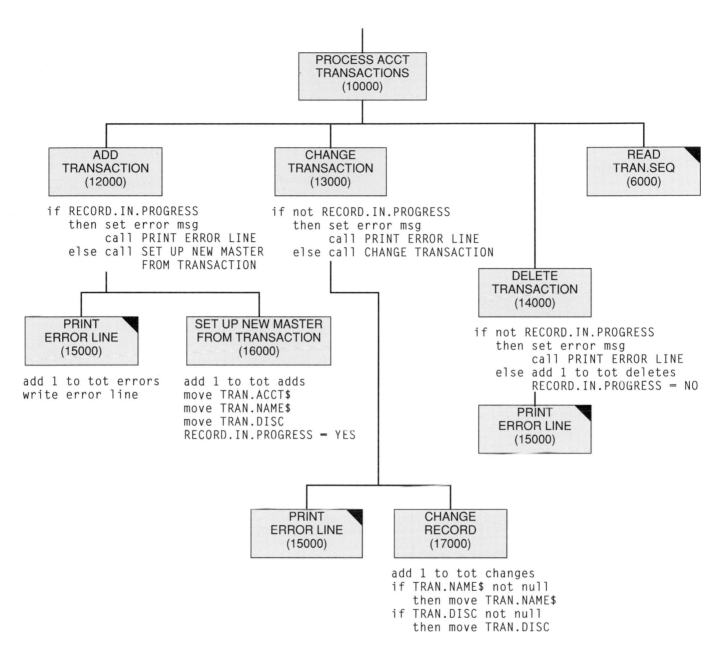

FIGURE 13.10 Logic design for Program 13.3

PROGRAM 13.3
```
1000 ' PROG13-3
1010 ' *****************************
1020 ' *     UPDATE MASTER FILE     *
1030 ' *     WITH ERROR REPORT      *
1040 ' *****************************
1050 '
1060 ' *****************************
1070 ' *          VARIABLES         *
1080 ' *****************************
1090 '
1100 ' TRAN.SEQ                 Transaction Input File
1110 ' Transaction Record:
1120 '     TRAN.CODE$
1130 '     TRAN.ACCT$
1140 '     TRAN.NAME$
1150 '     TRAN.DISC
```

PROGRAM 13.3   (continued)

```
1160 '
1170 ' OLDMAST.SEQ                   Old Master Input File
1180 ' Old Master Record:
1190 '     OLDMAST.ACCT$
1200 '     OLDMAST.NAME$
1210 '     OLDMAST.DISC
1220 '
1230 ' NEWMAST.SEQ                   New Master Output File
1240 ' New Master Record:
1250 '     NEWMAST.ACCT$
1260 '     NEWMAST.NAME$
1270 '     NEWMAST.DISC
1280 '
1290 ' CURRENT.KEY$                  Current account being processed
1300 ' MSG$                          Common message area
1310 ' RECORD.IN.PROGRESS            New master record being created
1320 '
1330 ' *****************************
1340 ' *        CONSTANTS          *
1350 ' *****************************
1360 '
1370    HIGH.VALUES$ = STRING$(4,CHR$(255))    'Highest possible value in
                                                 collating sequence
1380    MSG1$ = "ADD     - ACCOUNT ALREADY ON FILE"
1390    MSG2$ = "CHANGE  - ACCOUNT NOT ON FILE"
1400    MSG3$ = "DELETE  - ACCOUNT NOT ON FILE"
1410    NULL$ = ""                             'Empty string
1420    YES = -1                               'Value for true
1430    NO  =  0                               'Value for false
1440 '
1450 ' *****************************
1460 ' *    INITIALIZED VARIABLES  *
1470 ' *****************************
1480 '
1490    TOTAL.TRAN    = 0          'Total input records in TRAN.SEQ
1500    TOTAL.OLDMAST = 0          'Total input records in OLDMAST.SEQ
1510    TOTAL.ADDS    = 0          'Total new records added to Master File
1520    TOTAL.CHGS    = 0          'Total changes to Master File
1530    TOTAL.DELS    = 0          'Total deletions to Master File
1540    TOTAL.NEWMAST = 0          'Total output records in NEWMAST.SEQ
1550    TOTAL.ERRORS  = 0          'Total error records
1999 '
2000 ' *****************************
2010 ' *        CONTROL MODULE     *
2020 ' *****************************
2030 '
2040    GOSUB 3000                'Write Headings
2050    GOSUB 4000                'Update File
2060    GOSUB 5000                'Write Summary Lines
2070    END
2999 '
3000 ' *****************************
3010 ' *        WRITE HEADINGS     *
3020 ' *****************************
3030 '
3040    LPRINT TAB(25); "SEQUENTIAL FILE UPDATE"
3050    LPRINT
3060    LPRINT "RECORD IMAGE"; TAB(40); "ERROR MESSAGE"
3070    LPRINT
3080    RETURN
3999 '
4000 ' *****************************
4010 ' *          UPDATE FILE      *
4020 ' *****************************
4030 '
```

PROGRAM 13.3   (continued)

```
4040    OPEN "TRAN.SEQ"    FOR INPUT   AS #1
4050    OPEN "OLDMAST.SEQ" FOR INPUT   AS #2
4060    OPEN "NEWMAST.SEQ" FOR OUTPUT  AS #3
4070 '
4080    GOSUB 6000                              'Read TRAN.SEQ
4090    GOSUB 7000                              'Read OLDMAST.SEQ
4100    GOSUB 8000                              'Select Current Key
4110 '
4120    WHILE CURRENT.KEY$ <> HIGH.VALUES$
4140        IF OLDMAST.ACCT$ = CURRENT.KEY$
                THEN RECORD.IN.PROGRESS = YES: GOSUB 9000
                ELSE RECORD.IN.PROGRESS = NO
4160        WHILE TRAN.ACCT$ = CURRENT.KEY$
4170            GOSUB 10000                     'Process Acct Transactions
4180        WEND
4200        IF RECORD.IN.PROGRESS
                THEN GOSUB 11000                'Write New Master
4220        GOSUB 8000                          'Select Current Key
4230    WEND
4240 '
4250    CLOSE
4260    RETURN
4999 '
5000 ' ****************************
5010 ' *     WRITE SUMMARY LINES      *
5020 ' ****************************
5030 '
5040    LPRINT
5050    LPRINT USING "Records in TRAN.SEQ    = ##"; TOTAL.TRAN
5060    LPRINT USING "Records in OLDMAST.SEQ = ##"; TOTAL.OLDMAST
5070    LPRINT USING "Additions              = ##"; TOTAL.ADDS
5080    LPRINT USING "Changes                = ##"; TOTAL.CHGS
5090    LPRINT USING "Deletions              = ##"; TOTAL.DELS
5100    LPRINT USING "Records in NEWMAST.SEQ = ##"; TOTAL.NEWMAST
5110    LPRINT USING "Error records          = ##"; TOTAL.ERRORS
5120    RETURN
5999 '
6000 ' ****************************
6010 ' *          READ TRAN.SEQ        *
6020 ' ****************************
6030 '
6040    IF NOT EOF(1) THEN TOTAL.TRAN = TOTAL.TRAN + 1:
                        INPUT #1, TRAN.CODE$,TRAN.ACCT$,TRAN.NAME$,TRAN.DISC
                     ELSE TRAN.ACCT$ = HIGH.VALUES$
6050    RETURN
6999 '
7000 ' ****************************
7010 ' *          READ OLDMAST.SEQ     *
7020 ' ****************************
7030 '
7040    IF NOT EOF(2) THEN TOTAL.OLDMAST = TOTAL.OLDMAST + 1:
                        INPUT #2, OLDMAST.ACCT$, OLDMAST.NAME$, OLDMAST.DISC
                     ELSE OLDMAST.ACCT$ = HIGH.VALUES$
7050    RETURN
7999 '
8000 ' ****************************
8010 ' *      SELECT CURRENT KEY       *
8020 ' ****************************
8030 '
8040    IF TRAN.ACCT$ < OLDMAST.ACCT$
            THEN CURRENT.KEY$ = TRAN.ACCT$
            ELSE CURRENT.KEY$ = OLDMAST.ACCT$
8050    RETURN
8999 '
```

PROGRAM 13.3 (continued)

```
9000  ' *******************************
9010  ' *        SET UP NEW MASTER      *
9020  ' *          FROM OLD MASTER       *
9030  ' *******************************
9040  '
9050    NEWMAST.ACCT$ = OLDMAST.ACCT$
9060    NEWMAST.NAME$ = OLDMAST.NAME$
9070    NEWMAST.DISC  = OLDMAST.DISC
9080    GOSUB 7000                    'Read OLDMAST.SEQ
9090    RETURN
9999  '
10000 '*******************************
10010 '*   PROCESS ACCT TRANSACTIONS *
10020 '*******************************
10030 '
10040   IF TRAN.CODE$ = "A"              THEN GOSUB 12000
             ELSE IF TRAN.CODE$ = "C" THEN GOSUB 13000
             ELSE                          GOSUB 14000
10050   GOSUB 6000                   'Read TRAN.SEQ
10060   RETURN
10999 '
11000 '*******************************
11010 '*         WRITE NEW MASTER       *
11020 '*******************************
11030 '
11040   TOTAL.NEWMAST = TOTAL.NEWMAST + 1
11050   WRITE #3, NEWMAST.ACCT$,
                  NEWMAST.NAME$,
                  NEWMAST.DISC
11060   RETURN
11999 '
12000 '*******************************
12010 '*          ADD TRANSACTION        *
12020 '*******************************
12030 '
12040   IF RECORD.IN.PROGRESS
             THEN MSG$ = MSG1$: GOSUB 15000
             ELSE GOSUB 16000     'Set Up New Master
12050   RETURN
12999 '
13000 '*******************************
13010 '*        CHANGE TRANSACTION     *
13020 '*******************************
13030 '
13040   IF NOT RECORD.IN.PROGRESS
             THEN MSG$ = MSG2$: GOSUB 15000
             ELSE GOSUB 17000      'Change Record
13050   RETURN
13999 '
14000 '*******************************
14010 '*        DELETE TRANSACTION     *
14020 '*******************************
14030 '
14040   IF NOT RECORD.IN.PROGRESS
             THEN MSG$ = MSG3$: GOSUB 15000
             ELSE TOTAL.DELS = TOTAL.DELS + 1: RECORD.IN.PROGRESS = NO
14050   RETURN
14999 '
15000 '*******************************
15010 '*          PRINT ERROR LINE       *
15020 '*******************************
15030 '
15040   TOTAL.ERRORS = TOTAL.ERRORS + 1
15050   LPRINT TRAN.CODE$; TRAN.ACCT$; TRAN.NAME$; TRAN.DISC;
             TAB(40); MSG$
```

PROGRAM 13.3 (continued)

```
15060  RETURN
15999  '
16000  '*****************************
16010  '*      SET UP NEW MASTER     *
16020  '*       FROM TRANSACTION     *
16030  '*****************************
16040  '
16050  TOTAL.ADDS = TOTAL.ADDS + 1
16060  NEWMAST.ACCT$ = TRAN.ACCT$
16070  NEWMAST.NAME$ = TRAN.NAME$
16080  NEWMAST.DISC  = TRAN.DISC
16090  RECORD.IN.PROGRESS = YES
16100  RETURN
16999  '
17000  '*****************************
17010  '*           CHANGE RECORD    *
17020  '*****************************
17030  '
17040  TOTAL.CHGS = TOTAL.CHGS + 1
17050  IF TRAN.NAME$ <> NULL$
           THEN NEWMAST.NAME$ = TRAN.NAME$
17060  IF TRAN.DISC <> VAL(NULL$)
           THEN NEWMAST.DISC = TRAN.DISC
17070  RETURN
```

Test the Program

Figure 13.11 shows the new master file and the edit report produced by Program 13.3. Notice that the report includes only the records in error plus totals. If you want to provide an audit/error report, then you print each record and the action taken regarding it. Also, it is often helpful to know how many records were added, changed, and deleted, and how many additions, changes, and deletions were rejected. Figure 13.12 illustrates an alternative design, showing an audit/error report, more extensive control totals, and appropriate headings.

ON-LINE FILE UPDATING

Maintenance of small sequential files can be performed in program tables. One way to update a file on-line is to:

1. Load the master file into table(s). (More than one table may be required because the fields in the record may be of different data types.)

2. Present the user with a menu of options:
   a. Add a record
   b. Change a record
   c. Delete a record

3. If Add is selected:
   a. Request the key field (for example, the account number).
   b. Check the master file table for a matching key.
   c. Display an error message if a matching key exists.
   d. If the matching key does not exist:
      (1) Request and edit the new record.
      (2) Enter the new record into the master file table(s).
      (3) Log the transaction to a sequential file.

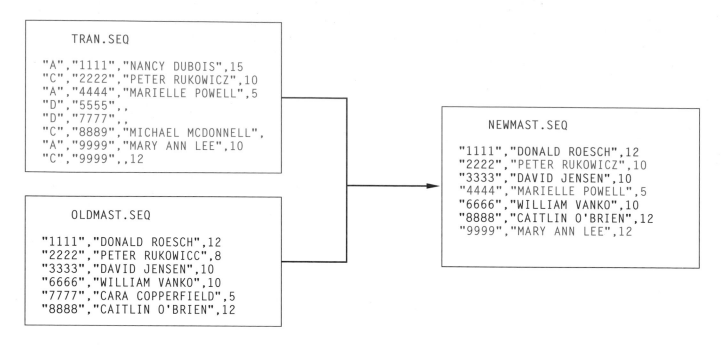

```
        TRAN.SEQ

"A","1111","NANCY DUBOIS",15
"C","2222","PETER RUKOWICZ",10
"A","4444","MARIELLE POWELL",5
"D","5555",,
"D","7777",,
"C","8889","MICHAEL MCDONNELL",
"A","9999","MARY ANN LEE",10
"C","9999",,12
```

```
        OLDMAST.SEQ

"1111","DONALD ROESCH",12
"2222","PETER RUKOWICC",8
"3333","DAVID JENSEN",10
"6666","WILLIAM VANKO",10
"7777","CARA COPPERFIELD",5
"8888","CAITLIN O'BRIEN",12
```

```
        NEWMAST.SEQ

"1111","DONALD ROESCH",12
"2222","PETER RUKOWICZ",10
"3333","DAVID JENSEN",10
"4444","MARIELLE POWELL",5
"6666","WILLIAM VANKO",10
"8888","CAITLIN O'BRIEN",12
"9999","MARY ANN LEE",12
```

The following report will print:

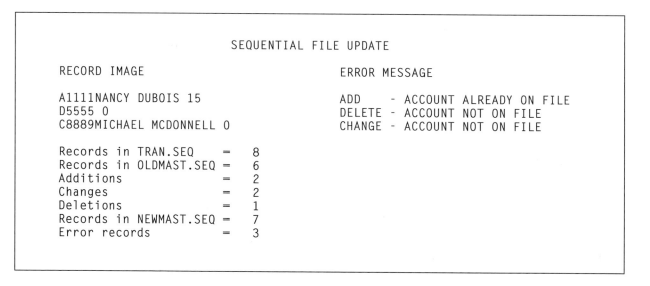

```
                    SEQUENTIAL FILE UPDATE

RECORD IMAGE                        ERROR MESSAGE

A1111NANCY DUBOIS 15                ADD    - ACCOUNT ALREADY ON FILE
D5555 0                            DELETE - ACCOUNT NOT ON FILE
C8889MICHAEL MCDONNELL 0           CHANGE - ACCOUNT NOT ON FILE

Records in TRAN.SEQ      =    8
Records in OLDMAST.SEQ   =    6
Additions                =    2
Changes                  =    2
Deletions                =    1
Records in NEWMAST.SEQ   =    7
Error records            =    3
```

FIGURE 13.11 Output of Program 13.3

4. If Change is selected:
   a. Request the key field.
   b. Check the master file table for a matching key.
   c. Display an error message if a matching key does *not* exist.
   d. If the matching key does exist:
      (1) Request and edit the change.
      (2) Change the master record in the table(s).
      (3) Log the transaction to a sequential file.

5. If Delete is selected:
   a. Request the key field.
   b. Check the master file table for a matching key.
   c. Display an error message if a matching key does *not* exist.
   d. If the matching key does exist:

```
SEQUENTIAL FILE UPDATE                                                    PAGE  ##
AUDIT/ERROR LIST                                                   MM-DD-19YY
                    BRIANA'S CUSTOMER MASTER FILE

UPDATE    ACCOUNT                              UPDATE
CODE      NUMBER   NAME                DISCOUNT ACTION    ERROR MESSAGE

     X    XXXX    XXXXXXXXXXXXXXXXXXXX    ##   ADDED
     X    XXXX    XXXXXXXXXXXXXXXXXXXX    ##   CHANGED
     X    XXXX    XXXXXXXXXXXXXXXXXXXX    ##   DELETED
     X    XXXX    XXXXXXXXXXXXXXXXXXXX    ##   REJECTED  ACCOUNT ALREADY ON FILE
     X    XXXX    XXXXXXXXXXXXXXXXXXXX    ##   REJECTED  ACCOUNT NOT ON FILE


Records in TRAN.SEQ       = ##
    ADDS                  = ##
        Processed         = ##
        Rejected          = ##
    CHANGES               = ##
        Processed         = ##
        Rejected          = ##
    DELETES               = ##
        Processed         = ##
        Rejected          = ##

    Total rejected        = ##

Records in OLDMAST.SEQ    = ##
Records in NEWMAST.SEQ    = ##
```

FIGURE 13.12   Alternate report design for Program 13.3

(1) Flag that entry in the table.
(2) Log the transaction to a sequential file.

6. When the file maintenance process is complete:
   a. Sort the master records in the table(s).
   b. Write the records from the table(s) to the new sequential master file, omitting any records in the table(s) flagged for deletion.

Instead of sorting the records after file maintenance is complete, you can adjust the table(s) containing the master file data as you do the maintenance. The table would then be in key order, and the sort would not be necessary.

Control is important in any data processing application, especially in such applications as master file updating, which require changing the data in important business files. If a problem occurs when Programs 13.2 and 13.3 are used to create the new file, the transaction and old master files are still available so that processing can be restarted.

If a problem occurs during an on-line update, however, the operator must reenter all the Add, Delete, and Change transactions. Consequently, a log file is often maintained during an on-line update. A *log file* or *journal file* is a sequential file containing a record for each transaction entered. Log files can be used as transaction files to update a master file. Log files also provide an audit trail to trace the history of an update to a master file.

The security of master file data is very important. If master files are lost or destroyed, a business or agency may no longer be able to function. To protect themselves, most firms keep copies of the original files. These copies are called *backup files*. Backup files are produced regularly, and sometimes backup and original files are kept at different sites.

Backup and recovery procedures are documented methods of reconstructing a file. For example, when a transaction file is used to update a master file, a new master file is created. The transaction file and the old master file are stored in case the new master file is damaged. The new master file can then be reconstructed from the transaction file and the old master file.

Summary

- A *master file* is a file whose records contain relatively permanent data. A file that contains data about individual events is called a *transaction file*. The process of changing a master file to reflect current conditions is *file updating*. The records in a transaction file provide the data to update the master file. There are two categories of file updating:

  1. *Posting* is the process of accumulating totals and updating the existing master file.

  2. *File maintenance* is the process of adding a record to a master file, changing a record in the master file, or deleting a record from the master file.

- In a sequential file update:

  1. There must be two input files, a transaction file and a master file.

  2. The transaction file and master file must be sorted on the same control field or key.

  3. The transaction file must include a code indicating what action the program should take to update the file.

  4. The output consists of a new master file and an audit/error report.

  5. Each record in the old master file must be rewritten to the new master file regardless of whether it is changed.

- To update a master file with new records, changes, and deletions, you need to:

  1. Read a record from the transaction file and the master file.

  2. Set the current key equal to the smaller key.

  3. If the current key is equal to the old master key:

     a. Move the old master data to the new master record.
     b. Read another old master record.
     c. Note that a record is in progress.

4. If the current key is equal to the transaction key, check for an addition, change, or deletion.

   a. If there is an addition, move the transaction data to the new master record and note that a record is in progress.
   b. If there is a change, check which fields to change and move the changes to the new master record.
   c. If there is a deletion, note that a record is not in progress.
   d. Read another transaction.
   e. Repeat until the transaction key does not equal the current key.

5. Write a new master record if a record is in progress.

6. Repeat steps 2–5 until all the records from both files are read.

- These problems in sequential file updating must be addressed:

  1. One master record may have more than one transaction.

  2. The user might attempt to add a record that already exists on the master file.

  3. The user might attempt to change a record that does not exist on the master file.

  4. The user might attempt to delete a record that does not exist on the master file.

- For small sequential files, file maintenance can be performed on-line by using program tables. Regardless of whether file maintenance is performed on-line or by batch processing, audit trails and error reports with control totals, log files, and backup files are critical to the survival of a business.

Review Questions

1. What is a master file?
2. What is a transaction file?
3. What is file updating?

4. What is the difference between file posting and file maintenance?

5. How many sequential files do you need for file updating?

6. During sequential file updating, do the files need to be in the same sequence?

7. Why must the transaction code in a transaction file be sorted?

8. What is file activity?

9. What is file merging?

10. Why is CHR$(255) used for high values to indicate the end of a file?

11. What is the meaning of the variable name HIGH.VALUES$? CURRENT.KEY$?

12. What problems can occur during file maintenance?

13. When can you update a sequential file on-line?

14. What is a log or journal file?

15. What is a backup file?

Problems

1. Modify Program 13.1 so that if the account number in a record in BILL1.SEQ is equal to an account number in BILL2.SEQ, the record in BILL1.SEQ is written to BILL3.SEQ before the record in BILL2.SEQ.

2. Modify Program 13.3 to print the report shown in Figure 13.12.

3. Customers order t-shirts from the Novelty T-Shirts mail order company. The order clerks at Novelty T-Shirts process the orders, and a transaction file is created with the following data for each order:

- Order Number
- Item Number
- Quantity Ordered

The master inventory file is updated by subtracting the number of items ordered from the quantity on hand. Each record in the master inventory file has the following fields:

- Item Number
- Item Description
- Unit Price
- Reorder Point
- Quantity On Hand

The transaction file contains the following data:

Customer Number	Item Number	Quantity Ordered
4322	801	1
6234	654	3
3452	989	7
7665	402	4
3001	586	2

The master file contains these data:

Item Number	Item Description	Unit Price	Reorder Point	Quantity On Hand
100	Bill Murray	6.98	50	65
378	Bill Cosby	6.98	70	80
402	Garfield	7.98	50	99
500	Snoopy	5.98	30	42
586	Joe Montana	8.98	65	66
633	Princeton Univ.	5.98	20	25
654	Johns Hopkins Univ.	8.98	40	52
700	Kermit	6.98	20	33
801	Dan Marino	7.98	65	80
989	Toronto Blue Jays	4.98	15	20

Pretend you are the computer and:

a. Sort the transaction file by item number. List the records after the sort.

b. List the records in the new master file after the transaction file has been used to update the current inventory master file.

c. Note any items that have reached the reorder point.

4. Using the following data, predict the output for Program 13.3.

```
TRAN.SEQ
    "D","1212",,
    "D","1500",,
    "A","2002","MARY DEY",12
    "C","4667",,15
    "A","5000","GARRETT JAKES",10
    "C","6001","MATTHEW PERRY",
    "C","6001",,15
    "A","8000","DREW PETERS",10

OLDMAST.SEQ
    "1212","JAMES JACKSON",15
    "2000","DANIEL KEARNEY",10
    "3434","PATRICK DODSON",12
    "4667","MARTHA MASON",10
    "5000","JANET DOTY",15
    "6001","DELLA STREET",10
    "8228","NAT CONSTANTINE",12
```

Program Assignments

1. Spencer Insurance Company (you wrote a program for them in Chapter 11) needs a program to merge three files. The input files are INS-IN1.SEQ, INS-IN2.SEQ, and INS-IN3.SEQ. The records in each file contain the following fields:

Field	Data Length	Data Type
Customer number	6	Numeric ######
Payment	7	Numeric ####.##
Payment date	6	Numeric *mmddyy*

Each file is sorted by customer number. The output file is INS-COM.SEQ, and each record has the following format:

Field Name	Data Length	Data Type
INS.CUST.NO	6	Numeric ######
INS.PAY	7	Numeric ####.##
INS.DATE	6	Numeric *ddmmyy*

(Notice the difference in the date formats of the two files.)

Using EDLIN, create three files for testing.

Extra credit: Add the logic to sequence check the input files. If a file is not in customer number order, alert the user. Make up appropriate test files.

2. Video World, a new video tape rental company, needs a program to update the inventory file of video tapes. The master file contains a tape number, tape description, quantity on hand, and tape category. The transaction file contains the transaction code, tape number, tape description, quantity, and tape category.

The format of the master file is:

VWMAST.SEQ   (sequential input file sorted by VWMAST.NUM$)

Field Name	Data Length	Data Type
VWMAST.NUM$	4	String
VWMAST.DESC$	20	String
VWMAST.QTY	2	Numeric
VWMAST.CAT$	1	String

VWMAST.CAT$ = 1 for new release
VWMAST.CAT$ = 2 for old release

The format of the transaction file is:

VWTRAN.SEQ   (sequential input file sorted by VWTRAN.CODE$ within VWTRAN.NUM$)

Field Name	Data Length	Data Type
VWTRAN.CODE$	1	String
VWTRAN.NUM$	4	String
VWTRAN.DESC$	20	String
VWTRAN.QTY	2	Numeric
VWTRAN.CAT$	1	String

VWTRAN.CODE$ = A   Add a new master record.

VWTRAN.CODE$ = C   Change a master record.

If VWTRAN.DESC$ or VWTRAN.CAT$ is not blank, change the field on the new master record.

If VWTRAN.QTY is not blank, increment the quantity field on the new master record.

VWTRAN.CODE$ = D   Delete the record.

The format of the new master file is:

VWNEW.SEQ   (sequential output file sorted by VWNEW.NUM$)

Field Name	Data Length	Data Type
VWNEW.NUM$	4	String
VWNEW.DESC$	20	String
VWNEW.QTY	2	Numeric
VWNEW.CAT$	1	String

Write a program to:

a. Update the VWMAST.SEQ file using the transactions in VWTRAN.SEQ.

b. If VWTRAN.CODE$ = "A", then add a record to the master file.

c. If VWTRAN.CODE$ = "C", then change the data in the matching master record.

d. If the VWTRAN.CODE$ = "D", then delete the record from the master file.

e. The output of the program is the new master file, VWNEW.SEQ, and the following totals displayed on the screen:

```
Total records in VWMAST.SEQ
Total records in VWTRAN.SEQ
Total adds
Total changes
Total deletes
Total records in VWNEW.SEQ
```

File contents (assume the data in both files are valid, but remember that there may be more than one transaction per master record):

VWMAST.SEQ

```
1000,Jane Fonda Workout,5,2
1229,Terms of Endear,3,2
1889,Beverly Hills Cop,5,1
2003,Footloose,2,2
2445,Risky Business,3,2
2667,Old Yeller,2,2
2778,Gandhi,4,2
3009,Romancing the Stone,5,1
3446,Karate Kid,3,1
3889,Animal House,3,2
3997,Amadeus,5,1
4005,Ghostbust,5,1
4115,Police Academy,4,2
4200,The Killing Fields,3,1
4300,Gremlins,4,2
4389,Rocky III,5,2
4568,Ordinary People,5,2
4699,Cloak and Dagger,3,2
5001,9 to 5,4,2
5025,Protocol,3,2
5546,Superman,6,2
5877,Four Seasons,4,2
5929,Max Dugan Returns,3,2
6001,Missing,4,2
6229,Tribute,3,2
6334,Conan the Destroyer,6,1
6445,Cross Creek,3,2
6557,Reds,7,2
6692,My Favorite Year,2,2
6789,On Golden Pond,8,1
6882,Yentl,5,1
6993,Auntie Mame,2,2
7001,Oh God!,8,2
7113,101 Dalmatians,4,2
7223,Herbie,4,2
7334,Shaggy D.A.,3,2
8001,A View to Kill,4,1
```

VWTRAN.SEQ

```
A,1109,Back to the Future,8,1
C,1229,Terms of Endearment,,
C,1889,,3,
A,2118,The Natural,4,1
C,3009,,,2
A,3122,The Breakfast Club,3,1
C,3446,,,2
D,3889,,,
C,4005,Ghostbusters,,
C,4005,,,2
A,4095,Rambo,5,1
C,4095,,4,
A,4111,Jewel of the Nile,5,1
C,4200,,,2
A,4310,Splash,3,1
```

```
C,4310,,2,
A,4450,Cocoon,9,1
C,5546,,2,
D,6229,,,
A,6589,Witness,2,1
D,6692,,,
A,9001,St. Elmo's Fire,4,1
```

3. Video World now would like to change the program that updates the VWMAST.SEQ file so that it handles the following possible errors:

a. Adding a record with a tape number that already exists on the file.

b. Changing a record that does not exist on the file.

c. Deleting a record that does not exist on the file.

Write a program to update the master file and check for the possible errors. Print an audit/error list report for Video World similar to the report design in Figure 13.12. Print 20 lines per page. Use the master file in program assignment 2 and the following VWTRAN.SEQ file (this new transaction file is labeled VWTRANX.SEQ on your data disk):

```
A,1000,Witch Mountain,3,2
A,1109,Back to the Future,8,1
C,1229,Terms of Endearment,,
D,1500,,,
C,1889,,3,
A,2003,The Natural,4,1
C,3019,,,2
A,3122,The Breakfast Club,3,1
D,3889,,,
C,4005,Ghostbusters,,
C,4005,,,2
C,4005,,3,
A,4095,Rambo,5,1
C,4095,,4,
A,4111,Jewel of the Nile,5,1
C,4200,,,2
A,4310,Splash,3,1
C,4310,,2,
A,4699,Cocoon,9,1
D,5000,,,
C,5546,,2,
D,6229,,,
A,6589, Witness,2,1
D,6692,,,
A,9001,St. Elmo's Fire,4,1
```

4. The payment file from program assignment 3 in Chapter 11 has been validated, and now Harley Clocks needs a program to update the balance and date fields in the master file.

The format of the master file is:

HCL-MAST.SEQ   (sequential file sorted by HCL-MAST.ACCT$)

HCL-MAST record:

Field Name	Data Length	Data Type
HCL.MAST.ACCT$	4	string
HCL.MAST.NAME$	20	String
HCL.MAST.BAL	8	Numeric #####.##
HCL.MAST.DATE	6	Numeric *yymmdd*
HCL.MAST.CR	5	Numeric #####

Check Chapter 11 for the contents of the master file.

The format of the transaction file is:

HCL-ARV.SEQ   (sequential file sorted by HCL-ARV.DATE within HCL-ARV.ACCT$)

HCL-ARV record:

Field Name	Data Length	Data Type
HCL.ARV.ACCT$	4	String
HCL.ARV.AMT	8	Numeric #####.##
HCL.ARV.DATE	6	Numeric *yymmdd*

a. Write a program to match the HCL-ARV record (payment record) with the HCL-MAST record (master record).

b. When a match is found, the program should subtract the payment from the balance and replace the balance field in the master record. Then it should replace the date field in the master record with the date field in the payment record.

c. All transactions have a matching master record.

d. Some master records have multiple transactions.

e. The output of this program is a new master file and the following totals displayed on the screen:

```
Total records in HCL-MAST.SEQ
Total records in HCL-ARV.SEQ
Total records in new master file
Total amount of the payments
     (total of HCL.ARV.AMT)
```

File contents:

HCL-ARV.SEQ   (This file is labeled HCL-ARVX.SEQ on your data disk.)

```
A100,100.55,890920
A250,200.62,890909
C260,6000.90,890930
J500,323.82,890930
K428,420.56,891020
M828,840.82,890930
M828,100,891010
```

```
M828,50.55,891020
N402,500,891010
N402,1500.80,891020
P492,487.62,890922
S378,320.62,890918
S460,500.30,891002
T600,960.82,890918
T600,960.82,890920
```

5. Harley Clocks now needs a program to update the name and credit limit on the master file. The company would like an on-line program that:

a. Loads the HCL-MAST.SEQ file into table(s).

b. Presents a menu with the following options:

```
Add a new record
Change the name or credit limit
Delete a record
```

c. If Add is selected:
  (1) Request the new account number.
  (2) Check the master file in the table for duplication of the account number.
  (3) Display an error message if the account already exists.
  (4) If the account does not exist:
      (a) Request and edit the name.
      (b) Request and edit the credit limit.
      (c) Place a zero in the HCL.MAST.BAL and HCL.MAST.DATE fields.
      (d) Enter the new account into the table(s).
      (e) Log the transaction to a sequential file (LOG.SEQ).

d. If Change is requested:
  (1) Request the account number.
  (2) Check the master file table for an existing account.
  (3) Display an error message if the account does not exist.
  (4) If the account is in the table:
      (a) Request and edit the name change.
      (b) Request and edit the credit limit change.
      (c) Change the master record in the table(s).
      (d) Log the transaction to a sequential file (LOG.SEQ).

e. If Delete is selected:
  (1) Request the account number.
  (2) Check the master file table for an existing account.
  (3) Display an error message if the account does not exist.
  (4) If the account is in the table:
      (a) Change the account number in the table to CHR$(255).
      (b) Log the transaction to a sequential file (LOG.SEQ).

f. When the file maintenance is complete:
   (1) Sort the records in the table(s) by account number.
   (2) Write a new master file.
   (3) Display the following totals:

```
Total records in HCL-MAST.SEQ
Total adds
Total changes
Total deletes
Total records in LOG.SEQ
Total records in new master file
```

The format of the log file is:

LOG.SEQ   (sequential output file)

LOG record:

Field Name	Data Length	Data Type
LOG.CODE$	1	String
LOG.ACCT$	4	String
LOG.NAME$	20	String
LOG.BAL	8	Numeric #####.##
LOG.DATE	6	Numeric *yymmdd*
LOG.CR	5	Numeric #####

```
LOG.CODE$ = A Add a record.
LOG.CODE$ = C Change name or credit limit.
LOG.CODE$ = D Delete a record.
```

Chapter Fourteen

Random Files

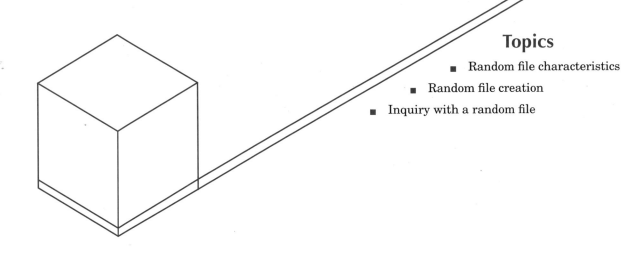

Topics

- Random file characteristics
- Random file creation
- Inquiry with a random file

BASIC Statements and Functions

```
CVD, CVI, CVS
FIELD #
GET #
LSET, RSET
MKD$, MKI$, MKS$
PUT #
```

INTRODUCTION

As you learned in previous chapters, sequential files work well for applications that access all of the records in a file in the order in which they are stored. They do not work well, however, when the user needs to access records randomly or needs to use only a few of the records in a file.

Sequential files do not work well in these situations because the system must read every record that precedes the record needed. After finding one record, the system must return to the beginning of the file and read through the file again to find a second record, even if the second is adjacent to the first.

Searching for information sequentially can be very slow. Consider how long it would take to find the name Zoe Zoom in the telephone book if you started on page 1 and looked at every name until you found Zoe Zoom. Also imagine how impatient you would become if, when you went to your bank to make a withdrawal, the clerk entered your account number into a computer terminal and required you to wait while the computer searched all the records prior to yours in the accounts master file.

Random files, sometimes called *direct-access files*, provide a way to avoid this problem. They allow the system to access a particular record in a file without reading the previous records. The process is analogous to turning directly to the last page of the telephone book to find Zoe Zoom's name. Random files are used extensively for information inquiry and on-line activities, such as banking, airline reservations, approval of credit card purchases, and mail-order applications. This process of working with individual records in random files is generally known as *inquiry* or *transaction processing*.

This chapter begins with an explanation of the characteristics of random files and then illustrates how to create and access a random file.

CHARACTERISTICS OF RANDOM FILES

A random file is a collection of records organized so that the system can retrieve or write any record without processing all the preceding records in the file. Two characteristics of random files make them especially useful for the applications mentioned in the introduction:

1. Given a method of determining where a particular record is, any record can be accessed in any order; the user can move backward or forward in the file.

2. After opening a file, the user can read from the file or write to it.

Like sequential files, random files contain records made up of fields. Unlike sequential files in BASIC, random files have fields of fixed length and thus the length of each record is the same. For example, the name field in a random file must be of the same length in all records. A short name is padded with spaces to fill the field; a long name is truncated to fit the field length. Numeric values are stored in a special compressed or packed binary format. For this reason, when you try to use the DOS TYPE command to display a random file, you often see strange-looking characters in the numeric fields shown on the screen.

Random files differ from sequential files in other important ways. You must read or write an entire record at one time in a random file, whereas you can access individual fields of a record in a sequential file. Also, in sequential files, fields are generally separated by commas or blanks (spaces), and quotation marks may delimit string characters. Because the fields and records in a random file are of a specified length, they need no separators or delimiters. Any unused portion of a field is filled with spaces.

A good way to picture a random file is as a table of information with the records as the rows and the fields as the columns. As Figure 14.1 shows, the row number is equivalent to the record number. Each record may be referenced by its relative position within the file. You can think of the entire table as being stored in random-access memory; any record in the table can be accessed by referring to its row number. In reality, only one record is in memory at any time; the rest of the table remains on the disk. The portion of memory in which the active record resides is called the file *buffer*. Records always pass through the buffer as they are read from and written to the file.

FIGURE 14.1
Table concept of random file

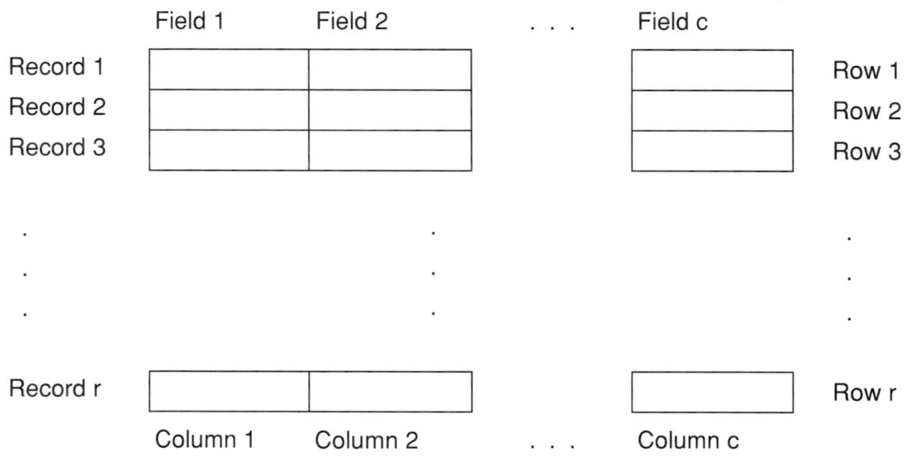

Advantages

Quick access to individual records is a major advantage of random files. For example, reading the 902nd record of a random file takes no longer than reading the 37th record; the only difference is the time necessary to move the read/write head on the disk drive. Random files may also be processed sequentially if all the records need to be accessed.

Random files generally require less disk space than sequential files because there are no excess commas, quotation marks, or extra spaces for delimiters and because numbers are stored in a more compact form.

Random files are simple to update because you can change any record without rewriting the entire file. Because records are accessed by their record number, they can be stored in a random fashion with no regard to order. This characteristic has given them the name "random files"; however, the less-used term *direct-access files* is more descriptive and more accurate.

Disadvantages

The procedures for storing and retrieving records from random files are more complex than those for sequential files.

RANDOM FILE APPLICATION

Amex Co-op is a small cooperative that maintains its own members' charge accounts. When Amex started, it was small enough that the clerks knew each member and handled charges and accounts informally. Now that Amex has over 100 members, Mr. Blake, the manager, says that it is too difficult for the clerks to remember who is a member, much less who is in good standing.

Mr. Blake wants an inquiry system programmed for their computer so that clerks can easily determine the status of a member's account. He would like the system to operate in the following manner:

1. When a member wishes to charge a purchase, the clerk enters the account number into the computer.

2. The clerk is then requested to enter the amount of the charge.

3. If the amount of the charge plus any amount owed (the previous month's balance due plus any current charges), exceeds the credit limit of the member, the system refuses the charge.

4. If the amount of the charge, plus any amount owed, is less than or equal to the member's credit limit, the system approves the charge.

5. If the charge is approved, the amount of the charge is added to the current charges.

6. After an inquiry is processed, the program displays a screen message asking for another account number.

The co-op currently keeps the following data about each member in a card file:

- Account number

- Name

- Balance due

- Current charges

- Credit limit

Before designing and writing the inquiry program, you need to create a random file containing the member data.

To keep the program simple, let the account number be the record number in the file, that is, account number 1 is record number 1, account number 2 is record number 2, and so on. In subsequent programs, you will use more realistic account numbers. The following values are to be stored in each record:

Item	Data Type	Data Length
First name	String	10
Last name	String	15
Balance due	Numeric	Single-precision (####.##)
Current charges	Numeric	Single-precision (####.##)
Credit limit	Numeric	Single-precision (####.##)

Describe the Output

The output is the random file of member data stored on the disk. The name of the file is MEM.RND. MEM (member) describes the contents of the file, and RND (random) describes the type of file.

Determine the Input

The input to the file creation program is information about each member, entered from the keyboard. Use the following list of names and credit information to test the program.

First Name	Last Name	Balance	Charges	Credit Limit
Joel	Carson	34.55	12.98	500.00
Willard Joseph	Potts	105.34	26.50	800.00
Richard	McCarty	45.60	25.98	800.00
Karen	Tempel	27.80	17.50	700.00
Bonnie J.	Baumgras	305.56	85.95	400.00
Bret	Murphy	45.60	9.85	800.00
Donald	Brown	45.36	0.00	800.00
Sally Ann	Pederson	190.10	50.67	500.00
Carline A.	Marino	55.47	12.35	300.00
Cheryl C.	Cruise	150.49	34.95	200.00

Design the Program Logic

This program consists of two level-1 modules. The first level-1 module, CREATE FILE, controls the task of creating the random file. The other level-1 module, WRITE END MESSAGE, displays a closing message on the screen.

After opening the file and defining the record, the module CREATE FILE calls three additional modules. INPUT ACCT NO displays a prompt on the screen requesting the member's account number. After the user enters the account number, the module INPUT DATA requests the remaining data needed to create the member's record. After the data are entered, the WRITE RECORD module writes the record to the file. This process is repeated until –9 is entered as the member's account number. Before exiting the CREATE FILE module, the system closes the random file.

Figure 14.2 shows the structure chart and pseudocode for Program 14.1.

Code the Program Instructions

The code in Program 14.1 implements the logic design of Figure 14.2. The program includes the following new BASIC statements and functions.

OPEN

Although the OPEN statement in line 3040 is not new, this is the first time you have seen it used with a random file. The form of the OPEN statement for random files is as follows:

```
[line#] OPEN <"R">, [#]<filenumber>,<"filename">,[recordlength]
```

"R" indicates a random file, and *filenumber* is the number of the buffer. *"Filename"* is the name for the random file (including the drive specification, if necessary), and *recordlength* is the number of bytes in each record.

When you open a random file that does not already exist, the system creates the file and opens a communication channel between the disk and the buffer. If you do not specify a record length, BASIC allocates a default record length of 128 bytes. The size of the random file buffer is always the same as the record length. If a record has more than 128 bytes, it is necessary to change the buffer size by loading BASIC with the /S: option. For example,

```
A>BASICA/S:212
```

sets the buffer to 212 bytes.

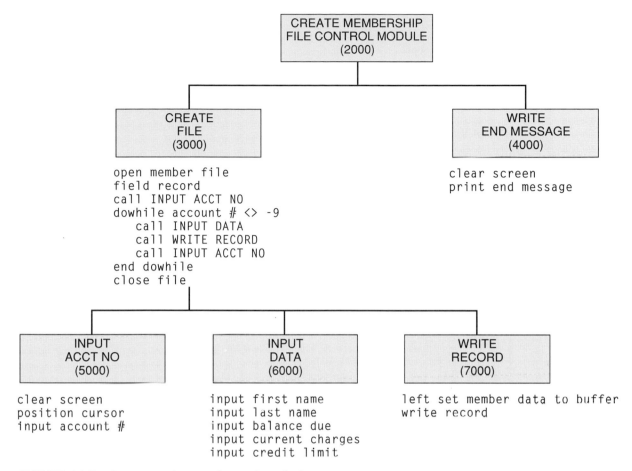

FIGURE 14.2   Structure chart and pseudocode for Program 14.1

PROGRAM 14.1

```
1000 ' PROG14-1
1010 ' *****************************
1020 ' *   CREATE MEMBERSHIP FILE   *
1030 ' *****************************
1040 '
1050 ' *****************************
1060 ' *         VARIABLES          *
1070 ' *****************************
1080 '
1090 ' MEM.RND                 Random data file
1100 ' Member record:
1110 '   Program Variable      Buffer Variable
1120 '     MEM.F.NAME$               MNF$          First name
1130 '     MEM.L.NAME$               MNL$          Last name
1140 '     MEM.BAL.DUE               MBD$          Balance due
1150 '     MEM.CUR.CHG               MCC$          Current charges
1160 '     MEM.CR.LIM                MCL$          Credit limit
1170 '
1180 ' MEM.ACCT.NO                                 Account number
1999 '
2000 ' *****************************
2010 ' *         CONTROL MODULE      *
2020 ' *****************************
2030 '
2040   KEY OFF
2050   GOSUB 3000                'Create File
2060   GOSUB 4000                'Write End Message
```

PROGRAM 14.1 (continued)

```
2070    KEY ON
2080    END
2999 '
3000 ' ******************************
3010 ' *          CREATE FILE          *
3020 ' ******************************
3030 '
3040    OPEN "R",#1,"MEM.RND",37
3050 '
3060    FIELD #1, 10 AS MNF$, 15 AS MNL$, 4 AS MBD$,
                    4 AS MCC$,  4 AS MCL$
3070 '
3080    GOSUB 5000              'Input Acct No
3090    WHILE MEM.ACCT.NO <> -9
3100        GOSUB 6000          'Input Data
3110        GOSUB 7000          'Write Record
3120        GOSUB 5000          'Input Acct No
3130    WEND
3140    CLOSE #1
3150    RETURN
3999 '
4000 ' ******************************
4010 ' *      WRITE END MESSAGE      *
4020 ' ******************************
4030 '
4040    CLS
4050    BEEP
4060    PRINT TAB(10); "FILE CREATION PROGRAM FINISHED"
4070    RETURN
4999 '
5000 ' ******************************
5010 ' *         INPUT ACCT NO          *
5020 ' ******************************
5030 '
5040    CLS
5050    LOCATE 10
5060    PRINT "ENTER ACCOUNT NUMBER"
5070    INPUT " (ENTER -9 WHEN FINISHED) ", MEM.ACCT.NO
5080    RETURN
5999 '
6000 ' ******************************
6010 ' *          INPUT DATA          *
6020 ' ******************************
6030 '
6040    INPUT "MEMBER'S FIRST NAME      ", MEM.F.NAME$
6050    INPUT "MEMBER'S LAST NAME      ", MEM.L.NAME$
6060    INPUT "BALANCE DUE             ", MEM.BAL.DUE
6070    INPUT "CURRENT CHARGES         ", MEM.CUR.CHG
6080    INPUT "CREDIT LIMIT            ", MEM.CR.LIM
6090    RETURN
6999 '
7000 ' ******************************
7010 ' *          WRITE RECORD          *
7020 ' ******************************
7030 '
7040    LSET MNF$ = MEM.F.NAME$
7050    LSET MNL$ = MEM.L.NAME$
7060    LSET MBD$ = MKS$(MEM.BAL.DUE)
7070    LSET MCC$ = MKS$(MEM.CUR.CHG)
7080    LSET MCL$ = MKS$(MEM.CR.LIM)
7090 '
7100    PUT #1, MEM.ACCT.NO
7110    RETURN
```

Keep in mind that a random file buffer does not work in the same way as a sequential file buffer does. You can use random file buffers for both input and output without closing and reopening the file. The OPEN statement does not specify a data transfer direction, as it does for sequential files in the FOR INPUT and FOR OUTPUT modes.

Consider this example of an OPEN statement:

```
3040  OPEN "R", #1, "MEM.RND", 37
```

It does the following:

1. Assigns buffer #1 a length of 37 bytes

Buffer #1

1 ...   37

2. Creates the random file MEM.RND on the disk in the default drive and opens a communication channel between the disk and the #1 buffer

Here are two more examples of OPEN statements for random files:

```
1000  OPEN "R", #2, "B:CLASS.RND", 68
```

This statement creates or opens the file CLASS.RND on drive B, links the file to buffer #2, and assigns a length of 68 bytes to the buffer.

```
1000  FILE$  =  "PERSON.RND"
1010  OPEN "R", #3, FILE$
```

This statement creates or opens the file represented by the string variable FILE$ (in this case, FILE$ = "PERSON.RND"), links the file to buffer #3, and assigns the default length of 128 bytes to the buffer.

Here is an alternate form for the OPEN statement for random files:

```
[line#] OPEN <"filename"> AS [#]<filenumber> [LEN=<recordlength>]
```

Line 3040 could have been written as

```
3040 OPEN "MEM.RND" AS #1 LEN = 37
```

FIELD #

Line 3060 defines the arrangement of data in the records of the random file MEM.RND. The FIELD # statement specifies how many bytes are reserved for each field in the record. It also specifies the order in which the fields are arranged in the record.

The general form of the FIELD # statement is:

```
[line#] FIELD [#]<filenumber>, <len1 AS var1$><,len2 AS var2$> . . .
```

Filenumber is the number assigned in the OPEN statement, *len*1 is the number of bytes assigned to the first variable or field name, *var*1$; *len*2 is the number of bytes assigned to the second variable, var2$; and so on. In this context, *field* is often used as a verb: to "field" or define the buffer area.

Keep the following information in mind when you allocate bytes to each fielded variable:

1. All integer variables require 2 bytes.

2. All single-precision variables require 4 bytes.

3. All double-precision variables require 8 bytes.

4. All string variables require 1 byte per character.

In Program 14.1, line 3060

```
3060  FIELD #1, 10 AS MNF$, 15 AS MNL$, 4 AS MBD$,
              4 AS MCC$,  4 AS MCL$
```

assigns the first 10 bytes of buffer #1 to the variable MNF$, the next 15 bytes to MNL$, the next 4 bytes to MBD$, the next 4 bytes to MCC$, and the last 4 bytes to MCL$. Buffer #1 would look like this:

MNF$ is 10 bytes because the first name can be 10 characters; MNL$ is 15 bytes because the last name can be 15 characters; and MBD$, MCC$, and MCL$ are 4 bytes because each of these buffer variables will hold a single-precision value.

Notice in lines 1120–1160 that each field in the random record is associated with two variable names: buffer variables and program variables. The FIELD # statement assigns the buffer variable names to the field. These are the names associated with the data while they reside in the buffer, a temporary holding place for the data as they are read from or written to the random file on disk. These field names are usually short, string variable names and indicate little more than position. Use these names only when you want to access the file. Never use the buffer variables to do calculations within the program; use program variables. There are two reasons for this. First, the buffer variables are string variables and cannot be used directly in numeric operations. Second, they are stored in a buffer location rather than a memory location, as regular variables are. Because buffer storage is fixed in length, any change in variable size could cause an error.

Sometimes you may want to define more than one FIELD statement for a random file buffer. For example, it is often convenient to write a header record to a file that might include a description of the file and the number of records in the file before the data records are written. That record might contain information of a different type than the data records contain.

To insert a header in MEM.RND, you could define the buffer an additional time as

```
3055  FIELD #1, 25 AS MHD$, 2 AS MNR$
```

MHD$ is the buffered variable associated with HEADER$, a 25-character (or less) description of the file. MNR$ is the buffer variable corresponding to the integer variable NO.OF.RECS. This statement divides the buffer into three fields. However, only the first two fields are used; the last 10 bytes remain unused but are needed because every record in this file must occupy 37 bytes. Now, when set up for a header record, buffer #1 would look like this:

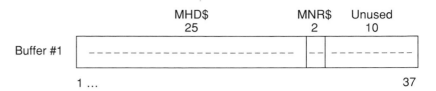

Keep in mind the following points about the FIELD # statement:

1. There may be more than one FIELD # statement for a random file.

2. Use only string variables in the FIELD # statement to define the buffer.

3. The FIELD # statement defines the position of the data fields in the buffer. It also defines the length of each data item (the number of bytes that each data item occupies).

4. The sum of the lengths of the variables listed in the FIELD # statement cannot be larger than the record length specified in the corresponding OPEN statement.

LSET AND RSET

The built-in functions LSET and RSET send the data from memory to the buffer in preparation for writing the data to the file. The general form of the LSET and RSET functions is:

```
[line#] LSET <fieldvar$  =  programvar$>
[line#] RSET <fieldvar$  =  programvar$>
```

Fieldvar$* is a string variable specified in the FIELD # statement, and *programvar$ contains the value to be inserted in the buffer.

Line numbers 7040 and 7050

```
7040  LSET MNF$  =  MEM.F.NAME$
7050  LSET MNL$  =  MEM.L.NAME$
```

transfer the information stored in the program variables MEM.F.NAME$ and MEM.L.NAME$ to the buffer variables MNF$ and MNL$, respectively. See Figure 14.3.

LSET left-justifies the data in the field. If the field is not large enough, the string is truncated on the right. If the field is larger than the string, the field is padded with blanks on the right. For example, if MEM.F. NAME$ = "Bonnie J." and MEM.L.NAME$ = "Baumgras", the buffer would look like this:

If MEM.F.Name$ = "Willard Joseph" and MEM.L.NAME$ = "Potts", then the buffer would look like this:

Notice that the first name, Willard Joseph, is truncated to Willard Jo because the field for first name can contain only 10 characters.

RSET right-justifies the data in the buffer field. If the field is not large enough, the data are still truncated on the right. If the field is larger than the data, the space to the left is filled with blanks.

Additional examples are:

```
1000   LSET C$  =   CITY$
2000   RSET Z$  =   ZONE$
3000   LSET B$  =   "Warehouse Number 302"
```

Some programmers use the convention of placing string data in the buffer with LSET and numeric data with RSET. In this chapter, LSET is used for both kinds of data, since there is no advantage to using RSET with numeric data.

MKI$, MKS$, and MKD$

To write numeric variables to the disk in a random file, you must first convert them to string values. You can do this with the MKI$, MKS$, and MKD$ functions. MKI$ is read as "make an integer variable a string variable," MKS$ as "make a single-precision variable a string variable," and MKD$ as "make a double-precision variable a string variable." MKI$ returns a 2–byte string; MKS$, a 4-byte string; and MKD$, an 8-byte string. In lines 7060–7080, the MKS$ function assigns the variables MEM.BAL.DUE, MEM. CUR.CHG, and MEM.CR.LIM to the buffer variables MBD$, MCC$, and MCL$, respectively.

Other examples of these functions are:

```
1000   LSET W$  =   MKS$(WAGE)
2000   LSET C$  =   MKI$(CODE%)
3000   LSET D$  =   MKD$(1223145634.678)
```

PUT

When you fill the buffer for a random file, the system does not automatically write the data to the disk; you must use the PUT statement to send the buffer values to the disk. The size of the sequential buffer file is a constant, 512 bytes. When creating a sequential file, the system writes information to the buffer. The information is stored there until the buffer is full, at which time the system transfers the data to the disk. The buffer might hold several records before a transfer becomes necessary. Similarly, when you open a sequential file for input, the system transfers enough records from the disk to fill the buffer, where they await an INPUT # statement.

Because random files may be used for either input or output, the program statements GET and PUT must direct the system to move data from a file to the buffer or vice versa. There is no way for the system to know automatically which way to move data.

In Program 14.1, the line

```
7100   PUT #1, MEM.ACCT.NO
```

is the statement that actually causes the data in the buffer to be written to the disk. The value of MEM.ACCT.NO determines what record number receives the contents of the buffer; for example, if MEM.ACCT.NO = 7, then the data in buffer #1 is written to record number 7. Notice in Figure 14.3 that space is reserved for the first six records. Those records do not need to be placed in the file before record 7, as they would if this were a sequential file.

The standard form of the PUT # statement is:

[*line#*]   PUT   [*#*] <*buffernumber*>[*,recordnumber*]

Buffernumber is the number assigned in the OPEN statement, and *record-number* is the particular record assigned. If you do not specify *recordnumber*, the system assigns one. The new record number is the last record number assigned plus 1. If the first PUT # statement has no record number, the system puts the contents of the buffer in record number 1.

```
PUT #1, MEM.ACCT.NO

  where
    MEM.ACCT.NO = 7
```

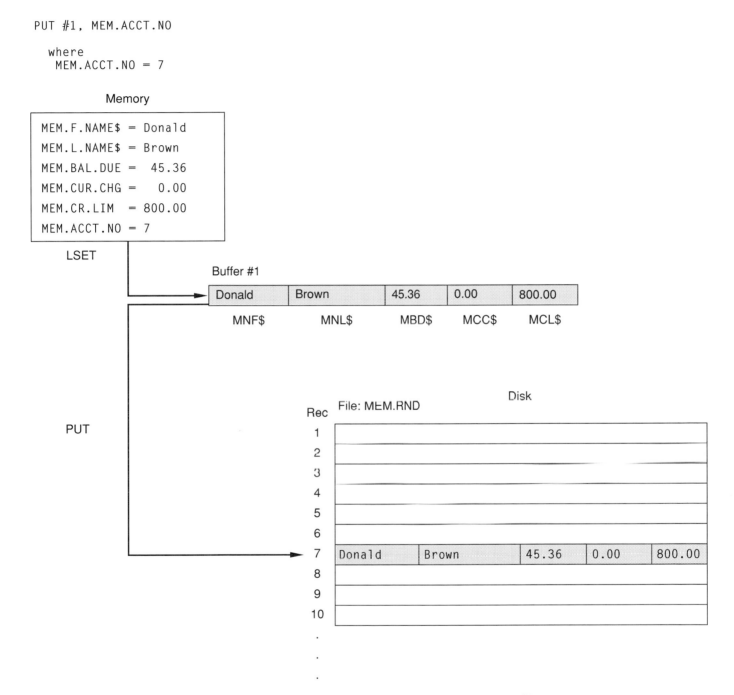

FIGURE 14.3   Transfer of a record from memory to the buffer and then to a random file

Other examples of the PUT # statement are:

```
1000   PUT #2, 35
2000   PUT #1, COUNT + 1
3000   PUT #3
```

Because no record number is indicated in the third example, the record number would be 1 more than the record number assigned the last time the statement was executed. For example, if the last record written to the file was 24, the data will be written to record location 25 the next time line 3000 is executed.

Test the Program

Using the data listed previously, the program will create the following random file:

Rec MEM.RND

Rec					
1	Joel	Carson	34.55	12.98	500.00
2	Willard Jo	Potts	105.34	26.50	800.00
3	Richard	McCarty	45.60	25.98	800.00
4	Karen	Tempel	27.80	17.50	700.00
5	Bonnie J.	Baumgras	305.56	85.95	400.00
6	Bret	Murphy	45.60	9.85	800.00
7	Donald	Brown	45.36	0.00	800.00
8	Sally Ann	Pederson	190.10	50.67	500.00
9	Carline A.	Marino	55.47	12.35	300.00
10	Cheryl C.	Cruise	150.49	34.95	200.00

Note: The numbers are actually stored in compressed or packed binary format.

RECORD RETRIEVAL

Now that the file has been created and the data have been entered, you can write the inquiry program to allow the clerks to look at any member's record in the file and determine if the amount to be charged is acceptable or not. Remember, if the system accepts the charge, it must add the charged value to the value of the member's current charges (MEM.CUR.CHG).

Determine the Input and Describe the Output

The input will be the account number entered from the keyboard (for the data listed previously, an integer from 1 to 10) and the amount of the charge. The output will be a message accepting or rejecting the charge. The record will be updated if the charge is accepted.

Design the Program Logic

This program consists of two level-1 modules. The first level-1 module, PROCESS FILE, controls the task of inquiries to the random file. The other level-1 module, WRITE END MESSAGE, displays a closing message on the screen.

After opening the file and defining the record, the module PROCESS FILE calls two additional modules. INPUT ACCT NO requests the user to enter an account number. If the account number is not –9, the PROCESS ACCT NO module is called.

For each account, the member's record is read and the name information is displayed on the screen. Next, the program requests the amount of the charge. The module VALIDATE CHARGE is called, and the sum of the balance due plus the current charges plus the amount of the charge is compared to the member's credit limit. If the charge is approved, the member's record is updated and a message is displayed; otherwise, the message "CHARGE DENIED" is displayed.

This process is repeated until the user enters −9 as the member's account number. Before exiting the PROCESS FILE module, the program closes the random file.

Figure 14.4 shows the pseudocode and structure chart for Program 14.2.

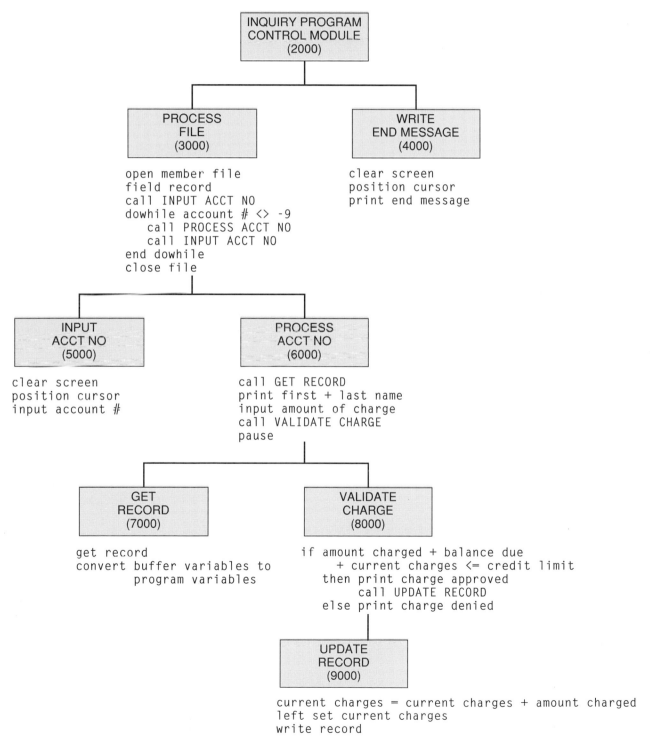

```
                    INQUIRY PROGRAM
                    CONTROL MODULE
                        (2000)


        PROCESS                          WRITE
         FILE                        END MESSAGE
        (3000)                          (4000)

open member file                   clear screen
field record                       position cursor
call INPUT ACCT NO                 print end message
dowhile account # <> -9
    call PROCESS ACCT NO
    call INPUT ACCT NO
end dowhile
close file


     INPUT                          PROCESS
    ACCT NO                         ACCT NO
    (5000)                          (6000)

clear screen                   call GET RECORD
position cursor                print first + last name
input account #                input amount of charge
                               call VALIDATE CHARGE
                               pause


            GET                          VALIDATE
          RECORD                         CHARGE
          (7000)                         (8000)

get record                     if amount charged + balance due
convert buffer variables to        + current charges <= credit limit
     program variables         then print charge approved
                                    call UPDATE RECORD
                               else print charge denied


                              UPDATE
                              RECORD
                              (9000)

                    current charges = current charges + amount charged
                    left set current charges
                    write record
```

FIGURE 14.4   Structure chart plus pseudocode for Program 14.2

PROGRAM 14.2

```
1000 ' PROG14-2
1010 ' ******************************
1020 ' *        INQUIRY PROGRAM         *
1030 ' ******************************
1040 '
1050 ' ******************************
1060 ' *          VARIABLES            *
1070 ' ******************************
1080 '
1090 ' MEM.RND                 Random data file
1100 ' Member record:
1110 '    Program Variable        Buffer Variable
1120 '       MEM.F.NAME$              MNF$              First name
1130 '       MEM.L.NAME$              MNL$              Last name
1140 '       MEM.BAL.DUE              MBD$              Balance due
1150 '       MEM.CUR.CHG              MCC$              Current charges
1160 '       MEM.CR.LIM               MCL$              Credit limit
1170 '
1180 ' AMT.CHG                                    Amount to be charged
1190 ' MEM.ACCT.NO                                Account number entered
1200 ' PAUSE$                                     Screen pause
1220 '
1230 ' ******************************
1240 ' *          CONSTANTS            *
1250 ' ******************************
1260 '
1270    MSG1$ = "CHARGE APPROVED"
1280    MSG2$ = "CHARGE DENIED"
1999 '
2000 ' ******************************
2010 ' *         CONTROL MODULE         *
2020 ' ******************************
2030 '
2040    KEY OFF
2050    GOSUB 3000              'Process File
2060    GOSUB 4000              'Write End Message
2070    KEY ON
2080    END
2999 '
3000 ' ******************************
3010 ' *          PROCESS FILE          *
3020 ' ******************************
3030 '
3040    OPEN "R",#1,"MEM.RND",37
3050 '
3060    FIELD #1, 10 AS MNF$, 15 AS MNL$, 4 AS MBD$,
                   4 AS MCC$,  4 AS MCL$
3070 '
3080    GOSUB 5000              'Input Acct No
3090    WHILE MEM.ACCT.NO <> -9
3100       GOSUB 6000           'Process Acct No
3110       GOSUB 5000           'Input Acct No
3120    WEND
3130    CLOSE #1
3140    RETURN
3999 '
4000 ' ******************************
4010 ' *       WRITE END MESSAGE         *
4020 ' ******************************
4030 '
4040    CLS
4050    BEEP
4060    LOCATE 10
4070    PRINT TAB(10); "FILE INQUIRY PROGRAM FINISHED"
4080    RETURN
```

PROGRAM 14.2 (continued)

```
4999 '
5000 ' ******************************
5010 ' *        INPUT ACCT NO        *
5020 ' ******************************
5030 '
5040   CLS
5050   LOCATE 10
5060   PRINT "ENTER ACCOUNT NUMBER"
5070   INPUT " (ENTER -9 WHEN FINISHED) ", MEM.ACCT.NO
5080   RETURN
5999 '
6000 ' ******************************
6010 ' *        PROCESS ACCT NO        *
6020 ' ******************************
6030 '
6040   GOSUB 7000                  'Get Record
6050   PRINT MEM.F.NAME$; SPC(1); MEM.L.NAME$
6060   INPUT "ENTER AMOUNT OF CHARGE "; AMT.CHG
6070   GOSUB 8000                  'Validate Charge
6080   LOCATE 22 : PRINT "PRESS ANY KEY TO CONTINUE"
6090   PAUSE$ = INPUT$(1)
6100   RETURN
6999 '
7000 ' ******************************
7010 ' *          GET RECORD          *
7020 ' ******************************
7030 '
7040   GET #1, MEM.ACCT.NO
7050 '
7060   MEM.F.NAME$   =   MNF$
7070   MEM.L.NAME$   =   MNL$
7080   MEM.BAL.DUE   =   CVS(MBD$)
7090   MEM.CUR.CHG   =   CVS(MCC$)
7100   MEM.CR.LIM    =   CVS(MCL$)
7110 '
7120   RETURN
7999 '
8000 ' ******************************
8010 ' *      VALIDATE CHARGE      *
8020 ' ******************************
8030 '
8040   IF (AMT.CHG + MEM.BAL.DUE + MEM.CUR.CHG) <= MEM.CR.LIM
         THEN PRINT MSG1$ : GOSUB 9000
         ELSE PRINT MSG2$
8050 '
8060   RETURN
8999 '
9000 ' ******************************
9010 ' *        UPDATE RECORD        *
9020 ' ******************************
9030 '
9040   MEM.CUR.CHG = MEM.CUR.CHG + AMT.CHG
9050   LSET MCC$ = MKS$(MEM.CUR.CHG)
9060   PUT #1, MEM.ACCT.NO
9070   RETURN
```

Code the Program Instructions	The code in Program 14.2 implements the logic design of Figure 14.4. The program includes the following new BASIC statements and functions:
GET #	The GET # statement gets a record from a random file and puts it in a buffer. In this program, line 5070 requests an account number. If the account number is not –9, the program transfers control to the module GET RECORD

(7000). Line 7040 gets the record corresponding to the value of the variable MEM.ACCT.NO and copies it to the buffer, where it is addressable with the variable names defined in the FIELD # statement. See Figure 14.5. If the value of MEM.ACCT.NO = 4, then Karen Tempel's record is placed in the buffer.

The general form of the GET # statement is:

[*line#*]   GET [#]<*buffernumber*>[, *recordnumber*]

Buffernumber is the buffer number assigned in the OPEN statement, and *recordnumber* is the number of the record the system is to fetch. If record number is omitted, the system gets the records in numeric order, starting with record 1.

Other examples of the GET # statement are:

```
1000   GET #1,24          Gets the 24th record
2000   GET #4,RECORD      Gets the record defined by RECORD
3000   GET #2,N + 1       Gets the record defined by N + 1
4000   GET #1             Gets the next record
```

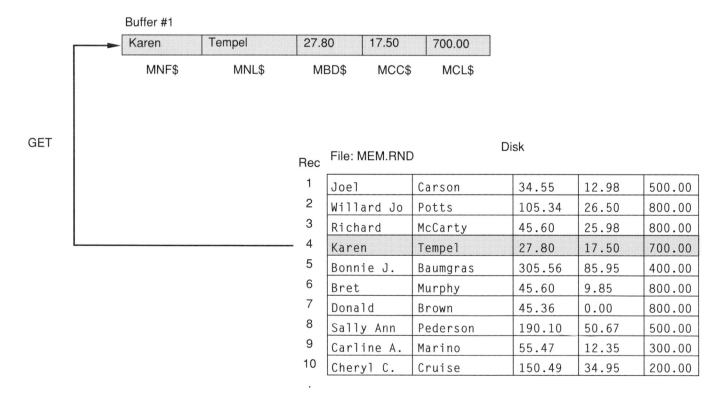

FIGURE 14.5   Transfer of a record in a random file to the buffer

CVI, CVS, and CVD

Once the program has retrieved a record from the disk file, it must change all of the fielded variables back to the program variables. This may require changing some string variables to numeric variables. Built-in BASIC functions CVI, CVS, and CVD do this job. The general forms of the functions are:

```
[line#] <var%  =  CVI(var$)>
[line#] <var!  =  CVS(var$)>
[line#] <var#  =  CVD(var$)>
```

Read CVI as "convert a string value to an integer value," CVS as "convert a string value to a single-precision value," and CVD as "convert a string value to a double-precision value." Lines 7080–7100 use the CVS functions to convert a string value to a single-precision value. Other examples of these functions are:

```
1000   CODE%  =  CVI(C$)
2000   WAGE!  =  CVS(W$)
3000   DEBT#  =  CVD(D$)
```

Comments about Program 14.2

For every record that the user requests, the buffer variables are converted to program variables and then the member's name is displayed. Line 6060 then asks the clerk to enter the amount of the charge. When the system has the charge value, the program transfers control to module VALIDATE CHARGE (8000), which checks whether the charge will make the member's outstanding charges larger than the member's credit limit.

The IF-THEN-ELSE structure in line 8040 checks whether the sum of the amount charged plus the balance due (unpaid charges from previous months) plus the current charges (previous charges in the current month) is less than or equal to the member's credit limit. If so, the message "CHARGE APPROVED" is displayed, and the program transfers control to the module UPDATE RECORD (9000). If the charge exceeds the limit, the message "CHARGE DENIED" is displayed, and program control is returned to line 6100 and then to line 3110, where the process begins again.

When program control passes to module UPDATE RECORD (9000), the variable MEM.CUR.CHG in line 9040 is incremented by the value of AMT.CHG. Line 9050 converts the value of MEM.CUR.CHG to a 4-byte string and then writes it to the buffer field MCC$. Note that line 9050 writes only the value of MEM.CUR.CHG to the buffer. All of the other data remains in the buffer; the value of only this one field changes. Line 9060 writes the entire contents of the buffer to the disk file. Remember, in this program record number is equal to the account number. Control then returns to line 8060, which transfers program control to line 6080.

Lines 6080–6090 keep the information on the screen until the clerk presses any key. Line 3110 calls the INPUT ACCT NO module and asks for another account number. The WHILE/WEND loop (lines 3090–3120) continues to be executed until the user enters –9 as the account number. When that happens, the loop is terminated and line 3130 closes the file. Execution passes to the CONTROL module, where an ending message is called, and the program ends.

Figure 14.6 shows the results of updating a record in the file MEM.RND.

Update Record #6 with a $30.00 charge.

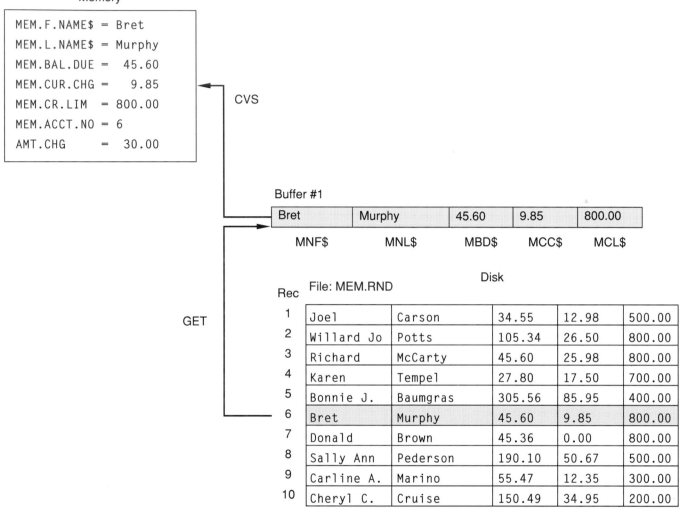

Memory

```
MEM.F.NAME$ = Bret
MEM.L.NAME$ = Murphy
MEM.BAL.DUE =  45.60
MEM.CUR.CHG =   9.85
MEM.CR.LIM = 800.00
MEM.ACCT.NO = 6
AMT.CHG     =  30.00
```

CVS

Buffer #1

Bret	Murphy	45.60	9.85	800.00
MNF$	MNL$	MBD$	MCC$	MCL$

Disk

File: MEM.RND

GET

Rec					
1	Joel	Carson	34.55	12.98	500.00
2	Willard Jo	Potts	105.34	26.50	800.00
3	Richard	McCarty	45.60	25.98	800.00
4	Karen	Tempel	27.80	17.50	700.00
5	Bonnie J.	Baumgras	305.56	85.95	400.00
6	Bret	Murphy	45.60	9.85	800.00
7	Donald	Brown	45.36	0.00	800.00
8	Sally Ann	Pederson	190.10	50.67	500.00
9	Carline A.	Marino	55.47	12.35	300.00
10	Cheryl C.	Cruise	150.49	34.95	200.00

FIGURE 14.6   Random file update (retrieving record)

Summary

- A random file is a collection of records organized so that any record may be retrieved or written without processing all the preceding records in the file.

- These are the characteristics of a random file:

  □ Given a method of determining where a particular record is, any record can be accessed in any order.

  □ After opening a file, the user can read from the file or write to it.

- To open a random file:

  □ Use the OPEN statement with the R mode; this opens the file for both input and output.

```
MEM.CUR.CHG = MEM.CUR.CHG + AMT.CHG
                 (9.85)     (30.00)
```

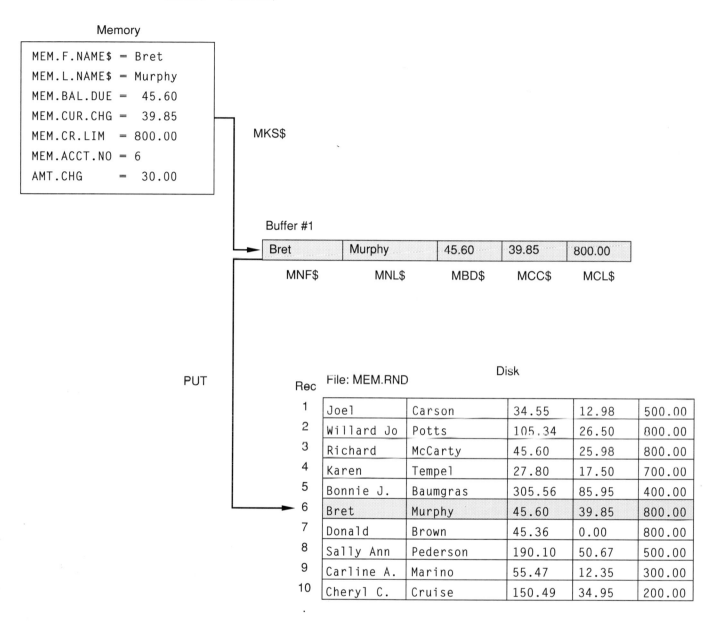

FIGURE 14.6   Random file update (replacing updated record)

□ Assign a buffer number (file number) to the file.

□ Specify the record length if you do not want the default length of 128 bytes.

■ Follow the OPEN statement with an appropriate FIELD # statement. Remember these points about FIELD #:

   □ There may be more than one FIELD # statement for a random file.

□ Use only string variables in the FIELD # statement to define the buffer.

□ The FIELD # statement defines the position of the data fields in the buffer. It also defines the length of each data item (the number of bytes that each data item occupies).

□ The sum of the lengths of the variables listed in the FIELD # statement cannot be larger than the record length specified in the corresponding OPEN statement.

- LSET and RSET are used to store data in the buffer. LSET left-justifies the data. RSET right-justifies the data.

- Two separate sets of functions are available to convert numeric data to and from string values for storage in and retrieval from random file buffers:

  □ MKI$, MKS$, and MKD$ convert numeric values to string values, allowing them to be stored in the buffer when the LSET or RSET command is given.

  □ CVI, CVS, and CVD convert string values from the buffer to numeric values so that they can be used in the program for calculations or other functions.

- The PUT # statement writes the data values stored in a buffer to the random file. For example, PUT #2 writes the contents of the #2 buffer to the next record position, whereas PUT #2,35 writes the contents of the #2 buffer to the 35th record position in the file.

- The GET # statement is used to retrieve a record from a random file and place it in the buffer. For example, GET #3 retrieves the next record from file #3, and GET #3,20 retrieves the 20th record from file #3.

- Chapter 14 describes the following new BASIC statements and functions:

CVD	A function that converts an 8-byte string to a double-precision value.
CVI	A function that converts a 2-byte string to an integer value.
CVS	A function that converts a 4-byte string to a single-precision value.
FIELD #n	A statement that defines the buffer for file #n, the variables contained in it, and their width.
GET #n	A statement that retrieves a record from file #n and places it in the appropriate buffer.
LSET	A BASIC built-in function that places data in the buffer positions, left-justified.
MKD$	A function that converts a double-precision value to an 8-byte string.
MKI$	A function that converts an integer value to a 2-byte string.
MKS$	A function that converts a single-precision value to a 4-byte string.

PUT #n	A statement that writes the data stored in the buffer to file #n.
RSET	A BASIC built-in function that places data in the buffer positions, right-justified.

Review Questions

1. What two types of file organizations are allowed in BASIC?

2. State one advantage and one disadvantage of random-access files.

3. What type of file is always opened for both input and output at the same time?

4. What statement must precede a FIELD # statement?

5. What parameter is generally included in an OPEN statement for random files but is not included in an OPEN statement for sequential files?

6. If the record length is not included in the OPEN statement for a random file, what is the default record length?

7. What do you do if you want to use a record longer than 128 bytes?

8. What is the purpose of the FIELD # statement?

9. What type of variables can be assigned in a FIELD # statement?

10. Once you open a random file, how many FIELD # statements can apply to it?

11. Is it possible to define the record length in the OPEN statement so that more than one record can be stored in the buffer?

12. Explain the purpose of the buffer for random files.

13. What does the LSET function do? The RSET function?

14. What does CVS(WAGE$) do?

15. What does MKS$(WAGE) do?

16. Why do you need all three of the functions CVI, CVS, and CVD? How about MIK$, MKS$, and MKD$?

17. Assume the last record accessed by a program was number 43 from file number 3. What record does each of the following statements apply to if they are executed consecutively?

    a. GET #3
    b. GET #3,78
    c. PUT #3
    d. PUT #3,102

18. From where does the GET # statement get a record? What happens to that record after it is retrieved?

19. From where does a PUT # statement get a record, and where does it place that record?

20. Can you use the TYPE (operating system) command to view the contents of a random data file? What will happen?

Problems

1. Which of the following statements are valid? Correct the invalid statements.

   a. 1000   OPEN "DATAFILE.RND",R,215

   b. 1000   OPEN "DATAFILE.RND"
   FOR RANDOM AS #1

   c. 1000   OPEN "R",#1,"DATAFILE.RND"

   d. 1000   OPEN "R",3,"B:DATAFILE.RND",123

   e. 1200   GET

   f. 1200   GET #2

   g. 1200   GET 2, 49

   h. 1400   PUT 3

   i. 1400   PUT 35, #2

   j. 1400   PUT

   k. 2000   LSET ID$ = CVS#(ID.NUMBER)

   l. 2000   CVS(WAGE$) = RSET WAGE

   m. 2000   DEPENDENTS = CVI(DEP$)

   n. 2000   RSET ED$ = MKD(EXPENSE)

2. Write a statement to open a random file named "EMPLOY.RND" that has records containing 69 characters (or bytes).

3. Write a FIELD # statement for the OPEN statement you wrote in problem 2 so that the file buffer can store data from the following program variables. Use appropriate buffer variables corresponding to the program variables.

EMP.NAME$	25 characters
EMP.POS$	15 characters
EMP.NUM	Integer value, 4 digits
EMP.SAL	Real value up to 99999.99
EMP.YRS	Integer value, 2 digits
EMP.IFO$	The remaining space available

4. Write the appropriate LSET or RSET statements to assign the program variables in problem 3 to the buffer.

5. Write the appropriate statement to place the buffer contents in problem 4 to the file as record #25.

6. Write a second FIELD # statement for the OPEN statement you wrote in problem 2 so that the file buffer can be used to write a header record at the beginning of the file. The header record should contain the name of the file, the number of fields, and the date it was created. Leave any space remaining at the end of the record blank.

7. For the following FIELD # statements, indicate what the record length for the random-access file should be.

   a. 1000   FIELD #1, 8 AS A$, 25 AS B$,
   4 AS C$, 12 AS D$

   b. 1000   FIELD #2, 36 AS A$, 2 AS B$,
   20 AS C$

   c. 1000   FIELD #3, 1 AS A$, 1 AS B$,
   4 AS C$, 10 AS D$

8. Using the following code, determine what is assigned to the buffer and then written as records to the file.

```
1000    OPEN "R", #1, "DATA.RND", 22
1010    FIELD #1, 16 AS HD$, 6 AS DD$
1020    FIELD #1, 6 AS ND$, 10 AS ID$,
                  2 AS QD$, 4 AS PD$
1030    DATE1$  =  "010186"
1040    HEADER$  =  "THIS IS A FILE"
1050    LSET HD$  =  HEADER$
1060    LSET DD$  =  DATE1$
1070    PUT #1,1
1080    NUMBER$  =  "517509"
1090    IDENTIFY$  =  "FLASHLIGHT"
1100    QUANTITY  =  9
1110    PRICE  =  4.98
1120    LSET ND$  =  NUMBER$
1130    LSET ID$  =  IDENTIFY$
1140    LSET QD$  =  MKI$(QUANTITY)
1150    LSET PD$  =  MKS$(PRICE)
1160    PUT #1,2
```

9. What does the following code do?

```
1000    OPEN "R", #2, "SQUARE.RND",4
1010    FIELD #2, 4 AS NS$
1020    FOR I  =  1 TO 100
1030        SQUARE  =  I^2
1040        LSET NS$  =  MKS$(SQUARE)
1050        PUT #2, 101 - I
1060    NEXT I
1070    CLOSE #2
```

10. Add a counter to Program 14.1 that will count the number of members when you create the membership file. Also add a header record to the file containing the name of the file and the

number of records. Print the value of the counter in the WRITE END MESSAGE module.

11. Add a routine to Program 14.2 to validate MEM.ACCT.NO. The value entered by the user must be a number between 1 and 10.

12. Write a program to list the records in MEM.RND sequentially on the screen.

Program Assignments

1. Styles School of Beauty keeps a card file containing the names, telephone numbers, and student numbers of current students. Write a program that will create a random-access file, STUDENT.RND, to store this information. Use the card number as the record number, i.e., card 1 will be record 1; card 2, record 2; and so on. Do not store the dash as part of the telephone number. Use the following data:

  1. Mary Smith, 567-7456, 3267
  2. Sara Ball, 567-1256, 4532
  3. Jonie Freeman, 567-3345, 4352
  4. Marty Denson, 567-9889, 3342
  5. Tara McCarty, 342-7666, 4456
  6. Karen Bolo, 567-9987, 4555
  7. Lea Cushing, 342-1123, 3890
  8. Max Learner, 567-1145, 3678
  9. Susie Maxwell, 567-3323, 3677
  10. Alice Melton, 342-1221, 3500
  11. Nadine Young, 342-9980, 3567
  12. Kathy Murphy, 567-7666, 4221

2. Write an inquiry program that will display the student name, telephone number, and student number. Retrieve the records using the card number. Since the dash is not included in the telephone number stored in the file, be sure to replace it when you display the information.

3. Write a program to create a random-access inventory file, SUPPLY.RND, for Better Houses Building Center. Each record in the file should contain the following information:

Item number	5 characters
Item description	25 characters
Item quantity	3 digits, integer
Item cost	7 digits, 2 decimal places
Item price	7 digits, 2 decimal places

Use the following data:

12345	hammer	23	5.85	9.95
54782	driver	12	1.29	3.98
34126	glue	28	.67	1.69
45111	square	5	9.50	17.95
33342	door	10	87.25	159.00
67234	window	9	42.50	99.99
44376	shelf	11	7.25	12.75
32117	switch	39	.48	1.09
98323	level	8	7.45	13.98
09567	door jamb	7	17.56	39.98
70656	ext. cord	17	3.79	7.95
89119	sink	8	29.45	62.50
37581	light	5	9.50	15.98

4. Write a program to produce an inventory report for the random file in programming assignment 3. The report should include five columns corresponding to the five fields contained in the record as well as two additional columns, quantity times cost and quantity times price. The program should total these last two columns, the total cost of items and the total retail value of items. Provide appropriate headings where necessary.

Chapter Fifteen

Random Files— Indexing, Inquiry, and Update

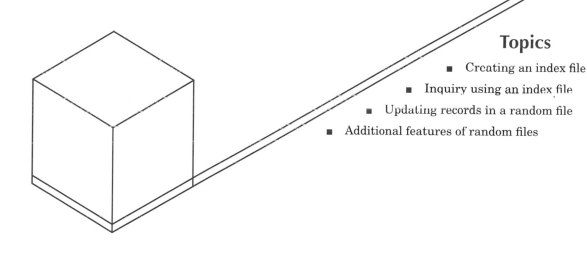

Topics

- Creating an index file
- Inquiry using an index file
- Updating records in a random file
- Additional features of random files

BASIC Functions

LOC(*n*)
LOF(*n*)

INTRODUCTION

In the Amex Co-op example in Chapter 14, the members' account numbers were integer values 1, 2, 3, and so on. This situation is not realistic. Few firms use the integer series 1, 2, 3, . . . to represent account numbers. Identification fields such as account numbers, employee numbers, or item numbers usually contain several digits and sometimes letters. These and other fields are seldom suitable keys from which you can directly assign record locations.

Some languages provide a third type of file organization known as an *index file*. In this type of file, the system automatically establishes a relationship between a record key and the record location. However, most BASIC systems do not provide index files. One solution to this problem is to create an index for the random data file. The index is a table that holds the key fields that are in the random file in the same order as they occur in the random file. The table is used to look up the record number, and after the record number (table row = record number) is located, access the random file. This concept is illustrated in Figure 15.1. This figure shows a random file of student numbers, names, and grades. The student numbers in the index table are in the same order as the student numbers in the random file. The steps to retrieve one record from the random file are:

1. The user enters the student number (for instance, 3016).

2. A table search produces a match (in this case, on the third row).

3. The record (in this case, record #3) is read from the file.

This table of key fields is usually saved in a sequential file, called an index file, between program runs. For each run of a program using a random file, the index file must be read into the table. At the end of the program run, the index table must be rewritten to the index file because the index table changes as records are added and deleted.

Program 15.1 creates a random file that is to be accessed by an index table, and Program 15.2 creates the initial index file. Program 15.3 is an inquiry program, and Program 15.4 is an update program. The last two programs access the random file using an index.

FIGURE 15.1
Random file access with an index table (Record Key = STUDENT NUMBER)

The user enters 3016.

		Index table of STUDENT NUMBERS		Random file STUDENT NUMBER	NAME	GRADE
3016 —No ►	Row 1	1984	Record 1	1984	Smith	A
—No ►	2	2846	2	2846	Jones	B
—Yes ►	3	3106	► 3	3106	Garcia	A
	4	4298	4	4298	Marsh	C
	5	4353	5	4353	Jackson	B
	6	5926	6	5926	Sanders	D

CREATE A RANDOM FILE

To use indexing in the Amex inquiry program, you need to change the structure of the random file, MEM.RND, to include an account number. Let the account number have five characters, a letter followed by four digits, for example, A3419 or G4315. In this program, the account number will be included in the record and will not be the record number.

The following changes and additions to Program 14.1 will produce the modified file (the same program structure applies). Note the changes in Program 15.1.

1. Change all occurrences of the numeric variable MEM.ACCT.NO to the string variable MEM.ACCT.NO$ (lines 1120, 3090, 5070, and 7040).

2. Change the OPEN statement to:

```
3040   OPEN "R", #1, "MEM.RND", 42
```

Use the same file name and increase the record length to 42 bytes (37 + 5 character account number = 42)

3. Change the FIELD # statement in line 3060 to:

```
3060   FIELD #1, 5 AS MAN$, 10 AS MNF$, 15 AS MNL$,
               4 AS MBD$,  4 AS MCC$,  4 AS MCL$
```

4. Add the following line to the WRITE RECORD module. This line writes the account number to the buffer.

```
7040   LSET MAN$  =  MEM.ACCT.NO$
```

5. Change the following line in the WRITE RECORD module:

```
7110   PUT #1
```

This places the first set of data in the first record, the second set of data in the second record, and so on. When you create a random file, you need not indicate the record number. The system places the records in the file in the order in which they are entered.

Since the logic design of Program 15.1 is almost identical to that of Program 14.1, there is no need to repeat it here. The only difference is that an account number is entered and included with the record in the file.

CREATE AN INDEX FILE

Using this new file, you can start to program the inquiry system around it. There is a problem, though: How do you determine which record number goes with which account number? For example, given that Donald Brown's account number is B1221, how can you find his credit information, since B1221 is not a record number? You could have the program search each record for his number, just as with a sequential file, but that would take too long, especially if Donald Brown's record is near the end of a long file.

Fortunately, there is a more efficient way to handle this situation. Use an index. Simply put the account numbers in a sequential file in exactly the order in which they appear in the random file. Then have the inquiry program read the sequential file of account numbers into an index table.

PROGRAM 15.1

```
1000 ' PROG15-1
1010 ' ******************************
1020 ' *    CREATE MEMBERSHIP FILE    *
1030 ' ******************************
1040 '
1050 ' ******************************
1060 ' *          VARIABLES          *
1070 ' ******************************
1080 '
1090 ' MEM.RND                      Random data file
1100 ' Member record:
1110 '   Program Variable           Buffer Variable
1120 '     MEM.ACCT.NO$               MAN$            Account number
1130 '     MEM.F.NAME$                MNF$            First name
1140 '     MEM.L.NAME$                MNL$            Last name
1150 '     MEM.BAL.DUE                MBD$            Balance due
1160 '     MEM.CUR.CHG                MCC$            Current charges
1170 '     MEM.CR.LIM                 MCL$            Credit limit
1999 '
2000 ' ******************************
2010 ' *          CONTROL MODULE          *
2020 ' ******************************
2030 '
2040    KEY OFF
2050    GOSUB 3000                    'Create File
2060    GOSUB 4000                    'Write End Message
2070    KEY ON
2080    END
2999 '
3000 ' ******************************
3010 ' *          CREATE FILE          *
3020 ' ******************************
3030 '
3040    OPEN "R",#1,"MEM.RND",42
3050 '
3060    FIELD #1, 5 AS MAN$, 10 AS MNF$, 15 AS MNL$,
                  4 AS MBD$,  4 AS MCC$,   4 AS MCL$
3070 '
3080    GOSUB 5000                    'Input Acct No
3090    WHILE MEM.ACCT.NO$ <> "-9"
3100       GOSUB 6000                 'Input Data
3110       GOSUB 7000                 'Write Record
3120       GOSUB 5000                 'Input Acct No
3130    WEND
3140    CLOSE #1
3150    RETURN
3999 '
4000 ' ******************************
4010 ' *          WRITE END MESSAGE          *
4020 ' ******************************
4030 '
4040    CLS
4050    BEEP
4060    PRINT TAB(10); "FILE CREATION PROGRAM FINISHED"
4070    RETURN
4999 '
5000 ' ******************************
5010 ' *          INPUT ACCT NO          *
5020 ' ******************************
5030 '
5040    CLS
5050    LOCATE 10
5060    PRINT "ENTER ACCOUNT NUMBER"
5070    INPUT " (ENTER -9 WHEN FINISHED) ", MEM.ACCT.NO$
5080    RETURN
```

PROGRAM 15.1 (continued)

```
5999 '
6000 ' ****************************
6010 ' *        INPUT DATA        *
6020 ' ****************************
6030 '
6040   INPUT "MEMBER'S FIRST NAME        ", MEM.F.NAME$
6050   INPUT "MEMBER'S LAST NAME         ", MEM.L.NAME$
6060   INPUT "BALANCE DUE                ", MEM.BAL.DUE
6070   INPUT "CURRENT CHARGES            ", MEM.CUR.CHG
6080   INPUT "CREDIT LIMIT               ", MEM.CR.LIM
6090   RETURN
6999 '
7000 ' ******************************
7010 ' *           WRITE RECORD      *
7020 ' ******************************
7030 '
7040   LSET MAN$ = MEM.ACCT.NO$
7050   LSET MNF$ = MEM.F.NAME$
7060   LSET MNL$ = MEM.L.NAME$
7070   LSET MBD$ = MKS$(MEM.BAL.DUE)
7080   LSET MCC$ = MKS$(MEM.CUR.CHG)
7090   LSET MCL$ = MKS$(MEM.CR.LIM)
7100 '
7110   PUT #1
7120   RETURN
```

The position of each account number in the index table (its row or subscript value) is the same as the number of the random file record with that account number.

The account number index is maintained on a sequential file because loading the index table from the sequential file takes less time than it does to load it from the random file each time the program is executed. When a clerk enters an account number, the program searches the index table to find that number. It uses the table row number (where it found the account number) in a GET # statement to retrieve the random file record. Figure 15.2 illustrates this process.

Design the Program Logic

The program to create the index file initially consists of four main functions:

1. *Initialize the index table.* An asterisk (or any character or set of characters that does not represent a valid account number) is placed in every row of the index table.

2. *Load the index table.* The random file is read sequentially, starting with the first record and continuing until the end-of-file marker is detected. As each record is read, the asterisk in the table is replaced with an account number.

3. *Write the index file.* The account numbers in the index table plus any remaining asterisks are written to the sequential file.

4. *Write the end message.* A message is displayed on the screen indicating the end of the program and the number of account numbers in the index file.

Figure 15.3 summarizes the design requirements of this program.

Disk

Random file named MEM.RND

Rec	ACCT NO	FIRST NAME	LAST NAME	BAL DUE	CUR CHG	CR LIMIT
1	A3412	Joel	Carson	34.55	12.98	500.00
2	A4523	Willard Jo	Potts	105.34	26.50	800.00
3	A5646	Richard	McCarty	45.60	25.98	800.00
4	B5434	Karen	Tempel	27.80	17.50	700.00
5	A9800	Bonnie J.	Baumgras	305.56	85.95	400.00
6	B1122	Bret	Murphy	45.60	9.85	800.00
7	B1221	Donald	Brown	45.36	0.00	800.00
8	A8878	Sally Ann	Pederson	190.10	50.67	500.00
9	A3343	Carline A.	Marino	55.47	12.35	300.00
10	A6656	Cheryl C.	Cruise	150.49	34.95	200.00

3.
Retrieve
record.

Memory

Index table of account numbers

Row	
1	A3412
2	A4523
3	A5646
4	B5434
5	A9800
6	B1122
7	B1221
8	A8878
9	A3343
10	A6656
11	*
12	*
13	*
14	*
15	*
.	
.	
.	
200	*

2.
Search table
for matching
account number.

Disk

Index file of account numbers

Rec	
1	A3412
2	A4523
3	A5646
4	B5434
5	A9800
6	B1122
7	B1221
8	A8878
9	A3343
10	A6656
11	*
12	*
13	*
14	*
15	*
.	
.	
.	
200	*

1.
Load account
numbers into
table.

*Asterisks indicate space for additional account numbers.

FIGURE 15.2   Indexing system for MEM.RND

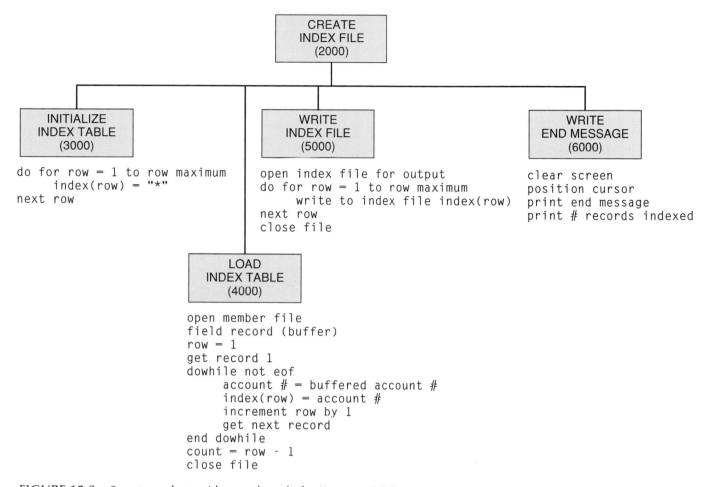

FIGURE 15.3   Structure chart with pseudocode for Program 15.2

Code the Program Instructions

Program 15.2 creates the index file. The INITIALIZE INDEX TABLE module places asterisks in each of the 200 rows of the index table (lines 3040–3060). The number 200 is an estimate of how many rows are required for existing account numbers plus projected new account numbers.

In the LOAD INDEX TABLE module, line 4040 opens the random file MEM.RND. Line 4050 defines the random buffer for the data record. Because the program will use only the random file account number, there is no need to include the rest of the variables in the FIELD # statement.

Line 4060 sets the variable ROW = 1. Line 4070 gets the first record from the random file. The WHILE/WEND loop in lines 4080–4130 gets each data record and assigns the account number from that record to the respective position in the index table, INDEX.TBL$. Thus, it assigns the account number in the first record of the random file to the first position in the index table, INDEX.TBL$(1); the account number in the second record to the second position, INDEX.TBL$(2), and so on. The loop continues until the end-of-file marker is read. Line 4140 assigns to the variable COUNT the number of records indexed. The random file is closed in line 4150. The priming read (line 4070) is necessary in this program because random files, unlike sequential files, do not bring in the end-of-file marker with the last record; the end-of-file marker is a separate record.

PROGRAM 15.2

```
1000 ' PROG15-2
1010 ' *****************************
1020 ' *       CREATE INDEX FILE       *
1030 ' *****************************
1040 '
1050 ' *****************************
1060 ' *           VARIABLES           *
1070 ' *****************************
1080 '
1090 ' MEM.RND                  Random file
1100 ' Member record:
1110 '   Program Variable        Buffer Variable
1120 '       MEM.ACCT.NO$              MAN$              Account number
1130 '
1140 ' INDEX.SEQ                Sequential index file
1150 ' Index record:
1160 '    INDEX.TBL$            Member account number
1170 '
1180 ' COUNT                    Number of records indexed
1190 ' ROW                      Table subscript
1200 '
1210 ' *****************************
1220 ' *       DEFINE INDEX TABLE       *
1230 ' *****************************
1240 '
1250    ROWMAX = 200              'Number of rows in table
1260    DIM INDEX.TBL$(ROWMAX)    'Table of member account numbers
1999 '
2000 ' *****************************
2010 ' *         CONTROL MODULE         *
2020 ' *****************************
2030 '
2040    GOSUB 3000               'Initialize Index Table
2050    GOSUB 4000               'Load Index Table
2060    GOSUB 5000               'Write Index File
2070    GOSUB 6000               'Write End Message
2080    END
2999 '
3000 ' *****************************
3010 ' *    INITIALIZE INDEX TABLE    *
3020 ' *****************************
3030 '
3040    FOR ROW = 1 TO ROWMAX
3050        INDEX.TBL$(ROW) = "*"
3060    NEXT ROW
3070    RETURN
3999 '
4000 ' *****************************
4010 ' *         LOAD INDEX TABLE        *
4020 ' *****************************
4030 '
4040    OPEN "R",#1,"MEM.RND",42
4050    FIELD #1, 5 AS MAN$
4060    ROW = 1
4070    GET #1,ROW
4080    WHILE NOT EOF(1)
4090        MEM.ACCT.NO$ = MAN$
4100        INDEX.TBL$(ROW) = MEM.ACCT.NO$
4110        ROW = ROW + 1
4120        GET #1, ROW
4130    WEND
4140    COUNT = ROW - 1
4150    CLOSE #1
4160    RETURN
```

PROGRAM 15.2   (continued)

```
4999 '
5000 ' ******************************
5010 ' *       WRITE INDEX FILE        *
5020 ' ******************************
5030 '
5040   OPEN "INDEX.SEQ" FOR OUTPUT AS #2
5050   FOR ROW = 1 TO ROWMAX
5060       WRITE #2,INDEX.TBL$(ROW)
5070   NEXT ROW
5080   CLOSE #2
5090   RETURN
5999 '
6000 ' ******************************
6010 ' *       WRITE END MESSAGE        *
6020 ' ******************************
6030 '
6040   CLS
6050   LOCATE 10
6060   PRINT TAB(10);"CREATE INDEX FILE PROGRAM FINISHED"
6070   PRINT TAB(10); COUNT ; "RECORDS INDEXED"
6080   RETURN
```

Line 5040 of the WRITE INDEX FILE module opens the sequential file INDEX.SEQ for output. Lines 5050–5070 write the 200 values stored in the index table to the disk. Any records that do not contain account numbers contain an asterisk. These records are available for new account numbers. Line 5080 closes the sequential file.

The WRITE END MESSAGE module signals the end of the program and displays a count of the number of records indexed.

INQUIRY PROGRAM USING AN INDEX FILE

Your task now is to use the index file to help the clerks answer inquiries about members' charges. The logic for this program is similar to that of the previous inquiry program, Program 14.2. The major change is the index table search for the account number. When a member's account number is located in the index table, its table row number is the same as the member's record number in the random file.

Design the Program Logic

Figure 15.4 presents the logic design for this program. Only the pseudocode for the modules that differ from the modules in Program 14.2 (the previous inquiry program) is shown in Figure 15.4.

Code the Program Instructions

Program 15.3 implements the design. The CONTROL module first calls the LOAD INDEX TABLE module (3000). The index file is opened for input in line 3050. Line 3070 reads the account numbers from the sequential index file into the index table. Since the entire table is contained in memory, the file can be closed in line 3090. Control then passes to the PROCESS FILE INQUIRY module (4000). In this module, the random file is opened and fielded (lines 4040 and 4050). Line 4060 calls the INPUT ACCT NO module (6000). Lines 6060–6070 request the user to enter an account number. When a clerk enters an account number, control returns to the PROCESS FILE INQUIRY module and line 4080 calls the CHECK FOR VALID ACCT module (7000), which determines whether that account number is valid.

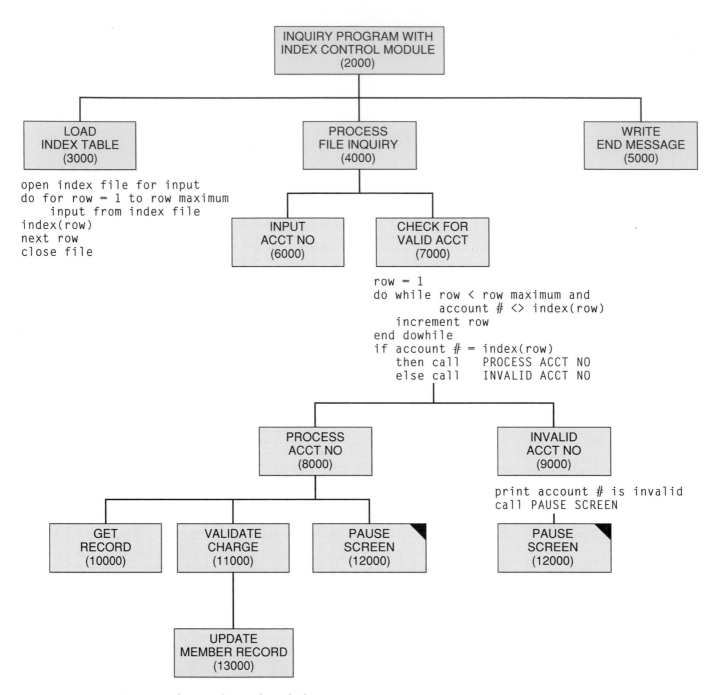

FIGURE 15.4   Structure chart and pseudocode for Program 15.3

PROGRAM 15.3

```
1000 ' PROG15-3
1010 ' *****************************
1020 ' * INQUIRY PROGRAM WITH INDEX *
1030 ' *****************************
1040 '
1050 ' *****************************
1060 ' *          VARIABLES          *
1070 ' *****************************
1080 '
1090 ' MEM.RND                 Random file
1100 ' Member record:
```

PROGRAM 15.3   (continued)

```
1110 '    Program Variables        Buffer Variables
1120 '      MEM.ACCT.NO$               MAN$         Account number
1130 '      MEM.F.NAME$                MNF$         First name
1140 '      MEM.L.NAME$                MNL$         Last name
1150 '      MEM.BAL.DUE                MBD$         Balance due
1160 '      MEM.CUR.CHG                MCC$         Current charges
1170 '      MEM.CR.LIM                 MCL$         Credit limit
1180 '
1190 ' INDEX.SEQ                 Sequential index file
1200 ' Index record:
1210 '    INDEX.TBL$             Member account number
1220 '
1230 ' ACCT$                     Account number entered from keyboard
1240 ' AMT.CHG                   Current purchase
1250 ' NEW.BAL                   Sum of amount owed + amount charged
1260 ' PAUSE$                    Screen delay
1270 ' ROW                       Table subscript
1280 '
1290 ' *****************************
1300 ' *          CONSTANTS        *
1310 ' *****************************
1320 '
1330   MSG1$ = "CHARGE APPROVED"
1340   MSG2$ = "CHARGE DENIED"
1350 '
1360 ' *****************************
1370 ' *      DEFINE INDEX TABLE   *
1380 ' *****************************
1390 '
1400   ROWMAX = 200              'Number of table entries
1410   DIM INDEX.TBL$(ROWMAX)    'Table of member account numbers
1999 '
2000 ' *****************************
2010 ' *         CONTROL MODULE     *
2020 ' *****************************
2030 '
2040   KEY OFF
2050   GOSUB 3000               'Load Index Table
2060   GOSUB 4000               'Process File Inquiry
2070   GOSUB 5000               'Write End Message
2080   KEY ON
2090   END
2999 '
3000 ' *****************************
3010 ' *       LOAD INDEX TABLE     *
3020 ' *****************************
3030 '
3040 '
3050   OPEN "INDEX.SEQ" FOR INPUT AS #1
3060   FOR ROW = 1 TO ROWMAX
3070       INPUT #1,INDEX.TBL$(ROW)
3080   NEXT ROW
3090   CLOSE #1
3100   RETURN
3999 '
4000 ' *****************************
4010 ' *     PROCESS FILE INQUIRY   *
4020 ' *****************************
4030 '
4040   OPEN "R",#2,"MEM.RND",42
4050   FIELD #2, 5 AS MAN$, 10 AS MNF$, 15 AS MNL$,
                 4 AS MBD$,  4 AS MCC$,  4 AS MCL$
4060   GOSUB 6000               'Input Account Number
4070   WHILE ACCT$ <> "-9"
```

PROGRAM 15.3 (continued)

```
4080        GOSUB 7000                'Check For Valid Account
4090        GOSUB 6000                'Input Account Number
4100    WEND
4110    CLOSE #2
4120    RETURN
4999 '
5000 ' *****************************
5010 ' *      WRITE END MESSAGE        *
5020 ' *****************************
5030 '
5040    CLS
5050    BEEP
5060    LOCATE 10
5070    PRINT TAB(10);"INQUIRY PROGRAM FINISHED"
5080    RETURN
5999 '
6000 ' *****************************
6010 ' *         INPUT ACCT NO          *
6020 ' *****************************
6030 '
6040    CLS
6050    LOCATE 10
6060    PRINT "  ENTER ACCOUNT NUMBER"
6070    INPUT " (ENTER -9 WHEN FINISHED) "; ACCT$
6080    RETURN
6999 '
7000 ' *****************************
7010 ' *     CHECK FOR VALID ACCT      *
7020 ' *****************************
7030 '
7040    ROW = 1
7050    WHILE (ROW < ROWMAX) AND (ACCT$ <> INDEX.TBL$(ROW))
7060        ROW = ROW + 1
7070    WEND
7080    IF ACCT$ = INDEX.TBL$(ROW)
            THEN GOSUB 8000
            ELSE GOSUB 9000
7090    RETURN
7999 '
8000 ' *****************************
8010 ' *        PROCESS ACCT NO         *
8020 ' *****************************
8030 '
8040    GOSUB 10000               'Get Record
8050    PRINT MEM.F.NAME$; SPC(1); MEM.L.NAME$
8060    INPUT "ENTER AMOUNT OF CHARGE "; AMT.CHG
8070    GOSUB 11000               'Validate Charge
8080    GOSUB 12000               'Pause Screen
8090    RETURN
8999 '
9000 ' *****************************
9010 ' *        INVALID ACCT NO         *
9020 ' *****************************
9030 '
9040    BEEP
9050    PRINT
9060    PRINT TAB(10);"ACCOUNT NUMBER "; ACCT$; " IS INVALID."
9070    GOSUB 12000               'Pause Screen
9080    RETURN
9999 '
10000 ' *****************************
10010 ' *          GET RECORD           *
10020 ' *****************************
10030 '
```

PROGRAM 15.3 (continued)

```
10040    GET #2,ROW
10050    MEM.F.NAME$ = MNF$
10060    MEM.L.NAME$ = MNL$
10070    MEM.BAL.DUE = CVS(MBD$)
10080    MEM.CUR.CHG = CVS(MCC$)
10090    MEM.CR.LIM  = CVS(MCL$)
10100    RETURN
10999  '
11000  ' ****************************
11010  ' *      VALIDATE CHARGE       *
11020  ' ****************************
11030  '
11040    NEW.BAL = AMT.CHG + MEM.AMT.DUE + MEM.CUR.CHG
11050    IF NEW.BAL <= MEM.CR.LIM
             THEN PRINT MSG1$ : GOSUB 13000
             ELSE PRINT MSG2$
11060    RETURN
11999  '
12000  ' ****************************
12010  ' *        PAUSE SCREEN        *
12020  ' ****************************
12030  '
12040    LOCATE 22
12050    PRINT TAB(10); "PRESS ANY KEY TO CONTINUE"
12060    PAUSE$ = INPUT$(1)
12070    RETURN
12999  '
13000  '****************************
13010  '*    UPDATE MEMBER RECORD     *
13020  '****************************
13030  '
13040    MEM.CUR.CHG = MEM.CUR.CHG + AMT.CHG
13050    LSET MCC$ = MKS$(MEM.CUR.CHG)
13060    PUT #2,ROW
13070    RETURN
```

If the account number is valid, ROW contains the value of the random file record number that matches the account number. If the account number is not in the index table, the IF statement in line 7080 is false, and module INVALID ACCT NO (9000) is called. Lines 9050 and 9060 print a screen message reporting that the account number is invalid. Control then passes to the module PAUSE SCREEN (12000), which requests the user to press a key to continue program execution. Program control then passes back to line 4090, where the INPUT ACCT NO module is called. It sends a message to the screen asking the user to enter another account number. At that time, a clerk can terminate the program by entering an account number of –9.

If the account number is valid, the IF/THEN/ELSE statement in line 7080 is true, so the PROCESS ACCT NO module (8000) is called. Line 8040 calls the GET RECORD module (10000). Line 10040 gets the random file record that corresponds to the value of ROW. Then lines 10050–10090 convert the buffer variables to program variables.

Next, program control passes to line 8050, which displays the first and last names of the account holder. The program then requests the clerk to enter the amount to be charged (line 8060).

Line 8070 calls the module VALIDATE CHARGE (11000), which determines if the amount to be charged exceeds the member's credit limit. Line 11040 sets the variable NEW.BAL equal to the sum of AMT.CHG, MEM. BAL.DUE, and MEM.CUR.CHG. If this value does not exceed the credit limit of the member, line 11050 prints the message "CHARGE APPROVED" and then calls the module UPDATE MEMBER RECORD (13000). If NEW.BAL exceeds the member's credit limit then line 11050 prints the message "CHARGE DENIED" and control passes back to line 8080, which calls the PAUSE SCREEN module.

In module UPDATE RECORD (13000), line 13040 adds the amount charged to the current charges. Then line 13050 converts the new value of current charges into a single-precision string and writes it to the buffer variable MCC$. Line 13060 puts the record back into its position in the random file. Notice that there is no need to write the other values of the record to the buffer; they are already there.

After line 13070, program control passes back to line 11060 and then to line 8080. When the user presses a key to continue, control passes to line 8090, then to line 7090, and then to line 4090, where the module INPUT ACCT NO is called. If the user enters an account number of –9 in response to the prompt of line 6070, the program returns to line 4100 and the loop defined by lines 4070–4100 is terminated. Line 4110 closes the random file. Processing returns to the CONTROL module, which calls the WRITE END MESSAGE module (5000), which in turn reports that the program is finished.

UPDATING THE RECORDS OF A RANDOM FILE

The last problem in this chapter is an example of updating and maintaining random data files. In Program 15.3, you changed members' records to incorporate their new charges. However, updating and maintaining records in a random file requires more than just changing one or more values in a particular record. You also must be able to add and delete records from the file.

The Amex Co-op accounting department would like to perform the following functions:

1. Display all the information in a member's record.

2. Add the record of a new member to the file.

3. Delete a member's record from the file.

4. Change the data in a member's record.

Design the Program Logic

To display a member's account record, the user must enter the account number. The account number is used to search the index table for a match, and then the record is retrieved and displayed.

To add a record to the random file, the user must again enter the new account number. The index table is searched to make sure there is *not* a match. If there is not a match, the first available row (a row with an asterisk) in the index table is used for the new account number. The rest of the data for the new account are entered, and the record is added to the random file using the row number in the table for the record number. See Figure 15.5.

To delete a record from the random file, the user enters the account number to be deleted. The index table is searched for a match. If a match is found, an asterisk is placed in that position of the index table. Any character string, however, could be used to denote a deleted record. The deleted record remains in the random file, but it can no longer be accessed through the index table. See Figure 15.6.

To change the data in the random file record, the user enters an account number. The index table is searched for a match. If a match is found, the user enters the changes, and the fields in the record are updated.

The user enters D4113.

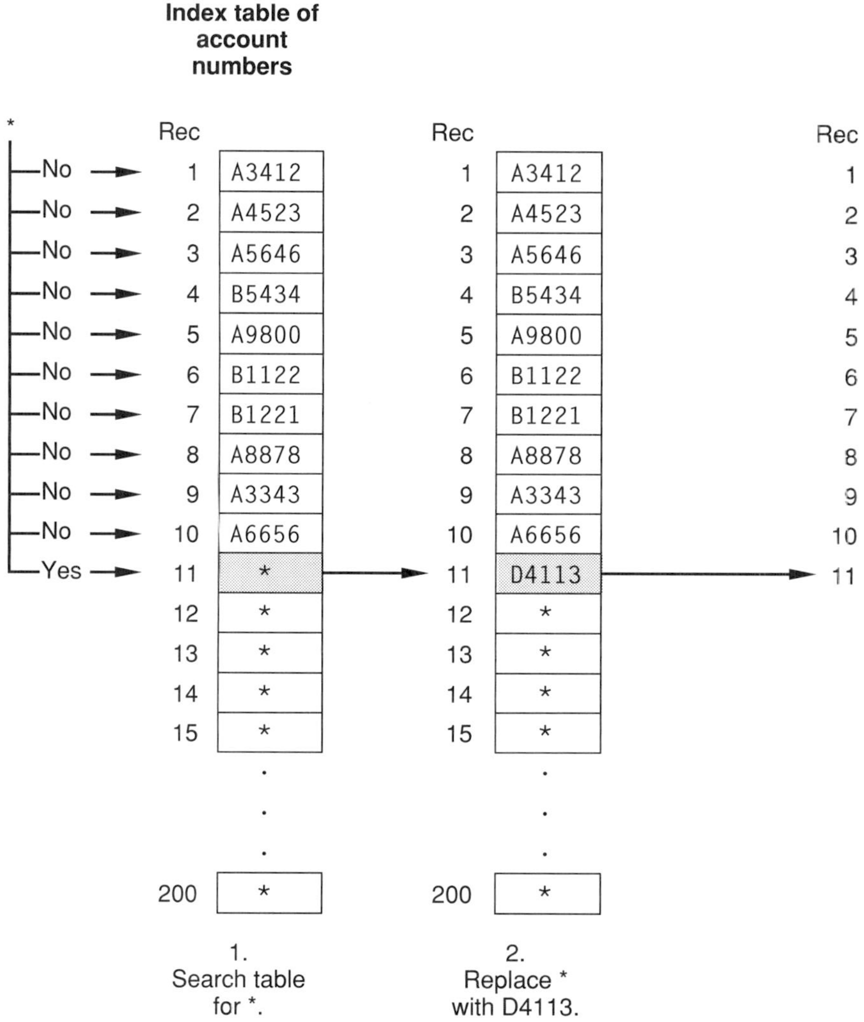

Disk

FILE: MEM.RND

Rec	ACCT NO	FIRST NAME	LAST NAME	BAL DUE	CUR CHG	CR LIMIT
1	A3412	Joel	Carson	34.55	12.98	500.00
2	A4523	Willard Jo	Potts	105.34	26.50	800.00
3	A5646	Richard	McCarty	45.60	25.98	800.00
4	B5434	Karen	Tempel	27.80	17.50	700.00
5	A9800	Bonnie J.	Baumgras	305.56	85.95	400.00
6	B1122	Bret	Murphy	45.60	9.85	800.00
7	B1221	Donald	Brown	45.36	0.00	800.00
8	A8878	Sally Ann	Pederson	190.10	50.67	500.00
9	A3343	Carline A.	Marino	55.47	12.35	300.00
10	A6656	Cheryl C.	Cruise	150.49	34.95	200.00
11	D4113	Cyd	McMullen	0.00	56.75	900.00

3.

Account number D4113 is added to the random file along with the other member data.

Index table of account numbers

Rec	
1	A3412
2	A4523
3	A5646
4	B5434
5	A9800
6	B1122
7	B1221
8	A8878
9	A3343
10	A6656
11	*
12	*
13	*
14	*
15	*

200 | *

No
No
No
No
No
No
No
No
No
No
Yes

*

1.
Search table for *.

Rec	
1	A3412
2	A4523
3	A5646
4	B5434
5	A9800
6	B1122
7	B1221
8	A8878
9	A3343
10	A6656
11	D4113
12	*
13	*
14	*
15	*

200 | *

2.
Replace * with D4113.

FIGURE 15.5   Adding a record

Disk

FILE: MEM.RND

Rec	ACCT NO	FIRST NAME	LAST NAME	BAL DUE	CUR CHG	CR LIMIT
1	A3412	Joel	Carson	34.55	12.98	500.00
2	A4523	Willard Jo	Potts	105.34	26.50	800.00
3	A5646	Richard	McCarty	45.60	25.98	800.00
4	B5434	Karen	Tempel	27.80	17.50	700.00
5	A9800	Bonnie J.	Baumgras	305.56	85.95	400.00
6	B1122	Bret	Murphy	45.60	9.85	800.00
7	B1221	Donald	Brown	45.36	0.00	800.00
8	A8878	Sally Ann	Pederson	190.10	50.67	500.00
9	A3343	Carline A.	Marino	55.47	12.35	300.00
10	A6656	Cheryl C.	Cruise	150.49	34.95	200.00
11	D4113	Cyd	McMullen	0.00	56.75	900.00

3.

Record 3 cannot be accessed using the index file even though the record still exists in the random file.

The user enters A5646.

Index table of account numbers

Rec	
1	A3412
2	A4523
3	A5646
4	B5434
5	A9800
6	B1122
7	B1221
8	A8878
9	A3343
10	A6656
11	*
12	*
13	*
14	*
15	*
.	.
.	.
200	*

A5646
- No
- No
- Yes

1.
Search table for A5646.

Rec	
1	A3412
2	A4523
3	*
4	B5434
5	A9800
6	B1122
7	B1221
8	A8878
9	A3343
10	A6656
11	D4113
12	*
13	*
14	*
15	*
.	.
.	.
200	*

2.
Replace A5646 with *.

FIGURE 15.6   Deleting a record

Figure 15.7 shows the logic design for the update program. Again, the pseudocode for any modules similar to any previous program modules is not repeated.

Code the Program Instructions

The code in Program 15.4 implements the logic design in Figure 15.7. The CONTROL module (2000) calls the LOAD INDEX TABLE (3000), PROCESS INQUIRY (4000), WRITE INDEX TABLE (5000), and WRITE END MESSAGE (6000) modules. When the PROCESS INQUIRY module is called and after the file is opened and fielded, the MENU module (7000) is called, and the user can select the appropriate menu function. After each inquiry is processed, the menu reappears on the screen until the user selects the "Quit" option.

When the program is run, the menu (lines 7050–7110) appears on the screen, and the user is asked to enter a value corresponding to one of the menu choices. If the operator enters an improper choice, control passes to the module INVALID SELECTION (14000), which displays a message reporting the invalid selection (line 14060). The user is again requested to select a menu choice.

When the user selects a valid menu number other than 5, program control returns to the PROCESS INQUIRY module. Line 4080 calls the module INPUT ACCT NO (8000). Line 8060 asks for a five-character account number. Once the user enters an account number, execution returns to line 4090, which calls module CHECK FOR VALID ACCT (9000). The index table is checked to see if it contains that account number (lines 9050–9070). If the number is in the table, ACC.OK is set to YES to indicate that the account number does exist; otherwise, ACC.OK is set to NO.

If the number is in the table, the WHILE/WEND loop terminates, and the value of the variable, ROW, is the record number the user needs. Program control then returns to line 4100 of the PROCESS INQUIRY module.

The program now calls one of the four menu modules, depending on the user's choice (line 4100). For simplicity, examine them in order. Remember that at this point the user has entered a valid menu selection, so CHOICE\$ is equal to one of the menu values and the value of ACC.OK is either YES or NO.

Display Record

If the value of CHOICE\$ is "1", execution continues with the module DISPLAY RECORD (10000). One of two situations can occur in this module. If the value of ACC.OK is YES, program control passes to module GET RECORD (15000). The record equal to the value of ROW is retrieved from the file, and the buffer variables are converted to program variables. Control then passes to the module DISPLAY DATA (16000), and the member information is displayed on the screen and remains there (because of the PAUSE SCREEN module) until the user elects to return to the main menu via the PROCESS INQUIRY module.

The second situation occurs when the value of ACC.OK is NO, indicating that the account number entered by the user is not in the table. In this case, program control passes to the module INVALID ACCOUNT (17000), which prints the message that the account number entered is invalid.

After the user signals the program to continue, control passes to line 10170, then to line 4110 of the PROCESS INQUIRY module, which calls the module to display the menu.

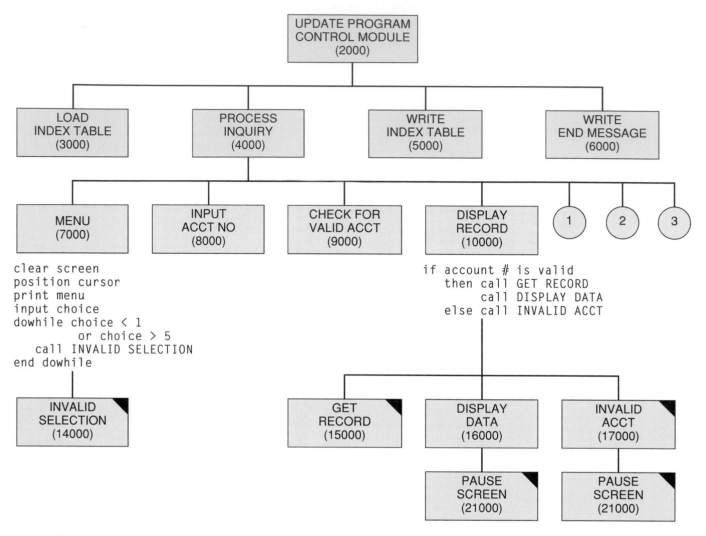

FIGURE 15.7   Structure chart and pseudocode for Program 15.4

PROGRAM 15.4

```
1000 ' PROG15-4
1010 ' ******************************
1020 ' *       UPDATE  PROGRAM       *
1030 ' ******************************
1040 '
1050 ' ******************************
1060 ' *         VARIABLES          *
1070 ' ******************************
1080 '
1090 ' MEM.RND                    Random file
1100 ' Member record:
1110 '    Program Variables       Buffer Variables
1120 '      MEM.ACCT.NO$            MAN$        Account number
1130 '      MEM.F.NAME$             MNF$        First name
1140 '      MEM.L.NAME$             MNL$        Last name
1150 '      MEM.BAL.DUE             MBD$        Balance due
1160 '      MEM.CUR.CHG             MCC$        Current charges
1170 '      MEM.CR.LIM              MCL$        Credit limit
1180 '
1190 ' INDEX.SEQ                  Sequential index file
1200 ' Index record:
1210 '     INDEX.TBL$             Member account number
```

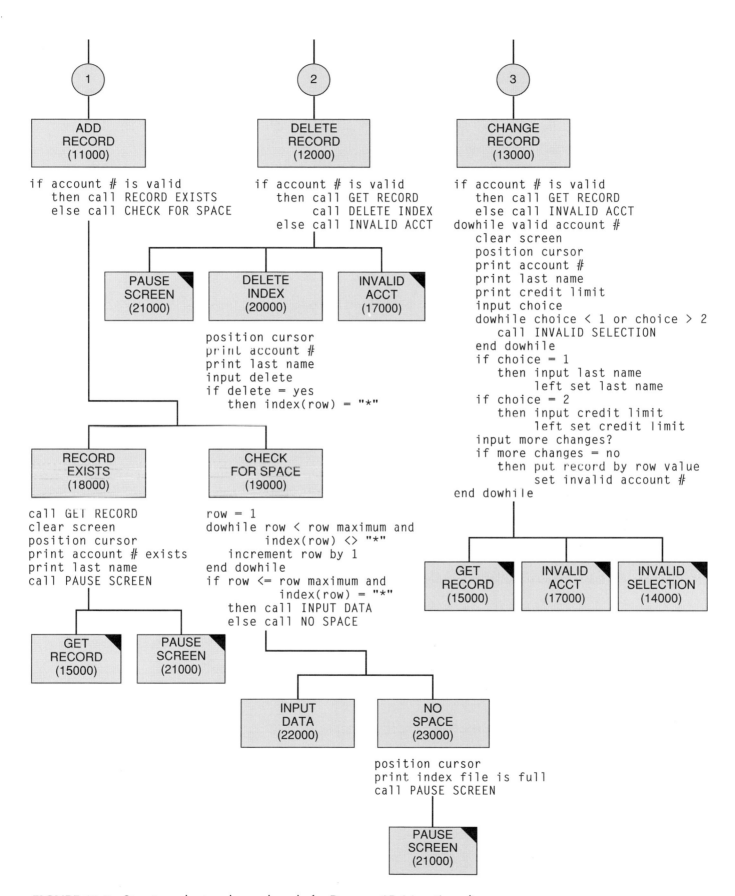

FIGURE 15.7 Structure chart and pseudocode for Program 15.4 (continued)

PROGRAM 15.4 (continued)

```
1220 '
1230 '    ACC.OK                  Account number flag
1240 '    ACCT$                   Account number entered from keyboard
1250 '    CHOICE$                 Value of menu selections
1260 '    DEL$                    Variable to delete a record, Y or N
1270 '    MORE.CHANGES$           Variable to indicate more changes, Y or N
1280 '    PAUSE$                  Screen delay
1290 '    ROW                     Table subscript
1300 '
1310 ' ****************************
1320 ' *        CONSTANTS         *
1330 ' ****************************
1340 '
1350   YES = -1                 'Value for true
1360   NO  =  0                 'Value for false
1370   MSG1$ = "PRESS ANY KEY TO CONTINUE"
1380   MSG2$ = "YOU MUST ENTER A PROPER SELECTION!"
1400   DETAIL.A$ = " \                    \   \                          \"
1410   DETAIL.B$ = " \                    \    $$##,###.## "
1420 '
1430 ' ****************************
1440 ' *    DEFINE INDEX TABLE    *
1450 ' ****************************
1460 '
1470   ROWMAX = 200             'Number of table entries
1480   DIM INDEX.TBL$(ROWMAX)   'Table of member account numbers
1999 '
2000 ' ****************************
2010 ' *      CONTROL MODULE      *
2020 ' ****************************
2030 '
2040   KEY OFF
2050   GOSUB 3000               'Load Index Table
2060   GOSUB 4000               'Process Inquiry
2070   GOSUB 5000               'Write Index Table
2080   GOSUB 6000               'Write End Message
2090   KEY ON
2100   END
2999 '
3000 ' ****************************
3010 ' *      LOAD INDEX TABLE    *
3020 ' ****************************
3030 '
3040   OPEN "INDEX.SEQ" FOR INPUT AS #1
3050   FOR ROW = 1 TO ROWMAX
3060      INPUT #1,INDEX.TBL$(ROW)
3070   NEXT ROW
3080   CLOSE #1
3090   RETURN
3999 '
4000 ' ****************************
4010 ' *      PROCESS INQUIRY     *
4020 ' ****************************
4030 '
4040   OPEN "R",#2,"MEM.RND",42
4050   FIELD #2, 5 AS MAN$, 10 AS MNF$, 15 AS MNL$,
                4 AS MBD$,  4 AS MCC$,  4 AS MCL$
4060   GOSUB 7000               'Menu
4070   WHILE CHOICE$ <> "5"
4080      GOSUB 8000            'Input Acct No
4090      GOSUB 9000            'Check For Valid Acct
4100      ON VAL(CHOICE$) GOSUB 10000,11000,12000,13000
4110      GOSUB 7000            'Menu
4120   WEND
```

PROGRAM 15.4   (continued)

```
4130    CLOSE #2
4140    RETURN
4999  '
5000  ' *****************************
5010  ' *      WRITE INDEX TABLE      *
5020  ' *****************************
5030  '
5040    OPEN "INDEX.SEQ" FOR OUTPUT AS #1
5050    FOR ROW = 1 TO ROWMAX
5060        WRITE #1, INDEX.TBL$(ROW)
5070    NEXT ROW
5080    CLOSE #1
5090    RETURN
5999  '
6000  ' *****************************
6010  ' *      WRITE END MESSAGE      *
6020  ' *****************************
6030  '
6040    CLS
6050    LOCATE 10
6060    BEEP
6070    PRINT TAB(10);"INQUIRY PROGRAM FINISHED"
6080    RETURN
6999  '
7000  ' *****************************
7010  ' *             MENU            *
7020  ' *****************************
7030  '
7040    CLS
7050    LOCATE 5  : PRINT TAB(25);"RANDOM FILE UPDATE MENU"
7060    LOCATE 8  : PRINT TAB(30);"1)   DISPLAY A RECORD"
7070    LOCATE 10 : PRINT TAB(30);"2)   ADD A RECORD"
7080    LOCATE 12 : PRINT TAB(30);"3)   DELETE A RECORD"
7090    LOCATE 14 : PRINT TAB(30);"4)   CHANGE A RECORD"
7100    LOCATE 16 : PRINT TAB(30);"5)   QUIT"
7110    LOCATE 19 : PRINT TAB(20);"ENTER YOUR SELECTION, 1, 2, 3, 4 or 5 ";
7120    INPUT CHOICE$
7130  '
7140    WHILE (CHOICE$ < "1") OR (CHOICE$ > "5")
7150        GOSUB 14000            'Invalid Selection
7160    WEND
7180    RETURN
7999  '
8000  ' *****************************
8010  ' *         INPUT ACCT NO       *
8020  ' *****************************
8030  '
8040    CLS
8050    LOCATE 10
8060    INPUT "ENTER A FIVE CHARACTER ACCOUNT NUMBER ", ACCT$
8070    RETURN
8999  '
9000  ' *****************************
9010  ' *     CHECK FOR VALID ACCT     *
9020  ' *****************************
9030  '
9040    ROW = 1
9050    WHILE (ROW < ROWMAX) AND (ACCT$ <> INDEX.TBL$(ROW))
9060        ROW = ROW + 1
9070    WEND
9080    IF ACCT$ = INDEX.TBL$(ROW)
            THEN ACC.OK = YES
            ELSE ACC.OK = NO
9090    RETURN
```

PROGRAM 15.4   (continued)

```
9999  '
10000 ' ******************************
10010 ' *        DISPLAY RECORD        *
10020 ' ******************************
10030 '
10040   IF ACC.OK THEN GOSUB 15000 :
                        GOSUB 16000
                    ELSE GOSUB 17000
10050   RETURN
10999 '
11000 ' ******************************
11010 ' *          ADD RECORD          *
11020 ' ******************************
11030 '
11040   IF  ACC.OK  THEN GOSUB 18000
                     ELSE GOSUB 19000
11050   RETURN
11999 '
12000 ' ******************************
12010 ' *        DELETE RECORD         *
12020 ' ******************************
12030 '
12040   IF  ACC.OK  THEN GOSUB 15000 :
                          GOSUB 20000
                     ELSE GOSUB 17000
12050   RETURN
12999 '
13000 ' ******************************
13010 ' *        CHANGE RECORD         *
13020 ' ******************************
13030 '
13040   IF  ACC.OK  THEN GOSUB 15000
                     ELSE GOSUB 17000
13050   WHILE ACC.OK
13060      CLS
13070      LOCATE 15
13080      PRINT TAB(10) "ACCOUNT NUMBER:        "; ACCT$  : PRINT
13090      PRINT TAB(10) "  1) LAST NAME:        "; MEM.L.NAME$ : PRINT
13100      PRINT TAB(10) USING "  2) CREDIT LIMIT:  $#,###.##"; MEM.CR.LIM
13110      PRINT TAB(10);
13120      INPUT "WHICH ITEM DO YOU WISH TO CHANGE, 1 OR 2"; CHOICE$ : PRINT
13130      WHILE (CHOICE$ < "1") or (CHOICE$ > "2")
13140         GOSUB 14000       'Invalid Selection
13150      WEND
13160      IF CHOICE$ = "1"
               THEN INPUT "ENTER NEW LAST NAME ", MEM.L.NAME$ :
                    LSET MNL$ = MEM.L.NAME$
13170      IF CHOICE$ = "2"
               THEN INPUT "ENTER NEW CREDIT LIMIT ", MEM.CR.LIM :
                    LSET MCL$ = MKS$(MEM.CR.LIM)
13180      PRINT
13190      INPUT "ANY MORE CHANGES?  (Y OR N) ", MORE.CHANGES$
13200      IF (MORE.CHANGES$ = "N") OR (MORE.CHANGES$ = "n")
               THEN PUT #2, ROW :
                    ACC.OK = NO
13210      WEND
13220   RETURN
13999 '
14000 ' ******************************
14010 ' *        INVALID SELECTION      *
14020 ' ******************************
14030 '
14040   LOCATE 20
14050   BEEP
```

PROGRAM 15.4   (continued)

```
14060    PRINT MSG2$ : LOCATE 19,58 : INPUT CHOICE$
14070    RETURN
14999 '
15000 ' *****************************
15010 ' *          GET RECORD           *
15020 ' *****************************
15030 '
15040    GET #2, ROW
15050    MEM.ACCT.NO$ = MAN$
15060    MEM.F.NAME$  = MNF$
15070    MEM.L.NAME$  = MNL$
15080    MEM.BAL.DUE  = CVS(MBD$)
15090    MEM.CUR.CHG  = CVS(MCC$)
15100    MEM.CR.LIM   = CVS(MCL$)
15110    RETURN
15999 '
16000 ' *****************************
16010 ' *          DISPLAY DATA          *
16020 ' *****************************
16030 '
16040    CLS
16050    LOCATE 8
16060    PRINT USING DETAIL.A$; "ACCOUNT NUMBER:", MEM.ACCT.NO$
16070    PRINT:PRINT USING DETAIL.A$; "NAME:", MEM.F.NAME$ + " " + MEM.L.NAME$
16080    PRINT:PRINT USING DETAIL.B$; "BALANCE DUE:", MEM.BAL.DUE
16090    PRINT:PRINT USING DETAIL.B$; "CURRENT CHARGES:", MEM.CUR.CHG
16100    PRINT:PRINT USING DETAIL.B$; "CREDIT LIMIT:", MEM.CR.LIM
16120    PRINT
16130    GOSUB 21000             'Pause Screen
16140    RETURN
16999 '
17000 ' *****************************
17010 ' *          INVALID ACCT          *
17020 ' *****************************
17030 '
17040    BEEP
17050    LOCATE 20
17060    PRINT TAB(10);"ACCOUNT NUMBER "; ACCT$; " IS INVALID."
17070    GOSUB 21000             'Pause Screen
17080    RETURN
17999 '
18000 ' *****************************
18010 ' *          RECORD EXISTS          *
18020 ' *****************************
18030 '
18040    GOSUB 15000             'Get Member Record
18050    CLS
18060    LOCATE 10
18070    PRINT "RECORD FOR ACCOUNT NUMBER "; ACCT$; " ALREADY EXISTS!"
18080    PRINT
18090    PRINT "NAME FOR ACCOUNT NUMBER: ";MEM.L.NAME$
18100    GOSUB 21000             'Pause Screen
18110    RETURN
18999 '
19000 ' *****************************
19010 ' *          CHECK FOR SPACE          *
19020 ' *****************************
19030 '
19040    ROW = 1
19050    WHILE (ROW < ROWMAX) AND (INDEX.TBL$(ROW) <> "*")
19060        ROW = ROW + 1
19070    WEND
```

PROGRAM 15.4 (continued)

```
19080    IF (ROW <= ROWMAX) AND (INDEX.TBL$(ROW) = "*")
             THEN GOSUB 22000
             ELSE GOSUB 23000
19090    RETURN
19999 '
20000 ' ******************************
20010 ' *          DELETE INDEX          *
20020 ' ******************************
20030 '
20060    LOCATE 12
20070    PRINT TAB(10);"ACCOUNT NUMBER: "; MEM.ACCT.NO$
20080    PRINT TAB(10);"NAME:          "; MEM.L.NAME$
20090    PRINT
20100    INPUT "DELETE? ( Y or N ) ",DEL$
20110    IF (DEL$ = "Y") OR (DEL$ = "y")
             THEN INDEX.TBL$(ROW) = "*"
20120    RETURN
20999 '
21000 ' ******************************
21010 ' *          PAUSE SCREEN          *
21020 ' ******************************
21030 '
21040    LOCATE 22 : PRINT MSG1$
21050    PAUSE$ = INPUT$(1)
21060    RETURN
21999 '
22000 ' ******************************
22010 ' *          INPUT DATA          *
22020 ' ******************************
22030 '
22040    CLS
22050    LOCATE 10
22060    PRINT "ACCOUNT NUMBER:        ",ACCT$
22070    INPUT "MEMBER'S FIRST NAME:   ",MEM.F.NAME$
22080    INPUT "MEMBER'S LAST NAME:    ",MEM.L.NAME$
22090    INPUT "PRESENT BALANCE DUE:   ",MEM.BAL.DUE
22100    INPUT "CURRENT CHARGES:       ",MEM.CUR.CHG
22110    INPUT "CURRENT CREDIT LIMIT:  ",MEM.CR.LIM
22120    GOSUB 24000                'Write record
22130    RETURN
22999 '
23000 ' ******************************
23010 ' *          NO SPACE          *
23020 ' ******************************
23030 '
23040    BEEP
23050    LOCATE 15
23060    PRINT "THE INDEX FILE IS FULL, YOU CANNOT ADD ANYMORE RECORDS!"
23070    GOSUB 21000                'Pause Screen
23080    RETURN
23999 '
24000 ' ******************************
24010 ' *          WRITE RECORD          *
24020 ' ******************************
24030 '
24040    LSET MAN$ = ACCT$
24050    LSET MNF$ = MEM.F.NAME$
24060    LSET MNL$ = MEM.L.NAME$
24070    LSET MBD$ = MKS$(MEM.BAL.DUE)
24080    LSET MCC$ = MKS$(MEM.CUR.CHG)
24090    LSET MCL$ = MKS$(MEM.CR.LIM)
24100 '
24110    PUT #2, ROW
24120    INDEX.TBL$(ROW) = ACCT$
24130    RETURN
```

Add Record

When the value of CHOICE$ is "2", program control passes to module ADD RECORD (11000). Three different situations can happen here:

1. The account number the user enters already exists.

2. The index table is full, and so the user cannot enter the record.

3. The account number is valid, and the index table is not full. In this last case, the user can add the account number and data to the file.

If ACC.OK = YES when control passes to this module, the user is trying to add an account number that already exists. When that happens, control passes to the module RECORD EXISTS (18000), which in turn calls the module GET RECORD (15000) and retrieves the conflicting record. The module RECORD EXISTS then displays a screen message telling the user that the account number is already in use and displays the last name of the member having that account number (lines 18070 and 18090).

The user must press a key to continue (PAUSE SCREEN module). The program then returns to line 11050, and then again to line 4110 of the PROCESS INQUIRY module.

When ACC.OK = NO, the account number entered is not presently being used. In this case, program execution passes to the module CHECK FOR SPACE (19000). The WHILE/WEND loop in lines 19050–19070 begins to search the index table to locate an asterisk in one of the rows.

If the search finds no asterisks, the IF statement in line 19080 transfers control to module NO SPACE (23000), which displays a message reporting that the index table is full and that the user cannot add the account number (line 23060). After the user presses a key, program control then returns to line 19090. This completes the module, and program control returns to line 4110 of the PROCESS INQUIRY module.

The last possibility is that the search conducted in the WHILE/WEND loop of lines 19050–19070 yields an asterisk. When this happens, the loop terminates, since one of its conditions for continuing becomes false. When the loop terminates, the value of ROW references a location that can hold the new record.

Since the IF statement in line 19080 is true, execution continues with the module INPUT DATA (22000), which displays the account number and requests the new account information (lines 22060–22110). Line 22120 calls the module WRITE RECORD (24000). Lines 24040–24090 write the data to the buffer, and line 24110 writes the buffer to the disk using the value of ROW as the record location. So that the index table will reflect the addition of this account number, line 24120 assigns INDEX.TBL$(ROW) the account number contained in ACCT$. In this way, the new account number is put in the index file.

Finally, execution returns to line 19090 and then back to line 4110 of the PROCESS INQUIRY module.

Delete Record

Menu selection 3 calls the module DELETE RECORD (12000). There are two possibilities in this module: either the account number entered is not in the table, or it is in the table and can be deleted.

If the value of ACC.OK is NO on entry into this module, control passes to module INVALID ACCOUNT (17000), which displays a message that the account number entered is invalid. When the user presses a key, control passes to line 12130, and then back to line 4110 of the PROCESS INQUIRY module.

If the value of ACC.OK is YES when control passes to this module, line 12040 calls the module GET RECORD (15000). This module gets the information about the record so that the user can confirm that it is the record to delete. Control passes to DELETE INDEX module (20000). Lines 20070 and 20080 display the account number and the member's last name, and line 20100 prints the question "Delete? (Y or N)". The user can then confirm that this is the record to be deleted by pressing Y or y. If the user enters anything else but Y or y, the record is not deleted.

Notice that the program does not actually remove the record from the random file. Instead, it replaces the account number in the index table with an asterisk (line 20110). The process of reorganizing the random file to remove the deleted records from the file is left as an exercise for you in program assignment 7.

Change Record

Menu selection 4 transfers control to module CHANGE RECORD (13000) so that the user can change the member's last name, the member's credit limit, or both. As in the other modules, the program displays an appropriate message if the user enters an invalid account number.

If ACC.OK = YES, line 13040 calls the module GET RECORD (15000). For valid accounts, the WHILE/WEND loop (lines 13050–13210) displays the account number, last name, and credit limit. The program then asks the user which item to change, 1 or 2 (line 13120).

If the user enters a response other than 1 or 2, control passes to module INVALID SELECTION (14000), which displays a message indicating the user's improper choice.

If the variable CHOICE$ contains "1", line 13160 asks the user to enter the new last name and writes the name to the buffer. If the value of CHOICE$ is "2", line 13170 asks the user for the new credit limit; it then converts the value to a 4-byte string and writes it to the buffer.

Line 13190 asks if there are any more changes. If the user enters Y or y, the WHILE/WEND loop continues, and the user can change the other item. If the user presses any character other than Y or y, line 13200 writes the record to the disk using the value of ROW as the record number. ACC.OK is set to NO, which terminates the WHILE/WEND loop, and control returns to line 4110 of the PROCESS INQUIRY module.

Review the CHANGE RECORD module for a moment. How could ON GOSUB be useful if more than two fields needed to be changed?

Quit

When the user selects choice 5, the WHILE/WEND loop in lines 4070–4120 terminates. Line 4130 closes the random file for use. Control passes to the CONTROL module, and the WRITE INDEX TABLE module (5000) is called. Because account numbers may have been added or deleted, the index file must be rewritten to the disk. Line 5040 opens the sequential index file for output, and lines 5050–5070 write the index table to the file. The file is closed in line 5080.

Control passes to line 2080, which calls the WRITE END MESSAGE module (6000). Line 6070 displays a message reporting the end of the program.

SOME ADDITIONAL FEATURES OF RANDOM FILES

Here are two other BASIC functions for use with random files:

```
LOC(filenumber)
LOF(filenumber)
```

Filenumber is the number assigned to the file in the OPEN statement.

LOC(n) returns the number of the last record that was moved in or out of the buffer with a GET or PUT statement.

LOF(n) returns the number of bytes in the file. The number is usually a multiple of 128, the default buffer size. If the record size (buffer size) is 128 bytes, then LOF(n) divided by 128 is the number of records in the file. If the record size is not 128 bytes, you can determine the number of records in the file by dividing LOF(n) by the record size defined in the OPEN statement.

Consider the following code:

```
1000    CLS
1010    OPEN "R", #1, "MEM.RND", 42
1020    FIELD #1, 42 AS RECORD$
1030    GET #1, 8
1040    PRINT "LAST RECORD ACCESSED IS "; LOC(1)
1050    GET #1, 2
1060    PRINT "LAST RECORD ACCESSED IS "; LOC(1)
1070    PRINT "NUMBER OF BYTES IN THE FILE IS "; LOF(1)
1080    PRINT "NUMBER OF RECORDS IN THE FILE IS "; LOF(1)/42
```

Line 1010 opens the random file "MEM.RND" with a record length of 42 bytes and assigns it buffer #1. Line 1020 defines the buffer to consist of one 42-byte string called RECORD$. The eighth record is retrieved in line 1030. Line 1040 prints the number of the last record accessed (which should be #8). Lines 1050 and 1060 repeat the process using record #2. The total number of bytes in the file is produced by line 1070. Line 1080 tells how many records are in the file (number of bytes in file divided by the record size). Figure 15.8 shows the results of executing this code.

One problem that you may encounter when using the LOF function on a file like MEM.RND is that LOF cannot distinguish between a valid record and a record marked for deletion in the corresponding index file, INDEX.SEQ. To determine the number of active records in the file, you need to remove all the records marked for deletion from the file.

FIGURE 15.8
Results of using the LOC and LOF functions on the random file MEM.RND

```
LAST RECORD ACCESSED IS  8
LAST RECORD ACCESSED IS  2
NUMBER OF BYTES IN THE FILE IS  420
NUMBER OF RECORDS IN THE FILE IS  10
Ok
```

Summary

- Unlike sequential file records, random file records can be updated without copying the file over. Using a sequential index file, an index table, and a random file, you can simulate an index file, an efficient type of file organization not available on most BASIC systems.

- With an index file, the key fields in a random file do not have to be the record number. The record number is determined by the record's position in the index file.

- Chapter 15 describes the following new BASIC statements and functions:

LOC — A function that returns the number of the last record moved into or out of the buffer.

LOF — A function that returns the number of bytes in the file.

Review Questions

1. Explain how you can simulate an index file in BASIC.

2. Why is the index table saved as a sequential file?

3. When you use an index table, what determines the size or dimension of the table?

4. Is it necessary for both the index file and the random file to contain the field that you are searching (that is, the field on which the index is based)?

5. In what ways does the index table not allow you to add a record to a random file?

6. When you use an index file, what is the most efficient way to delete a record?

7. What is the purpose of the LOC function?

8. What is the purpose of the LOF function?

Problems

1. A random file and an index file need to be created for a newspaper's dead article file. The records for the random file contain the following fields:

```
Article name, Date submitted, Reporter,
Reference number
```

State reasons why you can or cannot use any of the fields as the key in the index file.

2. A sequential file is composed of records that have the following fields:

```
Last name, First name, Address, City,
State, Zip code
```

If you create a random file from this sequential file, which field, if any, would make a good key for the index file?

3. Consider the following conditions:

- A directory of the disk shows that ARTICLE. RND contains 2592 bytes.
- The following code was just executed:

```
2330   OPEN "R", #3, "ARTICLE.RND", 72
2340   FIELD #3, 30 AS HDR1$,
                 42 AS HDR2$
2350   FILE.SIZE = LOF(3)
2360   REC = 37
2370   WHILE REC < 40
2380      GET #3, REC
2390      REC = REC + 1
2400   WEND
2410   CLOSE #3
2420   END
```

a. What values do the following have?

```
REC
FILE.SIZE
LOC(3)
LOF(3)
```

b. How many records are in the file?

Program Assignments

1. Write a program to create a random file, STK. RND, from STK.SEQ, the sequential file you created in program assignment 2, Chapter 7 (page 147). Create the index file IND-STK.SEQ at the same time you create the random file. Use STK.NO as the key for the index.

2. Write an inquiry program to access the random file STK.RND you created in program assignment 1, above. When the user enters the stock number (STK.NO), the stock name, number of shares purchased, and per share purchase price should be displayed on the screen.

3. Using STUDENT.RND, the random file you created in program assignment 1, Chapter 14 (page 390), complete the following assignments:

   a. Write a program that creates a sequential index file for the random file. Use the student number as the key.

   b. Using the index file you just created in program assignment 3a, write an inquiry program to access the random file. The user should enter the student number. If the number is valid, the program should return the name and telephone number.

   c. Write a program to change the telephone number in the random file. The user will enter the student number to access the particular record.

   d. Write a program to add and delete records from the random file. Be sure to update the index table when a record is added or deleted.

4. Write a program to create a sequential index file for the random file in program assignment 3, Chapter 14 (page 390). Use the item number as the key.

5. Write a program to update the random file in program assignment 3, Chapter 14. Use the index file you just created in program assignment 4, to locate a record. The update program should allow the user to display a record, add a record, delete a record, and change a record. The only fields that might need to be changed are the quantity, cost, and price fields. Be sure to update the index file when necessary.

6. Program 15.4 updates the member file of Amex Co-op. When a member's record is deleted from the random file, there is no provision in the program for flagging any amount owed by that member. Add a module to Program 15.4 that writes the record being deleted to a sequential file. Delete the account numbers A9800, B1221, and C2234 from the file. Because it is necessary to collect the amount due from the holders of these deleted accounts, write a program to produce a report from this sequential file showing the amount owed by each member who was deleted from the file.

7. Write a program to remove all deleted records from the random file MEM.RND. Compress the file; that is, move the subsequent records up to fill the space that the deleted record(s) occupied. You will either have to update the index file INDEX.SEQ at the same time, or you can run the Program 15.2, CREATE INDEX FILE, after you finish compressing the file.

Using the Data Disk

1. Insert the data disk into the disk drive.

2. Load BASIC (change the default drive if necessary).

3. Load PROG15-4.

   a. From the menu selections, display the following records and complete the following chart.

Account Number	Account Status	Credit Limit
A6656	_____	_____
A3412	_____	_____
B5434	_____	_____
A3343	_____	_____
C2221	_____	_____

   b. Add the following accounts to the file.

Acct No	First Name	Last Name	Bal Due	Cur Charges	Cr Lim
A6678	Paul	Williams	559.95	12.98	500
D4523	Ester	Dirks	0.0	135.89	800
A9800	Margie	Ashworth	79.65	56.70	1000
Z8809	Christopher J.	Johnson	209.43	0.0	900

   c. Delete the accounts numbered A9800, B4977, and A4523.

   d. Change the following records:

      (1) Change the credit limit of account number B1122 to 1500.00.
      (2) Change the last name field of account number A6656 to Dancer.
      (3) Change the last name field of account number D4412 to Smithfield.

   e. Select QUIT from the menu.

4. Type NEW to clear memory.

5. Enter the following code:

```
1000    OPEN "R", #1, "MEM.RND", 42
1010    FIELD #1, 42 AS HDR$
1020    FILE.SIZE = LOF(1)
1030    CLOSE #1
1040    PRINT "LOF(1) = "; FILE.SIZE
1050    END
```

   a. Type RUN.
   b. According to the code you just entered, how many records are in the file?
   c. Are all of these records valid? Why or why not?

Chapter Sixteen

Calling Program Modules from Disk

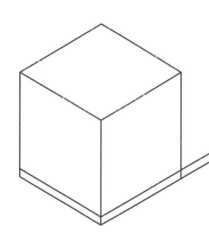

Topics

- Passing control from one program to another with BASIC's CHAIN command
- Passing Variables from a calling program to a chained program with BASIC's COMMON statement
- User-defined functions
- Combining programs with BASIC's MERGE command
- The use of random-access memory (RAM) for auxiliary storage to speed program run time

BASIC Statements and Commands

```
CHAIN
COMMON
DEF FN
MERGE
```

INTRODUCTION

Programs or modules saved on a disk may be chained. When modules are *chained*, a module in memory calls a module from disk; the disk module then replaces the program in memory and begins execution. All, some, or none of the variables in the first module may be passed to the module that replaces it.

Chaining is an especially useful technique when a program is too long to fit into available memory. Chaining also allows you to create a menu of programs. The user selects a program to perform one of several tasks. Then, when that job is finished, the menu is offered again.

Merging is similar to chaining in that it brings code resident on a disk into memory. Unlike chaining, merging combines the code from the disk with the code already in memory. This procedure is handy when you use the same blocks of code in many different programs.

Most versions of BASIC do not take advantage of all the available random-access memory of a microcomputer. Programs that frequently read from and write to random files run much faster when the file is stored in the computer's random-access memory rather than in secondary storage. Memory disks store files in memory that is otherwise unavailable to BASIC.

In addition to BASIC built-in functions, such as TAB and INT, functions can be defined by the programmer to help simplify programming. Long numeric or string expressions that are used often in a program do not have to be repeated. You can set them up once as user-defined functions, and then you need only specify the name of the function in later program statements.

This chapter begins with a discussion of chaining. Example programs demonstrate how to chain programs when no variables are passed between programs, when all of the variables are passed from one program to the next, and when only selected variables are passed. User-defined functions are used in a set of programs to calculate depreciation. These programs show how functions can be defined by the user. Another set of code illustrates merging code from disk into a program. The chapter ends with an explanation of how to use memory disks to speed programs that access random files frequently.

THE CHAIN COMMAND

BASIC's CHAIN statement allows you to use separate programs much as you use program modules and subroutines. Because the programs are in individual disk files, and not within the text of the program that calls them, they are usually referred to as *external subroutines*.

A program that is in memory and calls another program from disk is known as a *calling program*. The program that is being called from a disk file is the *chained program*. The chained program replaces the calling program in memory.

All, some, or none of the variables may be passed from a calling program to a chained program. Variables passed from the calling program to the chained program are common to both programs and are known as *common variables*. The basic CHAIN statement has the following characteristics:

1. It leaves open any files that were opened by the calling program.

2. It allows you to preserve variables, including tables.

3. It does not preserve variable types (DEF) or user-defined functions (FN).

4. It does not preserve the current OPTION BASE setting of the calling program.

Its general form is:

```
[line#] CHAIN <filespec>[,line#] [,ALL]
```

Filespec is the name of the chained program. The optional *line#* after *filespec* is the line number where program execution is to begin. ALL declares that all variables in the calling program are to be passed to the chained program. (You can use the COMMON statement to pass selected variables; this technique is discussed later in the chapter.) The following examples illustrate the use of CHAIN.

```
5000   CHAIN "PROG1.BAS"
```

Line 5000 loads and runs PROG1 starting from the first line. No variables are passed unless a COMMON statement has been executed.

```
6000   CHAIN "PROG1.BAS",1000
```

Line 6000 loads and runs PROG1 starting with line 1000. No variables are passed unless a COMMON statement has been executed.

```
7000   CHAIN "B:PROG1.BAS",1000,ALL
```

Line 7000 loads and runs PROG1 from drive B, starting with line 1000. All variables in the calling program are passed to PROG1.

```
8000   CHAIN PROG$,,ALL
```

If PROG$ = "PROG1.BAS", line 8000 loads and runs PROG1, starting with the first line. All variables are passed from the calling program to the chained program.

APPLICATION

A menu program that allows a user to choose among different applications is a very practical use of chaining. This first example shows how that is done.

Define the Problem

The firm of Lowell and Bauer needs you again. Mr. Lowell wants to run any of the programs, Client Listing (Chapter 6, Program 6.1), Create BILL.SEQ (Chapter 8, Program 8.1), or Client Billing Report (Chapter 8, Program 8.2) from a menu. That way, he does not have to load each program individually.

Because each of these programs is already coded and tested, you don't need to worry about them. You need only set up a calling module that displays a menu, allowing the user to select any one of the three programs. Because the programs are independent, there are no variables to pass from the calling program to the chained program.

After a program is chained and executed, the user will want to return to the menu program. Thus, you must add a CHAIN statement to each program to chain it back to the menu program. Figure 16.1 illustrates this chaining process.

FIGURE 16.1
Program flow in a chaining process

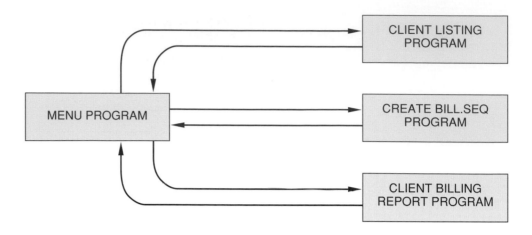

Describe the Output

The output, depending on the program called, is the client listing report, the sequential file for billing, or the client billing report.

Determine the Input

Program input depends on which program the user selects from the menu. Input will always be one of two files, the client file (CLIENT.SEQ) or the billing file (BILL.SEQ).

Design the Program Logic

This program must perform the following functions:

1. The program must allow the user to select which program will be called. From the menu, control must pass to the appropriate program. After the program ends, the menu must reappear on the screen so that the user can select another program or the Exit option. Figure 16.2 shows the menu displayed on a screen.

2. The program must allow the user to end the program by selecting the Exit option from the menu.

Figure 16.3 illustrates the structure of the program.

FIGURE 16-2
Menu for Program 16.1

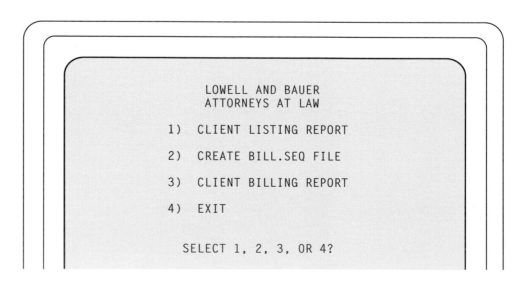

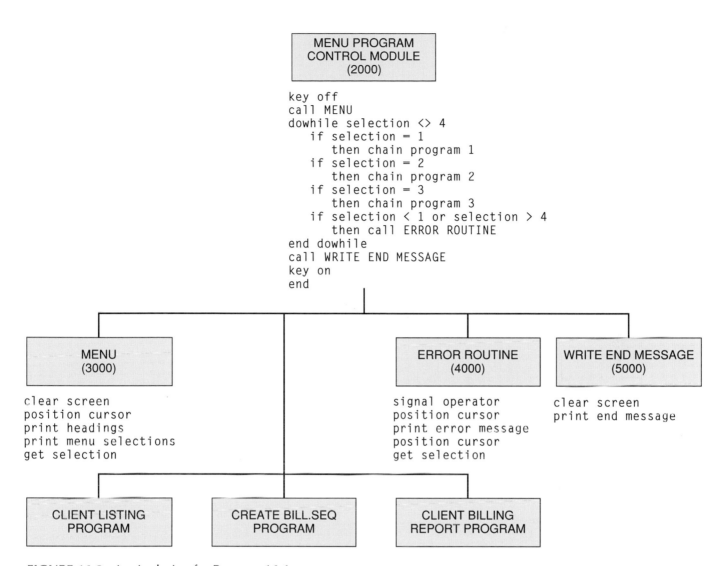

FIGURE 16.3   Logic design for Program 16.1

Code the Program Instructions

Program 16.1 contains the code to implement the design shown in Figure 16.3. Lines 1090–1140 list the chained programs and the files that each program uses. The CONTROL module (2000) calls the MENU module (3000). Lines 3040–3140 set up the menu and ask the user to select an option. When the user enters a selection, control passes to the CONTROL module, where one of the following happens:

1. If the selection is 1, 2, or 3, the appropriate program is called and executed.

2. If the selection is 4, the WRITE END MESSAGE module (5000) is called, ending the program.

3. If any other selection is made, the ERROR ROUTINE module (4000) is called.

When the user's selection is invalid, the computer beeps and prints a message (lines 4040–4060). The message remains on the screen while the user enters a new choice (line 4080).

PROGRAM 16.1

```
1000 ' PROG16-1
1010 ' *****************************
1020 ' *        CHAIN PROGRAM         *
1030 ' *****************************
1040 '
1050 ' *****************************
1060 ' *           FILES             *
1070 ' *****************************
1080 '
1090 ' CLIENT LISTING         (PROG16-2.BAS)    Chained Program One
1100 '     CLIENT.SEQ                           Client File
1110 ' CREATE BILL.SEQ        (PROG16-3.BAS)    Chained Program Two
1120 '     BILL.SEQ                             Billing File
1130 ' CLIENT BILLING REPORT  (PROG16-4.BAS)    Chained Program Three
1140 '     BILL.SEQ                             Billing File
1999 '
2000 ' *****************************
2010 ' *        CONTROL MODULE        *
2020 ' *****************************
2030 '
2040   KEY OFF
2050   GOSUB 3000                 'Menu
2060 '
2070   WHILE SELECT$ <> "4"
2080       IF SELECT$ = "1"   THEN  CHAIN "PROG16-2.BAS"
2090       IF SELECT$ = "2"   THEN  CHAIN "PROG16-3.BAS"
2100       IF SELECT$ = "3"   THEN  CHAIN "PROG16-4.BAS"
2110       IF (SELECT$ < "1") OR (SELECT$ > "4")
                THEN GOSUB 4000  'Error Routine
2120   WEND
2130   GOSUB 5000                 'Write End Message
2140   KEY ON
2150   END
2999 '
3000 ' *****************************
3010 ' *           MENU             *
3020 ' *****************************
3030 '
3040   CLS
3050   LOCATE 6
3060   PRINT TAB(30);"LOWELL AND BAUER"
3070   PRINT TAB(30);"ATTORNEYS AT LAW"
3080   LOCATE 10 : PRINT TAB(25);"1)  CLIENT LISTING REPORT"
3090   LOCATE 12 : PRINT TAB(25);"2)  CREATE BILL.SEQ FILE"
3100   LOCATE 14 : PRINT TAB(25);"3)  CLIENT BILLING REPORT"
3110   LOCATE 16 : PRINT TAB(25);"4)  EXIT"
3120   LOCATE 19 : PRINT TAB(27);"SELECT 1, 2, 3, or 4 ";
3130   INPUT SELECT$
3140   RETURN
3999 '
4000 ' *****************************
4010 ' *        ERROR ROUTINE        *
4020 ' *****************************
4030 '
4040   BEEP
4050   LOCATE 22
4060   PRINT TAB(15);"INVALID SELECTION,  ENTER A NUMBER 1 THROUGH 4"
4070   LOCATE 19,50
4080   INPUT "",SELECT$
4090   RETURN
4999 '
```

PROGRAM 16.1 (continued)
```
5000 ' *****************************
5010 ' *      WRITE END MESSAGE       *
5020 ' *****************************
5030 '
5040    CLS
5050    LOCATE 10
5060    PRINT TAB(25);"PROGRAM COMPLETE"
5070    RETURN
```

To return the menu to the screen, you need to chain the called program back to Program 16.1 so that execution of Program 16.1 begins anew. A change to Program 6.1, the CLIENT LISTING program, illustrates how the chained program returns to the calling program. The only change necessary is to change the END statement in line 2070 of Program 6.1 to a CHAIN statement:

```
2070    CHAIN "PROG16-1.BAS"
```

Now, when Program 6.1 is finished, line 2070 chains back to the menu program.

So that you wouldn't confuse this version of Program 6.1 with the original, it was saved in its modified form as Program 16.2. The following listing shows line 2070 in Program 16.2.

PROGRAM 16.2
```
1000 ' PROG16-2 (PROG6-1 revised)
1010 ' *****************************
1020 ' *      CLIENT LISTING        *
1030 ' *****************************
1040 '
        .
        .
        .
2040    GOSUB 3000             'Write Headings
2050    GOSUB 4000             'Process File
2060    GOSUB 5000             'Write End-of-Report Message
2070    CHAIN "PROG16-1.BAS"
2999 '
```

After similar modifications were made to Program 8.1 and Program 8.2, they were saved as PROG16-3.BAS and PROG16-4.BAS, respectively. Partial listings of Programs 16.3 and 16.4 follow:

PROGRAM 16.3
```
1000 ' PROG16-3 (PROG8-1 revised)
1010 ' *****************************
1020 ' *      CREATE BILL.SEQ       *
1030 ' *****************************
1040 '
        .
        .
        .
2040    GOSUB 3000             'Create File
2050    GOSUB 4000             'Write Summary Lines
2060    CHAIN "PROG16-1.BAS"
2999 '
```

PROGRAM 16.4

```
1000 '  PROG16-4 (PROG8-2 revised)
1010 ' ****************************
1020 ' *   CLIENT BILLING REPORT   *
1030 ' ****************************
1040 '
     .
     .
     .
2040     GOSUB 3000               'Write Headings
2050     GOSUB 4000               'Process File
2060     GOSUB 5000               'Write Summary Lines
2070     CHAIN "PROG16-1.BAS"
2999 '
```

When Program 16.1 is run, the menu appears, asking the user to select a program. See Figure 16.2. The selection of 1, 2, or 3 begins the chaining process. The selected program runs; when it ends, it chains back to the menu program.

CHAINING WITH COMMON VARIABLES

In Program 16.1, it was not necessary to pass the values of any variables to the chained programs. Sometimes it is necessary to pass values from the calling program to the chained program. The COMMON statement allows you to select the variables to be passed to the chained program. The general form of this statement is

[*line#*] COMMON <*var-1*> [,*var-2*, . . ., *var-n*]

where *var* represents any program variable. Tables are specified by appending adjacent open and close parentheses () to the right of the table name. For example

3400 COMMON NAME.TBL$()

A COMMON statement may appear anywhere in a program as long as it precedes the CHAIN statement. Multiple COMMON statements may be used in one program, but one variable name may not be repeated in a second COMMON statement.

Programs 16.5 and 16.6 illustrate the use of the COMMON statement.

PROGRAM 16.5

```
1000 '  PROG16-5
1010 '  The Calling Program
1020    COMMON ENDIT, TOTAL
1030    ENDIT = 4
1040    TOTAL = 0
1050    FOR CTR = 1 TO ENDIT
1060        TOTAL = TOTAL + 1
1070    NEXT CTR
1080    PRINT "TOTAL FROM PROG16-5 = "; TOTAL
1090    CHAIN "PROG16-6"
1100    PRINT "SUM = "; SUM
1110    END
```

PROGRAM 16.6

```
1000 ' PROG16-6
1010 ' The Chained Program
1020   COMMON SUM
1030   SUM = 0
1040   FOR CTR = 1 TO ENDIT
1050       READ NUM
1060       SUM = SUM + NUM
1070       TOTAL = TOTAL + 1
1080   NEXT CTR
1090   DATA 10, 20, 30, 40
1100   PRINT "TOTAL FROM PROG16-6 = "; TOTAL
1110   CHAIN "PROG16-5", 1100
```

When Program 16.5 is run, the following is displayed:

```
TOTAL FROM PROG16-5 =   4
TOTAL FROM PROG16-6 =   8
SUM =   100
Ok
```

Examine the flow of execution when Program 16.5 is run. After the variables ENDIT and TOTAL are initialized, the FOR/NEXT loop is executed, and TOTAL has the value of 4 at the completion of the loop. Line 1080 in Program 16.5 displays the current value of TOTAL. Line 1090 chains to Program 16.6, passing the variables ENDIT and TOTAL. At this point, both ENDIT and TOTAL have a value of 4. In Program 16.6, after SUM is initialized, the FOR/NEXT loop is executed. The four values in the DATA statement are read and summed. At the completion of the FOR/NEXT loop, SUM contains the value 100, and TOTAL contains the value 8. Line 1100 in Program 16.6 displays the current value of TOTAL. Line 1110 chains back to the calling program, passing the common variable SUM. Execution begins at line 1100 in Program 16.5. The value of SUM is displayed by line 1100.

CHAINING AND PASSING ALL VARIABLES

Mr. Young of Northwestern Sheetmetal Company uses a depreciation program on his microcomputer. One of his employees has written a routine to calculate depreciation by another method. The existing program calculates depreciation by the straight-line method, and the new routine calculates depreciation by the declining-balance method. He would like to chain the new routine to his program so that when he runs the first program and obtains the results, the declining-balance routine is loaded and executed using the same data. The code for calculating straight-line depreciation is shown in Program 16.7. The code for calculating declining-balance depreciation is shown in Program 16.8. The chaining statements needed for these two programs are explained on page 433.

USER-DEFINED FUNCTIONS

Program 16.7 introduces a new BASIC statement, the user-defined function, DEF FN. Lines 1320–1340 illustrate three user-defined functions. A user-defined function is defined by the user somewhere in the program before the function is used. User-defined functions often help to simplify programs. The general form of the user-defined function is:

```
[line#] DEF FNname[(arg [,arg] ...)]  =  expression
```

PROGRAM 16.7

```
1000 ' PROG16-7
1010 ' *****************************
1020 ' *         STRAIGHT-LINE         *
1030 ' *     DEPRECIATION PROGRAM      *
1040 ' *****************************
1050 '
1060 ' *****************************
1070 ' *          VARIABLES            *
1080 ' *****************************
1090 '
1100 ' ACC.DEP                  Accumulated depreciation
1110 ' COST                     Original cost
1120 ' DEP                      Amount depreciated per year
1130 ' DEP.AMT                  Total depreciation allowed
1140 ' DEP.BAL                  Amount of depreciation left
1150 ' SALV                     Salvage value
1160 ' YEAR                     Current year
1170 ' YEARS                    Number of useful years
1180 '
1190 ' *****************************
1200 ' *          CONSTANTS            *
1210 ' *****************************
1220 '
1230   HEAD.1$ = "\                          \    $$##,###.###"
1240   HEAD.2$ = "                   DEPRECIATION          ACCUMULATED"
1250   HEAD.3$ = "  YEAR              EXPENSE            DEPRECIATION"
1260   DETAIL$ = "   ##            ##,###.##           ###,###.##"
1270 '
1280 ' *****************************
1290 ' *      DEFINED FUNCTIONS        *
1300 ' *****************************
1310 '
1320   DEF FNSUM (X,Y) = X + Y
1330   DEF FNDIF (X,Y) = X - Y
1340   DEF FNQUO (X,Y) = X / Y
1999 '
2000 ' *****************************
2010 ' *       CONTROL MODULE          *
2020 ' *****************************
2030 '
2040   KEY OFF
2050   GOSUB 3000               'Input Data
2060   GOSUB 4000               'Print Headings
2070   GOSUB 5000               'Calculate Depreciation
2080   GOSUB 6000               'Write End Message
2090   KEY ON
2100   END
2999 '
3000 ' *****************************
3010 ' *          INPUT DATA           *
3020 ' *****************************
3030 '
3040   CLS
3060   LOCATE  6,20 : PRINT "ENTER THE FOLLOWING VALUES"
3070   LOCATE  8,20 : INPUT "COST                 : ",COST
3080   LOCATE 10,20 : INPUT "SALVAGE VALUE        : ",SALV
3090   LOCATE 12,20 : INPUT "YEARS OF USEFUL LIFE : ",YEARS
3100   RETURN
3999 '
4000 ' *****************************
4010 ' *        PRINT HEADINGS         *
4020 ' *****************************
```

PROGRAM 16.7   (continued)

```
4030 '
4040    CLS
4050    LOCATE 2,20 : PRINT "STRAIGHT - LINE - METHOD"
4060    PRINT
4070    PRINT USING HEAD.1$; "COST =", COST
4080    PRINT USING HEAD.1$; "SALVAGE =", SALV
4090    PRINT
4100    PRINT HEAD.2$
4110    PRINT HEAD.3$
4120    PRINT
4130    RETURN
4999 '
5000 ' *****************************
5010 ' *    CALCULATE DEPRECIATION   *
5020 ' *****************************
5030 '
5040    ACC.DEP = 0
5050    DEP.AMT — FNDIF (COST, SALV)
5060    DEP = FNQUO (DEP.AMT, YEARS)
5070    ACC.DEP = FNSUM (ACC.DEP, DEP)
5080    FOR YEAR = 1 TO YEARS
5090        PRINT USING DETAIL$; YEAR, DEP, ACC.DEP
5100        ACC.DEP = FNSUM (ACC.DEP, DEP)
5110    NEXT YEAR
5120    LOCATE 24,20 : PRINT "PRESS ANY KEY TO CONTINUE"
5130    PAUSE$ = INPUT$(1)
5140    RETURN
5999 '
6000 ' *****************************
6010 ' *        WRITE END MESSAGE     *
6020 ' *****************************
6030 '
6040    CLS
6050    LOCATE 10,30 : PRINT "PROGRAM FINISHED"
6060    RETURN
```

Name is a valid variable name, and *arg* is an argument, a variable that takes on assigned values. *Expression* defines the value that is assigned to the variable FN*name*. The type of the expression must match the type of the variable name.

A variable name that appears in the expression does not have to appear in the list of arguments. For example, consider the algebraic equation, $z = ax^2 + by^2$. A user-defined function can be written as follows:

```
DEF FNZ(X, Y) = A * X ^ 2 + B * Y ^ 2
```

Notice that the variables A and B are not defined in the function, they must be defined in the program before the first use of the function. If A has the value 5, and B has the value 4, then:

```
FNZ(2, 3) = 5 * 2 ^ 2 + 4 * 3 ^ 2
          = 5 * 4     + 4 * 9
          = 20        + 36
          = 56
```

In Program 16.7, line 1320

```
1320 DEF FNSUM(X,Y)  =  X + Y
```

defines the variable FNSUM as the sum of the arguments X and Y. For example, if you used this line in the program

```
9000   ADDITION  =  FNSUM(6, 9)
```

the value of ADDITION would be 15, the result of adding 6 and 9. In the program, this line

```
5070   ACC.DEP  =  FNSUM(ACC.DEP, DEP)
```

sets the value of ACC.DEP equal to the sum of ACC.DEP and DEP. In this example, the function is just a different way of writing the line

```
5070   ACC.DEP  =  ACC.DEP + DEP
```

Even though this use of the user-defined function is simplistic, such functions can be very useful. Suppose that the formula for the monthly payment of a loan is used several times in a program. Instead of coding the formula each time it is used, you can enter it just once as a user-function and call it when you need it. Suppose this is the formula:

$$Payment = \frac{rate\,(1 + rate)^n}{(1 + rate)^n - 1} \times loan$$

Rate is the monthly interest rate, *n* is the number of months necessary to pay off the loan, and *loan* is the amount of the original loan.

The user-defined function can be written as follows:

```
4500   DEF FNPAY(RATE, N, LOAN)  =
          RATE * ( 1 + RATE )^N / (( 1 + RATE)^N - 1 ) * LOAN
```

If the function is called with the following values

```
6000   PAYMENT  =  FNPAY(.01, 48, 9500)
```

the variable PAYMENT will contain the monthly payment for a loan of $9500.00 at 12% annual interest for 4 years.

Here is another example. The formula *Volume = length* x *height* x *width* can be defined in a DEF FNname function as follows:

```
4500 DEF FNVOL(L, H, W)  =  L * H * W
```

String variables can also be used in a user-defined function. For example, the lines

```
4500   DEF FNALPHA$(A$, B$)  =  LEFT$(A$, 5) + RIGHT$(B$, 4)
          .
          .
          .
6000   ANSWER$  =  FNALPHA$(C$, D$)
```

place the first five characters of C$ and the last four characters of D$ in the variable ANSWER$.

Now that you know about user-defined functions, you can continue with the solution to Mr. Young's problem. The straight-line method of determining depreciation provides for equal periodic charges to expense over the estimated life of the asset. To understand this method, assume that the cost of a depreciable asset is $25,000, its salvage value is $4000, and its estimated life is 7 years. The annual depreciation is computed as follows:

$$\frac{\$25000\ cost - \$4000\ salvage\ value}{7\ years\ estimated\ life} = \$3000\ annual\ depreciation$$

In Program 16.7, note the calculations in the CALCULATE DEPRECIATION module. Try to predict the results using the numbers given in the previous expression defining straight-line depreciation.

Program 16.8 is the code for the new routine that calculates the declining-balance depreciation. The declining-balance method yields a declining periodic depreciation charge over the estimated life of the asset. The most common technique is to double the straight-line depreciation rate and apply the resulting rate to the cost of the asset less its accumulated depreciation. Using the numbers given in the straight-line depreciation example, the first and second year depreciation values are

$$\textit{First year} \atop \textit{depreciation} = 2 \times \frac{1}{7 \; years} \times (\$25,000 \; cost - \$0.00 \; accumulated \; dep)$$

$$\textit{First year depreciation} = \$7,142.86$$

$$\textit{Second year} \atop \textit{depreciation} = 2 \times \frac{1}{7 \; years} \times (\$25,000 \; cost - \$7142.86 \; accumulated \; dep)$$

$$\textit{Second year depreciation} = \$5,102.04$$

In Program 16.8, note the calculations in the CALCULATE DEPRE-CIATION module. Try to predict the results using the previous numbers.

Notice in Program 16.8 that the user-defined functions are redefined in lines 1170–1190. (Recall that the chaining process does not preserve user-defined functions.) Line 1100 sets the variable ACC.DEP back to zero because Program 16.7 accumulates the depreciation for the first method, and the value will not be zero. This module also makes liberal use of the user-defined functions. If you chain these modules, execution begins at line 1000. All that is necessary is to add a CHAIN command to Program 16.7. To do that, insert line 2075 in Program 16.7 with the following statement:

```
2075  CHAIN  "PROG16-8", , ALL
```

A COMMON statement is not required because you are passing all of the variables.

Program 16.8 contains an END statement (line 3190) that terminates execution. If you wish to chain back to Program 16.7 and execute the WRITE END MESSAGE module (6000), then you should replace line 3190 of Program 16.8 with the following line:

```
3190 CHAIN "PROG16-7.BAS", 2080
```

When Program 16.7 runs, the user is asked to enter the values needed in the program. See Figure 16.4. Figure 16.5 shows the output of these two programs if the user enters the values 25000 for COST, 4000 for SALVAGE, and 7 for YEARS OF USEFUL LIFE. Now you can verify your predictions.

When you run Program 16.7, there is a time lag as the CHAIN command is executed. A disadvantage of chaining is the time it takes to load the chained programs.

FIGURE 16.4
Screen requesting input
values for Program 16.7

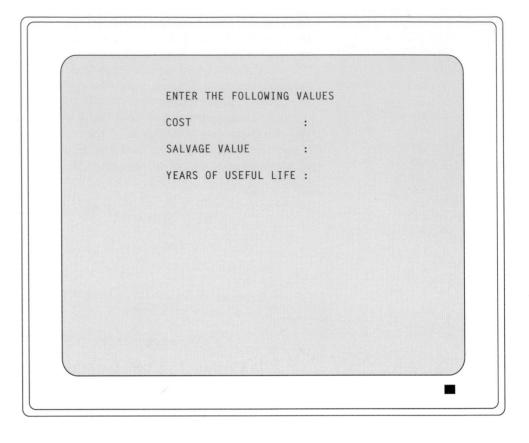

```
                    ENTER THE FOLLOWING VALUES

          COST                    :

          SALVAGE VALUE           :

          YEARS OF USEFUL LIFE :
```

FIGURE 16.5
Output of Program 16.7

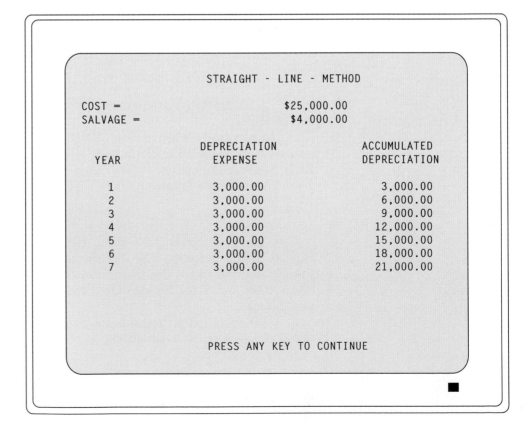

```
                        STRAIGHT - LINE - METHOD

          COST =                       $25,000.00
          SALVAGE =                     $4,000.00

                          DEPRECIATION            ACCUMULATED
              YEAR          EXPENSE              DEPRECIATION

               1            3,000.00                3,000.00
               2            3,000.00                6,000.00
               3            3,000.00                9,000.00
               4            3,000.00               12,000.00
               5            3,000.00               15,000.00
               6            3,000.00               18,000.00
               7            3,000.00               21,000.00




                        PRESS ANY KEY TO CONTINUE
```

FIGURE 16.5
Output of Program 16.8

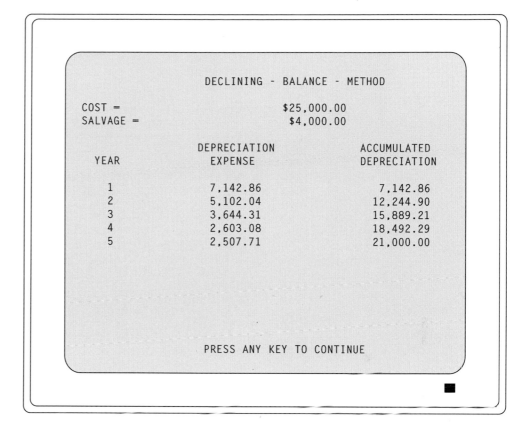

```
                    DECLINING - BALANCE - METHOD

     COST =                        $25,000.00
     SALVAGE =                      $4,000.00

                        DEPRECIATION          ACCUMULATED
        YEAR            EXPENSE               DEPRECIATION

          1             7,142.86                 7,142.86
          2             5,102.04                12,244.90
          3             3,644.31                15,889.21
          4             2,603.08                18,492.29
          5             2,507.71                21,000.00




                    PRESS ANY KEY TO CONTINUE
```

PROGRAM 16.8

```
1000 ' PROG16-8
1010 ' *****************************
1020 ' *     DECLINING-BALANCE     *
1030 ' *        DEPRECIATION        *
1040 ' *****************************
1050 '
1060 ' *****************************
1070 ' *   INITIALIZED VARIABLES   *
1080 ' *****************************
1090 '
1100   ACC.DEP = 0              'Accumulated depreciation
1110   YEAR = 1                 'Year counter
1120 '
1130 ' *****************************
1140 ' *     DEFINED FUNCTIONS     *
1150 ' *****************************
1160 '
1170   DEF FNSUM(X, Y) = X + Y
1180   DEF FNDIF(X, Y) = X - Y
1190   DEF FNQUO(X, Y) = X / Y
1999 '
2000 ' *****************************
2010 ' *       PRINT HEADINGS      *
2020 ' *****************************
2030 '
2040   CLS
2050   PRINT
2060   LOCATE 2,20 : PRINT "DECLINING - BALANCE - METHOD"
2070   PRINT
```

PROGRAM 16.8
(continued)

```
2080   PRINT USING HEAD.1$;"COST =", COST
2090   PRINT USING HEAD.1$;"SALVAGE =", SALV
2100   PRINT
2110   PRINT HEAD.2$
2120   PRINT HEAD.3$
2130   PRINT
2999 '
3000 '  *****************************
3010 '  *   CALCULATE DEPRECIATION   *
3020 '  *****************************
3030 '
3040   DEP.BAL = COST
3050   PERCENT = 2 * FNQUO(1, YEARS)
3060   WHILE  (FNDIF(DEP.BAL, DEP) > SALV)  AND  (YEAR < YEARS)
3070       DEP = PERCENT * DEP.BAL
3080       DEP = INT(100 * DEP + .5)/100
3090       DEP.BAL = FNDIF(DEP.BAL, DEP)
3100       ACC.DEP = FNSUM(ACC.DEP, DEP)
3110       PRINT USING DETAIL$; YEAR, DEP, ACC.DEP
3120       YEAR = FNSUM(YEAR, 1)
3130   WEND
3140   DEP = FNDIF(DEP.BAL, SALV)
3150   ACC.DEP = FNSUM(ACC.DEP, DEP)
3160   PRINT  USING DETAIL$; YEAR, DEP, ACC.DEP
3170   LOCATE 22,20 : PRINT "PRESS ANY KEY TO CONTINUE"
3180   PAUSE$ = INPUT$(1)
3190   END
```

MERGING PROGRAMS

As you write more programs, you will notice that some code is common to many different programs. In some cases, the code needed in different programs may be identical; in others, the code may vary only slightly.

BASIC's MERGE command allows you to insert program code saved on disk in ASCII format into a program in memory. Use MERGE with caution because, if the programs contain identical line numbers, the lines from the disk file replace the corresponding lines in memory. You need to treat the lines from the merged program just as you would newly entered code; the merged lines supersede any code with the same line numbers.

The general form of the MERGE command is

```
[line#] MERGE <filespec>
```

where *filespec* is the string expression for the file name.

You ordinarily issue the MERGE command from the keyboard. Because it is usually issued from the command level, no line number is needed. Here are some examples:

```
MERGE   "PROG1.BAS"
MERGE   "B:PROG2.BAS"
MERGE   PROG$              (where PROG$ = Basic program name)
```

The MERGE command can be helpful when several programmers are working on a program. Each person can code a portion of the program, and the program parts can then be merged into a complete program.

Caution! The disk code to be merged with the code in memory must first be saved in ASCII format. If the disk code has not been saved in ASCII format, the MERGE command will not work, and the system displays a "Bad File Mode" error message. When that happens, the program in memory remains unchanged. If the code you want to merge has not been saved in ASCII format, you can do the following:

1. Load the code to be merged.

```
LOAD "CODE1.BAS"
```

2. Save the code with the ",A" option (perhaps using another name, such as TEMP, so that the compact version of the program is still available as a backup).

```
SAVE "TEMP.BAS",A
```

3. Load the original program back into memory.

```
LOAD "ORIGINAL.BAS"
```

4. Now, merge the two programs.

```
MERGE "TEMP.BAS"
```

5. Memory now contains the two programs merged together.

Merging Code without Common Line Numbers

Consider the following two program modules that are saved under the names INPUTMOD.BAS and PRINTMOD.BAS on the default drive. The PRINTMOD.BAS code needs to be appended to the end of the INPUTMOD.BAS code. Notice that there are no duplicate line numbers.

PROGRAM 1
```
2000 ' INPUTMOD.BAS
2010 '
2020    INPUT "Enter Amount Invested ------> ", AMT
2030    INPUT "Enter Annual Interest Rate -> ", RATE
2040 '
```

PROGRAM 2
```
3000 ' PRINTMOD.BAS
3010 '
3020    INTEREST = AMT * RATE
3030    END.AMT  = AMT + INTEREST
3040 '
3050    PRINT "Amount Invested -------> "; AMT
3060    PRINT "Annual Interest Rate --> "; RATE
3070    PRINT "Amount At End of Year -> "; END.AMT
3080 '
```

To merge these two modules of code into one file, called COMBINED.BAS, you need to take the following steps while in BASIC:

1. LOAD "PRINTMOD"

2. SAVE "TEMP",A

3. LOAD "INPUTMOD"

4. MERGE "TEMP.BAS"

5. LIST
```
   2000 ' INPUTMOD.BAS
   2010 '
   2020    INPUT "Enter Amount Invested ------> ", AMT
   2030    INPUT "Enter Annual Interest Rate -> ", RATE
   2040 '
   3000 ' PRINTMOD.BAS
   3010 '
   3020    INTEREST = AMT * RATE
   3030    END.AMT  = AMT + INTEREST
   3040 '
   3050    PRINT "Amount Invested -------> "; AMT
   3060    PRINT "Annual Interest Rate --> "; RATE
   3070    PRINT "Amount At End of Year -> "; END.AMT
   3080 '
   OK
```

6. `SAVE "COMBINED"`

The combined code is saved on the disk under the name COMBINED.

Merging Code with Common Line Numbers

Consider two sets of code, FUNCTION.BAS and DISPLAY.BAS, saved on the default drive. Suppose you want to merge DISPLAY.BAS with FUNCTION.BAS but realize that the two modules have common line numbers. If you merge the modules as they are, the four lines of DISPLAY.BAS will replace the first four lines of FUNCTION.BAS.

PROGRAM 1
```
3000 ' FUNCTION.BAS
3010 '
3020    DEF FNVOLUME(X,Y,Z) = X * Y * Z
3030 '
3040    INPUT "Enter Length ---> ", L
3050    INPUT "Enter Width ----> ", W
3060    INPUT "Enter Height ---> ", H
3070 '
3080    FUNCT.VAL = FNVOLUME(L, W, H)
3090 '
```

PROGRAM 2
```
3000 ' DISPLAY.BAS
3010 '
3020    PRINT "The Volume of the Box Is "; FUNCT.VAL
3030 '
```

To merge these two modules of code into one file, you need to take the following steps while in BASIC:

1. `LOAD "DISPLAY"`

2. `RENUM 4000`

3. `SAVE "TEMP",A`

4. `LOAD "FUNCTION"`

5. `MERGE "TEMP.BAS"`

6. `LIST`
```
   3000 ' FUNCTION.BAS
   3010 '
   3020    DEF FNVOLUME(X,Y,Z) = X * Y * Z
   3030 '
   3040    INPUT "Enter Length ---> ", L
   3050    INPUT "Enter Width ----> ", W
   3060    INPUT "Enter Height ---> ", H
   3070 '
   3080    FUNCT.VAL = FNVOLUME(L, W, H)
   3090 '
   4000 ' DISPLAY.BAS
   4010 '
   4020    PRINT "The Volume of the Box Is "; FUNCT.VAL
   4030 '
   OK
```

7. `SAVE "DISFUNC"`

The combined code is saved on the disk under the name DISFUNC.

Replacing Lines of Code with the Merge Command

You can use the MERGE command to replace lines of code. Consider the following code saved in ASCII format on the default drive under the name REPLACE.BAS:

```
3020    DEF FNSURAREA(X, Y, Z) = 2*(X*Y + X*Z + Y*Z)
3080    FUNCT.VAL = FNSURAREA(L, W, H)
4020    PRINT "The Surface Area Is --> ", FUNCT.VAL
```

To put these lines in the place of existing lines 3020, 3070, and 4020 in the code you saved under DISFUNC.BAS, you need to do the following while in BASIC:

1. LOAD "DISFUNC.BAS"

2. MERGE "REPLACE.BAS"

3. LIST
```
3000 ' FUNCTION.BAS
3010 '
3020    DEF FNSURAREA(X, Y, Z) = 2*(X*Y + X*Z + Y*Z)
3030 '
3040    INPUT "Enter Length ---> ", L
3050    INPUT "Enter Width ----> ", W
3060    INPUT "Enter Height ---> ", H
3070 '
3080    FUNCT.VAL = FNSURAREA(L, W, H)
3090 '
4000 ' DISPLAY.BAS
4010 '
4020    PRINT "The Surface Area Is --> ", FUNCT.VAL
4030 '
OK
```

The three common lines from REPLACE.BAS have replaced the three lines in the copy of DISFUNC.BAS. in memory.

MEMORY DISKS

BASIC does not use all of the memory that is available in most computers. If your microcomputer has 640K of memory, you have approximately 540K of unused memory left after you load BASIC. If you use one of the products known as a *memory disk* (or ramdisk), such as the VDISK that comes with DOS 3.2, you can employ this unused memory to simulate a disk drive. These drives have the advantage of being very fast, even faster than a hard disk. Several of these products are available, and their cost is very reasonable. Public domain programs for this purpose are also available on many bulletin boards.

The operating system designates a memory disk, just as it designates any other drive, with a letter followed by a colon. The designation D: is used in the example that follows.

You can speed execution of programs that access data files frequently by transferring your data files to the memory disk; the program itself need not be transferred.

Caution! If the program changes the data file as it executes, then you must copy the data file back to the drive from which it was transferred to save the version permanently. If you shut off the computer without doing this, you lose the changes or additions you made to the file.

Returning to the system does not destroy the file in the memory disk. You can transfer it after you return to the system if you wish, but to be safe, you should make the actual transfer of the file(s) within the program.

Caution! If you reset the system, push the Reset button(s), or do a warm boot by pressing the Ctrl/Alt/Delete keys, the memory disk will cease to exist, as will any data it contained.

This process is illustrated in Program 15.3, the random file inquiry program for Amex Co-op members' accounts. If you have a memory disk, you can compare the difference in response time by running the program both ways on your system. The memory disk version of Program 15.3 is Program 16.9, shown in part later.

In the PROCESS FILE INQUIRY module (4000), you need to copy the random data file, MEM.RND, which resides on drive A, to drive D, the memory disk. You do not need to transfer the file INDEX.SEQ because the program accesses it only once as it reads it into memory.

Because copying a file is a system command, you need to use the SHELL command from within BASIC. Recall that the SHELL command allows you to execute a system command while you are in the BASIC subsystem. The system disk with COMMAND.COM must be on-line for the SHELL command to work. The data disk should be in drive A.

To do this, insert the following lines:

```
1025 ' *      USING MEMORY DISK      *
4035   SHELL "COPY A:MEM.RND D:"
```

Line 4035 copies the file to drive D, the memory disk, leaving the name of the file the same. If you cannot use the SHELL command, you can copy the file to drive D yourself before you load BASIC.

You need to change line 4040 to tell the computer where to find the file. So, change line 4040 from

```
4040   OPEN "R", #2, "MEM.RND", 42
```

to

```
4040   OPEN "R", #2, "D:MEM.RND", 42
```

Since changes will probably be made to the file MEM.RND, copy the file back to drive A at the end of the PROCESS FILE INQUIRY module (4000). The file is closed in line 4110, so insert line 4115, which copies the file back to drive A before the program ends:

```
4115   SHELL "COPY D:MEM.RND A:"
```

This procedure is actually very simple and must be seen to be appreciated. The COPY commands for the files do not need to be in the program. You can issue them from DOS before you load BASIC. Be sure to copy any changed files back to the disk when you are finished.

Here is a partial listing of Program 16.9:

PROGRAM 16.9

```
1000 ' PROG16-9
1010 ' *****************************
1020 ' * INQUIRY PROGRAM WITH INDEX *
1025 ' *      USING MEMORY DISK      *
1030 ' *****************************
1040 '
      .
      .
      .
3999 '
4000 ' *****************************
4010 ' *     PROCESS FILE INQUIRY     *
4020 ' *****************************
4030 '
4035   SHELL "COPY A:MEM.RND D:"
4040   OPEN "R",#2,"D:MEM.RND",42
```

PROGRAM 16.9
(continued)

```
4050    FIELD #2, 5 AS MAN$, 10 AS MNF$, 15 AS MNL$,
               4 AS MBD$,  4 AS MCC$,  4 AS MCL$
4060    GOSUB 6000              'Input Account Number
4070    WHILE ACCT$ <> "-9"
4080       GOSUB 7000           'Check For Valid Account
4090       GOSUB 6000           'Input Account Number
4100    WEND
4110    CLOSE #2
4115    SHELL "COPY D:MEM.RND A:"
4120    RETURN
4999 '
           .
           .
           .
```

You can speed the execution of programs that access random files frequently by storing the data file in a memory disk. Each time the program gets or puts a record, there is a delay while the computer positions the read/write head of the floppy disk drive. There is no delay, however, when you use a memory disk. If you often run programs that use random files, you should consider enhancing your system by adding a memory disk.

Summary

- *Chaining* is the process by which a program in memory calls a second program that replaces the original. None, some, or all of the variables may be passed between the two programs. Execution begins at the beginning of the called program or at the line number specified in the CHAIN command.

- *Merging* is the process of incorporating a program stored on a disk file into a program in memory. A program in a disk file can be merged into a program in memory only if the disk file is written in ASCII format. BASIC saves files in the ASCII format if the ",A" option is included in the SAVE statement, as in this example:

  ```
  SAVE "APROGRAM.BAS",A
  ```

- Merge programs with caution, because if the two programs contain identical line numbers, statements from the disk file will replace those already in memory.

- When extra memory is available, it can be used as storage space for data files during program execution. This memory is generally referred to as a memory disk or a ramdisk. Memory disks allow exceptionally fast file access. Placing random access data files in a memory disk speeds program execution. When using memory disks, be careful not to lose the data in memory before they are written back to a disk for permanent storage.

- In addition to using the built-in functions that BASIC provides, such as TAB and INT, the programmer can define functions to simplify programming. These functions are referred to as user-defined functions. The DEF FN statement permits the creation of a user-defined function. For example, in the following code, FNROUND can be used whenever a number is rounded to two decimal positions.

  ```
  100    DEF FNROUND(NUM) =
              INT(100 * NUM + .5)/100
         .
         .
         .
  800    PRINT FNROUND(GROSSPAY)
         .
         .
  900    PRINT FNROUND(NETPAY)
  ```

- Chapter 16 describes the following BASIC commands and statements:

  CHAIN A statement that, when used in the program in memory, calls another program from disk and executes it.

  COMMON A statement that specifies the variables that are in common use in two or more programs. It allows the variables to be passed between the programs.

DEF FN A statement that defines and names a function created by the programmer.

MERGE A command that combines a program or program module on disk with the program in memory.

Review Questions

1. Describe the processes involved in chaining programs.

2. During chaining, how can you pass variables from the calling program to the chained program?

3. Can user-defined functions be passed or transferred to a chained program?

4. Suppose a file is opened in one program and the program chains to another. What is the status of the file?

5. If a program in memory declares OPTION BASE 1 and then chains to a second program, what is the OPTION BASE setting of the second program if it does not contain an OPTION BASE statement?

6. Where in the program must you define user-defined functions?

7. Is it possible to pass dimensioned variables to a chained program? If so, do you have to dimension the table in both programs?

8. When you chain to another program, how can you specify where you want execution to begin?

9. What is the advantage, if any, of user-defined functions?

10. When you merge programs, what happens to statements in memory that have the same line numbers as statements on disk?

11. Explain what a memory disk is.

12. When you use a memory disk, what happens to data that reside there when you exit BASIC? Reset the machine? Perform a warm boot? When the power fails?

13. What precautions should you take to avoid losing data when you put a data file on a memory disk?

Problems

1. PROGRAMA.BAS resides in memory, and PROGRAMB.BAS resides on drive A. Write the BASIC instructions to meet the following conditions:

   a. PROGRAMA will call (chain) PROGRAMB. No variables need to be passed.
   b. PROGRAMA will call PROGRAMB, passing all variables.
   c. PROGRAMA will call PROGRAMB, and execution of B will start at line 3220. Only the single-precision variables COST, PRICE, and TAX need to be passed to PROGRAMB.
   d. PROGRAMA will call PROGRAMB, passing the table EXPECT.VAL, dimensioned 12 x 20, to PROGRAMB. Assume PROGRAMB resides on drive B in this one instance.
   e. PROGRAMA will call PROGRAMB, passing all variables. PROGRAMA opens the sequential data file DATA.SEQ, using buffer #1. PROGRAMB will read data from the file opened in PROGRAMA.

2. Consider the following three programs, which are chained together.

PROGRAM 1

```
1000  ' Program "ENTERDAT.BAS"
1010  '
1020  MAXROW  =  30
1030  ROW  =  1
1040  DIM GRADE(MAXROW)
1050  '
1060  CLS
1070  INPUT "Enter Grade, (-1 To Quit) ",
            GRADE(ROW)
1080  WHILE GRADE(ROW) <> -1
            AND ROW < MAXROW
1090     ROW  =  ROW + 1
1100     INPUT "Enter Grade, (-1 To Quit) ",
               GRADE(ROW)
1110  WEND
1120  '
1130  IF ROW  =  MAXROW
         THEN NUM.GRADES  =  ROW
         ELSE NUM.GRADES  =  ROW - 1
1140  '
1150  IF ROW <> 1
         THEN CHAIN "SUMDAT.BAS",,ALL
         ELSE END
1160  CHAIN "SUMDAT.BAS",,ALL
```

PROGRAM 2

```
1000  ' Program  "SUMDAT.BAS"
1010  '
1020  COMMON SUM, NUM.GRADES
1030  SUM  =  0
1040  '
1050  FOR ROW  =  1  TO NUM.GRADES
1060     SUM  =  SUM + GRADE(ROW)
1070  NEXT ROW
1080  '
1090  CHAIN "AVEDAT.BAS"
```

PROGRAM 3

```
1000  '   Program "AVEDAT.BAS"
1010  '
1020  AVERAGE  =  SUM / NUM.GRADES
1030  '
1040  CLS
1050  LOCATE 10
1060  PRINT "The average of the "; NUM.GRADES;
            " grades is "; AVERAGE
1070  END
```

What will the output be if you enter these data:

80,90,60,80,70,-1

3. By deleting some lines and renumbering each of the three programs in problem 2, merge the programs into one program that performs the same functions and produces the same output.

4. Consider the following programs, SUM.BAS and SQUARE.BAS.

Program SUM.BAS is the program in memory:

```
1000  '   Program to Sum Numbers
1010  '
1020  SUM  =  0
1030  INPUT "ENTER NUMBER, (0 TO END) ",NUM
1040  WHILE NUM <> 0
1050       SUM  =  SUM + NUM
1060       INPUT  "ENTER NUMBER, (0 TO END) ",NUM
1070  WEND
1080  PRINT "SUM  = "; SUM
1090  END
```

Program SQUARE.BAS is a partial program stored in ASCII format on drive A.

```
1000  '  Program to Sum Squares
1050  SUM  =  SUM + NUM^2
1080  PRINT "SUM SQUARED  =  ", SUM
```

a. What will the output be if you run the program in memory and enter the following data: 3,5,7,2,9,1,0

b. If you execute the following statement

```
MERGE "SQUARE.BAS
```

and run the program in memory, what will the output be when you use the data in a?

c. What code is in memory after the MERGE command is executed?

5. Create user-defined functions for each of the following formulas.

a. $s = a + 2b - c$
(Assume a, b, and c are real numbers.)

b. Effective interest rate $= \dfrac{interest\ for\ 1\ year}{principal}$

c. $S = P(1 + I/M)^{NM}$
(This formula gives the maturity value of an investment, where S = maturity value, P = investment, I = nominal rate of interest, N = time in years, and M = number of conversions per year.)

6. Given the following user-defined function

```
1000  DEF FNVALUE(A, B, C)  =
            5 + A - INT(B/C)
```

what are the values of the following?

a. FNVALUE(1, 1, 2)
b. FNVALUE(10, 20, 3)
c. FNVALUE(-2, 5, 2)
d. FNVALUE(3, 2, 0)
e. FNVALUE(2, 0, -1)

If the following statement is valid, what is its value?

f. FNVALUE(FNVALUE(1, 1, 2), 3, 2)

7. Given the following user-defined function and values

```
1000  PI  =  3.414
1010  FACTOR  =  5
1020  DEF FNGEOM(RADIUS) =
            FACTOR * PI * RADIUS ^ 2
```

what are the values of the following?

a. FNGEOM(1)
b. FNGEOM(3)
c. FNGEOM(-2)
d. FNGEOM(FACTOR)

Program Assignments

1. Program 16.1 is a menu-driven program that chains to any one of three billing programs. Add another choice to the menu: Program 11.3, the BILLING FILE EDIT program. Make the necessary changes in both Program 16.1 and Program 11.3.

2. A third method of computing depreciation is to use the sum-of-year's-digits method. This method results in larger deductions in the earlier years. The rate for each year is calculated as follows

$$Rate = \frac{N}{\text{sum-of-year's-digits}}$$

The denominator of the fraction is the sum of the year's digits $(1 + 2 + 3 + \ldots + n)$. The numerator, N, is at first the last year, n (the number of useful years), and is reduced by 1 for each successive year. The depreciation for the year is calculated as follows:

$$Depreciation = (Rate)(Cost - Salvage)$$

For example, if $n = 5$, the rates of depreciation for the five years are:

$$\text{First year rate} = \frac{5}{1 + 2 + 3 + 4 + 5} = \frac{5}{15} = \frac{1}{3}$$

$$\text{Second year rate} = \frac{4}{1 + 2 + 3 + 4 + 5} = \frac{4}{15}$$

$$\text{Third year rate} = \frac{3}{15} = \frac{1}{5}$$

$$\text{Fourth year rate} = \frac{2}{15}$$

$$\text{Fifth year rate} = \frac{1}{15}$$

It is possible to take all of the depreciation allowance before the number of useful years is up. This is a similar situation to the declining-balance method in the chapter example. Code the module and chain to it from Program 16.7. Test the program with the data given in the chapter example.

3. If you have a memory disk available, revise Program 16.1 so that the programs being chained reside on the memory disk. This should speed program execution. You will need to copy the programs to the memory disk and use the SHELL command if it is available. It will not be necessary to copy the programs back to the floppy drive when you are finished because you will not be changing any of the programs.

4. Enterprises Unlimited owns four stores. Each store has five departments. The table below represents the sales (in thousands of dollars) of each store during one week.

	Store 1	2	3	4
Department 1	12	9	8	11
Department 2	9	13	15	8
Department 3	7	6	10	10
Department 4	15	19	7	9
Department 5	5	18	6	14

a. Write a program module that stores the data as a sequential file.
b. Write a program module that adds the rows of the table using the file as input and prints the row totals.
c. Write a program module that adds the columns of the table using the file as input and prints the column totals.
d. Write a program module that produces a table whose entries are a percentage of the total of all sales.
e. Chain the modules together to produce the same output as in a, b, c, and d. You may need to delete or bypass some lines in some modules, and you will need to pass some or all variables.
f. By deleting unnecessary lines and renumbering the modules, merge them to produce one program with a control module.

5. Revise the random-access update program you wrote for Better Houses Building Center (Chapter 15, programming assignment 6, page 419). Use a memory disk to speed the inquiries. Transfer the data file to the memory disk with the SHELL command, if possible. Be sure to write the file back to the floppy disk when you have finished processing records.

Using the Data Disk

1. Insert the data disk into the disk drive.
2. Load BASIC (change the default drive if necessary).
3. Load program CH16-1.DD.

   a. Run the program and record the results (print screen).
   b. List the program.
   c. Add the following line to the program:

   ```
   1145   CHAIN "CH16-2.DD"
   ```

   d. Save the program as CH16-3.DD.
   e. Run the program and record the results (print screen).
   f. Load program CH16-2.DD.
   g. List the program.
   h. Replace line 1060 with

   ```
   1060   CHAIN "CH16-3.DD",1150
   ```

   i. Save the program as CH16-4.DD.

   ```
   SAVE "CH16-4.DD"
   ```

   j. Load program CH16-3.DD.
   k. Replace line 1145 with

   ```
   1145   CHAIN "CH16-2.DD", , ALL
   ```

   l. Run the program and record the results.
   m. Save the program as CH16-3.DD.

   ```
   SAVE "CH16-3.DD"
   ```

4. Load program CH16-2.DD.

   a. List the program.
   b. Delete line 1060.

   ```
   1060
   ```

   c. Renumber the lines starting with 2000.

   ```
   RENUM 2000
   ```

   d. Save the program in ASCII code as program CH16-5.DD.

   ```
   SAVE "CH16-5.DD",A
   ```

   e. Load program CH16-1.DD.
   f. Renumber lines 1150 through 1180 to 3000 through 3030

   ```
   RENUM 3000,1150,10
   ```

   g. List the program.

h. Merge program CH16-5.DD with this program in memory.

```
MERGE "CH16-5.DD"
```

i. List the program.
j. Run the program and record the results (print screen).
k. Save the program as CH16-6.DD.

Chapter Seventeen

Graphics

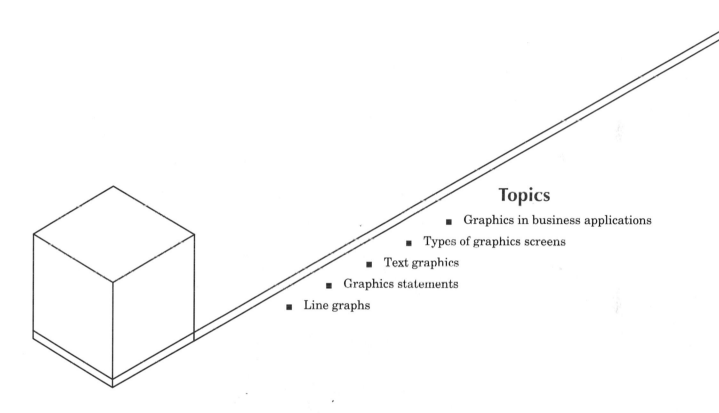

Topics

- Graphics in business applications
- Types of graphics screens
- Text graphics
- Graphics statements
- Line graphs

BASIC Statements

```
CIRCLE
COLOR
DRAW
GET
LINE
PAINT
PUT
PSET
SCREEN
WINDOW
```

INTRODUCTION

Businesses and government agencies collect vast amounts of data each day. These data usually find their way into reports in the form of lists and tables, but looking at row after row of numbers can overwhelm the reader and obscure the meaning of the figures. Graphs are one effective way to summarize data. "A well-drawn graph is worth a thousand numbers" is an apt paraphrase. The words *well-drawn* are the key. A graph that is too elaborate buries the information it means to convey. The graphic representation of data enables the reader to visualize the significant characteristics of the data easily. Even though graphs do not supply all the details of the raw data, they make it easy for readers to recognize trends and conditions. Microcomputers now provide a powerful tool for preparing various types of graphs.

Designs and blueprints can be moved and changed on the computer screen, where they can be evaluated and revised before the design is implemented or the item is manufactured. This step can help businesses avoid costly mistakes. Company logos can also be displayed on the screen to help viewers associate a company name with its products.

In this chapter, you will be introduced to computer graphics, and you will learn how to program some graphs and designs in BASIC. The chapter begins with a description of the BASIC graphics screens. Next, it describes some text screen applications. After you learn some background information and graphics statements, the chapter provides several examples, including programs to produce different types of graphs, logos, and animated designs.

SCREEN TYPES

Three different screens may be available for use with BASIC, depending on the type of hardware you use. SCREEN 0, the text screen (which is the screen you have been using), is available on all MS-DOS microcomputers. SCREEN 1, the medium-resolution screen, is available if your computer has a color/graphics interface card. SCREEN 2, the high-resolution screen, is also available with the addition of a graphics interface card. Color is available only if you have both the graphics interface card and a color monitor. The numbers 0, 1, and 2 are referred to as *screen mode values*. See Table 17.1.

SCREEN Statement

You select the desired screen with the SCREEN statement. The general form of the SCREEN statement is

```
[line#] SCREEN <n> [,burst] [,apage] [,vpage]
```

where:

n	has the value 0, 1, or 2.
	0 = text screen (default screen)
	1 = medium-resolution screen
	2 = high-resolution screen
burst	is a number to turn the color on (usually 0), or off (usually 1).
apage	selects the page written to by output statements. This parameter is valid only when *n* = 0.
vpage	selects the page to be displayed on the screen; *vpage*, too, is valid only when *n* = 0.

Table 17.1   Comparison of monitors, graphics cards, and screens available

MONITOR	ADAPTER CARD	SCREEN AVAILABLE	
Monochrome	MDA	0	
Monochrome	CGA	0,1,2	shades
RGB	CGA	0,1,2	colors
Monochrome	EGA	0[a]	shades
RGB	EGA	0,1,2[a]	colors
EGA	EGA	0,1,2[a]	colors

[a]Other screen modes (7–10) are available with BASIC 3.2 or later versions, but they are not covered in this book.

Because systems can be configured in many ways, it is up to you to determine the capabilities of the system that will run your programs. Be sure you find out this information *before* you begin designing the programs.

Note: To send graphics designs to a printer from SCREEN 1 or SCREEN 2, you must enter the GRAPHICS command from the system prompt before you load BASIC. Here is an example:

```
A>GRAPHICS
A>BASICA
```

After your program produces the graphic design on the screen, you can press the Shift/PrtSc keys to obtain a hard copy of the design.

TEXT SCREEN

The standard screen, the text screen, is available on all systems. It is defined by SCREEN 0, and it is the default screen when you enter BASIC. The designs produced on this screen are sometimes referred to as *text-mode graphics*. To produce graphics on this screen, you use the keyboard characters and the other printable ASCII characters. Appendix C lists all of the characters available to produce text graphics. If you are using a color monitor, you can display the characters in various colors.

WIDTH Statement

You can use the WIDTH statement to vary the number of columns on the screen. Its form is

```
[line#] WIDTH <n>
```

The parameter *n* is the number of characters per line, and its value may be either 40 or 80.

The screen will have 25 rows and 40 columns of character positions if you include the statement WIDTH 40 in a program. The characters will be as high as on an 80-column screen but will be twice as wide. For example, the statements

```
1000    WIDTH 40
1010    LOCATE 13,23
1020    PRINT CHR$(3)
```

position a heart in the 13th row and 23rd column of the screen. See Figure 17.1.

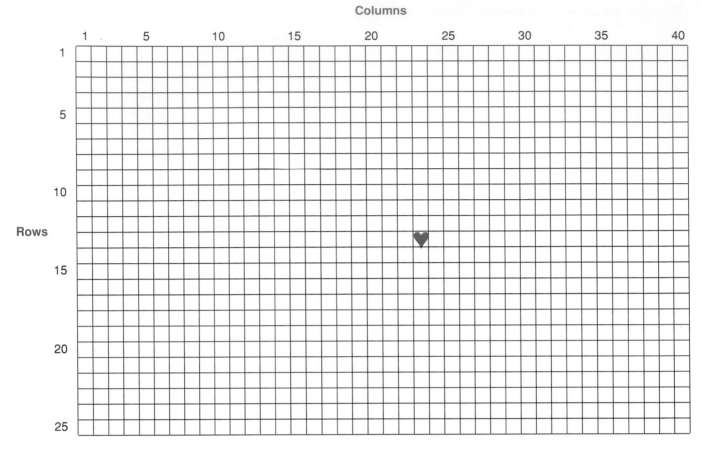

FIGURE 17.1 SCREEN 0, WIDTH 40, heart in location 13,23

COLOR Statement for Text Mode

The general form of the *text-mode* screen COLOR statement is

[*line#*]   COLOR   [*foreground*] [,*background*] [,*border*]

where:

foreground	is a number (0–31) representing the color of the text. Foreground values of 16–31 produce blinking characters, with the color of the character set by the foreground number minus 16.
background	is a number (0–7) representing the background color against which the text appears.
border	is a number (0–15) representing the color around the edge of the screen.

See Table 17.2 for color combinations.

Even if you do not have a color display or graphics adapter card, you can still use the COLOR statement to control the following screen functions:

Statement	Function
COLOR 0,0	Invisible characters
COLOR 0,7	Inverse video
COLOR 1,0	Underlined characters
COLOR 7,0	Normal characters (default condition)
COLOR 15,0	High-intensity characters
COLOR 23,0	Blinking characters
COLOR 31,0	High intensity, blinking characters

Table 17.2   Colors available for Screen 0

Foreground Number	Color	Background Number	Color	Border Number	Color
0	Black	0	Black	0	Black
1	Blue	1	Blue	1	Blue
2	Green	2	Green	2	Green
3	Cyan	3	Cyan	3	Cyan
4	Red	4	Red	4	Red
5	Magenta	5	Magenta	5	Magenta
6	Brown	6	Brown	6	Brown
7	White	7	White	7	White
8	Gray			8	Gray
9	Light blue			9	Light blue
10	Light green			10	Light green
11	Light cyan			11	Light cyan
12	Light red			12	Light red
13	Light magenta			13	Light magenta
14	Yellow			14	Yellow
15	High-intensity white			15	High-intensity white
16	Blinking black				
17	Blinking blue				
18	Blinking green				
19	Blinking cyan				
20	Blinking red				
21	Blinking magenta				
22	Blinking brown				
23	Blinking white				
24	Blinking gray				
25	Blinking light blue				
26	Blinking light green				
27	Blinking light cyan				
28	Blinking light red				
29	Blinking light magenta				
30	Blinking yellow				
31	Blinking high-intensity white				

Many of the programs in this text contain the following code to produce a screen pause.

```
3370    PRINT "PRESS ANY KEY TO CONTINUE"
3380    PAUSE$ = INPUT$(1)
```

In the following examples, you can display the message in different forms by adding two lines .

Inverse Video

```
3065    COLOR 0,7            'Set inverse video
3370    PRINT "PRESS ANY KEY TO CONTINUE"
3380    PAUSE$ = INPUT$(1)
3385    COLOR 7,0            'Return to normal display
```

Blinking Characters

```
3065    COLOR 23,0           'Set blinking
3370    PRINT "PRESS ANY KEY TO CONTINUE"
3380    PAUSE$ = INPUT$(1)
3385    COLOR 7,0            'Return to normal display
```

Blinking and High Intensity

```
3065    COLOR 31,0           'Set blinking & high intensity
3370    PRINT "PRESS ANY KEY TO CONTINUE"
3380    PAUSE$ = INPUT$(1)
3385    COLOR 7,0            'Return to normal display
```

Invisible Characters

The following program segment allows you to enter a "password" that is not displayed on the screen.

```
2250    PRINT "ENTER YOUR PASSWORD ";
2260    COLOR 0,0              'Invisible characters
2270    INPUT CODE$
2280    COLOR 7,0              'Return to normal display
```

A Text Graphics Application

Mr. Berg of Evergreen Products Company would like a design to appear on the screen of Evergreen's microcomputers when requested. Evergreen's computers are not equipped with color/graphics interface cards, and so only text graphics can be used. Mr. Berg has sketched a preliminary design. Figure 17.2 shows his sketch.

Program 17.1 produces the design shown in Figure 17.3. After the SET UP SCREEN module changes the width to 40 characters and clears the

FIGURE 17.2
Logo for Evergreen
Products

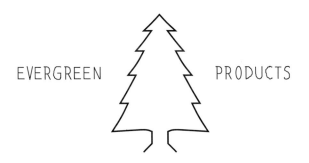

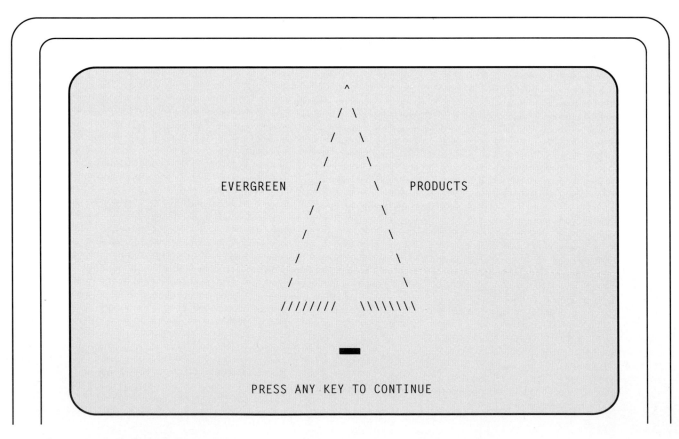

FIGURE 17.3   Output of Program 17.1

screen, the DRAW DESIGN module places the characters and text on the screen to form the Evergreen logo. The special characters used for the evergreen tree are assigned in the CONSTANTS section. Before the program ends, the screen is set back to the normal width of 80 in line 5050. It is always good practice to return the screen to the normal mode for the next user.

If you added the following statement to the program

```
3055    COLOR 2,7,4
```

the background of the screen would be white, the text would be green, and the screen would have a red border. Change Program 17.1 so that EVERGREEN PRODUCTS appears in yellow on a blue background and the message PRESS ANY KEY TO CONTINUE blinks on the screen.

PROGRAM 17.1

```
1000 ' PROG17-1
1010 ' ****************************
1020 ' *       TEXT SCREEN LOGO       *
1030 ' ****************************
1040 '
1050 ' ****************************
1060 ' *           VARIABLES          *
1070 ' ****************************
1080 '
1090 ' PAUSE$                    Screen pause
1100 ' ROW                       Counter in FOR/NEXT loop
1110 '
1120 ' ****************************
1130 ' *           CONSTANTS          *
1140 ' ****************************
1150 '
1160    P1$ = "^"
1170    P2$ = "/"
1180    P3$ = "\"
1190    P4$ = CHR$(219)          'Solid Block
1200    P5$ = CHR$(223)          'Horizontal Half Block
1999 '
2000 ' ****************************
2010 ' *          CONTROL MODULE      *
2020 ' ****************************
2030 '
2040    GOSUB 3000               'Set Up Screen
2050    GOSUB 4000               'Draw Design
2060    GOSUB 5000               'Write End Message
2070    END
2999 '
3000 ' ****************************
3010 ' *          SET UP SCREEN       *
3020 ' ****************************
3030 '
3040    KEY OFF
3050    WIDTH 40
3060    CLS
3070    RETURN
3999 '
4000 ' ****************************
4010 ' *          DRAW DESIGN         *
4020 ' ****************************
4030 '
4040    LOCATE 3,21 : PRINT P1$
```

PROGRAM 17.1 (continued)

```
4050    FOR ROW = 1 TO 7
4060        PRINT TAB(21-ROW); P2$; TAB(21+ROW); P3$
4070        PRINT
4080    NEXT ROW
4090    LOCATE 18,13 : PRINT STRING$(8,P2$); TAB(22); STRING$(8,P3$)
4100    LOCATE 19
4110    FOR ROW = 1 TO 3
4120        PRINT TAB(21); P4$
4130    NEXT ROW
4140    PRINT TAB(20); P5$; P5$; P5$
4150    LOCATE 10,4  : PRINT "EVERGREEN"
4160    LOCATE 10,30 : PRINT "PRODUCTS"
4170    LOCATE 25,9
4180    PRINT "PRESS ANY KEY TO CONTINUE"
4190    PAUSE$ = INPUT$(1)
4200    RETURN
4999 '
5000 ' *****************************
5010 ' *      WRITE END MESSAGE       *
5020 ' *****************************
5030 '
5040    CLS
5050    WIDTH 80
5060    KEY ON
5070    LOCATE 10,10 : PRINT "PROGRAM FINISHED"
5080    RETURN
```

Text Screen Graphs

Even without a color/graphics interface card, you can use ASCII characters to produce graphs. Mr. Berg would like a bar graph illustrating the weekly sales of the four major divisions of Evergreen Products. The divisions are Furniture, Cabinets, Doors, and Windows. See Figure 17.4 for a sample of this graph.

Program 17.2 produces the graph shown in Figure 17.4 if the user enters the following data:

Division 1	21200.00
Division 2	14300.00
Division 3	9045.00
Division 4	10700.00

The DRAW GRAPH module produces the graph on the screen. You can send ("dump") the screen output to the printer by pressing the Shift/Prtsc keys. Note that with the scale factor used (each block represents = $1000), the maximum number of blocks that will fit on the line is 29, or $29,000. (The width of the screen is 40, and "Furniture :" takes up 11 positions, leaving 29 available positions.) If sales of any division exceed $29,000, then change the scaling factor or increase the width of the line to 80.

In the DRAW GRAPH module, lines 5040–5080 place the heading on the screen. The FOR/NEXT loop determines how many blocks to print depending on the sales (line 5120), and then displays the name of the division (line 5130), the correct number of blocks (line 5130), and the sales amount (line 5140). After the graph is displayed, the message PRESS ANY KEY TO CONTINUE appears on the screen, allowing the user to view the graph as long as required.

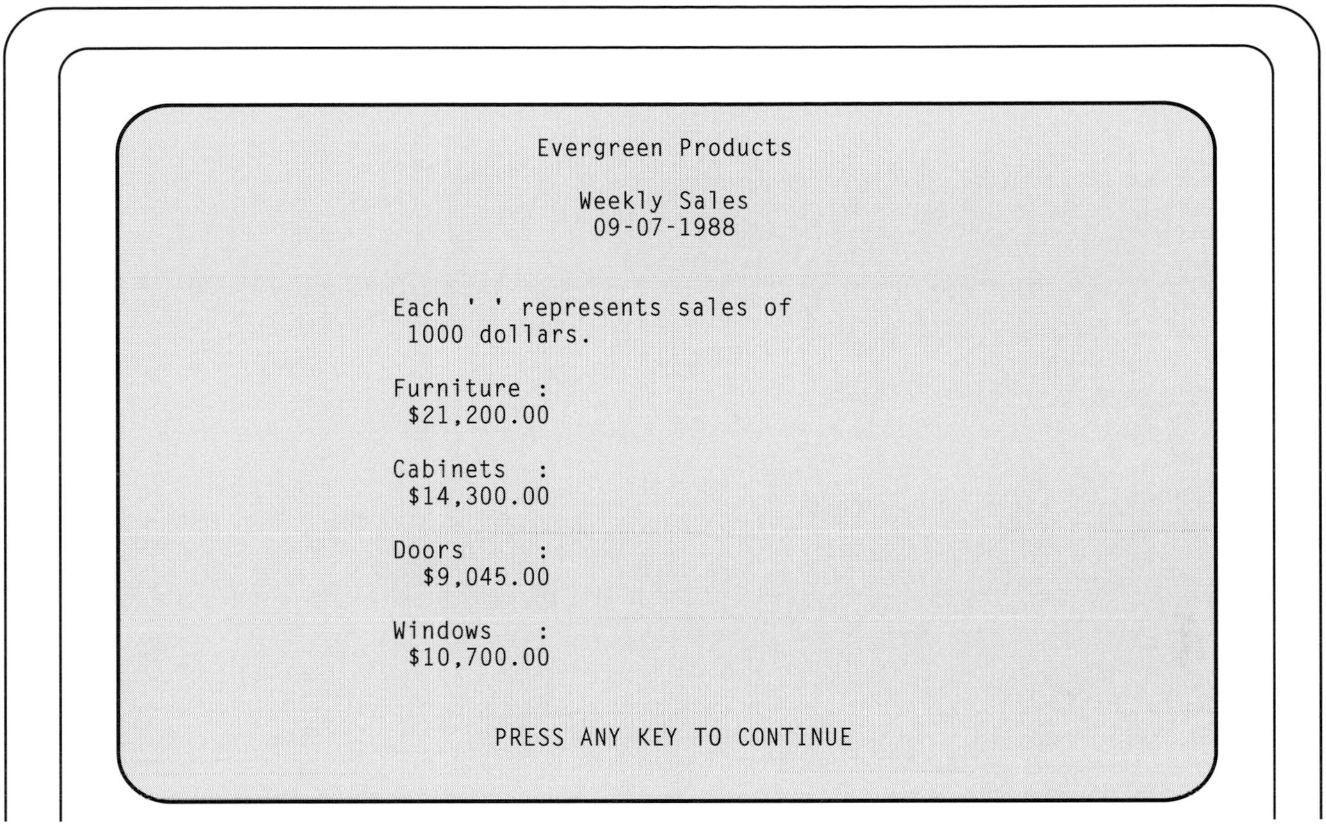

```
                      Evergreen Products

                        Weekly Sales
                         09-07-1988


             Each ' ' represents sales of
              1000 dollars.

             Furniture :
              $21,200.00

             Cabinets  :
              $14,300.00

             Doors     :
               $9,045.00

             Windows   :
              $10,700.00


                PRESS ANY KEY TO CONTINUE
```

FIGURE 17.4   Bar Graph showing Evergreen sales by division

PROGRAM 17.2

```
1000 ' PROG17-2
1010 ' *****************************
1020 ' *       TEXT BAR GRAPH      *
1030 ' *****************************
1040 '
1050 ' *****************************
1060 ' *         VARIABLES         *
1070 ' *****************************
1080 '
1090 ' NUM                      Divisional sales rounded to nearest thousand
1100 ' PAUSE$                   Screen pause
1110 ' ROW                      Table subscript
1120 '
1130 ' *****************************
1140 ' *       DEFINE TABLES       *
1150 ' *****************************
1160 '
1170   NO.DIV = 4               'Number of divisions
1180   DIM DIV.TBL$(NO.DIV)     'Table of division names
1190   DIM DIV.SAL.TBL(NO.DIV)  'Table of division sales
1200 '
1210 ' *****************************
1220 ' *     DATA FOR DIV.TBL$     *
1230 ' *****************************
1240 '
1250   DATA "Furniture :"
1260   DATA "Cabinets  :"
1270   DATA "Doors     :"
1280   DATA "Windows   :"
```

PROGRAM 17.2 (continued)

```
1999 '
2000 ' ******************************
2010 ' *         CONTROL MODULE        *
2020 ' ******************************
2030 '
2040    GOSUB 3000                 'Set Up Screen
2050    GOSUB 4000                 'Load Tables
2060    GOSUB 5000                 'Draw Graph
2070    GOSUB 6000                 'Write End Message
2080    END
2999 '
3000 ' ******************************
3010 ' *         SET UP SCREEN         *
3020 ' ******************************
3030 '
3040    KEY OFF
3050    CLS
3060    WIDTH 40
3070    RETURN
3999 '
4000 ' ******************************
4010 ' *         LOAD TABLES           *
4020 ' ******************************
4030 '
4040    LOCATE 6
4050    FOR ROW = 1 TO NO.DIV
4060       READ DIV.TBL$(ROW)
4070       PRINT "Enter Sales For "; DIV.TBL$(ROW);
4080       INPUT DIV.SAL.TBL(ROW)
4090    NEXT ROW
4100    RETURN
4999 '
5000 ' ******************************
5010 ' *         DRAW GRAPH            *
5020 ' ******************************
5030 '
5040    CLS
5050    LOCATE 2,11 : PRINT "Evergreen Products"
5060    LOCATE 4,14 : PRINT "Weekly Sales"
5070    LOCATE 5,15 : PRINT DATE$
5080    LOCATE 8 : PRINT "Each '"; CHR$(254); "' represents sales of"
5090    PRINT " 1000 dollars."
5100    LOCATE 11
5110    FOR ROW = 1 TO NO.DIV
5120       NUM = INT((DIV.SAL.TBL(ROW) + 500)/1000)
5130       PRINT DIV.TBL$(ROW); STRING$(NUM,CHR$(254))
5140       PRINT USING "$$##,###.##"; DIV.SAL.TBL(ROW)
5150       PRINT
5160    NEXT ROW
5170    LOCATE 24,8 : PRINT "PRESS ANY KEY TO CONTINUE"
5180    PAUSE$ = INPUT$(1)
5190    RETURN
5999 '
6000 ' ******************************
6010 ' *         WRITE END MESSAGE      *
6020 ' ******************************
6030 '
6040    CLS
6050    WIDTH 80
6060    KEY ON
6070    LOCATE 10,10 : PRINT "Program Finished"
6080    RETURN
```

MEDIUM-RESOLUTION GRAPHICS SCREEN

Instead of having character positions, the medium-resolution graphics screen is divided into points or *pixels*. The screen has 320 columns of 200 rows each for a total of 64,000 pixels. The upper left corner of the screen is always the position (0,0). See Figure 17.5.

You display your designs on this screen by turning individual pixels on and off. For example, you could use this statement to turn on the point at the intersection of column 215 and row 47:

```
1000  PSET (215,47)
```

This pixel is in the 216th column and the 48th row because the numbering of the columns and rows starts with zero. Note also that you must specify the column value first and then the row value. This is true of all of the graphics statements. Here is another example:

```
1000  LINE (25,30) - (175,130)
```

This statement draws a line from the point defined by column 25 and row 30 to the point defined by column 175 and row 130.

You can turn on pixels to generate characters, but you can also use any of the ASCII characters on this screen just as you would on the text screen. Any standard character that you use in this mode takes up a block of pixels that is 8 columns wide and 8 rows high. Notice that 320 columns

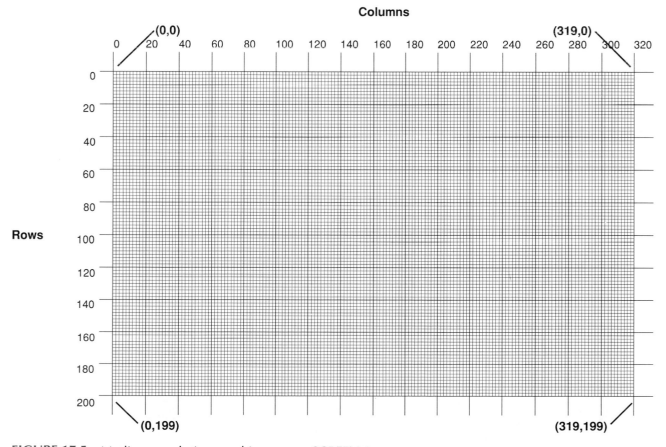

FIGURE 17.5   Medium-resolution graphics screen, SCREEN 1

FIGURE 17.6
Block of 8 x 8 pixels

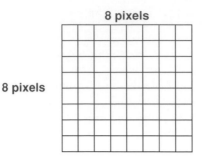

divided by 40 characters is 8 columns per character. The width for text characters is automatically set to 40 in SCREEN 1. Similarly, 200 rows divided by 25 rows is 8 rows per character. See Figure 17.6.

You can use the PRINT and PRINT USING statements to print text characters on the medium-resolution screen. You can also use the LOCATE statement. The LOCATE statement references an 8-by-8 block of pixels by row and then column. The statement

```
1000  LOCATE 15,20
```

refers to an 8-by-8 block of pixels in the 15th row and the 20th column of the screen. Notice that the graphics statements reference a pixel by *column-row*, and the LOCATE statement references a block of pixels by *row-column*.

HIGH-RESOLUTION GRAPHICS SCREEN

If your microcomputer has a high-resolution graphics board, you can call this third screen with SCREEN 2. The difference between SCREEN 1 and SCREEN 2 is that SCREEN 2 has twice as many pixels across the screen: 640 columns across and 200 rows down (128,000 pixels). See Figure 17.7. The greater number of pixels across the screen allows finer detail in graphs and designs. The "broken-line" effect is less noticeable on circles and curved figures.

Whereas several colors are available in SCREEN 1, only black, white, and shades of gray are available in SCREEN 2. Text characters printed on SCREEN 2 are only half as wide as on SCREEN 1 because the width of SCREEN 2 for text characters is set to 80, not 40. Otherwise, all commands and statements work the same in high-resolution graphics and medium-resolution graphics. Table 17.3 compares the types of screens available.

Table 17.3 Comparison of screens

Screen	Type	Horizontal Positions	Vertical Positions	Colors	
Screen 0 Width 40	Text	40	25	16 8 16	Foreground Background Border
Screen 0 Width 80	Text	80	25	16 8 16	Foreground Background Border
Screen 1	Graphics	320	200	3 16	Foreground Background
Screen 2	Graphics	640	200	Black and white	

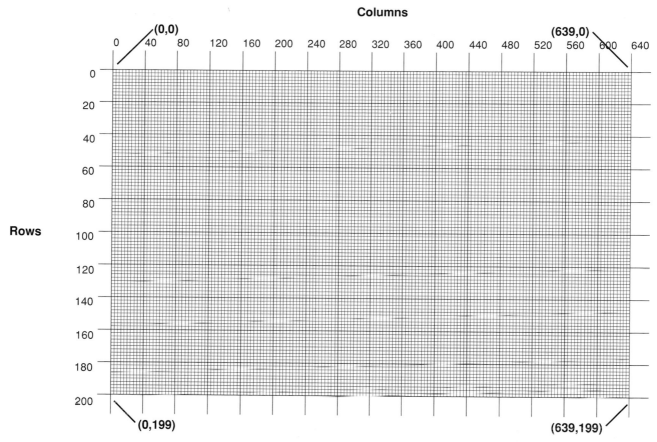

FIGURE 17.7   High-resolution graphics screen, SCREEN 2

GRAPHICS STATEMENTS

Before you attempt to write graphics programs using the medium-resolution screen, you need to learn some of BASIC's graphics statements. In general, if you omit any of the parameters in the statements, the values used in the previous statements are the default values.

COLOR Statement for Graphics

The general form of the *graphics* COLOR statement is

    [line#] COLOR [background] [,palette]

where:

> *background* is a numeric expression (0–15) specifying the background color.
>
> *palette* is a numeric expression that selects the palette of colors; palette is generally 0 or 1, but it can be any positive integer. Any even integer selects the even palette, and any odd integer selects the odd palette.

Table 17.4 lists the various colors that are available.

Table 17.4   Colors available for Screen 1

Background colors are denoted by a number from 0 to 15, as follows:

0	Black	5	Magenta	10	Light green
1	Blue	6	Brown	11	Light cyan
2	Green	7	White	12	Light red
3	Cyan	8	Gray	13	Light magenta
4	Red	9	Light blue	14	Yellow
				15	High-intensity white

When a color number is specified for the foreground in one of the graphics statements, the color used will depend on the active palette. The color numbers (0 through 3) below show the corresponding color used from the two palettes.

Color Number	Even Palette (0)	Odd Palette (1)
0	Background color	Background color
1	Green	Cyan
2	Red	Magenta
3	Yellow (brown)	White

If a color has not been designated, color number 3 from the even or odd palette is the default color.

Here are some uses of the graphics COLOR statement:

```
1000   COLOR  2,0
```
Sets the background color to green and selects palette 0, which makes the colors green, red, and yellow available.

```
1000   COLOR  4,1
```
Sets the background color to red and selects palette 1, which contains the colors cyan (greenish-blue), magenta, and white.

PSET Statement

The general form of the PSET statement is

```
[line#] PSET (x1,y1) [,color]
```

where:

(x1,y1)	are the coordinates of the pixel being turned on.
color	is the color of pixel from the active palette (0,1,2, or 3).

The statements

```
1010    COLOR 4,1
1020    PSET (20,30),3
```

turn on a white pixel in column 20 row 30 against a red background. The statements

```
1000    COLOR 5,2
1010    PSET (20,30), 1
```

turn on a green pixel in column 20 row 30 against a magenta background.

LINE Statement

The format of the LINE statement is

```
[line#] LINE [(x1,y1)] - <(x2,y2)> [,color#] [,B or BF]
```

where:

(x1,y1)	are the coordinates of the starting point.
(x2,y2)	are the coordinates of the ending point.
color#	selects the color from the active palette.
B	draws a rectangle having *(x1,y1)* and *(x2,y2)* as opposite corners.
BF	fills the rectangle with the color specified by *color#*.

The statement

```
1030  LINE (40,180) - (60,100), 2, B
```

draws a box 20 pixels wide and 80 pixels high. This statement

```
1040  LINE (140,80) - (180,120), 3, BF
```

draws a colored block centered on the screen. The statement

```
1050  LINE - (300,190), 2
```

draws a colored line from the current position to the pixel in column 300 row 190.

Figure 17.8 is a screen display showing the output produced by the following statements:

```
1000 SCREEN 1
1010 COLOR 9,1                             'light blue background
1020 FOR X = 20 TO 30 STEP 2
1030     PSET (X, X + 10),1                'cyan dots
1040 NEXT X
1050 LINE (40,160) - (75,90), 2, B         'magenta rectangle
1060 LINE (140,80) - (180,120), 3, BF      'white block
1070 LINE  - (300,190), 2                  'magenta line
```

FIGURE 17.8
Screen display of graphics statements (light blue background)

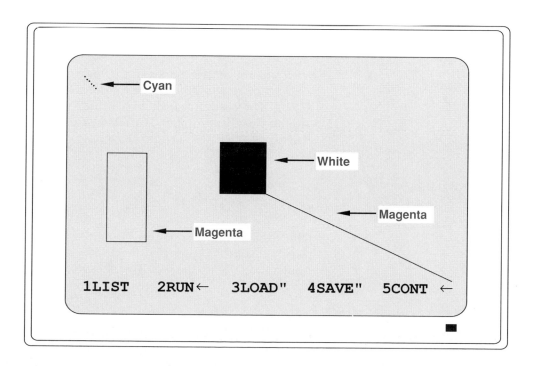

CIRCLE Statement

The general form of the CIRCLE statement is

[*line#*] CIRCLE <(*x,y*), *radius*> [,*color#*] [,*start*] [,*end*] [,*aspect*]

where:

(*x,y*)	is the point at the center of the circle.
radius	is the radius of the circle.
color#	is an optional parameter used to select the color from the active palette.
start,end	are optional parameters used to indicate where to start and stop drawing part of a circle. Values are in fractions of pi where pi is approximately 3.141593; 2*pi is a complete circle.
aspect	is an optional parameter used to determine the shape of the drawing. The default values that produce a circle are 5/6 (5 rows for every 6 columns) in medium-resolution mode and 5/12 (5 rows for every 12 columns) in high-resolution mode. You can vary the number of rows or columns to produce a vertical or horizontal ellipse.

Try different combinations of the CIRCLE statement to see what they do. For example,

```
1000    SCREEN 1
1010    COLOR 8,0
1020    CIRCLE (140,100), 75, 2, , , 2          'red ellipse
```

draws an ellipse in color centered in the screen.
The statements

```
1030    PI = 3.1416
1040    CIRCLE (80,50), 20, 3, 0, PI            'yellow semicircle
```

draw a semicircle in the upper left part of the screen. The following statements

```
1050    FOR RADIUS = 10 TO 50 STEP 10
1060        CIRCLE (270,150), RADIUS, , , , 1   'yellow circles
1070    NEXT RADIUS
```

draw five concentric circles in the lower right of the screen. Figure 17.9 shows a screen display of the circle examples.

The rest of this chapter contains programs illustrating various applications for the graphics statements. The examples use medium-resolution graphics (SCREEN 1) with color.

LINE GRAPHS

This first example produces a simple line graph representing the monthly sales of Amex Corporation for 1990. It includes a horizontal and a vertical axis and a title at the top. The axes are not labeled. The line graph is shown in Figure 17.10.

WINDOW Statement

The WINDOW statement is very useful when you use both medium-resolution and high-resolution graphics to draw line graphs. It is available only in more recent versions of BASIC. The WINDOW statement allows you to reset

FIGURE 17.9
Screen display of CIRCLE
statements
(gray background)

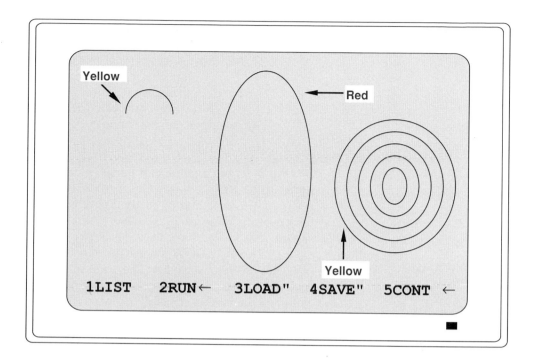

FIGURE 17.10
Output of Program 17.3
(red background)

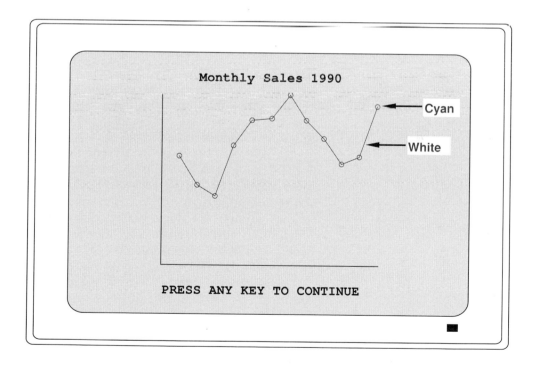

the coordinate system on SCREEN 1 and SCREEN 2 by specifying the coordinates of the opposite corners of the screen. The form of the statement is

$$(line\#) \text{ WINDOW } (\text{SCREEN})<(x1,y1) - (x2,y2)>$$

where:

$(x1, y1)$ mark the coordinates of the upper left corner of the screen.

<table>
<tr><td>(x2, y2)</td><td>mark the coordinates of the lower right corner of the screen.</td></tr>
<tr><td>(SCREEN)</td><td>is an optional parameter included only when you want to specify coordinates that increase from right to left and from top to bottom.</td></tr>
</table>

For example, the statement

```
1000  WINDOW (0,199) - (319,0)
```

sets up a screen that is 320 pixels wide and 200 pixels high with the coordinates (0,0) in the lower left corner of the screen. This statement simply reverses the coordinates of the default medium-resolution screen to adapt it for graphing. Figure 17.11 shows a comparison of this screen to the default screen.

The WINDOW statement can be very convenient when you design a program to draw graphs. The axes of a graph normally increase vertically and horizontally from the lower left; it is easier to position items on the screen if the screen coordinates increase in the same way.

The data for the graph are the monthly sales of Amex Corporation over the last year. The output is a line graph on the screen representing these sales. The horizontal axis represents the months, and the vertical axis represents the sales in thousands of dollars. Program 17.3 produces the graph in Figure 17.10.

Comments on Program 17.3

Notice the variables listed in lines 1090–1150. HEIGHT.FACTOR and LENGTH.FACTOR are the variables used to determine the scaling for the vertical and horizontal axes. Since a line graph of this type is constructed by drawing lines between two points, you can use (X1,Y1) for the first point and (X2,Y2) for the second point.

Because the data will have to be scaled to fit on the screen, the LOAD TABLE module determines the maximum monthly sales using the data in lines 1280–1310. In the SET UP GRAPHICS AREA module, line 4060 sets the screen to medium-resolution graphics. Line 4070 redefines the coordinate system so that the point (0,0) is the lower left corner of the screen. This redefinition simplifies the calculation of graph coordinates. In line 4080, the background color of the screen is set to red, and palette 1 is selected.

The DRAW AXIS module draws the axes and prints the title. Lines 5040 and 5050 locate and print the title in the first text row starting in column 11. Lines 5060 and 5070 use the graphics statement LINE. Line 5060 draws the vertical axis, connecting the point (56,40) to the point (56,180). Line 5070 connects the same point, (56,40), to the point (256,40). The point (56,40), at the bottom left corner of the screen, is the intersection of the two axes. There are now 20 pixels at the top of the graphing area, 56 pixels to the left of it, and 40 pixels below it. See Figure 17.12.

In the DRAW GRAPH module, the scaling factor for the vertical axis is determined from the number of available pixels and the maximum sales amount. The vertical axis starts on pixel 40 and ends on pixel 180, making it 140 pixels long. Line 6040 divides these 140 pixels by the variable MAX.SALES to produce the variable HEIGHT.FACTOR, ensuring that the largest monthly sales figure will fit in the graphing region. Because the horizontal axis starts on pixel 56 and ends on pixel 256, it is 200 pixels wide. These 200 pixels need to be divided over the twelve months of the year, and so the scale factor for this axis is 200 divided by 12. See line 6050.

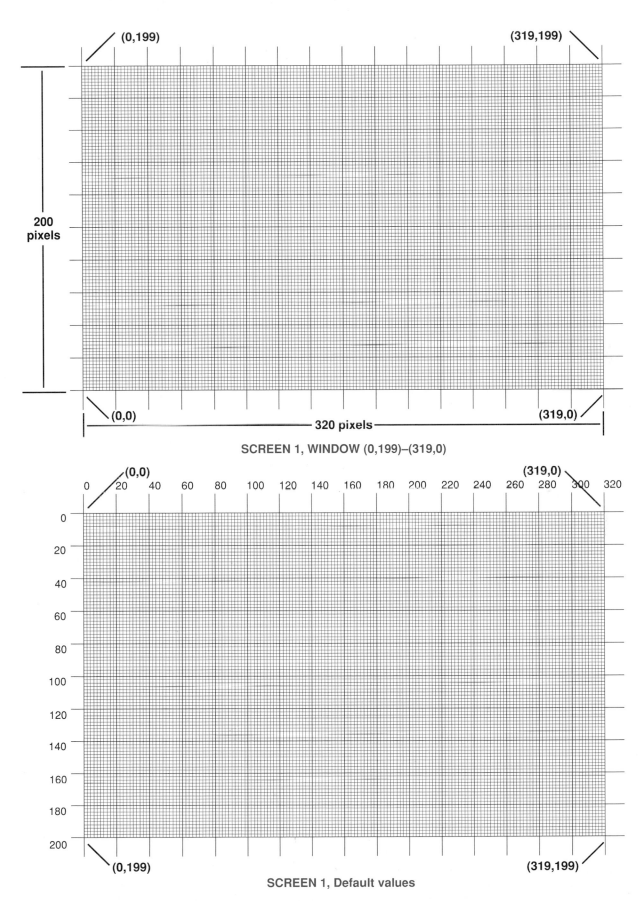

SCREEN 1, WINDOW (0,199)–(319,0)

SCREEN 1, Default values

FIGURE 17.11   WINDOW statement

PROGRAM 17.3

```
1000 ' PROG17-3
1010 ' *****************************
1020 ' *      BROKEN LINE GRAPH      *
1030 ' *****************************
1040 '
1050 ' *****************************
1060 ' *         VARIABLES           *
1070 ' *****************************
1080 '
1090 ' HEIGHT.FACTOR             Scaling factor for the vertical axis
1100 ' LENGTH.FACTOR             Scaling factor for the horizontal axis
1110 ' MAX.SALES                 Highest monthly sales of year
1120 ' MONTH                     Month of year
1130 ' PAUSE$                    Screen pause
1140 ' X1, Y1                    Coordinates of first point
1150 ' X2, Y2                    Coordinates of second point
1160 '
1170 ' *****************************
1180 ' *         DEFINE TABLE        *
1190 ' *****************************
1200 '
1210    MAX.MONTH = 12           'Number of months
1220    DIM SALES.TBL(MAX.MONTH) 'Table of monthly sales
1230 '
1240 ' *****************************
1250 ' *      DATA FOR SALES.TBL     *
1260 ' *****************************
1270 '
1280    DATA  675, 500,  425
1290    DATA  750, 900,  910
1300    DATA 1050, 890,  780
1310    DATA  630, 700, 1000
1999 '
2000 ' *****************************
2010 ' *         CONTROL MODULE      *
2020 ' *****************************
2030 '
2040    GOSUB 3000               'Load Table
2050    GOSUB 4000               'Set Up Graphics Area
2060    GOSUB 5000               'Draw Axis
2070    GOSUB 6000               'Draw Graph
2080    GOSUB 7000               'Return Text Screen
2090    END
2999 '
3000 ' *****************************
3010 ' *          LOAD TABLE          *
3020 ' *****************************
3030 '
3040    MAX.SALES = 0
3050    FOR MONTH = 1 TO MAX.MONTH
3060       READ SALES.TBL(MONTH)
3070       IF SALES.TBL(MONTH) > MAX.SALES
            THEN MAX.SALES = SALES.TBL(MONTH)
3080    NEXT MONTH
3090    RETURN
3999 '
4000 ' *****************************
4010 ' *     SET UP GRAPHICS AREA     *
4020 ' *****************************
4030 '
4040    CLS
4050    KEY OFF
4060    SCREEN 1
4070    WINDOW (0,199)-(319,0)
4080    COLOR 4,1
```

PROGRAM 17.3   (continued)

```
4090    RETURN
4999  '
5000  ' *****************************
5010  ' *           DRAW AXIS           *
5020  ' *****************************
5030  '
5040    LOCATE 1,11
5050    PRINT "Monthly Sales 1990"
5060    LINE(56,40) - (56,180)
5070    LINE(56,40) - (256,40)
5080    RETURN
5999  '
6000  ' *****************************
6010  ' *           DRAW GRAPH          *
6020  ' *****************************
6030  '
6040    HEIGHT.FACTOR = 140/MAX.SALES
6050    LENGTH.FACTOR = 200/MAX.MONTH
6060    FOR MONTH = 1 TO MAX.MONTH - 1
6070       X1 = 56 + LENGTH.FACTOR * MONTH
6080       Y1 = 40 + HEIGHT.FACTOR * SALES.TBL(MONTH)
6090       X2 = 56 + LENGTH.FACTOR * (MONTH + 1)
6100       Y2 = 40 + HEIGHT.FACTOR * SALES.TBL(MONTH + 1)
6110       CIRCLE(X1,Y1),2,1
6120       LINE(X1,Y1) - (X2,Y2)
6130    NEXT MONTH
6140    CIRCLE(X2,Y2),2,1
6150    LOCATE 23,8
6160    PRINT "PRESS ANY KEY TO CONTINUE"
6170    PAUSE$ - INPUT$(1)
6180    RETURN
6999  '
7000  ' *****************************
7010  ' *       RETURN TEXT SCREEN       *
7020  ' *****************************
7030  '
7040    SCREEN 0
7050    WIDTH 80
7060    KEY ON
7070    LOCATE 10,10 : PRINT "Program Finished"
7080    RETURN
```

After the scaling factors are set, the FOR/NEXT loop in lines 6060–6130 draws the twelve line segments. Since each line segment connects two points at a time, the loop continues for MONTH values from 1 to 11. When MONTH becomes 11, a line segment is drawn connecting the 11th and 12th months.

Lines 6070–6100 determine the values of the coordinates (X1,Y1) and (X2,Y2). For example, when MONTH = 1, the values of the points (to two decimal places) are

```
X1 =  56 + (200/12) * 1     = 72.67
Y1 =  40 + (140/1050) * 675  = 70.00
X2 =  56 + (200/12) * 2     = 89.33
Y2 =  40 + (140/1050) * 500  = 93.33
```

The line

```
6110 CIRCLE (X1,Y1), 2, 1
```

uses another of the graphics statements, CIRCLE. When this line is executed, a circle is drawn on the screen. The center is at the coordinate (X1,Y1), and the radius is 2 pixels. This very small circle, whose color is determined by the value 1, makes the point (X1,Y1) stand out.

FIGURE 17.12
Drawing the axis

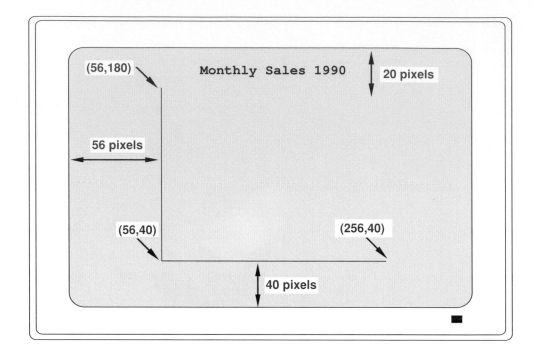

Line 6120 draws the line connecting the monthly sales values. In this case, the points are determined by (X1,Y1) and (X2,Y2). The FOR/NEXT loop continues until all twelve segments are drawn. When the loop finishes, line 6140 places the small circle around the last point.

Line 6170 produces a pause so that the user may view the results and print a copy of the graph before continuing.

Module RETURN TEXT SCREEN resets the screen to text mode for the next user. The SCREEN 0 statement returns the screen to text mode, and the WIDTH statement resets the width to 80.

One needed addition to this graph is a set of labels for the axes. The next example addresses that problem.

BAR GRAPHS

Rather than redo the broken line graph to label the axes, follow this program, which uses the same data to produce a bar graph. The vertical axis is scaled in thousands of dollars, and the horizontal axis is labeled with the first letter of the month.

Program 17.4 produces the graph in Figure 17.13. Since most of this program is identical to Program 17.3, only the labeling of the axes and drawing of the bars are discussed.

The FOR/NEXT loop in lines 5110–5150 prints the numeric value and marks the vertical axis. The program uses numbers that are multiples of 8 because the LOCATE statement in 5120 determines the location of an 8 by 8 block of pixels on one of the character lines on the screen. The printed value corresponding to the mark is the number of pixels up the axis divided by the HEIGHT.FACTOR.

Lines 5170–5200 label the horizontal axis. Again, multiples of 8 are used so that the LOCATE statement will place the character under the bar. All labels are printed on the 22nd character row of the screen. Since X goes from 64 to 256 by steps of 16 (line 5170), line 5180 becomes LOCATE 22,8, then LOCATE 22,10, and so on.

In the DRAW GRAPH module, lines 6040–6080 draw the bars for the twelve months. Line 6050 calculates the horizontal or x-value of the lower left corner of the bar. Line 6060 calculates the vertical or y-value of the upper right corner of the bar. The y-value of the lower left corner of the bar is always set at 40, the position of the horixontal axis. The x-value of the upper right corner of the bar is always the lower left x-value plus the width of the bar. Thus, the opposite corners of the bar are as shown in the LINE statement in line 6070, which draws and colors the respective bars by using the BF parameter with the LINE statement.

FIGURE 17.13
Output of Program 17.4
(red background)

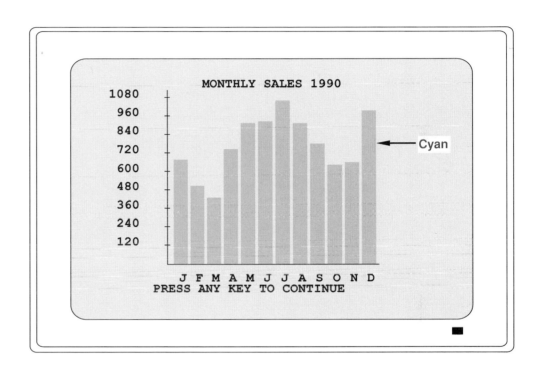

PROGRAM 17.4

```
1000 ' PROG17-4
1010 ' *****************************
1020 ' *          BAR GRAPH        *
1030 ' *****************************
1040 '
1050 ' *****************************
1060 ' *          VARIABLES        *
1070 ' *****************************
1080 '
1090 ' HEIGHT.FACTOR              Scaling factor for the vertical axis
1100 ' MAX.SALES                  Highest monthly sales for the year
1110 ' MONTH                      Month of the year
1120 ' PAUSE$                     Screen pause
1130 ' X                          Variable used to mark off x-axis
1140 ' Y                          Variable used to mark off y-axis
1150 ' X1,Y1                      Coordinate used to draw bar
1160 '
1170 ' *****************************
1180 ' *       DEFINE TABLES       *
1190 ' *****************************
```

PROGRAM 17.4 (continued)

```
1200 '
1210    MAX.MONTH = 12
1220    DIM MONTH.TBL$(MAX.MONTH)      'Table of months
1230    DIM SALES.TBL(MAX.MONTH)       'Table of monthly sales
1240 '
1250 ' *****************************
1260 ' *       DATA FOR TABLES      *
1270 ' *****************************
1280 '
1290    DATA J,  675, F, 500, M,  425
1300    DATA A,  750, M, 900, J,  910
1310    DATA J, 1050, A, 890, S,  780
1320    DATA O,  630, N, 700, D, 1000
1999 '
2000 ' *****************************
2010 ' *       CONTROL MODULE       *
2020 ' *****************************
2030 '
2040    GOSUB 3000                 'Load Tables
2050    GOSUB 4000                 'Set Up Graphics Area
2060    GOSUB 5000                 'Draw Axis
2070    GOSUB 6000                 'Draw Graph
2080    GOSUB 7000                 'Return Text Screen
2090    END
2999 '
3000 ' *****************************
3010 ' *         LOAD TABLES        *
3020 ' *****************************
3030 '
3040    MAX.SALES = 0
3050    FOR MONTH = 1 TO MAX.MONTH
3060       READ MONTH.TBL$(MONTH), SALES.TBL(MONTH)
3070       IF SALES.TBL(MONTH) > MAX.SALES
                 THEN MAX.SALES = SALES.TBL(MONTH)
3080    NEXT MONTH
3090    RETURN
3999 '
4000 ' *****************************
4010 ' *     SET UP GRAPHICS AREA    *
4020 ' *****************************
4030 '
4040    CLS
4050    KEY OFF
4060    SCREEN 1
4070    WINDOW (0,199) - (319,0)
4080    COLOR 4,1
4090    RETURN
4999 '
5000 ' *****************************
5010 ' *           DRAW AXIS        *
5020 ' *****************************
5030 '
5040    LOCATE 1,11
5050    PRINT "MONTHLY SALES 1990"
5060    LINE(56,40) - (56,190)       'Draw x & y-axis
5070    LINE(56,40) - (256,40)
5080    HEIGHT.FACTOR = 140/MAX.SALES 'Determine the scaling factor
5090    BAR.WIDTH = 12               'Set the bar width
5100 '
```

PROGRAM 17.4   (continued)

```
5110    FOR Y = 56 TO 190 STEP 16      'Scale & mark y-axis
5120        LOCATE 25-Y/8, 1
5130        PRINT USING "####"; ((Y - 40)/HEIGHT.FACTOR)
5140        LINE(54,Y) - (58,Y)
5150    NEXT Y
5160 '
5170    FOR X = 64 TO 256 STEP 16      'Scale & mark x-axis
5180        LOCATE 22, X/8
5190        PRINT MONTH.TBL$(X/16 - 4)
5200    NEXT X
5210    RETURN
5999 '
6000 ' *****************************
6010 ' *         DRAW GRAPH        *
6020 ' *****************************
6030 '
6040    FOR BAR = 1 TO 12
6050        X1 = 64 + (BAR - 1) * (192 / 12)
6060        Y1 = 40 + HEIGHT.FACTOR * SALES.TBL(BAR)
6070        LINE(X1,40) - (X1 + BAR.WIDTH, Y1), 1, BF
6080    NEXT BAR
6090    LOCATE 24,6
6100    PRINT "PRESS ANY KEY TO CONTINUE"
6110    PAUSE$ = INPUT$(1)
6120    RETURN
6999 '
7000 ' *****************************
7010 ' *     RETURN TEXT SCREEN    *
7020 ' *****************************
7030 '
7040    SCREEN 0
7050    WIDTH 80
7060    KEY ON
7070    LOCATE 10,10 : PRINT "Program Finished"
7080    RETURN
```

CIRCLE OR PIE CHARTS

Data can also be represented by pie charts or circle graphs. Program 17.5 produces a colored pie chart, centered on the screen and labeled. The chart illustrates the quarterly sales of Amex Corporation. The pie chart in Figure 17.14 was produced by Program 17.5.

This program sums the monthly values in each quarter and labels each quarter. The monthly sales values are in DATA statements.

There is no advantage to using the WINDOW command in the program since the only reference point is the center of the screen. The variables P.START and P.END indicate how much of the circle to draw. The line

```
5090 CIRCLE (160,100),75,2, P.START, -P.END
```

instructs the computer to start drawing a circle with a radius of 75 pixels in color 2 of the active palette. The circle should begin at the value of the angle P.START (in radians), which has an initial value of zero. The arc should be drawn to the angle value P.END (in radians). The minus (−) preceding the variable P.END indicates that the end of the arc is to be connected to the center of the circle. See Figure 17.15.

FIGURE 17.14
Output of Program 17.5
(blue background)

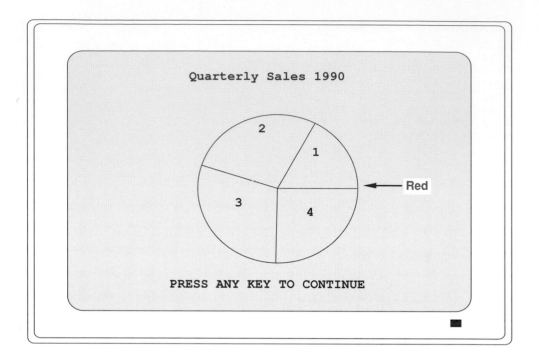

Line 5060 of Program 17.5 calculates the percentage each quarter's sales contribute to the total sales for the year. Line 5070 translates this percentage into an angle value in radians by multiplying the percent by 360 (degrees in a circle) and then dividing by 57.3 (the approximate number of degrees in 1 radian). Figure 17.16 shows how radians relate to degrees. Line 5070 could have been written as

```
5070 PERCENT = PERCENT * 2 * PI
```

Line 5100 calls the module that labels the quarter. Line 7040 averages the beginning and ending angles of the sector, giving the angle of a line through the center of the sector. Lines 7050 and 7060 compute the coordinates of the label. The formulas

$x = x\text{center} + \text{radius} \times \text{COS(Angle)}$
$y = y\text{center} - \text{radius} \times \text{SIN(Angle)}$

always give the coordinates (X,Y) of a point that lies on the center line through the sector at a distance from the center equal to the value of the variable RADIUS. These two formulas introduce two BASIC built-in trigonometric functions, the cosine and sine of an angle.

In line 7070, the values of X and Y are divided by 8, the number of pixels per character. These are used in the LOCATE statement to position the label in the PRINT statement.

When program execution returns to line 5110, the new starting angle for the next quarter, P.START, takes the value of P.END from the previous sector.

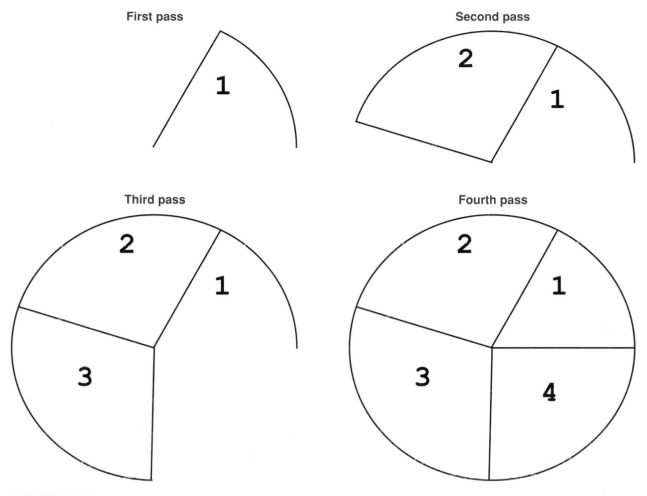

FIGURE 17.15   Drawing a pie chart

FIGURE 17.16
Comparison of radians and degrees

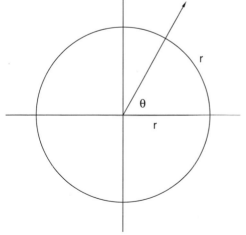

When the length of the arc described by an angle is equal to the radius of the circle, the measure of the angle is defined as 1 radian.

Circumference = $2\pi r$

Because 360° represent a complete circle, the radius of a circle can be measured off 2π times around the circle.

2π radians $= 360°$

1 radian $= \dfrac{360°}{2\pi}$

1 radian $\cong \dfrac{360°}{2(3.141593)} = 57.296°$

PROGRAM 17.5

```
1000 ' PROG17-5
1010 ' *****************************
1020 ' *          PIE GRAPH         *
1030 ' *****************************
1040 '
1050 ' *****************************
1060 ' *          VARIABLES         *
1070 ' *****************************
1080 '
1090 ' ANGLE                 Angle of the sector
1100 ' PAUSE$                Screen pause
1110 ' PERCENT               Ratio of quarterly sales to total sales
1120 ' P.END                 Angle for end of sector
1130 ' P.START               Angle for start of sector
1140 ' Q                     Table subscript
1150 ' SALES                 Variable for monthly sales
1160 ' TOT.SALES             Total sales
1170 ' X, Y                  Coordinates of label
1180 '
1190 ' *****************************
1200 ' *          CONSTANTS         *
1210 ' *****************************
1220 '
1230   PI = 3.1416           'Value of PI
1240 '
1250 ' *****************************
1260 ' *          DEFINE TABLE      *
1270 ' *****************************
1280 '
1290   NO.OF.QTRS = 4        'Number of quarters
1300   DIM QTR.TBL(NO.OF.QTRS) 'Table of quarterly sales
1310 '
1320 ' *****************************
1330 ' *       DATA FOR QTR.TBL     *
1340 ' *****************************
1350 '
1360   DATA  675, 500,  425
1370   DATA  750, 900,  910
1380   DATA 1050, 890,  780
1390   DATA  630, 700, 1000
1999 '
2000 ' *****************************
2010 ' *          CONTROL MODULE    *
2020 ' *****************************
2030 '
2040   GOSUB 3000            'Load Table
2050   GOSUB 4000            'Set Up Graphics Area
2060   GOSUB 5000            'Draw Graph
2070   GOSUB 6000            'Return Text Screen
2080   END
2999 '
3000 ' *****************************
3010 ' *          LOAD TABLE        *
3020 ' *****************************
3030 '
3040   TOT.SALES = 0
3050   FOR Q = 1 TO NO.OF.QTRS
3060      FOR MONTH = 1 TO 3
3070         READ SALES
3080         QTR.TBL(Q) = QTR.TBL(Q) + SALES
3090      NEXT MONTH
3100      TOT.SALES = TOT.SALES + QTR.TBL(Q)
3110   NEXT Q
3120   RETURN
3999 '
```

PROGRAM 17.5   (continued)

```
4000 ' *****************************
4010 ' *      SET UP GRAPHICS AREA    *
4020 ' *****************************
4030 '
4040   KEY OFF
4050   SCREEN 1
4060   COLOR 1,0
4070   CLS
4080   LOCATE 1,10
4090   PRINT "Quarterly Sales 1990"
4100   RETURN
4999 '
5000 ' *****************************
5010 ' *          DRAW GRAPH          *
5020 ' *****************************
5030 '
5040   P.START = 0
5050   FOR Q = 1 TO NO.OF.QTRS
5060      PERCENT = QTR.TBL(Q) / TOT.SALES
5070      PERCENT =  PERCENT * 360 / 57.3
5080      P.END = PERCENT + P.START
5090      CIRCLE (160,100), 75, 2, P.START, -P.END
5100      GOSUB 7000            'Label Quarter
5110      P.START = P.END
5120   NEXT Q
5130   LOCATE 23,8
5140   PRINT "PRESS ANY KEY TO CONTINUE"
5150   PAUSE$ = INPUT$(1)
5160   RETURN
5999 '
6000 ' *****************************
6010 ' *      RETURN TEXT SCREEN      *
6020 ' *****************************
6030 '
6040   SCREEN 0
6050   WIDTH 80
6060   KEY ON
6070   LOCATE 10,10 : PRINT "Program Finished"
6080   RETURN
6999 '
7000 ' *****************************
7010 ' *          LABEL QUARTER        *
7020 ' *****************************
7030 '
7040   ANGLE = (P.START + P.END) / 2
7050   X = 160 + 40 * COS(ANGLE)
7060   Y = 100 - 40 * SIN(ANGLE)
7070   LOCATE INT(Y/8), INT(X/8)
7080   PRINT Q
7090   RETURN
```

DESIGNS AND LOGOS

The suppliers of products and services often use a logo to symbolize their companies. This logo may appear on company software.

Peerless Aviation caters to the skydiving enthusiast. They take groups up for jumps and gives lessons in skydiving. Mr. McFarline of Peerless has purchased some computer-assisted instruction (CAI) materials so that prospective skydivers can go through the basic instruction on their own. He wants students to see the company name, Peerless Aviation, as they take these lessons. He has requested that an opening screen precede each lesson. Figure 17.17 is his sketch of how the design should look.

Program 17.6 produces the Peerless Aviation opening screen shown in Figure 17.18. The following statements are introduced in this program.

FIGURE 17.17
Hand sketch of an opening screen

FIGURE 17.18
Output of Program 17.6

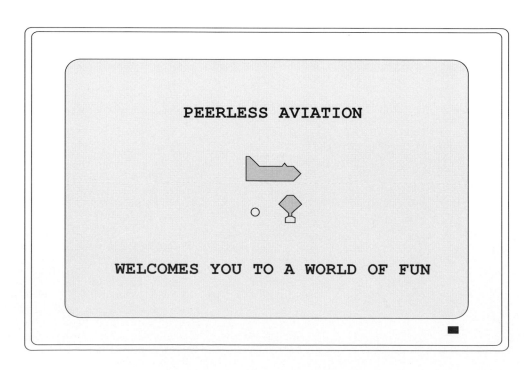

DRAW Statement

The general form of the DRAW statement is

[line#] DRAW <string variable>

where *string variable* is any string of movement commands. The DRAW statement executes a series of movement commands defined in the string variable. For example, line 4060 contains the statement DRAW PLANE$. Line 1160 defines the design to be drawn. The first part of the string PLANE$ is BM145,100. The letters BM simply cause the cursor to move to the coordinates (145,100)—nothing is drawn. The next movement command, R30, instructs the computer to draw a line 30 pixels long to the right. The remaining movement commands draw the rest of the airplane. The movement commands are summarized in Table 17.5.

For example, the line

1000 DRAW "BM50,75 R40 U20 L40 D20"

causes the pointer to move to the location defined by the coordinates (50,75). From this point, a line 40 pixels long is drawn to the right; then, from that position, a line 20 pixels long is drawn up. From this point, a line 40 pixels long is drawn to the left, and a line 20 pixels long is drawn down. Thus, a 40-by-20-pixel rectangle is constructed.

The lines

1000 DIAMOND$ = "E10 F10 G10 H10"
1010 DRAW "S12 XDIAMOND$"

cause a diamond whose sides are each 30 pixels long to be printed to the right of center. Line 1000 defines a diamond with sides of 10 pixels. In line 1010,

Table 17.5   Movement commands for the DRAW statement

Movement Commands

n represents a number.
b is a boundary color.
x,y are screen coordinates.
var represents a variable.

COMMAND	ACTION
U*n*	Move up *n* pixels
D*n*	Move down *n* pixels
L*n*	Move left *n* pixels
R*n*	Move right *n* pixels
E*n*	Move diagonally up and to the right *n* pixels
F*n*	Move diagonally down and to the right *n* pixels
G*n*	Move diagonally down and to the left n pixels
H*n*	Move diagonally up and to the left *n* pixels
M*x,y*	Move to the coordinates (*x,y*)
+M*x,y*	Move relative to the current position
B	Move without plotting
N	Move and then return to previous location
A*n*	Set the angle at which the figure is drawn (0 = 0°, 1 = 90°, 2 = 180°, 3 = 270°)
T*n*	Turn through an angle *n* for next drawing, -360° <= *n* <= 360°
C*n*	Determine the color of the figure from the active palette
P*n,b*	Color in an area bounded by color *b* using color *n*
S*n*	Determine the scale of the figure; the scale will be 1/4 of *n*
X*var*	Execute a subcommand, where *var* is a string variable containing additional commands

the scale factor is set to three times, denoted by S12. Recall from Table 17.5 that S*n* scales a figure by 1/4 of *n* (1/4 x 12 = 3). The X preceding the variable DIAMOND$ signals a set of movement commands defined by a string variable. So, DRAW "S12 XDIAMOND$" is a command to draw a figure three times the size defined by the movement commands in DIAMOND$.

PAINT Statement

The general form of the PAINT statement is

```
[line#] PAINT <(x,y)> [,paint#, boundary#]
```

where

(*x,y*)	are the coordinates of a point within the figure to be painted.
paint#	is an optional parameter denoting the number of the color used to paint the figure.
boundary#	is an optional parameter denoting the number that corresponds to the color of the edges of the area being painted.

Lines 4080 and 4100 in Program 17.6 contain examples of this statement. After a closed figure is drawn, you need only select a point within the figure to color or paint the entire interior.

Consider these lines:

```
1000 CIRCLE (200,70),20,2
1010 PAINT (210,80),1,2
```

Line 1000 draws a circle with a radius of 20 pixels centered at the point (200,70). The circle is drawn in color 2 of the current palette. Line 1010 locates the point (210,80) within the circle and paints the interior of the circle in color 1 of the current palette. The coloring proceeds until a boundary drawn in color 2 of the current palette is reached.

In the DRAW LOGO module of Program 17.6, after lines 4060 and 4070 draw the airplane, line 4080 uses the PAINT statement to color the plane by selecting a point (coordinates 160,98) within the plane. Line 4090 draws the parachute, and line 4100 colors the parachute.

PROGRAM 17.6

```
1000 ' PROG17-6
1010 ' ****************************
1020 ' *        LOGO PROGRAM         *
1030 ' ****************************
1040 '
1050 ' ****************************
1060 ' *          VARIABLES          *
1070 ' ****************************
1080 '
1090 ' PAUSE                Time delay
1100 '
1110 ' ****************************
1120 ' *          CONSTANTS          *
1130 ' ****************************
1140 '
1150    CHUTE$  = "BM165,115 E5 R3 F5 G9 D2 R5 U2 H9"
1160    PLANE$  = "BM145,100 R30 E4 H4 L4 H2 G2 L14 H6 L2 D14"
1180    TITLE1$ = "PEERLESS AVIATION"
1190    TITLE2$ = "WELCOMES YOU TO A WORLD OF FUN"
```

PROGRAM 17.6   (continued)

```
1200    WING$    = "BM165,96 L5"
1999  '
2000  ' *****************************
2010  ' *           CONTROL MODULE         *
2020  ' *****************************
2030  '
2040    GOSUB 3000                  'Set Up Graphics Area
2050    GOSUB 4000                  'Draw Logo
2060    GOSUB 5000                  'Return Text Screen
2070    END
2999  '
3000  ' *****************************
3010  ' *      SET UP GRAPHICS AREA      *
3020  ' *****************************
3030  '
3040    KEY OFF
3050    SCREEN 1
3060    COLOR 1,0
3070    RETURN
3999  '
4000  ' *****************************
4010  ' *              DRAW LOGO              *
4020  ' *****************************
4030  '
4040    LOCATE 8,13
4050    PRINT TITLE1$
4060    DRAW PLANE$
4070    DRAW WING$
4080    PAINT (160,98),2,3
4090    DRAW CHUTE$
4100    PAINT (175,115),2,2
4110    CIRCLE (150,120),2,2
4120    LOCATE 20,6
4130    PRINT TITLE2$
4140    FOR PAUSE = 1 TO 5000 : NEXT PAUSE
4150    RETURN
4999  '
5000  ' *****************************
5010  ' *         RETURN TEXT SCREEN        *
5020  ' *****************************
5030  '
5040    SCREEN 0
5050    WIDTH 80
5060    KEY ON
5070    LOCATE 10,10 : PRINT "Program Finished"
5080    RETURN
```

ANIMATION

Sometimes, animation is the best way to capture the viewer's attention. Animation is the process of sucessively placing and then removing a figure on the screen to give the illusions of movement. It usually involves the following steps:

1. Drawing a figure on the screen

2. Erasing the figure

3. Drawing it at another position

4. Erasing it again

5. Drawing it at yet another position

.

.

.

To reproduce the drawing over and over again, you should store the figure in memory so that the DRAW statements do not need to be executed each time the figure is drawn. The figure will be stored in an image array, which is nothing more than an integer array (or an integer table).

Application

Mr. McFarline liked the results of the last program, but he thinks his company's students would be more impressed if, after the first screen appears, they saw an image of an airplane moving across the screen and a parachutist skydiving. Program 17.7 produces this animated screen.

New BASIC instructions introduced in this program are the GET and PUT statements. Do not confuse these with the GET and PUT statements used for random-access files.

GET Statement

The GET statement reads the colors of the pixels in the specified screen area, a rectangular region defined by opposite corners, into an image array.

The standard form of the GET statement is

```
[line#] GET <(x1,y1)-(x2-y2)>, <variable name>
```

where:

$(x1, y1)$	are the coordinates of one corner of a rectangle that contains the figure.
$(x2, y2)$	are the coordinates of the opposite corner of the rectangle containing the figure.
variable name	is the array in which the pixels are stored.

If you store the figure in an integer array, then you can determine the size of the array by the following formula:

```
Number of bytes = 4 + INT((2 * length + 7) / 8) * height
```

where:

length	is the length of the rectangle in pixels that contains the figure.
height	is the height of the rectangle in pixels that contains the figure.

The statements

```
2110    DIM PIT%(44)
          .
          .
4550    GET (120,150) - (135,170), PIT%
```

reads the colors of the pixels in the rectangular region defined by opposite corners (120,150) and (135,170), and stores that image in the integer array PIT%. The length of the rectangle is 16 pixels (135–120+1) and the height is 21 pixels (170–150+1). If you use the formula on the rectangle defined by these coordinates, the number of bytes required is

$$
\begin{aligned}
\text{Number of bytes} &= 4 + \text{INT}((2 * 16 + 7) / 8) * 21 \\
&= 4 + \text{INT}(39/8) * 21 \\
&= 4 + \text{INT}(4.875) * 21 \\
&= 4 + 4 * 21 \\
&= 4 + 84 \\
&= 88
\end{aligned}
$$

Because an integer position can store 2 bytes, the dimension of PIT% needs to be 44.

PROGRAM 17.7

```
1000 ' PROG17-7
1010 ' ******************************
1020 ' *        ANIMATION PROGRAM          *
1030 ' ******************************
1040 '
1050 ' ******************************
1060 ' *            VARIABLES              *
1070 ' ******************************
1080 '
1090 ' PAUSE                      Time delay
1100 ' POSITION                   Counter for the position of plane and chute.
1110 ' X                          X coordinate of plane.
1120 ' X1                         X coordinate of chute.
1130 ' Y                          Y coordinate of chute.
1140 '
1150 ' ******************************
1160 ' *            CONSTANTS              *
1170 ' ******************************
1180 '
1190   CHUTE$  = "BM165,115 E5 R3 F5 G9 D2 R5 U2 H9"
1200   GROUND$ = "BM0,170 R35 E10 F10 E5 R40 E10 R10 D2 F5 R30 F10 R15 E10
               R30 U5 E10 F20 R50 E10 D40 L310 U27"
1210   PLANE$  = "BM145,100 R30 E4 H4 L4 H2 G2 L14 H6 L2 D14"
1220   TITLE1$ = "PEERLESS AVIATION"
1230   TITLE2$ = "WELCOMES YOU TO A WORLD OF FUN"
1240   WING$   = "BM165,96 L5"
1250 '
1260 ' ******************************
1270 ' *          DEFINE TABLES            *
1280 ' ******************************
1290 '
1300   DIM PLANE%(70)             'Table for airplane
1310   DIM CHUTE%(36)             'Table for parachute
1320   DIM PACK%(7)               'Table for pack
1999 '
2000 ' ******************************
2010 ' *          CONTROL MODULE           *
2020 ' ******************************
2030 '
2040   GOSUB 3000                 'Set Up Graphics Area
2050   GOSUB 4000                 'Draw Logo
```

PROGRAM 17.7 (continued)

```
2060    GOSUB 5000              'Get Images
2070    GOSUB 6000              'Animation
2080    GOSUB 7000              'Return Text Screen
2090    END
2999  '
3000  ' *******************************
3010  ' *     SET UP GRAPHICS AREA     *
3020  ' *******************************
3030  '
3040    KEY OFF
3050    SCREEN 1
3060    COLOR 1,0
3070    RETURN
3999  '
4000  ' *******************************
4010  ' *           DRAW LOGO          *
4020  ' *******************************
4030  '
4040    LOCATE 8,13
4050    PRINT TITLE1$
4060    DRAW PLANE$
4070    DRAW WING$
4080    PAINT (160,98),2,3
4090    DRAW CHUTE$
4100    PAINT (175,115),2,2
4110    CIRCLE (150,120),2,2
4120    LOCATE 20,6
4130    PRINT TITLE2$
4150    FOR PAUSE = 1 TO 2000 : NEXT PAUSE
4160    RETURN
4999  '
5000  ' *******************************
5010  ' *          GET IMAGES          *
5020  ' *******************************
5030  '
5040    GET (145,100)-(179,86),  PLANE%
5050    GET (165,126)-(179,110), CHUTE%
5060    GET (148,122)-(152,118), PACK%
5070    RETURN
5999  '
6000  ' *******************************
6010  ' *           ANIMATION          *
6020  ' *******************************
6030  '
6040    CLS
6050    CIRCLE (200,15),10          'Draw & paint the sun.
6060    PAINT (200,15),3
6070    DRAW GROUND$                'Draw & paint the ground.
6080    PAINT (55,180),1,3
6090  '
6100    FOR POSITION = 1 TO 7       'Start moving plane across the screen.
6110      X = POSITION * 17
6120      PUT (X,36),PLANE%         'Draw plane at current position.
6130      FOR PAUSE = 1 TO 600 : NEXT PAUSE
6140      PUT (X,36), PLANE%        'Remove plane from current position.
6150    NEXT POSITION
6160  '
6170    PUT (X+10,36),PLANE%        'Move plane and dump pack.
6180    PUT (X,50),PACK%
6190    FOR PAUSE = 1 TO 600 : NEXT PAUSE
6200    PUT (X+10,36),PLANE%        'Remove plane & pack.
6210    PUT (X,50),PACK%
```

PROGRAM 17.7   (continued)

```
6220    X1 = X                     'Set x coordinate for drop.
6230    Y = 60                     'Set y coordinate for drop.
6240 '
6250    FOR POSITION = 8 TO 16     'Finish moving plane and chute.
6260       X = POSITION * 17
6270       Y = Y + 10
6280       PUT (X,36),PLANE%       'Draw plane at current position.
6290       PUT (X1,Y),CHUTE%       'Draw chute at current position.
6300       FOR PAUSE = 1 TO 600 : NEXT PAUSE
6310       PUT (X,36),PLANE%       'Remove plane.
6320       PUT (X1,Y),CHUTE%       'Remove chute.
6330    NEXT POSITION
6340 '
6350    FOR PAUSE = 1 TO 1000 : NEXT PAUSE
6360    RETURN
6999 '
7000 ' *******************************
7010 ' *        RETURN TEXT SCREEN        *
7020 ' *******************************
7030 '
7040    SCREEN 0
7050    WIDTH 80
7060    KEY ON
7070    LOCATE 10,10 : PRINT "Program Finished"
7080    RETURN
```

FIGURE 17.19
Size of image array

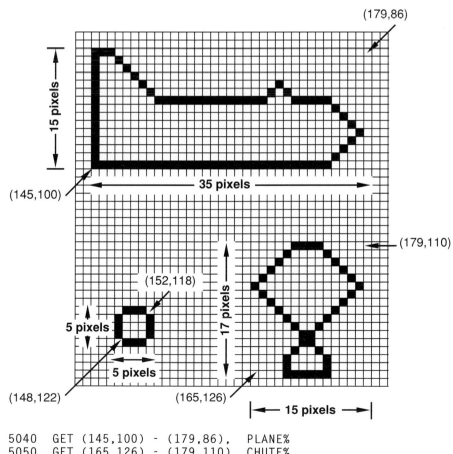

```
5040    GET (145,100) - (179,86),  PLANE%
5050    GET (165,126) - (179,110), CHUTE%
5060    GET (148,122) - (152,118), PACK%
```

Lines 5040–5060 of Program 17.7 represent the GET statements that store the rectangle containing the airplane, the pack, and the parachute. Lines 1300–1320 set the size of the arrays or tables that will hold the figures. You must reserve enough space to store the figure. The airplane is contained in a 35-by-15-pixel rectangle. By substituting these values into the formula, you get 139 as the number of bytes for the array PLANE%, which stores the airplane. See Figure 17.19. Likewise, the arrays CHUTE% and PACK% must contain 72 and 14 bytes, respectively. Because you are storing these images in integer arrays (and since an integer position can store 2 bytes) the dimensions are 70, 36, and 7, respectively.

PUT Statement

The PUT statement writes the colors of the pixels stored in an image array onto a defined area of the screen.

The standard form of the PUT statement is

```
[line#] PUT <(x,y)>, <variable name> [,action]
```

where:

(*x,y*)	are the coordinates of the upper left corner of the rectangle.
variable name	is the name of the array that is to be placed on the screen.
action	can be any of the following statements or logical operators:

1. PSET places the image on the screen.

2. PRESET is the same as PSET but reverses colors 0 and 3 and colors 1 and 2 from the active palette.

3. AND places the image at (*x,y*) only if some image is already there.

4. OR places an image at (*x,y*) without erasing the old image.

5. XOR is the default action. It places the image on the screen, or, if the same image is already there, then it erases the image.

The statement

```
5440   PUT (110,90), PIT%
```

places on the screen the figure stored in the integer array PIT%. The point (110, 90) is the upper left corner of the rectangle that contains the figure.

In Program 17.7, line 6120 puts the airplane on the screen. Line 6130 causes a brief pause, and line 6140 removes the plane. Line 6110 calculates a new x-coordinate, and the process is repeated. Lines 6170–6210 put the plane and pack on the screen and then remove them. Lines 6280–6320 put the plane and parachute on the screen and then remove them. This process is repeated until the plane moves off the screen and the parachute reaches the "ground."

Figure 17.20 shows the four images this program produces.

FIGURE 17.20
Four images produced by
Program 17.7

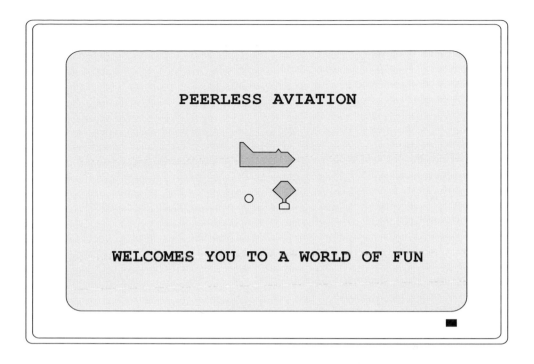

(1)

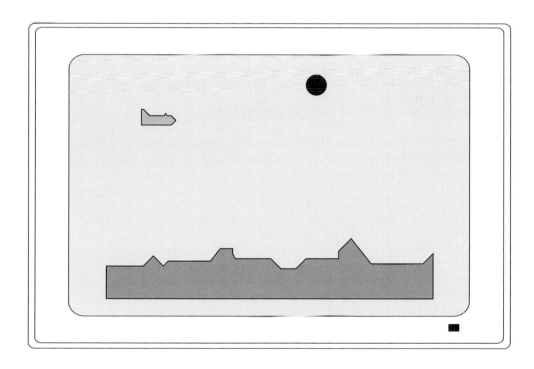

(2)

FIGURE 17.20
Four images produced by
Program 17.7
(continued)

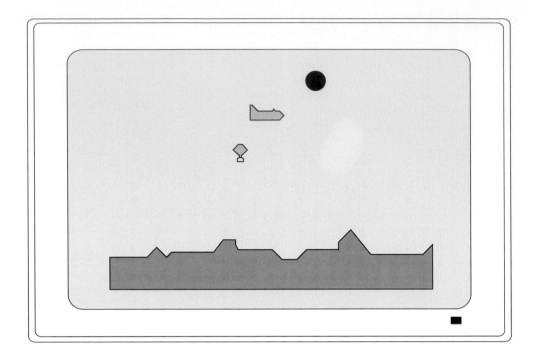

(3)

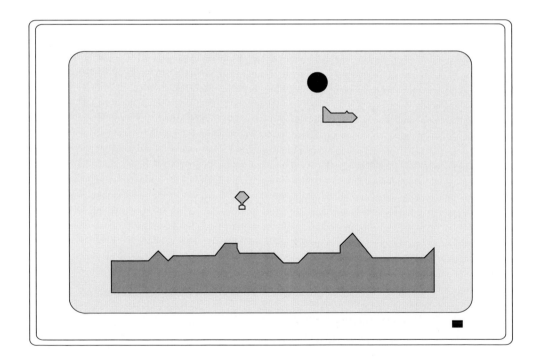

(4)

Summary

- Depending on your microcomputer's configuration, three types of display screen are available in BASIC.

  - SCREEN 0 is the standard 80-character text screen.

  - SCREEN 1 is the medium-resolution graphics screen.

  - SCREEN 2 is the high-resolution graphics screen.

- Any of the ASCII characters can be placed on SCREEN 0.

- SCREEN 0 and SCREEN 1 can have color capabilities, but SCREEN 2 does not.

- Any geometric figures—lines, circles, curves, rectangles, and so on—can be drawn on SCREEN 1 or SCREEN 2.

- Broken line graphs, bar graphs, and pie charts can be constructed using the graphics statements.

- To simplify graphing, use the WINDOW statement to change the coordinate system of SCREEN 1 and SCREEN 2.

- You can use the movement commands to construct designs and logos .

- You can use a GET statement to store a screen design in memory as an image array. You can animate a screen design by using successive PUT statements to place and remove the image array.

- Chapter 17 describes the following new BASIC statements.

CIRCLE	A statement that draws a circle, ellipse, or an arc given a center and a radius.
COLOR	A statement that selects the background color and a set of available foreground colors.
DRAW	A statement that executes a series of movement commands.
GET	A statement that retrieves a figure or design from the screen and saves it in memory as an image array.
LINE	A statement that draws a line between two points or that constructs a rectangle given two opposite corners.
PAINT	A statement that fills in the interior of a figure with color.
PSET	A statement that turns on a particular pixel (point) on the screen.
PUT	A statement that places a figure or design defined by an image array on the screen.
SCREEN	A statement that selects one of the three available screens for use.
WINDOW	A statement that redefines the screen coordinates.

Questions

1. What screens are generally available in BASIC?

2. How many rows and columns are available with SCREEN 0? With SCREEN 1? With SCREEN 2?

3. What kind of text can be used in the three different screens?

4. What are the hardware requirements for color graphics?

5. What are the default coordinate values for SCREEN 1 and SCREEN 2?

6. Fill in the blanks: The statement LOCATE X,Y refers to a position on the screen by its _____ value and then its _____ value. PSET(X,Y) refers to a position on the screen by its _____ value and then its _____ value.

7. What are the two major differences between SCREEN 1 and SCREEN 2?

8. How many pixels are required for a single character in SCREEN 1, WIDTH 40? In SCREEN 1, WIDTH 80?

9. How many pixels are required for a single character in SCREEN 2?

10. Name at least five geometric figures that can be drawn on the graphics screens.

11. Why do you need to scale most data before you can use them to construct a graph?

12. Does the COLOR statement select the actual colors used in a design? Explain.

13. When is the WINDOW statement useful?

14. Why is it necessary to use two trigonometric functions, SIN and COS, to plot the labels on a pie chart?

15. Movement commands are used in conjunction with the DRAW statement. Name at least eight of the commands and explain briefly what each does.

16. What is animation?

17. What is an image array?

18. What do the graphics GET and PUT statements do?

19. In which of the screens can you use the LO-CATE statement?

20. How would you save an image on the screen so that it can be used again later or just moved to another position?

Problems

1. Write the code to accomplish the following, using SCREEN 0 and WIDTH 40. Select an appropriate ASCII character(s).

   a. Draw horizontal lines across the screen at row 5 and row 20.
   b. Draw vertical lines up and down the screen at columns 5 and 35.
   c. Center a rectangle on the screen using the coordinates (10,10) and (15,30) as opposite corners of the rectangle.
   d. Print your first name centered in the rectangle.

2. Write the code to draw a tic-tac-toe grid centered in the following screens.

   a. SCREEN 0, WIDTH 40
   b. SCREEN 0, WIDTH 80
   c. SCREEN 1

3. Explain what the following program segments do.

   a.
   ```
   100 LOCATE 10,24
   110 PRINT CHR$(001)
   120 LOCATE 15,60
   130 PRINT CHR$(064)
   ```

   b.
   ```
   100 SCREEN 1
   110 LOCATE 10,20
   120 PRINT "BOX"
   130 LINE (50,100) - (80,140),,B
   ```

   c.
   ```
   100 SCREEN 1
   110 CIRCLE (120,100),50
   120 CIRCLE (120,100),25
   130 CIRCLE (120,100),15
   ```

   d.
   ```
   100 SCREEN 2
   110 WINDOW (0,200) - (600,0)
   120 LINE (150,250) - (60,40),,B
   130 CIRCLE (100,400),50
   ```

4. What are the coordinates of the corners of the screen when the following WINDOW commands are issued?

   a. `WINDOW (0,100) - (100,0)`
   b. `WINDOW (0,300) - (300,0)`
   c. `WINDOW (100,100) - (300,0)`
   d. `WINDOW (-100,100) - (100,0)`

5. Given the following code

   ```
   1000 SCREEN 1
   1010 WINDOW (0,200) - (300,0)
   1020 COLOR 1,2
   1030 PI = 3.141593
   ```

   describe what each of the following statements will produce.

   a. `1040 CIRCLE (75,80), 25,1`

   b. `1040 CIRCLE (75,80), 25,2,0,PI/2`

   c. `1040 CIRCLE (75,80), 25,3,PI,3*PI/2`

   d. `1040 LINE (50,50) - (70,70), 1`

   e. `1040 LINE (50,50) - (70,70), 2, B`

   f. `1040 LINE (50,50) - (70,70), 3, BF`

   g.
   ```
   1040 CIRCLE (100,100), 50,1
   1050 PAINT (110,110), 2,1
   ```

   h.
   ```
   1040 CIRCLE (100,100), 50,1
   1050 CIRCLE (100,100), 75,1
   1060 PAINT (110,110), 2,1
   1070 PAINT (160,160), 3,1
   ```

6. Write the code to draw the following figures on the screen. Use color if available.

   a.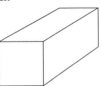

   b.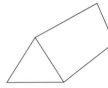

   c.

   d.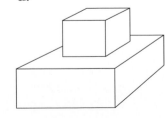

7. Using ASCII characters, place a border around the menu in Program 16.1, Chapter 16.

Program Assignments

1. Here is a random sample of the earnings per share of U.S. corporations reporting a first quarter 1990 operating profit:

```
.12  .31  .04  .28  .27 1.19  .96  .11  .02  .27  .33
.36 1.12  .45  .05  .19  .08  .12 1.11  .68  .52  .01
.48  .50  .35  .53  .10  .44  .13  .46  .05  .18  .96
.77  .56 1.21 1.05  .35  .47  .78  .19 1.25  .62 1.29
```

a. Write a program that counts the number of samples that fall into each of the following ranges listed below. Use DATA statements to store the earnings per share.

Range

```
0.00–0.14
0.15–0.29
0.30–0.44
0.45–0.59
0.60–0.74
0.75–0.89
0.90–1.04
1.05–1.19
1.20–1.34
```

b. Using text graphics, write a program to draw a bar graph indicating the number of samples in each range. In the same program, use text graphics to create a design that appears on the screen before and again after the bar graph appears. Incorporate the COLOR statement if possible.

2. Write a program that will place a border around the screen and then turn on 500 randomly selected pixels. Use the WINDOW command so that there are 300 positions across the screen and 200 positions down the screen. For each pixel, select a random integer between 0 and 300 as the horizontal position and a random integer between 0 and 200 as the vertical position. Once the coordinate is selected, turn the pixel on. If color is available, then plot the pixels in random colors. Use the RND (number) function to generate the random positions.

3. Given the following sales data in thousands of dollars

```
Division 1    920
Division 2    450
Division 3    780
Division 4    320
Division 5    830
```

write programs to do the following:

a. Produce a bar graph on SCREEN 0.
b. Produce a broken line graph on SCREEN 1.
c. Produce a bar graph on SCREEN 1.
d. Produce a pie chart on SCREEN 1.

Use colors, if available. If SCREEN 2 is available, write programs that use the high-resolution screen.

4. Write program modules to accomplish the following tasks. Use color if available. Label the output appropriately and include horizontal and vertical axes for the graphs in SCREEN 1.

a. Generate 200 integer values 0 through 9. Store the values in a table in memory. Count the number of times each integer appears in the table, i.e., how many 0's, how many 1's, and so on.
b. Draw a bar graph on SCREEN 0 to represent the number of occurrences of each integer. Scale the values if necessary.
c. Draw a bar graph on SCREEN 1 to represent the number of occurrences of each integer.
d. Draw a broken line graph on SCREEN 1 to represent the number of occurrences of each integer.
e. Chain the above modules together with a pause between them.

5. Write a program that places five stars on SCREEN 1 according to the following design. By assigning the stars the numbers 1 through 5, use a random number generator to make the stars blink on and off. Use GET and PUT statements, and not CLS.

6. Write a program that places a small car (approximately 20 pixels long and 10 pixels high) on the screen and then moves the car across the screen from left to right.

7. Write a program that moves a small rocket (approximately 5 pixels wide and 20 pixels long) from the lower left corner of the screen in an arc until it disappears at the upper right corner of the screen.

8. Write a program that draws the following logo centered on the screen. Keep the logo on the screen for approximately 10 seconds, then clear the screen and randomly move the logo around the screen. The logo should blink on and off at two-second intervals. The logo should always remain completely on the screen, i.e., you should always see all of it when it blinks on, not just part of it.

Using the Data Disk

1. Insert the data disk into the disk drive.

2. At the prompt type GRAPHICS

```
A> GRAPHICS
```

3. Load BASIC (change the default drive if necessary).

4. Use the PRINT statement with CHR$(002) to draw a square in text mode. Set the screen to a width of 40 columns.

5. Enter the following statements:

```
100   SCREEN 1
110   COLOR 1,0
120   CLS
200   PSET (50,60),0
210   PSET (51,61),1
220   PSET (52,62),2
230   PSET (53,63),3
```

   a. Run the program.

   b. Change the COLOR statement to COLOR 1,1 and run the program again.

   c. Add the following statements:

```
300   LINE (1,50) - (1,100),0
310   LINE (20,50) - (20,100),1
320   LINE (40,50) - (40,100),2
330   LINE (60,50) - (60,100),3
```

   d. Run the program.

   e. Change the COLOR statement to COLOR 7,0 and run the program again.

   f. Add the following statement to the program:

```
400   LINE (100,50) - (200,100),2,B
```

   g. Run the program.

   h. Change the B parameter to BF in statement 400 and run the program.

   i. Add the following statement to the program:

```
500   CIRCLE (280,160),10,1
```

   j. Run the program.

   k. Add the following statement to the program:

```
510   PAINT (280,160),2,1
```

   l. Run the program.

   m. Save the program as CH17-3.DD

6. Use the DRAW statement to display a box. Add a PAINT statement to color the box. Change the code so that the box is painted with a color and then erased (return the interior of the box to the background color) 10 times. Save the program as CH17-4.DD.

7. Load program CH17-1.DD

    a. List the program.

    b. Predict what the program will display.

    c. Run the program.

    d. Make a screen dump of the display to the printer.

    e. Press any key to return to SCREEN 0.

    f. List the program.

    g. Add the following lines to the program:

```
1090   CIRCLE (160,100), 90, 1
1100   PAINT (260,100), 1, 1
```

    h. Run the program.

    i. Change line 1040 to:

```
1040   COLOR 5, 0
```

    j. Run the program.

    k. Make a screen dump of the display to the printer.

    l. Save the program as CH17-5.DD.

8. Load program CH17-2.DD.

    a. Run the program.

    b. Make a screen dump of the display to the printer.

    c. Press any key to return to SCREEN 0.

    d. Add the following lines to the program.

```
1005   RANDOMIZE
1055   COLOR , 0
1085   C = INT((RND * 10) / 3)
1155   C = INT((RND * 10) / 3)
1225   C = INT((RND * 10) / 3)
1295   C = INT((RND * 10) / 3)
```

    e. Change lines 1090, 1160, 1230, and 1300 to

```
1090   LINE (20,Y) - (X,170), C
1160   LINE (X,170) - (300,Y), C
1230   LINE (300,Y) - (X,30), C
1300   LINE (X,30) - (20,Y), C
```

    f. Run the program.

    g. Make a screen dump of the display on the printer.

    h. Save the program as CH17-6.DD.

Appendix A

BASIC Reserved Words

Words marked with an asterisk are reserved words in versions 2.0 and later but not in earlier versions.

ABS	DELETE	INT	OPEN	SOUND
AND	DIM	*INTER$	OPTION	SPACE$
ASC	DRAW	*IOCTL$	OR	SPC(
ATN	EDIT	KEY	OUT	SQR
AUTO	ELSE	*KEY$	PAINT	STEP
BEEP	END	KILL	PEEK	STICK
BLOAD	*ENVIRON	LEFT$	PEN	STOP
BSAVE	*ENVIRON$	LEN	PLAY	STR$
CALL	EOF	LET	*PMAP	STRIG
CDBL	EQV	LINE	POINT	STRING$
CHAIN	ERASE	LIST	POKE	SWAP
*CHDIR	*ERDEV	LLIST	POS	SYSTEM
CHR$	*ERDEV$	LOAD	PRESET	TAB(
CINT	ERL	LOC	PRINT	TAN
CIRCLE	ERRR	LOCATE	PRINT#	THEN
CLEAR	ERROR	LOF	PSET	TIME$
CLOSE	EXP	LOG	PUT	*TIMER
CLS	FIELD	LPOS	RANDOMIZE	TO
COLOR	FILES	LPRINT	READ	TROFF
COM	FIX	LSET	REM	TRON
COMMON	FNxxxxxxxx	MERGE	RENUM	USING
CONT	FOR	MID$	RESET	USR
COS	FRE	*MKDIR	RESTORE	VAL
CSNG	GET	MKD$	RESUME	VARPTR
CSRLIN	GOSUB	MKI$	RETURN	VARPTR$
CVD	GOTO	MKS$	RIGHT$	*VIEW
CVO	HEX$	MOD	*RMDIR	WAIT
CVS	IF	MOTOR	RND	WEND
DATA	IMP	NAME	RSET	WHILE
DATE$	INKEY$	NEW	RUN	WIDTH
DEF	INP	NEXT	SAVE	*WINDOW
DEFDBL	INPUT	NOT	SCREEN	WRITE
DEFINT	INPUT#	OCT$	SGN	WRITE#
DEFSNG	INPUT$	OFF	*SHELL	XOR
DEFSTR	INSTR	ON	SIN	

DOS and EDLIN Commands

Your computer's disk operating system (DOS) is a group of programs that help you use your computer. DOS has its own vocabulary of commands, which you must master to use the operating system effectively. This appendix is an explanation of the commands used most often. When you are ready to use other commands, study your DOS reference manual or an MS/PC-DOS guidebook.

One of the programs DOS provides is a line editor, a type of editor that allows you to edit just one line at a time. This one is called, appropriately, EDLIN. EDLIN is handy for creating and editing text files. For a brief introduction to EDLIN see the end of this appendix.

STARTING DOS

You must run the DOS program named COMMAND.COM before you can do anything else with DOS or run any other programs. To run it, insert a disk containing COMMAND.COM in your default drive (drive C if you have a fixed disk, or the top or left drive, if you have two removable disk drives) and turn on the computer. Instructions in the computer's permanent memory cause the computer to search the default disk for COMMAND.COM and automatically run the program.

After the COMMAND.COM program is loaded in the computer's memory, the computer may prompt you to enter the date and time. (See the following discussion of DATE and TIME.) Then the DOS prompt appears on the screen. It is usually either A> or C>.

Sometimes your computer may "hang up" and do nothing at all in response to your entries from the keyboard. If so, you may be able to restart without turning the computer off. To do that, make sure the COMMAND. COM program is in the default drive and press the Ctrl, Alt, and Del keys simultaneously. This process is called a *warm boot*. If nothing happens then, you will have to turn the computer off and start over. (*Caution:* Some systems require that you wait several seconds before turning your computer on again. Check your instruction manual.)

Before you begin to study the specifics of using DOS, note that DOS does not distinguish between uppercase and lowercase letters. Thus, you may enter any DOS command all in uppercase, all in lowercase, or in any mixture of the two. The DOS commands are capitalized here only to make them stand out as you read them.

INTERNAL AND EXTERNAL COMMANDS

The code to execute some DOS commands is included in the COMMAND.COM program. These commands are called *internal* commands because they are always available in the computer's memory.

External commands have their own individual programs, so they must be accessible (on your fixed drive or on a diskette in the computer). The external commands described later in this appendix are DISKCOPY, FORMAT, and PRINT.

DESIGNATING DISK DRIVES

DOS uses letters to designate disk drives. For example, A refers to the system's default floppy disk drive, B to a second drive, C to a third, and so on. The letters may also refer to fixed (or hard) disks and memory disks; C is always used to refer to the primary fixed disk if there is one in the system.

You can change the default drive after running the COMMAND.COM program. At the DOS prompt, enter the letter designation for another drive followed by a colon. DOS changes the default drive and reminds you that it has been changed by displaying a new prompt, as these lines illustrate:

```
C>A:
A>
```

DIRECTORIES

Every disk has a main directory called the *root* directory. DOS automatically creates the root directory when it formats a new disk. You must create any other directories you decide to use. The symbol for the root directory is the backslash (\).

Directories are most useful on hard disks because these drives can contain thousands of files. You can think of directories as subdivisions of a disk and use them as you might use the various sections of a file cabinet. You could create directories for DOS, BASIC, your word processor, spreadsheet, data base, and other applications programs.

Each directory can have subdirectories, and those subdirectories can have subdirectories. For example, your word processor directory might have subdirectories for letters, reports, different projects, or any other group of documents you want to keep together.

Reference a directory by specifying the path that leads to it. A path is a list of directory names separated by backslashes. All paths begin at the root directory. The path to your word processor might be \wp, and the path to its subdirectories might be \wp\letter, \wp\report, and so on.

Several DOS commands help you use directories. Three of them are described in the "DOS Commands" section of this appendix. MKDIR creates a directory. RMDIR removes an empty directory. CHDIR changes from one default directory to another. Another command, PROMPT, allows you to change the prompt so that it displays not just the default drive but also the path to the default directory.

SPECIFYING FILES

Programs, data, letters—anything you store on a disk—must be stored in a file. You reference files by providing a file specification, a term abbreviated here and in DOS manuals as *filespec*.

A filespec begins with a drive designation referring to the drive where the file is located. Specify the drive by using the letter of the drive followed by a colon. If you omit a drive designation, DOS uses the current default drive. The second part of the file specification is a path. If you omit the path, DOS uses the current directory for the specified or default drive.

The remainder of the filespec is the file name. Every file must have a name. File names may have two parts. The first part may be 1 to 8 characters long and can contain any of these characters:

A–Z a–z 0–9 $ & # @ ! % ` ' ( ) - { } _ ^ ~

The second part of the name is called the extension. It is optional but, when present, consists of a period followed by 1 to 3 characters. All characters allowed in file names are allowed in extensions. You must include the extension when referring to a file that has an extension, but you can create a file without one.

Just as file names usually describe the contents of a file, file extensions usually describe the type of file. Here is a list of commonly used extensions.

.BAS	A BASIC program file.
.COM	Short for *command*; denotes a compiled program that you can run by entering the file name.
.EXE	Short for *executable*; like .COM, denotes a compiled program that you can run by entering the file name.
.BAK	Refers to *backup*; EDLIN and some word processors automatically create a file with this extension when you save a file after editing it.
.BAT	Stands for *batch* file; these files contain DOS commands that are executed when you run the file. You run a batch file by entering its file name.
.SEQ	Used in this text to refer to a *sequential* file.
.TXT	Another common extension for sequential files; refers to *text* files and the fact that they contain only characters in ASCII format.
.RND	Used in this text to refer to *random* or *direct-access* files.

Here are some examples of valid file specifications:

```
a:\command.com          c:\basic\prog1.bas
format.com              SAM
B:INVENTORY.SEQ         {^}.1
```

Global file name or *wildcard characters* can be useful when you specify file names. There are two such characters, ? and *. The ? in a file name or extension tells DOS that any character can occupy the position of the question mark. The * indicates that any character can occupy not only the position of the asterisk but also all the remaining positions in the file name or the extension. For examples illustrating how these characters can be helpful, see the discussion of the DIR command, later in this appendix.

DOS COMMANDS

This section introduces the most useful DOS commands. Many of the commands can be used in ways not described here. See your DOS manual to learn more about them.

CHDIR

Use the CHDIR command to change the default directory. Enter the command followed by the path to the new directory, as in this example:

```
C>CHDIR\BASIC
```

There is also a short form of the command, CD. This command produces the same result as the one in the previous example:

```
C>CD\BASIC
```

Entering the command

```
C>CD\
```

always returns you to the root directory.

The command CD.. takes you to the parent directory. For example, if the current directory is \BASIC, entering CD.. makes the root directory the default directory.

You can move to a subdirectory of the current directory without specifying a path. If the current directory is \WP, entering CD LETTER makes \WP\LETTER the current directory.

CLS

The CLS command does the same thing as the BASIC command of the same name: It clears the screen and displays the prompt in the upper left corner of the screen.

COPY

You can use the COPY command in several ways. The first one you need to learn is how to copy files from one disk to another. This is the general form for that command:

```
COPY <from-file> <to-file>
```

For example,

```
COPY a:prog1.bas  c:\basic\prog1.bas
```

copies the file prog1.bas from the disk in drive A to the basic directory on the fixed drive, C. You can get the same results by typing this shorter command:

```
COPY a:prog1.bas  c:\basic
```

There are two other handy uses of COPY. You need to know that DOS uses the letters CON to refer to the keyboard and the characters LPT1 to refer to the first printer connected to your machine. With this knowledge you can use COPY to write text at the keyboard and send it to the printer:

```
COPY CON LPT1
```

CON tells the system to get its input from the keyboard, and LPT1 tells it to send the output to the printer.

When you try this, notice that the text you enter does not go to the printer immediately. You must end the "file" first. To do that, you must press the Ctrl and Z keys simultaneously so that the last line of text contains the Ctrl-Z value. You can also enter the Ctrl-Z value by pressing the F6 key.

Use this version of COPY to send the contents of a sequential or text file to the printer:

```
COPY <filespec> LPT1
```

The following command creates a disk file directly from the keyboard:

```
COPY CON <filespec>
```

After entering the contents of the file, press F6 to end the file and write the contents to the disk.

When you need to copy several files, you may be able to avoid entering the file names one at a time by using the global file name characters with the COPY command.

DATE

The DATE command allows you to check or set the system date. If you enter the word DATE, the DOS response will be similar to this:

```
C>DATE
Current date is Fri 1-19-1990
Enter new date:

C>
```

If you do not enter a new date, as in this example, DOS skips a line, displays its prompt, and leaves the system date unchanged. If you want to change the date, enter it in *mm-dd-yy* format. You can enter all four digits of the year, if you wish, and you can use slashes instead of dashes.

When you start your computer, be sure to set the system date to the current date. Every time you create or revise a file, DOS records the date. That information can be very useful, but if it is always the system's default date, it won't do you much good.

DEL

The DEL command produces the same results as the ERASE command does. If you use ERASE rather than DEL, you are less apt to inadvertently type DEL for DIR and thereby erase one or more files by mistake.

DIR

Use the DIR command to list the information the system keeps about the files on your diskettes. If you enter DIR and nothing else, the system shows a complete listing of all information about the files in the default drive and directory. To obtain that listing for a disk in another drive, add a drive designation; for example,

```
C>DIR B:
```

To get the listing for another directory, specify a path, like this:

```
C>DIR \WP\LETTERS
```

You can use two optional parameters with this command. Often the list of files is too long to fit on the 25 lines of the screen. Use the /P parameter to display the list one screenful at a time:

```
C>DIR \BASIC /P
```

Alternatively, use the /W parameter to display a listing of just the file names and extensions in five columns on the screen:

```
C>DIR /W
```

This form of the command displays over 100 file names on a single screen.

You can use global file name characters with the DIR command. Suppose you have a series of BASIC programs on a diskette in drive B and you want to check which ones are there. If the programs are PROG-A.BAS, PROG-B.BAS, and so on, use the following entry to display information about all of the files in that series, including any backup files:

```
C>DIR B:PROG-?.*
```

Now suppose you want to display the directory information about all files in the default drive whose names begin with F and end with the extension .SEQ. Use the command

```
DIR F*.SEQ
```

DISKCOPY

DISKCOPY is an external command. You can use it only if you have a disk with the file DISKCOPY.COM in your computer.

DISKCOPY allows you to duplicate the contents of a diskette in one drive onto a diskette in a second drive. It also formats the second diskette if necessary.

The command

```
A>DISKCOPY A: B:
```

makes the disk in drive B a duplicate of the disk in drive A.

You cannot use DISKCOPY to copy a disk of one size to a disk of another size. For example, you cannot copy from a 5.25-inch disk to a 3.5-inch disk.

ERASE

ERASE removes files from a disk. Enter ERASE followed by a file specification. For example,

```
ERASE ASSIGN4.BAS
```

removes the file ASSIGN4.BAS from the disk in the default drive.

You can use the global file name characters with ERASE, but, be extremely cautious if you do use them! It is very easy to erase a file accidentally when you use the global characters.

FORMAT

FORMAT is an external DOS command. You must have the file FORMAT.COM on a disk in your computer before you can run FORMAT.

A new disk is similar to an unlined blank piece of paper in that it has no reference system. When you format a disk, you install the reference system DOS uses to tell one part of the disk from another part. The general form of the FORMAT command is

```
C>FORMAT [d:][/S][/V]
```

If you enter the command FORMAT A: with neither of the other two parameters, the system will respond in this way:

```
C>FORMAT A:
Insert new diskette for drive A:
and strike any key when ready
```

After you insert the diskette and press a key, formatting begins. Formatting takes a while, so be patient. When formatting is complete, your disk is ready to use.

Although the instructions tell you that the disk you format should be new, it need not be. You can format a disk over and over again, even though doing so serves no purpose. You may, however, wish to reuse old diskettes for another purpose; formatting them removes all the old files and directory data. Be careful when you format a used disk because all data on that disk are erased completely!

You can use the /S parameter with FORMAT to put the system files, including COMMAND.COM, on the disk you are formatting. Do this when you want to make a disk that you can use to boot the computer.

Before DOS lists the contents of a directory, it tells you the label on the disk. (If you want to check the label of a disk at other times, use the VOL command.) The /V parameter allows you to label a disk. After formatting is complete, DOS asks you to enter the label and tells you that it can be up to 11 characters long.

The following is an example of a screen display during the process of formatting a disk:

```
C>FORMAT B:/S/V
Insert new diskette for drive B:
and strike any key when ready

Formatting...Format complete
System transferred

Volume label (11 characters, ENTER for none)? BOOTDISK

   362496 bytes total disk space
    40960 bytes used by system
   321536 bytes available on disk

Format another (Y/N)?N
C>
```

Caution! Formatting a hard disk makes all the files on that disk inaccessible. *Never* enter FORMAT at a C> prompt unless you follow the command with another drive designation or you really intend to reformat the hard disk.

MKDIR

MKDIR creates a new directory. To use it, simply enter the command or its short form, MD, followed by the appropriate path, as this example illustrates:

```
C>MD \BASIC
```

If you do not enter a path, DOS creates the new directory in the current default directory. For example, assume \WP is the default directory. The command

```
C>MD LETTER
```

creates a directory named LETTER in the \WP directory.

PRINT

PRINT is an external command. You can use it only if you have a disk with a copy of PRINT.COM in your computer.

You can use PRINT to print a file (on the printer) at the same time you are using the computer to do something else. You use PRINT by entering the command name followed by a file specification, as in this example:

```
C>PRINT \BASIC\PROG-08.BAS
```

PROMPT

The PROMPT command allows you to change the DOS prompt. The command

```
PROMPT $P$G
```

changes the prompt so that both the default drive and the default directory are displayed. For example, instead of C>, the prompt might be

```
C:\BASIC>
```

RENAME

The RENAME command allows you to rename a file. Its form is:

```
RENAME <oldname> <newname>
```

You can type REN instead of RENAME and get the same result.

RMDIR

Use the RMDIR command to remove an *empty* directory by entering

```
RMDIR path
```

You cannot remove the root directory or the current directory.

TIME

The TIME command allows you to check or set the system time. If you enter the word TIME, DOS responds with this sequence:

```
A>TIME
Current time is 22:19:07.53
Enter new time:

A>
```

If you do not enter a new time, as in this example, DOS skips a line, displays its prompt, and leaves the system time unchanged. If you want to change the time, enter it in the format *hh:mm:ss.tt*. The seconds and hundredths of seconds are optional entries.

You may find the date records that DOS keeps in the disk directories more useful than the the time records, but, if you want them to be accurate, be sure that the current time is set whenever you start your computer.

TYPE

Use TYPE to display the contents of a file on the screen; simply enter the command TYPE followed by a file specification. If you want to stop the display of a large file before the end of the file, hold down the Ctrl key and press either the C key or the Break key.

VOL

Use the VOL command to learn the label on a disk. The form is

```
A>VOL d:
```

where *d*: refers to a drive designation.

EDLIN, THE DOS LINE EDITOR

EDLIN is an external DOS program, and for this reason it must be on a disk in one of your system's drives. Start the program with an entry like this:

```
A>EDLIN B:filename.ext
```

The file specification refers either to a file you want to edit or to one you want to create. EDLIN loads the file into memory, if the file exists. If it does not exist, EDLIN assumes that you are going to create a file by that name. Follow this simple example to learn how to create and modify a file using EDLIN.

Creating a File

You will create a sequential file of inventory records. Each record will contain an item name followed by a quantity number. Start EDLIN with this entry:

```
A>EDLIN B:INVEN.SEQ
New file
*
```

Notice that EDLIN responds with the comment that INVEN.SEQ is a new file because it was not on the disk in drive B. It then displays its prompt, an asterisk.

Next, you must tell EDLIN that you want to insert records into the file. You do that with the command I, for insert. (Most EDLIN commands are single letters.) When you enter I, EDLIN displays a line number followed by a colon and an asterisk, all indented from the original prompt:

```
*I
    1:*
```

Immediately after the asterisk, enter each line you want in the file. Assume you enter these four lines:

```
    1:*clips,398
    2:*pins,402
    3:*pots,33
    4:*tacks,519
    5:*^C
  *
```

EDLIN provides the new line number prompt each time you press the Enter key. When you have entered all the records (four, in this case) you need to return to the main prompt; do that by entering Ctrl-C (or Ctrl-Break) on a new line.

Saving a File

To save your newly created file you need only enter an E (for exit), and EDLIN writes the file from memory to the file specification you listed when you called EDLIN. This also ends your EDLIN editing session. If you want to do more, you must start EDLIN again.

Examining a File

EDLIN's L (for list) command displays up to 23 lines on the screen. If you enter L and nothing else, EDLIN displays 23 lines beginning 11 lines before the current line and ending 11 lines after the current line.

You can move from one line of text to another by specifying the number of the line you want to edit. Assume that you have just directed EDLIN to load B:INVEN.SEQ into memory and have listed the file's contents:

```
A>EDLIN B:INVEN.SEQ
End of input file
*L

        1:*clips,398
        2: pins,402
        3: pots,33
        4: tacks,519
```

The display is different this time. EDLIN's message "End of input file" indicates that there was room in memory for the entire file. The single asterisk indicates that the first line is the current line.

Editing a Line

To change a line, enter the line number. For example, if you enter 3, EDLIN makes line 3 the current line and displays the following:

```
    *3

        3:*pots,33
        3:*
```

The cursor is located just after the asterisk in the last line of the display, ready for you to enter the line in its new form. Suppose the correct number of pots in inventory is 38. Retype the line, replacing 33 with 38, and press Enter. The function keys F1 and F3 can help in the editing of a line. Pressing F1 duplicates the character above the cursor and pressing F3 duplicates the entire line. After you press the Enter key, EDLIN displays the asterisk prompt and awaits your next instruction.

Adding a Line

To add lines, enter the number of the line where the new data should appear and the letter I.' After EDLIN responds, enter the new lines. When they are all entered, press Ctrl-C to exit the insert mode. For example, the following display would appear as you add a record for mugs as the new second line in the sample file and then list the revised file:

```
    *2I
        2:*mugs,12
        3:*^C

    *L
        1: clips,398
        2: mugs,12
        3:*pins,402
        4: pots,38
        5: tacks,519
    *
```

Deleting a Line

To delete a line, simply enter the number of the line you want to delete followed by the letter D. For example, enter 2D to delete line 2. You can delete a range of lines by entering two numbers separated by a comma and followed by D; for example, enter 3,6D to delete lines 3 through 6.

Search and Replace

To replace all occurrences of a string with another string, enter the following:

```
[start#],[end#][?]Rstring1[ctrl-Zstring2]
```

The two numbers tell EDLIN which lines to search. If you omit the numbers, the search starts with the line following the current line and ends with the last line in memory.

The replacement of *string*1 with *string*2 is automatic unless you use the optional ? parameter. Use the ? parameter if you want to decide on an instance-by-instance basis which occurrences of *string*1 to change.

The R is the command symbol. *String*1 begins with the character immediately following the R, even if it is a space. *String*1 ends with the last character before the Ctrl-Z. *String*2 begins with the first character after the Ctrl-Z and ends with the last character before Enter.

This entry would change all names in INVEN.SEQ from plural to singular:

```
*1,5Rs<ctrl-Z>,
```

Quitting

If you want to leave EDLIN without writing the file back to the disk, enter Q. EDLIN asks if you want to abort the edit and waits for your confirmation before returning you to the DOS prompt.

Other Commands

There is more to learn about EDLIN than the commands described here, but you know enough to do basic work with files. If you want to explore other EDLIN commands, consult your DOS manual.

Appendix C

ASCII Character Codes

The following table lists all the ASCII codes (in decimal) and their associated characters. These characters can be displayed using PRINT CHR$($n$), where n is the ASCII code. The column headed "Control Character" lists the standard interpretations of ASCII codes 0 to 31 (usually used for control functions or communications).

Each of the characters can be entered from the keyboard by pressing and holding the Alt key, then pressing the digits for the ASCII code on the numeric keypad. Note, however, that some of the codes have special meaning to the BASIC Program Editor. It uses its own interpretation for the codes and may not display the special character listed here.

ASCII Value	Character	Control Character	ASCII Value	Character	Control Character
000	(null)	NUL	016	►	DLE
001	☺	SOH	017	◄	DC1
002	☻	STX	018	↕	DC2
003	♥	ETX	019	!!	DC3
004	♦	EOT	020	¶	DC4
005	♣	ENQ	021	§	NAK
006	♠	ACK	022	▬	SYN
007	(beep)	BEL	023	↨	ETB
008	■	BS	024	↑	CAN
009	(tab)	HT	025	↓	EM
010	(line feed)	LF	026	→	SUB
011	(home)	VT	027	←	ESC
012	(form feed)	FF	028	(cursor right)	FS
013	(carriage return)	CR	029	(cursor left)	GS
014	♫	SO	030	(cursor up)	RS
015	☼	SI	031	(cursor down)	US

ASCII Value	Character	ASCII Value	Character	ASCII Value	Character
032	(space)	079	O	126	~
033	!	080	P	127	⌂
034	''	081	Q	128	Ç
035	#	082	R	129	ü
036	$	083	S	130	é
037	%	084	T	131	â
038	&	085	U	132	ä
039	'	086	V	133	à
040	(	087	W	134	å
041	)	088	X	135	ç
042	*	089	Y	136	ê
043	+	090	Z	137	ë
044	,	091	[	138	è
045	-	092	\	139	ï
046	.	093	]	140	î
047	/	094	∧	141	ì
048	0	095	—	142	Ä
049	1	096	`	143	Å
050	2	097	a	144	É
051	3	098	b	145	æ
052	4	099	c	146	Æ
053	5	100	d	147	ô
054	6	101	e	148	ö
055	7	102	f	149	ò
056	8	103	g	150	û
057	9	104	h	151	ù
058	:	105	i	152	ÿ
059	;	106	j	153	Ö
060	<	107	k	154	Ü
061	=	108	l	155	¢
062	>	109	m	156	£
063	?	110	n	157	¥
064	@	111	o	158	Pt
065	A	112	p	159	ƒ
066	B	113	q	160	á
067	C	114	r	161	í
068	D	115	s	162	ó
069	E	116	t	163	ú
070	F	117	u	164	ñ
071	G	118	v	165	Ñ
072	H	119	w	166	ª
073	I	120	x	167	º
074	J	121	y	168	¿
075	K	122	z	169	⌐
076	L	123	{	170	¬
077	M	124	¦	171	½
078	N	125	}	172	¼

ASCII Value	Character	ASCII Value	Character	ASCII Value	Character
173	¡	201	╔	229	σ
174	«	202	╩	230	μ
175	»	203	╦	231	τ
176		204	╠	232	Φ
177	▒	205	═	233	Θ
178	▓	206	╬	234	Ω
179	│	207	╧	235	δ
180	┤	208	╨	236	∞
181	╡	209	╤	237	Ø
182	╢	210	╥	238	∈
183	╖	211	╙	239	∩
184	╕	212	╘	240	≡
185	╣	213	╒	241	±
186	║	214	╓	242	≥
187	╗	215	╫	243	≤
188	╝	216	╪	244	⌠
189	╜	217	┘	245	⌡
190	╛	218	┌	246	÷
191	┐	219	█	247	≈
192	└	220	▄	248	°
193	┴	221	▌	249	•
194	┬	222	▐	250	·
195	├	223	▀	251	√
196	─	224	α	252	ⁿ
197	┼	225	β	253	²
198	╞	226	Γ	254	■
199	╟	227	π	255	(blank 'FF')
200	╚	228	Σ		

File Transfers between BASIC and Popular Software Packages

Topics

- dBASE files   ⟵⟶   BASIC files
- Lotus files   ⟵⟶   BASIC files

Often you may want to use a data file from one software package in another one or in a BASIC program. If your data file is in Lotus format (or in the format of any other software package), you can change that file to ASCII format, the format of a BASIC sequential file, and use it in BASIC programs. Similarly, if you have a BASIC file in ASCII format, you can transfer its data to any of the popular software packages that accept ASCII data. This chapter describes techniques for these data transfers; it does not attempt to explain the use of any application programs.

If the data to be transferred to one of the application packages reside in a BASIC random-access file, then you must first convert the random-access file to a sequential file.

dBASE FILES TO BASIC FILES

Throughout this discussion, dBASE refers to both dBASE II, dBASE III, and dBASE III+. To learn how to convert dBASE to BASIC, consider a dBASE file with the structure shown in Figure D.1. If you list the file, you will see that it contains the records shown in Figure D.2. The first five-digit field is a record number supplied by dBASE and is not part of the data that you will transfer.

A dBASE file contains not only the data but also the structure for the file, that is, field names, lengths, and types. This structure is at the beginning of the file and should not be transferred to the BASIC file with the data.

To transfer the file, you need to do the following:

1. Make sure that you are in dBASE.

2. Call the file up for use by issuing the command.

```
.USE INVENTOR
```

You don't need to enter the extension .DBF.

3. Issue the following command to copy the contents (data items only) of the file:

```
.COPY TO INVENTOR.SEQ DELIMITED WITH "
```

This command copies only the data in the dBASE file INVENTOR.DBF to the file named INVENTOR.SEQ. The DELIMITED WITH parameter causes the COPY command to bypass the file structure during the copying routine. The double quotation marks in the command cause character data to be enclosed within double quotation marks and fields to be separated by commas.

Now, exit from dBASE to the system. At the system prompt, issue the command:

```
TYPE INVENTOR.SEQ
```

```
. use inventor
. display structure
Structure for database: B:inventor.dbf
Number of data records:      11
Date of last update   : 09/09/88
Field  Field Name  Type       Width     Dec
    1  STOCK       Character      4
    2  DESCRIPT    Character     20
    3  ON_HAND     Numeric        4
    4  COST        Numeric        6        2
    5  PRICE       Numeric        7        2
** Total **                      42

.
Command Line     <B:> INVENTOR              REC: 1/11              Num
                 Enter a dBASE III PLUS command.
```

FIGURE D.1　　Structure of the dBASE file INVENTOR.DBF

You should see the file displayed as in Figure D.3. Notice that it is in the same form as a BASIC sequential file.

```
    .
    .
    .
    .
. list all
Record #  STOCK DESCRIPT          ON_HAND   COST   PRICE
        1  8010  Coil Wire              15   1.75    3.45
        2  8011  Coil                    8  23.65   49.99
        3  9020  Carburetor              4  47.12  129.95
        4  7650  Antenna                12  12.95   25.99
        5  5000  Lock Out Hubs           3 218.55  519.99
        6  6010  Ring Gear               6  29.45   79.98
        7  3030  289 Engine Block        1 365.75  989.55
        8  3040  409 Engine Block        2 429.65 1085.85
        9  4041  Tachometer              4  65.42  149.95
       10  4052  CB Radio 415           19  89.95  198.99
       11  4065  Seat Cover             15  12.59   39.95
.
Command Line      <B:> INVENTOR          REC: EOF/11        Num

        Enter a dBASE III PLUS command.
```

FIGURE D.2   Records in the dBASE file INVENTOR.DBF

```
A>TYPE INVENTOR.SEQ
"8010","Coil Wire",15,1.75,3.45
"8011","Coil",8,23.65,49.99
"9020","Carburetor",4,47.12,129.95
"7650","Antenna",12,12.95,25.99
"5000","Lock Out Hubs",3,218.55,519.99
"6010","Ring Gear",6,29.45,79.98
"3030","289 Engine Block",1,365.75,989.55
"3040","409 Engine Block",2,429.65,1085.85
"4041","Tachometer",4,65.42,149.95
"4052","CB Radio 415",19,89.95,198.99
"4065","Seat Cover",15,12.59,39.95

A>
```

FIGURE D.3   Listing of the file transferred from the dBASE file

BASIC FILES TO dBASE FILES

For this conversion, use the following sequential data file, TRANSACT.SEQ. It is a transaction file for a checking account. The file contains the following data:

```
"D","3426","ABC Industries",678.54
"C","1902","First Federal",523.45
"C","1934","D&H Hardware",34.95
"C","1925","Union Oil",78.34
"C","1978","Wilder Shopping Center",39.45
"C","1894","American Heart Assoc.",10.00
"C","2003","Kmart",45.39
"C","1981","Amax Motors",205.55
"D","3427","Newmont Gold",887.45
"C","1976","Grant Medical Clinic",129.50
"C","2005","Cash",100.00
"C","1880","Shirley's IGA",50.00
"C","1903","Penny's",19.79
"C","1996","Sierra Pacific Power",56.89
"C","2010","Debbie Nelson",150.50
```

The first field is the type of transaction, the second is the transaction number, the third is the payee or deposit source, and the last is the transaction amount.

Before you can transfer data into dBASE, you need to create a dBASE file whose structure matches the arrangement of the data in the BASIC file. The above data require four fields; the first three contain character data, and the last contains numeric data. The first three fields should be 1, 4, and 25 characters long, respectively. The numeric field requires a maximum of eight positions including two decimal places.

Take the following steps to convert the BASIC file TRANSACT.SEQ to a dBASE file called TRANSACT.DBF.

1. Load dBASE.

2. Create the dBASE file TRANSACT.DBF so that it has the structure shown in Figure D.4.

3. Answer no to the dBASE prompt asking if you want to enter the data now. (You need not enter the data from the keyboard.)

4. Issue the following command:

   ```
   APPEND FROM TRANSACT.SEQ DELIMITED
   ```

   The parameter DELIMITED tells dBASE that the character fields are delimited with double quotes and that commas separate all fields. The dBASE message "00015 records added" tells you that the dBASE file now contains the data.

When you list the database file, you should see the records as they are displayed in Figure D.5. You can treat this file like any other dBASE file; you can edit records, append new ones, and prepare reports.

LOTUS 1-2-3 FILES TO BASIC FILES

Transferring files from Lotus 1-2-3 to BASIC is slightly more difficult than from dBASE. The transfer utility that comes with Lotus cannot be used to transfer Lotus files directly to ASCII files. Although you could transfer Lotus files to dBASE files and then convert the dBASE files to ASCII, this is not really desirable because to do so you must run dBASE and create a temporary holding file with the proper structure.

The best way to convert a Lotus data file to an ASCII file is to use the Lotus PRINT FILE command, which allows you to print the worksheet to a disk file in ASCII format. One problem with this technique is that the

```
. display structure
Structure for database: B:transact.dbf
Number of data records:        0
Date of last update   : 09/09/88
Field  Field Name  Type       Width    Dec
    1  TRANS_TYPE  Character       1
    2  TRANS_NO    Character       4
    3  TRANS_COM   Character      25
    3  TRANS_AMT   Numeric         8      2
** Total **                       39

.
Command Line    <B:> TRANSACT              REC: None              Num

             Enter a dBASE III PLUS command.
```

FIGURE D.4   Structure of the dBASE file TRANSACT.DBF

```
. append from transact.seq delimited with "
     15 records added
. list all
Record #  TRANS_TYPE TRANS_NO TRANS_COM               TRANS_AMT
       1  D          3426     ABC Industries             678.54
       2  C          1902     First Federal              523.45
       3  C          1934     D&H Hardware                34.95
       4  C          1925     Union Oil                   78.34
       5  C          1978     Wilder Shopping Center      39.45
       6  C          1894     American Heart Assoc.       10.00
       7  C          2003     Kmart                       45.39
       8  C          1981     Amax Motors                205.55
       9  D          3427     Newmont Gold               887.45
      10  C          1976     Grant Medical Clinic       129.50
      11  C          2005     Cash                       100.00
      12  C          1880     Shirley's IGA               50.00
      13  C          1903     Penny's                     19.79
      14  C          1996     Sierra Pacific Power        56.89
      15  C          2010     Debbie Nelson              150.50

.
Command Line    <B:> TRANSACT              REC: EOF/15            Num

             Enter a dBASE III PLUS command.
```

FIGURE D.5   Records in the dBASE file TRANSACT.DBF

individual fields in each line in the print file are not separated by commas, and character data are not enclosed in double quotes. The spacing is retained, however, and so the different fields can be distinguished. A short BASIC utility program can convert this print file to a comma-separated value file (CSV file).

To learn how this conversion works, use the same inventory worksheet that you used with dBASE; in Lotus it will be called INVENTOR.WK1. (In Lotus, the extension .WK1 is used for all worksheet files, and the extension .PRN is used for all print files.) The Lotus 1-2-3 display is shown in Figure D.6.

If you save the whole display as a print file, you get the titles and the two columns, T_COST and T_RETAIL, which do not need to be included in the print file. To avoid this, create a print file of the part of the worksheet in the cell range A3–E13 and save it under the name INVENTL.PRN. To do so, issue the following series of commands within Lotus 1-2-3.

```
/PRINT, FILE, INVENTL, RANGE, A3..E13, OPTIONS, MARGINS,
          TOP, 0, QUIT, GO, QUIT
```

Exit from Lotus to DOS and use the TYPE command to see what the file looks like. See Figure D.7.

To separate the values into a record that contains comma-separated values, two short BASIC programs utilizing the string functions will do the job.

Program D.1 reads a single record from INVENTL.PRN and prints its length. This is necessary since you need to know the length of each field.

```
A14: [W6]                                                    MENU
Worksheet  Range  Copy  Move  File  Print  Graph  Data  System  Quit
Global, Insert, Delete, Column, Erase, Titles, Window, Status, Page
      A            B          C        D       E        F        G
 1  STOCK      DESCRIPTION   ON HAND  COST    PRICE   T_COST   T_RETAIL
 2  =================================================================
 3    8010  Coil Wire          15     1.75     3.45    26.25     51.75
 4    8011  Coil                8    23.65    49.99   189.20    399.92
 5    9020  Carburetor          4    47.12   129.95   188.48    519.80
 6    7650  Antenna            12    12.95    25.99   155.40    311.88
 7    5000  Lock Out Hubs       3   218.55   519.99   655.65   1559.97
 8    6010  Ring Gear           6    29.45    79.98   176.70    479.88
 9    3030  289 Engine Block    1   365.75   989.55   365.75    989.55
10    3040  409 Engine Block    2   429.65  1085.85   859.30   2171.70
11    4041  Tachometer          4    65.42   149.95   261.68    599.80
12    4052  CB Radio 415       19    89.95   198.99  1709.05   3780.81
13    4065  Seat Cover         15    12.59    39.95   188.85    599.25
14
15
16
17
18
19
20
09-Sep-88  10:39 AM                                       NUM
```

FIGURE D.6   Lotus display for the file INVENTOR.DBF

```
A>TYPE INVENTL.PRN
     8010 Coil Wire                15      1.75      3.45
     8011 Coil                      8     23.65     49.99
     9020 Carburetor                4     47.12    129.95
     7650 Antenna                  12     12.95     25.99
     5000 Lock Out Hubs             3    218.55    519.99
     6010 Ring Gear                 6     29.45     79.98
     3030 289 Engine Block          1    365.75    989.55
     3040 409 Engine Block          2    429.65   1085.85
     4041 Tachometer                4     65.42    149.95
     4052 CB Radio 415             19     89.95    198.99
     4065 Seat Cover               15     12.59     39.95


A>
```

FIGURE D.7   Data in the file INVENTL.PRN

PROGRAM D.1

```
1000 ' PROGRAM D-1
1010 '
1020 ' OPEN FILE
1030 '
1040 OPEN "INVENTL.PRN" FOR INPUT AS #1
1050 '
1060 ' INPUT A RECORD
1070 '
1080 INPUT #1, A$
1090 '
1100 ' PRINT THE LENGTH OF THE RECORD AND THE RECORD
1110 '
1120 PRINT LEN(A$)
1130 PRINT "123456789 123456789 123456789 123456789 123456789 123456789 "
1140 PRINT A$
1150 '
1160 ' CLOSE FILE & END
1170 '
1180 CLOSE #1
1190 END
```

Running the program with the file produces the output shown in Figure D.8. You can tell from Figure D.8 that the first field in file INVENTL.PRN is in columns 1–5, the second is in columns 6–25, the third is in columns 26–32, the fourth is in columns 33–41, and the fifth is in columns 42–50. These values are needed in the string functions you will use in the following program.

Program D.2 converts the Lotus 1-2-3 print file INVENTL.PRN to the comma-separated value file INVENTL.SEQ.

PROGRAM D.2

```
1000 ' PROGRAM D-2
1010 ' OPEN FILES
1020 '
1030 OPEN "INVENTL.PRN" FOR INPUT AS #1
1040 OPEN "INVENTL.SEQ" FOR OUTPUT AS #2
1050 '
1060 ' CONVERT DATA AND REWRITE FILE
1070 '
```

PROGRAM D.2
(continued)

```
1080 WHILE NOT EOF(1)
1090     INPUT #1,A$
1100     STOCK = VAL(LEFT$(A$,5))
1110     DESC$ = MID$(A$,6,20)
1120     QUAN  = VAL(MID$(A$,26,7))
1130     COST  = VAL(MID$(A$,34,9))
1140     PRICE = VAL(RIGHT$(A$,9))
1150     WRITE #2,STOCK,DESC$,QUAN,COST,PRICE
1160 WEND
1170 '
1180 ' CLOSE FILES & END
1190 '
1200 CLOSE #1,#2
1210 END
```

From BASIC, execute Program D.2. Return to DOS and list the file INVENTL.SEQ. You will see the data file as it appears in Figure D.9. Notice that the length of the second field is 20 characters in all of the records. This fact affects neither the data in the file, nor the use of the file in a BASIC program. You can, however, add a routine to Program D.2 to delete the trailing spaces.

```
Ok
run
 50
123456789 123456789 123456789 123456789 123456789 123456789
8010 Coil Wire              15     1.75     3.45
Ok
```

FIGURE D.8 Output of Program D.1

```
A>TYPE INVENTL.SEQ
8010,"Coil Wire          ",15,1.75,3.45
8011,"Coil               ",8,23.65,49.99
9020,"Carburetor         ",4,47.12,129.95
7650,"Antenna            ",12,12.95,25.99
5000,"Lock Out Hubs      ",3,218.55,519.99
6010,"Ring Gear          ",6,29.45,79.98
3030,"289 Engine Block   ",1,365.75,989.55
3040,"409 Engine Block   ",2,429.65,1085.85
4041,"Tachometer         ",4,65.42,149.95
4052,"CB Radio 415       ",19,89.95,198.99
4065,"Seat Cover         ",15,12.59,39.95

A>
```

FIGURE D.9 Listing of the file INVENTL.SEQ

BASIC FILES TO LOTUS FILES

Use the BASIC file TRANSACT.SEQ to demonstrate transferring files from BASIC to Lotus. Recall that the file contains three character fields and one numeric field. The first record in the file is:

```
"D","3426","ABC Industries",678.54
```

You can use the File Import utility to bring this file into Lotus. The utility brings a print file from disk storage and superimposes it at a specified location in the current worksheet. You can import just text, just numbers, or both numbers and text that are enclosed in double quotes.

When you transfer a file to Lotus, the File Import utility requires that the file have the extension .PRN. Since the sequential file has the extension .SEQ, you must rename it before using File Import, as follows:

```
A>RENAME TRANSACT.SEQ TRANSACT.PRN
```

To transfer this file to Lotus, follow these steps:

1. Load Lotus 1-2-3

2. When the worksheet screen appears, position the cursor in cell A1 or in any cell at which you want the worksheet to start.

3. Enter the following series of commands:

```
/,File,Import,Numbers,TRANSACT
```

The result will be the spreadsheet shown in Figure D.10.

```
A1: 'D                                                            READY


         A        B        C        D        E        F        G        H
    1    D        3426     ABC Indus  678.54
    2    C        1902     First Fed  523.45
    3    C        1934     D&H Hardw   34.95
    4    C        1925     Union Oil   78.34
    5    C        1978     Wilder Sh   39.45
    6    C        1894     American    10.00
    7    C        2003     Kmart       45.39
    8    C        1981     Amax Moto  205.55
    9    D        3427     Newmont G  887.45
   10    C        1976     Grant Med  129.50
   11    C        2005     Cash       100.00
   12    C        1880     Shirley's   50.00
   13    C        1903     Penny's     19.79
   14    C        1996     Sierra Pa   56.89
   15    C        2010     Debbie Ne  150.50
   16
   17
   18
   19
   20
   10-Sep-88  03:51 PM                                       NUM
```

FIGURE D.10 Lotus spreadsheet for the file TRANSACT.PRN

Notice that the text items in column C are truncated. If you expand the width of column C to 25 characters, the data will appear in full. While in Lotus do the following:

1. Position the cursor at column C.

2. Type the following series of commands:

```
/,Worksheet,Column,Set-Width,25
```

The resulting worksheet is shown in Figure D.11.

If you want to transfer a BASIC file containing both character data and numeric data to Lotus, you must separate the data with commas and enclose the character data in double quotes. For example, if the record in the BASIC sequential file is

```
C,3449,Charles Greenhaw,375.95
```

you can either transfer only the numbers to the worksheet or transfer the entire record as a string of text. Neither of these is acceptable since you want to transfer all the data in a form that can be used in the worksheet. The data must be in a comma-separated value format (CVS) for the transfer to work properly.

```
C1: [W25] 'ABC Industries                                           READY


         A       B                 C              D        E       F
    1  D      3426    ABC Industries            678.54
    2  C      1902    First Federal             523.45
    3  C      1934    D&H Hardware               34.95
    4  C      1925    Union Oil                  78.34
    5  C      1978    Wilder Shopping Center     39.45
    6  C      1894    American Heart Assoc.      10.00
    7  C      2003    Kmart                      45.39
    8  C      1981    Amax Motors               205.55
    9  D      3427    Newmont Gold              887.45
   10  C      1976    Grant Medical Clinic      129.50
   11  C      2005    Cash                      100.00
   12  C      1880    Shirley's IGA              50.00
   13  C      1903    Penny's                    19.79
   14  C      1996    Sierra Pacific Power       56.89
   15  C      2010    Debbie Nelson             150.50
   16
   17
   18
   19
   20
   10-Sep-88  03:52 PM                                      NUM
```

FIGURE D.11   Lotus spreadsheet for TRANSACT.PRN with the width of column C set to 25

Debugging and Testing

The process of error removal, usually called *debugging*, is the first topic of this appendix. It also contains suggestions for te*sting* programs to help you determine when your code has problems and when it is doing what it is supposed to do.

The removal of errors from your code deserves as much attention as does the original design of a program. This attention to error removal is important not just because errors must be removed if the code is to work right but also because the error rate associated with debugging is very high. On the average, the correction of two errors results in the generation of a new error, a much higher rate than in new program coding.

Debugging and testing may never be as exciting as original coding, but they will be much less frustrating and time consuming if you are systematic in correcting mistakes in your code. The suggestions that follow will help you do that.

ERROR TYPES

Two types of errors, syntax errors and logic errors, appear in programs. A *syntax error* is caused by a misspelling or a violation of BASIC's rules for statement structure. A *logic error* is a mistake in a program algorithm that causes, under at least some conditions, the program to produce incorrect output.

When the BASIC interpreter detects a syntax or logic error, it displays a message reporting its interpretation of the problem. Table E.1 lists the more common error messages and explains what they mean.

CORRECTING ERRORS

Syntax errors are the easier of the two types to find and correct because BASIC displays each line in which one occurs. If you do not spot the error in the line immediately, check each word carefully for misspellings. If you find

Table E.1   Some of BASIC's Error Messages

Error Message	Comment
Bad file mode	Possible problems: A PUT or GET statement referenced a sequential or closed file. An OPEN statement executed with a file mode other than input, append, or random. An attempt to merge a file not in ASCII format.
Bad file number	Possible problems: The referenced file number is not open or is out of the range of specified file numbers. The device name in the file specification is too long or invalid. The file name itself is too long or invalid.
Can't continue	It is impossible to use CONT with a program because of an error, because the program was changed during the break in execution, or because the program is not loaded.
Can't continue after shell	While in the shell, a program remained resident in memory, preventing BASIC from recovering its workspace. Restart BASIC.
Device timeout	BASIC did not receive information from an input/output device (usually your printer) within its allowed time. Make sure that all cables are connected and that the device is turned on.
Direct statement in file	BASIC encountered a direct statement during a loading or chaining operation. This terminates the operation. If you are loading a program when this happens, you can list it to see where the program stopped loading.
Disk full	The disk that BASIC is trying to write to is full. Either use a new disk or erase some unneeded files from the full disk.
Disk not ready	Possible problems: The disk drive door is open. There is no disk in the drive.
Division by zero	After this message appears, the program continues running.
Duplicate definition	BASIC attempted to define the size of an array twice. Possible causes: The same array is defined in two DIM statements. A DIM statement for an array is encountered after BASIC has already established the default dimension (10) for that array. An OPTION BASE statement appears after BASIC has dimensioned an array.
Field overflow	Possible problems: A FIELD statement requested more bytes for the record length of a random file than were specified in the OPEN statement. The end of the FIELD buffer was encountered during sequential I/O to a random file.
File already exists	The file name in a NAME command duplicates the name of a file already on the disk.
File already open	Open a file only once as you write to it sequentially.
File not found	See that the file specification in the program matches the physical file name and its location.
FOR without NEXT	A FOR has no matching NEXT.
Illegal function call	Possible problems: An out-of-range parameter was passed to a system function. A subscript is negative or too large. There are instructions to raise a negative number to a power that is not an integer. A GET or PUT contains a negative record number. An argument to a function or statement is incorrect (such as TAB (5)). The user attempts to list or edit a protected BASIC program. The user tries to delete line numbers that do not exist.
Incorrect DOS version	The DOS command requires a different version of DOS than the one currently running.
Input past end	An INPUT# statement was executed after all the data in a sequential file were already read.
Internal error	An internal malfunction occurred in BASIC. Check your hardware. Try another copy of BASIC.
Line buffer overflow	A user attempted to enter a line with too many characters.
Missing operand	An expression contains an operator (AND, +, etc.) with no operand following it.
NEXT without FOR	A NEXT has no matching FOR.
Out of data	A READ statement tried to read more data than are in a program's DATA statements.

Table E.1 Some of BASIC's Error Messages (continued)

Error Message	Comment
Out of memory	A program is too large, has too many FOR loops or GOSUBs, too many variables, expressions that are too complicated, or painting that is too complex. Try using CLEAR at the beginning of the program to set aside more stack space or a larger memory area.
Out of paper	The printer is out of paper or is not on.
Out of string space	There is no more space to allocate for string variables.
Overflow	A number is too large to be represented in the BASIC number type being used. (Only integer overflow stops execution.)
Path/file access error	During an OPEN, RENAME, MKDIR, CHDIR, or RMDIR operation, the program referenced an inaccessible file or path. The operation is not completed.
Path not found	During an OPEN, MKDIR, CHDIR, or RMDIR operation, the program referenced a nonexistent path. The operation is not completed.
?Redo from start	You have responded to INPUT with too many or too few items, or with the wrong type value (letters instead of numbers).
RETURN without GOSUB	A RETURN statement has no matching GOSUB.
String formula too complex	A string expression is too long or too complex. Break it into shorter expressions.
String too long	A string exceeds 255 characters.
Subscript out of range	A table element has a subscript outside the dimensions of the table or with the wrong number of subscripts.
Syntax error	The BASIC editor automatically displays the line with the error, ready to be corrected.
Too many files	Possible causes: A program tried to create a new file (using SAVE or OPEN) but all directory entries on the disk were full. The file specification is invalid.
Type mismatch	A string data type is expected when a numeric type appears or vice versa.
Undefined line number	A program referenced a nonexistent line.
Undefined user function	A program referenced a function before the function had been defined with a DEF FN statement.
Unprintable error	An error was detected for which BASIC had no appropriate error message.
WEND without WHILE	A WEND has no matching WHILE.
WHILE without WEND	A WHILE has no matching WEND.
You cannot SHELL to Basic	BASIC cannot be run as a child process. Key EXIT.

none, look up the statement format in your text or in the BASIC manual, and make sure that the line conforms to BASIC's requirements.

Figure E.1 contains examples of BASIC's responses to two syntax errors, one a misspelling and the other an incorrect statement format. In the first case, the error is the misspelling of the word INPUT. When BASIC displays the line, notice that the cursor is under the first quotation mark, at the start of the first term following the error.

The format error in the second example is the omission of a colon separating the two statements in the THEN clause. Again, the cursor immediately follows the error; this time it is under the G in GOSUB.

Logic errors are more difficult to remove, because you must find them before you can correct them. If you develop and test your programs one module at a time, most errors will be confined to the new code. If your modules perform a single function, they will seldom be complicated or long, and finding errors and correcting them usually will be easy.

To deal with logic errors, begin by reviewing the pseudocode and structure chart to confirm that your program design is correct. If you find no

FIGURE E.1
BASIC's response to syntax
errors
(highlighted underscores
show cursor location)

Syntax Error Caused by Misspelling

```
1080   INPIT "Enter your name:   ", USER.NAME$
RUN
Syntax error in 1080
Ok
1080   INPIT "Enter your name:   ", USER.NAME$
```

Syntax Error Caused by Incorrect Format

```
1130   INPUT "Enter your age:   ", AGE
          .     .     .     .

2370   IF AGE >= 18 THEN PRINT "Adult"   GOSUB 6000
RUN
Enter your age:   23
Adult
Syntax error in 2370
Ok
2370 IF AGE >= 18 THEN PRINT "Adult"   GOSUB 6000
```

errors, compare the BASIC code with the logic documents. Try simulating the steps the computer will take in executing your program as you evaluate your logic. If you find that the code is not a faithful implementation of your design, rewrite the incorrect BASIC statements. However, if the errors still elude you, you will have to go hunting for them.

There are two helpful approaches to tracking down program errors. One is to use BASIC's trace facility. When the trace is turned on (TRON), BASIC displays the line number of each statement as it is executed. Figure E.2A shows an example trace of a code segment. The trace shows that the WHILE statement is executed but that the loop is never entered. Such a situation suggests a false value for the Boolean expression. In this example the expression will always be false; to correct it, insert NOT before the EOF(1) function in line 3930.

Another way to follow what is happening in a program is to use PRINT statements to trace the value of the program's variables. By printing the contents of variables, you can see how the program is changing them.

Figure E.2B illustrates this technique. The output of the PRINT statements (lines 2831 and 2861) inserted in the code indicates two problems: (1) The variable SCORE has not been assigned a value by the user when line 2830 is executed, and (2) the terminating value is being counted as a score.

FIGURE E.2
Tracing program execution

A. BASIC's trace facility

```
2230   OPEN "SMALL.SEQ" FOR INPUT AS #1
3920   CTR = 1
3930   WHILE EOF(1)
3940      INPUT #1, VALUE
3950      CTR = CTR + 1
3960   WEND
5870   PRINT CTR
TRON
Ok
RUN
[2230][3920][3930][5870] 1
Ok
```

FIGURE E.2
(continued)

B. Tracing with PRINT statements

```
1140   N = 0              ' Counter for number of scores entered
1150   TOTAL = 0       ' Accumulator for scores
2830   WHILE SCORE >= 0
2831 PRINT "Score"; N; "is";  SCORE  ' Temporary debugging line
2840      INPUT "Enter a score; negative number to quit:  ", SCORE
2850      TOTAL = TOTAL + SCORE
2860      N = N + 1
2861 PRINT "Score"; N; "is";  SCORE  ' Temporary debugging line
2870   WEND
2880   AVERAGE = TOTAL / N
2890   PRINT "The average of the"; N; "scores is"; AVERAGE
RUN
Score 0 is 0
Enter a score (negative number to quit):  89
Score 1 is 89
Score 1 is 89
Enter a score (negative number to quit):  90
Score 2 is 90
Score 2 is 90
Enter a score (negative number to quit):  -1
Score 3 is -1
The average of the 3 scores is 59.33333
Enter a score (negative number to quit):  -1
Score 4 is-1
The average of the 4 scores is 67.25
```

You can correct these problems by adding a priming INPUT statement and moving the INPUT statement in the loop so that it is the last line before the WEND. The revised code looks like this:

```
1140   N = 0              ' Counter for number of scores entered
1150   TOTAL = 0       ' Accumulator for scores
2820   INPUT "Enter a score (negative number to quit):  ",   SCORE
2830   WHILE SCORE >= 0
2840      TOTAL = TOTAL + SCORE
2850      N = N + 1
2865      INPUT "Enter a score (negative number to quit): ", SCORE
2870   WEND
2880   AVERAGE = TOTAL / N
2890   PRINT "The average of the"; N; "scores is"; AVERAGE
```

PROGRAM TESTING

So far, this discussion has focused on errors that are relatively obvious. Another important part of program development is testing the program to discover unobserved errors. A single set of sample data will be insufficient to unearth errors in all but the most trivial of programs. A good set of test data must be constructed systematically. Select data that will:

1. Exercise every THEN and ELSE in the program

2. Produce no passes as well as multiple passes through each loop

3. Include both valid and invalid values

To recognize the importance of testing all the possible choices in an IF statement, look again at the second example in Figure E.1. If the code were tested only with an age less than 18, the BASIC interpreter would not examine the THEN clause in 2370, and the programmer might assume that line 2370 was error free.

FIGURE E.3
An error when the loop is bypassed

```
1140   N = 0
1150   TOTAL = 0          ' Accumulator for scores
2820   INPUT "Enter a score; less than 0 to quit:  ", SCORE
2830   WHILE SCORE > 0
2840      N = N + 1
2850      TOTAL = TOTAL + SCORE
2860      INPUT "Enter a score; less than 0 to quit:  ", SCORE
2870   WEND
2880   AVERAGE = TOTAL / N
2890   PRINT "The average of the"; N; "scores is"; AVERAGE
Ok
RUN
Enter a score; negative number to quit:  -9
Division by zero
The average of the 0 scores is 1.701402E+38
Ok
```

Testing code with data that produce no passes through a loop may seem unnecessary; after all, the code in the loop is ignored, so how can an error turn up? To see what can happen with such a test, look at Figure E.3.

When a user enters a negative score in response to the prompt in line 2820, BASIC bypasses the loop and executes line 2880. Since N was set to 0 in line 1140, the division in line 2880 is zero divided by zero. An IF-THEN-ELSE statement in line 2880 would be an appropriate way to avoid this problem:

```
2880   IF N <> 0
              THEN AVERAGE = TOTAL / N
              ELSE PRINT "Error:  Value of divisor is zero"
```

Figure E.4 contains an example of a loop with an error that becomes evident only after more than one pass through the loop. In this case, the problem is a logic error: SCORE is used in lines 2850 and 2880 where TOTAL should be.

The following code and sample run illustrate the importance of testing with invalid data:

```
6030   INPUT "Enter the client's age:  ", AGE
7110   PRINT "The client's age is"; AGE
RUN
Enter the client's age:  seventeen
?Redo from start
Enter the client's age:
```

This can serve as a reminder to have your programs get all numeric input from users as strings and test the validity of the entry before assigning it to a numeric variable.

AVOIDING ERRORS

The best debugging technique is prevention. Code written in the United States for commercial applications averages two to four errors per 100 lines. You can do better if you follow the structured programming techniques presented in this text. In particular, strive to have all of the following be characteristic of your programs:

1. Understandable code with meaningful names, a readable format, and cohesive modules

2. Careful planning with structure charts and pseudocode

3. A preference for clear algorithms instead of clever ones

One Pass

```
LIST
1130   INPUT "Enter the number of tests: ", NUMBER.OF.TESTS
1140   TEST.NUMBER = 1
1150   TOTAL = 0          ' Accumulator for scores
2830   WHILE TEST.NUMBER <=  NUMBER.OF.TESTS
2840       INPUT "Enter a score:  ", SCORE
2850       SCORE = TOTAL + SCORE
2860       TEST.NUMBER = TEST.NUMBER + 1
2870   WEND
2880   AVERAGE = SCORE / NUMBER.OF.TESTS
2890   PRINT "The average of the"; NUMBER.OF.TESTS; "scores is"; AVERAGE
Ok
RUN
Enter the number of tests:  1
Enter a score:  98
The average of the 1 scores is 98
Ok
```

Two Passes

```
LIST
1130   INPUT "Enter the number of tests: ", NUMBER.OF.TESTS
1140   TEST.NUMBER = 1
1150   TOTAL = 0          ' Accumulator for scores
2830   WHILE TEST.NUMBER <=  NUMBER.OF.TESTS
2840       INPUT "Enter a score:  ", SCORE
2850       SCORE = TOTAL + SCORE
2860       TEST.NUMBER = TEST.NUMBER + 1
2870   WEND
2880   AVERAGE = SCORE / NUMBER.OF.TESTS
2890   PRINT "The average of the"; NUMBER.OF.TESTS; "scores is"; AVERAGE
Ok
RUN
Enter the number of tests:  2
Enter a score:   98
Enter a score:   100
The average of the 2 scores is 50
Ok
```

FIGURE E.4   A loop error evident only after more than one pass

The alternative to structured code is confusing code. If you lean in that direction, consider this advice from James McKelvey:

> A confused reader [of your program] is not likely to say, "Gosh, this is so complicated you must be a genius to understand it. How would you like a raise?" A more likely response is, "This program is so contorted and incomprehensible we'll never be able to maintain it. How good are you at filing and making coffee?"[1]

[1]*Debugger's Handbook*. Wadsworth Publishing Co. (Belmont, Calif. 1987), p. 39.

Sample Program Documentation

DOCUMENTATION FOR PROGRAM 4.1
(LIRE CONVERSION)

Programmer: Gail Yim
Bank of Glencoe

Date: 4 November 1990

```
Documentation for                                    Page 2
Program 4.1
```

PROGRAM DESCRIPTION

This program converts U.S. dollars to Italian lire. The input to the program is the dollar amount entered by the bank clerk. The output displayed is the current exchange rate, the lira equivalent, the charge for the conversion, and the total lire to be issued to the customer. The conversion charge is 5% of the lira equivalent.

INPUT

The input to the program is the dollar amount the customer wants to convert. This amount is entered by the user. There is a $999 limit on the amount that may be converted.

OUTPUT

The program displays the current exchange rate, the lira equivalent, the charge for conversion, and the total lire to be given to the customer. The screen design is illustrated on the following form:

Keyed by user

	1–10	11–20	21–30	31–40	41–50	51–60
01	Enter dollar amount		= ###			
02	Current exchange rate		= ####			
03						
04	Lire	#######				
05	Charge	- #######				
06						
07	Total lire	#########				
08						

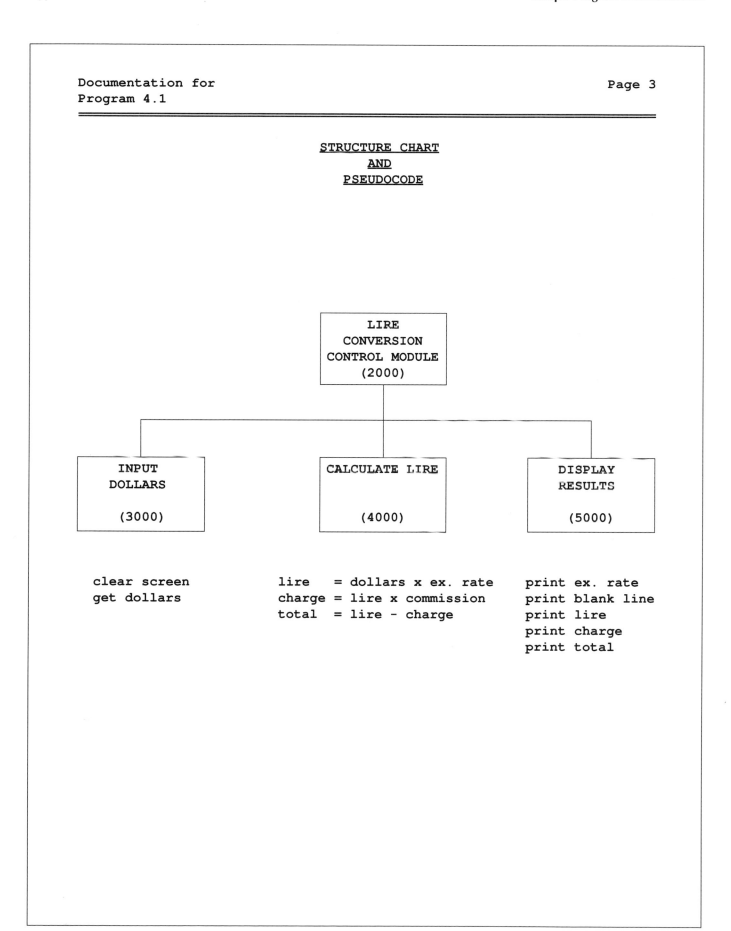

STRUCTURE CHART
AND
PSEUDOCODE

```
                    ┌─────────────────┐
                    │      LIRE       │
                    │   CONVERSION    │
                    │ CONTROL MODULE  │
                    │     (2000)      │
                    └─────────────────┘
```

INPUT DOLLARS (3000)	CALCULATE LIRE (4000)	DISPLAY RESULTS (5000)

```
clear screen          lire   = dollars x ex. rate   print ex. rate
get dollars           charge = lire x commission     print blank line
                      total  = lire - charge         print lire
                                                      print charge
                                                      print total
```

```
Documentation for                                    Page 4
Program 4.1
========================================================
```

SAMPLE RUN

```
        Enter dollar amount      = 500
        Current exchange rate    = 1280

        Lire              640000
        Charge          -  32000
        --------------------
        Total lire        608000
```

OPERATING PROCEDURES

1. Turn on the computer.
2. Select LIRE CONVERSION from the menu.
    (Enter 1 and press the Enter key)
3. The following prompt appears on the screen:

        Enter dollar amount   =

4. Enter the dollar amount requested by the customer.
5. Possible problems:

    a. The MESSAGE "?Redo from start" appears on the screen.

        You have entered a nonnumeric character. Reenter the
        amount pressing digits only. Be careful not to enter a
        dollar sign ($).

    b. The result is printed in exponential notation. For
        example: 1.28E+07

        You have entered a value larger than $999. Restart the
        program and enter another amount.

```
Documentation for                                        Page 5
Program 4.1

===============================================================


Program 4.1 listing

1000 ' PROG4-1
1010 ' *****************************
1020 ' *        LIRE CONVERSION        *
1030 ' *****************************
1040 '
1050 ' *****************************
1060 ' *          VARIABLES           *
1070 ' *****************************
1080 '
1090 ' CHARGE                  Charge for conversion
1100 ' DOLLARS                 Dollar amount entered by user
1110 ' LIRE                    Lira equivalent to dollar amount
1120 ' TOTAL                   LIRE - CHARGE
1130 '
1140 ' *****************************
1150 ' *          CONSTANTS           *
1160 ' *****************************
1170 '
1180   COMMISSION       = .05     '5% charge for conversion
1190   LIRE.PER.DOLLAR = 1280     'Exchange rate as of 5/21/88
1999 '
2000 ' *****************************
2010 ' *       CONTROL MODULE         *
2020 ' *****************************
2030 '
2040   GOSUB 3000                 'Input Dollars
2050   GOSUB 4000                 'Calculate Lire
2060   GOSUB 5000                 'Display Results
2070   END
2999 '
3000 ' *****************************
3010 ' *         INPUT DOLLARS        *
3020 ' *****************************
3030 '
3040   CLS
3050   INPUT "Enter dollar amount    = ", DOLLARS
3060   RETURN
3999 '
4000 ' *****************************
4010 ' *        CALCULATE LIRE        *
4020 ' *****************************
4030 '
4040   LIRE   = DOLLARS * LIRE.PER.DOLLAR
4050   CHARGE = LIRE * COMMISSION
4060   TOTAL  = LIRE - CHARGE
4070   RETURN
4999 '
5000 ' *****************************
5010 ' *        DISPLAY RESULTS       *
5020 ' *****************************
5030 '
5040   PRINT "Current exchange rate   ="; LIRE.PER.DOLLAR
5050   PRINT
5060   PRINT "Lire          "; LIRE
5070   PRINT "Charge       -"; CHARGE
5080   PRINT "--------------------"
5090   PRINT "Total lire    "; TOTAL
5100   RETURN
```

DOCUMENTATION FOR PROGRAM 6.1
(LOWELL and BAUER CLIENT LISTING)

Programmer: David Ryan
DDS, Inc.

Date: 17 September 1990

```
Documentation for                                          Page 2
Program 6.1
═══════════════════════════════════════════════════════════════
```

PROGRAM DESCRIPTION

This program produces a printed listing of Lowell and Bauer's clients.
Input to the program is from the firm's sequential client data file.

INPUT

The names of the firm's clients are read from the sequential client data
file, CLIENT.SEQ; the file is maintained on disks labeled "Client Data"
and "Client Data—BackUp". Each record in the file has the following
fields:

Field Name	Length	Data Type
CLIENT.ACCT$	3	String
CLIENT.NAME$	20	String

OUTPUT

The program prints a listing of names of the firm's clients. The report
design is illustrated in this print chart:

	1	2	3	4	5	6	7	8	9	10	11	12	13	14	15	16	17	18	19	20	21	22	23	24	25	26	27	28	29	30	31	32	33	34
1	C	L	I	E	N	T		L	I	S	T	I	N	G																				
2																																		
3	X	X	X	X	X	X	X	X	X	X	X	X	X	X	X	X	X	X	X	X														
4	X	X	X	X	X	X	X	X	X	X	X	X	X	X	X	X	X	X	X	X														
5	X	X	X	X	X	X	X	X	X	X	X	X	X	X	X	X	X	X	X	X														
6																																		
7	E	N	D		O	F		C	L	I	E	N	T		L	I	S	T	I	N	G													
8																																		

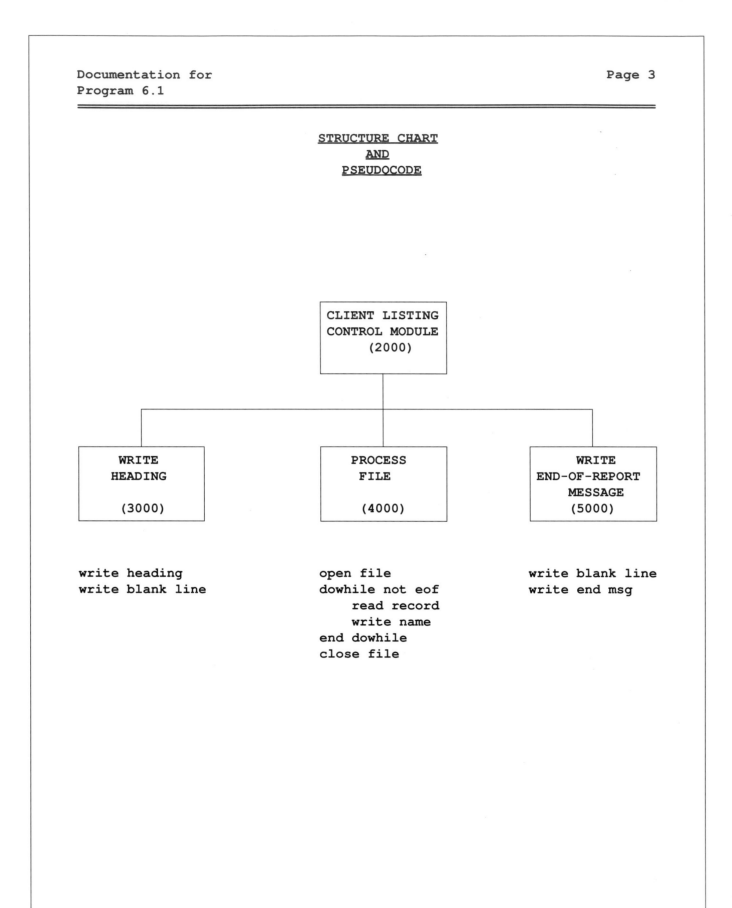

STRUCTURE CHART
AND
PSEUDOCODE

CLIENT LISTING
CONTROL MODULE
(2000)

| WRITE HEADING (3000) | PROCESS FILE (4000) | WRITE END-OF-REPORT MESSAGE (5000) |

```
write heading                open file                write blank line
write blank line             dowhile not eof          write end msg
                                 read record
                                 write name
                             end dowhile
                             close file
```

```
Documentation for                                    Page 4
Program 6.1
```

SAMPLE RUN

```
CLIENT LISTING

ALEXANDER BROWN
JEFFREY ARCHER
MARY HENDERSON
WELLINGTON GIFT SHOP
MARGARET CRAWFORD
RICHARD HAMILTON
COMPUTER SERVICES
HENRY CARLSON
MEGAN RYAN
PHILIP SPAULDING
FELICIA WILLIAMS
ELIZABETH STEWART
GIFT AHOY
JUSTIN MAILER

END OF CLIENT LISTING
```

```
Documentation for                                          Page 5
Program 6.1
```

Program 6.1 listing

```
1000 ' PROG6-1
1010 ' *****************************
1020 ' *        CLIENT LISTING       *
1030 ' *****************************
1040 '
1050 ' *****************************
1060 ' *          VARIABLES          *
1070 ' *****************************
1080 '
1090 ' CLIENT.SEQ                Client File
1100 ' Client record:
1110 '     CLIENT.ACCT$
1120 '     CLIENT.NAME$
1999 '
2000 ' *****************************
2010 ' *        CONTROL MODULE       *
2020 ' *****************************
2030 '
2040   GOSUB 3000                 'Write Heading
2050   GOSUB 4000                 'Process File
2060   GOSUB 5000                 'Write End-of-Report Message
2070   END
2999 '
3000 ' *****************************
3010 ' *         WRITE HEADING       *
3020 ' *****************************
3030 '
3040   LPRINT "CLIENT LISTING"
3050   LPRINT
3060   RETURN
3999 '
4000 ' *****************************
4010 ' *          PROCESS FILE       *
4020 ' *****************************
4030 '
4040   OPEN "CLIENT.SEQ" FOR INPUT AS #1
4050   WHILE NOT EOF(1)
4060       INPUT #1, CLIENT.ACCT$,
                     CLIENT.NAME$
4070       LPRINT CLIENT.NAME$
4080   WEND
4090   CLOSE #1
4100   RETURN
4999 '
5000 ' *****************************
5010 ' *     WRITE END-OF-REPORT     *
5020 ' *            MESSAGE          *
5030 ' *****************************
5040 '
5050   LPRINT
5060   LPRINT "END OF CLIENT LISTING"
5070   RETURN
```

Glossary

Accumulator A numeric variable incremented by successive values to obtain the sum of the values.

Algorithm An ordered list of actions that accomplishes a task.

Algorithm development The process of creating an algorithm.

Append The addition of records to the end of an existing file.

Applications program A program used for some purpose other than helping with the operation and management of a computer.

Argument A value passed to a function variable.

Arithmetic operator Any of the symbols used for arithmetic operations (^ * / \ + MOD).

Array Another name for a table.

Ascending order An arrangement of items so that their numeric or ASCII values increase continuously from the first to the last.

ASCII An acronym for the American Standard Code for Information Interchange; this is the code used by microcomputers to represent characters. (See Appendix C.)

BASIC An acronym for Beginner's All-purpose Symbolic Instruction Code; this is one of many high-level programming languages.

Binary search A search of an ordered table that begins with the median item in the table. If that item is the one being sought, the search stops. If it is not, the value of the median is compared with the search value and the process is repeated using only the half of the table that could contain the item. The process continues until the item is found or the list is exhausted.

Bit A BInary digiT (0 or 1).

Boolean expression An expression that is either true or false.

Buffer An area of memory (RAM) used to hold a record after it is read from disk or before it is written to disk.

Byte A set of 8 bits; it can represent a decimal number (in binary code) or a character (ASCII).

Character A letter, a number, or a symbol such as $ or #.

Choice structure Another name for a selection structure.

Code The statements in a program.

Coding (or program coding) The process of translating from thoughts, notes, or pseudocode to BASIC or another programming language.

Cohesive A term used to describe a single-function module.

Compiler A program that translates a high-level programming language to the machine format necessary for execution. Compilers convert the entire program before execution begins.

Computer An electronic device that can read data, transform them, and report results.

Computer program. An ordered list of instructions for a computer. The program may be written in machine language or a high-level language like BASIC that can be translated into a form the computer can recognize.

Computer programming. The process of developing a reliable, revisable program that accomplishes specific objectives.

Concatenation The process of combining two or more strings.

Constant A value in memory that does not change during program execution.

Control break A pause in the processing of detail lines (program records) because of a change in a field designated as the control field; the pause is often used to print subtotals.

Control field A field in a record designated as the field to signal a control break.

Control totals Totals used to verify a process or the contents of a file.

Counter A numeric variable incremented, usually by 1, during each cycle through a loop.

Cursor The blinking symbol that indicates where the next characters entered from the keyboard will appear on the screen and where deletions will occur.

Data The facts used by a program.

Data element A subdivision of a record; a field.

Data entry The process of entering data to create or update a data file.

Data validation The process of checking or editing data to correct errors.

Default drive The drive (usually A, B, or C) currently designated by the operating system to be used with any disk-access commands that do not specify a disk drive.

Descending order An arrangement of items so that their numeric or ASCII values decrease continuously from the first to the last.

Detail line A line that is displayed in a report for each record processed.

Direct-access file A file organized so that any record may be retrieved or written without processing all the preceding records in the file; often called a random file.

Disk operating system (DOS) A collection of programs that allow a computer to run applications programs and that provide computer users with tools for managing files and their contents.

Documentation Any information that can help a person understand how a program works. A complete documentation package for a program includes documentation for all steps in the program development cycle:

1. A narrative describing the purpose of the program (problem definition)
2. Input and output specifications
3. A structure chart with algorithms for program modules (program design)
4. A listing of the program and a sample run
5. A description of the testing that was done to verify that the program does what it is supposed to do
6. A user's manual with instructions for the user of the program

Double-precision number A BASIC numeric variable type that will store real numbers with an accuracy up to 17 digits.

Dowhile loop A section of code or pseudocode that is repeated as long as the conditions in the dowhile statement are true.

Dowhile structure Another name for a repetition structure.

Edit report A report that lists the contents of a file and prints an error message or code for each invalid field.

Endless loop A loop with no terminating condition or for which the terminating condition never occurs. A common cause of endless loops is omitting from the body of the loop a statement changing the value of the variable(s) tested in the WHILE statement. An improperly constructed Boolean expression is another frequent cause of loops that do not end.

End-of-file (EOF) marker A marker (usually ^Z) at the end of a file to indicate that no more records or text entries follow.

Execution The process of performing program instructions.

Field A subdivision of a record, also called a data element; it contains a group of related characters, such as a person's name or address.

File A collection of related records with all records having the same fields arranged in the same order.

File maintenance The process of adding a record, changing a record, or deleting a record in a master file.

File updating The process of changing a master file to reflect the current status of a business.

Firmware Software that is built into the hardware.

Flag A value used in a WHILE or IF statement to signal the occurrence of a condition. Such values are sometimes called terminating values or sentinel values.

Flowchart A graphic representation of program logic that uses a set of standard symbols. Flowcharts are useful for program planning and documentation.

Function A prewritten subroutine that performs an operation and returns a single value. Several functions are built into BASIC, but others can be written by the programmer.

Hard copy Output from a printer.

Hardware The physical parts of a computer system.

Hash total The sum of the entries in a numeric field that would not usually be totaled (such as account numbers or part numbers); the hash total is used to verify a process or the contents of a file.

Heading lines Lines at the top of a report that provide a title and identify columns.

Hierarchy chart Another name for structure chart.

Index file A file that serves as an index to records in another file.

Initial read An input statement that precedes a loop.

Input Data entered into a computer program.

Integer A positive or negative whole number. Also a BASIC numeric variable type for storing integers ranging between -32768 and +32767.

Interactive program A program that requires the user to enter (from the keyboard or other device) some or all of the input to the program.

Interpreter A program that translates program statements into machine instructions for execution. Interpreters convert and execute one statement at a time.

K A measure of computer memory or disk storage capacity; 1K (kilobyte) refers to storage for 1024 characters.

Line counter A numeric variable used to count the number of lines in a report.

Line number The number that begins a BASIC statement; the line numbers determine the order of statement execution.

Logical operators Symbols used to form Boolean expressions with multiple conditions; BASIC's logical operators used in this book are NOT, AND, and OR.

Logic error An error in a program's logic. As a consequence of the error, at least some of the program's output may be incorrect.

Loop A dowhile loop.

Maintenance The term for changing programs to reflect current user and system requirements. Program maintenance costs often exceed the costs of initial program development.

M or MB A measure of computer memory or disk storage capacity. 1MB (megabyte) refers to storage for approximately 1 million characters.

Master file A file that contains relatively permanent data.

Median The middle number in a list of numbers; half of the numbers are below and half are above it.

Memory sort A sort performed in a computer's memory (RAM).

Menu A screen display of functions that a program can perform and from which a user may select by making an appropriate keyboard entry.

Menu-driven program A program that can perform various functions that are executed as a user selects them from the program's menu.

Merge A process that combines two or more files of ordered records into a single file maintaining the same sorting sequence.

Mode The value or values that occur most often in a list.

Module A group of related code or pseudocode statements. A well-designed module performs a single function in the program and has a label or name reflecting its function.

Nested loop A loop contained within another loop.

Null string An empty string.

Numeric data A set of characters that includes the digits 0-9 and, optionally, a sign or decimal point.

Numeric variable A storage area (in RAM) for numbers; only numbers, including a sign and decimal point, may be assigned to a numeric variable.

Output Results reported by a computer program.

Page counter A numeric variable used to count the number of pages in a report.

Posting The process of accumulating totals and using them to update a master file.

Precision The number of digits that can be stored accurately in a numeric variable.

Priming read An input statement that precedes a loop.

Processing Manipulations of any sort that transform input to output.

Program Another name for computer program.

Program-control structures Statements that determine the order of execution of other statements in a program. The repetition or dowhile structure controls the repetition of statements, and the selection or choice structure controls which groups of statements are executed.

Program design The process of specifying program logic.

Program-development cycle The steps involved in planning and writing a program.

Program logic The set of algorithms that accomplish the purposes of a program.

Program maintenance (*See* Maintenance)

Programmer A person who codes and tests program instructions.

Prompt A message displayed by a program to request data or request an operator action.

Pseudocode A list of statements written to resemble computer language but with a more relaxed syntax. The exact form of the pseudocode will vary depending on the personal preference of the writer or the employer; it should, however, always be precise enough to describe what is to be done and clear enough to be understood by a person who is not a programmer.

Random-access memory (RAM) The working memory of a computer; the computer can read from it and write to it.

Random file A direct-access file.

Real number A number that may have a decimal component. In BASIC, real numbers can be stored only in single- or double-precision numeric variables.

Record A collection of related fields (data items) in a specific order and format.

Record key A control field within a record that identifies the record uniquely or classifies it as a member of a category of records within a file.

Relational operators Symbols used to combine a pair of numeric or character string data values to form a Boolean expression. BASIC's six relational operators are =, <>, >, <, >=, and <=.

Repetition structure This program structure controls the repetition of statements. In pseudocode, the statements between dowhile and end dowhile are to be repeated as long as the conditions that follow the dowhile are true. In BASIC, the statements between WHILE and WEND are repeated as long as the conditions that follow WHILE are true.

Reserved words The words that have a special meaning to BASIC and may not be used as variable names.

Selection structure The programming structure that evaluates a set of conditions and executes different sections of code depending on the value of the conditions. This structure selects sections of code to execute. IF, THEN, and ELSE are the BASIC key words used to implement the structure.

Sentinel value A flag.

Sequence structure A program segment in which one or more statements are executed in order, one after the other.

Sequential file A file in which records are stored in consecutive order and from which records must be retrieved in that same order.

Serial (sequential) search A search that starts at the beginning of a table and during which items are examined one at a time until a matching value is found or the end of the table is reached.

Single-precision number A BASIC numeric variable accurate up to 7 digits; it is stored in one byte.

Soft copy Program output that is sent to the screen.

Software Computer programs.

Sorting The process of arranging records in some order.

Source document. A form used for the initial recording of data prior to entry into a computer data file.

String data A set of characters consisting of letters, numbers, and other symbols.

String variable BASIC's nonnumeric variable type, which stores a group of from 0 to 255 characters. The characters may be letters, numerals, and other symbols.

Structure chart A graphic display that shows the purpose of a program, identifies the general steps, or functions, required to solve the programming problem, and shows the relationship of those functions to one another. Structure charts are also called hierarchy charts and visual tables of contents.

Structured design An approach to problem solving in which complex problems are divided into simpler subproblems. The process is repeated for each of the subproblems until the only problems remaining cannot be subdivided again. Usually, it is easy to describe the solutions to the remaining problems.

Structured program A program with all of the following characteristics:

1. Program logic developed with structured program design techniques.

2. Appropriate documentation at the beginning of the program

3. Descriptive labeling of program modules

4. Program execution controlled only with the standard programming structures

5. Program statements indented or aligned wherever appropriate.

6. Each program statement on a separate line

Structured walk-through A process for reviewing program design in which colleagues scrutinize the design, making sure that it meets all requirements and that the logic is correct.

Subscript A numeric value or variable identifying the location of a particular data item in a table.

Summary lines Lines at the end of a report; often they contain totals and end-of-report messages.

Syntax errors Violations of the grammar rules of a programming language.

Systems design The process of specifying what each program in a system is supposed to do. In particular, the specification of the products each program is to produce and the data and information required so that the program can produce those products.

Table A collection of related string or numeric data items referenced by a single variable name.

Terminating value A flag.

Testing The process of correcting errors in program logic and code.

Top-down design A problem-solving approach that begins at the "top" with the original problem and works "down," decomposing problems into subproblems until only relatively simple problems remain.

Top-down testing The testing of each module of code as it is added to a program. This way of testing is advantageous because it is much easier to find logic errors in a relatively small, single-function module than it is in a complete program.

Transaction file A file that contains data about individual events or transactions, such as the removal of an item from inventory or a room reservation.

Transaction processing The processing of transactions as they occur rather than in batches.

User A person who operates a computer or who uses information produced by a computer.

Variable A storage location in memory, the contents of which may change during program execution.

Visual table of contents (VTOC) Another name for structure chart.

Index